HUMAN NEUROPSYCHOLOGY

HUMAN NEUROPSYCHOLOGY

HENRI HECAEN

Ecole des Hautes Etudes en Sciences Sociales
E. R. A. #274 au C.N.R.S.
Unité de Recherches Neuropsychologiques et Neurolinguistiques (U. 111)
I. N. S. E. R. M.
Paris, France

MARTIN L. ALBERT

Department of Neurology
Boston University Medical School
and
Veterans Administration Hospital
Boston, Massachusetts

A WILEY-INTERSCIENCE PUBLICATION

JOHN WILEY & SONS, New York · Chichester · Brisbane · Toronto

Library of Congress Cataloging in Publication Data

Hécaen, Henri, 1912–
  Human neuropsychology.

  "A Wiley-Interscience publication."
  Bibliography: p. 1
  Includes index.
  1. Neuropsychology. 2. Aphasia. 3. Apraxia.
I. Albert, Martin L., joint author. II. Title.
[DNLM: 1. Psychophysiology. WL102 H445h]
QP360.H39   616.8   77–14158
ISBN 0–471–36735–4

Printed in the United States of America

1 0 9 8 7 6 5 4 3

FOREWORD

While it is always pleasant to be invited to write a foreword, to have been invited to prepare the introduction to a volume authored by Henri Hécaen is not merely a pleasure but an honor.

One needs only to review the history of the higher functions to appreciate the special position occupied by Professor Hécaen. Before World War I this field occupied a central position in neurology, and nearly all the great figures who created the discipline made contributions to the understanding of the more advanced functions of the human brain. After the great war, however, there was a sharp decline in interest, and only a corporal's guard of isolated and courageous scholars maintained the fragile thread of the great tradition. At the end of World War II only a handful of investigators were devoting themselves to this area. Henri Hécaen was one of the new pioneers who revivified the field. His contributions have become so much a part of our basic everyday thinking that it is paradoxically easy to forget his role.

Even in the period when the foundations of this field were established, the functions of the right hemisphere had been neglected. Hécaen was one of those who were instrumental in correcting this major gap in our knowledge. The conventional wisdom of earlier generations of aphasiologists had taught that the brain of the left-hander was the mirror image of the right-hander. Hécaen has been a leader among those who have taught us not only that left-handers as a group have a quite different cerebral organization from right-handers but also even within the left-handed population there are clear-cut subgroups. These findings represent one of the first approaches to the study of the individual differences in brain organization, which will undoubtedly be one of the major frontiers in the field of brain-behavior relationships.

The linguistic features of aphasia had been a central interest of several workers in the classic period of aphasia, and Wernicke himself had used linguistic analysis as a major criterion separating the speech performances of patients with anterior and posterior lesions. But whereas such authors as Pick, Salomon, and Bonhoeffer had continued this tradition, linguistic analysis has attained a position of focal importance in aphasiology only in the past 20 years. Hécaen has again been in the vanguard of those who have forged a link between the modern revolution in linguistics and the study of the focally damaged brain.

Finally one should recall that Hécaen's detailed studies of such clinical entities as alexia without agraphia stood out in an era when the dominant teaching denied the existence of delimited disorders of the higher functions. The great analytic power of modern psychological and linguistic techniques would have been seriously diminished without the renewed awareness of the existence of separable syndromes that can be related to the anatomic organization of the brain.

This listing of Professor Hécaen's personal contributions to the field of the higher functions is only a partial one, as the reader of this book will soon discover. What the reader may not appreciate is his major role as a public scientific figure. In the 1950s the field of brain-behavior relationships was, in effect, despite its major importance in the history of neurology from 1860 to 1914, barely more than a struggling infant, and all of the significant investigators in the world could easily have been assembled in one small room. Much of its modern growth must be attributed to Hécaen's efforts. He has trained a large number of junior collaborators who have gone out to spread knowledge of this area in many countries. He was a founder of the International Neuropsychological Symposium, whose early meetings were attended by a mere handful of participants. Its success was the result not only of its wide geographic distribution but also of its total disregard of disciplinary boundaries.   Neurologists, psychologists, linguists, neurophysiologists, anatomists, students of animal behavior, and others, have all been brought together in isolated and beautiful locations to listen, learn, and above all to argue into the late hours of the night. This meeting is a monument to Hécaen's total freedom from two of the common vices of science, national chauvinism and the even more pernicious and insidious blight of professional chauvinism, that unfortunately often still persist as barriers to scientific advancement.

He founded what was probably the first journal, *Neuropsychologia*, devoted primarily to the disorders of human higher functions. His energetic and scholarly management of this journal was a major factor in restoring the field of human brain-behavior relationships to its rightful eminence in the world of science.

I will not speak here of Henri's personal qualities as a friend and supporter of the young investigator. I cannot, however, forgo the opportunity to say that I have little doubt that, when Olympic prizes are awarded for excellence as a grandparent, Henri will surely walk off with the first gold medal.

My pleasure in writing this foreword can only be increased by the fact that I have long had a special relationship with the coauthor, Dr. Martin Albert. He carried out his neurological training in my department, and I think there is little doubt that his contact during that period with the Aphasia Research Unit of the Boston Veteran's Administration Hospital played a major role in his subsequent career orientation. My colleagues and I welcomed and made possible his plan to work in Hécaen's unit. In the postwar period the Aphasia Unit established by Fred Quadfasel, in which he was joined by Harold Goodglass and Robert Sparks, had been one of the very few centers in the world where the scientific study of aphasia was carried on. It was therefore more than pleasing to those of us who worked there to have Dr. Albert go to Paris to link two of the major traditions in modern behavioral neurology and psychology. The fruitfulness of this cross-fertilization will be obvious to any reader of this book.

NORMAN GESCHWIND, M.D.
James Jackson Putnam Professor of Neurology
Harvard Medical School

Boston
August 1977

PREFACE

The accumulating facts of science have literally overrun the ability of the scientist to deal with them. This statement is equally true for the field of neuropsychology. Even as we were writing this book, we realized that new facts and new theories were spilling out onto the scientific marketplace. At the risk of being incomplete, and in full knowledge of being incomplete, we have selected, organized, and interpreted facts and theories from the almost overwhelming body of literature on adult human neuropsychology. We have made a sincere effort to present a balanced overview of the field. In many specific areas within the general field, contradictions abound, both in fact and in theory. We have not hesitated to present our own opinion. At the same time we have tried to present not only the hypotheses but also the supporting evidence of others whose opinions differ from our own, so that the reader could fairly draw his own conclusions.

This book is not intended to be a comprehensive "review of the literature." We have incorporated our combined clinical and research experience in selection, organization, and interpretation. In many sections we have included material not published elsewhere. As a result of this approach we have specifically excluded from the text consideration of several important aspects of neuropsychology properly belonging to the field but with which we have had insufficient personal research contact. These topics include dementia, neuropsychological aspects of attention and emotion, and developmental neuropsychology (with the exception of childhood aphasia, which we have included in the text). At times we introduce a topic by discussing anatomic or physiological evidence from human or animal experimentation. These discussions are not intended to provide a complete background to the topic. Rather, they are designed to serve as indicators of the types of basic neuroscientific research that can contribute to a greater understanding of adult human neuropsychology.

The human brain and its relation to human behavior are not subjects that lend themselves easily to categorization. In this book we have arbitrarily selected as our basis for categorization the broadly accepted neuropsychological syndromes, for example, aphasia, alexia, apraxia, and so forth, with the exception of those syndromes related to frontal lobe dysfunction. As yet, these latter syndromes are poorly defined behaviorally. Consequently we have elected to look at the frontal lobes as anatomic regions that, if damaged, may be associated with certain specific behavioral defects, rather than, as in the remainder of the book, to start with the behavioral defects and seek their neurological basis.

This book is a personal statement relating to the state of the art of adult human neuropsychology as we see it. If we have been successful, the book will serve as an introduction to the field for those with little previous exposure, as a point of reference for those already working in the field, and as a challenge to specialists who wish to understand and to explain the human brain and to resolve its apparent contradictions.

We took as a point of departure Hécaen's *Introduction á la Neuropsychologie,* published in 1972 by Larousse. However, all chapters in that book were completely rewritten, and several new chapters have been added.

We gratefully acknowledge the assistance of colleagues who offered advice on different sections of the manuscript: in particular, Drs. Edith Kaplan, Harold Goodglass, and D. Frank Benson.

Some of the work in this book was supported by the Foundations Fund for Research in Psychiatry; NIH Grant #NS-06209; the Ecole des Hautes Etudes en Sciences Sociales; CNRS; INSERM; and the Aranne Laboratory for Human Psychophysiology, Department of Neurology, Hadassah University Hospital, Jerusalem.

HENRI HÉCAEN
MARTIN L. ALBERT

Paris, France
Boston, Massachusetts
August 1977

CONTENTS

HUMAN
NEUROPSYCHOLOGY

ONE
INTRODUCTION

Human neuropsychology is the study of neural mechanisms underlying human behavior. The discipline is based on a systematic analysis of disturbances of behavior following alterations of normal brain activity by disease, damage, or experimental modification.

Human neuropsychology may be divided into adult neuropsychology, the study of disturbances of established patterns of behavior, and developmental neuropsychology, the study of disturbances of the acquisition of cognitive functions regardless of the pathological origin (e.g., lesions acquired before or after the establishment of the function). Neurolinguistics represents a major subdivision of neuropsychology, dealing with disturbances of verbal performance following cortical lesions. Neurolinguistics may, itself, be divided into the study of language pathology of adults and that of children.

Neuropsychology is at the intersection of the neurosciences (neurology, neuroanatomy, neurophysiology, neurochemistry) and the behavioral sciences (physiological psychology, developmental psychology, psycholinguistics, and linguistics). Clinicoanatomic correlation forms the indispensable base: the knowledge of the nature, extent, and evolution of brain lesions; the means of demonstrating these lesions; the significance to accord them; and the associated constellation of signs and symptoms of localizing value. Neuroanatomy adds the essential structural knowledge—the architectonic maps of cortical regions; the pathways that connect cortical areas to each other or to subcortical structures; the limits of neuronal mechanisms or systems. In addition to the study of human neuroanatomy, comparative anatomy allows an understanding of behavioral differences in various species. Anatomic studies following animal experimentation aid in defining the structures involved in a functional system.

1

Neuroanatomy and neurophysiology are complementary within the field of neuropsychology and cannot be interpreted independently. Physiological technology leads us toward an understanding of fundamental mechanisms, reveals their profound complexity, and encourages a certain prudence in the interpretation of behavioral phenomena. Neurophysiology and physiological psychology tend more and more to overlap, defining, in the process, physiological correlates of animal behavior and cellular reactions to sensory inputs. For example, the technique of evoked potentials, despite technical difficulties in its application and interpretation, can be used with man. This allows evaluation not only of the sensory modality but also of the quality and internal effect of a stimulus.

Neurochemistry has introduced another perspective, although the ultimate adaptability of this science to behavioral studies remains to be proved. For example, the work on the role of macromolecules in the consolidation or transfer of memory has encouraged further study in this direction. It is also possible to see potential benefits of studies demonstrating control of behavior by specific cerebral regions by the intermediary of neurohumoral mechanisms. Histochemical analysis attempts to isolate specific neural systems responsible for specific behavioral activities, for example, the dopaminergic system, with its role in the integration of movement; the noradrinergic pathways, with their role in arousal, vigilance, emotion, and the reward system.

Neuropsychology also depends on the behavioral sciences. From physiological psychology neuropsychology borrows models and methods, adapting them as necessary. Similar use is made of the techniques and models of psycholinguistics and general linguistics. Starting from these bases neuropsychology establishes typologies of observed pathological performances. To these sciences, in return, neuropsychology offers a means of testing hypotheses; the brain lesion often impels the use of new strategies in the performance of an otherwise habitual task.

In addition to systematized observations of abnormal behavior, neuropsychology offers the possibility of determining cerebral localization of function. Independence or interdependence of behavioral functions may be established by observing their associations to specific foci of brain dysfunction. Neuropsychology affirms its specificity as a scientific discipline by presenting its own hypotheses derived from its own evidence. Between inputs and outputs, studied in an increasingly precise manner, neuropsychology attacks the problem of the "black box"; effort is given to establishing correlations between observed deficiencies and lesional localization. The anatomic map of the brain is thus being replaced by a functional map.

Although neuropsychology, originally a purely clinical specialty, is now a structured and systematic discipline, it neither denies nor rejects its clinical attachments. Every observation of a single brain-damaged individual represents an opportunity for the clinician, an opportunity to reinterpret mechanisms of function such that ultimately an understanding of the bases of disordered function will benefit the brain-damaged subject himself. Derived from such clinical observation and tentative interpretation, neuropsychology proceeds by attempting to verify clinical intuition, formulating hypotheses and developing experimental techniques capable of yielding quantifiable and reproducible results.

Since the Second World War neuropsychology has undergone considerable development, transformation, and extension. However, it is not at all a new science. Tentative first steps in the creation of the discipline are seen as far back as the introduction of phrenology by Gall and Spurzheim (1810–1819), in the publication on cerebral dominance for language attributed to Marc Dax (1836), and in the earliest works about language by Bouillaud (1820s–1830s). Definitive establishment of the specialty was made by Broca (1861), who clearly demonstrated the relationship of a lesion in a particular region of the brain to the alteration of a particular function—in this case the production of language.

In tracing the history of neuropsychology in subsequent chapters we shall observe the development and elaboration of theories of cerebral localization, of "image" centers and their connecting pathways, and of the innumerable brain diagrams designed to explain brain function. In parallel with the development of such concepts came the ideas of asymboly (Finkelnburg 1870), of agnosia (Freud 1891), and of apraxia (Liepmann 1900). The effectiveness of analyses of higher cortical functions was somewhat diminished by the rigid propositions of the "diagram makers" of the turn of the century. The attempts to explain all cognitive phenomena by reference to simple but rigid theoretical diagrams led to the little-publicized reactions of Bergson (1896) and Jackson (1864) and, finally, to the more famous frontal assults by Marie (1906a,b,c), Head (1926), and Von Monakow (1928).

It was, however, the development of the Gestalt theories that radically modified existing modes of thought concerning cerebral localization. The very bases of the localizationist theories were overturned. The distinction between primary or elementary functions and secondary or higher functions was no longer acceptable. According to Gestalt theory the loss of one fundamental attribute of brain function could account for disturbances of recognition (agnosia), of language (aphasia), or gestures (apraxia). This attribute, lost following any brain lesion, is the ability to form gestalten, the differentiation of a figure from its background. Accompanying these radical changes in theories of higher cortical functions, new results of animal experimentation appeared, adding further weight to the arguments against strict localizationist theories. The work of Karl Lashley strongly suggested that cerebral organization was not rigidly dependent upon structural peculiarities of specific regions of the brain. Rather, it seemed that cerebral organization required the participation of large masses of nervous tissue in brain functions. Anatomic specialization was accepted only for projection areas. Intelligence was conceived of as a dynamic and nonspecialized function of the brain acting in its entirety. From this viewpoint a diminution of intelligence was considered to be directly dependent on the mass of nervous tissue destroyed, with little or no consideration given to the localization.

The associationist and localizationist period demonstrated a basic approach: the isolation of deficits, their analysis, and their regrouping into syndromes according to particular lesional localizations. Clinical observation was at the basis of this work and thus formed the specialty of neuropsychology. However, the importance of unique, individual cases was overestimated and the value of negative cases insufficiently considered. Despite these faults, mention should be made of the remarkable insight of Wernicke (1874). His anatomopsychological approach resulted in the elucidation of models of brain function that have continued to be supported by subsequent experimentation.

The Gestalt theory represented a necessary movement that was, nonetheless, retrograde and dangerous on several counts. In particular it substituted psychological concepts for explanations. However, the introduction of this theory did produce new methods of observation and demanded consideration of total behavior, and not simply an isolated performance in a single domain. By stressing the notion of total organization Gestalt theory aids the understanding of clinical facts. The extreme localizationist views must be rejected and weight given to the evidence of general disturbances caused by isolated lesions.

At the experimental level Lashley's conclusions in favor of the role of "mass action" and equipotentiality of brain function profoundly influenced neurological thinking. It has been only since Lashley that rigor and precision in neuropsychology have developed: experimentation added to observation, quantification of facts, strict anatomic control of preparations, use of control groups, and statistical verification of results. It was the application of these techniques that allowed Lashley's students subsequently to reaffirm the importance of the principle of cerebral localization in the study of the higher cortical functions.

In the period between the two world wars the two major neuropsychological tendencies continued to develop. The defenders of localizationism adopted progressively rigid attitudes. Myelotectonic and cytoarchitectonic maps of the brain proliferated (Campbell, 1905; C. and O. Vogt, 1919; Brodmann, 1909; von Economo and Koskinas, 1925), and for each anatomically defined brain area a specific psychological function was sought. This atomism found

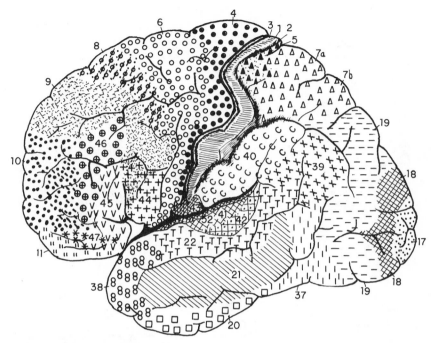

Cytoarchitectonic areas of the brain (Brodmann, 1903–1908). Copyright 1960 by Masson & Co., Paris. Reproduced by permission.

its most ardent enthusiasts in Henschen (1920–1922), Kleist (1933), and Nielsen (1946).

At approximately the same time Pavlov (1949) was opening the route to an objective method for study that was ultimately to be extremely productive. For Pavlov cerebral function was a mosaic of analyzers in reciprocal interaction reflecting reality from reflex arcs. One should mention that this sytematization of Pavlov was a translation into physiological terms of older associationist postulates.

The two main schools of thought, globalist and localizationist, came to lose all heuristic value by their detachment from concrete facts and their reliance on *a priori* conceptual notions. From this period, however, special attention should be given to the innovative methodology of L. S. Vygotsky (see review, 1965). Refusing to be boxed in between holistic and atomistic theories, he considered the question of cerebral localization from an approach to the higher cortical functions as if they were themselves a significant functional system. He posed three principles as working hypotheses: (1) the existence of plastic, modifiable, interfunctional relationships; (2) the existence of dynamic

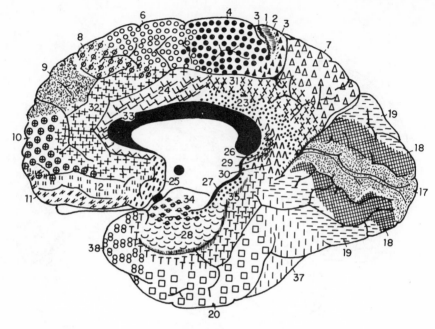

Cytoarchitectonic areas of the brain (Brodmann, 1903–1908). Copyright 1960 by Masson & Co., Paris. Reproduced by permission.

functional systems considered as being the result of the integration of elementary functions; and (3) the reflection of reality on the human mind.

For the first principle identical syndromes can be determined by differently located lesions in the child and the adult. Conversely lesions in identical locations in the adult and the child can give rise to different syndromes. The second principle rejects the notion that the whole and all of its parts are equivalent in cerebral activity. The function of the "whole" is an integration of the complex and dynamic interrelations of differentiated and hierarchically organized isolated zones. Specific function, on the other hand, is not based solely on the activity of a limited zone. The third principle was derived from research conducted on the purely human aspects of cerebral functions in their relationship to cerebral localization.

Following the Second World War new scientific developments produced new facts incompatible with any of the pre-existing theories. Sudden technological advances appeared in neurophysiology and neuroanatomy; these were applied to animal species higher in the phylogenetic scale than those previously used in animal experimentation. In conjunction with conditioning techniques, more precise observations, and the adoption of quantitative methods

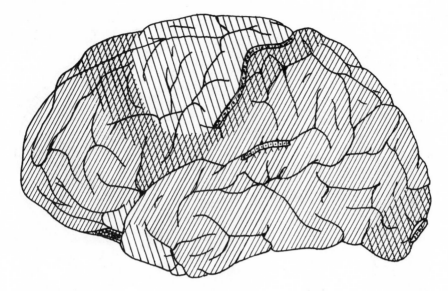

Architectonic regions of the brain (Bailey and von Bonin, 1951). Copyright 1951 by the University of Illinois Press, Urbana. Reproduced by permission.

of study of the abnormal behavior of large series of human beings with war-induced brain injuries, they rendered suspect all general theories not support-ed by experimental verification. Owing to a neopositivism desirous of demon-strating processes and structural relationships rather than isolated facts, the problem of cerebral localization began to change character. The interpreta-tion of results now required systematization following the rules of these newer disciplines.

Neurophysiology, for example, with the techniques of evoked potentials, is transforming our available information about the brain and its functional heterogeneity. This technique aids in defining the cortical topography of the zones of reception and projection, in pointing out the somatotopic organiza-tion, and in demonstrating the functional complexity of individual areas. With the use of microelectrodes and single-cell recording, the specificity of the different cells within a single receptive area can also be determined, allowing for psychophysical correlations. In addition, electrophysiological techniques permit the identification of association areas, areas of integration and convergence of polysensorial activity. Whereas previously the integrative functions of subcortical structures were emphasized, the significance of corti-cal control of behavioral activity and the importance of intrahemispheric and interhemispheric connections can now be reevaluated.

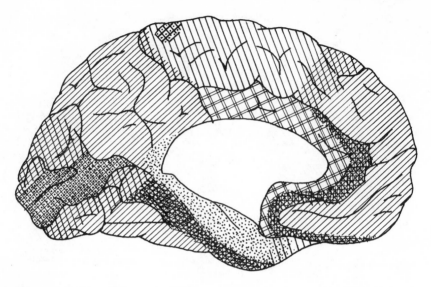

Architectonic regions of the brain (Bailey and von Bonin, 1951). Copyright 1951 by the University of Illinois Press, Urbana. Reproduced by permission.

These technological advances have resulted in a reaffirmation of the importance of the principle of cortical localization but at the same time have led to a rejection of the rigid diagrams of cortical function still lingering from the end of the nineteenth century. Functional organization of the brain may be seen as being a dynamic combination of complex systems, of brain areas with specific and nonspecific functions with multiple interconnections. Before the cortical regions are reached and interpretation takes place, the messages received peripherally are progressively transformed and progressively integrated. By a balance of inhibitory and excitatory activity the central nervous system accepts or rejects innumerable messages delivered from the external world.

As for neuroanatomy a strong reaction set in against the efforts being made to chop the brain into countless specific centers. Not only has the number of architectonic areas been reduced by newer studies, but also their limits are no longer considered as being abruptly defined. Such work as that by Walker (1938) and by Bailey and von Bonin (1951) supports the principle of cerebral localization, although the extent of the functional cortical zones is increased. Attention is also being given to the connections between these larger cortical zones and the subcortical nuclei.

Thus the study of the cortical projections of the thalamic nuclei has resulted in a modification of the notion of association areas in the sense defined by

Fleschig (1901) when he distinguished them from projection areas. The areas called associative by Fleschig also receive thalamic projections. Rose and Woolsey (1949) and Pribram (1960a,b) propose that the distinction be made instead between "extrinsic" and "intrinsic" areas. Extrinsic areas, which would correspond to primary projection areas, receive fibers coming from extrinsic thalamic nuclei, which in turn receive fibers of known origins. Intrinsic areas, which would correspond to the association areas, receive afferent fibers from the intrinsic thalamic nuclei, for which the primary source of afferent fibers is not well known.

In physiological psychology the work of Jacobsen (1936), Bard (1938), Kluver and Bucy (1939), and others, had already demonstrated the significance of ablation of certain cerebral regions in the production of abnormal behavior. However, with the work of Pribram, Chow, and Semmes, students of Lashley, it was clearly established that limited and well-defined posterior cortical lesions situated outside of primary projection areas could cause sensory deficits distinguishable from those produced by destruction of the sensory areas themselves. These behavioral alterations involved single sensory modalities and were determined by the site of ablation. Comparison of these results with those of similar and renewed studies of frontal lobe ablations showed some basic differences. Anterior ablations did not demonstrate deficits limited to single sensory modalities; rather, they showed deficits of a type that were independent of a single sensory modality.

In recent years continued experimentation has confirmed these earlier findings, progressively enriching our knowledge of functional localization. However, this new information brings with it new questions—the role of the subcortical structures, the true nature of a deficit observed in a particular performance, the role of the orienting reactions, their specificity or their global nature, the role of transfer phenomena, and the study of types of behavior called instinctive: emotional, sexual, alimentary, and aggressive. Functional localization may be different depending on the species studied or the developmental phase.

The significance of Lashley's earlier results has been modified. Newer experiments on the rat, the animal that Lashley had studied the most, show that the "mass effect" depends on the extension of the lesions toward specific critical regions in different loci in the cortex. It is the disturbance of these regions, and not simply the effect of mass, that results in the deficit on a particular test, for example, orientation in a maze (Gross, Chorover, and Cohen 1965). This does not, however, minimize the importance of the mass effect on general functioning of the brain. The combined efforts of anatomists and physiologists, for example, Rose and Woolsey (1949) on auditory areas, is permitting the correlation of cytoarchitectonic divisions with various areas of sensory representation. Special impregnation techniques have been used with secondary neuronal degeneration in animals having received localized cortical ablations. Such studies in these animals, which have also been studied with neurophysiological and behavioral tests, aid in the discovery of the anatomic and functional connections of these zones.

In parallel with these newer experimental findings in animals has been the development of the study of human behavior following brain damage. New and more precise descriptions and new facts have rendered the pure globalist positions less and less tenable. In particular, evidence has been accumulating that functional hemispheric asymmetry is not limited to language; lesions of one or the other hemisphere determine agnosic and apraxic syndromes that are now possible to diagnose clinically. Experimental psychological techniques associated with human neurosurgery (ablation and stimulation) have also been important in this regard, as well as classical anatomoclinical studies and newer electroencephalographic procedures permitting the association of particular paroxysmal disturbances to dysfunction of defined cerebral regions.

Neuropsychology, at this stage in its development, wanted to seek an understanding of the nature of the functions for which deficits had been demonstrated, to verify proposed hypotheses according to scientific criteria, and to confront anatomic observations in humans with those from animal experimentation. It became evident that the study of human cortical pathology could not progress without the application of methods from related disciplines. In this regard the importance of the research of H. L. Teuber (1959), transposing to human pathology the methods of experimental psychology, should be underlined. His approach has helped lead to results that can support or refute theories based on classical anatomoclinical observations. He introduced tests that reduce the verbal element to a minimum, proposed new hypotheses verifiable by experimentation, and, in addition, stimulated experimental psychologists to study pathological human behavior with their own methodology.

Equally important to the contemporary development of the study of higher cortical functions has been the research of Geschwind (1965). He has forced a reconsideration of certain aspects of the classical literature, in particular the role of the connections between a small number of functional regions of the brain and their significance in the learning of complex activities. As a result of this work experimentation has started in laboratories of neurophysiology and neuroanatomy, as well as in research sections working on artificial intelligence and cybernetics, that will ultimately lead to new and valuable information for the neuropsychologist.

Luria (1964), in the Soviet Union, influenced by the ideas of Vygotsky and Pavlov, has been using methodology of structural linguistics with a large series of subjects suffering from war injuries to the brain to create an anatomolinguistic typology. In addition, from a collection of simple and ingenious tests, he is trying to elucidate the nature of the different factors responsible for the observed abnormal behavior, factors he considers to have been described previously with a terminology of vague psychological notions.

Behavioral studies of split-brain patients, that is, patients with complete or partial section of forebrain commissures, have provided a dramatic opportunity for evaluation of functional hemispheric asymmetries (Sperry, 1968b; Bogen, 1969; Gazzaniga, 1970).

The domain of neuropsychology is vast. Engaged in the study of the pathology of human communication due to abnormalities of brain structure, it attempts to define the nature of deficits to different codes: linguistic, perceptual, gestural. For this it will be necessary to have knowledge of the relationship of the defect not only to its anatomophysiological substrate but also to its own semiotic system. In addition, to deal properly with the codes of specific systems, it is equally important to understand the role of the various levels of memory, as well as the nonspecific or supramodal functions such as alerting and attentional activities, programming functions, and spontaneity.

Disturbances of instinctual, affective, and motivational behavior are unquestionably within the realm of neuropsychology, influencing cognitive performance directly. Animal experimentation has been able to define some of the mechanisms of hunger and thirst and of sexual or aggressive behavior. In man more and more clinical and experimental observations are succeeding in clarifying the relationship between anatomic and physiological alterations and affective disorders. Research on temporal lobe epilepsy has contributed greatly to this field. The important role of subcortical structures, the archipallium, and endocrinologic interaction is being stressed.

Despite the brevity and highly schematic quality of this introductory chapter, it is nonetheless possible to follow the course of development of modern neuropsychology. Within the realm of the neurological sciences neuropsychology progressively affirmed its autonomy, establishing closer and stronger links with those disciplines that study the same functions in normal human beings and in other animals, as well as with those fields of basic science that underlie the higher cortical functions. No scientific discipline has abrupt limits. Necessities of research may, however, temporarily isolate a field of study by requiring that unique hypotheses, methodology, and means of interpreting results be developed.

TWO
DISORDERS
OF LANGUAGE

THEORETICAL FRAMEWORK FOR THE STUDY
OF LANGUAGE DISORDERS

Chapter 1 stressed the three-sided foundation for the contemporary discipline of human neuropsychology: neurology, psychology, and linguistics. Nowhere is the interdependence of these three fields more evident than in the study of aphasia. In this chapter we consider each of the three fields from the point of view of its particular relevance to the study of language disorders. It is arbitrary, indeed, to discuss one field separately from the others; however, by isolating each, one may see more clearly its dependence on others.

This chapter deals with disorders of language, not disorders of speech. Speech refers to the mechanical process of articulation; such a process can be disturbed by weakness, slowness, or incoordination of the muscles of the glossopharyngeal apparatus; and disturbances would be termed dysarthria, dysphonia, or mutism. Language refers to a process of verbal symbolic communication. This system of communication can, of course, be defined only in terms of the model used for its description. Aphasia may be defined as a disorder of language due to brain damage.

Neuropsychology has often dealt with aphasia by means of criteria extrinsic to specific linguistic perturbations, for instance, by reference to associated clinical symptoms or gross anatomoclinical correlations. The methods and concepts of linguistics have provided additional criteria for the study of aphasia, criteria by means of which language disorders and speech disorders may be more clearly distinguished. Thus conceived, aphasia represents a disruption in the use of a particular linguistic rule or code.

Neuropsychology and Aphasia

The written history of aphasia extends back to 2500 *BC;* in the Ebers Papyrus we have the record of a man who, as the result of head injury, "lost his ability for speech without paralysis of his tongue." The early history of aphasia represents isolated and anecdotal descriptions of patients with language disorders (Benton and Joynt, 1960).

The birth of the "neuropsychology of language" occurred in the beginning of the nineteenth century in Europe, when anatomoclinical correlations between cerebral lesions and language pathology were first considered (see the historical reviews by Head, 1926; Kleist, 1933; Weisenburg and McBride, 1935; Nielsen, 1946; Brain, 1965; Hécaen and Angelergues, 1965; Hécaen and Dubois, 1969; Hécaen, 1972a). The specialists who forged the early theories of aphasia, their schools and beliefs, the currents and countercurrents have been well described elsewhere and are reviewed only briefly here.

From the time of Gall and Spurzheim in 1809 to the time of World War II there have been two main streams of thought concerning the study of aphasia: localizationist, with its major subcategory of associationism, and globalist. Gall, by introducing the concept of phrenology, was the first to propose a systematic relationship between specific psychological components of human behavior and specific cerebral regions. Although many of his conceptions slid over the scientific borderline into the realm of fantasy, his neurobehavior-oriented, phenomenological approach left a powerful legacy.

Thus Bouillaud (1825), remaining faithful to Gall's conceptions, attempted to provide anatomoclinical proof that the "legislative organ of speech" resided in the anterior lobes of the brain. Bouillaud's influence should not be

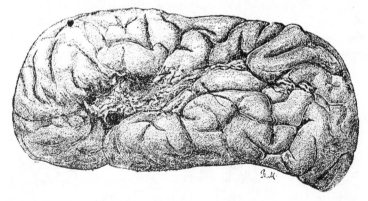

Broca's autopsy of the left cerebral hemisphere of Leborgne (Drawing by Pierre Marie). Copyright 1960 by Masson & Co., Paris. Reproduced by permission.

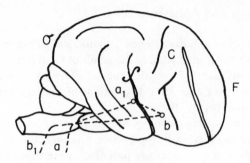

Wernicke's (1874) diagram of the organization of language in the brain. a = point at which acoustic pathway enters brainstem; a_1 = cortical termination of acoustic pathway; b = center for verbal motor images; b_1 = brainstem exit for centrifugal motor pathways; o = occipital pole; F = frontal pole; C = central fissure; S = Sylvian fissure. Aphasia could be caused by any lesion of the a–a_1–b–b_1 pathway, but the clinical picture would vary according to precise locus of the lesion.

minimized, since one of his most devoted students was Paul Broca. The localizationists can date the beginning of their movement as April 18, 1861, when Broca described a patient who had lost the "faculty for articulated language" and who had a left hemispheric lesion. Broca concluded that the posterior-inferior portion of the frontal lobe controlled this behavioral "faculty." In 1865 Broca reaffirmed the principle of left hemispheric dominance for the "faculty of articulated language." Wernicke, in 1874, demonstrated that a lesion in a region different from that described by Broca produced a different form of language disturbance: a lesion in the posterior portion of the first temporal gyrus provoked a loss of memory for the "auditory images" of words. This lesion produced a clinical syndrome manifested by loss of verbal comprehension with preservation of the capacity to speak; writing was also impaired, and was considered to be an activity dependent on oral language.

These two regions—Broca's area and Wernicke's area—came to be considered primary centers for production and reception of oral language; other regions were subsequently located as the controlling centers for aspects of written language. With centers being isolated for the control of certain components of language behavior, the connections or associations between the various centers became of important theoretical interest, since lesions of the centers could produce one type of language disorder, while disruption of the connections could produce other types. The names of Bastian (1869, 1898), Finkelnburg (1870), Kussmaul (1877), Exner (1881), Lichtheim (1884, 1885), and Charcot (1887), among others, are frequently cited as key representatives of the "school of associationism," which flourished during this period. Dejerine (1892, 1914) provided anatamoclinical evidence to support many of the theoretical claims of the "diagram makers."

Even at the time that the localizationists and associationists were brandishing their explanatory diagrams, a countercurrent of thought was developing. This, the globalist school, contended that language was a dynamic process derived from the integrated function of the entire brain. With greater or lesser variation on this basic theme, globalists denied the value of a localizationist approach. Thus Jackson (1864–1932) in England, Freud (1891) in Austria, and Bergson (1896) in France claimed that individual memory images were not lost following cerebral damage; rather, what occurred was the interruption of a continuous process by which the memory developed.

Marie (1906,a,b,c) fired a broadside attack against the localizationists. For Marie there was only one aphasia, Wernicke's aphasia. The various forms described by others were nothing more than artifacts of examination or products of preconception, and motor disturbances were not a part of language at all. In addition this true aphasia was not the result of a sensory deficit, word deafness, but was a specific form of intellectual dysfunction. It is of some interest that Marie, who is remembered for his holistic approach, did not completely maintain this belief in later years. Studying war-injured soldiers, he distinguished different forms of aphasia according to the lesion site within Wernicke's area.

From its early stages the holistic approach to aphasia gathered momentum and adherents. Pick (1913), in a brilliant series of studies, based his conclusions on the differentiation of propositional and nonpropositional activity reminiscent of Jackson. The progression from thought to its verbal expression

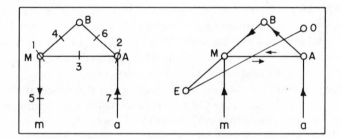

Diagram of Lichtheim (1885).
A = Auditory verbal center; B = center for intellectual elaboration; M = center for verbal articulation; aA = pathway carrying auditory verbal stimulation; Mm = pathway connecting the center for articulation to the lower motor centers; O = center for visual representation; E = center for writing. Lesions at 1, cause cortical motor aphasia; 2, sensory aphasia; 3, conduction aphasia; 4, transcortical motor aphasia; 5, subcortical motor aphasia; 6, transcortical sensory aphasia; 7, word deafness.

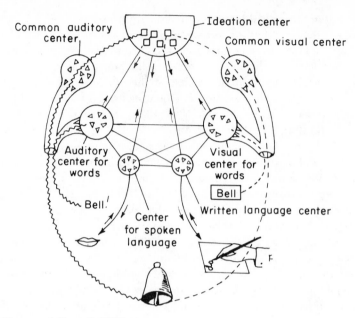

The Bell Diagram of Charcot (1890).

passed through four successive stages: a mental attitude in which thought is undifferentiated, a period of structured thought in which differentiated ideas have not yet received verbal representation, the formulation of the structure of the sentence, and then the selection of words. To this series of stages Pick added Jackson's distinction between voluntary and emotional language. Head (1926) also reflected the conceptions of Jackson, considering language to be a voluntary and symbolic activity with distinction to be made between automatic and propositional language. Von Monakow (1910), von Monakow and Mourque (1928), and van Woerkom (1921) further elaborated the holist conception of aphasia and its relation to disorders of intelligence.

Theories of Gestalt psychology, which were being developed at that time (e.g., Gelb and Goldstein, 1920; Gelb, 1933) and which were finding support in laboratories of neurophysiology (Lashley, 1923), were applied to theories of aphasia. Emphasis was placed on the difference, within language activity, between sensorimotor processes, which constituted the instrumentalities of language, and psychological processes, evaluated in terms of a thought-language dialectical relationship. Since language was an integral part of the total human organism, aphasia could not represent a specific deficit; rather, aphasia must be a part of the general defense system by which the organism responds to a particular stress. The functional disorganization of the organ-

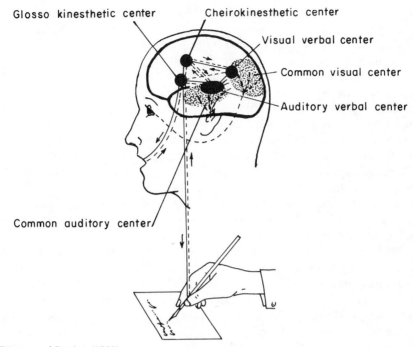

Diagram of Bastian (1898).

ism, and therefore the syndrome that appeared, was always a representation of the global reaction of adaptation.

By way of response to the prevailing trends the localizationist approach to aphasia reappeared at this time in extreme form (Henschen, 1926; Kleist, 1933). For these authors, each aspect of language production corresponded to a specific and precise anatomic center. The brain, thus functionated behaviorally and anatomically, resembled again the phrenological diagrams of Gall.

In an attempt to break away from tradition-bound preconceptions, Weisenburg and McBride (1935) provided a major impetus to neuropsychological studies of aphasia. Using a systematic descriptive analysis of large numbers of aphasic patients, they presented results of an empiric, quantitative research project. They compared the findings of controls, of brain-damaged subjects without aphasia, and of aphasic subjects with unilateral hemispheric lesions. In this way they isolated four major types of aphasia: expressive, receptive, expressive-receptive, and amnesic. Their study represents the first major attempt to apply statistical techniques to the analysis of behavioral defects of brain-damaged patients.

The Second World War and subsequent international conflicts provided brain-damaged patients in abundance. Conrad (1947, 1949, 1954) and Bay (1952, 1962) studied large numbers of brain-damaged patients, aphasic and nonaphasic, continuing to support globalist conceptions of language disorders. Ombredane (1951) maintained the beliefs of the Gestalt theorists but added an attempt to define the specific factors responsible for the various aphasic syndromes and to relate them to underlying physiological mechanisms. In line with the holist tradition Schuell and Jenkins (1959) found a single defect underlying all aphasia. A factor analysis of aphasia test scores revealed a general language factor—word-finding ability—to be impaired in all cases of aphasia. Against the conceptions of the holists, and armed with analyses of large numbers of brain-damaged patients, Nielsen (1946) presented an atomistic point of view, according to which lesions of small collections of cortical neurons (centers) would be directly responsible for specific functional deficits.

With the two major trends of aphasia theory (localizationism and globalism) vying with each other for primacy, contemporary studies of split-brain patients (Geschwind and Kaplan, 1962; Geschwind, 1965; Gazzaniga, Bogen, and Sperry, 1965) revived the concepts of associationism. The earlier proposals of Wernicke, Dejerine, and other associationists have gained new credibility in light of the anatomoclinical studies of the corticocortical disconnection syndromes (Geschwind, 1965, 1969; Goodglass and Kaplan, 1972; Benson and Geschwind, 1972; Goodglass and Geschwind, 1976).

However, despite the theoretical appeal of such an "anatomico-associationistic" model of language, fully satisfactory anatomic supporting evidence has not yet been provided. Thus many authors consider it most useful at present to correlate symptoms or symptom clusters with language zones (Hécaen and Angelergues, 1965; Brain, 1965; Luria, 1970; Hécaen, 1972a). Lesions within the general borders of this region would result in a particular cluster of language symptoms characteristic for that zone.

Neurolinguistics and Aphasia

Neurolinguistics is a discipline that attempts to relate neurological activity and linguistic behavior. It would seem natural, therefore, that the study of language pathology due to brain damage should occupy a prominent portion of basic linguistic research. Until recently, however, the opposite has been the case; the application of linguistic theory and technique to the study of aphasia is a relatively new development (see Goodglass and Blumstein, 1973, and Whitaker, 1970, for a more detailed elaboration of this point). Although systematic studies of phonological errors by aphasic subjects date back to the mid-1920s (Bouman and Grunbaum, 1925; Ombredane, 1926), and occasional reference is found to other studies of articulatory errors of aphasics (Alajouanine, Ombredane, and Durand, 1939; Grewel, 1951; Schenk, 1953), it was not until the work of Jakobson and Halle in 1956 that the field had its distinctive beginnings.

Already in 1941 Jakobson, a theoretical linguist, had emphasized the parallels between the order of dissolution of phonemic distinctions in aphasia, their order of development in the process of language acquisition by the child, and their universality in the languages of the world. Luria, in 1947, presented an analysis of different varieties of posttraumatic aphasia, considering linguistic principles in his analysis. However, Jakobson established the field of neurolinguistics with his publication of *Fundamentals of Language* with Halle in 1956.

In this basic work Jakobson and Halle presented a theoretical analysis of aphasic disorders. The point of departure was a bipolarity of the structure of normal language. In the normal structure of linguistic activity, paradigmatic and syntagmatic linguistic signs were present; the breakdown of language was such that one of these two systems was used to the exclusion of the other. They believed their analysis of aphasic patients revealed either one or the other of these two aspects of language, but not both. Thus aphasia could be reduced to either a disorder of similarity (paradigmatic) or a disorder of contiguity (syntagmatic). All varieties of aphasia oscillated between the metaphoric and the metonymic poles.

Disorders of similarity were manifested by impairments in the ability to select and to substitute. Language became entirely reactive, and verbal selection could be made only by reference to the context. Words most closely linked to syntactic context were most likely to remain for this type of aphasic, while key words disappeared or were replaced by more general terms. In tests of naming, the name of the presented object would neither be pronounced nor even repeated by the aphasic, for whom the presentation of the object implied the uselessness or redundancy of its naming. Semantic groupings would be guided by factors of spatial or temporal contiguity, that is, by recourse to metonymy, rather than by factors of similarity.

Disorders of contiguity were manifested by impairments in the ability to form propositions and to combine simple linguistic units into more complex linguistic entities. Here one found a deficiency of context, not a loss of words; syntactic rules were disrupted. Word order became chaotic, with grammatical function words disappearing first. This variety of aphasia resulted in production of childlike sentences and even sentences of single words. They believed that the gradual regression of the structures of linguistic sounds was parallel, but in reverse order, to the order of phonemic acquisition of the child. The loss of contiguity and of the capacity to maintain correct linguistic hierarchies resulted in attempts to produce approximative metaphoric identifications.

This analysis was valuable in stimulating further linguistic research in aphasia but was too far removed from clinical realities. Fry (1959) and Shankweiler and Harris (1966) demonstrated a lack of parallelism between the sounds failed by children and those most difficult for aphasics. Furthermore, by referring only to problems of verbal emission, Jakobson and Halle automatically excluded other varieties of language disorder from consideration.

On the other hand other psycholinguists have been able to find experimental support for many of Jakobson's contentions. Goodglass and his collaborators (1958–1974) studied linguistic aspects of aphasia by selecting patients on the basis of the presence or absence of agrammatism. The agrammatic aphasic (disorder of contiguity) was found to be characterized primarily by his syntactic, rather than morphemic, defect; the aphasic without agrammatism (disorder of similarity) was characterized by, among other factors, an inability for key-word evocation. Goodglass, in the later studies, refined these distinctions, highlighting those areas of correspondence and of noncorrespondence between his observations and the theories of Jakobson.

Blumstein (1973, 1974), using the Jakobson and Fant concepts of "distinctive features" and of "markedness" in phonological studies of aphasic subjects, found that both of these theoretical concepts had predictive value in determining the direction of articulatory errors. Aphasics make many more substitutions of consonants varying by a single distinctive feature from their target than differing by two or more distinctive features. In addition the unmarked or more basic member of a contrasting consonant pair is more stable than the marked form.

In 1964 Luria presented an anatomolinguistic classification of language disorders. The general principle underlying this classification was that language is a complex, hierarchical system of codes for which each level maintains its own functional organization. The totality of the anatomolinguistic system depends on the combined activity of several different cortical zones, each of which makes specific contributions to the development of the whole. Six varieties of aphasia, each dependent on a different cerebral lesion, were distinguished: (1) sensory aphasia (left temporal lesion) reflects disorders of acoustic analysis and phonemic discrimination; (2) kinesthetic or afferent motor aphasia (postcentral lesion) depends on disorders of kinesthetic analysis of the movements of speech; (3) kinetic or efferent motor aphasia (lesion anterior to the motor strip) indicates a defect in passing from one articulation to another and a perturbation of verbal sequences; (4) semantic aphasia (parietal lesion) is a manifestation of the inability to organize isolated elements into a coherent whole; (5) acoustic-amnesic aphasia (temporal lesion) suggests a deficit in retention of audioverbal traces; and (6) dynamic aphasia

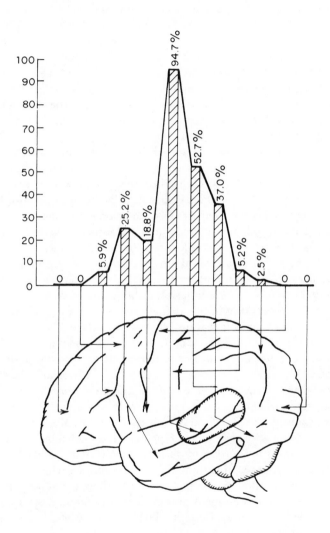

Deterioration of auditory phonemic perception according to lesion localization (Luria, 1947). Bars represent percentage of errors of different groups corresponding to lesion localization. Copyright 1970 by Mouton & Co., The Hague. Reproduced by permission.

(frontal lesion) refers to an impairment in the contextual organization of inner speech.

On the basis of Luria's classification, Jakobson (1964) proposed an additional theoretical construct for aphasia. For Jakobson the six varieties of aphasia proposed by Luria could be reclassified, according to the pattern of verbal behavior, into disorders of encoding and of decoding. They could thus be seen corresponding to the contiguity-simultaneity dichotomy proposed by Jakobson and Halle in 1956: dynamic aphasia, afferent motor aphasia, and efferent motor aphasia correspond to disorders of combination (syntagmatic defect); the other three forms correspond to disorders of selection (paradigmatic defect). By means of an analysis somewhat more refined than in his prior studies Jakobson suggested that the disorders may be considered along the lines of a new dichotomy: sequence-concurrence, or in the terms of Saussurien linguistics: successivity-simultaneity.

Since 1962, Hécaen, Dubois, and their collaborators have developed a combined neurological, neuropsychological, and neurolinguistic approach to the study of aphasia (1962–1974). Their major efforts have been directed toward an anatomoclinicolinguistic classification of aphasic disorders. The research team has incorporated into its conception of the domain of neurolinguistics the following elements: description of disorders of verbal performance following focal cortical lesions, identification of similarities and differences between linguistic performances of separate brain-damaged groups, study of factors responsible for disturbances of verbal performance, and study of patterns of interaction according to task specificity and sensory channel.

Their major observations have defined several varieties of aphasia, each with its particular linguistic features, each with its dependence on damage to a specific cerebral zone. Of particular interest is the observation that patterns of linguistic structures remain stable during the resolution of the aphasic syndrome. This observation is used by the Paris school as a basis for the hypothesis that aphasic patients with focal cortical lesions retain the fundamental integrity of knowledge of the system of linguistic rules necessary for linguistic competence. The classification developed by this group has many points in common with the clinical typologies most commonly accepted: expressive aphasia with disorders of phonemic realization; conduction aphasia with defective sentence programming; sensory aphasia with its three major aspects—disorganization of semantic relations, failure of auditory decoding of phonemic units, and attentional disorganization; and amnesic aphasia with multiple underlying mechanisms, of which one is a prototype of Jakobson's defect in paradigmatic choice.

We believe that neurolinguistics should not be limited simply to the application of linguistic methodology to the study of language disorders. If such were the case, neurolinguistics would be nothing more than an attempt to prove or disprove a given linguistic theory, and bias would be introduced by the very selection of a linguistic method (and its associated theory) for the study in question. This attitude was prevalent during the initial stages of collaboration between linguists and aphasiologists.

Issues in neurolinguistics may be considered from another point of view. Aphasic language is a manifestation of an ensemble of factors that have been disrupted either in isolated or in combined manner; these factors are basic elements of the rules governing the relationship between sound and meaning. Pathological verbal behavior concerns more than linguistic structures alone; it concerns alterations in such components of behavior as memory, attention, vigilance, perception, and sound emission. Neurolinguistics must concern itself with disturbances in all of these factors, and the ways in which they may interfere with the efficient and effective application of the grammatical mechanism.

Application of mathematical and statistical principles, word-frequency concepts (Rochford and Williams, 1962), and distributional models of language has allowed the development of quantitative neurolinguistics. Wepman and Jones (1966) compared the frequency distributions of different sections of discourse by aphasics with those of normal people. Geschwind and Howes (1964) used word-frequency distribution analyses to distinguish basic operations underlying word production. Lhermitte, Lecours, and Ouvry (1967) and Lecours and Lhermitte (1969), basing their work on models of structural linguistics, performed a series of qualitative and quantitative psycholinguistic analyses of aphasic discourse to extrapolate linguistic interpretations of normal language.

The generative and transformational model of language (Chomsky, 1965) has been applied to the study of aphasia. For Weigl and Bierwisch (1970) investigation of aphasic speech provides a means of relating linguistic theories to language performance. The observations of these authors may be considered according to level of linguistic disturbance (morphological, semantic, syntactic), as well as according to specific theories of language. Thus, for example, they discuss the case of an aphasic patient who had been unable to write to dictation. By means of a "deblocking" technique, in this case copying the model of a simple sentence, the patient could then write to dictation transformationally related sentences—questions, passives, and so on. They used this evidence to comment on the important role of transformations in relating deep and surface structures, concluding that linguistic performance is impaired in aphasia, while linguistic competence remains intact. But Weigl and Bierwisch's use of the competence-performance distinction is not quite the same as that ordinarily used in linguistic theory (Chomsky, 1965). According to them competence refers to the individual's tacit knowledge of his language, and performance refers to his access to this knowledge.

Adhering more to the standard linguistic notion of the competence-performance dichotomy but nonetheless finding his observations in accord with those of Weigl and Bierwisch, Hécaen (1972a) suggests that the distinction between competence and performance may serve as a useful criterion for separating disorders of verbal behavior seen in aphasics (due principally to loss of linguistic performance) from those seen in more general disturbances of cognitive function, such as the dementias (due principally to loss of linguistic competence). A counterargument is proposed by Goodglass and Blumstein (1973). They indicate that both competence and performance may be impaired in aphasia. They suggest that gaps in the aphasic's imperfectly retained competence may be temporarily restored by cuing or deblocking, with the result that adequate performance becomes possible.

Neurolinguistic studies of aphasia and the development of neurolinguistic classification schemes have led to further studies designed to uncover the neurophysiological mechanisms underlying the language disorders. The syndrome of phonetic disintegration (Alajouanine, Ombredane, and Durand, 1939) has been described as an articulatory disorder of speech (Tikofsky, 1965; Lehiste, 1968). An opposing view has also been presented. In a well-controlled study of five expressive aphasics, each with a major residual deficit in articulation, Shankweiler and Harris (1966) attempted to explore the phonemic characteristics of this syndrome and determine its underlying cause. These authors analyzed word repetition, using a test battery balanced for equal occurrence of phonemes in initial, medial, and final position. More errors occurred with phonemes in the initial position than in either of the other two positions, and consonants produced many more errors than vowels. This led the authors to conclude that the syndrome of phonetic disintegration was not the result of a primary dysfunction of speech muscles or of the articulatory apparatus but rather was "a disturbance in the process by which phonological units are encoded for production."

Additional studies on encoding and decoding of phonetic and phonemic signals have been conducted by the members of Haskins' laboratory in an attempt to evaluate the processes of successive conversion leading from the sentence to the final stage of acoustic analysis (Liberman, Cooper, Shankweiler, and Studdert-Kennedy, 1967; Shankweiler et al, 1967, 1968). The model developed suggests that the different phonemes in a verbal emission are represented by a series of successive subphonemic traits and that these traits exist in the nervous system as implicit instructions destined for separate and independent segments of the motor system. Central neural rules regulate the motor system in such a manner as to adjust the amplitude and to coordinate these instructions temporally, which are subsequently directed to the muscles of the articulatory apparatus. The central nervous system signals are presumed to be in one-to-one correspondence with the multiple dimensions of subphonemic traits; this correspondence occurs at a stage prior to the conversion of these signals into commands for muscular contraction. At the moment of muscular contraction another signal conversion takes place in the form of the vocal apparatus by the intermediary of articulatory rules. The onset of each new series of muscular contractions (in terms of central nervous system instructions for these contractions) begins before the completion of the preceding series. Thus each form of the vocal apparatus represents at any instant the emergence of the effects of past and present contractions. The final conversion, from the form of the vocal apparatus to the sound emission, is controlled by elementary physicoacoustic rules.

The same research team (Liberman et al, 1967) has also provided a concept concerned with perception of the speech code: the "motor theory of speech perception." For these authors a purely auditory mechanism for extraction of phonemic sequences is unlikely. They proposed a mechanism by which the listener may use the same processes used by the speaker in the realization of the encoding operations necessary to verbal emission. Perception is realized by the intermediary of the neuromotor correlates of articulatory gestures, and language decoding reproduces the successive stages necessary for language encoding but in the reverse order.

As for the question of liaison between the processes of encoding and decoding, a feedback system is invoked. The feedback of each articulatory movement (in terms of nervous signals) can provide information for the decoding mechanism. However, this information could as well come from corollary discharges (Teuber, 1968); that is, information is directed toward the reception zones at the same moment that the signals for motor commands are sent to the muscles. Thereby the corollary discharge signals could permit a reevaluation of the sensory input. In either case it is necessary to predicate the constitution of a "memory" allowing the comparison between sounds and motor engrams and permitting the listener to decode language immediately, without the necessity for encoding. Preliminary evidence for such a "memory" within the auditory system has been provided (Massaro, 1972).

At present neurolinguistic research on aphasia has not provided a complete verification of the motor theory of speech perception, although considerable concordance has been shown. Referring to this model, one may consider three types of liaison between the mechanisms of encoding and those of decoding. In the first there is a direct liaison between the zone from which the motor commands leave and the zone of acoustic decoding. That is to say, at every moment the motor command provides information to the perceptual mechanisms in such a manner that they may function to isolate the phoneme from the acoustic stream. In this case any lesion that provokes a disturbance in phonological production should, at the same time, cause a perturbation in phonetic discrimination. In clinical experience, in general, aphasic disturbances have not been sufficiently pure to allow for the discovery of such an association in an isolated manner.

In the second type there would be a zone superimposed on both the encoding area and the decoding area; this region would be responsible at the same time for providing both the neural pattern for phonemic realization of the word to be emitted and the neural code required to apply to the sounds of the word to be received. In such a case the syndromes of "pure" motor aphasia or "pure" word deafness could be predicted. However, one should also observe clinically a complex syndrome in which disorders of phonological emission and discrimination coexisted.

Clinical studies of aphasia thus seem to impose a third solution, that of a "memory" that could store the information about the motor commands and about their acoustic results. Such a memory would permit the immediate decoding of the acoustic stream into discrete and discontinuous units. A lesion of this "memory" zone could produce a syndrome of pure word deafness without necessarily provoking concurrent disorders of verbal emission. This last possibility is supported by the rare cases of pure word deafness reported in the literature.

The fundamental problems of classification in aphasia and elucidation of basic mechanisms underlying various aphasic patterns are often envisaged in terms of a particular theory of language. Theories of distributional and structural linguistics have highlighted the qualitative differences of the several hierarchically organized linguistic structural systems whereby basic elements at one level combine to produce the units of a superior level. By consequence, breakdowns in this process may be manifested as aphasic syndromes corresponding to different levels (phonemes, morphemes, sentences). In this theoretical construct the unity of aphasia may be seen only in the context of accepting language as an integrative synthesis of a collection of different functions. Aphasia may thus appear as a unitary disorder, since it results from a disruption of this integrative synthesis, although the manifestations may vary according to the structural level involved.

Generative and transformational linguistics defines language as an innate knowledge, of which "competence" is the abstract linguistic system available to an idealized speaker-hearer, and "performance" is the putting into action of this competence, based on a set of factors pertaining to a particular subject and a particular situation. According to this model the neurolinguistic aspects of aphasia present a different appearance. There cannot be a veritable disorder of language unless the competence component, the intuitive linguistic knowledge, is affected. However, a variety of aphasic syndromes may be found following disruption of the performance components.

We believe that the interplay of anatomoclinical evaluation and psycholinguistic technique may provide a complementary methodology that will allow a more precise and descriptive analysis of the complex verbal performances found in the diverse aphasic syndromes. Based on a linguistic typology of verbal behavior, the study of anatomoclinical correlations may provide a satisfactory semiology of neurolinguistics.

Neurology and Aphasia

The Anatomic Basis of Language

In the early associationist period of the history of aphasia, clinical studies and theoretical conceptions were reinforced by postmortem examinations of brains of aphasic patients. Dejerine (1914) defined the topography of the "zone of language" after long and detailed study by macroscopic and microscopic analysis of large numbers of such brains. He described three primary regions within the "zone of language": (1) an anterior portion, Broca's area, consisting of the posterior portion of the foot of the third frontal convolution, the frontal operculum, and the immediately adjacent cortical zone (tip of F_3 and foot of F_2), not including the rolandic operculum (this region extending as far as the anterior portion of the insula); (2) an inferior or temporal portion, Wernicke's area, consisting of the posterior portion of the first and second temporal gyri (this region representing the center for verbal auditory images); and (3) a posterior portion corresponding to the angular gyrus (this region representing the center for verbal visual images).

Marie (1926), who denied the neuropsychological conceptions of the localizationists and associationists and who specifically concluded that "the foot of the third frontal convolution played no role in aphasia" (1906), provided his

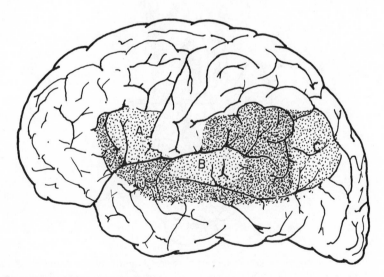

Dejerine's "zone of language" (1914).
A = Broca's area; B = Wernicke's area; C = angular gyrus.
Copyright 1960 by Masson & Co., Paris. Reproduced by permission.

own anatomic correlations. For Marie there was only one aphasia, and this always corresponded to a lesion of Wernicke's area, even if the symptoms could be variable. Broca's aphasia was conceived of as a combination of Wernicke's aphasia plus anarthria. This anarthria, which was not a part of the true aphasia, resulted from a lesion somewhere within the confines of a subcortical quadrilateral zone. This "quadrilateral of anarthria" had the following anatomic limits: in front, by a verticofrontal plane passing through the fissure that separated F_3 from the insula and descending in depth to the head of the caudate nucleus; in back, by a plane limiting the insula posteriorly and descending in depth to the posterior extremity of the lenticular nucleus. He emphasized that this quadrilateral zone was always involved and that the foot of the third frontal convolution was frequently uninvolved in the presence of motor disturbances of language.

The battle was thus begun, and violent criticisms were heard on both sides. Dejerine (1908), on the basis of further and more precise anatomic data,

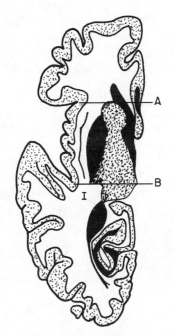

Marie's quadrilateral space (1926): lesions between A and B produce anarthria; lesions behind B cause true (Wernicke's) aphasia; lesions at I may cause Broca's aphasia (Wernicke's aphasia plus anarthria); lesions in front of A cause no true aphasia. Copyright 1960 by Masson & Co., Paris. Reproduced by permission.

argued that if lesions of Marie's quadrilateral space were associated with aphasic phenomena, it was only because such lesions disrupted the fibers descending from the anterior portion of the zone of language (frontal opercu- lum, foot and tip of F_3). Subsequently Marie and Foix (1917) admitted, despite Marie's earlier affirmations concerning the unity of aphasia, that a separate variety of aphasia, with a prominent disturbance in reading ability, resulted from a lesion of the angular gyrus.

Each localizationist who followed presented his own anatomic refinement to the argument (e.g., Henschen, 1926; Kleist, 1933; Nielsen, 1946). While providing more detail, and occasionally elaborating additional centers, espe- cially for aspects of visual language (i.e., reading and writing), these authors consistently located their centers within the general topographic region origi- nally outlined by Dejerine.

Even Goldstein (1948), the best known of the globalists, after first asserting the impossibility of localizing the functions of language, finally admitted its possibility. He described the existence of disorders of the instrumentalities of language, with specific defects of auditory, visual, and motor gestalten. These defects, which corresponded neuropsychologically to the specialized varieties of aphasia described by the classical authors, corresponded anatomically to the different cortical foci as well. Nonetheless, Goldstein affirmed that the capacity for inner speech, closely tied to the faculty for abstraction, remained dependent on "the central regions of the cortex."

In the mid-1960s, Geschwind (1965), reviving and reinforcing the anatom- ic conceptions of Wernicke and Dejerine, provided a compelling theoretical argument concerning the region of the angular gyrus as a critical anatomic development in the evolution of language. By means of its crucial location, abutting the association cortices of three sensory regions (auditory, visual,

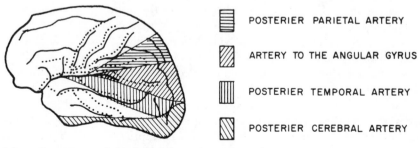

POSTERIER PARIETAL ARTERY

ARTERY TO THE ANGULAR GYRUS

POSTERIER TEMPORAL ARTERY

POSTERIER CEREBRAL ARTERY

Schematic representation of arterial supply to posterior sylvian regions (C. Foix, 1928). Copyright 1960 by Masson & Co. Paris. Reproduced by permission.

and somesthetic), and by virtue of its dense polysynaptic connections, the angular gyrus region was able to foster the formation of corticocortical, non-limbic, cross-modal associations necessary for certain aspects of human language.

Neurological Diseases and Aphasia

The study of patients with vascular lesions has played a major role in the elaboration of classical aphasiological doctrine. Geschwind (1970b) contends that the best type of pathological material for the study of aphasia comes from discrete vascular lesions that have destroyed circumscribed cerebral areas. Nonetheless, whereas vascular lesions are common, patients with isolated lesions who have undergone detailed premortem neuropsychological evaluation and whose brains have been subjected to detailed postmortem study are not common.

The work of Dejerine and his school was based primarily on the anatomic study of vascular lesions. Special mention, in this regard, should be given to Foix (1928), whose systematic study of the different vascular territories of the brain led to the establishment of a map of these territories of aphasia and of the clinical syndromes that depend on the destruction of these territories. A complete perisylvian infarction produced a dense Broca's aphasia; a superficial perisylvian infarction produced a milder form of Broca's aphasia; a deep sylvian lesion caused either Broca's aphasia or anarthria. Incomplete, superficial sylvian infarctions produced different patterns, depending on the location of the lesion: (1) A lesion in the anterior territory caused anarthria due to involvement of the pediculofrontal region, with almost constant involvement of the quadrilateral space; (2) a lesion in the posterior territory caused either a Wernicke's aphasia (large posterior infarction), or a milder Wernicke's aphasia with a prominent alexia (infarction of the parietal-angular gyrus region), or a Wernicke's aphasia (infarction of the temporal-angular gyrus region). Infarction in the distribution of the posterior cerebral artery, either complete or in its posterior portion, produced alexia.

In a detailed anatomoclinical correlational study Critchley (1930) described the existence of aphasia and dysarthric disorders, usually transitory, resulting from thrombosis of the anterior cerebral artery of of the dominant hemisphere.

Head injuries, from war wounds and accidents, have provided large numbers of patients for neuropsychological study. Although the anatomic localization of the lesions in these cases could only be approximate, their great, and ever-increasing, number and ready availability have prompted many large-scale statistical studies. Following World War I, Marie and Foix (1917) reported their observations. They distinguished four anatomoclinical forms of posttraumatic aphasia: temporal aphasia (pure Wernicke's aphasia); aphasia of the supramarginal gyrus (moderate, but global, aphasia); aphasia of the angular gyrus (moderate Wernicke's aphasia with prominent alexia); and various minor aphasic syndromes due to superficial lesions or lesions marginal to the zone of language.

World War II was followed in its turn by several major studies. Schiller (1947) studied 46 brain-damaged, aphasic soldiers with penetrating missile wounds and formulated the following conclusions. Frontal lesions produced mainly disorders in the initiation of speech, a slowing of speech once started, impairment of articulation, and impairment of vocal inflection. Temporal lesions disturbed the comprehension of spoken language and caused paraphasias, jargon, and agrammatism. Posterior temporal and temporoparietal lesions affected reading especially. With parietal lesions, perseverative phenomena and even stuttering were frequent, as well as distortions of words and sentences. As for amnesic aphasia, Schiller concluded that there was no single site responsible, the syndrome never appearing in a pure form isolated from other aphasic symptoms. In addition to the observations with localizing value, Schiller noted that the severity and extent of intellectual deficits were proportional to the amount of tissue destroyed.

Conrad (1947, 1949) studied 216 brain-damaged aphasic soldiers. His findings are consistent with those of other authors. A specific addition was his observation that pure motor aphasia and Broca's aphasia did not result from different lesions but rather resulted from the severity of the lesion in the anterior language zone.

Luria based his anatomolinguistic classification of 1947 on studies of aphasics with war-induced head injuries. He divided subjects into the following groups: aphasia with phonemic disintegration due to lesions in the posterior portion of the temporal lobe, aphasia with deficits in the ability to communicate relations (space, time, logicogrammatical forms) due to parieto-occipital lesions, aphasia with loss of capacity to synthesize successive elements in a continuous series due to frontotemporal lesions, and dynamic aphasia due to frontal lesions. Additional studies by Alajouanine et al (1957) and Russell and Espir (1961) present similar conclusions, although with minor variations in the names and proposed mechanisms of the syndromes.

In particular the different authors confirm the classical anatomy of the zone of language while, at the same time, emphasizing the importance of the role of the volume of brain tissue destroyed with respect to the intensity, persistence, and more or less global character of the language disorder. All of these studies with posttraumatic aphasia have in common the explicit or implicit tendency to deny any localizing value to the problem of disorders of naming.

Brain tumors producing language defects have also been a source of patient material for neuropsychological study. In such studies most authors have made allowance for the lack of precision of lesion boundaries, as well as for the behavioral defects due to increased intracranial pressure that may be added to the focal symptomatology. Of particular interest regarding the relationship of brain tumors to language pathology has been the commonly made observation that word-finding difficulty is frequently the presenting system regardless of the localization of the tumor, and this difficulty may remain in isolated fashion for a considerable period of time. According to Botez (1962) the naming disorder associated with brain tumors may be of two types: one he calls anomia, the other, amnesic aphasia. In anomia a patient cannot find the name of an object on confrontation, but he does not try to substitute any other word; he simply does not respond. For Botez anomia may be found in the early stages of any left hemispheric tumor, but its persistence in isolated form often suggests the presence of a frontal lobe tumor because of inability to initiate action for speech. In true amnestic aphasia the patient attempts to give a verbal description of the object by reference to its usage. This variety, especially in the early stages, is thought to have localizing value (temporal or temporoparieto-occipital regions).

Hécaen and Angelergues (1964) presented a quantitative analysis of the correlations between signs of aphasia and lesion localization in 214 right-handed patients with left hemispheric lesions of diverse etiologies, principally tumors or trauma. An initial observation was that the volume of the lesion, as well as the location, played a major role in producing aphasic symptoms; the greater the lesion volume, the more severe the symptoms. The several symptom patterns of language disorganization varied according to lesion localization. No purely motor aphasic syndromes were found, although rolandic lesions seemed particularly responsible for articulatory disorders. Lesions affecting the temporal or parietal lobes caused various symptom clusters within the general category of sensory aphasia. The relative degree of severity of agraphia or alexia varied with lesion localization: in temporo-occipital lesions, alexia predominated; in parieto-occipital lesions, agraphia was more marked than alexia. As for naming defects these were present regardless of lesion localization. Intensity of naming defect was increased if the lesion was large or if it involved the temporal lobe.

Cortical and Subcortical Stimulation and Destruction

The electrocortical stimulation studies of Penfield and Jasper (1954) and Penfield and Roberts (1959) have provided additional information concerning language disorders. By stimulating different cortical regions in awake subjects, these authors could provoke disturbances of vocalization, speech arrest, and even aphasic-like symptoms. The expressive disturbances were caused by stimulation of either hemisphere; the aphasic-like symptoms (e.g., word-finding difficulty) were found only following stimulations in the dominant hemisphere. Three specific cortical regions were associated with speech and language: (1) inferior frontal region corresponding to Broca's area, (2) the temporoparietal region, and (3) the supplementary motor zone.

Penfield and Roberts (1959) performed cortical excisions and observed the effects on language. Although ablation of many different cortical regions was done, provoking signs similar to those seen with cortical stimulation, the speech and language defects were most striking if the lesions were made in the same three cortical regions found to be important in stimulation studies. The defects were never permanent, however, and the authors concluded that aphasia persists in a permanent manner only when the tissue remaining after the operation functions abnormally.

The surgical procedure of deep subcortical (usually thalamic) destruction of tissue as a treatment for Parkinson's disease has led to an analysis of speech and language defects due to such lesions. Already in 1959, on the basis of their cortical stimulation and ablation studies, Penfield and Roberts had

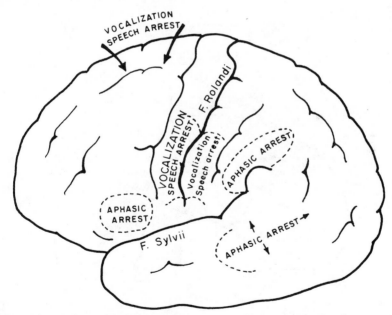

Summary of areas in the dominant hemisphere in which electrocortical stimulation may interfere with speech, or produce vocalization (Penfield and Rasmussen, 1950). Copyright 1950 by MacMillan, New York. Reproduced by permission.

proposed that the three cortical regions responsible for speech and language were themselves dependent on specific projections from different segments of the thalamus. Guiot et al (1961), Hassler (1966), and van Buren (1963) have observed arrest or acceleration of speech and confusion associated with thalamic, caudate, or pallidal stimulation. These speech disorders have not, however, involved phonemic organization but have been disruptions of the rhythm or spontaneous initiation of verbal emission. More convincing has been the work of Ojemann et al (1968a,b), who found anomia, paraphasia, and verbal memory disturbance following stimulation of the left pulvinar and posterocentromedian portion of the ventrolateral nucleus. No such defects were found with stimulation of the right pulvinar or other portions of the thalamus. Also of interest are the subcortical stimulation studies of Fedio and van Buren (1975). Stimulation in the left pulvinar caused transient aphasia and a retrograde loss of recent memory for verbal material. Comparable stimulation in the right pulvinar caused no verbal defect.

These results raise the index of suspicion concerning the possibility that subcortical stimulation or damage can cause aphasic symptomatology. Whether true, permanent aphasic syndromes result from purely subcortical lesions is a subject of controversy. On the one hand are the studies against the

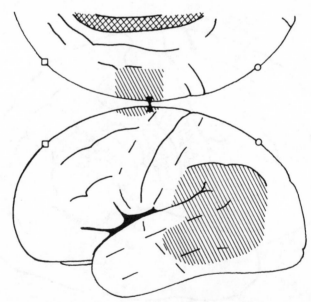

Summary of cortical stimulation studies outlining the speech areas of the dominant hemisphere (Penfield and Roberts, 1959). Copyright 1959 by Princeton University Press, Princeton. Reproduced by permission.

possibility. For example, Dubois et al (1966), in a neurolinguistic analysis of the language of 20 Parkinsonians before and after stereotaxic surgery, found no disruption of the linguistic code. Van Buren (1975) reviewed the anatomo-clinical evidence regarding the thalamic role in speech and language and advised caution in assigning to the dominant thalamus more than a minor role in the total speech mechanism.

On the other hand are the case reports and statistical studies in favor of the possibility. For example, Mohr et al (1975) described the behavioral effects of left thalamic hemorrhage in a total of six cases and concluded that a peculiar state of logorrheic paraphasia resembling delirium was sufficiently distinctive to warrant isolation as a language disorder separate from traditional aphasic syndromes. Psychometric studies of patients with surgically induced thalamic lesions have indicated that thalamic nuclei, especially ventrolateral and pulvinar, may play a role in verbal functions (e.g., Riklan, Levita et al, 1969a,b; Riklan and Cooper, 1975).

The psychometric studies have demonstrated defects primarily in fluency (for which the left thalamus tends to be dominant). It is known that thalamic nuclei participate in alerting or arousal aspects of verbal and nonverbal behavior. It may be the alerting feature that influences psychometric results, and not linguistic features. This observation does not deny the obvious and significant interrelation between thalamic structures and specific cortical sensorimotor regions that underlie verbal behavior. Thalamic lesions could disrupt this interrelationship and produce aphasic signs. In such a case one might expect the language dysfunction to be transitory, for the cortical structures remaining intact could eventually readjust to the new intracerebral situation.

Summary—The Anatomy of Language

The wide variety of clinical, anatomopathological, and electrophysiological studies of the past 75 years seems to confirm, with minor exceptions and qualifications, the earlier work of Dejerine. It is reasonable to talk about a "zone of language" present in the dominant hemisphere, situated in the perisylvian region, excluding the frontal and occipital poles and the superior and inferior regions of the hemisphere, and to which must be added the supplementary motor zone. However, rather than refer to the limited and rigid concept of a cortical "center" for behavioral function, one should consider the concept of functional zones. A central zone, the classical Wernicke's area, may be essential to all modalities of language. Related to this central zone, a certain number of functional poles may be defined: an anterior motor pole, situated in the classical Broca's region, but perhaps extending to the postcentral rolandic region as well; a posterior parieto-occipital pole concerned with reading and writing; and a superior pole (parietal) concerned with gestural activity.

Both lesion volume and lesion localization influence language. In addition, inherent in the concept of functional zones is the belief that a supple and dynamic organization of activity underlies the language function for which each zone is preferentially responsible and thus allows for the often considerable recovery of function seen following aphasia-producing lesions.

THE APHASIAS—DISORDERS OF SPOKEN LANGUAGE

"Expressive" Aphasia

Pure Motor Aphasia

The "pure" aphasias have in common the feature of affecting only a single input or output modality while leaving language intact in all associated modalities. Pure aphasias are quite rare (Goodglass and Kaplan, 1972). Pure motor aphasia, occasionally called subcortical motor aphasia or aphemia, is an isolated disorder of articulation in which auditory comprehension, reading, and writing are intact. In the early stages of this syndrome the patient may be unable to produce any speech sounds, although the capacity for phonation may be preserved.

Dejerine (1914), while accepting the existence of the syndrome, denied that it had a single anatomic correlate, since the syndrome could be found following cortical (foot of F_3) and subcortical lesions. Hécaen and Consoli (1973) studied 19 subjects with anatomically verified lesions limited to Broca's area. Within this group, a subgroup with lesions restricted to the cortical surface had a cluster of signs that corresponded to pure motor aphasia: decreased verbal fluency and dysprosody (slowness, dysrhythmia, and syllabication), even in the absence of dysarthric deformations. Reading, writing, and auditory comprehension were within normal limits, although spelling was impaired. When the lesions extended beyond the cortical surface, disorders of reading, writing, and auditory comprehension were seen.

Disorders of Phonemic Production

The neurolinguistic syndrome described here corresponds to the classical term *motor aphasia*, and to the terms *anarthria* of Pierre Marie (1926); *verbal aphasia* of Head (1926); *expressive aphasia* of Weisenburg and McBride (1935); *syndrome of phonetic disintegration* of Alajouanine, Ombredane, and Durand (1939); *efferent motor aphasia* of Luria (1966); and *nonfluent aphasia* of Benson and Geschwind (1972). In addition to the phonemic disturbance this syndrome is associated with agraphia, although the severity of the written disorder does not necessarily parallel that of the spoken.

In the most severe forms language emission may be impossible. The patient, unable to verbalize, begins to gesticulate wildly to indicate the impossibility of speaking. This disorder is not infrequently associated with psychological depression (Benson, 1973), since the patient is aware of his defect. Occasionally the patient emits an unintelligible grunt or groan. In a modification of this severe variety the patient is able to produce only a limited range of meaningless phonemes or syllables, referred to as verbal stereotypies. Of particular interest is that this limited, meaningless phonemic production may often be fluent. Thus Broca's patient had the syllables "Tan, Tan" at his disposal, and no others. Occasionally these sounds may be strung together with meaningful modulation or intonation, rarely even with rhythm patterns representing normal sentence syntax.

With less severe involvement the patient may use a reduced verbal stock; here the production is consistently nonfluent (Benson, 1966; Geschwind, 1972a) and effortful. The lexical items contain multiple deformations, called phonemic paraphasias, that correspond to disorders based in the phonetic structure of the item.

In general, prosody, that is, expressive intonation, rhythm, and accent, is not impaired, although Monrad-Krohn (1947) has called attention to the occurrence of dysprosody in motor aphasia, dysprosody occasionally being the only residual feature of the disorder. This perturbation of prosodic elements of speech may confer a "foreign accent" quality. The dysprosody may also be manifest simply by a slowing of speech with scanning whereby each utterance is pronounced syllable by syllable, each syllable representing an autonomous articulation. Spectrographic and clinical analysis (Marcie, 1972) suggest that dysprosody may result from an overcorrection of the difficulties of phonemic production by means of auditory and/or kinesthetic feedback. Thus it would seem unlikely that simple "cortical dysarthria" (Bay, 1952) is responsible for the disorder; the pattern is more consistent with a defective phonemic programming.

Naming of objects to confrontation is often nil. Comprehension of spoken language may be severely impaired in the earliest stages of this syndrome but usually recovers rapidly, often to nearly normal. In the pure varieties of this syndrome, reading comprehension is not disturbed, although the ability to read aloud is defective.

By contrast spontaneous writing is almost always impaired, with manifestations of agrammatism and spelling errors with literal paraphasias (paragraphias). This agraphia is also seen on writing to dictation, although the ability to copy is preserved. Spelling is severely disturbed.

Singing of melodies is generally well preserved. The preservation of melodic intonation has given rise to new programs of therapy (Albert et al 1973b, Sparks et al, 1974).

In addition to disorders of language, defective calculating ability is also frequently seen. The degree to which this syndrome is accompanied by buccofacial apraxia has been diversely commented on by various authors (Johns and Darley, 1970; Goodglass and Kaplan, 1972). We believe apraxia to be a common, although not obligatory, accompaniment. The evolution of buccofacial apraxia is not necessarily parallel to that of other, more general apraxia disturbances. From a general neurological point of view right hemiplegia or right brachial monoplegia with facial involvement is the rule, at least at the onset. Sensory disorders on the right half of the body are not infrequently seen.

This variety of aphasia is thus characterized by disturbance of spoken and written expression. To speak of a disorder of phonemic production presupposes the acceptance of a linguistic taxonomy in which the structural level of phonemes is distinguished from other levels. Two models of grammar must also be implicit: operations for phonemic emission and reception are separable. These distinctions are clinically demonstrable, since patients with this syndrome are able to provide adequate morphemic transformations, while phoneme production remains disturbed. Such distinction between phonemes and morphemes may also be demonstrated in these patients by their differential abilities with monosyllabic versus polysyllabic words on one hand, and with nonsense words versus meaningful words on the other. The length of the phonetic program is significant: monosyllabic words are better produced than disyllabic, independently of the phonetic composition; nonsense words are better produced than meaningful words of the same length. In either test the length of the item or the complexity of the new articulations is the critical factor.

It is possible to analyze the distribution of errors according to distinctive features (in terms of articulatory points). Cohen et al (1963) have found preservation of vocalic systems with deficits most prominent on fricatives and liquids, less on occlusives; with perturbations of consonant groups and modifications of vowel formants by consonant transitions; with phenomena of vocalic or consonant—even syllable—anticipation; and with perservation. These authors concluded that the basic phonological system was preserved, although the distribution of errors was variable. Shankweiler and Harris (1966) analyzed the phonemic errors of five subjects with this clinical syndrome and confirmed these observations. They noted a variability in substitutive errors and the absence of a systematic error pattern referring to articulatory locus. These observations led to the conclusion that the mechanism underlying the defect could not be muscle paresis or spasticity; rather there must be a disorganization of the processer by which phonological units are encoded. Thus motor aphasia could not be considered a form of subcortical dysarthria (Marie, 1926) or cortical dysarthria (Bay, 1952).

Darley and his colleagues have attempted to describe and define the nature of the language output disorders seen in motor aphasia (Darley et al, 1968; Darley et al, 1969a,b; Johns and Darley, 1970; Trost and Canter, 1974) and in other neurological states (Darley, 1975). These authors indicate that disturbances of motor speech programming are commonly observed in patients with motor aphasia and that these articulatory problems are distinct from those based on defective neuromotor projection systems (dysarthria) and from those due to sensory or perceptual impairment. Admitting the existence of terminological controversy, these authors call the defect "apraxia of speech" and have described the distinctive characteristics of this syndrome (see especially Johns and Darley, 1970). In particular the authors note the presence of alterations of volitional articulation manifested by variability of phoneme production; anticipatory errors; unrelated and additive substitutions, repetitions, and blocks; *conduite d'approche;* and dysprosody.

As for the disturbance of written expression a number of features are discernible (Hécaen et al, 1963; Hécaen, 1972a). Letter production itself is rarely more than minimally impaired. However, at the level of morphemes, literal paragraphias are almost constant. These consist of inversions of letter positions, additions, omissions, substitutions, and, less frequently, incomplete words. Writing is often reduced to isolated words. When sentences are completed, a striking absence of grammatical-function words is noted. This form of agraphia is characterized by three main features: (1) copying ability is almost always preserved; (2) single and multiple digits are generally well written; (3) writing of meaningful items to dictation is better than writing of nonsense words.

Disorders of Syntactic Production: Agrammatism

The symptoms and signs manifested in this condition are an extension and variation of the previously described syndrome. The psycholinguistic aspects of agrammatism have been extensively studied by Goodglass (1958–1974) and others (Pick, 1913; Isserlin, 1922; Cohen and Hécaen, 1965). The essential clinical features are seen in the effortful production of isolated, substantive words, with relative absence of grammatical-function words. Phonemic paraphasias, while present, are less prominent, usually appearing more in repetition tasks than in spontaneous discourse.

The defects of agrammatism are situated at the level of the immediate constituents of a sentence—noun phrase and verb phrase. Contrasts between syntactic variants are suppressed. In this manner agrammatism differs from that variety of motor aphasia in which the deficit focuses principally on phonetic productions, since the constituent morphemes may be produced without error in spontaneous speech (Cohen et al, 1963). As with other motor aphasics, running speech is nonfluent; however, for the preserved elements of speech, expressive intonation and accent may be maintained.

For Hécaen (1972b) the features of agrammatism may be grouped into two major categories: the impoverishment of utilizable syntactic rules and the preservation of lexemes but with the reduction of lexical stock. The linguistic economy of agrammatism is manifested by a general reduction of speech output with a specific reduction in grammatical-function words.

For Goodglass and Geschwind (1976) disturbances of grammar and syntax also fall into two clinically distinctive categories, but these are defined differently from those above. One involves the loss of relational and inflectional terms and fragmentation of grammatical structure. The other consists of confusions of inflectional and other small grammatical terms and the disruption of syntax by means of semantically anomalous juxtapositions.

In 1956 Jakobson attempted a theoretical interpretation of agrammatism. He cited three major characteristics: reduction in sentence variety, loss of ties of grammatical coordination and subordination, and reduction of words endowed with purely grammatical functions.

Tissot, Mounin, and Lhermitte (1973) provided a detailed analysis of agrammatism based on a study of linguistic performance of 19 subjects with this form of syntactic disorder. The analysis was based primarily on Martinet's principles of functional linguistics. Results obtained from these agrammatic subjects were compared with results on similar tests from a group of subjects with sensory aphasia.

The authors, rejecting prior interpretations of the syndrome of agrammatism, emphasized its unity, defining the basic problem as an inability to dominate grammar. Thus one could understand agrammatism as a "syndrome of grammatic disintegration," in contrast to the "syndrome of phonetic disintegration" of motor aphasics. Patients with the syndrome of grammatical disintegration have reduction of language as a necessary condition and can be divided into three subgroups: (1) agrammatism with a morphological predominance, (2) agrammatism without major morphological disturbance but with marked syntactic defects, and (3) pseudoagrammatism with dysprosody.

The authors start their descriptions of linguistic abnormalities by referring to the theoretical descriptions of normal syntax provided by Martinet. They conclude, however, by referring to a model of transformational grammar. In essence they consider that the two true forms of agrammatism they have discerned reflect the relative independence of morphological and syntactic mechanisms. In the form of agrammatism with relative sparing of morphology, the syntactic disorder is a manifestation of deep-structure abnormality. In the form of agrammatism in which syntax is relatively spared, technical aspects of transformation, and in particular those dependent on morphology, are defective; these features relate more to surface structure.

In a series of psycholinguistic studies on the grammar of aphasics Goodglass (1973) observed a similarity of aphasic performance irrespective of clinical type. These results were analogous to those found by Blumstein (1973) on the phonological level. Goodglass and Blumstein (1973) suggested that the hierarchy of agrammatical errors revealed with structured psycholinguistic testing of aphasics may not reflect a purely linguistic disturbance. Performance factors such as sentence length, word frequency, and especially stress were found to contribute significantly to the patients' apparent grammatical defect. They concluded that linguistic impairments in aphasia cannot be explained exclusively by reference to linguistic theories of derivational or transformational complexity but must be considered in terms of a performance model. Zurif and his collaborators (Zurif et al, 1972, 1975) have pursued this issue and have demonstrated that the agrammatic subject has impaired "performance." They conclude from this that agrammatism is not simply an economizing measure to circumvent articulatory problems; rather it reflects a language limitation.

Disorders of Sequential Programming: Conduction Aphasia

Wernicke postulated, without proving, the existence of a clinical aphasic syndrome subsequently called conduction aphasia (Konorski, 1967; Hécaen et al, 1956; Geschwind, 1965), central aphasia (Goldstein, 1919, 1948; Stengel and Lodge-Patch, 1955), and afferent motor aphasia (Luria, 1966). Although a sufficient number of clinical observations has been reported to permit acceptance of the syndrome as a clinical entity (Benson et al, 1973), for some authors the syndrome represents a fortuitous association of symptoms or a stage in regression from sensory aphasia (Liepmann and Pappenheim, 1915; Kleist, 1916, 1933). The clinical features of the syndrome include disturbance of repetition ability, phonemic paraphasias, impaired ability to read aloud, disorders of writing, and defective spelling, all in the presence of preserved comprehension of written and spoken language. Often the syndrome appears in the process of recovery from sensory aphasia; occasionally it appears in isolated fashion. Not uncommon in frequency when due to vascular etiology, it has been found to occur in 12% of all cases of aphasia seen on a large aphasia service (Albert, unpublished data).

Clinical evaluation further indicates that paraphasias are often determined by telescoping of words, plus paraphonia (confusions of words phonetically close). The patient, fully aware of his deficits, attempts to correct them by successive approximations (conduite d'approche). Serial speech, days, months, alphabet, and so forth, by contrast, are often well produced, especially for the early portion of the series. No articulatory disturbances are seen in phoneme production. Length of words or sentences plays a definite role in the repetition disorder; the longer the word or sentence, the more likely the repetition defect.

For some authors (Howes and Green, 1972) naming disorders are frequently associated. For others (Hécaen, 1972b) naming disorders may be seen early in the course of the syndrome but pass more or less quickly. Phonemic discrimination and verbal comprehension are not impaired. Although reading comprehension is within normal limits, reading aloud is severely impaired, with frequent paralexias, especially for longer or less well-known words. Spontaneous writing to command or to dictation is always perturbed, but copying ability may be normal. Of interest is the fact that these patients may be able to transpose block letters to script in a normal manner.

Associated with the language disorders are other defects: acalculia, inability to reproduce heard rhythms, and asomatagnosias (especially finger agnosia). Constructional or indeomotor apraxia may also be seen. Sensory or motor defects are not prominent features of the syndrome.

A neurolinguistic analysis of six pure cases of conduction aphasia by Dubois et al (1964) has provided a basis for understanding the structural basis of this syndrome. The distinctive feature was found to be a persistent tendency to transpose or substitute phonemes. The syndrome is exclusively an expressive aphasia that affects the emissive (encoding) system. The various tasks testing the decoding of linguistic messages were well performed. However, even in their most severe form, disturbances of output were different from those observed in motor aphasics. In motor (anterior) aphasia, output defects involve the second articulation (the phonemic level in Martinet's terms); in conduction aphasia, defects involve the first articulation (the morphemic level in Martinet's terms). Spontaneous expression is characterized by disturbances at the level of syntagm or syntagmatic combination, and not at the level of phonetic programming. The syndrome is caused by a disorganized execution of the encoding program, and this disorder in verbal programming depends on the information load faced by the speaker at each instant in his performance. Errors appear in the spoken chain at the very point at which sudden variations in the amount of information occur. One sees a pathological exaggeration of the pausal phenomena documented in normal readers by Goldman-Eisler (1961a). It may be possible, nonetheless, that, in addition to being an expressive aphasia, the syndrome involves a delay of self-regulation through auditory feedback, at least in the early stages.

Agraphia is constant in conduction aphasia but is never total. In particular, individual letters and numbers are well preserved, beyond the ability to write the name and address. Ability to copy is also intact, as well as the ability to transpose from block print to script. Spelling, on the other hand, is always impaired, both for recognition of orally spelled words and for spelling aloud.

Dubois et al (1964) concluded that the neurolinguistic features are sufficiently distinctive to warrant considering this an autonomous syndrome, representing neither a variant of the expressive aphasic syndrome, which we have called "disorder of phonemic production," nor a regressive stage of sensory aphasia. However, the isolation of a single basic difficulty (disturbance of repetition, of expression, or of auditory control over output; phonemic paraphasias; or difficulty with inner speech) fails to take into account the totality of the phenomena. They consider this to be a form of disorder in which relationships between elements are more important than the elements themselves.

Warrington and her collaborators (1969, 1970, 1971) in a series of studies presented a different point of view. They provided evidence that auditory-verbal short-term memory could be selectively impaired, that there is a correlation between this selective deficit and lesions of the dominant angular and supramarginal gyri, and that their three patients with these lesions and memory defects resembled other patients who had been diagnosed as having conduction aphasia. In particular they had severe impairment of repetition, together with intact comprehension. These results challenge the conceptions of Dubois, Hécaen, et al (1964).

Faced with these contradictions, Tzortzis and Albert (1974) studied the question: is there a single neuropsychological defect causing the impairment of repetition seen in conduction aphasia, and, if so, is this defect a selective deficit in auditory-verbal short-term memory or a deficit in verbal sequential programming? Short-term memory was evaluated in three patients with conduction aphasia. Even though these patients could reproduce the items presented, they could not recall the correct order of the items. It was concluded that the disorder underlying the repetition defect in these three patients with conduction aphasia was an impairment of their memory for sequences. An additional conclusion was, however, that there is more than one neuropsychological defect that can underlie impaired repetition following brain damage.

This latter conclusion was reinforced by results of another study on the repetition defect in conduction aphasia. Strub and Gardner (1974) studied a single patient in detail and determined that the patient's errors in repetition were primarily paraphasic and sequential. They observed that, although his defect could be explained on a linguistic basis, mnemonic factors could not be absolutely ruled out.

Amnesic Aphasias—Disorders of Morpheme Selection

Nonmodality-Specific Forms

Probably all aphasics have a reduced stock of words available for speech, or a reduced access to a preserved stock, or a reduced access to a reduced stock (Schuell and Jenkins, 1959; Goodglass and Geschwind, 1976). Thus, naming deficit and word-finding disturbance are regular features of the aphasic syndromes, and various theories have been proposed to account for the several different varieties of naming disorder observed clinically (cf. reviews of the subject by Geschwind, 1967b; Luria, 1973).

However, one group of aphasic subjects seems to be isolable from other groups by manifesting a selective loss of lexical items, in the presence of fluent articulation, preserved grammar, and intact comprehension. This selective impairment is called anomia, and the syndrome within which this impairment is found is called anomic, amnestic, or amnesic aphasia (also called "nominal" aphasia by Head, 1926; "semantic" aphasia by Wepman, 1961).

Pitres first claimed clinical autonomy for this syndrome in 1898, asserting the basic defect to be a simple forgetting of words. Dejerine (1914), while accepting the existence of word-finding difficulty, felt that an isolated anomic syndrome was quite rare. For him an anomic syndrome was more usual as the beginning stage or the end of recovery stage of motor or sensory aphasia. Marie (1926) recognized the syndrome only as a residual defect of Wernicke's aphasia. But no general review of aphasia since Pitres has failed to take note of the syndrome in one manner or another.

Clinically one sees rambling but uninformative and circumlocutory speech. Discourse, while essentially fluent, may be punctuated by pauses during which the patient attempts to find the correct word. Indefinite nouns and verbs take the place of the precisely correct lexical item desired and may be used repetitively. Periphrases, descriptions of a word rather than the word itself, and even explanatory gestures substitute for the target word. Tests of naming demonstrate a hierarchy of difficulty, nouns being most severely impaired, and verbs and adjectives next.

An essential question to be resolved is whether the deficit in morpheme selection is a single neuropsychological deficit, regardless of the clinical context in which it appears, or whether it represents different defects with a common clinical manifestation. For Goldstein (1948) true amnesic aphasia results from an underlying defect in abstract attitude, and this syndrome should be distinguished from other disorders in which word-finding defect is present. As causes for these other disorders of word-finding ability one would find either a deficit of the instrumentalities of language or a general disorder of memory. True amnesic aphasia, on the other hand, translates a basic loss of orientation to words as symbols that stand for concepts. These patients have an associated difficulty in understanding abstract concepts and fail on tasks that require sorting by category. Yamadori and Albert (1973) provided a striking example of a patient who had a nonmodality-specific anomia coupled with a comprehension defect limited to words in specific semantic categories. By demonstrating that semantic categories may have an independent existence in the process of decoding for meaning, these authors provided, at the same time, both partial support and partial refutation of Goldstein's hypothesis.

Neurolinguistic studies are beginning to clarify the picture of naming disorders. Newcombe, Oldfield, and Wingfield (1964) demonstrated that word frequency is a significant variable. This result was similar to that of Wepman et al (1956), who had earlier found an overuse of high-frequency words, regardless of grammatical class, in the speech of aphasics. On the other hand, for Fraisse et al (1962) familiarity of a word (because of daily contact with certain objects) played as great a role as word frequency.

Ramier (1972b) studied naming in 83 subjects with left hemispheric lesions, contrasting them with a large series of control subjects. She used an extensive battery of naming tests and evaluated responses according to the typology established by Goldblum (1972a) in a similar, previous study. This typology considered naming responses with reference to a large number of linguistic variables.

From both statistical and clinical evidence Ramier was able to demonstrate the existence of a true, pure syndrome of amnesic aphasia. The syndrome was rare (3 cases out of 83) and was characterized by a unity or similarity of defective naming performances, regardless of the type of stimulus material or the modality of presentation, while all other aspects of verbal behavior were entirely normal.

The types of errors were for the most part failures to respond, or claims of not knowing, or forms of verbal predication. When verbal substitutions were made, they were always semantically close to the target. Phonological cuing facilitated response. Word-finding deficits in spontaneous speech were not necessarily linked to the naming disorder. Recovery in these pure forms of amnesic aphasia was always rapid. Lesions were located in the temporal lobe in all three.

Other studies have provided evidence that word-finding ability may be a function of the semantic category of the word involved (Yamadori and Albert, 1973; Goodglass and Geschwind, 1976). Goodglass et al (1966) examined the order of difficulty of naming visual stimuli in several different semantic categories in several aphasic groups. Objects were most often the hardest category to name and letters the easiest. In auditory comprehension of spoken names, however, this relationship was reversed, a finding that eliminated the word-frequency concept as the sole explanation of the findings.

Also to be considered in the process of naming is the amount of information available in the sensory input. For the visual modality (Bisiach, 1966) and for the tactile modality (North, 1971), reduction of total information available (e.g., by obscuring the drawing of an object with extraneous lines) reduced the ability of aphasics to name the objects, even though recognition by multiple choice was intact.

Modality-Specific Forms

Naming difficulty may be limited to stimuli presented in a single sensory modality while being preserved for stimuli presented in other modalities. Thus Freund (1888) described a case of optic aphasia in which the naming disorder appeared with stimuli in the visual modality but not with stimuli in the auditory modality. Geschwind and Kaplan (1962) demonstrated modality-specific tactile aphasia in the left hand of a patient with callosal transection. After studying the dissociation of visual and tactile naming in a group of aphasics, Spreen et al (1966) concluded that, although word-finding difficulty is ordinarily nonmodality specific, some aphasic patients have a clear dissociation of naming ability depending on the modality of stimulus presentation.

Explanation of the syndrome of optic aphasia has been based on two anatomic lesions, one being a left occipital lesion producing a right homonymous hemianopia, the other a lesion of the splenium of the corpus callosum. The naming disorder would result from a disconnection of the right occipital lobe—the only region capable of receiving visual inputs—from the language centers in the left hemisphere (Geschwind, 1965). As with optic aphasia, tactile aphasia also represents a callosal disconnection syndrome.

A highly demonstrative case of optic aphasia was reported by Lhermitte and Beauvois (1973). Naming disorders were limited to stimuli presented in the visual modality. Evocation of names (word finding) in response to oral description of an item was preserved. This subject had a coexistent agnosic alexia and an agnosia for colors. The authors believed that the term *visuoverbal disconnection* both described the syndrome and provided an adequate explanation for its cause. Error analysis revealed that semantic errors predominated; that is, the subject, in misnaming items presented visually, used the name of a word in the same semantic field as the target item. The visual stimulus no longer evoked the specifically correct name but rather a more diffuse pattern sharing the diverse traits characteristic of the target. If structural complexity of a pictured object was reduced, for example, errors diminished. Lhermitte and Beauvois concluded that, wherever the lesion might be (corpus callosum, left occipital lobe, temporo-occipital region), it prevented a visual message that had already been processed in the visual system from reaching the zone of language. They do not deny, however, the possibility that visuoperceptual deficits might play some role.

Not all authors have accepted the explanation of visuoverbal disconnection to account for optic aphasia. Occasional observations of modality-specific aphasias associated with temporal lobe lesions permit one to conclude that callosal disconnection cannot be the only explanation for all cases of this syndrome.

Sensory Aphasias

General Clinical Features

Sensory aphasia (also called syntactic aphasia by Head, 1926; receptive aphasia by Weisenburg and McBride, 1935; acoustic aphasia by Luria, 1966; and Wernicke's aphasia) is characterized primarily by a disorder in verbal reception and comprehension, although other associated defects are the rule. Since the original descriptions by Bastian (1869) and Wernicke (1874) the clinical features have been frequently commented on. Spontaneous speech output is fluent, or indeed hyperfluent, with an increased rate of words per minute and an inability to bring a sentence to a close ("press of speech"). Intonation pattern and facial and gestural expression remain normal, even while the content of the utterance is incomprehensible. This incomprehensibility of verbal output is due, not to a deformation of the word in its motor production (as in motor aphasia), but rather to a substitution of an incorrect lexical item for a correct one (paraphasia), without the patient himself being aware of this substitution. Multiple paraphasias added to the circumlocutory speech due to word-finding difficulty result in a verbal output, called jargon-aphasia, that permits of virtually no meaningful communication. Repetition is impaired but to varying degrees, depending on the type of sensory aphasia. Naming and word finding are defective.

Comprehension defect, the hallmark of the syndrome, may vary from mild to total and is seen for both spoken and written language. Evaluation of auditory comprehension in terms of the linguistic level at which the comprehension defect occurs—phonemic, semantic, syntactic—has permitted a more refined delineation of separable syndromes within the general category of the sensory aphasias.

A number of studies have provided convincing evidence that the disorder of comprehension, previously considered to be global and unitary, can be dissociated. The Sentence Ordering Test of von Stockert (1972) was one of the early studies suggesting this dissociation. The test requires the subject to reconstitute a sentence that has been written onto a card, the card then being cut in several places, and the elements of the sentence being presented in a meaningless order. This test was presented to a patient with Broca's aphasia and to one with sensory aphasia with alexia. The alexic with impaired verbal comprehension had preserved knowledge of structural relations, since he could reconstruct the sentence grammatically but not semantically. The patient with Broca's aphasia without verbal comprehension defect was not better than the other subject. Consequently von Stockert suggested that these results indicated the possibility that lexical meaning and lexical structure could be dissociated in language and that these separate processes could be selectively disturbed in certain types of aphasia.

A different approach to the same problem by Zurif et al (1972) has provided additional support for the notion that one level of language (phonemic, morphemic, or semantic) can be selectively impaired in certain types of aphasia. The subject is required to demonstrate appreciation of syntactic relatedness of words in sentences. Qualitatively identical responses were obtained for verbal reception and verbal production performances by a group of agrammatic aphasics. The issue of "economy" as a verbal strategy in such patients was thus proved to be an insufficient explanation of the entire linguistic abnormality. Agrammatic subjects based their judgments on a hierarchical schema that permitted exclusion of nonessential elements (i.e., grammatical words) in the sentence. By contrast, control subjects relied more on syntactic markers in the surface structure of the sentence.

A similar dissociation within disorders of comprehension was found in a study by Kremin and Goldblum (1975). Subjects with unilateral right or left hemispheric lesions were asked to reconstitute cut-up sentences of two forms: either the sentences were complete (with all normal elements of surface structure), or they were telegraphic (with only lexical items). With both sentence forms, cut-up pieces of the sentence were displayed in a random horizontal array. Two groups of aphasics could be distinguished on the basis of distinctive performance patterns with the two sentence forms. The first group, composed of motor and mixed aphasics, had difficulty primarily with grammatical elements of the complete sentences but had no difficulty reconstituting the logical order of sentences limited to lexical items. The second group, composed of sensory and mixed aphasics, had opposite performances on the two sentence types. Their principal difficulty was with the correct ordering of lexical items; when they were given all surface structure elements, they could produce a syntactically correct sentence. Correlational analyses demonstrated two sets of correlations: (1) between syntactic-type deficits and disturbed word repetition and (2) between lexical-type deficits and disturbed object-naming ability.

Variations in the clinical pattern of comprehension defect from one sensory aphasic to the next led Hécaen and his colleagues (1968, 1969, 1972, 1974) to attempt a systematic evaluation of the various factors seen in sensory aphasia in large groups of subjects. A provisional series of studies has allowed a regrouping of the sensory aphasias into three main types, each with a set of distinctive characteristics but with a tendency for overlap among types. One subtype has word deafness as a major feature and probably represents a disorder of phonemic decoding. Another subtype results from an impairment in semantic comprehension. These two subtypes of sensory aphasia represent the clinical verification for the tentative suggestion of Yamadori and Albert (1973) that there may be a two-step mechanism in the process of the comprehension of spoken language: word-sound perception and word-meaning comprehension. Hécaen's third subtype results from a nonlinguistic attentional disorganization. These separate subtypes of sensory aphasia are further discussed below.

Reading aloud, by contrast with reading comprehension, is sometimes possible, although paralexias may be frequent. Writing of name, address, and some words or short phrases may be adequate; however, paragraphic errors are abundant. Longer phrases and sentences cannot be written. The writing disorder, in fact, seems to us to reflect precisely the character and intensity of the oral-language disorder. Copying ability, on the other hand, may be reasonably well preserved. Spelling is impaired.

Associated, nonlinguistic defects may often include ideomotor, ideational, and constructional apraxias; acalculia; visual recognition defects; and finger agnosia. These defects are not constant, however. General neurological examination may show nothing more than a right hemianopia or quadrantanopia.

Pure Word Deafness

Word deafness refers to an inability to identify the sounds of language, although hearing is intact and the ability to identify nonverbal meaningful sounds is preserved. The clinical picture is characterized by markedly impaired auditory comprehension of the sounds of letters and words; repetition is also defective. Spontaneous speech, spontaneous writing, reading, and naming are intact. Writing to dictation is impaired.

In its pure form the syndrome is exceedingly rare. Ordinarily it occurs as an evolutionary stage progressing toward or recovering from global sensory aphasia (Lichtheim, 1885; Dejerine and Serieux, 1897; Barrett, 1910; Zeigler, 1952; Klein and Harper, 1956; Gazzaniga et al, 1973). Emphasis should be placed on the following clinical observation. Pure word deafness is not necessarily associated with impaired ability to understand the meaning of heard nonverbal sounds. Dissociation of deficits of auditory perception may occur in which a patient has lost his ability to appreciate the significance of nonverbal sounds but can understand spoken language; the converse may also occur (e.g., Albert et al, 1973b; Albert and Bear, 1974).

From the point of view of anatomic localization two main groups appear. One relates the syndrome to a single, left hemispheric, subcortical lesion, especially involving T_1 (Shuster and Taterka, 1926; Hoff, 1961); the other speaks of bilateral, temporal, corticosubcortical lesions disconnecting the outputs of both primary auditory centers from an intact Wernicke's area (Hoff, 1961; Lhermitte et al, 1973a; Goodglass and Geschwind, 1976).

From a pathophysiological point of view Okada et al (1963–1964) demonstrated a defective identification of language sounds. Hécaen (1972a) underlined the importance of inattention to acoustic stimuli with indifference to words. Lhermitte et al (1973a) reported three cases of auditory agnosia of which two had anatomoclinical correlation. The recognition deficit in these cases involved words and verbal sounds, nonverbal meaningful sounds, and melodies. Language defects were primarily in auditory reception, although phonemic paraphasias and reduction of lexical stock were apparent. Auditory inattention was prominent, but audiometric analysis confirmed the absence of significant peripheral deafness. Psychoacoustic studies, especially in one of the three subjects (Chocholle et al, 1975), demonstrated the following impairments: fragility for brief sonoric stimuli, disturbed appreciation of sound rhythms, defective sound localization, augmentation of homolateral and contralateral masking effect, and differential frequency and intensity thresholds. By contrast, fusion thresholds were relatively spared. Albert and Bear (1974) studied a word-deaf patient whose defective comprehension of spoken language improved dramatically when the examiner spoke at an abnormally slow rate; that is, their patient had a rate-dependent linguistic processing defect limited to the auditory modality. They found impaired auditory temporal resolution to be a critical factor in the production of this syndrome.

Disorders of Phonemic Decoding

A quantitative analysis of a series of patients with sensory aphasia allowed Hécaen et al (1968), and Hécaen (1972b) to construct cliniconeuropsychological profiles of verbal performance. Two main groups were clearly delimited. One group had predominant features of word deafness (due, perhaps, to disorders of phonemic decoding), and the other group had predominant features of defective verbal semantic comprehension. Additional experimental studies have tended to confirm these observations (Goldblum and Albert, 1972).

The sensory aphasics with the predominance of features of word deafness had the following profile. Spontaneous speech output, while logorrheic and paraphasic, nevertheless maintained a relative thematic coherence and a moderate degree of comprehensibility. Paraphasias were not prominent and were linked to context, as for example, by phonic approximations. Neologisms were more frequent than word substitutions.

On repetition tests these patients were equally bad on words and nonsense syllables, and the severity of repetition defect was high. Performance output was rarely related to the target stimulus, the dissociation between stimulus and response being striking.

Comprehension of spoken language was totally impossible, the patients being incapable of making any phonemic discriminations. Decoding of the written message was, however, always better than that of the spoken message. Reading aloud demonstrated abundant paralexias that increased with increasing length and complexity of text.

On tests of writing a dissociation was seen between spontaneous writing and writing to dictation. Though containing errors, spontaneous writing remained possible, and some thematic coherence was preserved. Of interest was that patients were usually aware of their errors in written expression, although they were unable to correct them. Writing to dictation was overrun with paragraphias. The ability to copy was ordinarily retained.

Disorganization of Semantic Relations

The sensory aphasics whose predominant clinical features were in a disturbance of verbal semantic comprehension had the following profile. Spontaneous speech output was abnormal in prosody and rhythm; sentence segments could be well spoken, but the whole collection of segments was poorly strung together. Substitutive semantic paraphasias were more frequent than neologisms. Agrammatical substitutions punctuated the discourse, producing an apparently abnormal syntactic structure called paragrammatism. Anosognosia, unawareness of illness, was particularly prominent.

On tests of repetition, performance varied with the linguistic nature of the material. Meaningful words were better reproduced than nonsense words. Errors in response were close approximations of the target. Repetition of sentences and carrying out of oral commands clearly distinguished these two clinical subtypes of sensory aphasia. In the predominantly word-deafness variety neither of these tasks could be accomplished, because of the lack of perception of words as sounds. In the predominantly semantic comprehension variety, repetition of sentences was only mildly impaired. In effect, repetition of the sentence by the subject sometimes facilitated the comprehension.

In general, comprehension was severely impaired for both written and oral commands, although phonemic discrimination was only mildly disturbed. The severity of the comprehension defect was parallel for written and spoken inputs. Paralexias were abundant in reading aloud.

As for writing, the dissociation observed in the predominantly word-deafness form was reversed in this form of sensory aphasia. Writing of words to dictation, while not completely normal, was satisfactory. Writing of nonsense syllables was marred by frequent graphemic substitutions. By contrast to the relative preservation of the writing of words to dictation, spontaneous writing was filled with abundant paragraphias.

This description effectively corresponds to that for transcortical sensory aphasia, first postulated by Lichtheim (1881) and subsequently described by Wernicke (1903). The meaning of the word is lost, although appreciation of the verbal sound is intact. For this reason one can account for the preserved capacity for repetition (even echolalia) without evocation of word significance. Spoken language is always at least mildly disturbed, because the patient is unable to monitor its adequacy. Reading aloud may be fluent but without understanding. Writing to dictation may be relatively spared, but spontaneous writing is full of paragraphic errors. (See below, section on transcortical sensory aphasia, for discussion of proposed pathophysiology.)

Attentional Disorganization

Hécaen, Dubois, and Marcie (1967) evaluated the effects of disordered attentional mechanisms on linguistic performance. They observed two disorders, distractibility and perseveration, that played a role in both expressive and receptive performance. In spontaneous speech the patients were unable to carry a sentence to completion. Parenthetical thoughts would intrude and lead the sentence from one point to another, with no single thought ever being fully expressed. Circumlocutory, meaningless ("empty"), but grammatically correct speech output was the result. Perseveration manifested itself by a moderately severe echolalia and by the character of the paraphasias, which were perseverative at both the phonemic and semantic levels.

In commenting on the linguistic defects found in patients with acute confusional states, Chedru and Geschwind (1972) noted especially a word-finding difficulty and a severe dysgraphia.

Transcortical Aphasias

Basing their proposals on earlier work by Goldstein (1948), Benson and Geschwind have defined two major subdivisions of aphasia (1972): those with repetition defect, due ordinarily to perisylvian lesions; and those without repetition defects, due ordinarily to lesions in the border zone surrounding the classical zone of language. The aphasic syndromes with repetition defects correspond to a greater or lesser degree to the classical varieties of aphasia. The aphasic syndromes without repetition defect are called transcortical aphasias.

There are two main types of transcortical aphasia: transcortical motor aphasia, called dynamic aphasia by Luria (1966), due to a lesion in the anterior portion of the border zone; and transcortical sensory aphasia, due to a lesion in the posterior portion of this zone. A combined form, called "the syndrome of isolation of the speech area," has also been recognized (Geschwind et al, 1968).

Transcortical Motor Aphasia

The chief clinical features of this syndrome are an impairment in the ability to initiate speech and a severe nonfluency in spontaneous and conversational speech, in the presence of normal or nearly normal repetition (Goldstein, 1917; Luria and Tsuectkova, 1967; von Stockert, 1974). The patient retains the ability to reply with one-word answers to common questions. Word-finding capacity in response to questions may be impaired, but confrontation naming is ordinarily preserved. Comprehension of written and spoken language is normal. Reading aloud may be normal but is occasionally defective. We have observed several patients with this syndrome who exhibited a peculiar "warming-up" phenomenon. After 10 or more minutes of questioning by the examiner these patients seemed to develop an increased capacity for self-initiation of speech. This increased fluency, although never reaching the limits of normal, persisted throughout the remainder of the examination but disappeared within minutes after the examination was completed.

Luria (1964, 1966) has proposed that this form of aphasia represents a malfunctioning of the normal regulatory activity of the frontal lobes for all forms of responsive behavior and is not a specific linguistic disorder. Of interest in this regard are the several studies of verbal fluency that demonstrate impairment following frontal lobe lesions (Milner, 1962; Benton, 1968; Ramier and Hécaen, 1970; Perret, 1974).

Transcortical Sensory Aphasia

In this syndrome the patient may have fluent spontaneous speech with abundant phonemic and verbal paraphasias, severe disturbance of comprehension of spoken and written language, impaired naming, defective writing, but normal repetition, often with a tendency to echolalia. Thus the clinical pattern is similar to that of the classical Wernicke's aphasia, except for the remarkable preservation of repetition. (A more detailed clinical description has already been presented. See above, in section on disorganization of semantic relations.)

One proposed mechanism underlying this syndrome (Geschwind et al, 1968; Benson and Geschwind, 1972; Goodglass and Kaplan, 1972) is that, because the perisylvian zone of language is intact, Wernicke's area can perform its normal operations of auditory analysis and classification and pass its information forward to an intact Broca's area to permit repetition. However, the anatomic separation of the intact zone of language from the rest of the brain prevents the associations necessary for comprehension. An alternative interpretation may also be considered: repetition may be taking place because of activity of the nondominant hemisphere.

Goldstein (1948) accepted the reality of this form of aphasia but rejected the associationist explanation provided by Lichtheim (1881) and Wernicke (1903), according to which the center for auditory verbal memory images was disconnected from the center for concepts. For Goldstein the disorder derived from an inability to use the instrumentalities of language, which were themselves, however, intact. The causes of the defect were a diminution of attention and acoustic memory and a mild disturbance in the relationship between instrumentalities of language and nonverbal performance; word concept formation depended on this relationship. Goldstein proposed a vague suggestion of lesional localization for this syndrome: a temporal lesion sparing the region responsible for verbal reception but more or less destroying the posterior portion of the left hemisphere.

DISORDERS OF WRITTEN LANGUAGE

Alexia

Alexia refers to an acquired inability to comprehend written language as a consequence of brain damage. Benton (1964) credits the earliest observation of alexia to Valerius Maximus, who in 30 *AD* described a man who was struck on his head by an axe and lost his memory for letters but had no other defects. Sporadic case reports appear from the 1500s to the mid-1800s [Mercuriale, 1588, Schmidt, 1676, Gesner, 1769–1776, Gendrin, 1838, (cited in Benton and Joynt, 1960), Trousseau, 1864; Wernicke, 1874; Kussmaul, 1884], Mercuriale (1588) noting "a truly astonishing thing; this man [following a seizure] could write but could not read what he had written." In 1887 Charcot presented a detailed clinical description of a typical case. It was, however, Dejerine who provided the impetus for further study of the syndrome by his publications in 1891 and 1892 of two clearly defined case reports including postmortem findings. For Dejerine alexia in its pure form was a specialized variety of aphasia.

Since the early period numerous studies have been devoted to the topic (see the reviews by Hécaen, 1967b; Benson and Geschwind, 1969; Dubois-Charlier, 1970, 1971; Hécaen and Kremin 1976). Despite theoretical and nosological dispute most authors agree that the alexias may be subdivided on an anatomoclinical basis into three major groups: (1) alexia associated with sensory aphasia, due to lesions of the dominant posterior temporal lobe; (2)

alexia with agraphia, due to lesions of the angular gyrus; (3) alexia without agraphia (also called pure alexia and, by some, agnosic alexia).

Pure Alexia (Alexia without Agraphia)

The Anatomy of Pure Alexia   Dejerine (1891, 1892) described two different varieties of alexia that he attributed to lesions interfering with the normal reading process at different stages. One type, pure word blindness, he said was due to destruction of fibers connecting the calcarine region to the angular gyrus, with the focus of the lesion in the white matter of the lingual lobule. Pötzl (1928), who considered this syndrome to be a variety of optic agnosia, agreed with Dejerine's anatomic localization.

The role of a lesion of the posterior portion of the corpus callosum, the splenium, in the production of this syndrome had been noted by Dejerine but was first stressed by Quensel (1931). Foix and Hillemand (1925) had already indicated that pure alexia resulted from disturbance in the territory of the posterior cerebral artery, rather than of the middle cerebral artery, which had been found to be the territory responsible for oral language disorders. They asserted having found alexia in two patients with combined lesions of occipital lobe and splenium of the corpus callosum, while a third patient who had occipital but not callosal damage did not have alexia. The significant role played by the combination of lesions including the lingual and fusiform gyri of the dominant occipital lobe and the splenium of the corpus callosum has been stressed by most authors ever since (Vincent et al, 1930; Gloning et al, 1955; Geschwind, 1962–1965; Benson, Segarra, Albert, 1974; etc.).

But pure, nontransitory alexia may occur even in cases in which the splenium is intact (Hécaen and Gruner, 1974). And callosal disruption does not seem to be a satisfactory explanation for those cases of pure alexia without hemianopia (Hinshelwood, 1900; Hoff and Pötzl, 1937; Peron and Goutner, 1944; Alajouanine and Lhermitte, 1960; Ajax, 1967; Goldstein, Joynt, and Goldblatt, 1971; Greenblatt, 1973).

Varieties of Pure Alexia   Pure alexia is an accepted clinical syndrome, although the basic mechanisms are still disputed. For Dejerine (1891, 1892) and many of his followers it represented a specialized form of aphasia. For Marie (1926), Pötzl (1928), and others, it represented a specialized variety of optic agnosia. For Goldstein (1948) and Conrad (1947–1954) it represented the expression of a fundamental disorder: the loss of the structuring of forms. Wechsler, Weinstein, and Antin (1972) spoke of a "complex disturbance in the relationship between visual and language functions."

Clinically, in addition to the impaired comprehension of written language, one often finds impairment of ability to copy and acalculia. By contrast oral language is normal, except for a mild naming disturbance; writing and spelling are normal. Visual agnosias for objects and colors are occasionally found. Right homonymous hemianopia is an almost constant accompaniment.

Evaluation of the reading disorder has demonstrated different subsets within the main syndrome; however, these varieties of alexia have often been considered to be variations in intensity of the basic disorder. Hécaen (1967b), Dubois-Charlier (1970, 1971, 1972b), and Hécaen and Kremin (1976) have conducted neurolinguistic analyses of pure alexia, determining the structural (linguistic) basis of the several varieties: literal, verbal, sentence, and global. By this means they have determined that the different varieties of alexia represent, not degrees of severity of a single process, but rather, distinctive, although overlapping, disorders. These conclusions have now been confirmed in other laboratories (Benson et al, 1971a; Albert et al, 1973a).

Literal alexia refers to the inability to read letters, despite the relative preservation of the ability to read words. In this variety of alexia, letter blindness is virtually never complete. Among words that may be read, lexical items are better preserved than grammatical-function words or· nonsense words. Paralexias are frequent in reading aloud, especially paralexias-insphere, that is, in the same semantic category (Beringer and Stein, 1930). Simple commands may be read and carried out; however, complex commands are incompletely understood. Reading a paragraph, either aloud or for comprehension, is totally impossible. Reading of numbers seems more impaired than in verbal alexia.

Associated disorders are common. The ability to copy is severely impaired, often taking the form of a slavish reproduction of apparently meaningless forms, with no ability to transpose from cursive script to block print. Writing spontaneously or to dictation is more or less impaired, although the ability to write isolated words may be preserved. Writing of multiple-digit numbers is impaired. Recognition of pictures and colors is defective but usually to a minor degree. Mild praxic and somatagnosic difficulties may be seen. Right homonymous hemianopia is common, but not absolute, as in verbal alexia.

An essential feature of this form of alexia is the inability to read by spelling out the word. Some words may be captured globally. For others, mistakes may occur in the whole word because the patient reads the first syllable and guesses at the rest.

In a quantitative and qualitative study of paralexic errors Marshall and Newcombe (1966) reported results approximating the description of literal alexia given above. Errors were selectively grouped according to the grammatical classes the words presented. The order of difficulty was nouns (easiest to read), then verbs, then adjectives, and finally grammatical-function words. Error type for nouns was semantic; for adjectives and verbs error types were "visual" (e.g., "next" instead of "exit") or "completion" (e.g., "gentleman" instead of "gentle"). Regardless of paradigmatic class or paralexic error type, responses tended to be nominal.

By contrast with literal alexia, verbal alexia manifests itself as an inability to read words as a whole, despite the ability to read letters. As in the preceding form neither the inability to read words nor the ability to read letters is complete. Difficulties arise in letter reading especially if the letters are presented in an oblique or inverse position. By slowly reading letter by letter, the patient is often able to arrive at a correct word. Nonsense words, as well as meaningful words, may be spelled out and read in this way. In mild forms the patient may be able to decipher simple commands, but complex commands and the meaning of a paragraph are never successfully achieved.

Isolated digits and numbers containing up to three digits are always well read, difficulties appearing in larger numbers. Calculations are often erroneous. Other associated findings include an impaired ability to copy; however, in this form, unlike in literal alexia, transposition from cursive script to block printing is possible. Minimal paragraphic and dysorthographic errors are found in writing spontaneously and to dictation, except for numbers, which are always well produced. Visual agnosia for colors and pictures is often found, and right homonymous hemianopia is constant.

An additional variety of alexia called alexia for sentences has been proposed as a separate category (Hécaen et al 1967; Dubois-Charlier, 1970, 1971; Hécaen, 1972; Hécaen and Kremin, 1976). The ability to read letters and words is largely preserved, along with the ability to read single and multidigit numbers. Errors become numerous, however, with the reading (and comprehension) of simple commands. As the commands or sentences to be read for meaning become longer and more complex, the deficit becomes exaggerated. Given the theoretical interest of this variety of alexia, it would be useful to have these observations confirmed in other laboratories.

Global alexia is the inability to read either letters or words, despite the relatively normal ability to read single and multidigit numbers. In this variety of alexia the patient can compensate by kinesthetic feedback. Thus, as noted in the earliest reports (Charcot, 1877; Dejerine, 1892; Westphal, 1908), these subjects can "read" letters and even words by actively tracing the letters with their fingers or by having the examiner move their arms in the air in the pattern of the letter. Spontaneous writing and writing to dictation remain normal. Associated disorders have been variously reported. These may include difficulties with arithmetic operations and with recognition of musical notation (Hécaen, 1972b) and agnosia for colors (Pötzl, 1928). Right homonymous hemianopia is a constant finding.

Hécaen and Kremin (1976) reexamined this classification scheme for the alexias by administering a battery of reading tests to a series of patients with left hemispheric lesions, as well as to three patients with pure alexia. Statistical analysis of results demonstrated not only a quantitative but also a qualitative difference between reading disorders of the type that accompanies aphasic syndromes and reading disorders characteristic of pure alexia. With respect to the pure alexias the classification of literal, verbal, and sentence alexia seemed to be supported, in the forms described above, but with the following modifications. Three contrasting tendencies were noted to affect reading style: recognition versus reading of items; meaningfulness versus meaninglessness of stimulus material; and combinatory versus global apprehension of stimulus material. Examined from this point of view, the results indicate that the several neurolinguistic varieties of alexia may depend on the isolated or combined expression of different neuropsychological mechanisms manifesting themselves more or less specifically at different stages in the reading process.

Alexia with Agraphia

To separate this syndrome clinically from the combination of alexia and agraphia associated with sensory aphasia, one must find impaired ability to read and write in relative isolation from disorders of oral language and calculations (Dejerine, 1891; Wolpert, 1930; Nielsen and Raney, 1938; Alajouanine et al, 1960; etc.). A lesion of the angular gyrus in the language-dominant hemisphere is accepted as the anatomic locus underlying this syndrome (Benson and Geschwind, 1969; Hécaen, 1972b), and this syndrome is even called "parietal alexia" by some (Quensel, 1927; Pötzl, 1927; Hoff et al, 1954).

Recognition of letters is generally better preserved than that of words, while context often facilitates the understanding of a sentence. Nonetheless, with longer or more complex sentences, comprehension fails. Disorders of graphic expression of language, while present, may not parallel the severity of the alexia. Of significance in this variety of alexia is the loss of the perceptual strategies for reading, as defined for normal persons (Haslerud and Clark, 1957), which tend to be intact in the pure alexias.

Associated disorders include, almost invariably, a mild to moderate anomia. Often, but not always, one may see elements of the Gerstmann syndrome: dyscalculia, dysgraphia, right-left spatial disorientation, and impairment in the ability to recognize or identify fingers (Gerstmann, 1930). Although this is not frequently reported in the literature, we have found it to be common. Hemianopia is not necessarily present. Kinesthetic feedback does not benefit these patients.

In 1904 Dejerine and Thomas reported a case of alexia with agraphia that was distinguished from other varieties of alexia by preserved ability to spell words orally and to recognize orally spelled words, unlike the usual variety of alexia with agraphia. These authors did not regard this as a separate type of alexia but interpreted it as a combination of pure word blindness with a separate lesion disconnecting motor control of the left hand from the language areas of the dominant hemisphere and thereby producing agraphia. Albert et al (1973a) observed a similar case, and by means of a series of matching and forced-choice tests, demonstrated a virtually intact perception of written words and a striking preservation of semantic understanding of written words. Caplan (1972) also reported a case of an alexic patient who was able to demonstrate a surprisingly intact comprehension of the meaning of written language when appropriate cues were given.

Several possible explanations may be proposed for these observations. These subjects may have retained the capacity for semantic reading in their dominant hemispheres, while at the same time suffering a functional disconnection between the visual linguistic and the auditory-oral-motor processes of language. Another possibility is that, although the dominant hemispheric language zones are impaired, the nondominant hemisphere retains some capacity for comprehending written verbal material. Split-brain studies (Gazzaniga, 1970; Sperry et al, 1969; Gazzaniga and Hillyard, 1971; Gazzaniga, 1973) tend to support the latter alternative.

Agraphia

The term *agraphia* refers to a disorder of expression of written language due to brain damage. In dealing with the graphic or written expression of language and its disorders, one must take into account the distinction between the

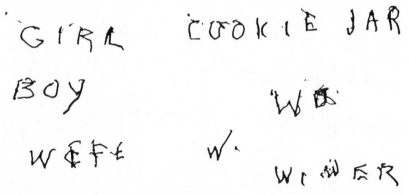

Agraphia from a patient with anterior aphasia. The task was to describe in writing a picture in which a mother is washing dishes; water is splashing out of the sink onto the floor; a boy is standing on a stool trying to reach cookies on a high shelf; a girl is standing on the floor near the boy and the stool is about to fall. The picture is taken from the Boston Diagnostic Aphasia Examination of Goodglass and Kaplan, 1972.

elementary ability to write, which involves primary motor and perceptual functions, and the symbolic content and linguistic characteristics of the material to be expressed. The graphic code cannot be considered as a simple transcription of the oral code. Graphic expression provides a system of symbols in the spatial sphere, derived from a distinct set of linguistic rules. These rules condition the production of graphemes and their linkage in manuscript writing so as to preserve the individuality of graphemic signs within a broad range of idiolectal variants. At the level of syntax these rules provide the structure within which graphic output can indicate segmentation and thus avoid the loss of information that in oral expression may be transmitted by nonsegmental elements, such as intonation, facial and manual gestures, and situational context. These conditions both allow and require a high degree of redundancy for the transmission of grammatical and semantic information.

Graphic activity represents an autonomous model of linguistic performance, closely linked nonetheless to the performance model of oral expression. The relationship between these two performance models may be seen at different stages of writing. For example, aside from their independent significance, graphemic signs have specific articulatory referents with respect to the phonological system of the language under consideration. In addition written sentences may have a deep structure identical with that of spoken sentences despite different sets of performance rules.

RIGHT IN THE PICTURE IS BROS.
AND SIS(I)TER WITH MOTHER.
THERE AT TIPPED TIER?
AND AT MOTHER THERE
IS A SPILL(E)(B) WATER
AT THE SIN(K)(E)

Agraphia from another patient with anterior aphasia.

From the foregoing considerations it may be concluded that separable varieties of agraphia may occur, each resulting from breakdown at a different level within one of the several neuropsychological systems upon which graphic symbolic expression depends—motor, perceptual, linguistic, and so forth. Disorders of written expression may be categorized into clinical subgroups of agraphia: pure, apraxic, spatial, and aphasic. In this section we consider the first three varieties, aphasic agraphia having been discussed in the appropriate sections dealing with aphasia.

Pure Agraphia

Anatomic Considerations By pure agraphia is meant disorders of written language expression in the absence of disorders of oral language, reading, or praxis. In 1865 Benedikt suggested that the elements underlying written and spoken language may have separate anatomic localizations, but he did not specify a precise locus. In 1881 Exner presented evidence in favor of the anatomic localization of an independent graphic center in the foot of the second frontal gyrus, separate from Broca's area. Henschen (1920–1922), from the anatomoclinical study of five cases, suggested there was a motor graphic center located in Exner's area and a sensory graphic center in the angular gyrus.

Very few well-studied cases of pure agraphia with lesions localized to the foot of the second frontal gyrus have been reported, and the localizing value of these cases is diminished by the fact that the pathology was always tumor or trauma (e.g., Gordinier, 1899). However, Penfield and Roberts (1959) observed transient agraphia following surgical excision of F_2 and F_3. In 1969 Dubois, Hécaen, and Marcie described six cases of pure agraphia, four of which were due to frontal lesions, although a more precise intrafrontal locus could not be adduced. Assal et al (1970) described a patient with pure agraphia due, presumably, to a dominant frontal lobe vascular lesion; again it was impossible to be more specific regarding the anatomic locus.

Starting from the anatomic rather than the clinical point of view, Hécaen and Consoli (1973) analyzed language disorders associated with lesions of Broca's area. The lesions were verified either surgically or at postmortem examination and included the foot of the third frontal convolution but did not extend past the rolandic gyri posteriorly or the sylvian fissure inferiorly. In their group of 19 subjects, 4 had lesions involving F_2 as well as F_3. Three of these 4 subjects had no language disorder at all, written or spoken. Of the total group of 19 subjects, 5 had deficits limited to a mild agraphia, combined with a minimal dysprosody. These 5 subjects had lesions restricted to the cortex of the foot of the third frontal convolution.

Boy and girl want to eat from cookies. The boy slips out to EL STOOL.

The woman is thinking girl and forgetting. The water on the basin runs on the floor, the shoes are wet. The faucet opens to water to fall. The plate is cleaned. The window is open.

Agraphia from a patient with posterior aphasia.

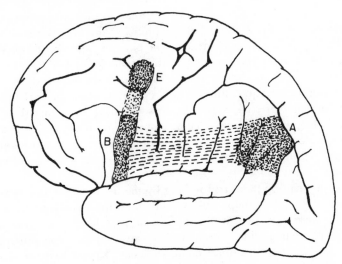

Nielsen's (1936) concept of writing centers. A lesion in any of the shaded areas or connections would cause agraphia. E is Exner's writing center at the foot of the second frontal convolution. B is Broca's area. A is the angular gyrus. Copyright 1965 by Harper and Row, Publishers, Hagerstown, Maryland. Reproduced by permission.

A novel form of agraphia, selective for written spelling, was described by Kinsbourne and Rosenfield (1974). The patient had a dissociation between his ability to spell by writing and manual sorting (which was impaired) and his ability to spell orally (which was relatively spared). The authors postulated that the programs that translate letter choice into visual terms for purposes of written (as distinct from oral) spelling may be related to a specific cerebral location and that this location, possibly the left posterior parasagittal parietal area, could be selectively impaired by a focal lesion.

Chedru and Geschwind (1972) contend that an isolated disorder of writing occurs in the presence of acute diffuse brain dysfunction. They do not accept the syndrome of pure agraphia as a specific language output disorder, stating that writing is a delicate, fragile task that may appear when a wide variety of pathophysiological processes affects general cerebral activity.

Neuropsychological and Neurolinguistic Aspects   Several detailed reports of the clinical and neurolinguistic aspects of isolated disorders of writing have been published (Hécaen et al, 1963; Dubois et al, 1969; Assal, 1970; Chedru and Geschwind, 1972). Dubois, Hécaen, and Marcie (1969) studied six patients with this syndrome. They found no disorder of oral language or of constructional ability. All of their patients had acalculia and four had general intellectual deterioration.

Analysis of graphic output revealed the following features. Formation of letters was normal, although dysorthographia was marked. Even while misspelling the words in written expression, the patients were able to spell aloud the same words correctly. No significant differences in total errors were noted between single digits and letters or multidigit numbers and words. Ability to copy was essentially intact, although errors crept in when the patient had to change from one expressive code (e.g., cursive script) to another (e.g., block print). Morphographemic rules of expression were normally maintained, and the correspondence of letter to sound (morphographemic-to-morphophonological relationship) was preserved. Perseverative errors were found in only one patient.

Writing in script by hand and writing by the use of anagram letters were compared. In half the group, writing in manuscript was worse; in two patients errors were equivalent with either method. Spelling errors were further analyzed. Error types, aside from the perseverative errors of one patient, were errors of combination and of selection, the central portion of the item accounting for the most errors.

From these observations the authors concluded that pure agraphia consisted of two main forms of graphic defect. One was a spatiotemporal disorganization specific to graphic activity, isolated from constructional apraxia; the other was a disorder of grapheme selection, even in the absence of impaired ability to name letters. Except for the findings in one patient the remaining observations were similar to those seen with the graphic disturbances that accompany that particular variety of aphasia manifested by a disorder of phoneme production. Hécaen (1972b), drawing on personal experience, commented on observations of patients with similar graphic disturbances in the presence of minimal defects in oral expression. On the basis of these different sets of observations he proposed that pure agraphia may represent the extreme, and isolable, end of a spectrum found with a symptom complex in which disorders of oral and graphic expression are associated with variable intensity.

Apraxic Agraphia

Disturbance of gestural capacity has long been recognized as a causative factor in many cases of agraphia. These agraphias have been linked primarily to parietal apraxia, and numerous authors have studied both the motor and the kinesthetic limbs of this practic activity. As early as 1867 Ogle referred to "ataxic agraphia," a term that Kussmaul (1884) borrowed in describing disorders of writing due to damage to the centers of coordination between spoken and written language. Henschen (1920–1922) underlined the relationship of agraphia and apraxia to each other and to parietal lesions.

Kleist (1933) distinguished separate varieties of apraxic agraphia. One was an agraphia due to disturbance in the ability to manipulate writing implements, such as paper and pencil, but independent of general ideomotor apraxia; one was an apraxia for written discourse, with preservation of the ability to write letters and words, due to a loss of opticokinesthetic associations; and one was a constructional agraphia due to a loss in the ability to form letters correctly. Goldstein (1948) accepted two major forms of writing disorder: those he called apractoamnesic agraphias and the aphasoamnesic agraphias. Travenec (1958) evaluated the effect of kinesthetic disturbances on writing and observed a "passive kinesthesiolexia" in which the patient could not identify writing movements through which his own hand was moved passively by the examiner. He found such defects especially following lesions of the dominant, inferior, posterior parietal region.

Apraxia produces agraphia by impairing the ability to form normal graphemes, inversions and distortions appearing in their stead. The disorder is seen in all modalities of writing (spontaneous, to dictation, and by copying), although infrequently the ability to spell or compose words with alphabet blocks is retained. Two main forms of apraxic agraphia may be seen clinically: agraphia associated with unilateral ideomotor apraxia and apraxic-alexic agraphia.

In agraphia associated with unilateral ideomotor apraxia no direct relationship between a global impairment of gestural capacity and the ability to write can be assumed, since in this uncommon syndrome the apraxia is limited to the left arm and hand, while the agraphia is limited to the right hand (Pitres, 1884). In cases of this type that we have seen personally, the agraphia occurs without disorders of spoken language and in the absence of alexia. Although apraxic, the left hand is able to spell and compose words with alphabet blocks, albeit with some spelling errors.

This disorder is difficult to explain. We have found the right-hand agraphia to be part of a general, frontal lobe type of motor tone and reflex disturbance, with grasp reflex and avoidance response being prominent in the left hand and agraphia in the right. Heilman et al (1973) studied agraphia and apraxia in a left-handed patient and suggested that dominance for language and dominance for handedness could be represented separately in the two hemispheres in some individuals, language in the left, and handedness in the right. If this were correct, disorders of praxis and disorders of graphic linguistic expression could be found in separate hands.

The more common variety of apraxic agraphia represents a combination of elements from the syndrome of parietal apraxia and that of alexia with agraphia and is sometimes called parietal agraphia. A disturbance in both encoding and decoding of written language is found, although the severity of the defect is not necessarily parallel in the two. Frequently associated with this syndrome are disorders of spoken language, especially amnesic aphasia and mild comprehension difficulty.

The characteristics of this agraphia reflect the apraxic influence; distortions and inversions of graphemes are prominent. The use of alphabet blocks often improves the situation but never completely. Spelling errors are numerous, with abundant iterations. When there is only a moderately severe a-graphia, a short sentence may be reasonably well produced, although paragraphic errors would still be found. Agrammatism is not seen, since it is in the written production of anterior aphasics. Unlike the writing performance of patients with sensory aphasias, writing in this syndrome has recognizable semantic value. The ability to copy is always perturbed. Writing of numbers is impaired, except for occasional single digits or small, multidigit numbers. Spelling is always defective and usually to a marked degree.

We consider this variety of agraphia to be distinctive and not assimilable into aphasia-linked agraphias. Nor can apraxia alone entirely explain the findings. This syndrome represents a basic disorder of written language, to which have been added elements of disordered gestural behavior. The essential defect is in the programming of the graphic message, at the level of both gestural performance and organization of linguistic symbolic structures. The defect manifests itself primarily in the graphic production of morphemes, the correspondence between phonic and graphic structures being disrupted.

Spatial Agraphia

This is a disturbance of graphic expression due to an impairment in visuospatial perception resulting from a lesion in the nonlanguage-dominant (i.e., minor) hemisphere. It represents one of the several features of the "nondominant-hemisphere syndrome" (Hécaen et al, 1956) and usually results from a lesion involving the right parietotemporo-occipital regions. The syndrome is frequently associated with spatial alexia and spatial acalculia; and the char-acteristic features clearly distinguish this type of agraphia from those type related to dominant hemispheric pathology.

Graphemes are well formed, and morphosyntactic components of writte expression are preserved. Four major features define this clinical syndrom((1) Some graphemes are produced frequently with one, two, or even mor extra strokes, the letters m, n, and u being especially duplicated. (2) The lin of writing are not horizontal but slant at variable angles of inclination to tl top or bottom of the page. The axis of the line, with reference to a straig line between the first and last letters, undulates or takes more complex co figurations, such as stepwise. (3) The writing occupies only the right-ha part of the paper. (4) Blanks are inserted between the graphemes that ma up the word, disorganizing the word and destroying its unity.

In a quantitative study of the graphic performance of 82 right-handed patients with unilateral lesions, Hécaen and Marcie (1974) observed the following. Only the iteration of strokes and letters and enlargement of the left-hand margin were significantly associated with right hemispheric lesions. By contrast left hemispheric lesions caused a loss of continuity in the writing of words. The enlargement of the left-hand margin seems clearly related to the presence of unilateral spatial neglect. The repetition of letters and portions of letters was considered to be a perseverative phenomenon linked specifically to the spatial aspects of writing.

LANGUAGE AND THE RIGHT HEMISPHERE

Crossed Aphasia

In 1899 Bramwell introduced the term *crossed aphasia,* by which he meant either right hemiplegia and aphasia in a left-handed individual or left hemiplegia and aphasia in a right-hander. Since the study of cerebral dominance in left-handers has revealed more or less satisfactory explanations for aphasia in left-handers with left-brain damage (Goodglass and Quadfasel, 1954; Hécaen and de Ajuriaguerra, 1963; Gloning et al, 1969; Hécaen and Sauguet, 1971) the term *crossed aphasia* in modern times has come to refer to language disorders in right-handers with damage to the right hemisphere.

The presence of aphasia following a right hemispheric lesion in a right-handed patient is difficult to reconcile with the concept that language resides exclusively in the left hemisphere. One is forced to conclude that some language capabilities are mediated by right hemispheric function, at least in some people, if not in all. Nevertheless the syndrome of crossed aphasia is sufficiently rare that one may agree with Zangwill (1967b) that there may be something "special" about such patients.

That the syndrome exists, however rare or unusual it may be, is indisputable. Estimated incidence varies; Zangwill (1967b) reports a 2% figure; Gloning et al (1963a), 1%; Benson and Geschwind (1972), less than 1%; and Hécaen et al (1971), 0.4%. Of interest is the "negative" proof of Boller (1973), who reported the case of a right-handed man with destruction of his dominant Wernicke's area with no language disability. The absence of aphasia in this case suggests that language may have been controlled by the right hemisphere.

Zangwill (1967b) and Hécaen (1972b) raised the question of the type of language disturbance in crossed aphasia. The aphasic symptoms do not seem to cluster within one of the recognized patterns. In a critical review of the subject Hécaen et al (1971) note that various authors have included nonlinguistic symptoms in the clinical picture, for example, confusion, memory defects, attentional disorders, personality changes, perseveration (Marinesco et al, 1932; Stone, 1934). As for the language disorders described, agrammatism and agraphia in particular, they seem to arise regardless of the lesion localization (Ettlinger et al, 1955; Angelergues et al, 1962; Barraquer-Bordas et al, 1963; Clarke and Zangwill, 1965; Brown and Wilson, 1973). Comprehension and naming, for the most part, are preserved or only mildly impaired.

As for etiology Boller (1973) indicates that only 23% are vascular, contrasting with the frequency of vascular accidents as a cause for aphasia in the general population, while the majority of reported cases of crossed aphasia are of tumoral or traumatic etiology. Boller cautions against overinterpretation of aphasia-like symptoms in right-brain-damaged right-handers when the etiology is tumor or trauma.

Effects of Left Hemispherectomy

Although a large number of children with infantile hemiplegia have been subjected to a left hemispherectomy relatively few adults have been subjected to this procedure. These few cases in adults may be analyzed to determine the nature and extent of preserved linguistic capacity.

Zollinger (1935) and Crockett and Estridge (1951) described patients whose survival following operation was of relatively short duration. Language behavior in these patients was markedly restricted. All that remained of expressive capacities were "automatic" speech, expletives, and words of over-learned songs. The case reported by Hillier (1954) was that of a 14-year-old child; thus comments regarding language performance would be of uncertain value. Of the patients with left hemispherectomy described by French et al (1955) one, who had been aphasic since 12 years previously when he had undergone an operation for brain tumor, was able to ask simple questions and had a good degree of comprehension. The patient described by Smith (1966), unlike the other reported patients, had a significant return of language function. Six months after the operation he could produce well-constructed, if short, sentences, and verbal comprehension was fairly good. Writing remained quite poor. This patient was right-handed, and there was no left-handedness in the family.

Smith and Sugar (1975) have reviewed the literature on patients with left hemispherectomy for infantile hemiplegia and presented a 15-year follow-up on one of their own patients. This patient demonstrated superior language and intellectual abilities on a battery of neuropsychological tests. The authors stressed the capacity of the right hemisphere to provide necessary substrata for linguistic skills; they also emphasized the importance of repeated, long-term follow-up in neuropsychology.

Despite the undoubted interest of these cases, it would be difficult from so few to draw general conclusions about the language capacity of the right hemisphere.

Effects of Right Hemispheric Damage

Few neuropsychological studies have been devoted to language performance following right hemispheric damage, primarily because no obvious aphasic signs had been found, and absolute left hemispheric dominance for language had been a generally accepted rule. Nonetheless, since Jackson (1864) there has been a continuous stream of suggestions relating the right hemisphere to language in one way or another (Marie, 1926; Liepmann and Pappenheim, 1915; Kleist, 1933; Nielsen, 1946; Goldstein, 1948).

In 1961 Eisenson described an analysis of language dysfunction associated with right-brain damage. By contrast with controls, subjects with right-brain damage were impaired on certain verbal tests. He concluded that this impairment resulted from decreased ability for generalization and conceptualization. Critchley (1962) commented on the following disorders resulting from right-brain damage: (1) disorders of articulation, often transitory; (2) impairment of literary creativity; (3) hesitations and even blocking in word finding with circumlocutions; (4) difficulty in learning new linguistic material; (5) nonaphasic misnaming; (6) impaired comprehension of the meaning of pictures, as one manifestation of a disorder in symbol formation. Weinstein and Keller (1963) also observed nonaphasic misnaming in such patients.

Marcie et al (1965) conducted a detailed neuropsychological analysis of the linguistic performance of 28 right-brain-damaged subjects. On overall review their findings supported the results of previous workers; in particular they did not find language defects comparable to those of patients with lesions in the left hemispheric language zone. However, three main types of language disorder were revealed: (1) Disorders of expression, mainly dysprosody and problems of repetition, were associated with rolandic or frontorolandic lesions. (2) Disorders of syntactic transformation and vocabulary selection were associated with parietal or parieto-occipital lesions. These defects seemed to be perseverative in origin. (3) Disorders on a specially designed test of sentence production, using words provided by the examiner; separate study with this test revealed defects associated with temporal lobe, especially temporal tip, lesions (Assal and Ramier, 1970).

In 1971 the results of an international symposium on "language and the right hemisphere" were summarized by Gazzaniga. Two major conclusions reached were that none of the studies completed to date revealed more than a mildly limited linguistic capacity of the right hemisphere following injury and that, with time, effort, and imagination, more functions might be found for which the right hemisphere was responsible.

Split-Brain Studies

In a patient whose posterior corpus callosum had been surgically sectioned but whose visual fields were intact, Tresher and Ford (1937) observed failure to recognize and understand letters or words presented to the left visual field alone, while the patient was able to read stimuli presented to his right field. The authors conjectured that stimuli to the left visual field were received in the visual cortex of the right hemisphere, but because of the section of the splenium of the corpus callosum, they were unable to reach that portion of the left hemisphere responsible for comprehension of written symbols. This syndrome of hemialexia was subsequently described in more detail by others (Maspes, 1948; Wechsler, 1972).

Suggestions that the neocortical commissures played a significant role in neurobehavioral function were rejected by Akelaitis (1942, 1944), who examined a series of patients with partial or complete surgical lesions of the corpus callosum. However, new impetus was given to the study of the syndromes of hemisphere disconnection by the so-called split-brain animal studies of Myers (1961) and Sperry (1961). These animal studies proved that the corpus callosum and other neocortical commissures were necessary for the interhemispheric transfer of learning and memory and for certain motor and sensory interhemispheric integrations. The newly revived interest in disconnection syndromes was rewarded by the observations of such syndromes in human beings (Bogen and Vogel, 1962; Gazzaniga et al, 1962; Geschwind, 1962; Geschwind and Kaplan, 1962). Detailed reviews of the disconnection syndromes in animals and man and the methods for evaluating these syndromes appear elsewhere (Geschwind, 1965; Sperry, Gazzaniga, and Bogen, 1969; Gazzaniga, 1970; Geschwind, 1970c; Dimond, 1972; Dimond and Beaumont, 1974; Kinsbourne, 1975a). In this section we consider primarily the split-brain data concerning language and the right hemisphere.

With respect to the language capacity of the right hemisphere a major distinction has been drawn between language production and language comprehension. The right-handed commissurotomized patient is generally unable to express in speech or writing things felt with the left hand or seen in the left half of the visual field (Gazzaniga and Sperry, 1967). The presumed mechanism for this defect in linguistic expression is that somesthetic and visual function in the right hemisphere are disconnected from the language-expression-dominant left hemisphere. This explanation receives support from two lines of evidence. When stimuli are presented to the right hand or the right half of the visual field, verbal expression is normal. Also, when simple manual or other nonverbal responses are requested, the right hemisphere can demonstrate comprehension.

As for language comprehension in the right hemisphere, split-brain studies

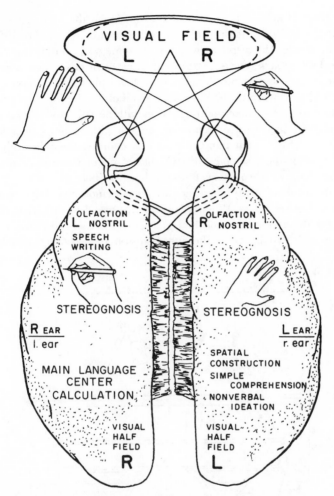

Sperry's (1970) schema of the way in which visual, tactile, auditory, and olfactory stimuli may be projected to the hemispheres of a split-brain subject. Copyright 1973 by McGraw-Hill, New York. Reproduced by permission.

demonstrate understanding of both written and spoken words (Gazzaniga and Sperry, 1967; Sperry et al, 1969; Dimond, 1972). Auditory comprehension was demonstrated by the capacity of the subjects to retrieve with the left hand an object named aloud by the examiner and hidden among a group of test objects. In this manner nouns and a few adjectival forms (e.g., geometric shapes) could be understood by the right hemisphere. This was true not only when the object was named directly but also when the object was described by definition. However, in such instances in which the language-dominant left hemisphere also hears the auditory verbal stimuli, it would be difficult to insist that the left hemisphere was not in some way aiding the right, for example, by feedback effects, subcortical transfer, or cross-cuing strategies.

Visual verbal comprehension in the right hemisphere was demonstrated by flashing a printed word to the left visual hemifield and asking the split-brain patient to retrieve the corresponding object with his left hand from a group of hidden objects. In converse technique, after a hidden test object had first been palpated by the left hand, the patient could successfully indicate the correct name of the test object from a list of printed names or a series of printed names flashed successively to the left hemifield.

Right-hemisphere comprehension was best demonstrated for nouns and with nonverbal responses. When a subject was asked to mimic or carry out simple acts, the performance of the right hemisphere was less satisfactory. In testing syntactic capabilities of the right hemisphere, Gazzaniga and Hillyard

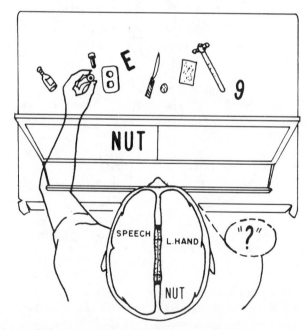

Names of objects flashed to the left half-field of a split-brain subject can often be read and understood but not spoken. The subject may be able to retrieve the named object by touch with the left hand but not with the right hand (from Sperry, 1970). Copyright 1973 by McGraw-Hill, New York. Reproduced by permission.

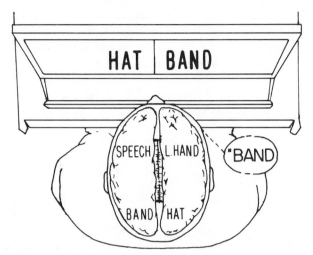

The name flashed to the left visual field is not consciously perceived by the subject, while the name flashed to the right visual field is read and reported verbally (from Sperry, 1970). Copyright 1973 by McGraw-Hill, New York. Reproduced by permission.

(1971) administered a series of pictorial-verbal matching tests and found only the affirmative-negative to be present. They concluded that, while a moderate semantic capability exists in the right hemisphere of the right-handed split-brain patient, little or no syntactic capability is present.

Using a newly devised technique with contact lenses that exclude a desired portion of the visual field while permitting ocular movement, Zaidel (1976, 1977) studied linguistic capacity of the right hemisphere in split-brain subjects and those with hemispherectomy. Auditory vocabulary of the disconnected right hemisphere was found to be equivalent to that of normal subjects. Picture vocabulary was similar to that of a group of (unclassified) aphasics. Word frequency was as important a factor for vocabulary of the right hemisphere as of the left. The right hemisphere was able to understand verbs and names of actions, as well as nouns. By contrast auditory comprehension of language, judged by the token test, was severely impaired in the right hemisphere, the level corresponding to that of a 4-year-old child.

Analysis of errors indicated that linguistic competence of the right hemisphere could not be compared with (i.e., was different from) that of children and that of aphasics. The right hemisphere seemed to be more sensitive to perceptual and mnestic (auditory verbal short-term memory) constraints, and the left hemisphere (in the aphasic group) more sensitive to linguistic variables.

Components of each sentence in the test were understood by the right hemisphere, but they were not integrated into a single, higher level verbal short-term memory for sequences. This limitation prevented the development of a processing strategy based on access to a stored abstract linguistic code of the message. The right hemisphere was superior to the aphasics on the syntactic dimensions of the test (functional words) because it was able to understand isolated words and a normal message, if redundant; but the right hemisphere failed in direct relation to the length of the test sentence.

LANGUAGE AND INTELLIGENCE

The relationship between deficits of intelligence and disorders of language has been a major focus of concern since the earliest studies on aphasia. The dogma of Bastian (1869) that "we think in words" has been defended, in various ways and with greater or lesser success, to the present, resulting in the widespread belief that symbolic, cognitive activity is language dependent. One argument has been that there is a fundamental defect that underlies all symbolic behavior (Head, 1926) or that may bring about the loss of the abstract attitude necessary for cognitive activity in any domain (Goldstein, 1948, 1953). Recognition that apractic and agnosic syndromes may occur following damage to the "minor" hemisphere has not reduced the intensity of belief that symbolic activity may be language dependent.

Various neuropsychological approaches have been used to evaluate the relationship of disorders of language to disturbances of cognitive activity. One method starts with subjects who have general deterioration of intellectual activity, as in dementia, and looks at linguistic performance. Another looks at the behavior of subjects with localized unilateral cerebral damage, with and without aphasia, and studies performance on various tests designed to evaluate linguistic and other symbolic capacities. In this chapter we consider both of these approaches.

Language in Dementia

A major attempt to describe the language behavior of patients institutionalized for a variety of illnesses affecting higher cognitive activity was made by Seglas in 1892. However, no characteristic linguistic patterns emerged. Goldstein (1948), Critchley (1964), and Stengel (1964), tried to systematize linguistic performance of patients with simple dementia. A primary characteristic found was incoherence of language output, manifested by a breakdown in logical associations of spoken discourse and inappropriate verbal responses in conversation; these suggested an inability to adapt to changing contextual conditions of communication. Another characteristic observed was echolalia, a reflex automatism of verbal response, providing an empty, stereotyped quality to speech. The pseudocoherence of some conversations did not mask the existence of a message without a meaning. A third characteristic was reduction of lexical stock, often with use of vague generic terms in place of the specifically appropriate item. A fourth characteristic was a loss of effective control over verbal output; incoherence or word-finding difficulty provoked no anxiety in the demented patient. A fifth characteristic was the augmentation of the verbal production disorder the longer the conversation continued. A sixth characteristic was an impairment in verbal comprehension.

In 1967 Irigaray performed a psycholinguistic analysis of the language of 40 demented patients with and without aphasia. An ensemble of linguistic features provided evidence that these patients had relatively preserved linguistic competence for syntactic patterns and capacity for transformations but had lost the ability for semantic interpretation. Morphological rules for production were disturbed only when dementia was accompanied by aphasia. However, rules of discourse were disrupted, as shown by logical contradictions and diffluence of speech. Perseveration was found at all linguistic levels. Behavioral reactions, such as refusal to respond to commands, were present, as were memory disorders and reduced vigilance. A close interdependence existed between disorders of language and disorders of general behavior and cognitive activity. (See also Irigaray, 1973).

Aphasia in Dementia

Two main varieties of dementia are considered in this section: presenile dementia and dementia due to cerebral arteriosclerotic disease.

In patients with cerebral arteriosclerosis, encephalomalacia affecting the "zone of language" may provoke an aphasic syndrome that is exaggerated and modified by cognitive, nonlinguistic defects. Aphasia may appear suddenly in a previously demented patient; or aphasia may precede the general intellectual impairment, which develops slowly in stepwise fashion; or, on a background of intellectual deterioration, minor pathological vascular events may occur repeatedly in the left hemisphere, producing a slowly evolving aphasic picture that generally begins by verbal amnesia.

The language disorder may appear at first to be more severe than it actually is; the patient may often perform better after stimulation. Nonetheless mental activity remains reduced and the stock of ideas is limited. Sentences are started and not finished; perseveration is intense. In spontaneous or responsive speech the features of dementia may mix with paraphasias and verbal amnesia to the point of total jargon aphasia and to such an extent that it becomes impossible to distinguish the two orders of impairment. And facial expression, intonation, and gesture of limbs do not facilitate communication.

Defects of equal severity are also seen in writing and in auditory comprehension.

Another observation often reported as one of the features of aphasia in dementia is echolalia. The closely related phenomenon of completion of a sentence left incomplete by the examiner is also seen. For Stengel (1964) these are not automatized reflex responses; rather they are attempts at communication. Alternative explanations are also possible: these signs may be evidence of a disinhibition of the neural mechanisms controlling language (Hécaen, 1972b) or a mixed transcortical aphasia due to isolation of an intact language zone from the rest of the brain (Goldstein, 1948; Geschwind, Quadfasel, and Segarra, 1968).

When the aphasia is primarily of a motor type, the patient may remain in an apathetic, semimute state interrupted sporadically by outbursts of anger manifested verbally by meaningless jargon or expletives.

In patients with presenile dementias the pattern of aphasia may be different according to whether one is dealing with Pick's or Alzheimer's disease. Delay and Brion (1962) have described anatomic and clinical differences between these two diseases. The experienced clinician will readily admit, however, that clinical differentiation of these two varieties of presenile dementia is difficult at best and that the diagnosis of Pick's disease is rarely made in life. The following descriptions should be viewed in this light.

In Pick's disease the occipital lobes and the posterior third of the superior temporal gyrus (Wernicke's area) are usually free from atrophy. Prefrontal and temporal lobe (other than Wernicke's area) atrophy are striking. One may expect characteristic linguistic, cognitive, and affective disturbances that correspond with the neuroanatomic distribution of lesions. Ideation and memory stock are reduced. Spontaneity is lacking and psychomotor retardation is prominent. Echolalia, echopraxia, verbal iterations, absence of facial expression, and even mutism may be seen. Word-finding difficulty is the principal language disorder. Spontaneous speech may be reduced to a small number of words used over and over again (verbal stereotypies). Naming may be severely impaired, the patient having recourse to circumlocutory phrases and words without specific semantic value. The verbal amnesia may be quite marked before any evidence of comprehension defect appears. A characteristic course could be a general reduction of language and progressive deterioration of speech resulting eventually in total mutism.

According to Tissot et al (1975) true disorders of language are exceptional. In those cases in which true language defects occur, they are always discrete, corresponding to lesions of the temporal convexity. Reduction of language output is common and may proceed to mutism. This defect, as well as verbal stereotypies, echolalia, and palilalia, would result from frontal lesions.

From an anatomic point of view, Alzheimer's disease is characterized by cortical atrophy affecting primarily the frontal and parietotemporo-occipital association regions and sparing the primary sensory projection areas. On a background of general intellectual deterioration appear disorders of instrumentalities: apraxias, agnosias, and aphasia. Sjogren et al (1952) found aphasia in one of its forms in every case of Alzheimer's disease. Regarding specific defects they found amnesic aphasia in 100%, sensory aphasia in 83%, agraphia in 83%, and alexia in 77%. Perseveration was present in almost every case. By contrast with the clinical picture of Pick's disease this syndrome is one of a sensory aphasia superimposed on general intellectual deterioration; it resembles the pattern seen in patients with generalized cerebrovascular disease with lesions in the dominant temporal lobe.

Disorders of Language and Disorders of Intellectual Functioning

The two preceding sections dealt with one aspect of the complex issue of the relationship of disorders of language and disorders of intelligence. In this section we analyze an additional aspect: whether or not the human brain has a capacity for cognitive functioning that is independent of verbal mediation. Piercy (1964, 1969) and Zangwill (1964) have extensively studied the influence of cerebral lesions on intellectual functioning and have proposed that psychological theories on the nature of intelligence may be used for understanding how intellectual skills are organized in the cerebral cortex.

Trousseau (1864), in opposition to the opinion of Broca (1861b), considered that intellectual deterioration was a necessary accompaniment of aphasia. For Jackson (1932) language was an inseparable feature of thought, to the extent that language was necessary for "making propositions." These opinions were followed in their extreme by Marie (1906a,b,c), for whom aphasia was nothing other than a specialized variety of intellectual deficit. Also for Head (1926) aphasia represented an impairment in a basic capacity for symbolic behavior. With the writings of the Gestalt psychologists (e.g., Gelb and Goldstein, 1920; Gelb, 1933; Goldstein, 1948, 1953) the intimate linking of language and intelligence was firmly established. For these authors aphasia was a modification of cerebral functioning that affected the entire organism, producing regression toward a less abstract, less rational, more immediate, and more concrete behavior.

Presenting results founded more rigorously in empirical data obtained by the administration of standardized tests of cognitive function to normal and brain-damaged subjects, Weisenburg and McBride (1935) showed that performance on nonverbal tasks was impaired by the presence of aphasia. However, they also found pieces of contradictory evidence. Some patients had nonverbal performance disturbed to a degree that could not be accounted for by the degree of aphasia, and some aphasic patients had normal nonverbal performance. These authors concluded that under ordinary circumstances thought is verbally mediated but that in some cases aspects of intellectual behavior may be altered by brain damage even in the absence of aphasia. For Weisenburg and McBride there is an indirect link between language and intelligence; to analyze this link it is necessary to evaluate quantitatively both verbal and nonverbal symbolic behavior.

Large-scale psychometric studies of subjects with right or left cerebral hemispheric damage with or without aphasia were undertaken. Initial analyses of studies using the Wechsler-Bellevue battery revealed the following. Subjects with left hemispheric lesions had impaired performance on verbal tests; subjects with right hemispheric damage had impaired performance on visuospatial tasks. McFie and Piercy (1952a) found left-brain-damaged patients to be more impaired than right-brain-damaged patients on tests of abstraction whether these tests were verbal or nonverbal. Similar results were found in other laboratories (DeRenzi et al, 1966; Archibald et al, 1967).

Once the role of cerebral hemispheric dominance for different behavioral functions was established, the question of the influence of aphasia on tests of abstraction was posed. McFie and Piercy (1952) demonstrated a deficit of intellectual functioning in a group with left-brain damage, by contrast with right-brain-damaged subjects, but found no correlation with aphasia. These observations were consistent with those of Meyers (1948), Bauer and Beck (1954), Teuber and S. Weinstein (1956), and S. Weinstein (1962).

These results emphasized the relationship of intelligence to specific cerebral regions rather than that of intelligence to language. Zangwill (1964) reinforced these observations with his results of a study in which he administered the Raven's Progressive Matrices to brain-damaged subjects. Even in the most severe cases of aphasia, performances were relatively good. On the other hand a high correlation was found between disorders of constructional ability (constructional apraxia) and poor performance on this test. Tissot et al (1963) also found apraxia to be a significant functional defect associated with impairment on intelligence tests.

Teuber (1964a) tested brain-damaged subjects with nonverbal tasks derived from those used with monkeys, for which task requirements and responses could be given without words. A selective deficit was found among aphasics on a complex conditioned-reaction test. With the Gottschaldt Hidden Figures Test, Teuber and S. Weinstein (1956) found impairment regardless of the location of brain damage but a significant impairment among aphasics by comparison with nonaphasic brain-damaged subjects. Thus defects on nonverbal tasks could clearly be associated with aphasia. These results were confirmed by Basso et al (1973).

In a series of studies DeRenzi and his collaborators have evaluated the neuropsychological evidence for the existence of cerebral areas critical to the performance of intelligence tasks. In an earlier study (DeRenzi et al, 1966) they found a correlation between performance on the Weigl Card Sorting Test and the presence of Wernicke's aphasia. Although they invoked the possibility of a deficit in abstract thought among this group of aphasics, they preferred the suggestion that the impaired abstracting ability was not necessarily linked causally to the aphasia. They proposed that a cerebral region in the left hemisphere may be responsible at the same time for linguistic and for symbolic intellectual activity.

In another study they looked at the ability of brain-damaged patients to deal with colors on a conceptual level (DeRenzi et al, 1972). Patients with aphasia were more significantly impaired than any other brain-damaged group. The influence on coloring performance of disorders of language, conceptual thinking, and color perception was assessed by introducing scores on various tests designed to evaluate these behavioral capacities. The authors concluded that the inability of aphasics to call the representation of colors to mind could be considered one aspect of a more general disorder of conceptualization associated with, but not directly dependent on, the language derangement. Taken together with results of earlier work by the same research team (DeRenzi et al, 1968c; Faglioni et al, 1969c) these results could suggest that aphasics have, in addition to their language defect, a difficulty with nonverbal associative tasks. DeRenzi et al (1972) proposed that two left hemispheric retrorolandic areas that overlap anatomically may be individually related to linguistic and intellectual function.

In a later study (Basso et al, 1973) these authors presented the Raven Colored Matrices to control and brain-damaged subjects, grouped according to hemispheric side of lesion, presence or absence of visual field defect, and presence or absence of aphasia. Groups found to be significantly impaired were right-brain-damaged patients with visual field defects, and left-brain-damaged patients with aphasia, with or without visual field defects. Statistical analyses confirmed that the right-brain-damaged group with visual field defects did not fail because of visuoperceptual impairment. The aphasic group did not fail because of language disorder, since almost zero correlation was found between Raven scores and measures of oral comprehension. Nonspecific factors such as lesion size and speed of performance did not play a role. From this evidence the authors drew the following conclusions. The brain is not equipotential for intelligence; there are at least two areas that are critical in this respect. One, in the right hemispheric retrorolandic region, is specialized for the processing of visual data. The other, in the left hemisphere, overlaps the language area and is involved in the performance of several different intellectual tasks, both verbal and nonverbal.

The study by Tissot et al (1963) on the "intellectual status of aphasics" also concludes that there is no statistically significant correlation between aphasia and general intellectual impairment. They did, however, find the presence of semantic paraphasias to be correlated with disorders of performance on Piagetian tests suggestive of a regression to operational levels characteristic of stages in the behavioral development of the child.

From the various studies just cited one may glean indications of a set of relationships between aphasia and disorders of intelligence in which intellectual defects may be correlated with specific linguistic defects. Of particular interest in this regard is the frequently reported association of disorders of general intellectual functioning with impaired auditory comprehension or with the presence of semantic paraphasias, suggesting a special relationship between Wernicke's aphasia and defective intellectual capacity. From a different point of view, however, if Wernicke's aphasia may be considered to represent a clinical symptom complex with diverse underlying mechanisms, then one would be justified in expecting to find individual patients with this syndrome without intellectual deficit.

SPECIAL VARIETIES OF APHASIA

Aphasia in Polyglots

Aphasia in polyglots presents a special challenge to neuropsychological analysis since a clinical situation may arise in which a patient is aphasic in one language and not in another; yet both languages ostensibly use the same sensory and motor channels. In 1895 Pitres proposed a rule regarding recovery from aphasia: the polyglot patient first regains comprehension of his most current language (usually his mother tongue), even though he may be unable to speak. Next he recovers ability to speak this language, even though he is unable to speak or understand other languages. Only later is the patient able to understand adopted or secondary languages and, occasionally, to speak them.

Prior to Pitres, Ribot (1883) had established the "rule of primacy," which stated that, in any damage to memory, the oldest material remains less affected than the later acquired material. Ribot's rule was adopted by some as an explanation for patterns of recovery in bilingual aphasia.

These rules have been honored as much by being broken as by being followed. In many cases of aphasia in bilinguals the patient recovers one language earlier than the other language. In some patients one language recovers, while one never does. In some patients one language recovers first, and then it regresses as a second language starts to recover. A few cases have even been reported in which a single patient presents different aphasic syndromes in each of his different languages at the same time (Bychowski, 1919; Albert and Obler, 1975; Obler et al, 1975). In most cases, however, languages are lost and regained in parallel.

Studies on the subject have been predominantly clinical (van Thal, 1960; Minkowski, 1963; Lebrun, 1976) or anatomoclinical (Pötzl, 1930; Stengel and Zelmanowicz, 1933; Leischner, 1948) and have emphasized correspondence or divergence from the rule of Pitres. In a review of the topic Minkowski (1963) accepted, in general, Pitres' rule, but pointed out that the many exceptions are due to a variety of factors: affective considerations; the method of language learning, visual or auditory; social factors; and so forth. A review by Albert and Obler (1975) of 92 published case reports of aphasia in polyglots revealed no single characteristic rule or pattern for recovery.

Few psycholinguistic studies have been done on aphasia in ployglots. In 1959 Lambert and Fillenbaum studied aphasia in bilingual French and English speakers. Following Weinreich (1953) and Ervin and Osgood (1954a,b), they agreed that the degree of dissociation between the two languages depended on the similarity of the context in which the languages had been learned. "Compound" languages were those learned in a common environment; these were unlikely to be dissociated. "Coordinate" languages were those acquired in different environments; these were more likely to be dissociated.

Lhermitte et al (1966) applied linguistic techniques to the analysis of language behavior of eight aphasic polyglots. No differences were found in linguistic typology between languages. Characteristic patterns of aphasic disturbance were found in all languages. With expressive aphasias the autonomy of linguistic systems remained the same as that seen in normal persons. With sensory aphasia, however, interference of one language with another was severe. Interference, which took the form of telescoping of words and substitutions both in syntax and in lexicon, was in the direction of the older (more stable, more familiar) language toward the newer. The authors stressed that the linguistic characteristics and mode of recovery were relatively independent of psychosocial and affective factors.

Obler et al (1975) described results of a dichotic listening test presented in each of the natural languages to groups of Hebrew-English bilinguals. Although all groups had a predominantly right-ear effect for each language, there was a significant asymmetry of dominance between Hebrew and English. Analysis of data suggested the possibility of a "language-learning" effect, in which the right hemisphere contributed actively to the process of aquisition of the second language (English or Hebrew), and a "language-specific" effect, in which English seemed to be dominantly organized in the left hemisphere and Hebrew seemed to be organized in a more bilateral fashion. Results of tachistoscopic studies with Hebrew-English bilinguals (Gaziel, Obler, and Albert, in press) are consonant with the dichotic listening results.

Childhood Aphasia

A distinction should be drawn between developmental (congenital) aphasia in children and acquired aphasia in children. In the latter, which we discuss in this section, language disorders develop after the child has already achieved the capacity for language comprehension and verbal expression.

The clinical pattern of acquired aphasia of childhood has several essential differences from that of adults (Bernhardt, 1885; Guttmann, 1942; Basser, 1962; Lenneberg, 1967; Hécaen, 1975). As early as 1885 Bernhardt observed that acquired aphasia in childhood was relatively frequent, transient, and predominantly expressive. Freud (1897) clearly distinguished acquired aphasia from developmental language retardation, emphasizing that it occurred with much greater frequency after right hemispheric lesions than acquired aphasia in adults did. In 1942 Guttmann presented the first detailed and systematic analysis of childhood aphasia, describing 16 of his own cases. Most subsequent authors, with occasional exceptions, have tended to agree on the main clinical features. Regardless of lesion localization the spontaneous speech is nonfluent. Mutism is common initially. Subsequently there are reduced initiative for speech, hesitations, dysarthria, and an impoverishment of language with reduced lexical stock. Disturbances of writing are constant. The reported frequency and severity of comprehension defects vary with the study. For Guttmann (1942) and Branco-Lefevre (1950) disorders of comprehension are rare; for Alajouanine and Lhermitte (1965) and Collignon et al (1968) they can be found in one-third of cases of childhood aphasia and may be quite severe.

Hécaen (1975) also studied the relation between different aspects of the language disorder and lesion localization. Mutism appeared chiefly in association with anterior (frontal or rolandic) lesions. It was present in three of the four cases with anterior lesion, and in one of four cases with temporal lesion (though in this case there was also involvement of the brain stem). Articulatory disorders were similarly noted in all four anterior cases, and in two of the four cases of temporal lesion, though again, one of these patients had subcortical involvement. Conversely disorders of auditory verbal comprehension were found only with temporal lesions (three of four cases). There were no localizing features of the disorders of naming, writing, or reading, at least during the acute period. This difference of the clinical picture according to localization was present in both the youngest and oldest children in the series.

Recovery from aphasia also presents characteristics special to the developing brain. Motor aphasia, the usual variety, may have a good prognosis, recuperation often being complete in 4 weeks (Guttmann, 1942). But the prognosis in mixed motor and sensory aphasia remains more guarded.

In his studies of cerebral dominance for language in the child Lenneberg

(1967) attempted to define a critical period for the acquisition of language, a period corresponding to the development of cerebral dominance. Age of onset of cerebral injury was used as a guide. If aphasia was acquired prior to age 3, recovery was rapid and complete. Before 10 years of age, a true aphasia would develop, but slow recovery was the rule. If the child was between 11 and 14 when brain damage occurred, recovery was less likely. Lenneberg concluded that a period roughly between 2–3 years of age and puberty was critical. During this time a state of cerebral plasticity existed; following this period the hemispheres have achieved their final specialization.

Recently the conclusions of Lenneberg have been disputed by Krashen (1973). This author lowered the end of the period during which transfer between the hemispheres is still possible to 5 years of age. He pointed out that in the series of Basser (1962) there were no instances of aphasia with a right-sided lesion occurring after age 5. Similarly, in this same series, left hemispherectomy performed in five cases in which the lesion occurred after language acquisition, but no later than the 21st month, was followed by a dysphasia in only one instance, and in this case it resolved in 2 months. Krashen compared the frequency of right-sided lesions in several series of childhood aphasias where the lesion occurred before or after 5 years with the frequency of right-sided lesions producing aphasia in adults. He noted that in the older children the percentage of right-sided lesions producing aphasia was similar to that observed in adults. Krashen found support for this argument as well in the results of studies of dichotic listening, particularly those of Kimura (1963) and Knox and Kimura (1970). The superiority of the right ear—that is, the predominance of the left hemisphere—in the reception of verbal material (digits) appears toward the age of 6, and that of the left ear (right hemisphere) for familiar sounds toward age 5. Since this work Nagafuchi (1974) and Ingram (1974) have found a right-ear superiority for verbal sounds (words) as early as 3 years of age. Statistical analyses in the Hécaen (1975) series tend to support the Krashen argument.

Findings from studies of aphasia in childhood thus support the notions that very young children have hemispheric equipotentiality for language and that cerebral dominance is established in the course of maturation. There does appear to be a critical period during which each hemisphere may support verbal activity, but this critical period may be of shorter duration than had been suggested by Lenneberg (1967). Nevertheless, as we see later, arguments have also been presented in favor of the notion that hemispheric specialization is innate.

Of considerable interest to clinicians in recent years has been the repeated observation of an unusual aphasic syndrome in childhood that may be related more to electrophysiological abnormality than to gross anatomic damage. Motor aphasia is present, associated with clinical or subclinical (elec-

troencephalographic) evidence of a convulsive disorder (Landau and Kleffner, 1957; Worster-Drought, 1971; Gascon et al, 1973; Sato and Dreifuss,
1973). A clinical neurophysiological study of three children with this disorder
found marked bilateral spike-wave discharges with a temporal lobe predominance when the aphasia was most severe (Shoumaker et al, 1974). The severity of aphasia paralleled the electroencephalographic abnormalities. As the
paroxysmal discharges were reduced by appropriate anticonvulsant therapy,
language performance improved. Correction of aphasia lagged some 2
months behind correction of the electroencephalographic abnormality.

Aphasia in Left-Handers

As abundantly demonstrated in this chapter, the left hemisphere is dominant
for language in the overwhelming majority of right-handed adults. Cerebral
dominance for language in left-handed adults is not so clearly established. At
the same time that Broca was attempting to establish the theory of cerebral
dominance, which stated that the left hemisphere is dominant for language in
right-handed individuals, he was also proposing the converse doctrine, which
stated that the right hemisphere is dominant for language in left-handers.
Cases of crossed aphasia reported during and shortly after the studies of
Broca, were in contradiction to his doctrine. (At the time, crossed aphasia
referred to left-handers with left-sided lesions.) Nonetheless these cases were
considered to be merely rare exceptions to the basic rule. Finally, in 1936
Chesher proposed that these cases were not simple exceptions; rather, he
asserted that cerebral representation for language was basically different for
left-handers and right-handers.

   This early work was followed by several large-scale, systematic studies of
language function in left-handed subjects with unilateral cerebral lesions
(Conrad, 1949; Humphrey and Zangwill, 1952; Goodglass and Quadfasel,
1954; Penfield and Roberts, 1959; Hoff, 1961; Russell and Espir, 1961;
Hécaen and de Ajuriaguerra, 1963). These studies demonstrated that cortical
organization is different for left- and right-handers. The conclusions of Goodglass and Quadfasel (1954) effectively summarized the various reports: it is
not correct to establish a direct and necessary correlation between handedness and cerebral lateralization for language functions; left cerebral dominance for language is more frequent than right-handedness, and right cerebral dominance for language is much less frequent than left-handedness. A
résumé of most series reveals that 20–30% of left-handed aphasics have right
hemispheric lesions.

   Additional studies (Subirana, 1952, 1969; Hécaen and Angelergues, 1964:
Luria, 1970), together with previous reports, repeatedly suggested that aphasia was milder, although more frequent, in left-handers than in right-handers,

regardless of the hemisphere damaged. Also, left-handers recovered more quickly and more thoroughly from aphasia than right-handers did. In 1969 Gloning et al studied a large series of left- and right-handed subjects matched for site of lesion. They found that for left-handers a lesion in either hemisphere was as likely to produce aphasia as a left-sided lesion in a right-handed patient. These various observations are consistent with the hypothesis that left-handers have a cerebral ambilaterality for language representation.

However, observations made in large series of subjects with unilateral hemispheric lesions indicate that left-handers do not form a homogeneous group regarding functional hemispheric asymmetry, as right-handers do. The role of a familial history of left-handedness and the relationship of this history to cerebral organization for language was first invoked by Kennedy (1916), who pointed out that right-handers who developed aphasia after a right cerebral lesion were likely to be members of a left-handed family. As methodological tools in neuropsychology improved, this topic became more suitable for systematic study.

In 1960 Wada and Rasmussen described the effects of injecting barbiturate into a single carotid artery and thereby producing transient signs of unilateral hemispheric dysfunction. By means of this test, known as the Wada test, Milner, Branch, and Rasmussen (1966) studied cerebral dominance for language in a large scale group of right- and left-handed epileptics. Unlike the findings expected by studies of patients with known cerebral lesions, the findings in this report were that only 90% of right-handers had left cerebral dominance for language, while 70% of left-handers had left hemispheric dominance.

A more recent review of their records has, however, prompted a modification of these conclusions (Milner 1974b). In a group of 262 subjects (140 right handed, 122 left handed) language was considered to be represented in the left hemisphere in 96% of the right-handers and in 70% of the left-handers (15% bilateral, 15% in the right hemisphere). When, however, lesions occurred at a young age, the percentages were different. In 31 right-handers who had suffered early cerebral damage, 81% had representation of language in the left hemisphere, 13% in the right, and 6% bilateral. Of 38 left-handers with early cerebral damage, 30% had language dominance on the left, 51% on the right, and 19% had cerebral ambilaterality.

The dichotic listening test has been another important laboratory tool for investigating lateralization of cortical function (Broadbent, 1954; Kimura, 1961a,b). Simultaneous presentation of different verbal stimuli to each ear results in superior reports of right-ear information for right-handers. Simultaneous stimulation of each ear with competing nonverbal signals, for example, musical tones, demonstrates a left-ear superiority (Kimura, 1964). The application of this test to left-handed subjects results in a diminution of perceptual asymmetry by comparison with right-handed subjects (Bryden, 1965; Curry and Rutherford, 1967; Satz et al, 1969). When statistical analyses take into account the presence or absence of a familial history of left-handedness, this diminution in perceptual asymmetry is primarily found with left-handers with a family history of left-handedness (Zurif and Bryden, 1969). According to Satz et al (1969) dichotic listening test results support the hypothesis that in the group of left-handers with a family history of left-handedness the cerebral representation of language is on the same side as the dominant hand.

Over a period of years Hécaen and his collaborators have studied neuropsychological aspects of left-handedness (Hécaen and de Ajuriaguerra, 1963; Hécaen and Angelergues, 1964, 1965; Hécaen and Sauguet, 1971; Hécaen, 1972b). Both qualitative and quantitative alalyses were done, with the following main conclusions. The left hemispheric syndrome in left-handers maintains many of the features of the left hemispheric syndrome of right-handers. However, disorders of auditory comprehension, of writing, and of spelling are significantly less frequent in left-handers than in right-handers, while alexia and spatial dyslexia are more frequent. The disorganizations of linguistic, practic, and gnostic behavior found in left-handers with left hemispheric lesions are, in the main, similar to those found in right-handers with left hemispheric lesions. However, some of the neurobehavioral abnormalities found with right hemispheric lesions in right-handers are also seen in left-handers with left hemispheric lesions.

The right hemispheric syndrome in left-handers is characterized by a significantly increased frequency of disorders of spoken and written language expression by comparison with those abnormalities in right-handers with right hemispheric lesions. Left-handers also have an increased frequency of alexia and spatial dyslexia.

Comparison of right and left hemispheric syndromes in left-handers shows fewer differences than comparison of similar syndromes in right-handers does. The main differences are nonlinguistic and lie in the realm of visuospatial perception and constructional abilities. The results are consistent with the hypothesis that left-handers have less hemispheric specialization or more cerebral ambilaterality than right-handers do. These studies may be summarized as follows. Neuropsychological syndromes due to unilateral hemispheric lesions in left-handers present a varied and atypical character by comparison with such syndromes in right-handers. Symptoms may be found that correspond to functions of either hemisphere, disorders are less intense, and regression is rapid and often marked.

Hécaen and Sauguet (1971) reexamined these issues in 49 brain-damaged left-handers, taking into account the presence or absence of a family history of left-handedness. In the "familial" group of left-handers comparison of performance scores of subjects subdivided into those with left and those with right hemispheric lesions showed no significant differences. By contrast significant differences were found for the group with "nonfamilial" left-handedness, depending on which hemisphere was damaged. This group corresponded more closely in performance to right-handers, since there were virtually no language deficits following right-brain damage. More recent studies by Newcombe et al (1974) have not supported the existence of cerebral ambilaterality for "familial" left-handers.

When the performance of familial and nonfamilial left-handers, both with left hemispheric lesions, was compared in the Hécaen and Sauget (1971) study, no significant differences were found with respect to spoken language and reading, although writing was more impaired in the familial group. Scores on both spoken and written language tests were similar for familial left-handers, whether the lesion was on the right or on the left. Writing was more impaired than oral language for nonfamilial left-handers with left-sided lesions. Deficits were almost totally absent with right-sided lesions in this group of nonfamilial left-handers. The absence of significant differences in oral language and reading for these two groups of left-handers is not consistent with the contention that familial left-handers have a greater degree of cerebral ambilaterality. One would expect the deficits to be more severe in the nonfamilial group, for whom cerebral dominance for language should be restricted to the left hemisphere. Nonetheless an argument may be put forth that cerebral organization for behavioral functions in familial left-handers is not only bihemispheric but also less focal than in the nonfamilial group or in right-handers. This argument remains to be confirmed.

RECOVERY FROM APHASIA

Recovery from aphasia has not ordinarily been a subject of great enthusiasm for many clinicians. Nonetheless, for survivors of strokes, aphasia may be the only factor limiting successful social adjustment. Sarno (1970), in a succinct review, traced the history of efforts in aphasia reeducation and described the various methods employed, from Bateman in 1890 to present-day specialists. Darley (1975), referring to traditional methods of language retraining, correctly indicated that claims of success in aphasia therapy may seem to outweigh actual proof of such success but that, by careful patient selection, judicious choice of therapy modality, and concern for the patient, many patients can benefit from speech therapy. Shankweiler (1970) observed that, although there can, as yet, be no categorical answer to the question of whether speech therapy works in aphasia, "specific treatment programs which grow out of an analysis of the salient features of a particular disorder, can and should be subjected to scientific study." It is along the lines of this latter suggestion that neuropsychologists and aphasia therapists have been combining forces to develop and evaluate unconventional methods for language retraining.

In 1973 Albert et al reported results in three aphasic subjects with a new form of aphasia therapy that they called melodic intonation therapy (Albert, 1973b). Of particular interest was the rapid return of expressive language abilities in these patients who had been specifically selected because they had had severe, long-term, stable language defects and because other forms of therapy had been tried in vain. The therapy program involves embedding short phrases and sentences in a simple, nonlinguistically loaded melodic intonation pattern that resembles, to a certain extent, the normal prosodic line of a sentence (Sparks et al, 1974). As the aphasic patient improves, the melodic aspect of the program is faded.

The theoretical basis for the successful results so far seen is uncertain. The authors suggest that the damaged left hemisphere may still be exerting its influence on language production and thus causing the aphasia. If the right hemisphere is dominant for melodic intonation, as has been suggested by a number of studies (e.g., Milner, 1962; Bogen and Gordon, 1971), it may be that, by attaching melodic intonation to propositional language, one may be increasing the relative influence of the healthy right hemisphere on the bihemispheric interaction affecting language, and in this way one may be reducing the deleterious influence of the damaged left hemisphere.

Studies on the teaching of language to subhuman primates have provided the basis for additional unconventional approaches to language retraining in aphasic patients. During the past half century several efforts have been made to teach human language to a chimpanzee (Kellogg and Kellogg, 1933; Hayes and Hayes, 1951, 1952, 1955; Gardner and Gardner, 1969; Rumbaugh, et al, 1974). The Gardners have succeeded in teaching their chimpanzee Washoe to communicate in the American Sign Language with her fingers and hands (1969).

Since 1966 Premack has been teaching a chimpanzee, Sarah, to read and write with variously shaped and colored pieces of plastic (1971). Sarah has a vocabulary of about 130 terms that she uses with a reliability of between 75 and 80%. However, her understanding goes beyond the meaning of words and includes the concepts of class and sentence structure, including negative, interrogative, conditional (e.g., if, then), and others.

From the concepts introduced by the teaching of language to Sarah the chimpanzee, Glass, Gazzaniga, and Premack (1973), with the assistance of M. Sarno, have attempted to assess natural language and to undertake artificial language training in seven globally aphasic patients who had sustained left hemispheric damage. Initial assessment of natural language showed some semantic knowledge but no syntactic or grammatical ability. Words could be distinguished from nonwords, and words could be spelled in the absence of semantic comprehension. The authors felt the initial observations to be consistent with a prelinguistic coding of verbal stimuli as visual gnostic units. Despite the severe deficits in natural language, their aphasic patients were able to learn an artificial language system consisting of cut-out paper symbols for words. Various levels of competence were obtained, ranging from simple statements of action to the expression of relations between objects. Other tests of conceptual-cognitive capacity revealed potential for abstraction and conceptual thought.

Gardner and Zurif (1975) and Baker et al (1975), in a therapy research project based on similar fundamental hypotheses, have also been successfully teaching an artificial language system to a small number of severely globally aphasic patients. Of eight patients given sufficient opportunity to learn this new visual communication system, five demonstrated significant capabilities in communication, although their ability to communicate using natural language was severely restricted. These authors believed that cognitive operations entailed in natural language may persist in the face of destruction of natural language capabilities.

THREE
DISORDERS OF GESTURAL BEHAVIOR —THE APRAXIAS

Although each special variety of apraxia requires a separate description and explanation, apraxia in general may be considered as an impairment of the ability to carry out purposeful movements by an individual who has normal primary motor skills (strength, reflexes, coordination) and normal comprehension of the act to be carried out (no agnosia, no general intellectual impairment). A wide range of severity is seen, from an inability to perform pretended actions out of context to an inability to manipulate everyday objects. This range of severity may be quantitative, in which case the disorganized behavior represents a different degree of dysfunction of the same basic neuropsychological defect, or qualitative, in which case the various abnormal functions observed may reflect different basic defects. In this chapter we consider the classification of gestural behavior, clinical varieties of apraxia, and neuropsychological studies concerned with underlying mechanisms.

CLASSIFICATION OF GESTURAL BEHAVIOR

A major obstacle to the goal of understanding the physiological basis of gestural behavior and its breakdown has been the absence of a comprehensive and systematic classification of gestures as a system of signs. If such a semiotic system of gestural behavior could be established, the relationship of gestures to linguistic activities could be more clearly established.

Experiments by Kimura (1973a,b) on manual activity during speaking demonstrate steps being used to try to relate gestural and speech behaviors.

Studying groups of normal right- and left-handed subjects, she classified their overt motor activity into seven categories. Of these categories, two occurred with a frequency great enough to warrant reporting: free movements and self-touching movements. For the group of right-handed subjects her findings suggested that speaking is strongly tied to other motor behaviors, as evidenced by a greater motor activity during speaking than during nonspeaking activities. A specificity of association was found between speaking and free movements of the hand opposite the speech hemisphere (as determined by dichotic listening studies); self-touching movements showed no such asymmetry. One conclusion of this study was, therefore, that there is some system common to control of both free movements and speaking and that this system is based primarily in the left hemisphere of right-handers.

A number of classification schemes have been proposed for gestural behavior. One such system is derived from observations of brain-damaged subjects with varied disturbances of voluntary motor function. In this system separate status has been accorded to gestures with and without objects present, to graphic gestures, and to constructional gestures. Gestures in the absence of objects may be further classified: those that in a highly codifed form take the place of language, for example, sign language or gesture language of deaf-mutes; those that are less highly codified but that characteristically accompany language; those that represent conventional symbols, for example, sign of the cross; meaningful expressive gestures that are more or less conventional, for example, threat or supplication; descriptive gestures relating to bodily activities; and gestures simulating object usage. Ideomotor apraxia in classical terminology results from disorders involving gestures in these categories.

Among those acts of voluntary motor behavior relating to manipulation of real objects, a subdivision has been made for those that do not have a direct relation to the body (breakdown in this system is called ideational apraxia) and for those that do have a direct relation to the body (breakdown in this system may be seen in dressing apraxia).

Pierce (1932) proposed a tripartite classification scheme of gestures based on a logical division of signs: (1) symbolic gestures, (2) iconic gestures, and (3) indicative gestures. Symbolic gestures are either highly codified and organized into a system or are less rigorously organized (conventional symbols) and represent a link of artificial contiguity between the gesture and its intended meaning. Iconic gestures are expressive reactions or pantomime behavior in which the liaison between gesture and meaning is created by similarity. Indicative gestures are descriptive of object use, and the link between gesture and meaning is served by real, rather than artificial, contiguity.

In accepting this classification scheme, Jakobson (1964) added that a description of gestures must also take into account their successive or simultaneous characteristics. Successivity would mark substitutive gestural languages and certain of those gestures related to object manipulation—with or without the presence of the object. By contrast, simultaneity would mark gestures of conventional symbolic behavior and most expressive gestures.

The two preceding approaches to the classification of gestures may be more easily understood with reference to the following table (Hécaen, 1967a).

Division of Signs	Temporal Relation
1. Symbolic gestures	
A. Codified, substitutive language	Successive
B. Conventional symbols	Primarily simultaneous
2. Iconic expressive gestures	Simultaneous
3. Indicative gestures	
A. Description of object usage	
1. Simple	Simultaneous
2. Sequential	Successive
B. Manipulation of real objects	
1. Simple	Simultaneous
2. Sequential	Successive

With respect to this classification scheme we would add two additional considerations. First, intermediate forms may exist. Second, spatial factors, as well as temporal, are equally important in gestural behavior.

An additional classification scheme may be provided, based on the nature of the stimulus. Gestures may be executed in response to verbal command, in imitation of gestures of the examiner, in response to or in imitation of passively imposed stimulation (kinesthetic inputs), or as a descriptive response following visual, auditory, or tactile presentation of an object. In all classification schemes gestures may be further subdivided as transitive or intransitive, and meaningful or meaningless.

Piaget (1960) discussed the development of systems of coordinated movements in children with respect to result or intention. He elaborated three psychogenetic stages: (1) level of sensorimotor coordination; (2) intermediate level, at which stage the symbolic function of gestures appears; and (3) level of representation, with figurative and operative aspects. These three developmental stages correspond to the three major groups of gestural disorganization described by de Ajuriaguerra et al (1960) in a study of brain-damaged subjects: sensorikinetic apraxia, somatospatial apraxia, and apraxias of symbolic formulation.

The disorders that comprise the last clinical group seem to correspond to at least two different gestural capacities. One is related to problems of gestural language, that is a codified system directly related to a given sociocultural level but without formal convention. This form of gestural capacity may correspond to Piaget's figurative activity; breakdown in this capacity may be found in the ideomotor apraxias with disturbance of symbolic gestures and iconic, expressive gestures. The second subgroup is represented by defective propositional usage of objects (Denny-Brown, 1958) or disorders in the programming of sequential gestures; this form of gestural capacity may correspond to Piaget's operative activity.

Another valuable developmental study is that of Kaplan (1968), who conducted a large-scale, systematic evaluation of gestural representation of implement usage by children of different ages. According to her observations one of the critical factors involved in the acquisition of representational skills is the factor of distance. For example, up to age 8, but usually not above this age, children have a strong tendency to represent the use of an implement by making the hand or finger take the role of the implement and come into direct contact (reduced distance) with the object of the action. Apraxic adult subjects have been found to manifest this "body-part as object" behavior (Goodglass and Kaplan, 1963).

The gestures that accompany language seem to pose a special problem of classification and, as such, have not previously been dealt with in great detail. Although it is difficult to assign them a slot in the Pierce–Jakobson classification table described earlier, they have particular significance by virtue of their intimate association with language. Clinical observations reveal that such gestures may be relatively well preserved even in the presence of severe aphasia. Since 1969 Hécaen and his associates have been painstakingly studying the gestures that accompany language in normal and brain-damaged subjects. Although their study is still in progress, early and tentative observations may be summarized as follows.

Reduction or abolition of gestures that accompany language was never found associated with ideomotor or ideational apraxia (Goldblum, 1972b). With respect to the gestures of aphasics, once again no abolition of motor activity was found; however, modifications of the normal pattern of gestures were observed. These modifications did not seem to represent compensatory phenomena for the language disorders. During spontaneous speech, gestural behavior adapted to and reflected the language defect. For example, patients with anterior aphasias had an overall reduction in the total quantity of gestures. The majority of gestures accompanied meaningful words and were figurative. By contrast, patients with posterior aphasias had fluent gestures, as well as fluent speech. Their gestures seemed to represent the converse of those found with anterior aphasias. With the posterior aphasics figurative gestures accompanying meaningful words were rare; the reduction of meaningful content and the abundance of paraphasias in spoken discourse did not routinely give rise to a gestural compensation. The gestures produced were not linked to the meaningfulness of lexical constituents taken in isolation; rather, they seemed to be related to the syntactic formulation of the utterance, and they corresponded well to the melodic contour of the sentence. Units comprising the gestural structure seemed more to articulate with grammatical elements of the sentence, such as conjunctions and prepositions.

Distributional analysis of gestures in normal subjects according to the part of the body involved showed both qualitative and quantitative differences. The right hand of right-handers executed more gestures than the left hand. The gestures produced by the right hand were more directly linked to the linguistic content of spoken sentences than those produced by the left hand were. Gestures of the left hand functioned more as indicators of intensity. These observations are similar to those of Kimura (1973a,b), who used a different approach to obtain corresponding results. The differences observed between gestures of right and left hand in normal persons were not so evident in posterior aphasics, even in those with no motor defect (Goldblum, 1972b).

Despite the difficulties posed by such an undertaking, it would nonetheless seem possible that, by methodological examination of pathological gestures in brain-damaged subjects, a more rational map of the relationships between different types of gestural behaviors and different aspects of verbal performance may be drawn. In this manner we may come closer to understanding the various intricate relations between symbolic and motor capacities of the nervous system and the systems of abstract rules that apply to linguistic behavior and that may apply, to some degree, to gestural behavior.

CLINICAL VARIETIES OF APRAXIA

Historical Background

Although Liepmann (1900, 1905, 1908) justifiably receives credit for establishing apraxia as a distinctive neuropsychological category, other authors had already described clinical conditions with similar findings and had even introduced the term. Stendhal (1870, cited in Hécaen, 1972b) was probably the first to apply the label *apraxia* to disorders, not of primary motor skills (e.g., strength, coordination), but of the "relationship between movements and the objects with which the movements were concerned." Gogol (1874), used the term *apraxia* for impaired ability to use objects. For Gogol, however, apraxia resulted from a gnostic disturbance. Other authors at the end of the nineteenth century provided clinical descriptions of apraxic syndromes, without attempting methodical analyses of their observations.

Prior to Liepmann, the concept of "asymbolia" had been introduced (by

Finkelnburg, 1870) and described as a generalized disturbance in the capacity to express or comprehend symbols in any modality, including linguistic and gestural symbols. In subsequent work Finkelnburg expanded the concept, incorporating disorders of the recognition of place, persons, and objects. Thus disorders of the voluntary control of intentional movements became part of a central communication disorder related to defective capacity for recognition. Jackson (1932) similarly discussed gestural behavior (pantomime) in the context of "words and other symbols."

Meynert, in 1890, accepted two major varieties of asymbolia: sensory asymbolia, which had been called "agnosia" by Freud (1891), and motor asymbolia. Motor asymbolia was found in patients who could not manipulate objects or who could not initiate or release neural activity related to "images of innervation of the upper limb." Unfortunately for Meynert the clinical case that he presented to support his analysis had too many other problems (cortical blindness, paralysis, ataxia) for his position to be clear and generally acceptable. But this conception of motor asymbolia corresponded precisely with Liepmann's conception of apraxia, as Liepmann himself indicated.

Among other precursors one should cite Wernicke (1884, 1895), who attributed the impossibility of certain movements in some of his nonaphasic patients to the abolition of motor images (representations, memories) for these movements. Nothnagel (1887) introduced the term *psychic paralysis* to cover states that were both akinetic and apractic and that occurred in one limb or one side of the body during regression from hemiplegia. De Ruck (1899, cited in Hécaen, 1972) considered the disorders of motility (which he called parakinesias) of one of his patients to have resulted from a dissociation (disconnection) of the center for ideation from the motor projection centers.

The question of disorders of the voluntary control of movements was thus confused, terminology was overabundant, and clinical references were disparate and poorly described by the time at which Liepmann (1900) provided his first report on apraxia. This was the famous case of Imperial Counsellor, M. T., who had defective gestural behavior affecting the right arm and leg, and the head, face, and tongue, while the left hand was normal for movements to verbal command and imitative gestures, with or without objects. No visual recognition disorder was present, verbal comprehension was good, and general intellectual capacity was "to a large degree preserved." To the general term *apraxia* Liepmann added the qualifying term *motor* to specify this disturbance. For this case Liepmann provided a detailed anatomoclinical analysis, concluding that the lesions related to the apraxia were located subcortically in the frontorolandic region with destruction of the corpus callosum and also in the left posterior parietal area. For Liepmann, apraxia represented a dissociation between the idea of the movement and its motor execution.

In a detailed and systematic study of 89 brain-injured patients Liepmann (1905) reported a high incidence of apraxic difficulty with the left hand ("sympathetic apraxia") in subjects with motor aphasia and right hemiplegia. A much lower incidence of apraxia was found in the left arm of right hemiplegics without aphasia, and no apraxia was found in the right arm of left hemiplegics.

In the same year Pick (1905) described a 43-year-old aphasic subject, who, although able to understand simple verbal commands, was unable to manipulate common objects, even though he could name and describe the objects and their use. For example, he used a razor as if it were a comb and tried to write with a pair of scissors. Pick called this disorder ideomotor apraxia.

Subsequently Liepmann (1908), on the basis of his own observations plus those of selected authors, such as Bonhoeffer (1903), Pick (1905), and Strohmayer (1903), elaborated a clinical, anatomic, and psychopathological synthesis of apraxia in its various forms. For Liepmann, apraxia was a unitary phenomenon, a disturbance in the voluntary control of purposive movements, the different varieties resulting from dysfunction at different levels of the same basic mechanism. Following is his overall analysis.

1.—*Melokinetic apraxia* (called innervatory apraxia by Kleist, 1911) represented the loss of kinetic memories for a single limb; this resulted from a mild lesion in the cerebral motor cortex insufficient to produce paralysis.

2.—*Bilateral ideomotor apraxia* (primitive motor apraxia) resulted from isolation of the sensorium (left parietal region) from the zones of execution. If the lesion involved the corpus callosum, isolating only the right hemispheric zone of execution, one could find a unilateral left ideomotor apraxia.

3.—*Ideational apraxia* (called ideomotor apraxia by Pick, 1905) referred to disorders of gestural behavior at a more abstract or "ideational" level. In this form the sequential kinetic activity remained functional, but the overall conception of the nature of the movement to be carried out was lost. This resulted from lesions that were more diffuse and that included a posterior parietal locus.

In addition to these specific attributions Liepmann added that a complete memory of a complex movement could not be considered to be related exclusively to a single cerebral region; visual, tactile, acoustic, and kinesthetic elements were essential components of the overall memory image of the complex act. A circumscribed cerebral lesion could not, therefore, bring about the total loss of a motor memory except in unusual situations.

This basic analysis by Liepmann has remained the standard against which other theories have been measured and tested. In 1914 von Monakow opened the path to additional explanations of apraxia by rejecting the idea that apraxia in any of its forms could be related to specific anatomic regions of the brain and by refusing to consider apraxia simply as a loss of motor image-memories. Goldstein (1948) carried these nonlocalizationist tendencies further, believing that a general loss of abstract behavior could be manifested by the inability to execute pretended actions.

Sittig (1930) affirmed a physiological theory of apraxia in which all possible intermediate forms of movement disorder could exist between complete motor paralysis and the different varieties of apraxia. For this author apraxia was closer to hemiplegia than hemiplegia was to peripheral nervous system paralysis. Sittig asserted that the dissociation between the preservation of automatic movements and the abolition of voluntary movements (considered by Liepmann to be characteristic of apraxia) was also seen, albeit to a lesser degree, in cortical paralyses.

In addition to general arguments about the mechanisms of the apraxias, additional varieties of apraxia were separated from the main syndrome. Kleist (1911) isolated innervatory apraxia, and Strauss (1924) and Kleist (1930, 1934) described and defined constructional apraxia. The relation of apractic and agnosic phenomena was explored by Poppelreuter (1914–1917), Foix (1916), Morlaas (1928), Schilder (1935), Lhermitte (1939), and others. This relationship was granted a special label—apractagnosia (Grunbaum, 1930), and the apractagnosic syndrome was subjected to neuropsychological examination (Hécaen et al, 1956). Brain (1941a,b) characterized the syndrome of dressing apraxia, and disorders of constructional activity due to right hemispheric lesions with visuospatial defects were elaborated (McFie, Piercy, and Zangwill, 1950; Hécaen, de Ajuriaguerra, and Massonet, 1951; Piercy et al, 1960, 1962).

Review of the history of apraxia thus reveals three major approaches to the subject. In one, for example Liepmann (1908), apraxia represented an isolated neuropsychological defect of gestural behavior, related to other defective symbolic functions but not dependent on them. In another, for example Finkelnburg (1870), Jackson (1932), and Brain (1965), apraxia was a component of a central communication defect, and gestural disturbance was a direct correlate of aphasia. In the third, for example Bastian (1898), Goldstein (1948), gestural deficiency resulted from nonspecific intellectual deterioration, rather than from localizable disturbances either of movement or of communication. In the next sections we describe clinical features of the apraxias and discuss neuropsychological studies designed to support one or another of these three approaches.

Major Forms of Apraxia—Bilateral Apraxias

Classically the major forms of apraxia include ideomotor apraxia, ideational apraxia, constructional apraxia, and dressing apraxia. Other forms of apraxia pose special problems and are considered separately. By contrast with

the four major varieties the others are distinguished by the difficulty of defining the limits between them and primary motor or psychomotor defects, by
their segmental character with respect to the body part involved (face, limb),
by their unilateral aspect, and/or by the fact that hemispheric lateralization
of the lesion does not seem to play a determining role.

Ideomotor Apraxia

The disorder is limited to simple, single gestures, while the level of ideation
necessary for complex gestures is preserved. All complex acts can be executed; however, their constituent elements are disturbed. The disorder is only
rarely seen in spontaneous activity and must often be looked for by special
tests, either of verbal command or of imitation. There may be a clear distinction between the response to verbal command and the response by imitation,
response by imitation being better than that to command. In all instances, for
the defect to be considered apractic, evidence that the patient has understood
the command must be clear. An additional criterion for apraxia, and one
used to distinguish this defect from aphasia, is that on imitation some movements may be restored, but on the whole performance remains defective.

Simple gestures used to demonstrate the apraxia may be classified as follows: expressive gestures with more or less symbolic value (e.g., wave good-
bye, threaten, blow a kiss); gestures of conventional symbolic value (e.g.,
military salute, sign of the cross); gestures descriptive of object use without
the presence of the object (e.g., pretend to stir coffee with a spoon, pretend to
hammer a nail into a block of wood); imitation of meaningless gestures (e.g.,
unusual positions of the hand). This descriptive classification has often been
considered to represent a progression of difficulty for the apractic subject,
expressive gestures being the easiest to reproduce, imitation of meaningless
gestures being the most difficult.

The pattern of behavior of the apractic patient may have several forms.
Either the desired response may be totally absent; or the patient may produce diffuse, amorphous, confused movements that represent the desired response in abridged and deformed manner; or the appropriate movements of
two or more gestures may be incorporated into a single gesture. Additional
elements characteristic of apractic behavior may also be observed, including
gestural enhancement, pantomimed context, body part as object, and vocal
overflow (Goodglass and Kaplan, 1963). Gestural enhancement is the drama-
tizing or emphasizing of a gesture by accompanying the required movement
with additional expressive facial or bodily movements. Pantomimed context
is the pantomiming of a situational setting in which the desired movement is
embedded. Body part as object is the use of a part of the body to serve as an
object in a pretended action, as in hammering with a fist or stirring sugar

with an index finger. Vocal overflow occurs in spite of instructions to refrain from speaking when the subject accompanies the gesture with an explanatory or exclamatory vocalization.

A detailed neuropsychological study by Hécaen (1975) has perhaps helped clarify the issue of clinical classification of ideomotor apraxia. He studied 249 subjects with left hemispheric lesions and analyzed their performance according to four categories (see Hécaen, 1967a, and introduction to this chapter): conventional symbolic gestures, expressive gestures, descriptive bodily gestures, and object utilization gestures. Commands were given verbally or by physical representation (demanding an imitation response).

An initial conclusion was that disorders of gestural behavior in response to verbal command could not easily be dissociated from disorders of language. The subsequent conclusions were based entirely on disturbances of gestural behavior on imitation. When apraxic behavior was correlated with other neuropsychological disturbances, two distinctive clinical clusters could be identified. In one, impairments of conventional symbolic gestures and of expressive gestures could be grouped together as disorders of a single system of signs. Descriptive gestures, whether they related to the body or to object use, belonged to another category. Disturbances in this latter category seemed to be caused by a motor sequencing defect.

In general, ideomotor apraxia is bilateral. In the early and famous case described by Liepmann, only the limbs on the right side of the body were involved, but this seems to have been an exception to the rule. The special problem of ideomotor apraxia involving only the left side of the body is considered below.

Ideational Apraxia

Ideational apraxia is seen when an apraxic subject attempts to carry out a complex gesture: although the individual elements of the total act are executed correctly, there is disruption in the logical and harmonious succession of separate elements. The overall act is inaccurately performed because the normal sequence is altered. Since ideational apraxia is a disturbance in the realization of a complex motor act, and not a disturbance in the realization of any of the components of that act, the disorder is bilateral and general, rather than segmented with respect to body parts. The patient with ideational apraxia is unable to establish the plan of action necessary to accomplish the intended goal, even though segmental kinetic capacity remains intact.

In ideomotor apraxia isolated gestures are disturbed, but the overall plan of action may be preserved; the converse is true for ideational apraxia. One may see, for example, a patient unable to complete the task of lighting a candle with a match, although the acts of removing the match from the box or striking the match may be normal. In such a complex act one is as likely, however, to see the patient strike the match against the wrong side of the box, or attempt to strike the wrong end of the match, or even attempt to strike the candle against the box, or present an unlit match to the candle. The patient is unable to conceive the desired action as a whole and organize the diverse partial acts that constitute the whole in their temporal and spatial relations.

The pattern of behavior of the subject with ideational apraxia may have several forms. The apractic may stop after the first, partial act has been completed; he may substitute a similar action for the desired action; or he may confound the order of the steps, omitting one or several intermediate steps. As the desired action becomes longer with more steps, the disorder becomes more severe. Complex acts that have become automatized by overlearning may be carried out normally. The defect is characterized by variability and may intermittently diminish in response to increased attention or need. These subjects can imitate sequential actions of the examiner if the total action is neither too long nor too complicated. However, the imitated gesture may be reproduced in a denatured or deformed manner. Perseveration of one action into another is common.

The relationship between ideomotor and ideational apraxia is still uncertain. Ideomotor apraxia is seen most often in the absence of ideational apraxia; however, there is considerable dispute over whether ideational apraxia can occur in the absence of ideomotor apraxia. Liepmann (1908) reported 6 cases of ideational apraxia in a series with 24 cases of ideomotor apraxia. Hécaen and Gimeno (1960) reported 8 cases of ideational apraxia in a series with 47 cases of ideomotor apraxia. In the latter series 3 cases of ideational apraxia without ideomotor apraxia were described; however some doubt is cast on the acceptance of these 3 cases because these subjects had difficulty with bimanual coordination. Associated clinical symptomatology is the same for both syndromes, although more frequent with ideational apraxia. This includes aphasia, constructional apraxia, intellectual deterioration or confusion, sensory disorders, and finger agnosia.

Discussion of these two syndromes concerns whether they represent two separate disorders or simply different degrees of severity of the same basic problem, as maintained by Liepmann (1908) and Kleist (1930, 1934). Ideational apraxia has been considered by some authors to be a defect in the handling of objects; others have considered a defect in object handling to be a severe form of ideomotor apraxia. Ideational apraxia has also been defined as a defect in the performance of a serial movement; others have considered this to be a defect in memory. Denny-Brown (1958) believed that both syndromes resulted from a single conceptual disturbance: the loss of the propositional usage of objects. Liepmann had gone further in his analysis: ideomotor apraxia was the manifestation of a dissociation between the sensorimotor components of a gesture and the control of these components by the ideational concept; ideational apraxia was a disturbance within the ideational concept itself.

Foix (1916) and his student Morlaas (1928) inferred that the essential difference between ideomotor apraxia and ideational apraxia did not lie between complex and simple acts, but rather between acts involving the use of objects and acts not involving the use of objects. Thus, Morlaas considered ideational apraxia to be an "agnosia of object utilization"; that is, the subject could name the object and give a verbal description of its use but could not actually use the object. For practical neuropsychological testing DeRenzi et al (1968a) accepted Morlaas's definition of ideational apraxia as the inability to demonstrate the use of real objects.

Sittig (1930, 1931) and Zangwill (1960, 1967a) wondered if ideational apraxia might not represent so severe a stage of ideomotor apraxia as to involve even the easiest gestures, such as those requiring the use of objects. Zangwill asserted that it was difficult, if not impossible, to find in the literature a detailed clinical description of a patient with ideational apraxia who did not also have ideomotor apraxia.

Heilman (1973) believed that ideational apraxia represented a distinctive entity. He described three patients with anomic aphasia who, unlike patients with ideomotor apraxia who perform poorly to command but often with appropriate motions, were unable to respond to command with any but the most irrelevant gestures. They appeared perplexed and said they could not carry out the command, and yet they could demonstrate verbally that they understood and also could choose the correct movement on multiple choice. Unlike patients with ideomotor apraxia who improve slightly with imitation but still perform abnormally, these patients performed flawlessly on imitation. He hypothesized that the defect was in the verbally mediated motor sequence selector responsible for choosing appropriate motor sequences.

Constructional Apraxia

In 1912, during the epoch following Liepmann's elaboration and classification of apraxia, Kleist isolated a separate variety that he subsequently named "constructional apraxia" (Kleist, 1922). For Kleist constructional apraxia was a disorder of formative activities in which the spatial part of the task was disturbed, although single movements were not affected. The precise locus of the defect, in the chain of production of voluntary movements, was neither visuoperceptive nor motor; the defect was to be found in the transmission of information from visual perception to the appropriate action. In 1917 Poppelreuter described a patient with disturbance of constructional activity of such a nature that visual perception by the patient not only did not rectify the problem but also served to exacerbate it. Since the earliest clinical descriptions (Kleist, 1912, 1922; Poppelreuter, 1914–1917; Seelert, 1920; Strauss, 1924) constructional apraxia has been generally accepted as an independent syndrome; discussion has concentrated on the issue of underlying mechanism(s). The argument has been whether the defective performance is executive, resulting from a motor impairment for complex or sequential activities, or perceptual, resulting from a defect in visuospatial perception.

Clinical characteristics may be elicited by giving the patient drawing or constructional tasks, by verbal command, or by imitation. Drawing tasks may be simple and two dimensional or complex and three dimensional. Constructional tasks have often used cardboard puzzles, sticks of wood, or blocks. Specific constructional or drawing defects may include any or several of the following: simplification of the model; expanded reproduction with scattering of parts; the closing-in phenomenon, in which the drawing or the construction is placed very close to the model, often even overlapping the model (Mayer-Gross, 1935, 1936); misalignment on the page; and spatial disorientation with reversals, rotations, and disruption of vertical and horizontal axes. The defect may be variable for the same task at different times, or it may not appear except when the task requirement is complex and three dimensional.

Benton (1962, 1969a) has stressed that the different tests used to define constructional apraxia are biased by the implicit assumption that there is a

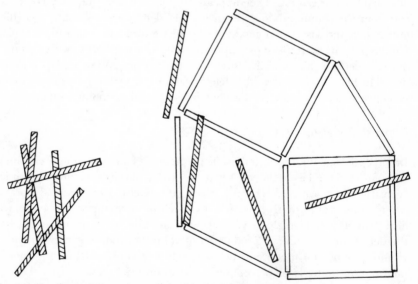

Constructional apraxia in a demented subject. Note the "closing-in" effect.

unitary disorder that can be uncovered by one or another of these tests. By means of a systematic neuropsychological exploration of 100 subjects with cerebral damage he found that intercorrelations between the performances of these subjects on four tests of constructional ability did not support such an assumption; performances related to drawing were distinguishable from performances related to assembling. He concluded that constructional apraxia is the manifestation of at least two separate neuropsychological defects.

This conclusion is supported by the results of a study by Benson and Barton (1970). They evaluated the performance of subjects with localized cerebral lesions on six tests of constructional ability. They found that constructional defects occurred with lesions in all areas but that different combinations of constructional defects occurred depending on the location of the lesion.

Systematic observations of patients with lesions localized to a single hemisphere clearly demonstrated that constructional apraxia could follow lesions limited to the speech-dominant hemisphere (Kleist, 1933) and also limited to the speech-nondominant hemisphere (Paterson and Zangwill, 1944; McFie et al, 1950; Hécaen et al, 1951). It was now left to subsequent research to determine if the syndromic differences observed following damage to one or the other hemisphere were quantitative or qualitative.

For one group of authors the differences of constructional capabilities seen following right or left hemispheric lesions reflected differences in frequency and severity of the same basic disturbances (e.g., Piercy and Smith, 1962). A study by Piercy et al (1960) demonstrated a significantly greater frequency of practic defects following right hemispheric lesions than following left hemispheric lesions (22.3% vs. 11.6%), as well as a greater severity of disorder. Arrigoni and DeRenzi (1964) argued that the greater frequency and severity of practic defects seen after right hemispheric lesions were probably due to the fact that lesions of the right hemisphere are larger than those of the left, since lesions of the left hemisphere are detected earlier because of the associated symptoms of aphasia.

An increasing number of neuropsychological studies have supported the hypothesis that a qualitative difference in practic defects results from lesions of different hemispheres. Patterson and Zangwill (1944) called attention to the "piecemeal" approach of patients with right hemispheric lesions in the reproduction of the model. Hécaen et al (1951) noted that following right hemispheric lesions patients had difficulty especially with complex or three-dimensional models, that the spatial orientation of their drawings was askew, and that these patients tended to neglect the left side of their drawing. Piercy et al (1960) compared performances of subjects with left or right hemispheric lesions on tests for constructional apraxia. In the group with left hemispheric

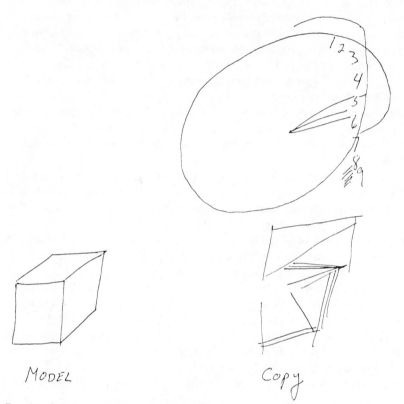

clock drawn to command

MODEL   Copy

Drawing deficit in a patient with right parietal lesion

lesions the structure of the drawing was simplified and the number of lines used was reduced by comparison with the model. In the group with right hemispheric lesions, the number of lines used was greater than that seen in the other group occasionally exceeding the number of lines in the model. Warrington et al (1966) studied drawing disabilities in relation to lateralization of the cerebral lesion. In the apraxias caused by right hemispheric lesions there was a diminution in the angle size in the copy of a star; no increase in the number of corners in the copy of a cube; an increase in details on a test of free design; and no improvement with learning during the test procedure. In the apraxias caused by left hemispheric lesions the exact opposite of the these findings was observed. These authors concluded that constructional apraxias following right-brain damage were due to a defect in visuospatial perception, but constructional apraxias following left-brain damage were due to a defect in motor executory control, a defect in programming the action (see also Warrington, 1969).

Split-brain studies have also contributed to our understanding of constructional apraxia, indicating that the right hemisphere plays a dominant role in visuoconstructive activities (Gazzaniga, Bogen, Sperry, 1965, 1967; Bogen, 1969; Gazzaniga, 1970; Dimond, 1972). For right-handers with hemispheric separation resulting from callosal section it is difficult, and often impossible, to copy a three-dimensional model, such as a cube, with the right hand, although the left hand is capable of performing this task. The inferiority of the left hemisphere in controlling the ability of the right hand to copy may be overcome by the examiner's giving verbal instructions to the subject.

Hécaen and Assal (1970) compared constructional defects in groups of subjects with right and left hemispheric lesions. If cues were given for the reproduction of models, subjects with left-sided lesions improved, but subjects with right-sided lesions did not improve and even deteriorated in some cases. These findings provide systematic neuropsychological verification of similar observations made previously by Poppelreuter (1914–1917) and more recently by von Dongen and Drooglever-Fortuyn (1968). The significant point is that patients with constructional apraxia with left hemispheric lesions are aided by visual cues while those with right hemispheric lesions are not. This observation supports the hypothesis that lesions in the left hemisphere disrupt the execution of the action (Duensing, 1953; Warrington et al, 1966; Zangwill, 1960, 1967a) or more specifically the planning of the action (Warrington, 1969). Visual cues appear to compensate for the deficit by providing a program for the action. Additional findings (Warrington et al, 1966; Hécaen and Assal, 1970) indicate that performance improves with learning for the group with left-sided, but not for the group with right-sided lesions.

Neurobehavioral symptoms associated with constructional apraxia are different according to the hemisphere damaged. Following left-sided lesions the most frequently associated clinical defects are the several varieties of posterior aphasia; also seen are elements of the Gerstman syndrome, or the entire syndrome (acalculia, apraphia, right-left disorientation, and finger agnosia). Following right-sided lesions disturbance in the recognition of corporeal space and extracorporeal space are the main associated symptoms. For Costa and Vaughan (1962) constructional apraxia seen following right hemispheric defects is part of a larger ensemble resulting from visuospatial disorganization.

The studies and arguments just summarized tend to support a general hypothesis: constructional apraxia may result from a breakdown in different underlying neuropsychological mechanisms, depending on the hemisphere damaged. Following left hemispheric lesions the disorder may be a defect of execution due to the inability to establish the program for the desired action. Visual information and learning may attenuate the severity of the disorder. Following right hemispheric lesions the apraxia, which is intimately associated with visuospatial disturbances, is not benefited, and may even be aggravated, by visual cues and learning.

Dressing Apraxia

In 1922 Marie et al described two patients with "planotopokinesia" (an inability to orient themselves in a two-dimensional plane) who were unable to dress themselves properly although they were not otherwise apraxic. In 1941 Brain isolated the syndrome and applied the name *dressing apraxia*. Hécaen and de Ajuriaguerra (1942–1945) indicated that isolated disturbances in dressing resulted from lesions in the nonspeech-dominant hemisphere.

Clinically the subject has great difficulty orienting and correctly disposing clothing with respect to his own body. He manipulates the clothes incoherently, turning and reversing them and handling them haphazardly. If, by accident, he successfully accomplishes the task of laying out the clothes properly, prior to putting them on, he is unable to organize the gestures necessary to establish the appropriate relationship between his clothes and his body. The semiautomatic motor capacity for dressing oneself is lost. In mild cases clothes may eventually be put on properly, after a series of fruitless attempts and after long reflection. Even in these cases, however, the patient is unable to tie a necktie or shoelaces.

Dressing apraxia appears in conjunction with the same symptom complex of visuospatial-constructive defects due to right hemispheric lesions—sensory, spatial, and somatognosic. Dressing apraxia is much less frequent than constructional apraxia (in a ratio of 1 to 4). Piercy (1964) suggests that such a proportion is probably the result of what Teuber has called the "order of fragility" of two activities, in this case dressing ability being more resistant to disrupting influences than constructional activites.

When the dressing disturbance occurs without constructional apraxia, it seems to depend on another deficit, hemiasomatognosia, and may be unilateral. It seems that these are the cases to which Denny-Brown has referred (1958, 1963) when he reduced the syndrome of dressing apraxia to a subcategory of "unilateral kinetic apraxia of the repulsive type" related to amorphosynthesis. According to this conception avoidance reactions prevent the subject from normally adjusting clothing to that side of the body with the motor reflex disturbance.

Poeck (1969) also denies this syndrome the independent status of apraxia, claiming that the disorder results from one of several underlying symptoms, including ideomotor apraxia, spatial disorientation, or neglect of one side of corporeal or extracorporeal space. This explanation would not, however, answer the question of why only gestures of dressing are impaired in isolated fashion in some cases, and not also object manipulation of conventional symbolic gestures, or the question of why dressing apraxia is frequently bilateral, while neglect of space is generally found to be unilateral. There is no doubt that some cases of dressing apraxia are associated with, and may even be dependent on, hemiasomatognosia. But in these cases the dressing apraxia is unilateral. We would sooner suggest that the specificity of bilateral dressing apraxia as a syndrome is difficult to reject, and the causes of this syndrome may be searched for in the conjunction of neuropsychological factors relating gestural behavior to one's own body.

Unilateral and Segmental Apraxias

Melokinetic Apraxia

This syndrome represents a form of movement disorder intermediate between paresis and apraxia. The clinical manifestations include an impairment in the rapidity, skill, and delicacy of complex or serial movements, such as rapidly pressing and releasing a button repeatedly. The disorder is ordinarily confined to a small muscle group, is unilateral, and is contralateral to a mild lesion situated in the premotor area. Kleist (1911, 1933) considered the defect to be exclusively executive, resulting from an impaired ability to link or to separate closely related but independent muscle groups having separate innervations.

In practice it is difficult to define the limits between this disorder and muscle weakness. Ethelberg (1951) demonstrated that automatic, reflexive movements were equally as impaired as voluntary movements, while awareness of the action to be accomplished was fully intact. He concluded that the syndrome was not apraxic.

In 1908 Wilson described a disturbance of tonic (reflexive) innervation that he indicated was related to motor apraxia. Mayer-Gross (1935, 1936) believed that perseveration of tonic, reflexive behavior was a major factor in apraxia. These concepts were further developed by Denny-Brown (1958), who described "kinetic apraxia" in relationship to the "magnetic" syndrome seen in patients with frontal lobe damage. These patients with a grasping reflex of the hand or foot have an irresistible tendency to follow objects that touch their hand. This fixation prevents the patient from shifting his focus of attention and thus interferes with the execution of gestures. Considered in these terms, melokinetic apraxia would not be acceptable as a true apraxia (Denny-Brown, 1958).

Buccofacial Apraxia

This variety of apraxia was first described by Jackson (1932), who discussed a patient who was unable to stick out his tongue on command but was able to use his tongue to remove a breadcrumb from his lip. The disorder reflects a disturbance in buccofacial motor activities not linked to speech and is characterized by an inability to perform voluntary movements in the presence of a preserved ability to perform automatic and reflexive movements with the same muscle groups.

Clinically one observes that these patients are able to eat, chew, swallow, blow out a match, smile, and so forth while at the same time they are unable to perform to verbal command tasks involving use of the same motor pathways, such as stick out the tongue, blow, suck, chew, and smile. In any individual case, aspects of motor disorders—tonic, spastic, paralytic—may be seen. Reproduction of facial expression by imitation is ordinarily preserved. Voluntary activity of the upper half of the face is usually not defective, and these subjects can respond to verbal commands by frowning, closing their eyes, raising their eyebrows, and so on. Facial paralysis frequently accompanies this disorder; however the paralysis is unilateral, while the apraxia is bilateral.

Theoretically the distinction between cortical facial diplegia and buccofacial apraxia should be easy, because the diplegia should affect reflex and automatic movements, as well as voluntary movements. In practice, however, a dissociation between automatic and voluntary movements may also be seen in cortical facial diplegias, for instance, in cortical pseudobulbar syndromes. In general, preservation of automatic movements is limited to chewing and swallowing. Thus the distinction between motor disturbance and buccofacial apraxia is often difficult to make. By means of glossograms Bay (1957) has observed movement abnormalities of the tongue in patients with buccofacial apraxia even when they were moving the tongue unintentionally. Denny-Brown (1963) has called attention to the presence of an automatic sucking reflex in patients with severe buccofacial apraxia.

The frequency of buccofacial apraxia, partly because of the anatomoclinical difficulties just cited, is difficult to ascertain. This syndrome, although associated with ideomotor and ideational apraxia, may be independent; it seems to be most highly correlated with ideomotor apraxia. Of 19 of their patients with ideomotor apraxia, de Ajuriaguerra el al, (1960) found 8 with buccofacial apraxia. In the same study each case of unilateral kinetic apraxia of the "magnetic" type (see sections on melokinetic apraxia and unilateral apraxia for an explanation of this term) was also accompanied by buccofacial apraxia.

The relationship between motor aphasia and buccofacial apraxia was underscored by Liepmann (1908), who considered disorders of verbal expression as an apraxia of the speech muscles. Nathan (1947) and Bay (1957) maintained a similar position, using the term *cortical anarthria* or *apraxic dysarthria*. Alajouanine and Lhermitte (1960) found buccofacial apraxia to be constant in the initial stages of anarthria; however, they observed that the two clinical conditions did not regress at the same rate, apraxia disappearing even while anarthria persisted. Our own position on the mechanisms underlying disorders of verbal expression is detailed in the chapter on aphasia.

According to Denny-Brown (1963) the cortical aphasia of Broca is an apraxia of speech manifested by the inability to begin a word that reappears at each new syllable with contaminations and perseverations from the preceding syllable. Always associated with buccolinguofacial apraxia at the beginning, the phonetic disintegration persists longer than the buccofacial apraxia. Nonetheless the different patterns of regression are insufficient, according to Denny-Brown, to deny that the expressive aphasia is really a disorder of praxis. The difficulties in producing labial movements necessary for the production of certain phonemes, such as occlusives, are of the same type as the automatic sucking reflexes seen following frontal lesions. The disorder represents, for Denny-Brown, a kinetic apraxia complicated by disorders of rhythm and perseveration.

Our personal clinical experience is not consistent with this interpretation. We have not observed a constant association between disorders of phonemic expression and buccolinguofacial apraxia for nonlanguage movements. We have found disorders of phonemic expression independent of buccofacial apraxia, and we do not consider it possible to affirm an absolute relationship between these two disorders.

Unilateral Limb Apraxias

In the famous case of Liepmann (1900) the practic disorder was limited almost entirely to the right side of the body. In subsequent reports Liepmann emphasized either bilateral ideomotor apraxias or unilateral apraxias involving the left arm. Regarding unilateral left-sided apraxia, Liepmann indicated two types. The first he called sympathetic apraxia. In a large proportion of cases this was associated with a right hemiplegia and motor aphasia. The disorders of gestural behavior in the left arm and leg were quite marked and were present both to command and on imitation, although there was improvement on imitation.

The second type resulted from an anterior callosal lesion that interrupted the anatomic connections between the left sensorimotor cortex and the right hemispheric zone for execution of commands and thus deprived the right motor cortex of verbal commands coming from the left hemisphere. In this variety of apraxia orders given verbally may be carried out by the right hand but not by the left hand. Despite this, the left hand can manipulate objects well and can even correctly imitate gestures of the examiner, without being able to describe the usage of the object by means of movements (Geschwind and Kaplan, 1962). In addition the left hand has writing difficulties of an aphasic type and cannot transpose printed letters to script, although the right hand writes normally. The results of split-brain studies on human beings (Sperry et al, 1967; Bogen, 1969; Gazzaniga, 1970; Dimond, 1972) confirm the reality of this syndrome of disconnection between the language zone and the right motor area.

Denny-Brown (1958, 1963) clearly distinguished bilateral apraxias from unilateral kinetic apraxias, which affect the limbs on one or the other side of the body, depending on the hemisphere damaged. Normal movements are determined by tactile, visual, and proprioceptive factors that function both in concert and in competition; the removal or reduction of one of these factors may result in hyperactivity of the others, as well as in the appearance or inhibition of instinctual reflexes. A cortical lesion may thus produce a rupture in the equilibrium between the contact reactions and the avoidance reactions. Following this line of reasoning, Denny-Brown recognized two types of kinetic apraxia. One, kinetic apraxia of the magnetic type, corresponded to the release of reactions of contact and prehension. The other, kinetic apraxia of the repulsive type, corresponded to the release of avoidance reactions. Brain damage may cause the release of primitive reflexes and automatic motor behaviors, for example, contact, avoidance, prehension, which contaminate all gestures.

From a review of the literature plus extensive personal observations Hécaen (1972b) and Gimeno (1960) concluded that three major forms of unilateral left-sided ideomotor apraxia could be defined. The first form was characterized especially by inertia, an absence of spontaneous activity of the left extremities. Voluntary movements were amorphous; expressive gestures were less well performed than descriptive gestures. Object manipulation was generally well preserved, and actions requiring bimanual collaboration were well executed (Maas, 1910). This form of apraxia seemed to be related to posterior right hemispheric lesions, as suggested by the associated symptomatology of hemiasomatognosia, dressing apraxia, unilateral spatial agnosia, astereognosis, and/or left hemianopia. However, other cases had associated symptomatology suggestive of left hemispheric localization for the lesion, and anatomoclinical correlation was not established. This form of unilateral disturbance of gestural behavior seems most closely related to a defect in recognition of the contralateral (to the lesion) half of one's own body. The gesture, shorn of its corporeal reference, loses its significance if a real object is not available to provide concrete cues.

The second form was characterized especially by phenomena of tonic perseveration, abnormal movements, and/or crural monoplegia, left or right, strongly suggesting a lesion on the medial surface of the frontal lobe. Postmortem and surgical studies have confirmed the clinical impressions of left or right hemispheric anterior cerebral artery infarctions or frontocallosal tumors. Forced prehension is sometimes seen on the same side as the apraxia. In Hécaen's series all movements were disturbed on the involved side, indicating that this form of apraxia corresponds to Denny-Brown's "magnetic" type of kinetic apraxia.

The third form was characterized by a motor disturbance with associated signs of the avoiding reaction; however the abnormal instinctual avoiding reflexes were not necessarily found in the apraxic limbs but may have been seen in the nonapraxic limbs. Object manipulation was normal, but coordinate activity of the two hands was impaired. This type of apraxia was found to result from lesions in the posterior part of the cerebral hemisphere ipsilateral to the apraxic limbs.

Studies with unilateral apraxias thus reveal two major underlying problems. One relates to a disconnection between the zone of execution in the right hemisphere and the zone of language in the left hemisphere; gestures of the left hand are possible if the orders are not given verbally, but not possible in response to verbal command. The other relates to psychomotor defects (reactions of prehension, avoidance, or motoric hemiaspontaneity) that contaminate the gesture regardless of the stimulus modality or the type of gesture.

Apraxia of Gait and Whole-Body Movements

Gait disturbances, called frontal ataxia, had been related to frontal lesions and had been considered a motor disorder resulting from disturbance of the frontopontocerebellar pathways until 1926, when Gerstmann and Schilder represented them as a true apraxia of the lower limbs. According to van Bogaert and Martin (1929) apraxia of gait consisted essentially of a diminution or loss of the normal capacity to dispose the legs appropriately for the act of walking, despite absence of any paresis or other gross motor defect. Clinically one finds various degrees of the disturbance from loss of initiative (see the chapter on frontal lobe disorders), to maladroit performance, to an impossibility of voluntary movement with perseveration of impulsive movements. For van Bogaert and Martin (1929) the disorder represented a stage in the regression of static motor function that ended in complete static atonia.

Following the reasoning of Denny-Brown (1958), Meyer and Barron (1960) reviewed the question in a clinicophysiological study, concluding that apraxia of gait was like a double kinetic apraxia of the magnetic type. Movements of walking were affected by interference of tonic phenomena, of oppositional rigidity, and of perseveration of the forced prehension reaction. The ground seemed to exert a magnetic attractive force on the feet. The greatest difficulty was seen in the initiation of movement, especially when voluntary movements of an "abstract" nature were requested, for example, pretend to kick a football, write a number with a toe. Once the movement began, performance improved.

Apraxia of gait is often accompanied by what has been referred to as "trunco-pedal" apraxia, that is, apraxia of global, whole-body movements, such as lying down, sitting, rising, rolling over. Regarding apraxia of gait and of whole-body movements, Geschwind (1965, 1973) rejects the former and indicates special features of the latter. Geschwind prefers the term *frontal gait disturbance* to *apraxia of gait,* since he believes that the disorder of gait that follows frontal lesions reflects impairment of motor mechanisms and does not satisfy the criteria of apraxia.

As for whole-body movements Geschwind has stressed not so much the impairment of such activities as their preservation in patients with otherwise widespread apraxic dysfunction. He described the clinical situation in which a patient may have severe buccofacial apraxia and severe bilateral limb apraxia but could nonetheless carry out in good, if not perfect, manner movements affecting the whole body, such as standing up, turning around, and assuming various typical poses, for example, the position of a boxer. Our clinical observations with apraxic patients tend to support this suggestion regarding the preservation of whole-body responses in apraxic patients. Geschwind proposed that the corpus callosum is not necessary for the integration of this type of bodily movement and that walking and other whole-body activities may be controlled as integrated acts at the level of the brain stem. Commands may descend unilaterally to this integrating system to set it in action.

Selective Apraxias

In the chapter on disorders of language we indicated the effect that apraxia could have on certain types of graphic performance even though constructional ability might not be disturbed.

Motor amusia or avocalia, that is, the inability to sing, whistle, or hum, either spontaneously or on imitation, both for isolated notes and for melodies, may result from apraxic defects. Kleist (1933) described a tonal mutism due to apraxia of the movements of the face, tongue, and larynx. In this case isolated musical sounds could not be reproduced, while the rhythm of melodies could be. Kleist stated that the reverse situation could also be observed.

Various authors who have written on this topic suggest a left or right posterior frontal localization for the lesion.

Personal observations by Denckla have called attention to a selective apraxia for the movements of the head related to saying "yes" and "no," that is, nodding and turning the head from side to side. The observation refers to a consistent and striking dissociation between the vocal utterance of the patient and the accompanying head gesture; for example, the patient says "yes" while shaking his head "no" and vice versa. Whether this "yes-no apraxia" is a true, independent syndrome or an artifact of the testing situation remains to be confirmed.

MECHANISMS OF THE APRAXIAS

Anatomoclinical Correlations

The dissociation of apraxic phenomena is seen not only at the clinical level but also at the antomoclinical level, where anatomic localization and hemispheric lateralization vary according to the modality of gestural disturbance. In this section we consider the relationship of anatomy to function by considering the behavioral changes that occur following lesions in specific regions.

Posterior Left Hemispheric Lesions

Ideomotor and ideational apraxia are the major apraxic syndromes that depend unequivocally on lesions in this region. In a series of 415 cases with retrorolandic hemispheric lesions these two varieties of apraxia were not found unless the lesions were in the left hemisphere or bilateral (Hécaen, 1962, 1972b). In the study of ideational apraxia by DeRenzi et al (1968a) disorders of object manipulation were found following left-sided lesions.

Foix (1916) suggested that these two forms of apraxia corresponded to involvement of two different vascular territories: ideomotor apraxia was an element of the syndrome of the parietal branch of the artery to the angular gyrus; ideational apraxia was an element of the syndrome of the temporal branch of the artery of the angular gyrus. De Ajuriaguerra, Hécaen, and Angelergues (1960) found ideomotor apraxia to be associated with parietal and temporal lesions, and ideational apraxia with large posterior (parietal, temporoparietal) lesions. As we have already indicated, constructional apraxia with primarily executive or planning defects also result from lesions in these areas.

We may thus conclude that dominant hemispheric posterior parietal and temporoparietal lesions (supramarginal and angular gyri) play an important role in the production of ideomotor, ideational, and constructional apraxia.

Nonetheless, in a statistical study, Hécaen (1969a) did not find significant correlations between the specific posterior lobe involved and either ideomotor or ideational apraxia, although constructional apraxia was significantly related to the parietal lobe. However, the role of frontal lesions in the production of any of these three types of apraxia was significantly excluded.

Posterior Right Hemispheric Lesions

Lesions in these areas produce constructional apraxia and dressing apraxia. The lesions producing these defects are localizable to the temporoparieto-occipital junction. However, a mass effect is more marked in this hemisphere than in the language-dominant hemisphere; the three retrorolandic lobes of the right hemisphere seem to have more of a tendency for equipotentiality of function than those of the left hemisphere. Despite this general observation some lobe-specific differences were found in a study of subjects with verified lesion localizations (Hécaen and Assal, 1970). A significant correlation for constructional apraxia was found only for parietal lobe lesions; a significant correlation for dressing apraxia was found for lesions of the parietal and occipital lobes. Again, frontal lobe lesions were significantly excluded as causes of either of these two types of apraxia.

Frontal and Callosal Lesions

Lesions in these regions have been found to produce melokinetic, buccolinguofacial, and unilateral apraxias. For melokinetic apraxia Kleist (1930, 1933) had proposed as the responsible lesion site the contralateral, anterior portion of the motor cortex. Nielsen (1946) proposed areas 4 and 6. We find these suggestions to be more in keeping with a primarily motor, rather than apractic, disorder. Fulton (1937) demonstrated motor defects of a "melokinetic" type in chimpanzees with ablations of area 6.

Buccolinguofacial apraxias have also been associated with lesions of the anterior portion of the frontorolandic operculum (Nathan, 1947), and many other authors have referred to lesions of F_1 and F_2. Lesions of the left hemisphere have been most frequently considered responsible for this form of apraxia, especially because of the frequent association of motor aphasia and right facial paralysis. However, some observations in which the lesion was lateralized to the right hemisphere have also been reported (Hartmann, 1907; Rose, 1908; Goldstein, 1909). Geschwind (1965) has proposed the following anatomoclinical explanations for the production of buccolinguofacial apraxia. The lesions may occur either in the motor association cortex anterior to the motor region for control of the face near Broca's area or in the region of the supramarginal gyrus. Facial movements would not be executed, either in response to verbal command or on imitation of the examiner's movements.

In the case of the posterior lesion the buccolinguofacial apraxia would result from a disconnection of the posterior language areas from the anterior association cortex. In the case of the frontal lesion apraxia would occur because the connections between the motor face area on the left and the origins of the callosal fibers to the face area on the right were destroyed. However, following tactile stimulation the right motor cortex could act to cause facial movements; the right motor cortex would also be able to function for overlearned actions.

As for unilateral apraxias various anatomoclinical correlations have been noted by different authors. Sympathetic apraxia, associated clinically with motor aphasia, results from frontal lesions that extend subcortically beneath the left motor strip and beneath Broca's area, destroying the origin of fibers that pass across the corpus callosum to the right motor strip.

Unilateral kinetic apraxia of a magnetic type depends on frontal lesions identical to those that release the forced-grasp reflex, that is, area 8. These lesions may be found in either hemisphere, in the superior or medial portions of the frontal lobe, with or without involvement of the corpus callosum. Unilateral kinetic apraxia of a repulsive type depends on parietal lesions that produce an avoidance reaction. Denny-Brown (1958), by means of ablation studies with monkeys, has demonstrated exaggerated exploratory responses with frontal lesions and avoidance responses with parietal lesions.

Split-Brain Studies

The relationship of natural and surgical lesions of the corpus callosum to unilateral apraxia requires special consideration. Liepmann (1900, 1905, 1908a) had emphasized the role of corpus callosum lesions in the production of left-sided ideomotor apraxia. This conclusion, generally accepted as a result of Liepmann's and then Goldstein's (1909) observations, fell into disregard subsequently. Early split-brain studies with animals did not support the human clinical observations, and human subjects with surgical section of neocortical commissures were reported to have no remarkable behavioral changes (Akelaitis et al, 1942). Nonetheless a clinical report with anatomic verification published in the early sixties (Geschwind and Kaplan, 1962) seemed to support the earlier Liepmann argument and contradict that of Akelaitis.

Studies on split-brain patients by Gazzaniga, Bogen, and Sperry (1967) and experimental studies by Dimond (1972) shed new light on these conflicting reports. Support for both positions was provided. In the immediate postoperative period Gazzaniga et al (1967) noted antagonistic movements of the two hands in one of their nine patients. These movements were similar to those called diagnostic dyspraxia by Akelaitis. With one hand the patient might attempt to pull on his trousers, while with the other hand he would lower his trousers. With the right hand he might beckon to or enlist aid from his wife, while with the left hand he would push her away aggressively.

Sperry et al (1960) emphasized the marked variation in motor control from one patient to another in the immediate postoperative period. Nonetheless, with the exception of one patient who had received a left hemispheric operation, all split-brain subjects had a unilateral apraxia to verbal command involving the left limbs, while motor control of right limbs was good. These defects disappeared by the end of the first postoperative week, except in one patient who retained the unilateral apraxia for 5 years following commissurotomy.

In the later postoperative period, study of gestural behavior evaluated the effective hemispheric control of the contralateral or ipsilateral limbs. Left hemispheric control of the right arm was normal. Left hemispheric control of the left arm was normal for the proximal portion of the limb but was mediocre, at best, for the distal portion, especially for fine movements of the hand. Thus, in response to visual stimuli to the left hemisphere or to oral verbal stimuli, the left hand could point to objects and trace their external contours, could write words, and could carry out arithmetic operations. However, writing, which was crude and hesitant, became impossible if proximal arm movements were impeded.

Right hemispheric control of the left hand was normal for all nonverbal tests. Right hemispheric control of the right hand was the most deficient, poor performance being found on all but the simplest pointing-to-object and outline-tracing tests. Again, successful motor control of the ipsilateral limb seemed to predominate for the proximal segment of the limb.

Regardless of the hand involved, all tests that required a motor response to verbal stimuli presented to the right hemisphere were performed poorly. One should not assume that these failures represented a loss of motor control; it is more likely that they resulted from poor degree of verbal comprehension by the right hemisphere.

Interhemispheric conflict was also manifest; the motor control of an ipsilateral limb by one hemisphere could be overcome by sending contradictory signals to the contralateral hemisphere. For example, if the right hemisphere received a visual stimulus of a triangle, the right hand could draw the outline of the triangle. If, however, at the same moment that the right hemisphere was receiving the triangle, the left hemisphere received a circle, the right hand would draw a circle. Despite manifestations of interhemispheric competition, the two hands normally worked together in a well-coordinated manner. Akelaitis had noted that one of his split-brain patients could type or play a piano. When conflicting tasks were demanded, the motor disturbance became apparent.

Further exploring independent hemispheric control of motor function, Gazzaniga et al (1967) found that each hemisphere could also function simultaneously on separate tasks. Split-brain subjects could perform two tasks (e.g., response to color discrimination vs. response to brilliance discrimination) with the same reaction time for both as it would take normal subjects for either one alone.

Sperry, Gazzaniga, and Bogen (1969) concluded that the possibility of hemispheric control of motor behavior, both contralateral and ipsilateral, may be preserved if the callosal section is pure; that is, if there are no hemispheric lesions. However, hemispheric control of the ipsilateral limbs is inefficient and incomplete, especially for distal movements and movements requiring delicate control. Any complication, whether from preoperative or perioperative lesions or phenomena of diaschisis, may interfere with the mechanism of control of the ipsilateral limb, while that for the contralateral limb is more solid. Variations in the clinical picture may result from different combinations of these factors.

Long-term motor effects of cerebral commissurotomy in man have also been studied. Examining eight subjects having undergone commissurotomy 6 to 8 years previously, Zaidel and Sperry (1977) noted the persistence of a mild left-sided dyspraxia and impaired ability to copy with the right hand. An additional observation was that these subjects had no performance deficit, although they were slower in performance on tests of motor coordination and dexterity than normal persons; they were even slower than subjects with unilateral hemispheric lesions. However, with tests demanding interdependent manual coordination or with alternating bimanual movements, the split-brain subjects were clearly impaired.

Neuropsychological Considerations

Apraxia and Disorders of Language

Can the voluntary control of gestural behavior be considered an independent neuropsychological system, or is the behavioral capacity language dependent? One approach to this question has been to study the relation of apraxia and aphasia.

Although Liepmann's chief legacy to neuropsychology is that apraxia is essentially a movement disorder, nonetheless, in 1905, he indicated that sympathetic apraxia was related to aphasia. Since then, the role of left hemispheric lesions in the production of aphasia and apraxia has been the subject of numerous studies (de Ajuriaguerra et al, 1960; Goodglass and Kaplan, 1963; DeRenzi et al, 1968a; etc.), but the relationship between aphasia and apraxia remains an open question. Two main possibilities have been hypothesized. Either these two disorders are independent and often occur together because of the neuroanatomic proximity of those cerebral regions responsible for language and gestural behavior, or the two disorders are linked by virtue of an underlying, global defect of communication affecting linguistic and paralinguistic activity. This latter formulation resembles the concept of asymbolia originally proposed in the 1800s by Finkelnburg (1870). In asymbolia disorders of gestural behavior are elements of an ensemble of defects representing the capacity to understand or express symbols.

Goodglass and Kaplan (1963) studied these questions by testing groups of aphasic and brain-damaged nonaphasic subjects matched for age and IQ with a battery of quantifiable tests of gestural behavior, including natural expressive gestures, conventional gestures, simple and complex narrative pantomime, and descriptions of objects and of object usage. They found disorders of gestural behavior to be significantly more severe in the aphasic group; however, there was no clear relation between the severity of apraxia and that of aphasia. Essentially the aphasics differed from the nonaphasics in that the performance of the aphasics did not improve with imitation. This suggests a disorder of voluntary control of movements and not a disorder of symbolic formulation. In the absence of aphasia left hemispheric lesions produced more impaired gestural movements than right hemispheric lesions did. The authors concluded that the gestural deficiency of aphasics was an apraxic disorder due to left hemispheric lesions and was not an aspect of a general communication disorder. Of interest to note, however, is their observation that gestural ability was impaired in direct relation to the loss of intellectual efficiency in brain-damaged patients, whether or not they were aphasic.

The relations between ideational apraxia, language disorders, and general intellectual dysfunction seem to be strong. De Ajuriaguerra, Hécaen, and Angelergues (1960) found a high degree of association of these disorders: of 11 subjects with ideational apraxia, 10 had aphasia and 9 had either a confusional state or a state of general intellectual deterioration.

DeRenzi et al (1968a) studied the capacity for object manipulation in a large group of subjects with unilateral cerebral lesions (45 right hemispheric, 160 left hemispheric, of which 127 were aphasic) and in a group of normal controls. Deficient object use was found in 34% of aphasics and 6% of subjects with left hemispheric lesions without aphasia, but this defect was not found following right hemispheric lesions. Correlational studies revealed a high degree of correlation between ideational apraxia (defined as impaired object use) and impaired verbal comprehension but a relatively low correlation between ideational apraxia and general intelligence level or ideomotor apraxia. The results of this study confirmed the previously observed relationship between left hemispheric lesions, ideational apraxia, and aphasia. On the other hand, no support was found for the belief that ideational apraxia is dependent on impaired general intellectual functioning, attention, or memory. These authors proposed that the defective ability to associate an object with its corresponding action may be related to the defective ability of aphasics to associate designs of common objects with their corresponding colors or with their corresponding sounds. All of these defects represent an impaired ability to associate different aspects of the same concept. For DeRenzi et al (1968a) this impairment, a defect in concept formation, may be inherent to aphasia. Nonetheless these authors do not completely reject the possibility that the liaison between these disorders and aphasia may be anatomic proximity.

This same study clearly demonstrated the neuropsychological independence of ideomotor and ideational apraxia, since 11 of the subjects with ideational apraxia did not have ideomotor apraxia. Such evidence runs counter to the opinion of those (e.g., Sittig, 1931) for whom ideational apraxia represents the most severe stage of ideomotor apraxia. The DeRenzi et al (1968a) study employed tests of object manipulation and tests of conventional symbolic or expressive gestures; however, the subjects were not asked to pretend to manipulate objects that were not present. We would propose the hypothesis that a neuropsychological dissociation may occur between these two categories of gestural behavior, that is, conventional symbolic or expressive gestures on one side, and gestures descriptive of object use on the other, whether or not the object is present. This hypothesis conforms to previous observations and conclusions by Hécaen (1972b). However, Zangwill (1967a) described subjects who were able to simulate object use in the absence of the object but who were unable to demonstrate correct usage of the actual objects or to describe verbally the sequence of actions necessary for using these objects. For Zangwill these patients have lost memories of the necessary patterns of action. Although there is a frequent finding of general intellectual impairment in these subjects, Zangwill did not consider this impairment to be the determining factor of the apraxia.

There is no clear and definite relationship between constructional apraxia and aphasia. In the de Ajuriaguerra et al (1960) series disorders of language were present in only 72% of cases of constructional apraxia due to left hemispheric lesions. We have also observed patients with severe sensory aphasia who did not have constructional apraxia. These observations suggest the possibility of an indirect, rather than direct, association of constructional apraxia and aphasia. The nature of this association may be further analyzed by reference to additional observations of the same 1960 study. Constructional apraxia following left hemispheric lesions was found in 72% of subjects who also had ideomotor apraxia but in 100% of subjects who also had ideational apraxia. We have already commented on the observation that constructional apraxia due to left hemispheric lesions may result from a programming defect. Similarly a programming defect is evident in ideational apraxia. Hécaen

(1972b) has advanced the hypothesis that a fundamental defect underlying both constructional apraxia and ideational apraxia is a defect in programming that results from a lesion in a specific region of the dominant hemisphere—the region of supramarginal and angular gyri. The differing frequencies of appearance of these two syndromes would result from different "orders of fragility." Since ideational apraxia results from extensive dominant hemispheric lesions that include the region of the supramarginal and angular gyri, it is not surprising that aphasia is so often found as well. One might, however, propose that the association of these two syndromes results from the anatomic proximity of cerebral zones responsible for programming and for verbal activities.

Ettlinger (1969) has used evidence from cases of brain bisection to propose that apraxias be considered as language-dependent disorders of movement. Why else, he asks, has it been impossible to reproduce apraxia in the experimental animal? He suggests that apraxia may consist of two separate conditions. One, true apraxia, would be a language-dependent disorder caused by left hemispheric lesions in which the subject cannot carry out commands given verbally. The other would be a disorder of dexterity resulting from bilateral hemispheric lesions. The fact that split-brain patients can still use objects or imitate gestures with their left hand is not reconcilable with the hypothesis that these movements are under the exlusive control of the left hemisphere. As a result, Ettlinger concluded, every case of bilateral ideomotor or ideational apraxia in which the subject is unable to imitate gestures must be due to bilateral lesions. We believe that the existence of case reports of bilateral ideomotor or ideational apraxia following unilateral left hemispheric lesions (e.g., Foix, 1916; Marie and Foix, 1922; Bremer, 1921) makes Ettlinger's opinion diffucult, if not impossible, to accept. Nonetheless his conclusion raises the important issue of the possibility that learned, skilled movements may be subject to bilateral hemispheric control. This opinion is not far from that of Denny-Brown (1958), who proposed that cerebral lesions could bring about a dissociation between ideation and dexterity.

Clinical and Physiological Correlations

In an attempt to explain the breakdown of control of gestural behavior, many, if not most, authors have tended to blur distinctions between anatomy, physiology, and psychology. Often psychological explanations are given in terms more appropriate to anatomy or physiology and vice versa. Despite these often serious problems in terminology, attempts at synthesis have been made.

Denny-Brown (1958) has provided the following accounts to explain the apraxias. Unilateral kinetic apraxias, of either the magnetic or the repulsive type, are not determined by specific lateralization of the lesion. These are psychomotor phenomena that are manifestations of defective cortical control of primary motor reflexes. Ideational apraxia, on the other hand, represents disruption at both the physiological and the psychological (ideational, conceptual) levels. Dressing apraxia, limited to that side of the body affected by amorphosynthesis, is the result of a lesion in the contralateral parietal lobe. Constructional apraxia may be due to lesions in either hemisphere and is caused by the loss of cortical control of automatic movements plus the loss of summation of spatial stimuli. Buccolinguofacial apraxia and expressive aphasia both reflect a release of primitive relexes interfering with the complex motor act of speech; even though this act is highly conditioned, it nonetheless becomes automatic at a physiological level.

The "disconnection theory" approach, elaborated in detail by Geschwind (1965), in support of Liepmann's earlier theories, provides partial answers to the question of how one might find apraxia when a lesion is located in a particular site within a hemisphere. The underlying concept of the disconnection theory holds that the idea of the action is prevented from attaining (i.e., is disconnected from) the motor cortex responsible for the muscles in the action. However, this theory becomes less secure when lesions are pure and are limited to the corpus callosum. The reviews by Sperry et al (1969), Gazzaniga (1970), and Dimond (1972) indicate that, in such cases, although language should be cut off from motor systems, there nonetheless seems to be ipsilateral hemispheric control allowing for some degree of motor output. We believe that the disconnection theory may be clearly applicable to certain disorders of visual perception (see the chapter on agnosia) but should not be accepted uncritically as the sole explanation of the apraxias.

As is the case for the agnosias, however, the disconnection theory may provide the best explanation for certain types of apraxia. For example, corticocortical disconnections interfering with visuomotor control may underlie certain unilateral apraxias. Haaxma and Kuypers (1975) showed that, in split-brain monkeys, transection of occipitofrontal corticocortical connections at the parieto-occipital junction caused impairment of visual control of the contralateral limb. Similar defects were found in split-brain monkeys with occipital lobectomy. But split-brain monkeys with transection of occipitofrontal fibers retained their ability for visual discrimination on orientation tasks. In human beings, in certain cases of unilateral apraxia, especially those with associated optic ataxia, the same underlying pathophysiology may be present. Tzavaras (1975) studied a subject with a parietal lesion who had optic ataxia and unilateral apraxia contralateral to the cerebral lesion. This patient, who had neither a hemianopia nor a motor defect, was unable to use his affected hand for fine, detailed movements. (He could not use his apraxic fingers in a delicate grasping manner to retrieve small objects located in a recessed container, especially when these objects were not directly in front of him. He could perform this task without difficulty with his other hand.) These findings in the human being were similar to those described by Haaxma and Kuypers (1975) in the monkeys with disconnection syndromes.

Other interpretations than that depending on the disconnection theory may, however, be provided to explain the observations of Tzavaras (1975). The posterior parietal association cortex of monkeys contains cells that relate to motor and sensory functions of the opposite side of the body and for a certain sector of space (Hyvarinen and Poranen, 1974). These cells discharge only when a sensory stimulus of interest to the animal becomes the object of manual search, manual manipulation, or ocular pursuit. A percentage of these cells do not discharge until there is a convergence of tactile and visual stimuli. The authors considered these neurophysiological data to be important for the understanding of visuospatiomotor deficits in human beings with posterior parietal lesions.

Constructional apraxia and dressing apraxia are best considered in connection with associated disorders of higher cortical function. Following lesions of the right hemisphere in right-handed individuals, constructional apraxia is linked to a complex of defects of spatial organization. These include unilateral spatial agnosia, loss of topographical memory, spatial dyscalculia, spatial dysgraphia, spatial dyslexia, and metamorphopsia. Experimental studies have demonstrated a significant correlation between right hemispheric lesions and visuospatial disorders (Newcombe, 1969; Hécaen, 1972a,b), and a detailed study of the practic defects due to right hemispheric lesions shows a strong effect of this disturbed visuospatial activity. Visual cues impede, rather than improve, performance. Constructional apraxia, basically a defect in sensorimotor coordination, may vary in its clinical appearance, depending on the predominance of visual, proprioceptive, or vestibular factors. When dressing apraxia involves both sides of the body, it is intimately linked to constructional apraxia and represents the incapacity of placing corporeal and extracorporeal space in proper relationship to each other.

Afferent and Efferent Apraxias

The experiences of the Soviet effort in the area of apraxia have been reviewed and synthesized by Luria (1948, 1965a, 1966). The conceptual approach and terminology, while often differing from those of non-Soviet neuropsychologists, are always dynamic and challenging. For Luria the cerebral cortex is a highly differentiated system of zones, working together, upon which complex forms of behavioral processes are based. The higher psychological functions, of which the voluntary control of motor activity is one, are complex functional systems that may be disturbed by lesions of any link in the collectively working dynamic complex. Afferent apraxias result from disorders in the input limb of the systems concerned with voluntary control of movement; efferent apraxias result from disorders in the output limb.

Detailed syndromic analyses were done on individual patients with disorders of gestural behavior. A general conclusion was that disturbances of voluntary movement and practic activity associated with lesions in different localizations are different in character. Following is a description of the major varieties of apraxia according to Luria.

Voluntary movement and activity are processes based on a complex group of afferent systems (optic, tactile-kinesthetic, auditory, and motor) whose relative importance may differ in various pathological conditions. The afferent apraxias follow lesions affecting these systems. Important parts of the cortical and of the visuospatial analyzer lie in the parieto-occipital regions of the brain. Lesions in these regions cause a disturbance of the analysis of spatial coordinates within which movement takes place. For this reason a patient with such a lesion finds it difficult to perform practic activity. For example, such a patient would lay a blanket crosswise on a bed, hold a spoon vertically instead of horizontally, confuse his directions while walking, and, in general, perform poorly on tasks requiring a coordinated arrangement of spatial relationships. Action disintegrates but only with respect to the spatial organization of the action.

The postcentral divisions of the parietal regions form a part of the cortical end of the proprioceptive analyzer. Disturbance of cutaneous and deep sensation resulting from lesions in these regions leads to a disturbance of the proprioceptive afferent basis of movement. Impulses directed toward muscles may not reach their exact destination. A result of this impairment in cortical analyzer function is the loss of the selection of fine, differentiated movements necessary for the performance of detailed gestures requiring careful control.

The interaction between afferent and efferent aspects of voluntary movement is intimate; the frontal and prefrontal divisions of the cortex have both afferent and efferent function. The premotor division of the brain is responsible for the "denervation of the individual links of a complex motor act and for the smooth flow from one motor link to another" (Luria, 1947, 1966). Lesions in this region do not affect the spatial arrangement or accurate direction of motor impulses; rather, they affect the organization of motor processes in time. "Pathological inertia of the individual motor links" develops, and the "kinetic melody," which is the distinguishing feature of highly automatized skilled movements, is disturbed.

The frontal and prefrontal divisions of the cortex are related to the preservation of complex patterns of afferent integration (Anokhin, 1949), are responsible for the regulation of action by speech (Luria, 1948, 1966), and are concerned with comparison of a motor act and its intention (Luria, 1966).

Lesions in these regions of the brain, in addition to producing behavioral changes known as the frontal syndrome (see the chapter on frontal lobe syndromes), may result in replacement of the goal-directed motor act by isolated impulsive movements or inert sterotyped actions, often losing all connection with the initial purpose. Defective object manipulation may be seen in this form of apraxia.

From this descriptive and correlational analysis Luria concluded that voluntary movement is the result of the combined activity of the whole brain. He did not wish to imply, however, that all parts of the brain are equally important in this activity. Rather, each segment of the brain plays its own distinctive part in the organization of the voluntary control of movement.

Teuber (1966a) has summarized the main features of what he calls Luria's "bold generalizations." Luria has proposed that lesions affecting parietal and occipital lobes in the dominant hemisphere may interfere with "simultaneous synthesis," while lesions anterior to the fissure of Rolando interfere with "successive synthesis." "Simultaneous synthesis" refers to the simultaneous neural organization of visual or auditory input, or the corresponding requirements for spatial orientation in such complex human activities as constructional tasks. "Successive synthesis" refers to maintenance of serial order in behavior. Only by understanding such a sequential-versus-simultaneous dichotomy can the multifaceted interconnections of human psychological processing be understood.

Luria (1965a, 1966) has presented his own views as follows. In the early stages of development kinesthetic and optic afferent impulses play a major role in influencing a child's movements and actions (Zaporozhets, 1960). In later developmental stages the spoken instructions of adults become increasingly important in the formation of voluntary movement and action. Subsequently the child's own speech plays a major role (Vygotsky, 1962). Speech provides the afferent system distinguishing human voluntary motor behavior from the motor behavior of animals. The creation of voluniary motor acts, that is, a system of goal-directed movements, involves the coordinated interaction of a complex group of afferent and efferent systems, including optic, tactile-kinesthetic, auditory, motor, and speech. Speech provides the indication of the goal toward which the action is directed and formulates a definite intention and appropriate mode of action. In later stages of development, complex motor actions may become automatized.

A characteristic feature of voluntary motor behavior is that the performance of each act is determined by the "motor task" (Bernstein, 1947, 1957). This "motor task" represents a visual or verbal image that pro·ides direction and selectivity to the action. Another essential feature is that voluntary movements and activities require the constant comparison of the intended actions with the efforts achieved. This means that a continuous feedback of signals must occur from the performed movement and from the organization of the afferent systems involved in the performed movement, and these feedback signals must be constantly compared with the plan of action. In this way there is a constant corrective principle, providing for the possibility of deviation from a given plan of action. Any disorder of this self-regulating mechanism may deprive voluntary movement and activity of their directed and selective character and may lead to their replacement by inadequate or irrelevant acts, as seen in the apraxias. The creation of a "motor task," that is, a plan of action, by the preceding action, and the presence of an afferent feedback system that permits constant comparison of the plan with the effect actually achieved are considered by Luria to be the two most important and interconnected conditions for the performance of the voluntary motor act.

Relating these concepts of the ontogenetic development of gestural behavior to the breakdown of this behavior following cerebral lesions, Luria stresses the features summarized above by Teuber. Many afferent systems are involved in the construction of voluntary acts. Visual and auditory imputs, haptics, and speech are associated with the recoding of the spatial coordinates of planned movements into proprioceptive signals. This activity, by means of simultaneous synthesis, takes place in specific regions of the brain. Depending on which afferent system is affected by the cerebral lesion, simultaneous synthesis may be disrupted and one or another variety of afferent apraxia may occur.

Proprioceptive signals ensure the accurate direction of impulses to specific muscle groups. Motor activity also requires the "perceptual denervation" of the individual links of the movement as other links are brought into play. This creates a consecutive series of motor stereotypes of "kinetic melodies" by means of successive synthesis. Such activity takes place in anterior regions of the brain, and cerebral lesions here produce varieties of efferent apraxia.

Finally, voluntary movement and activity require the accurate formulation and prolonged retention of the "motor task" created by a visual or speech association, and the continual comparison of actual performance with original intention, by evaluation of how closely the actual gestural behavior corresponds with or deviates from the intended goal. Either frontal or posterior lesions may interfere with these mechanisms at different stages and for different reasons and thereby produce additional, distinctive varieties of apraxia.

Cerebral Dominance and the Voluntary Control of Movement

The original hypothesis of Liepmann for ideomotor apraxia stated that apraxia is primarily a movement disorder; the syndrome appears as a manifestation of the disturbance of a system in the left hemisphere that is concerned with the control of "purposive" movements, that is, learned, goal-directed movements. The frequently observed relationship between apraxia and aphasia was due to the anatomic proximity of cerebral regions responsible for the control of language and of gestural behavior. A series of research reports studying cerebral dominance and the voluntary control of movement seems to support Liepmann's hypothesis.

Wyke (1967, 1971) studied the effects of brain lesions on the rapidity and skill of unilateral and bilateral arm and hand movements. In both studies she compared subjects with left and right hemispheric lesions and normal subjects. She found that repetitive alternation of hand movements with the hand ipsilateral to the cerebral lesion was significantly slower only in subjects with left-sided lesions. With tests of bilaterally synchronous tapping movements and of movements of manipulative skill, she found that left-brain damage caused a significant decrease in the rapidity of repetitive movements for both the ipsilateral and contralateral hands, whereas right-brain damage caused a decrease in the rapidity of repetitive movements only for the contralateral hand.

Carmon (1971) studied sequenced motor performance in patients with unilateral cerebral lesions. Repetitive motor performance, sequenced for locus and pace, was evaluated in two separate experiments. For both locus and rate, brain-damaged subjects did significantly worse than controls. No effect was found to be related to side of lesion when the locus was sequentially changed. However, when the rate of tapping was changed, a side-of-lesion effect was noted. At a fast pace left-sided lesions caused more deficiency than right-sided lesions; at a slow pace a reverse trend occurred.

Heilman (1973) also studied tapping performance in brain-damaged subjects, but he divided his groups clinically. He compared the performance of a group of left-brain-damaged subjects having ideomotor apraxia with that of a group of left-brain-damaged subjects without apraxia. The left-hand tapping performance of the apraxics was significantly slower than that of the nonapraxics.

Kimura and Archibald (1974) found that lesions of the left hemisphere, by contrast with lesions of the right hemisphere, impaired the performance of complex motor sequences, regardless of whether the sequences were meaningful or not. Patients with left-brain damage were impaired relative to patients with right-brain damage on a task in which they copied unfamiliar, sequential movements of the hand and arm. The difficulty in copying movements was unrelated to the presence or absence of hemiplegia, except that the hemiplegic limb could not be tested. The impairment was bilateral and equal in both hands in patients without hemiplegia. The same patients who showed a disorder of copying sequential movements showed no difficulty in producing isolated finger flexion or in copying a static hand posture. Correlational analyses showed that isolated finger flexion tasks and copying of sequential movements were not related.

Further analyses showed no statistical correlations between the movement disorders induced by left hemispheric lesions and disorders of language or disorders of perception of movement. The authors concluded that the deficiency was an impairment of motor control, unrelated to representational content. They proposed the interesting speculation that the unique functions of the left hemisphere, in speech as well as in voluntary control of movement, might be related to motor sequencing, rather than to symbolic or language function. In a similar direction Heilman et al (1975) demonstrated defective motor learning in ideomotor apraxia. Of a group of patients with right hemiplegia, only those with ideomotor apraxia had significant impairments in retention of a recently learned visuomotor task.

From our point of view, it would seem difficult, in light of the current status of the problem, to accept a unitary basis for apraxia, as originally envisaged by Liepmann, even if we excluded certain apraxias limited to one side of the body or restricted to specific body parts. The very fact that different behavioral effects are caused by different lesional lateralizations prevents the adoption of such a hypothesis. However, perhaps a unitary basis for disorders of gestural behavior may be found in the possible existence of an underlying neuropsychological deficit, such as defective sensory guidance of fine motor behavior, which might represent a necessary, if not sufficient, condition for apraxia. The conjunction of such a disorder, which could be called prepraxic, with a deficit linked preferentially to the damaged hemisphere (of spatial organization on the right, of sequential organization on the left) could perhaps explain the dissimilarity of apraxic patterns found following right or left hemispheric lesions. Factors within each hemisphere such as extent of lesion or lesional localization could perhaps account for additional diversity of apraxic syndromes.

FOUR
DISORDERS OF
VISUAL PERCEPTION

It is not our intention to review in detail the neurophysiology and neuroanatomy of each sensory system. Rather, as in the other chapters, we attempt to analyze breakdowns in these systems and the relationship of these perceptual disorders to their neurological substrates. Nonetheless, in the rapidly expanding field of sensory physiology, certain key issues must be considered, to aid in the understanding of pathological states. In Chapters 4, 5, and 6 we introduce each sensory system by referring briefly to some of these key anatomic and physiological issues.

ANATOMIC AND PHYSIOLOGICAL CONSIDERATIONS

Visual-Motor Coordination

Vision is not a passive process. Normal vision involves more than the progressive extraction of critical spatial and temporal features of an input. It involves an active motor system component. Active movement of the eyes ordinarily leaves the perceived world stable, but passive movement renders the perceived world unstable. Von Holst (1950, 1957) Sperry (1950, 1952) and Teuber (1961a,b) have provided a hypothetical explanation for this phenomenon. At the moment a voluntary movement is initiated, an efferent signal (Teuber's "corollary discharge") is produced. This efferent signal is in addition to the efferent signal sent to the muscles involved in the voluntary action. This additional signal joins the reafferent signal coming from sensory receptors stimulated by the act of voluntary muscle displacement. The combination of the reafferent signal and the efferent corollary discharge signal conditions (or presets) central processing mechanisms both for perception and for subsequent response. Thereby stability of the perceived external world is maintained.

When objects or scenes are displaced in the visual world and when the animal does not move, the corollary discharge is not produced; absence of central corollary discharges permits the animal to accept the displacement of objects and scenes as real. If all or a portion of the animal's body is moved passively, no efferent signal (i.e., corollary discharge) is produced to counteract the sensory reafferent impulse. Absence of this efferent corollary signal renders the control system less efficient, the result being an impaired, but not totally absent, adaptation to the novel environment. The animal may then experience an illusion of instability of the external world.

In the case of vision for a moving animal the corollary discharge prepares visual reception centers and provides information that, whatever the movement of the retinal image, there has been no objective displacement of the external world. Thus perceptual constancy is preserved. If this sensorimotor correlation is modified, a perceptual illusion may be produced. If a voluntary movement is intended but cannot be performed (as would be the case, for instance, if a subject with a recent sixth nerve lesion tried to look laterally), the corollary discharge would be produced, in the absence of a sensory reafferent signal. In such a case, at least during the acute phase, the subject would have the illusion that the external world was moving in the direction of intended ocular movement.

This hypothesis thus implies that normal rearrangement compensation is dependent on the corollary discharge, that the corollary discharge is produced when the subject is active, and that compensation does not occur if movement is exclusively passive. The function of the corollary discharge is to preset sensory systems for changes in the input that are the anticipated consequences of the willed movement.

Neurophysiological and neuropsychological evidence both pro and con has been provided with respect to the corollary discharge hypothesis. Research by Held (1961, 1965, 1968) on perceptual rearrangement (modification of vision by wearing prismatic lenses) and by Freedman on perceptual changes in sensory deprivation (1961, 1965) tends to support the hypothesis. Bizzi (1968) studied frontal eye field neurons during saccadic and following eye movements in unanesthetized monkeys and observed that these cells discharge when the head and eyes reach a certain position and only after initiation of movement or at the moment movement stops. This evidence favors the hypothesis, because these frontal cells, which serve as indicators of eye position, do not discharge when eye movement is passive. Also in favor of the hypothesis are the results of Bossom (1965), who found that bifrontal or basal ganglion lesions caused great impairment in the capacity of monkeys to adapt to prisms. Jeannerod and Sakai (1970) observed that ocular movement potentials from posterior cortical and geniculate ganglion regions were independent of all visual or proprioceptive inputs. These potentials may be entirely of central origin, linked to motor mechanisms responsible for eye movement and reflecting activity of oculomotor mechanisms en route to sensory centers.

Other studies are not, however, consistent with the corollary discharge hypothesis. Wurtz (1969a,b) argued that, if corollary discharges existed, differences within the visual system should be registered in response to the following two conditions: either the retina moves in front of a stationary image or an image moves in front of a stationary retina. He found, in fact, that, in the case of rapid eye movement before a stationary stimulus, some striate cortex neurons gave an excitation response, some a suppression response, and some no response; in the case of rapid movement of the stimulus in front of fixed eyes, the responses were similar to those obtained with ocular movement. Wurtz stressed the fact that Bizzi (1968) had been unable to demonstrate changes in single-cell activity of lateral geniculate body neurons in the unanesthetized monkey associated with rapid eye movement. If the corollary discharge exists, he concluded, it functions in different regions of the central nervous system (CNS) than the striate cortex or lateral geniculate bodies, or else it is associated only with slow pursuit movements.

Michael and Ichinose (1970) found no modification of receptor field organization in the lateral geniculate body associated with oculomotor activity; however, visual evoked responses were different if oculomotor activity was present or not. Thus one may conclude that an interaction between processing of visual information and oculomotor activity exists at some point in the nervous system. This point may turn out to be striate cortex, despite the studies of Wurtz (1969a,b); other studies (e.g., Orban et al, 1970) have shown an influence of brain stem oculomotor stimulation on single-unit activity in the visual cortex. Later studies by Wurtz and Goldberg (1971) again support the corollary discharge hypothesis. They found responses of cells in deep layers of the superior colliculus that preceded ocular movements. They suggested that these neuronal discharges might represent corollary discharges of the oculomotor system toward the sensory system.

Of interest are the observations of Burchfiel and Duffy (1972) with isolated brain preparations in the monkey. They noted that ocular saccades occurring in the dark are associated with an inhibitory influence on resting activity or neurons in area 17. This inhibitory effect was not seen with geniculate cells. Since the inhibition was dependent on the direction of the saccade and since the temporal characteristics of development of inhibition corresponded with the temporal characteristics of supression of saccades, the authors concluded that the inhibition of neurons in the visual cortex supressed visual perception when voluntary eye movement was being performed. Additional supporting evidence relating visual cortical cells to saccadic movements has been found in the cat (Noda et al, 1972).

By contrast, studies by Jeannerod and Chouves (1972) provide evidence about sensorimotor function that does not need explanation by a corollary discharge hypothesis. These authors presented coupled flashes with abrupt displacement of visual patterns across the retina of curarized cats. Movement of the image across the retina, whether the field moved and the eyes were stationary or vice versa, was a factor sufficient to modify visual perception concomitantly.

The extensive research by Held (1961, 1965, 1968, 1974) and his associates on plasticity in sensorimotor systems has effectively demonstrated that information provided by movement plays a significant role in maintenance of perceptual constancy, whatever the circumstances of retinal image displacement. An initial series of experiments showed that compensation for perceptual distortion in adults did not appear unless the subject had the possibility for active movement. Another series showed that, in the earliest phases of development, voluntary movement was essential for normal acquisition of sensorimotor coordination.

The experiments with adults dealt with compensation to perceptual distortion of lines by subjects wearing prismatic lenses. It had been known for many years that after a certain length of time the distortions and spatial displacements of objects brought about by wearing prisms became corrected to such a degree that voluntary movements could finally be directed correctly in space (Helmholtz, 1867, Stratton, 1897, Kohler, 1951). This return to perceptual-motor accuracy was generally thought to result from a process of progressive correction of errors. Held et al (1965) rejected this assumption, since a partial adaptation to displacement produced by vision with prisms could occur even without the subjects' knowledge. The new experiments confirmed the role of sensorimotor feedback in adaptation; active movements allowed compensation. When movements were entirely passive, no adaptation occurred. Such adaptation that occurred with active movement was incomplete. Steinbach (1969, 1970a,b) has established that the differences of visuo-motor adaptation following active or passive movements are more quantitative than qualitative.

We might add that other interpretations may also be provided to account for differences of adaptation with active or passive movements. Peripheral proprioceptive mechanisms must play a role in recalibration of a movement with no visual displacement.

The experiments with immature animals provided means for judging the respective roles of experience and maturation in the acquisition of spatial information and the development of capacities for visually guided behavior. Visuomotor feedback was shown to play an essential role in the acquisition of these behavioral skills. Previous studies of sensory deprivation in young animals had given results that were difficult to interpret, perhaps because of anatomic changes caused by the deprivation that led to an underuse of sensory structures. Nonetheless, Riesen (1958) had already found that kittens raised in the dark except for brief periods of exposure to patterned light had difficulties with form discrimination, interocular transfer, and orientation. Meyers and McLeary (1964) showed that kittens raised in diffused light, with no exposure to patterned light, could discriminate patterns and movement if they could respond without having to orient their bodies toward the stimulus. Kittens raised in normal light but placed in a restraining apparatus manifested difficulties with visual control of behavior. Held (1961) interpreted these results as indicating a poor correlation between visual stimulus and movement, and this hypothesis was confirmed by several experimental studies (Held, 1965; Hein, 1972; Bossom, 1965). In one experiment, for example, pairs of kittens were raised in darkness for 8 to 12 weeks. Subsequently they were placed inside a large drum whose interior wall was painted with vertical stripes. One kitten of a pair could walk freely; the other was placed in a container that moved only under the action of the first kitten. Following variable degrees of exposure time within the drum, kittens who could move freely had normal visually guided reactions (visual placement, blinking to threat, etc.), while kittens who were moved passively had abnormal visually guided reactions. Thus, although both kittens in each pair had been exposed to identical visual stimulation, movement within the visual setting had varied, being active for one, passive for the other. It would seem, then, that changes in visual stimulation must be associated with active movement for the development of normal visually guided behavior.

The same test was carried out under conditions of alternating monocular vision; one eye was open during active movement, the other was open during passive movement (Hein, 1972). Deficits on spatial visuomotor tasks were limited to the eye that was open during passive movement. Other studies with cats and monkeys demonstrated that eye-hand coordination was dependent on the possibility of looking at the moving hand but that each eye alone could control head and body orientation (Held and Hein, 1963; Held and Bauer, 1967, 1974).

To complicate the issue further, it has been noted that the absence of active movement is insufficient to cause the failure of establishment of a visually induced extension reaction (Hein, 1968). Kittens with head and body immobilized develop a visually induced extension response if they are exposed to patterned or diffused light during development. Thus feedback of body movement is not indispensable to the establishment of this visuomotor reaction. Hein (1972) concludes from this, and from the previously cited experiments, that the failure of visuomotor coordination to become normally established is due to a "dyscorrelation" between movements of the subject and variations in visual stimulation.

It seems, as well, that visually induced extension reactions develop in conditions that differ from those in which visually guided placement reactions develop. For these movements to develop, the animal's own movements must be accompanied by movements of images across the retina. The extension reaction produced by visual stimulation, according to Hein (1972), is organized subcortically. When a sensorimotor feedback system is established subcortically, a cortical control mechanism is superimposed on this system, and the primitive response is incorporated into the corticosubcortical system of visually guided placement. Following ablation of occipital cortex, but not of temporal cortex, of kittens raised in normal conditions, the extension reaction to visual stimulation is preserved, but visually guided placing reactions are lost. Subsequently, after exposure to 14 days of normal light, these lesioned kittens perform the same as normal ones. In other kittens with visual cortex ablations kept in the dark, the extension reaction persists but not the visually guided motor control. Next, placed in normal light but immobilized, these kittens do not regain visual control of motor behavior. Free to move, but without being able to see their limbs, they develop the capacity to avoid the deep end of a visual cliff but not the capacity for visually guided limb placement. Total recuperation occurs if the animals are allowed to move freely and to look at their limbs.

Experiments with raising kittens under variable conditions of exposure to visual stimuli or modification of visuomotor feedback have demonstrated the relative independence of certain components of visually guided behavior. Acquisition of this behavior may be limited to a single limb, to one eye without transfer to the other, and even to the photopic or scotopic system independently (Hein and Diamond, 1971). According to Hein and Diamond (1971a,b) a specific sequence of acquisition may be necessary for the various feedback loops to be used properly. For example, kittens must have learned visually guided locomotion before they can acquire a visual reaching capacity. It seems that the kittens possess a "body centered map of visual space in which objects can be localized."

Research by Held and Bauer (1974) on the development of manual seizure of an object by monkeys prevented from looking at their hands or body during the first weeks of life supports the conclusions of studies with kittens. The ability to guide the hand visually with the usual precision requires the activation of a system of coordinates for motor response within visual space.

Prior exposure seems essential for the constitution of such a map of visual space coordinates. Ocular movements also seem to represent a necessary component of visuomotor feedback implicated in the development of visually guided behavior (Vital-Durand, 1975).

Two Visual Systems

The previous section on sensorimotor coordination indicated that one mode of treatment of visual information required integration of visual feedback derived from movement. This variety of information processing permits the animal to orient itself to objects by relating body movements to object positions in space. Meyers and McLeary (1964) demonstrated that this particular visual processing system could be disturbed without affecting ability for visual recognition of forms. Subsequent experimental evidence (some of which is reviewed below) has established the existence of two different systems of visual processing, different both in anatomy and in function. One system involves geniculostriate pathways, the other, extrastriate (tectopulvinar) pathways.

It should be added, however, that visual integrity for perception of forms after deafferentation and disruption of visuomotor feedback is still an open question (Wiesel and Hubel, 1965; Hubel and Wiesel, 1970; von Noorden et al, 1970; Dews and Wiesel, 1972; Ganz et al, 1972; Ganz and Haffner, 1974). Visual perception in such cases may not be normal, even when recuperation seems complete. Rather, the preserved vision may be the result of an improved use of information by the remaining cells (Hubel and Wiesel, 1970), or of the use of movements of the head to obtain information about form (Rizzolati and Trabardi, 1971), or of the use of contours or luminance as indices for building a perception (Ganz and Haffner, 1974).

As for the secondary visual system comparative studies in several different animal species are in general agreement. We may summarize the main issues by reference to work by Schneider (1967, 1969) on the golden hamster. He found fundamentally different types of visual processing defects produced by lesions in visual areas of cortex and tectum. Undercutting the superior colliculus abolished the hamster's ability to orient toward an object but not the ability to identify it, according to tests of pattern discrimination learning. Destroying visual cortex destroyed the ability to identify an object but not the ability to orient toward it. Similar results supporting the notion of two visual systems have been found in the goldfish (Ingle, 1967), in the cat (Blake, 1959; Sprague, 1966), in the rat (Barnes et al, 1970), and in the monkey (Denny-Brown and Chambers, 1955, 1958; Denny-Brown, 1962; Humphrey and Weizkrantz, 1967).

Extensive studies have been done on the tree shrew, an animal whose brain could be considered a phylogenetic precursor of that of primates, although characteristics of insectivores are still present (Snyder and Diamond, 1968; Diamond and Hall, 1969; Killackey et al, 1972; Diamond, 1972; Ware et al, 1974; etc). Tree shrews with total ablations of striate cortex can easily discriminate between two simple patterns presented simultaneously or successively. Thus these animals can identify patterns in the absence of striate cortex. They can also learn reversal tasks and localize objects in space. They cannot, however, discriminate patterns incorporated within another form. Ablation of the cortical ring encircling striate cortex causes a delay in learning a visual discrimination task and an inability to learn reversal tasks, although camouflaged patterns can now be discriminated.

On the basis of anatomical-behavioral studies, Snyder and Diamond (1968) proposed that two visual pathways reached the cortex. One pathway was the primary visual system with direct projection to lateral geniculate nuclei and from there to striate cortex. The other was the secondary visual system, projecting indirectly to the pulvinar by the intermediary way station of the tectum and reaching, finally, the circumstriate cortex. If the cortical targets of the two visual systems are removed, the tree shrew is severely incapacitated in learning simple habits based on pattern differences (Ware, Diamond, and Casagrande, 1974). The specific functional capacities of the tectum have yet to be fully clarified but probably include color and some aspects of form perception (Schilder, Pasik, and Pasik, 1971).

Studies by Tervarthen (1968) on split-brain monkeys also favor the existence of two visual systems. One system is cortical and deals with identity resolution by means of successive fixations of focal vision. The other is mesencephalic and deals with ambient, movement-related vision, the animal obtaining information about space by moving head, eyes, and body, and sending the information centrally for visuomotor coordination.

It seems clear to us that normal visual perception must involve an interaction of the two visual systems. Despite results of visual rearrangement studies that have for the most part demonstrated independence of these two systems, it must be remembered that only certain aspects of form discrimination have been shown to be modified, while others remain unchanged, even though total visuomotor system adaptation occurs following visual field distortions by prisms. Although interocular transfer of form discrimination is excellent in newborn cats raised in unpatterned, diffused light, interocular transfer of visually guided behavior does not occur.

It seems difficult to distinguish formally between these two visual systems and to conceptualize them in a hierarchical manner anatomically and functionally at the same time. On the one hand arguments are presented that one system is superior and phylogenetically more recent, and the other, inferior and older. On the other hand arguments are presented in favor of a process of telencephalization: certain aspects of visual function performed by lower animals by the mesencephalon are performed by telencephalic structures in higher animals. To the mesencephalon are attributed the following functions—discrimination of certain aspects of visual function performed by lower animals by luminous flux, brilliance, simple patterns, colors, and detection of speed. The cortex is credited with complex discriminations.

Berlucchi et al (1972) studied visual discrimination in split-brain cats with inputs limited to a single hemisphere. Isolated or combined cortical or subcortical lesions were placed. With lesions of the pretectum and superior collicular region the animals were unable to learn a form discrimination task, although retention of a preoperatively acquired discrimination was preserved. Defects in luminous-flux discrimination were mild, at worst. The pretectal region and superior colliculi seemed to form a single functional unit, and their combined destruction had an additive effect. In considering recovery of function, we might comment that, when one of these two structures is damaged and the other spared, a reorganization of function may occur, and deficits may be mild.

Various other combinations of lesions and effects were created, allowing some general conclusions. First it seems that the cortex and mesencephalon do not function independently in visual activity. Without question the contributions of these two anatomic regions to visual function are not identical. This has clearly been shown from single-cell studies, as well as from ablation studies. We would, however, agree with Berlucchi that cortex and mesencephalon interact in the performance of (even complex) visual function. A two-tiered, hierarchical system must be rejected, at the present time, as an explanation for visual activity.

Second it seems that visual function may be preserved, although in a deficient manner, even with large lesions within the visual system. It has now been confirmed in several animal species—rat, cat, monkey, man—that small remnants of visual cortex or of the pretectal-superior colliculus complex may be sufficient to preserve some function.

Finally it seems that the two visual systems are interdependent in that a lesion in one system may modify activity in the other. For example, receptive fields of superior colliculus cells may be considerably modified by visual cortex ablations (Wincklegren and Sterling, 1969). This interaction had been demonstrated by ablation studies in the cat (Sprague, 1966) and was confirmed in the monkey (Schiller et al, 1974). The effect was not found, however, with animals under general anesthesia (Rizzolatti et al, 1970a; Hoffman and Straschill, 1971).

Sprague (1966) interpreted his results as suggesting that each superior colliculus received facilitatory inputs from ipsilateral cortex and inhibitory inputs from contralateral cortex by the intermediary of the intercollicular commissure. A cortical lesion disrupts the equilibrium and renders the colliculus nonfunctional. Destruction of the contralateral colliculus or section of the commissure permits return of function. More recent studies have confirmed the earlier observations (Sherman, 1974a; Wood et al, 1974).

To interpret the various experimental results that demonstrate the possibility of a recovery of function, Berlucchi et al (1972) speak of diaschisis. The "effect at a distance" in the case of visual functions can be demonstrated in either direction—cortex toward mesencephalon or vice versa. Diminution of this effect with time following the ablation precedure is accompanied by disappearance of deficits. The deficits return and become permanent if a second ablation is done on the structure inhibited by the first ablation.

This model is well adapted to experimental results in lower animals, but it is more difficult to accept for primates. It is true that ablation of primary visual cortex in the monkey does not necessarily wipe out all visual capacity. Humphrey (1970), for example, by studying the long-term evolution of visual defects in a monkey with striate cortex removed, documented the return of visually guided motor behavior, such as orientation in space. However, in primates new cortical centers may take over the visual activity of the damaged visual cortex.

A certain complementary activity may exist between two cortical regions with respect to a particular complex of behaviors. This has been demonstrated in the monkey for the anterior and posterior zones of the inferotemporal area (Iwai and Mishkin, 1969) and in the tree shrew for the temporal and striate regions (Kaas et al, 1972).

These complementary functions may be the natural result of specialization during evolution. The original common visual center (tectum) first guaranteed all visual function (memory, attention, perception, etc.). Following appearance of the neocortex and its anatomic subdivisions, all old and new centers continued to participate in different psychological categories of vision, but a complementary relation developed among them. In the tree shrew each center receives its inputs from its own thalamic relay, but in the monkey destruction of the pulvinar does not cause lesions similar to those caused by inferotemporal lesions, even though inferotemporal areas receive pulvinar connections (Mishkin, 1972). By contrast, in the tree shrew, destruction of the pulvinar causes a deficit similar to that produced by temporal ablation (Diamond and Hall, 1969). In the monkey a double dissociation is obtained when lesions are placed in the extrastriate centers within the temporal lobe; in the tree shrew one of the lesions must be in the striate cortex itself.

In a study with split-brain human beings, Trevarthen (1970) found experimental evidence for a brain stem contribution to visual perception in man. These commissurotomized subjects could integrate separate moving visual stimuli presented to each hemifield, despite the independence of each geniculostriate system. As have others (e.g., Ware et al, 1974), Trevarthen proposed that visual perceptual integration may involve mesencephalic mechanisms linked by means of the pulvinar to extrastriate visual areas in each hemisphere.

Feature Detection Mechanisms

Neurophysiological studies of the visual system during the past decade, especially studies using single-cell recordings, have provided valuable data to the neuropsychologist. Lettvin et al (1959) and Hubel and Wiesel (1962, 1963, 1965, 1968, 1970) have contributed and have stimulated others to contribute to our understanding of how the visual system, from the retina to the cortex, responds to various stimuli. A clear picture is gradually emerging of the manner in which elementary information is transformed and retransformed at different levels of the visual system and of how the most complex information is finally extracted by means of what Teuber (1972) calls a "cascade specification of inputs." No single cell by itself responds to a complex stimulus; the projection onto single cells of a long chain of single cells from periphery to cortex results in the final integration of complex information.

At the retina, cells may be grouped into three types, according to their responses; "on-cells" discharge in the presence of light, "off-cells" discharge in darkness, and "on-off cells" discharge in light and in darkness. The receptive field of a retinal cell is that portion of retina whose stimulation influences activity of the cell. The receptive field of a cell is surrounded by a field of inhibition that corresponds to the receptive fields of cells with opposite activities. At the geniculate bodies receptive fields of single cells are more or less similar to those of retinal cells. In cortical area 17, two types of cells appear: simple cells that respond to orientation of a slit of light in their receptive fields (this provides discrimination of verticality, horizontality, and obliqueness of lines) and complex cells that respond to form and orientation of a luminous stimulus. The simple cortical cell integrates information from certain geniculate cells that were activated by certain retinal cells. Complex cells integrate information from simple cells. At this level a single complex cell has a large receptive field, integrates responses of directionality and edges, and can thereby detect forms.

· Hypercomplex cells of two types are found in areas 17, 18, and 19. Lower order hypercomplex cells receive information from several simple cells. Higher order hypercomplex cells receive projections from the lower order group. Area 18 contains 90% complex cells and 10% lower order hypercomplex cells. Area 19 contains 58% hypercomplex cells of which some are higher order. Hypercomplex cells can respond to forms, such as angles, light, or dark, by a process of inhibition or excitation within their receptive field, after visual

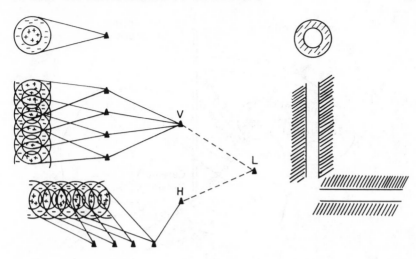

Schematic diagram of principle of cascade specificity of visual inputs. From left to right: receptor fields, retinal neurons, first order and higher order cortical neurons; optimal stimulus. From top to bottom: retinal contrast detectors combine with cortical detectors of verticality or horizontality (from Teuber, 1966). Copyright 1971 by Masson & Co., Paris. Reproduced by permission.

stimuli have been already hierarchically processed (Hubel and Wiesel, 1962–1970).

Dow (1974) has stressed the necessity of distinguishing subclasses of complex cells according to the properties of their receptive fields. Each subclass has a specified, corresponding laminar distribution. It may also be possible that they project to different cortical regions. Dow (1974) envisages several systems treating visual information in parallel, rather than a single chain extending from simple to hypercomplex cells to extract successively the progressively increasing complexities of visual information.

Cortical visual cells are disposed in long, narrow columns, perpendicular to cortical layers (Mountcastle, 1957; Colonnier, 1966). Cells in a single column have receptive fields of the same orientation and often of the same organization. Simple cells project to complex cells that are ordinarily in the same column. The ratio of cortical cells to geniculate is about 1350 to 1, implying that each retinal field has multiple cortical representations from one column to another for different orientations of light stimuli. This multiple representation is even greater for central regions of the retina. Hubel and Wiesel (1968) observed that in the monkey visual cortex there exists a form of vertical organization composed of two independent systems of functional columns, one containing cells responding to line orientation, the other containing cells

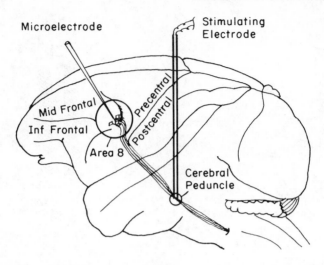

Microelectrode positioned in area 8 with apparatus for antidromic stimulation of efferent fibers (from Bizzi and Schiller, 1970). Copyright 1971 by Masson & Co., New York. Reproduced by permission.

with a monocular preference. A horizontal organization corresponding to the horizontal disposition of cortical layers has also been found. This system is hierarchical; complex and hypercomplex cells are found in superficial and deep layers, and simple cells in layers III and IV.

The visual cortex thus appears to be organized in different ways in its vertical and horizontal dispositions. In the vertical system, with its vertical columns of cells possessing common traits, the stimulus dimensions (orientation of lines and ocular dominance) are represented in a series of superimposed semi-independent mosaics. The horizontal system isolates the cells in a hierarchical manner within cortical layers. Hypercomplex cells permit an increase in response selectivity. Position and dimension are dealt with by lower order hypercomplex cells, while the higher order cells generalize from the basic form information provided by the lower order cells.

Such a neurophysiological analysis of the visual system explains not only how a particular form is "recognized" by a cell but also how general knowledge of a particular form is elaborated, independently of its position or its dimensions. In addition to cells that detect the specific features of visual stimuli (movement, direction, orientation, size, position in the visual field), there seem to be other cells capable of responding to what is specific to each experience; they are available for each new experience and respond in each instance to a new and different stimulus (Spinelli and Barrett, 1969).

The cat has cells that respond specifically to line orientation and also to light intensity (Hoeppner, 1974). The same responses of a given cell can be obtained by various combinations of light intensity and line orientation. It would seem, then, that, at least for some cells, the message may remain equivocal. This ambiguity diminishes, however, when the relative activity among various neurons and the temporal features of the response are taken into account. The hierarchical model, with its ultimate consequence of a pontifical terminal cell, no longer appears inevitable for identification of a complex stimulus. Cells that may serve more than one class of information have also been found in the monkey (Bartlett and Doty, 1974).

Poggio et al (1975) have demonstrated cells in the foveal and parafoveal striate cortex of the macaque with selective responses to stimulus orientation similar to those described by Hubel and Wiesel, and also cells that lack this selectivity to orientation. The cells lacking this selectivity comprise half of the cells of the foveal region and one-third of cells of the parafoveal region. The majority of these cells receive monocular inputs, either entirely or predominantly.

This observation makes it difficult to accept that the visual system is composed of cells linked in a hierarchical sequence. Two systems, independent both anatomically and functionally, seem to be present in the striate complex: one for ocular dominance, the other for selectivity to orientation.

Abundant information has been obtained in recent years concerning the treatment of color stimuli. Cells of the geniculate body respond in opposing manner (excitation or inhibition) to flashes of monochromatic light of differing wave lengths (DeValois, 1973) or on the basis of organization of their receptive fields (Wiesel and Hubel, 1965); there are other cells that respond to light of any wave length. Inputs from three types of cones arrive at "nonopponent" cells. The cells of the lateral geniculate bodies seem to be able to process many aspects of color vision.

Treatment of color stimuli at the level of the striate cortex is less well established. Dow (1974) has indicated that 30% of foveal striate cortex cells may respond to color; Poggio et al (1975) reported 70% in the foveal cortex and 40% in the parafoveal. In addition DeValois (1973) suggested that cells categorized as not responding to specific color information may in fact generalize from any color, which would allow them to recognize forms, independently of their colors. Poggio et al (1975) demonstrated the presence of cells, which they called luminosity cells and which respond in variable manner to brilliance of luminous stimuli, procuring also a spectral reference for the color and for color contrasts.

Gouras (1970a) defined three categories of cells receiving inputs from three cone mechanisms. The first category comprised spatial opponent cells responding specifically to luminous lines of precise orientation coupled with synergistic inputs from cone channels sensitive to red or to green. These cells were specific, not to the color per se, but to different types of color contrasts. The second consisted of color opponent cells receiving antagonistic inputs from different cone channels. The third group of cells had both color-opponent and spatial-opponent properties. These three groups of cells had different distribution patterns in the different cortical layers. Because of the existence of different classes of complex cells in the striate cortex and their variations in laminar distribution, Dow proposed that colored and noncolored stimuli were treated by different mechanisms.

Evidence has been provided in the macaque for a region in visual area IV that contains a high concentration of color-coding cells. Most of these cells also respond to form and orientation, provided that the color has a specific wave length (Zeki, 1973a). The tendency is for cells responding to the same wave length both to be grouped in the same region and to be organized in columns. This specialized region receives afferents from areas 18 and 19. The existence of a region so highly evolved for coding color information has considerable importance for the interpretation of pathological data in man.

There are other cells in the visual cortex that receive converging projections from diverse sensory inputs (Jung, 1961; Murata et al, 1965). Experiments in the cat have demonstrated modification of receptive fields of some visual cortex cells associated with rotation of the head or tilting of the body (Denney and Adorjani, 1972; Horn et al, 1972). These results suggest that visuovestibular convergence can be highly specific and may function in maintenance of perceptual constancy. According to Morrell (1967) nearly all of the cells in visual area III of the cat (i.e., the area that corresponds to area 19 in man), possessing visual response characteristics, are activated not only by the complex preferential visual stimulus but also by acoustic and/or tactile stimuli. In addition the response pattern of each of these single units was different for each type and modality of stimulation. When a preferential visual stimulus combined with stimuli from other sensory modalities, the response pattern became quite complicated; the pattern could not in most cases be attributed to a simple linear summation. For 90% of these cells, if the original preferential visual stimulus was again presented, the regular original response pattern for this stimulus was again obtained. For the remaining 10% the response pattern to a repeated presentation of the original preferential visual stimulus did not return to its original form; it retained a form similar to that obtained under conditions of combined sensory stimulation. This effect persisted for 20 to 30 minutes. These cells with modifiable responses were also found to have a grouped columnar organization.

Morrell contends that this transitory modification of response patterns of single cells is specifically related to particular past experiences. If a cell that is located in the receptive field for a specific visual stimulus also responds to stimuli from other sensory modalities, that does not imply that the monosensory information is lost. The arrival of the same acoustic information at two different visual cells may modify the response patterns of these cells in two completely different ways. A cell capable of polysensorial activation may nonetheless maintain a discharge pattern specific to the stimulus.

Morrell studied cells in visual area III. One could deduce that these plastic, modifiable cells represent the highest level of visual system function, receiving information from hypercomplex cells. In fact there is already some evidence to suggest that these cells that respond to diverse sensory stimuli in a modifiable manner are widely distributed in the neuraxis. In addition Jung (1961) has found cortical cells that can be activated by retinal stimulation only if they are also activated by nonspecific influx.

From these various studies one could suggest that the role of "context" may be manifested at each step in the process of feature detection. Sensory encoding may be realized not only by immediate polysensorial coordination integrating a specific response but also by recourse to past experience.

Activity of thalamic and reticular formation structures should not be ignored when one considers feature detection mechanisms. These anatomic regions influence sensory control by means of selection, e.g., selective attention can influence use of one channel over another (Hernandez-Peon, 1961). Cortical cells may also play a role in visual attention and orientation (Dow and Dubner, 1969).

Since different cells in the visual system respond specifically and preferentially to different stimuli, one could conceive that species-specific perceptual characteristics depend on the feature extraction systems present in each species. In the frog, for instance, certain cells exist that respond only to small dots in movement—what Lettvin et al (1959) have called "bug-detectors." According to Sutherland (1969) the varying capacities for visual form discrimination in different species depend on different proportions and distributions of feature-detecting cells. However, the manner in which the rules of form recognition are transferred into memories may also be a factor related to these perceptual specificities.

In the face of the increasing body of neurophysiological data concerning visual perception, prudence is warranted to avoid overinterpretation. Warren (1969), for example, argued that performances of cats on a task of discrimination of mirror images were qualitatively similar to those of rats, octopuses, monkeys, and human infants. Cats discriminated vertical mirror images more rapidly than horizontal. Given similarities of performance across different animal species, it would be difficult to accept that the differences of discrimination found in various species could depend only on relative differences in distribution of visual cortical cells that have specific receptive fields for the different orientations.

More likely a process similar to the following occurs. Certain specific stimuli may act as liberators of innate behavioral patterns characteristic of each species, but to be effective, the stimuli must appear during a particular period of development. Feature detectors exist from birth, but they must be stimulated during development. These feature detection cells seem to be especially vulnerable during a critical developmental stage. Although an inborn system of rules and operations exists for each species, learning intervenes at a critical stage for normal development. Experience might be the liberating process permitting the education of visual attentional mechanisms vis-à-vis information (i.e., subsequent visual stimuli). Learning would not function as a process of enrichment so much as a means of differentiating specific features of stimulus invariants reaching the organism (Gibson, 1966). The animal would not construct reality, as Piaget (1935) has proposed; rather, there would be a development of possibilities for detection of critical features of stimuli and an expansion of attention span.

VISUAL ILLUSIONS AND HALLUCINATIONS

These disorders of perception are usually paroxysmal; they frequently appear in association with each other; and in Jacksonian terms, they represent positive symptoms of perceptual disturbance. Visual illusions and hallucinations ordinarily have an organic rather than "functional" or psychiatric basis, and the pathology is usually cortical rather than subcortical. Not only does cortical localization of lesion play a key role in producing these disorders but also hemispheric lateralization influences the form of the disturbance. Experimental manipulations by means of electrocortical and subcortical stimulation, administration of drugs, and sensory deprivation have provoked illusions and hallucinations. As we shall see below, it has become possible to simulate the disorders and evaluate the relative importance of different factors that influence their development.

Visual Illusions (Metamorphopsias)

Under this rubric we consider only those visual perceptual modifications concerning form, contour, size, number, or movement of objects or people, and also, by extension, modifications of colors of objects. We do not include those illusions dependent on a particular affective state such as strangeness or familiarity. In these latter states the disorder is not truly perceptual; affective disturbance influences visual experience. Dreamy state phenomena may be associated with true metamorphopsias, but in our opinion, in contrast with the opinions of Penfield (1958a,b) or Critchley (1953), these two sets of abnormal phenomena must be clearly distinguished.

Metamorphopsias have been long recognized as clinical neuropathological conditions, after first having been studied as psychiatric conditions. The work of the Viennese school, in particular that by Pötzl (1928) and Hoff (1935a), detailed and elaborated the clinical descriptions, as well as provided information on lesion sites responsible for the syndromes. Bender and Teuber (1947) studied these perceptual deformations with respect to their relationship to visual field defects. Critchley (1953) provided a complete clinical classification. The important role of hemispheric lateralization, already suggested by the studies of the Viennese school, was subsequently established with certainty (Mullan and Penfield, 1959; Teuber et al, 1960; Hécaen and Angelergues, 1963, 1965). Finally experimental studies with drug administration and sensory deprivation were used to help explain the syndrome with reference to the von Holst theory of reafference (Teuber, 1961b; Held, 1965; Freedman, 1961, 1965).

Clinical Features

Metamorphopsias are mainly paroxysmal, appearing as manifestations of epilepsy, as auras or epileptic equivalents, more rarely as migraine attacks. When they are persistent, the cause is usually a peripheral ophthalmologic problem or craniocerebral trauma in the acute phase. In describing the clinical features we use a modified version of Critchley's classification (1953). Although we divide the symptom clusters for convenience of description, it should be stressed that different varieties of visual illusion often appear together.

Two major categories may be discerned: elementary illusions and complex illusions. Elementary metamorphopsias modify perceptual qualities of an object, while complex metamorphopsias are characterized by alterations of three-dimensional visual space.

Elementary illusions have several varieties: (1) modification of object size (increased size is called megalopsia or macropsia; decreased size is called micropsia); (2) modification of object size in a single dimension (stretching, flattening); (3) obliquity of vertical or horizontal components or of both; (4) inverted image of object; (5) blurring and irradiation of outlines; (6) modification of object colors (e.g., disappearance of color is called achromatopsia; instead of losing color, objects may acquire a uniform tint); (7) fragmentation of contours; and (8) illusion of movement of stationary objects, illusion of increasing movement of objects moving at a steady pace, and decrease or loss of appearance of real movement.

Different varieties of complex illusions are also found: (1) telescoping of objects, whereby they seem small and far away; (2) pelopsia, in which objects seem to approach the subject and become larger; (3) loss of stereoscopic vision; (4) visual perseveration (palinopsia); (5) optic alloesthesia, or displacement or false localization of objects in space; and (6) metamorphopsia affecting only a portion of a visual scene. In a series of 83 patients with metamorphopsia Hécaen (1963) found that 71 could be classified into four groups: (1) deformation of objects, (2) illusory movements, (3) polyopia, and (4) macropsia or micropsia. The other 12 subjects had splitting and separation of objects (4 cases); reversed image of objects (1 case); complex visual illusions (1 case); and 6 cases with metamorphopsias limited to human faces.

Deformation of objects may have a variety of manifestations, and subjects may have difficulty characterizing the deformations. "It is misshapen such that I cannot recognize it." "It is like a mirror in an amusement park distorting all shapes." Occasionally the object is "stretched" in length, occasionally in width. An object may suddenly assume a sinusoidal shape; this is especially true for long objects. Objects may curve in one direction only, assuming a "bent over" appearance. At times one object may penetrate another, even without giving the sensation of movement in the process. Objects may appear to be one inside another to such an extent that the subject cannot determine the number of objects or items present. This variety of metamorphopsia is seen especially in reading, with letters appearing to be telescoped together, rendering comprehension impossible. Visual deformations often involve only one category of objects, the category being defined either by the specific characteristics of items (e.g., graphic characters) or by perceptual similarities (e.g., all box-shaped objects). It has been our impression that this type of illusion appears in isolated fashion relatively often by comparison with other varieties of illusion.

Illusions of movement are also varied. Most often a subject has the impression that an object is oscillating in different planes of space, giving the illusion that the "objects are continuously jumping from one place to another." Sometimes the objects seem to be "jumping in place." An illusory movement may be unidirectional along a single spatial coordinate (e.g., sliding toward the right or left; approaching or receding without change in size). This movement of the object may be accompanied by another movement related to the object itself, most frequently a rotation upon itself. The perceptual illusion may be limited to movements of the object alone, without the object's being displaced in space. One subject, for example, complained that he saw children moving, while in fact they were immobile. The illusion may be somewhat amorphous, "like a flag waving" or "like a poorly adjusted television set." In Hécaen's series this type of illusion was always associated with other symptoms (vertigo, dreamy state, visual hallucinations, etc.).

Polyopia or monocular diplopia caused by cerebral lesions was extensively studied by Hoff and Pötzl (1937). They described different types: images multiply in the sagittal or frontal planes or even in a concentric manner (Gloning et al, 1968). Of 19 cases reported by Hécaen (1972), most often seen was triplopia, and less often, monocular diplopia or quadriplopia, but image multiplication could extend almost to infinity.

Phenomena of macropsia and micropsia are frequent (Hécaen et al, 1963, 1965; Mullan and Penfield, 1959). These illusions of enlargement or shrinkage of objects or people may or may not be associated with sensations of moving closer (pelopia) or further away (teleopia). Certain features of an object may become smaller even while the whole object in general is getting larger. Ordinarily this illusion involves only some objects or some parts of the entire visual scene; occasionally it is global and encompasses the totality of the perceived environment.

The illusion of splitting of an object into two parts may occur along a horizontal or vertical axis and may be accompanied by separation of the parts, such that they do not touch.

Among the more complex visual illusions are loss of stereoscopic vision, which may be limited to the vertical meridian of the visual world (Pötzl, 1928). Optic alloesthesia occurs when an object located in one visual field is perceived as if it were located in an homologous portion of the other visual field (Herrmann and Pötzl, 1928). Illusions of reversed images have been longer lasting rather than paroxysmal, although only a small number of cases have been reported. Palinopsia or visual perseveration should also be included in this group of complex visual illusions. Critchley described visual perseveration as the reappearance of perceptions after removal of the object that was the basis of the original perception. He also used this term to refer to the illusory extension of visual perception to a greater area than what the stimulus would normally have provoked. Examples of palinopsia include the patient who continued to see cobblestones moving, after the vehicle in which he was riding had stopped (Le Beau and Wolinetz, 1958), and the patient who continued to see someone walking by the foot of his bed, although the person walked by only once (Holmes, 1918a). Bender et al (1949a,b) asserted that palinopsia was always associated with other optical illusions and that it was related to visual afterimages of the normal subject. They found visual perseveration to occur mainly in cases with mild visual field defects and to disappear when the field defect became severe or when the field defect improved.

In addition to these varieties of visual illusion, we should mention certain phenomena close to those of metamorphopsia and often associated with the metamorphopsias. These include modifications in appearance of object colors. The objects may abruptly or progressively lose their color (achromatopsia) or acquire a monochromatic tint, regardless of the nature or number of objects; this latter is most commonly reddish (erythropsia). Another associated illusion is that affecting time: all real movements appear in an accelerated or slowed rate (Hoff and Pötzl, 1937). The illusion of acceleration may also concern auditory perceptions; the illusion of slowing may proceed to complete arrest of movement. Metamorphotaxis refers to a tactile impression of deformation of a grasped object that may be perceived as being larger or smaller; metamorphotaxis may accompany metamorphopsia.

Clinicoanatomic Correlations

Lesions at any level in the visual system from the eye to the cortex may be associated with perceptual distortions producing illusions. Illusion may also be caused by disorders of ocular motility, intrinsic or extrinsic, as well as by dysfunction of vestibulocerebellar connections due to brain stem lesions. If one excludes illusions due to toxic states, to use of hallucinogenic drugs, or to effects of partial or complete sensory deprivation, visual illusions of all types are most frequently caused by cortical lesions.

From the earliest clinicopathological studies of Hoff and Pötzl (1935a, 1937) an increased frequency of illusory phenomena had been found with right rather than left hemispheric lesions. Studies of patients with traumatic head injuries (Teuber et al, 1960), with lesions of varied etiologies (Hécaen and Angelergues, 1963), and by means of electrocortical stimulation (Mullan and Penfield, 1959) confirmed the importance of right hemispheric lateralization for visual illusions. In one series, for example, with verified cortical lesions in right-handers, metamorphopsias were found in 10.3% of 194 subjects with right hemispheric lesions and in 5.8% of 292 subjects with left hemispheric lesions (Hécaen and Angelergues, 1965).

As for intrahemispheric localization Hoff and Pötzl (1935a, 1937) emphasized the importance of the parieto-occipital region. In the Teuber et al (1960) series, lesions causing metamorphopsias were principally located in the occipital or temporo-occipital regions. By electrocortical stimulation studies, visual illusions were most often produced by stimulation of temporal lobe (Mullan and Penfield, 1959). In the Hécaen and Angelergues (1963) study, of 18 cases of metamorphopsia due to verified right hemispheric lesions, the occipital lobe was involved 13 times, of which 5 were isolated occipital lesions; the temporal lobe was involved 8 times, of which 3 were isolated temporal lesions; and the parietal lobe was involved 9 times, of which 1 was an isolated lesion. Of 13 cases of metamorphopsia due to verified left hemispheric lesions, the occipital lobe was involved 11 times, of which 3 were isolated occipital lesions. In the left hemisphere a parieto-occipital lesion seemed most common.

Lesion localization seems to vary according to the type of illusion, although clinicoanatomic data are not sufficient to confirm this observation with certainty. For two types of illusions, however, a clear anatomic differentiation has been found. Illusions of movement are associated with temporal lesions;

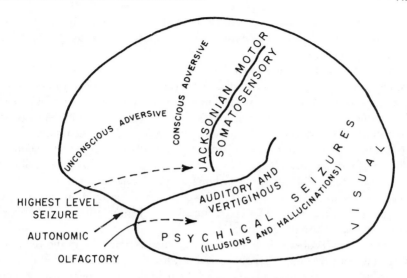

Location in left hemisphere for production by electrocortical stimulation of auditory, vertiginous, and psychomotor seizures with illusions, hallucinations, dreams, and memories (from Penfield and Rasmussen, 1950). Copyright 1950 by Macmillan Co., New York. Reproduced by permission.

polyopsia is associated with occipital lesions. On reviewing published cases of visual perseveration, we find this disorder to result almost exclusively from right occipital or parieto-occipital lesions.

If one compares percentage of illusions with percentage of visual field defects according to topography of the lesion, a clear parallelism is seen, both for right and for left hemispheric lesions. A parallel is also found between percentage of illusions and percentage of disorders of perception of visual coordinates (horizontal and vertical) according to lesion site, with the following exceptions. Metamorphopsias are rare with temporoparietal lesions; in the left hemisphere the parallelism is found only with occipital and parietooccipital lesions.

Theoretical Considerations

The earliest studies of the Viennese school emphasized the importance of a vestibular component in the production of metamorphopsias. Subsequent research confirmed the earlier contentions. Vestibular stimulation causes visual illusions in subjects with parieto-occipital lesions, in subjects with paroxysmal hallucinations, and even in normal subjects under certain conditions. It has been shown that the parietal cortex represents the site of cortical projection for the vestibular apparatus (Fredrickson et al, 1968). Clinically we find that vertiginous sensations are the most frequent symptomatic accompaniment of metamorphopsias.

In addition to the influence of the vestibular component Pötzl (1928) proposed another interpretation, at least for certain visual illusions. He proposed that illusions of accelerated movement resulted from a central deficiency in fusion due to disturbance of ocular kinetics. An occipital lobe lesion causes a dysequilibrium, a deviation of fixation resulting from the predominant activity of the normal occipital lobe. Bender and Teuber (1947, 1949) modified this interpretation for polyopia and monocular diplopia. Because of deviation of fixation, they said, extrafoveal points on the retina receive rapid and repeated stimulation. This results in the activation of multiple functional centers corresponding to the different points of retinal stimulation, and therefore multiple images are produced.

Bender and Teuber (1947, 1949) also studied systematically the relationship between perceptual distortions and localized visual field defects. Perceptual distortions seem to polarize toward the field defect. Under certain experimental conditions (e.g., prolonged fixation, simultaneous exposure in different portions of the visual field, tachistoscopic presentation) these perceptual alterations could be exaggerated or reduced. Such experimental conditions can also be used to produce milder degrees of perceptual distortions in normal subjects. In this regard Bender and Teuber pointed out the analogies between their results with brain-damaged subjects and the results of Kohler and Wallach (1944) with normal subjects. The latter authors submitted one portion of the visual field to prolonged gaze on a single stimulus and found that all neighboring portions became "satiated" by this procedure. In such a state any two-dimensional item introduced into the neighboring regions tended to be distorted and was almost always displaced along a third dimension.

Results of studies using experimentally induced drug intoxication or sensory deprivation have provided data useful for theoretical considerations of visual illusions. Long periods of sensory deprivation may produce hallucinations, depersonalizations, states of delirium, distortions of body image, and perceptual distortions (Hebb, 1966). These perceptual distortions may be illusions of fluctuation and displacement of objects and surfaces; changes in positions of objects according to head and eye movements; distortion of forms, lines, and angles; changes in brightness or saturation of colors; or modifications of size constants. Milder degrees of similar illusions have also been found following shorter periods of partial or complete sensory deafferentation (Courtney et al, 1961; Freedman, 1961, 1965; Zubek, 1970). Studies using such drugs as mescaline or LSD have reported qualitatively similar and quantitatively more intense effects.

Because similar perceptual distortions may be produced by cortical lesions, by drug intoxications, and by sensory deprivation or experimentally induced perceptual rearrangements, one may consider that a common mechanism is responsible for these perceptual defects in the various conditions. We suggest that a model derived from the theory of reafference of von Holst may provide the common mechanism. (We have previously discussed this model in the section on visual-motor coordination for the interpretation of sensory readaptation to experimental perceptual rearrangement.) Teuber (1961b) adopts this model for interpretation of metamorphopsias caused by cortical lesions.

Metamorphopsia may be conceived of as an illusion resulting from a disorder of sensorimotor coordination. The corollary discharge, destined to provide information to a cortical region about the intention to move, provides false information if the subject has paralysis of the muscles involved in that particular movement. An illusion of movement with abducens paralysis is an example of such a case. Or, by contrast, false information of constancy may be provided. For example, micropsia is produced in some subjects after ocular application of atropine. If this subject looks in the distance and then attempts to accommodate on a near object, a reduction in size of the visual background occurs. Macropsia may be produced by intraocular instillation of physostigmine, which causes accommodation spasm. If this subject tries to accommodate on a distant object, everything in the distance appears to grow larger. In the normal state, despite increase or decrease of the visual angle, size constancy is maintained, according to this model, because of information feedback to central regions that then act to compensate for the changing visual angle. In the presence of accommodation paralysis or spasm, central compensation continues but inappropriately. Constancy becomes illusion (Teuber, 1961b).

With metamorphopsias of cortical origin it is the central processing component that functions abnormally. Wyke (1960), studying alternations of size constancy associated with brain lesions in man, provided evidence in support of this hypothesis. Size constancy is especially disturbed following parietal lesions of either hemisphere. No correlation was found between disorders of size constancy and visual field defects. Consequently it was presumed that there was a central perceptual dysfunction, the parietal lesion preventing a correct cortical interpretation of information arriving from ocular muscles during convergence together with information arriving from the retina when the visual stimulus is displaced.

Illusions produced by cortical lesions probably depend essentially on defective sensorimotor coordination. In our opinion, however, other factors, especially vestibular and oculomotor, also play a role. Cortical lesions producing metamorphopsias are situated in regions that are responsible for oculomotor coordination and that receive vestibular projections. Abnormal vestibular inputs may provide incorrect information about bodily movements, with no corollary discharge being produced; thus the sensory distortion cannot be corrected. Other factors, relating for example to lesion localization, may also play a role in determining the particular variety of visual illusion that may appear.

Visual Hallucinations

Some authors consider that hallucinations, at least when they are no longer elementary, should not be thought of as perceptual disorders; complex hallucinations, they argue, should be classified with the cognitive or affective disorders. Perhaps this distinction can be justified for hallucinations in other sensory modalities. With visual hallucinations, however, it seems to us that a basic disorder of esthesis, or capacity for sensation, may be found to underlie the varied symptomatology. Nonetheless it is evident that any analysis of hallucinatory phenomena that depends on declarations of patients runs a risk of double interpretation—that of the patient and that of the examiner. Only an examination as systematic and as nonsuggestive as possible can diminish, without altogether eliminating, this risk.

Clinical Features

We attempt in this section to describe and categorize different forms of visual hallucination. Our evidence is clinical and is based on declarations of patients made to us in personal observation. In a subsequent section we attempt a clinicoanatomic correlation. The outline of clinical varieties of visual hallucination that we propose is as follows.
1. Elementary hallucinations
2. Complex hallucinations
   a. Esthesic
   b. Associated with dreamy states
   c. Oneirism
   d. Associated with ophthalmologic lesions
   Elementary visual hallucinations are described as simple visions, such as ephemeral lights, flashes of light, sudden brightenings, appearance of colors, etc., barely patterned. Certain terms used by the patients correspond more to a manner of speaking than to a real description of hallucination. Simplest forms appear as luminous points, lights, stars, sparkling visions, floating objects (e.g., little butterflies). The patient may at one time be struck by the intensity of the light, at another time by the multiplicity of light sources ("as if there were a thousand candles"). Often, color is an important feature, especially reds, then green, blue, and violet. Perhaps only one color is involved, but not rarely the colors are multiple and simultaneous.

Elementary hallucinations are characterized by the absence of pattern. Nonetheless, occasionally a geometric form is described, horizontal lines, circles, half-hexagons, and so forth. These hallucinations are often animated by movements that vary the forms, especially zigzag or rotatory movements. In some cases a vibratory movement may seem to be animating real objects. The hallucinatory image may move in space, usually in a horizontal direction, more rarely in a vertical.

Elementary hallucinations are most often seen in a single hemifield, although they may occur throughout both visual fields. These hallucinations may precede complex hallucinations.

Psychophysiological studies have been done to analyze the characteristics of phosphenes produced by electrical stimulation of cortical and subcortical regions. Chapanis et al (1972) studied patients with electrodes chronically implanted in the thalamus but traversing the occipital lobe and optic radiations. In general the characteristics of phosphenes produced by stimulation at a particular point were reproduced by repeated stimulation of the same point, not only in the same session, but also from one session to another. Pulse frequency influenced both threshold for phosphene production and phosphene characteristics. Good constancy of visual angle was regularly found for a given phosphene. Eye movements seemed, however, to be related to phosphene movement.

Additional studies on the characteristics of visual sensations produced by occipital lobe stimulation have been a tangible result of efforts to devise visual prostheses for the blind (Brindley, 1972; Dobelle and Mladejorsky, 1974a,b). Brindley and Lewin placed 80 electrodes on the pole and medial surface of the occipital lobe of a blind subject. By means of radio transmission one electrode could be activated. The phosphene produced in this way consisted most often of a point of flickering light. With a person who had been blind for a longer period of time, the phosphenes were larger and more diffuse. The position of a phosphene was consistently located in the field contralateral to an electrode, regardless of the stimulus force or frequency.

The map of the visual field that could be constructed by means of phosphene production corresponded in general to the classical anatomicofunctional maps: posteriorly placed electrodes produced central phosphenes; anteriorly placed electrodes produced peripheral phosphenes. Despite their fixed position in a visual field, phosphenes moved each time the eye moved.

Dobelle et al (1974a,b) placed electrodes on the medial surface of the occipital lobe in sighted and blind subjects. In the sighted subjects, area 17 was most efficient in phosphene production. These phosphenes were never greater in size than a large coin held at the end of one's outstretched arm. Increasing stimulus intensity produced multiple phosphenes. Eye movements were associated with phosphene displacement. Phosphene brilliance was affected by pulse amplitude. Again, position of phosphenes in the visual field corresponded to classical projections of visual field to cortex.

The Dobelle studies were done on sighted or newly blind subjects and produced somewhat different results from those of Brindley and Lewin with subjects who had been blind for longer periods of time. Long-standing blind subjects perceived phosphenes with parastriate as well as striate stimulation. Also, with long-standing blindness, phosphenes were achromatic, while colored phosphenes were seen in some of the acute cases.

Complex hallucinations of an esthesic type may be defined by the fact that the vision contains elements that appear nearly real. These qualities of the hallucination encourage a belief such that the patient may consider the hallucination as one of the possible perceptual choices among real stimuli. Reduction of level of consciousness is minimal in these cases; lucidity is preserved. In general, patients describe the hallucinated image as possessing size, shape, detail, and color of real objects. The affective state of the subject at the moment of the hallucination corresponds, in general, to the nature of the hallucinated scene.

Occasionally the behavior of the subject, his acts and words, bear witness to his belief in the reality of what he sees. Foerster (1928), for example, reported on a patient who tried to catch a hallucinated butterfly that appeared before him when his cortical area 19 was electrically stimulated. Hécaen and de Ajuriaguerra (1952) described the case of a man with posttraumatic epilepsy who had the hallucinatory image of a dog shortly after his cortical scar was electrically stimulated; the patient called to and whistled to the dog and insisted, against the contrary opinions of the surgeons, "He is there because I see him."

These hallucinations project most often into the entire visual field, rather than into one hemifield. Classically it has been taught that these hallucinatory visions move from the periphery toward the center and disappear when they reach the fixation point. In fact, however, they may not undergo this central displacement. They may remain totally immobile, or they may be animated by movement appropriate to the entire visual scene.

The subject generally retains a precise recollection of his hallucinatory experience. After the event he may be able to describe the experience in great detail and thereby attest to the absence of confusion or alteration of consciousness at the time of the event. In this way, especially when a particular hallucinatory experience is repeated in stereotyped fashion, initial belief in the reality of the hallucination gives way to acceptance of its unreality. Additional factors leading to a disbelief in the reality of the hallucination, other than stereotyped repetition of the hallucinated scene, include the incompleteness or inadequacy of the image in its relation to the real situation and the previous occurrence of elementary hallucinations.

This group of hallucinations may thus be considered as homogeneous on the basis of the subject's lucidity, his belief in the hallucination, the esthesic quality, and the lack of modification of primary affectivity. This is not a relived experience but an entirely new one (or a fragment of a new visual scene). Elements of the hallucination may be borrowed from prior experience, but the patient never identifies the scene as a memory. Frequently the hallucinated image relates to perceptual experiences of the recent past, but these perceptions will have been reworked, disassembled, and rebuilt to provide a new experience. Based on fragments of prior perceptual experience a new event—the esthesic hallucination—is created in a relatively coherent form, adapted more or less to the perceptual reality of the moment.

Certain phenomena are especially common with esthesic hallucinations. These include lilliputian-type hallucinations, micropsias, macropsias, and metamorphopsias associated with the hallucinated image. By contrast the coexistence of hallucinations in other sensory modalities together with esthesic hallucinations does not seem frequent.

Complex visual hallucinations associated with a dreamy state or associated with phenomena of hallucinatory rememorization form another clinical category. In this category the hallucinatory phenomena arise in the context of a particular variety of modification of consciousness: the dreamy state. Sentiments of strangeness, nonfamiliarity, *déjà vu, jamais vu,* or *déjà vécu* envelop the subject, and he suddenly feels as if he were in an unreal situation. Very often the subject assimilates the hallucination into the dreamlike experience that envelops him. No true oneiric structure is present; rather, the subject simply attempts to translate the profound sensation of unreality that he grasps from the total experience, whether or not a hallucination is present. These states occur as part of the syndrome of uncinate fits and may thus be associated with other psychosensory phenomena.

Two subgroups are found. The first is characterized by the sentiment of living in an unreal, unhabitual, and strange situation; the second, by the delusion of reliving a prior experience, with recognition that the delusion is in some way related to memory of past events. Penfield et al (1950, 1958a, 1963) described this latter group under the term *recollection*. These two subgroups with different clinical features have elements in common, especially a disbelief in the reality of the phantasm. It is the sentiment accompanying the hallucination that gives it its distinctive characteristics, by contrast with esthesic hallucinations, in which the affective aspect derives from the character of the hallucination itself.

In the first subgroup a sentiment of strangeness, of the bizarre, of living in a dream accompanies and often precedes the hallucination. Esthesis is minimal, the image being poorly defined, imprecise, and fantastic. The sense of unreality pervades the hallucination. The sentiment to which the patient reacts ranges from anguish to exaltation and colors his visions. Memory for the hallucinated sense is poor: the patient remembers blurred, imprecise images that quickly pass from memory. Subjects are aware of the unreality of the situation ("It is happening in my imagination," "It is as if I am seeing things," "I see it and feel it at the same time"). The esthesic quality is uncertain, fluctuating. One finds all possible stages between a true hallucination (active mental representation) and the simple sentiment of unreality. "I know it is not real," recounted one patient, "I have the impression of entering another world."

In the second subgroup the hallucinations have different manifestations. Clarity of the scene is a hallmark; details exist; esthesis is more pronounced. One is not, however, dealing here with purely visual phenomena. The scene is relived in all of its prior forms. Here we have an event that already existed for the subject, who has the sudden ineluctable sentiment of *déjà vu*. With each new attack the hallucination may be repeated with stereotyped regularity, or different hallucinations may appear each time. "Not like a dream; not like a movie;" one patient declared; "it is as if it existed." But the patient does not believe in the reality of these images, even though they may seem real. The subject is invaded by the impression of *déjà vu*, the impression of living through an already lived-through event, often with an affective state similar to that experienced at the time of the first event. At times another affective mood interacts with the former: that of anguish or disgust and paradoxically *jamais vu*.

Although clearly related to the hallucinations of the first subgroup, those in this subgroup are distinguished from the former by their visual clarity and by their close correspondence with the previously experienced real events. The hallucinated scene is complex, precise, well defined; people move about and act in expected ways. At times these hallucinated people speak, producing correct speech that may be accompanied by a sentiment of having been heard before. Often the subject sees himself in these episodes. He sees again a scene of the past in which he had participated; he sees himself moving and acting as he did then.

The two subgroups of this category of complex hallucinations correspond detail for detail with the distinction made by Penfield in his descriptions of "psychic illusions of an experiential response type" with or without hallucinatory phenomena. In one type—recollections—the subject is suddenly aware of a previous experience. In the other the responses of the subject have an interpretative nature that alters the perception of current experience such that present events are imbued with a sense of familiarity, strangeness, or amusement (Penfield and Perrot, 1963).

With oneirism the hallucinations have clinical features distinguishable from those in the previous two categories of complex hallucinations. Modifications of consciousness are prominent and vary from simple wandering of attention, such as may be seen in drowsiness, to confusional states associated with temporospatial disorientation, incoherence, and emotional disturbances, usually anxiety. Hallucinated visions are most often organized and rich, integrating with the external world and frequently deforming this world. Hallucinations in other sensory modalities join the visual to provoke a motor and/or emotional response on the part of the subject, who usually understands these hallucinations to be a threatening reality. In severe oneiric states, such as may be seen in delirium tremens, the disorder of consciousness is maximal, and belief in the hallucination is total. Following such episodes, amnesia is complete.

These hallucinations are mainly visual and are analogous to dreams; the same vividness of unrolling of events with the active participation of the patient occurs. *Hypnagogic imagery* is also close to that of dreams, but because of at least partial preservation of contact with reality, the subject may at times act as if he is a spectator observing the spatially projected image.

Hypnagogic phenomena of milder intensity have, by virtue of the localization of lesions that produce them, been called peduncular hallucinosis (Lhermitte, 1939; van Bogaert, 1927). They are also frequent in the Gelineau syndrome associated with cataplexy or narcolepsy. According to Lhermitte (1939) these hallucinoses have objective sensorial qualities with relation to the subject's own body and the space around him. The subject believes he is perceiving objects, animals, and people, often rich in color, multiple, and mobile. In *peduncular hallucinosis* the emotional reaction may be absent or minimal, or the subject may observe his visions with pleasure and curiosity. The subject may be aware of the unreality of his visions unless he becomes obtunded, at which time he may believe the hallucinations are real. Disbelief returns with the return to consciousness. This form of hallucination occurs most often at late evening, when drowsiness begins and attention starts to wander.

The distinctive characteristics common to oneirism, hypnogogism, and peduncular hallucinosis are related to the scenic nature of the hallucinations: colored, rich, mobile, projected into space, integrated into the external world, and continuous with it. In all, there is an impression of reality that exceeds the visual field. Both the real world and the hallucinations are susceptible of deformation. Although less frequent in occurrence, hallucinations of other sensory modalities may appear, in general fitting into the visual scene. Participation of the subject in this hallucinatory world is the rule, as soon as level of consciousness starts to drop.

Hallucinations associated with ophthalmologic lesions are a heterogeneous group. If we exclude oneiric phenomena in relation to sleep disturbances that may occur in such patients, two principal varieties may be isolated: the Charles Bonnet syndrome and the syndrome of monocular hallucinations with positive scotomata.

The Charles Bonnet syndrome refers to a group of hallucinatory phenomena associated with decreased visual acuity and named after the naturalist who compiled the self-observations of his grandfather. The hallucinations are often continuous or almost continuous, occasionally for many years. At the onset elementary hallucinations occur, but with time the visions may become figured, multiple, rich, and changing. Lilliputian people, animals, and objects are not rare. Polychromasia, vivacity of colors, and brilliance of phantasmic images are the rule. Movement and animation of the hallucinated scenes are common. Scintillation effects may be superimposed. Themes may be fixed and stereotyped, although more frequently there is variety. Visions are generally projected into the entire visual field, although their presence on one side only (usually before the eye that is more severely afflicted) is not rare. An aspect of reality is commonly present with objectification of the images in space. However, overall, the subject rejects the reality of the hallucination. These abnormal phenomena may be initiated, arrested, or modified by eye movements, eye closure, increased light, and mental activity, although the influence of these variables differs for each subject. Regardless of ophthalmologic etiology, these hallucinations are linked to impaired visual acuity, the necessary, if not sufficient, cause. Blindness may not be complete, but there is always a rather severe and relatively acute decrease in vision when these hallucinations occur.

Monocular hallucinations with positive scotomata have been isolated from oneirism as an independent syndrome in delirium tremens (Morel, 1933). The positive scotomata have an elliptical form and are centrally located. The exterior borders are blurry; the spot is composed of small, tightly textured elements, rarely dense. The scotoma separates from the background, mainly grey in appearance, occasionally colored, almost never black. The colors may vary during a single hallucinatory experience. Hallucinations occur only during the day; eye closure and darkness suppress them. Both the scotoma and the hallucinations have variable dimensions depending on their projected distances. That is, they will appear to be larger if they are projected at a distance; as they approach the patient, they decrease in size, always by abrupt stages. Movements of hallucinated images may also occur in a horizontal direction, in which case the movements tend to be sliding. A positive scotoma of optic neuritis can easily be understood to provoke such hallucinations during an attack of delirium tremens. It may also be seen with other optic nerve or retinal diseases. When the patient returns to lucidity, two features of the clinical condition become clarified: the hallucination has interfered with visual perception of distant objects; with eye closure, the patient perceives his scotoma as a spot.

Clinicoanatomic Correlations

If one attempts to correlate visual hallucinations and lesion sites responsible for the hallucinations without first categorizing the abnormal visual phenomena following a detailed analysis of their clinical characteristics, one would meet with failure. The results of such an effort would justify the long-standing skepticism concerning the localizing value of hallucinations. Although the prominent role of occipital and temporal lesions was often stressed, many studies with large numbers of subjects suffering from cerebral tumors concluded that no specific highly focal locations could be correlated with hallucinations. Thus, for example, reporting on findings in 439 patients with cerebral tumors, Hécaen and de Ajuriaguerra (1956) observed 36 cases with visual hallucinations. Of these, 17 had posterior cortical lesions; the others had frontal, mesodiencephalic, and even posterior fossa localizations. Taken globally, these results confirm antilocalizationist conclusions of previous studies. However, when Hécaen attempted anatomoclinical correlations after regrouping hallucinatory phenomena according to their structural aspects, a clearer correlational pattern emerged. In addition to anatomoclinical studies, cortical stimulation studies in man have been conducted in which hallucinations were experimentally produced and the sites responsible for their production were defined (Lowenstein and Borchardt, 1918; Krause, 1924; Foerster, 1928; Penfield and Rasmussen, 1950; Penfield, 1958; Penfield and Perrot, 1963).

In this section we present etiologic and pathological data for each of the clinical categories we have described already. The first three categories are related to cortical lesions; the last two, to subcortical or peripheral lesions.

Elementary Hallucinations   These are associated primarily with occipital lesions but may also be found with temporal lesions. For many years authors have insisted that occipital tumors provoke hallucinations that are almost exclusively elementary. With electrocortical stimulation of occipital areas Penfield and Rasmussen found only this type of hallucination. Chapanis et al (1972) observed that phosphenes could be produced by stimulation of geniculostriate pathways, as well as of striate cortex. This observation confirmed results of an earlier study (Marg and Dierssen, 1965). Dobelle et al (1974) also noted production of phosphenes with parastriate stimulation.

Elementary hallucinations have been found with temporal lesions (Sanford and Bair, 1939; Lund, 1952; Hécaen and de Ajuriaguerra, 1956) and temporal stimulation (Penfield and Rasmussen, 1950), although less frequently than with occipital lesions. When cortical stimulation of temporal lobes has caused elementary hallucinations, the stimulation either has used currents of high intensity or has been deep. In our experience elementary hallucinations of temporal origin generally appear in the entire visual field, by contrast with those of occipital origin, which usually appear in the hemifield contralateral to the lesion (Parkinson et al, 1952; Hécaen and Garcia Badacco, 1956a,b). According to Penfield, with stimulation of calcarine areas, subjects especially report hallucinations of colored light spots moving from one point to another, while stimulation of areas 17 and 18 produces hazy glimmerings of variously colored lights that flash on and off.

Complex Esthesic Hallucinations   For Penfield occipital lesions can produce only elementary hallucinations, while complex hallucinations arise from temporal lesions and represent experiential responses or rememorizations. Hécaen and Garcia Badacco (1956a,b), in clinical and anatomoclinical studies, formed a different conclusion. For these authors, patterned complex hallucinations of an esthesic type result from lesions of occipital convexity. The Paris group used Penfield's own observations to support their conclusion. Penfield described the results of stimulating patient R. W. in the cortical region representing the "border between visual and mnestic cortex." He obtained a response that started with an elementary visual hallucination and progressed to a vision of "people coming towards him" or of two people that he knew, a girl and a boy, carrying rifles.

Thus, by stimulating points situated on the lateral occipital surface, Penfield obtained hallucinatory responses whose characteristics corresponded to the findings of Hécaen and Garcia Badacco. No sentiment of strangeness, no mnestic aspect was observed. We may be justified in asking if the transit zone between anterolateral occipital cortex and posterior temporal cortex, a region recognized by Penfield himself as being responsible for elaboration of visual perception, may not be responsible for complex visual perceptual processing in relative isolation from mnestic elements. The feeling of reliving the visual event may not be present, and thereby a sense of reality may be accorded the phantasm.

Russell and Whitty (1955), in a study of visual phenomena secondary to head injury, had similar conclusions. They asserted that complex visual hallucinations could originate from two distinct areas; one situated in the temporal lobe (associated with sentiments of reminiscence and *déjà vu*); the other, in the posterior parietal or parieto-occipital region (associated with visual imagery and visual memory).

Complex Hallucinations Associated with Dreamy State and with Hallucinatory Rememorizations   For this type of hallucinations whose essential nature resides in the sentiments that accompany the visual phenomena, a lesion localization in the temporal lobe has been accepted since the earliest studies on the dreamy state (Jackson, 1932). Subsequent studies confirmed the localizing value of "uncinate fits" (Kennedy, 1911; Cushing, 1922; Horrax, 1923; Wilson, 1917). In particular Penfield has studied these visual and dreamy state phenomena with interoperative electrocortical stimulation. For Penfield experiential or interpretative psychic responses are caused by stimulation of the superior and lateral surface of the temporal lobe. This surface includes the superior bank of the Sylvian fissure and the neighboring portions of the insula. He did not find such responses with stimulation of uncus or hippocampal gyrus.

As for hemispheric lateralization Mullan and Penfield (1959) noted a predominance for temporal occurrence of visual phenomena associated with right-sided stimulations not only for perceptual illusions but also for rememorization and interpretative responses. In later studies Penfield observed that the points for which stimulation determined visual experiential responses varied in the two hemispheres. In the hemisphere dominant for language the points were almost entirely limited to the superior surface of T_1, whereas in the opposite hemisphere the points were widely spread over the entire temporal lobe but were especially prominent in the posterior zone (that is, in the area that, in the left hemisphere, develops for representation of language).

Hécaen and Angelergues (1965) analyzed the frequency of appearance of hallucinatory phenomena in a large series of right-handed subjects with proved retrorolandic lesions in one or the other hemisphere. Taking hallucinations globally, they found that, of 179 subjects with left-sided lesions, 23 (13%) had visual hallucinations; of 125 subjects with right-sided lesions, 26 (21%) had visual hallucinations. This study provided additional evidence of the predominant role of the right hemisphere in visual hallucinations; however, this role varied according to the different clinical categories of hallucinatory phenomena. Of the 23 subjects with hallucinations due to left hemispheric lesions, 16 had elementary types, 4 had complex esthesic types, and 3 had "experiential" types, or respectively 8.5%, 2%, and 1.6%. Of the 26 subjects with hallucinations due to right hemispheric lesions, 12 had elementary, 12 esthesic, and 2 experiential types, or respectively 9.5%, 9.5%, and 1.6%.

Functional hemispheric asymmetry was thus found only for one type of hallucination—the complex figured visual hallucination with realistic sensorial qualities—which was more prominent with lesions of the nondominant hemisphere. The discordance between these results and those of Penfield and Perrot (1963) can perhaps be explained by the fact that, in the stimulation studies, of 38 visual responses classified as experiential, only 14 were accepted by the patients as having formed a part of their past experience.

Anatomic correlations in the Hécaen and Angelergues (1965) study showed that elementary and complex hallucinations were closely linked to occipital lesions, either isolated or in association with temporal or parietal lesions.

Oneirism This syndrome, especially frequent in infections or toxic-metabolic disorders, may also be seen with certain subcortical lesions. Lhermitte (1923) and van Bogaert (1927) pointed out that hallucinoses constituting a milder form of oneirism characterized by a lesser degree of disturbed consciousness could result from peduncular lesions. Association of this form of hallucinosis with narcolepsy and cataplexy further implies a subcortical origin.

In the series of patients with cerebral tumors described by Hécaen and de Ajuriaguerra (1956) eight patients with mesodiencephalic lesions had this

variety of hallucination. They were always accompanied by decreased consciousness and sometimes by elements of Korsakoff's syndrome. Visual hallucinations resulting from frontal lobe tumors were also of this type (except in
those cases in which the frontal tumor caused bilateral optic atrophy). In
cases of frontal tumors the symptoms may have been secondary to cerebral
edema or to the fact that the frontal lobe acts as association cortex for a
variety of subcortical structures (Nauta, 1971; Hécaen and Albert, 1976).

No definite statements can yet be made concerning the locus of action of
hallucinogenic drugs. Some indications exist, however, that LSD has an influence on temporal lobe activity. Administration of this drug may be associated with electrical activity recorded from the medical temporal region that
resembles electrical activity of temporal lobe epilepsy. In a study using chimpanzees, when LSD was administered, Baldwin and Hofman (1969) found
the animals to act in a "psychotic" way. This was true for normal chimpanzees and for those with cortical ablations; however, with bitemporal ablations, no psychotic reaction was obtained.

Hallucinations Associated with Ophthalmologic Lesions   Ocular lesions, as
well as lesions of optic nerve or chiasm, can produce hallucinatory symptoms.
Suppression of visual acuity seems to be the responsible factor. The question
remains, however, whether these ophthalmologic lesions, although necessary,
are sufficient. Some authors maintain that a cerebral lesion, or at least a
transient cerebral dysfunction, is necessary for appearance of hallucinations
(Lhermitte and de Ajuriaguerra, 1936; Burgmeister et al, 1965). Naturally,
since these symptoms develop often in elderly subjects, the probability of
cerebral dysfunction is high. Nevertheless we have observed such disorders in
relatively young subjects in whom the probability of cerebral lesion was low.
The symptomatology of these hallucinations also seems to distinguish them
from hallucinations that occur following known cerebral damage.

Theoretical Considerations

We consider visual hallucinatory phenomena to have both an underlying
unity of causation and a diversity of clinical manifestation. To attempt an
explanation of mechanisms responsible for the production of hallucinations,
one must account for experimental, as well as anatomoclinical evidence. This
evidence derives from cortical and subcortical stimulation studies, from the
variety of lesion sites depending on the clinical aspect under consideration,
from the factor of functional hemispheric asymmetry, from the hallucinogenic effect of drugs, from studies of sensory deprivation, and from experimental
studies on sleep and dreams.

Experimental intoxications (mescaline, LSD, etc.) cause perceptual illusions analogous to those described in studies of sensory deprivation. Perceptual illusions mark the onset of the intoxication, followed by richly colored elementary visual hallucinations, and finally by complex hallucinations, vivid and well exteriorized. Analogies with effects of sensory deprivation, such as those described by Hebb and others at McGill, are too impressive to allow one to escape the conclusion that underlying mechanisms are similar.

Hallucinatory phenomena such as those reported by the subjects studied by the Montreal group were, however, less frequent and less dramatic in other series of experiments. (These other experiments involved partial sensory deprivation or total deprivation for shorter periods of time.) Currently the tendency is to put more weight on the role of observer suggestion (Zubek, 1964, 1970) or to consider that the visual imagery results from a reduced level of attention. Reduction in level of attention, even in normal conditions, may provoke visual imagery (Ziskind and Ausburg, 1967).

The relationship between sleep, dreams, and the perceptual disorders we have described in this chapter must also be considered. The earlier studies of Dement and Kleitman (1957) showed that dreams did not occur in all stages of sleep but only in those accompanied by rapid eye movements. This is the so-called paradoxical sleep stage in which one finds, in addition to rapid eye movements, a low-voltage rapid activity on the electroencephalogram and a hypotonia of nuchal muscles. Studies of paradoxical sleep in the cat (e.g., Jouvet, 1967, 1969) suggest a rhombencephalic origin for this activity. On the electroencephalogram one sees cortical activation associated with regular hippocampal activity with spikes along a pontogeniculo-occipital pathway. This observation suggests that there exists an ascending projection from pontine tegmentum toward the geniculate body and then to occipital cortex. Following destruction of the caudal part of the locus ceruleus, one may find an increased number of spikes in the geniculate body associated with a behavior pattern simulating fear or rage, even though the animal does not respond to external visual stimuli. These have been called "hallucinatory-like states." Thus, from rhombencephalic regions one may release paradoxical sleep together with its oneiric component. In man a certain similarity of events occurs: a relationship exists between the direction of eye movements and the direction of movement of dream activity as reported by subjects who have been awakened immediately after observation of their eye movements.

The question of the origin of oneirism still presents several obstacles to complete answer; nonetheless the previously cited evidence provided strong indications in favor of an explanation. It is clear that this evidence may be related to hallucinatory episodes of the narcolepsy-cataplexy complex and to those of brain stem lesions (peduncular hallucinosis). Thus one basic element in disordered visual psychosensory phenomena is that they may be considered as disturbances of one of the components of the sleep mechanism. Another is that activation of the geniculostriate system is necessary for their appearance.

Whatever the variety of visual hallucination, its essential nature seems to us to be dependent on the esthesic quality present. The element of sensory projection seems primordial. A visual hallucination is a sensory fact, whether or not the subject believes what he is seeing. Activation, by lesion or otherwise, of projection pathways and centers of the visual system is an essential feature of visual hallucinations. Here is the unifying basis of visual hallucinatory phenomena, whatever their origin and however varied their clinical manifestations. From this basis certain constants may be abstracted from the variety of clinical forms. For example, hallucinations associated with ophthalmologic lesions are variously described, with progressive enrichment, multiplicity, and circumstantiality. Yet analysis of these descriptions permits detection of constants of form, despite their apparent complexity. Kluver (1942) proposed that these various hallucinations may be the descriptions afforded by different subjects to modifications of a limited number of fundamental forms: (1) grillwork, filigree, honeycomb, and checkerboard; (2) spider's web; (3) tunnel, tube, and cone; and (4) spiral. With hallucinations of calcarine cortex origin these basic forms may be easily discerned, since these hallucinations do not become transformed, as a rule, into more complex patterns and figures. By contrast the abruptness and brevity of appearance of complex patterned hallucinations of lateral occipital origin renders discovery of these constants of form more difficult. Of interest in this regard is the study of Bazhin et al (1973) demonstrating that patients with visual hallucinations due to occipital lesions have difficulty with visual information processing; they cannot easily distinguish signal from noise. Constants in visual hallucinations are not limited to form. We think that characteristics of brilliancy and luminosity can be interpreted in the same way. Kluver (1942) also believes that constants other than those of form exist, independently of the etiology of the hallucination. He lists tendencies to reduplication of images, to modifications of size and shape, and to alteration of spatial relations of the hallucinated images. Because of these constants Kluver (1942) suggested that there might exist several fundamental mechanisms for hallucinations, each related to a different level of the nervous system. He proposed three levels of constants within hallucinations: of form, of multiplication and deformation of images, and of modifications of temporospatial relationships. These constants are not specific to hallucinations but are also found in other visual, and also nonvisual, phenomena. They represent a general structure of neuropsychological behavior.

It may be interesting to consider the concept that multiplication and deformation of images may be a neuropsychological constant, since, as we have already seen, experimental evidence is available to support this view. The relationship between visual illusions and complex figured hallucinations is apparent, whether at the cortical level, where the factor of hemispheric asymmetry influences both sets of phenomena; or following experimental intoxications; or with hallucinations associated with ophthalmologic lesions. Following administration of certain drugs, for example, one finds a progression from distortions to movement of real objects, to micropsias or macropsias, to movements of objects toward or away from the subject, to color modifications with elementary hallucinations, and finally to complex hallucinations derived from the preceding events, retaining many of the aspects of the preceding events.

It is also easy, at times, to capture the transition from certain metamorphopsias of cortical origin to complex hallucinations. There is, thus, only a difference of degree (spatial or temporal) between a visual perseveration (palinopsia) or visual alloesthesia and a hallucinatory phenomenon. Occasionally it becomes difficult to classify a paroxysmal visual event as illusion or hallucination. A patient described by Hécaen (1972b), for example, had both a disturbance in visual perception of real colors (he saw pink as mauve) and hallucinatory visions of brightly colored red and yellow animals jumping about; his hallucinated images were blurred and distorted (twisted dogs, cats with bizarre shapes).

The esthesic nature and the hallucinatory constants forge the underlying unity of hallucinations of all types. At the same time they link hallucinations to other sensory phenomena. In this way, according to the specific conditions that determine the various phantasmic states, one can understand both the unifying thread and the wide variability of manifestation. If we consider hallucinations of the rememorization and strangeness variety, the role of visual involvement becomes less evident, to the same degree that the affective aspect becomes more prominent. In such cases association with metamorphosias may reflect a disorder of sensorimotor coordination.

The visual hallucinations of oneirism pose similar problems of interpretation. Modifications of temporospatial relations seem to be most important in these hallucinations. Disorders of consciousness are a principal element in this syndrome, whose prime mover seems to depend on activation of the geniculostriate system, as with normal dreams. It may be that tonic changes that accompany paradoxical sleep also contribute to disruption of the sensorimotor link.

The visual hallucination, in all of its forms, seems to derive from functional or pathological activation of the visual system. Spontaneous activity of the visual system normally inhibited by peripheral stimuli or by systems of attentional control may be liberated by several factors. Among these are lesions situated in visual pathways or centers, physiological or pathological lowering of alertness, and suppression or distortion of stimuli arriving from the external world. According to the level of the visual system at which modifications of function occur, other mechanisms (mnestic, sleep-wake mechanisms, sensorimotor coordination mechanisms) may interfere with liberation of spontaneous visual activity to provide special characteristics to the hallucinatory phenomena.

CORTICAL BLINDNESS

It has traditionally been taught that bilateral destruction of striate areas in man causes total blindness. However, the rapid development of research on residual vision in animals after ablation of occipital areas has thrown the classical doctrine into doubt. Recent research on the possibility for certain kinds of preserved visual capabilities in the "blind" field of human beings with occipital lesions seems to be opening a new chapter.

Experimental Background

Although it had long been known that bilateral posterior neocortical ablations in cats, dogs, and monkeys caused blindness, some doubts persisted about the capacity of these animals to distinguish light from dark. Experiments by Lashley (1935) confirmed that the rat with posterior neocortical ablation could make no visual pattern discriminations, but at the same time, these studies established that the rats could relearn a light versus dark discrimination and could distinguish positions and perhaps also distances. Marquis (1934) found that, although dogs with bilateral occipital ablations acted as if they were blind (bumping into objects, not responding to threat or presentation of food), they could still learn a lightness versus darkness discrimination, albeit with a reduced threshold by comparison with their preoperative skill.

In the cat, experiments in the past decade have again shown that animals with visual cortex removals are unable to relearn a visual pattern discrimination, if the luminous flux and contours had been equalized. It may, however, be that capacity to reestablish this type of discrimination is present but requires a greater number of trials (Spear and Braun, 1969). The variables of contrast and stimulus configuration, and duration of postoperative learning all seem to be factors that influence the capacity to establish visual pattern discrimination by cats with bilateral occipital lesions. It is possible that discrimination of visual patterns by cats without visual cortex takes place by usage of cues that the normal cat does not use. Dalby et al (1970) refer to this as a capacity of the cat to appreciate how space is filled.

Doty remains skeptical about the visual potential of cats operated on at birth or in adulthood "if in addition to marginal, splenial, post lateral, and lingual gyri (to remove all of areas 17 and 18 and some of area 19), the posterior ectosylvian plus middle and posterior suprasylvian gyri are included." In such cases "complete blindness is produced." Even in such cases the ability to discriminate intensity or modifications of flicker fusion speed remains. Murphy et al (1975) confirmed the existence of severe deficits in acquisition of pattern discrimination by adult cats with almost total ablation of visual areas. These deficits were not present, however, in cats operated on as infants.

Anatomic and electrophysiological studies on cats suggest that the lateral suprasylvian and ectosylvian fields are particularly important for pattern discrimination. These ancillary visual areas receive inputs directly from the lateral geniculate bodies, as well as from the striate and prestriate cortex (Doty, 1973). However, large ablations in the medial and posterior suprasylvian gyri or in the posterior suprasylvian and ectosylvian gyri, without involvement of primary visual cortex, caused severe deficits in acquisition of a multiple-object discrimination task (Hara et al, 1974). Lesions limited to posterior suprasylvian and ectosylvian gyri produced deficits in repeated reversals using spatial or visual cues. Wood et al (1974) have demonstrated that suprasylvian gyri in the cat, while playing only a small role in normal pattern discrimination, are important with respect to residual capacity in the animal with visual cortex ablations.

In the cat, ablation of posterior neocortex and superior colliculi causing total degeneration of geniculate bodies does not prevent the possibility of relearning a lightness-darkness discrimination (Urbaitis and Meikle, 1968). Thus, as we have discussed in a previous section (on two visual systems), one is led to consider the role of the pretectum in residual visual functions after cortical lesions. Sprague et al (1970) noted that pretectal lesions involving superior colliculi, while not disturbing lightness-darkness discriminations, impair both visually guided responses to moving stimuli and form discrimination. Addition of cortical lesions limited to area 17 did not aggravate these deficits.

In the monkey the classic studies by Klüver (1942) showed that the macaque with bilateral striate cortex lesions could discriminate stimuli only on the basis of their differences in luminous energy. After effective elimination of geniculostriate function, brilliance, surface, color, distance, and form were no longer stimulus variables that could be used for determining responses to visual stimuli. Kluver was able to demonstrate that the apparent responses to factors of brilliance, distance, and position in space were in fact responses to changes in luminous-flux density to which the visual stimuli were subjected under different conditions. Ablation of occipital cortex brought about a loss of constants and thereby created for these monkeys a remarkable degree of stability of the visual world. With the geniculostriate system destroyed, the eye behaved as a simple photoelectric cell, and all possibility of transformation of constants and evaluation of equivalences was abolished. However, other authors (e.g., Denny-Brown and Chambers, 1955) found that, despite bilateral ablation of area 17, monkeys preserved the capacity to localize moving objects, even under conditions of low illumination.

In a series of studies on extrageniculostriate vision in monkeys Pasik and Pasik (1968, 1973a,b) proved that monkeys with bilateral occipital lobe ablations could discriminate light from dark and also could discriminate transilluminated figures under conditions either of differences in brilliance and luminous flux but with equal surface dimensions or of difference in brilliance and surface dimensions but with equal luminous flux. These discriminative capacities were abolished by addition of bilateral lesions in the lateral sections of the mesodiencephalic junction. Isolated lesions in the same mesodiencephalic regions did not disrupt acquired capacities for visual discrimination if striate cortex were present. This region, and particularly the paralemniscal nucleus situated anterior to the inferior colliculi and lateral to the medial lemniscus, seemed important to these authors in extrageniculostriate vision (secondary visual system).

According to Pasik and Pasik (1973) the accessory optic system may be the critical structure in the macaque that permits visual function in the absence of striate cortex. Monkeys were able to perform a gross luminous-flux discrimination following total ablation of striate cortex and partial ablation of areas 18 and 19, of temporal neocortex, and of parahippocampal and retrosplenial allocortex, and also following ablation of pulvinar or superior colliculi. Only when the lesion involved the lateral pretectal region and caused degeneration of the nucleus of the accessory optic tract was the visual discrimination task completely abolished.

In other studies on the relationship of the superior colliculus to "higher visual function" in the monkey, it was shown that destruction limited to superior colliculi caused no deficit in detection of differences of total luminous flux or of movement, or of pattern or color discrimination, and no change in frequency threshold for flicker fusion (Anderson and Symmes, 1969). A disturbance in capacity for discrimination of differential speed of movement was found, although some compensation for this deficit could occur. Destruction of superior colliculi does not prevent reacquisition of a discrimination learned preoperatively but does destroy the possibility of acquiring a new discrimination (Anderson and Williamson, 1971). If cortical striate lesions are added to collicular lesions, visual defects become severe. It would seem that isolated pretectal or posterior thalamic lesions may cause mild deficits in pattern or color discrimination that, when coupled with striate lesions, become quite marked.

Weiskrantz (1963) confirmed that under certain conditions the young monkey with striate cortex ablations can discriminate visual stimuli only if they differ in luminous energy. Under other conditions, however, the same animal could discriminate certain patterned stimuli. The conditions that permit a monkey with bilateral area 17 lesions to make visual discriminations relate to differences in luminous flux and differences in total degree of spatial or temporal variation of stimuli. Total length and movement seem to be the spatial and temporal dimensions for which such monkeys retain discriminative skills. Capacity to discriminate the distribution of these spatial or temporal variables seems to be lost. In subsequent research Humphrey and Weiskrantz (1967) found that young adult monkeys with ablation of striate cortex also retained the capacity to detect and even to touch by hand moving objects and blinking lights.

Further research by Humphrey (1970) has demonstrated additional, unexpected capacities of the monkey with occipital cortex ablation. Using a technique in which the monkey was allowed to reach for stimuli under free-choice conditions, Humphrey found that the monkey could see and touch stationary stimuli. In addition he found that it was possible to determine and measure those factors that render discriminability easier; he called these factors the salience factors of the stimulus. Salience could be measured as a function of variation of stimulus dimension. Among determinants of salience, Humphrey found that increasing size produced a parallel linear increase in salience. Brilliancy contrasts were similar in salience to size, and the degree of salience for a given degree of contrast was greater for positive than for negative contrasts. Color contrasts, on the other hand, contributed little or nothing to stimulus salience. Form did play a role, however. Humphrey discovered that if two stimuli were equilibrated for degree of salience, the monkey could not discriminate between them. Similar findings have been reported from other laboratories (Keating and Horel, 1972).

For these observations Humphrey provided the following interpretations. The monkey deprived of its cortex preserves an intact sensorial field but loses its "visual world" (in Gibson's sense). All sensory details are perceived, but the animal can no longer abstract the attributes (form, color, etc.) and use the abstracted attributes as the basis of perceptual classification. The animal sees each item but does not recognize it; the animal is, in fact, agnosic. This does not imply that the visual field is entirely without structure. The normal process of figure-ground differentiation continues, allowing the separation of distinct gestalten. The factors involved in this separation are movement of the figure relative to its background, brilliancy contrasts, and nature of the form. Color contrasts are not helpful. Humphrey contends that by means of this experimental approach an animal model is provided that may be used to understand determinants of the figure-ground relationship provided in theoretical fashion in earlier years by proponents of the Gestalt school of psychology.

We might comment that the monkey with striate cortex ablated possesses information about the localization of an object in space (since he is able to grasp the object). Perhaps perception is not taking place at this stage. Perhaps eye-hand control is established by an internal circuit dependent on cross-cuing mechanisms related to ipsilateral eye-hand control factors, assisted by eye movements guided directly by figures in the visual field. Such ipsilateral eye-hand control mechanisms and cross-cuing activity have been demonstrated to occur in split-brain monkeys (Gazzaniga, 1969).

For Humphrey, in the normal monkey the extrageniculate visual system provides an articulated visual field that permits the animal to become aware of and to orient toward (and fix on) figures in the field. Higher order visual processing may then take place because of feature analyzers located within the geniculostriate system. This higher visual processing involves the imposition of a disjunctive classification on the nondisjunctive flow of information, with final description of the visual world as discrete entities each with its own specific sensorial properties.

Humphrey (1970) pursued his studies of the same monkey with striate cortex removal, extending his observations for a period of 8 years before the animal was sacrificed. Evolution of the animal's behavior showed a remarkable recuperation of spatial functions. Not only was the monkey able to localize objects in space and reach out and touch them in a precise fashion, but also it was able to avoid bumping into obstacles placed in natural and artificial settings. Humphrey posed the question of whether these capacities reflected true spatial perception or whether, because movements of ocular fixation preceded any manual grasp activity, the monkey obtained information by command signals from eye movements. As for the ability to avoid obstacles, this may depend on persistence of ambient vision (in the sense proposed by Treverthen, see above), all focal vision being lost. As for focal vision, virtually no recovery was seen; the monkey continued to be unable to make any visual discrimination other than that based on object salience.

From the anatomic point of view Humphrey's monkey was found to have preserved a small island of striate cortex in the left hemisphere in the depth of the calcarine fissure. A small region of normal cells in the anterioventral portion of the lateral geniculate body corresponds to the patch of preserved cortex. It is difficult to imagine that all remaining visual capacity can be related to the undamaged cortex.

Despite the remarkable recovery of the monkey with almost its entire striate cortex removed, visual discrimination 8 years after surgery did not surpass that found in earlier studies with the same animal. It is worth recalling, however, the observations of Schilder, Pasik, and Pasik (1971), who noted the capacity for form and color discrimination by monkeys with striate cortex removals, even when precautions were taken to prevent cuing by changes in luminous flux. This capacity disappeared when areas 18 and 19 were added to the lesion.

Lepore et al (1975) studied the question from a different point of view. First they determined spectral sensitivity curves for photopic and scotopic vision. Then they ablated striate cortex in two monkeys (area 17 and most of area 18). Monkeys with these lesions had normal curves of scotopic sensitivity, but the photopic curve was displaced toward the scotopic. These results, which confirm those obtained by Malmo (1966) with a monkey with partial destruction of striate cortex, indicate that visual information coming from cones is treated by the geniculostriate system, while that coming from rods is treated primarily by subcortical centers. Anatomic research to date has not demonstrated direct foveal representation in the colliculi, although electrophysiological studies have suggested a collicular representation for the central visual field.

These striking observations were not reproduced by Cardu et al (1975) in a similar study in which the superior colliculi were destroyed. Scotopic and photopic sensitivity curves were equally normal. From this one may conclude either that the geniculostriate system can treat visual information coming from both cones and rods or that other mesencephalic structures are responsible for scotopic vision.

As we have discussed above (see section on "two visual systems"), Humphrey's observations with monkeys, together with those from other animal species (e.g., hamster, tree shrew), provide evidence in favor of the anatomofunctional notion that there is a secondary visual system in addition to the geniculostriate system. The secondary system includes superior colliculus, pretectal regions, and, perhaps, prestriate cortex. It is relevant to note, as does Humphrey (1970), the analogy between the optically guided manual reach and grasp capabilities of monkeys without visual cortex and the prey-catching behavior of the toad, an amphibian without visual cortex. In the latter case, response is also dependent on stimulus size and brilliance (Ewert, 1970).

Anatomoclinical Aspects

The onset of cortical blindness may be acute and total, or cortical blindness may develop in two steps, the final loss of vision occurring in a subject who already had hemianopia. Blindness of cortical origin is distinguished from that of peripheral origin by the integrity of the globe and fundus and by the preservation of pupillary reflexes. In addition, neighborhood signs of cortical damage are often, although not always, present.

It has generally been taught that blindness of cortical origin is absolute, "equivalent to a bilateral enucleation or to bilateral optic nerve atrophy" (Magitot and Hartmann, 1927). This notion has not yet been replaced by a newer one, although in many case reports the authors observe that patients can distinguish lightness from darkness (e.g., Brindley et al, 1969; Hécaen, 1972b). Of interest is the autopsy report by Brindley and Janota (1975) that some occipital cortex was preserved in one of these cases.

In those cases in which optokinetic nystagmus has been studied, no positive abnormalities were noted (Velzeboer, 1952; Bergmann, 1957; Teuber et al, 1960), except in one case in one series (Brindley et al, 1969, 1975). Eye movements, both reflex and voluntary, are made normally.

Ordinarily, internal visual representation for imagery and dreams is retained (Magitot and Hartmann, 1927), although in some cases, evocation of visual memories is almost impossible (Graveleau, 1956). Dissociations of the qualities of these visual memories have been reported. Thus Lhermitte and Nicolas (1923) stressed that cortically blind patients often could not call to mind the visual image of colors.

Electroencephalographic recordings of patients with cortical blindness routinely demonstrate abolition of normal occipital rhythm with absence of response to intermittent photic stimulation (Bergmann, 1957) and absence of the alerting response in the same leads (Graveleau, 1956). Visual evoked responses from occipital derivations are also abolished (Kooi and Sharbrough, 1966).

Two major categories of functional disorder are frequently associated with cortical blindness: visual hallucinations and confusional states. Visual hallucinations may be either elementary or complex, transient or longer lasting. Hallucinations in other sensory modalities may also occur. The general mental abnormalities that often, although not always, accompany cortical blindness consist of confusion with temporospatial disorientation, disorders of attention, and, especially, memory defects.

A syndrome of anosognosia has been described concerning certain patients who are cortically blind but who deny or refuse to recognize their loss of vision. Denial of sensory defect was clearly described by Anton (1898, 1899), who reported on three such patients with cerebral lesions and sensory defects; one of these patients had visual system involvement. Cortical blindness with denial of blindness has subsequently been called Anton's syndrome, although such a symptom complex had already been described by Dejerine and Vialet (1893) and von Monakow (1897). For Anton the general disturbance of intellectual functioning that often accompanies cortical blindness was insufficient to explain the full syndrome. Many other authors have described and attempted to explain the syndrome (Lhermitte and Nicolas, 1923; Magitot and Hartmann, 1927; Redlich and Dorsey, 1945; Nobile and d'Agata, 1951; Angelergues et al, 1960; etc.).

The general clinical pattern of these anosognosic patients is similar from one to the next; the wide variability of symptoms found in patients with somatic anosognosia is not found here. The visual anosognosic refuses to admit his blindness, acts as if he could see, and persists in this behavior despite all evidence to the contrary. He obstinately refuses to learn to accept that he is blind, even though his incapacity disorients him, disrupts his pattern of living, and even injures him (by virtue of obstacles lying in his way that he cannot see). This clinical pattern may be transitory, lasting hours or days, or it may be permanent. Occasionally the anosognosia is manifested by simple indifference to the blindness, with lack of complaints on the part of the patient concerning his disability. Occasionally, to explain away the visual disorder, the patients invent excuses related to the environment: poor lighting, poor glasses, dust in the eye, and so forth. Some subjects react angrily that one should suspect them of having visual deficits. In some cases the denial of blindness is reinforced by the presence of visual hallucinations.

As a rule, disorders of recent memory accompany visual anosognosia, and confusional states are common. These facts have led to the interpretation of the syndrome as a manifestation of general mental dysfunction. According to some authors, denial of blindness never occurs in the absence of defects of memory and orientation; the denial represents confabulation. In such circumstances the anosognosic syndrome would be similar to, if not identical with, Korsakoff's syndrome (Redlich and Dorsey, 1945). Although this may be a correct explanation for some cases of visual anosognosia, it cannot explain them all. Denial of blindness may occur with the visual defect resulting entirely from peripheral causes, with no intracranial, cortical lesion. Certainly one cannot equate denial of blindness in these cases with Korsakoff's syndrome. Other authors have also rejected the argument that visual anosognosia results from a general defect in intellectual functioning. Bychowski (1920) described a patient who had posttraumatic blindness with indifference and euphoria but with no defect of intellect, memory, or attention. It has occasionally been suggested that the peculair affective state resembles hysteria.

The coexistence of visual hallucinations has also been invoked to account for denial of blindness. In one demonstrative case the patient denied his blindness at the same moment that hallucinatory images appeared (Lagrange et al, 1929). This explanation cannot, however, apply to all cases, since not all patients develop hallucinations.

According to Magitot and Hartmann (1927) unawareness of blindness is similar to unawareness of hemianopia. Any lesion of the visual cortex produces both a visual field defect and the loss of awareness of existence of this defective sector of the visual field. They considered this to be a reduction of the internal perceptual field.

Some authors contend that the bilaterality of lesions and large volume of tissue destruction that cause cortical blindness produce a state of neurological deficiency that is responsible for the anosognosia. Anton (1899) rejecting this explanation, felt that interruption of long association fibers prevented the patient from becoming aware of his perceptual defect; the visual disorder, by virtue of having its substrate isolated from the rest of the brain, would not be recognized and would therefore be denied. Bychowski (1920) accepted this interpretation, especially for acute cases: the subject, suddenly becoming unable to elaborate new visual impressions, continues to see previously elaborated visual images without being able to criticize his errors regarding the source of the stimuli.

For those patients who have an acute confusional state associated with cortical blindness, we believe that the sudden sensory deprivation caused by the occipital lesion, together with the possible liberation of previously inhibited visual imagery, together with the reduction in level of consciousness, combine to account for the development of visual anosognosia. We might add, by way of speculation, that in view of the studies demonstrating "blindfield" vision in human beings with occipital lesions (Weiskrantz et al, 1974; Perenin and Jeannerod, 1975), it is not impossible that subjects with cortical blindness who deny their blindness may really have retained some capacities for visual perception, but because they have damaged striate cortex necessary for higher perceptual processing, they do not recognize or are not aware of what they see.

Cortical blindness may occur as a paroxysmal event, representing epileptic equivalents or migraine or transient ischemic attacks. It may also develop following head injury, in which case it is only rarely permanent (Marie and Chatelin, 1915; Teuber et al, 1960). When associated with vascular lesions, cortical blindness is generally longer lasting, extending to months (Anton, 1899; Bergmann, 1957; Monbrun and Gautrand, 1920) and even years (Saenger, 1919; Terbraak et al, 1971; Brindley et al, 1969, 1975).

Recovery from cortical blindness ordinarily follows a characteristic, stepwise pattern: perception of light, then movement, then colors, then forms. The last two steps—recovery of colors and forms—may occur simultaneously, or forms may return before colors. Pötzl (1928) defined three stages of evolution from cortical blindness: (1) sensation of darkness with or without hallucinations; (2) grayness and blurring of objects, hazy perception of light, scintillating sensations, colors perceived as dirty and washed out (red is the first color to return, blue the last); (3) blurry vision like that of a myopic, diplopia with fusion difficulties, rapid fatigability, asthenopic dyslexia, and metamorphopsias. At this stage, difficulty in object perception could simulate agnosia. As Faust (1955) had indicated, these pseudoagnosias are particularly manifest when presentation time is prolonged (cerebral asthenopia).

Recovery in monkeys has so far proved to be considerably different from that in man. As early as the 11th postoperative day a rhesus monkey with bilateral occipital ablations began to follow a moving light with its eyes (Weiskrantz, 1963), whereas, as we have pointed out, almost total blindness may persist in man for years. Two factors, and others unknown, may account for these differences. First the monkeys were young, and the human beings were adult. Second, in the absence of precise anatomic information concerning lesion localization in man, one cannot rule out the possibility that human beings with permanent or long-lasting cortical blindness have lesions both in striate and in retinomesencephalic structures. Only the stage of repression from cortical blindness in which the patient experiences an undifferentiated sensation of light, with neither form nor color, can be compared to the response to differences in total luminous flux of the monkey with occipital cortex removed.

From the point of view of anatomy, lesions producing cortical blindness are located bilaterally in the occipital lobes, destroying both banks of both calcarine fissures and the subjacent white matter. Vascular lesions are most often the cause of complete destruction of both striate regions. These are usually thromboses located in the basilar artery, or in both posterior cerebral arteries, or in a posterior cerebral artery on one side and a sylvian vessel on the other. Certain diffuse lesions, such as leukoencephalitis, demyelinating diseases, and carbon monoxide poisoning, may also cause cortical blindness. Tumors less frequently cause this blindness. Trauma is a relatively infrequent cause in adults but a more common cause in children. As for children the disorder is more frequent than is usually thought. Anoxia is a common cause, and the syndrome is generally transient (Barnet et al, 1970).

Anatomic considerations should be taken into account for explaining the general mental disturbances that are so often a part of the syndrome; amnesia, confabulation, and perhaps anosognosia. The territory of irrigation of the posterior cerebral arteries includes not only posterior cortical structures but also posterior thalamic and medial temporal structures. That is, bilateral lesions may affect the hippocampal-mamillary-thalamic-cingulate circuit. Lesions in this circuit may produce signs of the Korsakoff syndrome, that is, recent memory defect with confabulation. Anosognosia for blindness could then be at least partially explained by this combination of defects. Effects of sensory deprivation, liberation of visual images, and reduction of consciousness could complete the picture.

A new and exciting development in the study of the visual system has been the observation of residual vision in the cortically blind hemifields of human beings. It has been suggested by Weiskrantz (1972) that the monkey with striate cortex removal may be capable of residual, even normal, pattern vision but with reduced visual acuity. Drawing on methodological techniques from the experimental laboratory, Weiskrantz et al (1974) studied the potential for vision in the blind hemifield of a 34-year-old man with surgical removal of his right occipital lobe "including the major portion of the calcarine cortex." Even though this patient had no awareness of "seeing" in his blind field, he was nonetheless able to respond to visual stimuli in a limited manner. He could reach for visual stimuli accurately, he could differentiate the orientation of a vertical line from a horizontal, and he could differentiate an *X* from an *O,* provided the stimuli exceeded a critical size.

These results confirmed the findings of Poppel, Held, and Frost (1973) that residual vision remained after brain wounds involving the central visual pathways in man. In this study a weak but significant correlation was found between target position and eye fixation for loci out to 30° eccentricity in the "blind" field.

Perenin and Jeannerod (1975) tested residual visual ability by means of patterned afterimages in perimetrically blind regions of the visual field in six subjects with postgeniculate lesions and two with pregeniculate lesions. None of the subjects detected an afterimage. However, subjects with postgeniculate lesions were able to point to the origin of a luminous source with good accuracy, although subjects with pregeniculate lesions could not.

We have observed a 62-year-old man who became cortically blind following infarction in the distribution of both posterior cerebral arteries. Inconsistently he would deny his blindness. Although he himself would occasionally state that he was "unable to see anything" and although he was considered totally blind by the attending physicians and nurses, he was able to grasp an object in motion and to indicate the direction of motion (horizontal, vertical, or diagonal). He was unable to see an immobile object, even if it was larger than the moving objects that he could see. This is an example of the Riddoch effect, first described in 1917 (Riddoch, 1917).

These various observations suggest that the visual capacity remaining after damage to striate cortex in man may be greater than has been generally believed. Botez (1975), after an extensive review of animal and human studies of visual perception, concluded that, in certain clinical syndromes related to damage of visual cortex in man, parts of the preserved primitive (tectopulvinar) system may remain to compensate loss of visual perception.

VISUAL AGNOSIAS: DISORDERS OF VISUAL RECOGNITION

By the term *visual agnosia* we refer to a series of disturbances of perceptual function concerning identification and recognition of objects, faces or their representations, meaningful or meaningless forms, colors, and spatial information by the visual modality. At this point we do not further define visual agnosia, preferring to let experimental and clinical evidence unfold first. The notion of agnosia as a specific perceptual disorder limited to appreciation of the meaning of a stimulus, despite intact primary sensory modalities and normal higher cortical function ("a percept stripped of its meaning," Teuber, 1966a), has been subjected to abundant criticism. Presentation of the evidence will allow clarification of the issues.

We precede descriptions of the various disorders of visual recognition by a historical review that traces the course of development of the classical notion of agnosia and shows how this notion has been modified by different psychological theories. The influence of these theories has affected not only the concept of agnosia itself but also the descriptions of agnosia as provided by pathologists.

Historical Background

Associated with the earliest studies on aphasia, disorders in recognition of people and places were little by little isolated as a separate problem. Finkelnburg (1870) provided the term *asymbolia* as a global designation of defective recognition of conventional symbols. For Finkelnburg asymbolia represented the loss of a basic human faculty, the *"facultas signatrix"* of Kant, a faculty independent of the two other basic human faculties for knowledge: sensorial and intellectual. Asymbolia referred to the inability both to identify objects and to use them. Meynert (1900) divided the single notion into two subdivisions: sensory asymbolia and motor asymbolia.

Results of animal experimentation conducted during this period of intense neuropsychological activity provided arguments in favor of the reality of disorders of recognition appearing in a particular sensory modality and linked to disorganization of a specific system. On the basis of his ablation studies with dogs Munk (1890) introduced the term *psychic blindness,* as distinguished from cortical blindness, which referred to the loss of all visual sensation. The animal subjected to ablation of a zone of about 1½ centimeters in the gray matter of the posterior and superior regions of the two occipital tips had the following behavioral features. "No abnormalities of hearing, taste, smell, motricity, or sensation. The dog walks freely about the room without bumping into objects. If one blocks his path, he avoids or adroitly jumps over obstacles. But within the psychic domain of vision a distinctive defect exists: he pays no attention to water or food, even if he is hungry and thirsty. He seems to be indifferent to everything he sees; threats do not frighten him. One can bring a lit match up to his eyes without him backing away. Seeing his master or seeing other dogs leaves him impassive." Munk concluded that "the dog has psychic blindness, that is, he has lost memory images acquired by previous visual perceptions such that he no longer knows or recognizes that he sees. He has reverted to the state of a young dog." We should append to this observation the fact that the dog was capable of relearning; at the end of several weeks he again behaved like a normal animal.

Appearing coincidentally with newly developing theories of symbolic behavior, Munk's experiments gave rise to violent arguments either because in research of others the same effects were not reproduced or because the effects he found were attributed to an amblyopia associated with disturbance of general "intelligence" with no particular relationship to the specific hemispheric lesion (Goltz, 1892).

The interpretation of perceptual processes propounded by Wernicke (1894) with respect to tactile identification of objects was founded on the sensualist and associationist theories of the epoch and were directly influenced by his earlier (1874) interpretation of sensory aphasia. According to Wernicke the observed data reflect the loss of memories necessary for the comprehension of objects. Subjects could see clearly, hear, and feel objects by palpation with no loss of manual dexterity with respect to object manipulation. But the sensory impressions they received were foreign to them and useless. The subjects had lost the faculty of recognizing objects. Thus Wernicke went further than Munk and extended the notion of asymbolia to the loss of ability to synthesize different perceptual modes. He considered perception to be the result of two successive processes: primary and secondary identification. Primary identification refers to the arousal of an image by a real sensory impression arriving in the same sensory channel; a visual impression aroused a visual image. Primary identification evoked other sensory images related to the object in the course of prior experience. The ensemble of these memory images constituted the concept of the object, derived from secondary identification. A lesion of a sensory center interfered with primary identification by this channel and suppressed the development of associated sensory images required for elaboration of the concept of the object. A lesion of association pathways prevented secondary identification, by isolating the sensory center responsible for primary identification from other sensory centers. Asymbolia, according to this interpretation, is thus the loss of the capacity to establish the concept of the object by disruption of the process of secondary identification. This systematization of disorders of identification, together with experimental research, had a major impact on clinical research, and ever-increasing numbers of more detailed clinical observations began to appear (Charcot, 1883c; Bernheim, 1886; Wilbrand, 1887, 1892; Freund, 1888; etc.)

At the same time a major step in the history of psychic blindness was being taken by the work of Lissauer (1890). This author provided the first truly demonstrative anatomoclinical case report of psychic blindness in man and attempted to analyze the psychophysiological elements. After having determined that perception (*empfindung*) and apperception (*warhnehmung*) were related by a series of imperceptible transitions, Lissauer proposed that "apperceptive blindness" should be distinguished from "associative blindness," all the while admitting that these two forms of visual agnosia were not separated by essential differences. Apperceptive visual agnosia was characterized by a basic defect in visual perception, manifested by the loss of ability to recognize differences that distinguish two similar objects; by a difficulty in focusing attention and by an inability to reconstruct visual forms in one's mind and to articulate an overall plan in such a way as to construct coherent ensembles. By contrast, associative visual agnosia was characterized by a defective ability to evoke representations, that is, memory images or engrams of people and things. From the physiological point of view, this conceptualization implies the rupture of connections linking perceptual centers with representational centers that are repositories for the maintenance of memory images, engrams, or sensory representations. From the anatomic point of view Lissauer's hypothesis suggests that apperceptive psychic blindness was dependent on lesions of occipital cortex, while associative blindness resulted from destruction of subcortical pathways that spared the centers but involved their connections.

Liepmann (1908b) developed a theory of perceptual disorders that approximated that of Lissauer. He referred to "dissolutional agnosia," due to disruption of representational complexes; and "disjunctive" or "ideational agnosia," due to fractionation of representations into primary elements. The second type was related to alterations in the centers themselves, while the first was related to lesions in the conducting pathways necessary for representational groupings. As these analyses developed, the model of angosia was perfected. Perfection of the model, in turn, encouraged new clinical observations and descriptions, isolating and correlating with greater and greater precision the clinical syndromes and anatomic substrates.

At the turn of the century reaction set in. Von Monakow (1905) rejected the notion of cortical centers as repositories for memory images. Underlining the complexity and great variability of disorders called gnostic, he insisted on the diversity of phenomena encompassed by this term. From the anatomic point of view he preferred to speak of a functional modification of the entire brain, rather than of behavioral defects related to specific centers. Von Stauffenberg (1914) developed similar antilocalizationist, antiassociationist theories and ushered in the notions of Gestalt. Agnosia was never an isolated loss of a single neuropsychological function. According to this view psychic blindness resulted from dysfunction of two fundamental factors: one was a disorder of central synthesis of visual impressions, interfering with their coming into meaningful form (*formgestaltung*); the other was a general defect in ideational capacity, such that more or less well-formed optic elements could not be harmonized with previously stored sensorial complexes, rendering impossible the final analytic process of recognition.

The revolution brought about by Gestalt theory was fully developed by the clinicopathological studies of Gelb and Goldstein (1920, 1924). According to these authors any cortical lesion situated outside of a primary reception zone caused a funadmental defect: "the dedifferentiation of figure from back-ground," and this disorder was manifested in all domains. The specificity of agnosias was nothing more than the result of a preconceived observation artificially isolating one particular type of performance. Rather, a general noetic disorder, "the loss of abstract attitude," could account for recognition defects in all sensory modalities.

On the basis of a particularly well-detailed observation of their patient, Schn., Gelb and Goldstein accepted the existence of pure apperceptive optic agnosia (of Lissauer), considering this disorder to depend on a deficit in the ability to form elementary visual gestalten in the absence of primary defects in visual reception. Their patient, although able to perceive colors and light, was unable to recognize even the most simple forms or to evoke a single visual memory. "Everything for him was chaos, within which he could identify only black and white spots." In such cases, the authors argued, one cannot be dealing with isolated functional defects; observation of the behavior of such patients, if done without preconceived ideas, allows one to discover the funda-mental disorder in several sensory domains. For example, the patient, Schn., presented with a "loss of abstract spatial relations," although in concrete situations requiring motor responses he was sufficiently capable of orienting himself.

According to Goldstein (1939) the problem of localization of functional defects following cortical damage must be considered in a different manner for "peripheral cortex" (i.e., for that part of the cortex in correspondence with peripheral elements) and for "central" portions of the cortex. With lesions of "peripheral cortex" the only field of performance deficiency noted is that affected by the process of dedifferentiation. With lesions of "central cortex," in which higher cortical functions are affected, all fields of perfor-mance are affected to a greater or lesser degree. Thus Goldstein did not really deny that a lesion of a specific cortical region may have a special importance with respect to the development of a particular complex of signs and symp-toms. He was able "to envisage, although with some reservation, that each performance corresponds to the excitation of a definite cortical region, the excitation spreading to the rest of the cortex and not limiting itself to a specified region. It is this that should be understood as localization."

During approximately the same period Poppelreuter (1914–1917, 1923), agreeing that the complexities and varieties of perceptual disorders covered by the term *psychic blindness* could not be interpreted simply by anatomoclini-cal or associationist terms and not wanting to offer a new theory of agnosia, attempted to define the levels of perceptual defects. Beginning with a tachis-toscopic study of normal perception, he described a series of stages in the normal perceptual process, as follows: (1) The basic fact is the visual field, pure and simple, that is, a formless extent. (2) An initial differentiation distinguishes stimuli according to their position, right or left, in the visual field, without further differentiating form and without clear borders between light and dark. (3) A surface is differentiated, without distinct dimensions, without verticality or horizontality, but with equal dimensions on all sides. (4) The mass possesses an orientation in the visual field. (5) Extent and principal dimensions are distinguished, in this stage the indeterminate form is perceived as being long, small, horizontal, and so on. (6) Discrimination of several separate forms in the visual field occurs. (7) Strict perception of the form takes place by discrimination of lines, geometric figures, and so forth.

According to Poppelreuter lesions of the visual system may be considered in three ways: (1) in terms of functional divisions, by distinguishing light, color, space, movement, and direction; (2) in topographical terms, according to the region of visual field affected; and (3) in terms of the principle that the ordinary visual defect resulting from central lesions is amblyopic, not amaurotic, and is related to degree of visual imperfection, not with loss of vision of a stimulus but with deficient differentiation of the stimulus.

By applying these three principles by which lesions may affect visual perception to the stages of normal visual perception described above, one can discern six stages of pathological disorganization of visual function: (1) stage of purely quantitative, formless luminous perceptions; (2) perception of an indeterminate mass, whose size is independent of the retinal area stimulated; (3) perception of indeterminate forms of which the object may be appreciated with respect to its general dimensions, but not with respect to its specific contours and not by analysis of its details; (4) discrimination of two lights or of two distinct objects; (5) stage of mild amblyopia; (6) stage of normal vision.

Thus optic agnosia would be a pathological entity neither well delimited nor theoretically based but rather linked to the extraordinarily complex processes of higher order visual recognition. Breakdown of these processes would result in a wide variety of isolated defects in visual differentiation. Poppelreuter excluded purely sensorimotor defects, especially visual field defects, from the notion of optic agnosia. He stressed his observations that an object that is not specifically recognized may be generically appreciated (a swallow may be identified as a bird) and that this notion of categorization confers an indisputable authenticity to optic agnosia with respect to and as separable from disorders of sensory discrimination. He also indicated that agnosia often gave rise to false recognitions that may correspond to the real stimulus, the similarities appearing in the error of identification (e.g., a dog for a lion); the patient may incorrectly respond to a global conception of the stimulus (e.g., a four-footed animal) while ignoring the characteristic detail (e.g., an elephant's trunk).

The classical, anatomically based notion of agnosia derived from associationist theories of perception was thus, in the period following the First World War, subjected to attack from two directions. The Gestalt theorists tended to dilute the specificity of agnosia, incorporating the defect within a more fundamental disorder inherent in all cortical lesions. A second group, even more radical than Poppelreuter, reduced agnosia to a disorder of visual discrimination dependent on a lesion at any level of the sensory system. Within these two perspectives anatomic considerations disappear, since disorders of recognition are determined, for the former group, by any central cortical lesion, and for the second group, by any lesion of the sensory system involved in the production of symptoms.

Extreme Gestaltist conceptions were maintained, for example, by Conrad (1932), for whom any cerebral lesion caused a halt in performance at a pregestalt level, at which the characteristic pattern of performance was of a "protopathic" type, that is, a state of unending fluctuation and dependence with respect to the stimulus. From a more physiological point of view, referring to the field of cortical forces and to the work of Kohler and Wallach (1944), Bender and Teuber (1947) proposed descriptive hypotheses for the various disorders of spatial perception.

At the other extreme Stein (1926) and Weizsacker (1928) proposed an explanation of the various disorders of visual recognition by reducing perception to sensation. They introduced the notion of functional modifications (*Funktionswandel*) and related perceptual defects to alterations in excitation thresholds, lability of thresholds, sensory perseveration, sensory delay, and so forth. Agnosia could not be defined except by precise analyses of the variations in relationships between differing sensory defects, all taken as a function of time. Bay (1950, 1952, 1953) became a more recent protagonist of this point of view, providing this hypothesis systematic support. For Bay agnosia translated at the perceptual level a series of dynamic disturbances of sensory processes, from peripheral receptors to central projection zones.

One and the other of these theoretical tendencies combined in the rejection of any question of localizationism of the so-called agnosic phenomena. This rejection of cortical functional specialization, outside of primary reception or projection areas, was reinforced by results of experimental psychology. Franz (1902, 1912) paved the way in his attack against the "new phrenology" by asserting that no experimental evidence allowed localization of mental processes in the brain. Lashley (1923), after extensive and detailed study with the rat, and after a review of published anatomoclinical cases, formally rejected the principle of cerebral specialization, opting instead for the principle of cerebral equipotentiality. He also rejected the reflex theory and the theory of transcortical connections. Influenced by Gestalt theory, he accepted the equivalence of sensory stimuli and demonstrated the equivalence of motor reactions. Cerebral organization, for Lashley, should be described in terms of relative mass and of spatial dispositions of large cerebral segments, with equivalence between these segments; one should speak of direction of gradients and of sensitization of final common pathways to models of excitation. "Patterning" activity was established at the projection areas, permitting the distinction of an object from its background, of spatial orientation, of what is and of what is not. Lashley did not assume that these patterning activities were the property of specific cortical regions; he stressed the importance of relationships between these projection areas and subcortical structures. Spatial models of perceptual organization would be subjected to transformation into spatial and temporal models of motor activity, not by simple direct relationships but by a series of steps involving subliminal activity producing specific patterns of facilitation.

The classical concept of optic agnosia as a high-order perceptual defect involving specific categories of the external world and determined by focal cortical lesions was thus submerged under the weight of clinical, experimental, and theoretical counterargument. The specificity of agnosic facts was denied, its clinical reality being debunked as observer artifact. As for focal lesions, their role was minimized. The presence of negative cases (that is, a focal lesion not producing the predicted functional defect), the rarity of anatomoclinical cases, and the inadequate study of such cases, either from the clinical or from the anatomic point of view, seemed sufficiently weighty as arguments to compel total rejection of the anatomoclinical experience of the preceding period. This is not to say that certain localizationist positions were not maintained; in fact, they were even exaggerated by some authors to the point of atomism (e.g. Henschen, 1920–1922; Kleist, 1933; Nielsen, 1937, 1946). These authors, generally in the minority of theorists on the topic, conceived of the cerebral surface as a mosaic of centers, the destruction of any one of which would produce a precise and limited functional defect.

In the course of the past two decades neuropsychological conceptions of perceptual disorders have again undergone transformation. The problem of cerebral localization of function is being raised in new ways; theoretical discussions are at a different level. As a result of the growing awareness of specific defects related to the so-called minor hemisphere, previously considered mute and passive, hemispheric functional asymmetry is coming to be accepted. Disorders of visual recognition may thus differ according to the hemisphere damaged. As disorders of visuospatial activity came to be reported more and more with right hemispheric lesions, studies of large series of patients selected on the basis of hemispheric lateralization of lesion began to replace individual case studies selected on the basis of symptoms. The frequency of the different functional disorders could then be established with respect to hemispheric lateralization of lesion or to intrahemispheric localization. Also, associations could be established between the functional defects and the symptomatic contexts in which they occurred.

On the basis of studies conforming to the pattern described above, Hécaen and Angelergues (1957, 1961, 1962, 1963, 1965) distinguished three separate but related aspects of visual agnosia.

1. *Selectivity.* This refers to an essential clinical fact; it is difficult, if not impossible, to accept that a functional defect limited to a specific type of visual recognition could be due to a general intellectual defect or to a sensory defect. Two groups of visual recognition disorders may be discerned, according to the principle of selectivity: disorders in recognition of objects, colors, and letters; and spatial agnosia and agnosia for faces. These two groups appear to be mutually exclusive to a statistically significant degree. Analysis of individual observations also demonstrates the same dissociation. Thus no unitary hypothesis can be invoked to account for visual agnosia.

2. *Specificity of associations (symptom complex) for each type of optic agnosia.* Statistical analyses of symptomatic contexts associated with each of these two groups confirms the validity of their separation. With the first group of agnosias (objects, colors, letters) the essential association is a defect in language. With the second group (spatial agnosia, prosopagnosia) the context is represented by somatosensory defects.

3. *Hemispheric lateralization of lesion.* The same dissociation noted above in items (1) and (2) is again found here. The first group of visual recognition defects is associated with left hemispheric lesions; the second, with right-sided lesions.

By studying intrahemispheric localizations, one finds a different functional lesion pattern according to the hemisphere damaged. In the left hemisphere, lesions producing agnosias tend to be more focal, and the role of the occipital lobe is clear. In the right hemisphere, lesions producing agnosias may be more widespread, suggesting that mechanisms underlying visual and other sensory recognition processes and also praxis are diffusely organized. A mass effect at the parietotemporo-occipital junction clearly influences development of symptoms with right hemispheric lesions. This difference of functional organization of the two hemispheres seems to exist for less complex functions as well, for example, somesthesis (Semmes et al, 1955, 1960) and elementary visual processing (Goldman et al, 1968).

Quantified data, derived from the methodologies of experimental psychology and applied to the study of the effects of cortical lesions, have appreciably reduced observer subjectivity and have thereby contributed to newer conceptions of cerebral localization and perceptual disorder. Research conducted with brain-injured subjects (Teuber and Weinstein, 1956) and with epileptics subjected to temporal lobe resections (Milner, 1958, 1965, 1968b) has resulted in refinement of detail in our understanding of disorders of visual recognition. Studies using sophisticated statistical analyses were done with subjects grouped by lesion localization and compared with controls to determine the relative influence of cerebral lesions on degree of intensity of defect.

From such studies Teuber (1966a) refused to accept the term *agnosia*, because the term probably covered defects with different underlying mechanisms. In his studies of American soldiers injured in the Korean War he attempted to clarify by experimental means the degrees of deficit ranging from specific to nonspecific. He concluded that the classical definition of agnosia as a disorder of recognition by a single sensory channel could not encompass all aspects of the true defect. For example, subjects with parietal lesions may have a deficient ability to manipulate topographic information both by haptic and by visual means.

In the epileptic subjects with temporal lobectomies Milner (1958–1968) found that right-sided ablations were associated with defects in visual recognition of complex, nonfigurative forms, while left-sided ablations were associated with visual recognition defects related to verbal material. She found that hemispheric lateralization of lesion influenced performance according to the verbal or nonverbal nature of the material, not only for recognition tasks but also for recall and learning tasks, regardless of the sensory modality.

DeRenzi et al (1966a,b; 1967; 1968b,c; 1969a,b; 1970a,b; 1972) also determined that qualitatively different defects occurred depending on whether the damaged hemisphere was right or left. They deemphasized the verbal-nonverbal dichotomy, however, and spoke of a perceptual-discriminative versus associative-semantic one. With right hemispheric lesions the defect of visual recognition mainly concerns identification of complex patterns.

These various approaches to defects in visual recognition, while casting the whole question of visual agnosia in a new light, nevertheless at least partially confirm classical conceptions derived from observation of individual cases. In particular they demonstrate that, according to the hemisphere damaged, disorders of visual recognition depend, at least in part, on the nature of the material to be perceived.

Disorders of Visual Perception in Animals

The rapid development of experimental research in the animal has also contributed to our understanding of perceptual defects in man, especially by demonstrating the importance of well-defined cortical zones and the specificity of defects according to sensory modality. However, differences between evidence from human pathology and evidence from animal experimentation should not be underestimated; in fact they should be emphasized. To our knowledge of anatomic and behavioral particularities of various animal species, we must add the appearance of language and hemispheric specialization to understand human neuropsychology.

We have seen that animal experimentation has a long history and that the very notion of psychic blindness was derived from experimental observations of dogs with partial occipital lobe ablations (Munk, 1890). Subsequent experiments with dogs, cats, and monkeys produced contradictory results, especially as concerns the anatomic locus for these disorders of visual perception, some authors insisting on a parieto-occipital locus. Much later the experimental studies of Lashley (1923) led him to reject the principle of specialization of cerebral tissue, apart from primary motor and sensory zones. He accepted the principles of equipotentiality and mass action. The studies of Kluver and Bucy (1937, 1939) contributed to our knowledge of cerebral localization. Following bilateral temporal lobectomy in the monkey, these authors observed, in the middle of a characteristic modification of general behavior, a disorder resembling psychic blindness. The monkeys seemed to have "entirely lost the capacity to recognize the meaning of objects with the aid of optic criteria." Ades and Raab (1946a) made similar observations, but with temporopreoccipital excisions.

All of these facts remained imprecise and debatable. Kluver himself thought that the visual defects might have arisen from a nonspecific underlying general defect in behavior. It was only following the studies of Chow, Pribram, and Blum-Semmes over a period of several years that disorders of visual discrimination in the monkey were definitively placed in relationship to bilateral lesions of parietotemporal-preoccipital zones. In the initial studies the visual deficits were found to be heterogeneous from the point of view of psychological complexity. Rapidly in subsequent work it was shown that the cerebral region specifically linked to these visual functions was limited to the inferotemporal area. Differences between effects of inferotemporal lesions and those of visual cortex ablations were demonstrated. Inferotemporal lesions produced no visual field deficit (Cowey and Weiskrantz, 1967), no disorder of critical flicker fusion threshold (Symmes, 1965), and no disturbance of visual sensitivity (Bender, 1973). Only complex discriminative functions necessary for learning visual problems were related to inferotemporal areas. By contrast, lesions of striate cortex caused defects of visual acuity, of visual field, and of visual threshold, even though these animals had better performances on complex discriminative tasks than monkeys with inferotemporal lesions did (Cowey and Weiskrantz, 1967).

Experiments performed since 1950 have established that a limited area, localized to the inferotemporal region, is responsible for the processes of learning in tasks of visual discrimination. Bilateral ablation of this area causes a visual modality-specific learning defect. Other zones have been found to be specific for other sensory modalities, while the frontal lobes have been found responsible for general learning, not linked to a specific modality.

The deficit of visual discrimination due to inferotemporal lesions is not complete; one of its characteristics is its quantitative nature. It has been shown, for example, that color discrimination is less disturbed than form discrimination (Mishkin, 1954), that discrimination of objects is less disturbed than that for patterns (Riopelle et al, 1953), that simple problems can be learned even though learning set is lost (Chow, 1954), that these problems are retained if they have been overlearned (Orbach and Fantz, 1958), and that, with tasks in which differences between stimuli are large, there is less deficit than with tasks having small differences between stimuli (Mishkin and Hall, 1955). As for the nature of this inferotemporal deficit many interpretations have been offered: deficit in sensory capacities, learning deficit, defect in selective attention, defective choice and search among opposing cues and among distinctive features of an isolated stimulus, and deficit of visual categorization. No interpretation has yet been definitively established.

More anatomic detail has profoundly modified the issue. The role of preoccipital regions, excluded by Lashley (1923), has been reaffirmed by Mishkin (1966). This author, in a series of ablation studies, demonstrated that this zone does not interact with subcortical structures but does interact with other cortical zones by means of corticocortical, connections. The prestriate area thus represents a transmission terminal between various cortical components of the visual system. Elaboration of higher order visual mechanisms begins here. Mishkin found that, following bilateral inferotemporal ablation, the monkey could relearn the discrimination, whereas subsequent bilateral ablation of prestriate cortex prevented any relearning. Ablation of superior temporal gyri, for purposes of comparison, did not impair retention of the visual task. The results were the same even if the sequence of operations was reversed. We should stress that prestriate ablations caused deficits only when associated with inferotemporal resections; this observation of Mishkin was confirmed in a separate study by Pribram (1969). However, Butler (1966) and Butter (1969) found that monkeys with lateral striate lesions had a deficit, not of initial learning, but of reacquisition of a visual discrimination task. Mishkin stressed the difficulty of totally ablating prestriate tissue without involving visual radiations in the lesion and thereby causing primary visual defects.

In a series of studies with Iwai, Mishkin (1972) studied prestriate cortex while sparing much of the inferotemporal region (70–80% of geniculate bodies were not degenerated). The monkey, although preserving an adequate visually guided behavior, was unable to relearn a pattern discrimination. When bilateral prestriate ablation was done in two stages, the first ablation, which involved the lateral portion, caused no defect of relearning. Addition of the ventral portion to the lesion produced the deficit. According to Mishkin the number of pathways in this region is so great that no partial destruction could be sufficient to prevent passage of visual information. An indirect

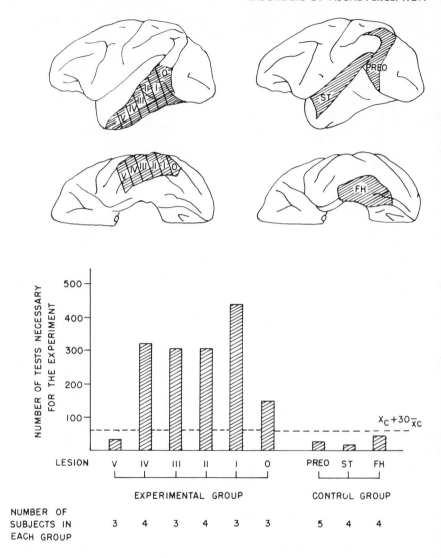

Schematic representation of six different 5 millimeter lesions produced in the inferotem-poral convexity of the monkey and of control lesions. Preo = preoccipital; ST = superior temporal; FH = fusiform and hippocampal gyri. Histograms indicate the mean number of trials necessary to obtain relearning for each group (from Iwai and Mishkin, 1969). Copy-right 1969 by Academic Press, New York. Reproduced by permission.

proof of the significance of corticocortical pathways in transmission of visual information was provided by results of a study in which bilateral destruction of more than 90% of pulvinar produced no deficit of visual discrimination learning (Mishkin, 1972).

Isolation of the monkey's temporal lobe, either from its visual inputs by cortical section of occipitotemporal pathways or from its outputs by section of corticosubcortical pathways in white matter of medial temporal lobe, produced permanent deficits of visual discrimination and other elements of the Kluver-Bucy syndrome (Horel and Misantone, 1974). The authors suggested that the cortical lesion prevented visual information from arriving at the necessary processing zone and that the subcortical lesion prevented processed visual information from being transmitted to regions necessary for expression of behavior.

The deficit of visual discrimination was not found when lesions involved other structures that receive inferotemporal projections (frontal cortex, dorsomedial nucleus of the thalamus, pulvinar, amygdala, superior colliculus, pretectum). Destruction of two specific regions did produce comparable defects of visual discrimination: tail of caudate nucleus (Divac et al, 1967), and caudoventral putamen (Buerger et al, 1974). In the latter case it was possible to demonstrate modality specificity of the defect, since the same lesion caused no disorder of auditory discrimination or of delayed alternation.

Two separate anatomofunctional zones have been distinguished in the inferotemporal region, with a continual interaction occurring between them (Iwai and Mishkin, 1969). The anterior zone is more responsible for retention of correct responses; the posterior zone, for appreciation of complex stimuli. The posterior zone has been defined with precision; it begins at the anterior segment of the inferior occipital sulcus, includes the posterior bank of this sulcus, and extends forward by 2 centimeters to the posterior end of the anterior medial temporal sulcus. This zone may be further subdivided into two regions corresponding to areas *TE* and *TEO* of Bailey and von Bonin (1951).

Iversen and Weiskrantz (1964, 1967) observed both quantitative and qualitative differences in the defective visual discrimination, depending on whether the lesion was limited to the inferotemporal region or whether a hippocampal lesion was adjoined. The inferotemporal lesion caused a perceptual disorder in visual categorization; the hippocampal lesion added a mnestic element. Cowey and Gross (1970) also discerned two types of deficit within the "classical" inferotemporal syndrome. Lesions limited to anterior inferotemporal areas corresponded to the anterior lesions in the experiments of Iwai and Mishkin (1969); lesions of the foveal prestriate cortex corresponded to the ventrolateral portion of the circumstriate belt receiving cortical projections of foveal representation (Zeki, 1969, 1970; Cragg and Ainsworth, 1969). In the case of visual discrimination of complex models learned preoperatively, the postoperative defects were greater in the monkeys with foveal prestriate lesions. Defective postoperative acquisition of a difficult discrimination was also greater in this group. In the case of discrimination of simple objects learned simultaneously in the postoperative period, inferotemporal monkeys were inferior. If, however, the animals learned each of the discriminations separately before having to resolve the problems of simultaneous presentation, no differences were found between groups. If new visual discrimination tasks were added to the first, learned separately, the inferotemporal group was again more severely impaired.

In summary, animals with foveal prestriate lesions were much more impaired on tasks of acquisition and retention of complex visual discriminations than inferotemporal monkeys were. Animals with inferotemporal lesions had defects in concurrent discriminations requiring simultaneous acquisition of several simple discriminations.

The significance of effects of foveal prestriate ablations contrasts with the absence of effects of lesions in foveal striate cortex. In the latter case animals or men use the extrafoveal portion of the retina for visually guided behavior such that the extrafoveal prestriate cortex may treat the information. With a foveal prestriate lesion the monkey may continue to fix with its fovea, and information projected to foveal striate cortex may not reach its usual central site in the prestriate region.

This series of experiments confirms earlier conclusions: anterior inferotemporal lesions modify the associative or mnestic stage of visual learning, while foveal prestriate lesions disturb perceptual or attentional mechanisms necessary for detecting differences among stimuli. In the latter situation one cannot argue that the defect is at the level of elementary sensation, for ablation of the macular projection of the striate cortex does not disturb visual discrimination of stimuli.

The hypothesis advanced by Pribram (1969) reverses the direction of influence: he proposed that the inferotemporal zone has an efferent corticofugal effect on the striate cortex. Thus continuous stimulation of the inferotemporal area brings about modifications of evoked potentials over the primary visual cortex by producing a prolongation of recovery time. These cells seem to remain occupied for a longer than normal time; each new stimulus has fewer visual cortical cells at its disposition; redundancy is reduced. By contrast inferotemporal ablations increase redundancy in the system; stimulus inputs find a greater number of receptor cells at their disposition.

Other studies do not, however, support Pribram's contention that the inferotemporal region has an efferent influence on the striate cortex (Schwartzroin et al, 1969; Vaughan and Gross, 1969). Gross et al (1969, 1974) showed that responses of inferotemporal cells, even though being analagous to those of complex and hypercomplex cells of the striate and prestriate cortex, were characterized by a very large receptive field, a long latency, and a rapid disposition after repeated stimuli. Three-dimensional objects were most commonly the adequate stimuli. (Several rare cells showed, in addition, a particular specificity by responding only to highly complex stimuli, such as the shadow of a monkey's hand.) These characteristics are similar to unit responses of the posterior pulvinar system. The authors emphasize the anatomic connections between pulvinar and inferotemporal cortex previously demonstrated by Kuypers et al (1965).

Rocha-Miranda et al (1975) noted that inferotemporal neurons that respond exclusively to visual stimuli cease responding after bilateral ablation of striate cortex. After unilateral ablation of striate cortex, cells of the inferotemporal region respond only to stimuli projected in the field contralateral to the intact striate cortex. When the anterior commissures are cut, neurons of each inferotemporal region respond only to stimuli in their own contralateral field.

Thus it may be suggested that the inferotemporal cortex, which receives afferent influx from striate and prestriate cortex (geniculostriate system) and from the pulvinar (superior collicular-thalamic system), represents the integrating mechanism for visual information arriving from the two visual systems. One system provides visual information about the nature of the stimulus; the other, about the location of the stimulus within the visual world.

Butter (1974a,b) studied visual discrimination impairments in rhesus monkeys with combined lesions of superior colliculus and striate cortex. With such lesions the monkey has deficits in learning pattern discrimination but not brilliance discrimination. Combined foveal prestriate and inferotemporal lesions produce defects in retention of pattern discriminations and partial defects in size discrimination. Butter interprets these results as supporting the hypothesis that visual function of the inferotemporal prestriate region results from the capacity of this region to combine inputs from striate cortex and colliculus. Nevertheless Butter accepts the possibility that interaction between striate cortex and superior colliculus may occur without recourse to another cortical zone.

By contrast with Iwai and Mishkin (1969), who see the role of the inferotemporal region as combinatory (for visual memory and visual perception), Wilson (1968) proposed a model whereby this region facilitates a process of trade-off between discrimination and encoding of the stimulus input. Anterior and posterior inferotemporal regions would be complementary: whatever has been memorized determines what will be perceived, and whatever has been perceived determines what has to be memorized. She accepts two types of stimulus redundancy: schematic, when the problem contains a single pertinent dimension facilitating codability, and discriminative, when stimulus pairs differ along several dimensions. One form of redundancy increases when the other decreases.

In subsequent studies this same author attempted to clarify the trade-off model (Wilson et al, 1968, 1969). She found that, by contrast with normal monkeys, those with inferotemporal lesions were unable to impose limits on memorization of redundant traits. This evidence favors the Pribram hypothesis, which states that inferotemporal regions function to reduce redundancy. However, the manner in which normal animals used redundancy in discrimination but not in retention prompted Wilson to propose a system of cortical transformations rather than that of an efferent effect on subcortical processes.

This system may be related to visual attention. Soper et al (1975) showed that inferotemporal lesions in monkeys caused selective attentional deficits that are manifested when too many stimuli are present and that can be overcome if the number of stimuli is reduced. Paying attention to newly presented information limits the inferotemporal monkey in its capacity to use previously stored information, and vice versa.

Rocha-Miranda et al (1975) observed that most inferotemporal cells have a receptive field extending to both visual fields. They proposed that the convergence of inputs from hemiretinae for both visual fields represent a mechanism for ensuring equivalance of both sides. Bilateral inferotemporal ablation impairs this convergence, and different discrimination habits become established concurrently for each variation of conditions of discrimination (e.g., different viewing angles). Thus discrimination of a stimulus pair can no longer be mastered.

Humphrey and Weiskrantz (1969) presented an alternate interpretation of inferotemporal function. They found an impairment in appreciation of size constancy by monkeys with inferotemporal ablations. These animals continued to respond to stimulus size but incorrectly. Their perception of size corresponded to a "calculation error" applied to information reaching the retina. The authors suggested that perception of true size depends on the combination of retinal information about largeness of the stimulus and distance, according to the formula: perceived size $= K$ (largeness of image $\times$ distance). With disturbances of the normal mechanism that uses this formula, a compromise may obtain: perceived largeness no longer depends on the combination of these two types of information but only on one, with an arbitrary value fixed for the other. From then on, perception could oscillate between use of the correct formula and use of either of the two partial strategies. This interpretation provides an analogy between the perceptual disorders of inferotemporal monkeys and the visual illusions produced in man by parietotemporal lesions. In man disturbance of the mechanism for maintaining constancy seems the most likely explanation for these illusions (see above, section on visual illusions).

Pohl (1973) summarized an interesting series of experiments that demonstrated dissociation of spatial discrimination deficits following frontal and parietal lesions in man. Three groups of monkeys with ablations respectively of inferotemporal, dorsolateral prefrontal, and posterior parietal were compared with control monkeys on tests of orientation: egocentric, based on body position, and allocentric, based on the position of an external referent. Inferotemporal and posterior parietal monkeys were impaired on the allocentric tests. Frontal monkeys were impaired on the egocentric tasks. Only inferotemporal monkeys were impaired on a nonspatial test of reversal of object discrimination.

Mishkin (1972) interpreted Pohl's results by postulating two parallel visual systems: one (fovea-geniculate body-striate cortex) concerned visual acuity and served to identify *what* the object is; the other (parafoveal-collicular pretectal region-pulvinar-parastriate cortex) was visuospatial and served to appreciate *where* the object is.

Whichever interpretation one might wish to use to explain the nature of the defect caused by inferotemporal lesions in the monkey, certain aspects of lesions in this zone may be generally accepted. Lesions in the inferotemporal region impair processing of visual information and learning of visual discrimination tasks, even though elementary visual functions are not affected. Two different sections of the inferotemporal region may be distinguished, with either combinatory or complementary functions (learning and associative or perceptual discrimination). The prestriate zone functions as an association or interconnection area in learning and in visual discrimination. Inferotemporal cortex is an association zone whose ablation causes perceptual difficulties specific to a single sensory modality: vision.

When we consider disorders of visual recognition in man, it will be necessary to keep these animal data in mind, with the proviso that in man the evolutionary additions of language and functional hemispheric specialization necessarily modify our approach.

Disorders of Visual Recognition in Man—Visual Agnosias

By the term *visual agnosia,* which we retain despite the criticisms leveled against it, we refer to disorders of visual recognition that cannot be explained by a general disturbance of mental functioning or by a defect of elementary visual sensory function. We cannot accept the notion that usage of this term should interfere with the search for underlying neuropsychological mechanisms that may explain the specific perceptual defects observed clinically. Indeed the classical meaning of the word *agnosia* rather nicely defined a type of abnormal perceptual behavior situated at an intermediate stage between primary sensory defect and general intellectual dysfunction. Regardless of interpretation, the evidence from clinical behavioral studies, experimental studies in human beings and animals, and anatomoclinical correlations justifies the presentation of the visual agnosias as a special group of perceptual defects (see historical review, above). On this basis we describe and discuss form agnosias, color agnosias, and spatial agnosias.

Disorders of Recognition of Forms

Visual Object Agnosia

Clinical Aspects The expression "visual object agnosia" refers to a specific variety of perceptual defect: a brain-damaged patient can see an object shown to him but cannot appreciate its character or meaning. Not only is he unable to name the object or demonstrate its use, but he also cannot remember ever having seen it before. If, however, an appeal is made to his understanding through another sense such as touch, he can immediately name or use the object correctly. Implicit in the definition is the contention that there is no visual sensory defect, no aphasia, and no general intellectual impairment.

Lissauer (1890) provided a classical clinical description. His patient was unable to recognize objects (associative blindness) but could visually discriminate designs that were quite similar in appearance—two squares, for example, one with a cross inside, the other without. This subject did not have general signs of mental deterioration, but he did have memory disturbance. He had a right homonymous hemianopia, but visual acuity in the remaining field was nearly normal. The patient could perceive and distinguish colors, but he was unable to make the appropriate connection between perceived color and color name. Although he was more or less able to draw the objects, he was still unable to recognize them. Initially he was totally alexic; subsequently the alexia diminished. He was never agraphic. Spatial orientation returned to nearly normal from an initial stage of disorientation in space. The recognition defect was nearly complete; however, at times the patient could make out the significance of an object corresponding to a design representing that object. Nevertheless, even on this test he was often wrong. Lissauer noted that it was more difficult for the patient to discern differences than similarities.

Unquestionably object agnosia is a rare syndrome, at least in a state sufficiently pure to allow useful description. In a series of 415 cases of patients with cortical lesions Hécaen and Angelergues (1963) found object agnosia four times, only one of which was pure. In a series of 124 patients with unilateral hemispheric lesions DeRenzi and Spinnler (1966a) found one case of object agnosia. The very rarity of the syndrome has cast doubt on the reality of its existence, the few reported cases being explained away by reference to disorders of language, sensation, or general intellectual function. Rare though it may be, we believe that there has been a sufficient number of published cases since Lissauer to justify the clinical reality of a disorder of recognition of the meaning of objects limited to the visual modality. Four recently published cases, described in exhaustive detail, support this viewpoint (Rubens and Benson, 1971; Lhermitte et al, 1973b; Hecaen et al, 1974; Albert et al, 1975a).

These subjects are able to describe the shape, outline, and interior parts of the object without being able to name it or describe its usage verbally or by gesture. If the object has a characteristic sound, and the subject hears the sound, or if the subject is allowed to palpate the object, or if the object has a characteristic odor that the subject smells, he can immediately name it. Spatial information may be normally appreciated and familiar faces readily recognized, even from small photographs. Thus, for example, one patient called a hat, a "little pot"; a ball was misidentified as "a round block of wood"; a bicycle was called "a pole with two wheels, one in front, one in back." He could describe the clip of a penholder or the band of a cigar without apprehending their meaning, and the pen and cigar were called "cylindrical sticks of variable length." All objects were immediately identified as soon as he palpated them.

Certain features of the syndrome seem to be common to all reported cases and may be useful to consider from the point of view both of understanding the defect and of determining which functions are spared. The dimensions of the object do not seem to influence recognition; objects are not better recognized, for instance, if they are large or small. The general outlines of objects are often appreciated. Movement of the object may facilitate its identification (matches taken from a box, a dollar taken from a wallet). Placement of an object within its normal appropriate context may also aid in its recognition. For example, one patient could identify his bedroom slippers when they were placed under his bed but not in other situations.

By contrast with these cases, in the form of agnosia called apperceptive by Lissauer (1890), of which a recent example was described by Benson and Greenberg (1969), no element of form can be grasped. Matching, naming, describing, drawing are all impossible. On the other hand these are cases in which geometric figures may be identified but not objects.

In those cases in which the general form or elements of detail may be described out loud by the patient, he may ultimately succeed in deducing the nature of the whole by a process of adding successive pieces together. One such patient, for example, was shown a Star of David (✡). He said, "It is something holy. It is made up of two sets of closed, three-sided figures which interlock. Therefore it must be a Star of David." He was then asked "Do you recognize it as a Star of David?" and replied, "Not exactly. But it is the most logical conclusion" (Albert et al, 1975a). By contrast with the situation of deduction for identification, one single element of the object, called the critical detail by Birkmayer (1951), may be sufficiently meaningful to the patient to permit identification of the entire object. For example, de Buscher's patient identified a boat by the presence of its mast.

These different aspects of meaningfulness that aid object recognition (movement, context, addition of details, inference from single elements) may also give rise to false recognition. For example, a patient described by Hécaen and de Ajuriaguerra (1956), seeing the examiner bring a spoon to his lips, and having previously mistaken the spoon for a pencil or pen, declared, "There, that thing you are bringing to your mouth, it must be a cigar or cigarette; something you bring to your mouth like that."

At times these patients, even though unable to recognize the item, may remember having seen the item during a previous examination (Lissauer, 1890; von Stauffenberg, 1918; Heidenhain, 1919; Adler, 1944, 1950). A certain degree of learning may be manifested in the repetition of recognition tests, but if an isolated object is thereby identified, it is necessary only for the examiner to place the object in the midst of others for the patient to lose again his ability to identify the item (Davidenkoff, 1956).

Perseverative phenomena may be present; one may then speak of a veritable intoxication by the object. Adler (1944), for instance, concluded that errors of recognition resulted in part from the superposition of successive optic impressions. It is also important to note the variability of performance from one day to the next, even during the course of a single examination (Lissauer, 1890; Lange, 1936).

Anatomic Aspects   An initial point to consider is that the vast majority of anatomically verified cases of visual object agnosia have had bilateral, extensive, and even diffuse lesions. Von Stauffenberg (1918), after reviewing published cases, concluded that most cases had bilateral but asymmetrical lesions situated in the white matter of the lateral occipital gyri around the lateral ventricles. He thought the symptoms to be more marked if the lesion was larger in the left hemisphere and if it extended more ventrally into the occipital lobe. He remarked that the corpus callosum was affected in some cases. Hoff and Pötzl (1935a,b) drew similar conclusions. For these authors psychic blindness resulted from lesions that destroyed the left occipital lobe, descending into the white matter, and often affecting the right hemisphere as well. In addition they observed that object agnosia, color agnosia, and alexia were more marked if the destruction extended to compromise the ventral surface of the occipital lobe. They felt that the necessity of damaging basal occipital regions accounted for the rarity of agnosias in cases of head injury; trauma that would produce such lesions in occipital regions would also affect the adjacent brain stem, causing death. Other authors (Kleist, 1933; Faust, 1955) concur with these anatomic localizations.

From these various studies, as well as from personal observations, we may

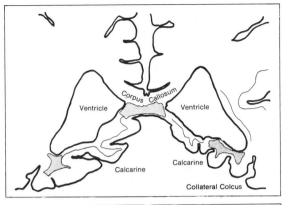

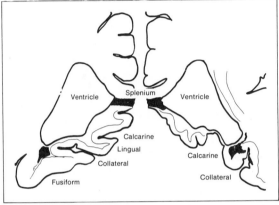

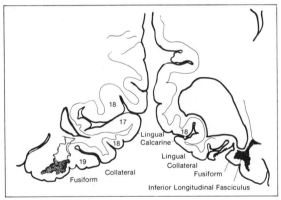

Schematic representation of coronal sections of brain of patient with prosopagnosia (from Benson, et al, 1970). Top: Occipital lobes at level of splenium of corpus callosum. Middle: 1 centimeter behind previous section. Bottom: 1 centimeter behind splenium. Damage is noted in splenium of corpus callosum and in fusiform lobes, but not in areas 18. The inferior longitudinal fasciculus and other occipitotemporal connections are interrupted. Copyright 1970 by American Medical Association Publications, Chicago. Reproduced by permission.

summarize opinions concerning anatomic location of lesions responsible for optic agnosia. Left occipital lobe lesions seem indispensable, with extension of the lesion into subcortical white matter; bilaterality of occipital lobe lesions seems to be important, with peristriate, angular gyrus, and lingual and fusiform lobule involvement. More recently a detailed clinicopathological correlational study of visual agnosia was reported (Benson et al, 1974). Occlusive vascular disease of the posterior cerebral arteries had produced infarction destroying the left medial occipital area, the splenium of the corpus callosum, and the right inferior longitudinal fasciculus. Particular stress was placed on the bilaterality and involvement of the nondominant inferior longitudinal fasciculus.

By contrast some authors implicate the dominant occipital lobe only. Nielsen (1937, 1946) accepted that a unilateral left occipital lesion in area 02–03 was sufficient to cause visual agnosia. This opinion is reinforced by case reports of patients with visual object agnosia without spatial disorders or prosopagnosia who had a left occipital lobectomy (Hécaen and de Ajuriaguerra, 1956; Hécaen et al, 1974).

Because of the rarity of visual object agnosia, at least in its pure form, the anatomopathological conditions for its production must be difficult to obtain. These may be the following: a posterior left hemispheric lesion large enough to involve visual structures and also partially affecting angular gyrus; small enough to spare language regions; deep enough to involve subcortical white matter, and perhaps, at least partially, corpus callosum; and, to the extent that right hemisphere may be involved, small enough to spare those regions responsible for perception of shape, faces, and spatial information.

Recognition Defects for Drawn Stimuli   This group of disorders cannot be considered homogeneous. Deficits have been observed in the recognition of a variety of drawn stimuli, but these deficits are not necessarily correlated with each other. They include defective recognition of realistic representations of simple objects or complex scenes, schematic reproductions of objects, geometric figures, meaningless forms, incomplete figures, and abstract drawings.

Hécaen and Angelergues in 1963 distinguished two groups of drawn stimuli for which defective recognition was correlated: realistic representations of objects, and drawn symbols—that is, drawings of meaningful items with high association values. Visual field defects and general mental deterioration seemed to form a part of the overall symptom complex. From the point of view of hemispheric lateralization these authors found that defective recognition of drawn objects was most likely to be linked to lesions of the right hemisphere, while agnosia for drawn symbols was significantly more common with bilateral than with left-sided lesions, but the difference was not significant between bilateral and right-sided lesions. With respect to intrahemispheric localization, agnosia for pictured objects was correlated with left hemispheric occipital lesions and right hemispheric temporal lesions; no significant anatomic correlations were found for defective recognition of symbols.

Impaired recognition of pictured objects or scenes seems to be present in all cases of visual object agnosia. It may be that this disorder in isolated form represents a mild version of object agnosia, or perhaps the same neuropsychological defect that underlies this disorder is also present in cases with visual object agnosia. But exceptions to this rule are also found.

When considering disorders of visual recognition of complex meaningful pictures or drawings, one must be concerned with the issue of simultaneous agnosia or *simultanagnosia,* first described by Wolpert. This syndrome refers to the inability of a subject to interpret the totality of a complex pictured scene despite preservation of the ability to apprehend individual portions of the whole. Details are perceived, but they cannot be grouped into a meaningful whole; at times, small details are perceived but not large ones. Wolpert provided the example of a patient, looking at a postcard scene that was familiar to him, who replied, "It is a dog." The scene in fact included a dog crossing a street. According to Wolpert the syndrome also includes dyslexia of a particular type: the patient can read words only by spelling them out letter by letter. Wolpert interpreted this disorder as being a unitary defect in the capacity of perceiving a whole as the sum of its parts.

Kinsbourne and Warrington (1962b) studied two patients with the combined syndrome of simultanagnosia and dyslexia. On a tachistoscopic study the recognition threshold for isolated forms was normal. When, however, items were presented in pairs, a long interval was necessary for perception of the second item. These authors concluded that the defect was a limitation of simultaneous perception of visual forms. One of their patients was found to have a left occipital lesion.

It seems to us that, although functional disorders of this type are seen relatively often in clinical neuropsychology, the specification of these disorders as autonomous "agnosic" syndromes is open to question. In the first place we believe that a distinction should be made between simultanagnosia and defective recognition of complex pictures for which an approximate, overall, or general understanding may be appreciated, although no true description can be given. In this regard the study by Ettlinger (1960) is of interest. By presenting pictures tachistoscopically to brain-damaged subjects, he found two recognition processes: one in which the subject described the pictures by enumeration of items, the other in which interpretation was achieved by assembling the different elements.

A variety of neurological and neuropsychological defects has been proposed to account for simultaneous agnosia. For example, central and paracentral scotomata, especially on the background of general impairment of consciousness or intellectual deterioration, may produce a clinical picture resembling simultaneous agnosia. Also considered basic by some is an inability to grasp the figure-ground relationship. In addition there is no doubt that the oculomotor disorder found in Balint's syndrome (see below) causes the eyes to fix on individual elements of the picture, preventing simultaneous perception. Luria (1959, 1963) has provided examples of both syndromes. Another factor that may be invoked is that of disorders of spatial perception (see below), which, by impeding appreciation of spatial relations among different elements, impair understanding of the overall sense of the presented scene.

The clinical condition called *cerebral asthenopia* may simulate the pattern of simultanagnosia (Faust, 1955). The essential features of these pseudoagnosias are derived from two major issues: first, visual performance is globally impaired; second, the factor of time is critical. In these subjects a number of different disorders of visual perception appear after a relatively long examining session; these disorders include impairments in reading, object recognition, facial recognition, and simultaneous perception of a situation. Disorders of spatial recognition are not prominent. In extreme cases continuation of the examination results in total suppression of optic function. These functional alterations may be induced commonly under conditions that cause visual fatigue, such as in bright light or dim light, with presentation of moving pictures, with detailed work requiring constant visual control, and also under general conditions of excessive effort, fatigue, or emotional stress. But the functional defect remains limited to visual activity and does not affect other neuropsychological functions such as language. Even under conditions that provoke failures in visual recognition, the routine ophthalmologic examination may be negative. By contrast, special tests of visual function, such as critical flicker fusion, the Cibis-Bay test of local adaptation, or certain tachistoscopic tests, demonstrate dynamic modifications of optic function. In fact, it is the poor performance on these special tests of optic function that forms the basis of interpretations of defects of visual recognition by those authors who reject the very notion of agnosia. For example, Bay (1950, 1952, 1953) asserts that disorders of visual recognition represent the translation of dynamic disorders of elementary visual system mechanisms from retina to cortex.

When quantitative analyses of visual recognition defects are done, we find that, whatever the type of drawn, pictured, or written stimulus, and whatever the hemispheric lateralization or intrahemispheric localization of lesion, performances are always impaired in brain-damaged subjects by comparison with normal persons.

In addition, results of various studies converge to indicate that visual recognition defects are more severe following right than left hemispheric lesions (see the excellent review by Newcombe, 1969). The role of the right hemisphere in these disorders has been shown for story interpretation (without words), estimation of dots shown tachistoscopically, recognition of meaningless patterns (Milner, 1958; Kimura, 1963; Milner and Teuber, 1968; Meier, 1970), interpretation of projected pictures (Ettlinger, 1960), and recognition of complete or overlapping figures (DeRenzi and Spinnler, 1966a;

Warrington and James, 1967). Milner (1968b) has asserted that these deficits are present regardless of the task (recognition, recall, learning). For her the essential element of these right-hemisphere-induced deficits is the nonverbal character of the material. DeRenzi et al (1966, 1969) have argued that the nature of the material is less relevant than the mode of information processing. The right hemisphere, according to this view, would be better than the left on tasks involving complex discriminations.

Other neuropsychological studies have provided evidence for a contribution to visual form perception from either hemisphere, and not just the right. Poeck et al (1973) evaluated impairments with circumscribed hemispheric lesions. Aphasics performed more poorly than left-brain-damaged subjects without aphasia but as poorly as right-brain-damaged subjects. Statistical analyses indicated that the defect in the aphasic group was not due to the presence of aphasia per se or to severity of lesion. Rather, the presence of aphasia indicated a locus of lesion critical for the performances tested. The authors concluded that "there is a common underlying functional disturbance of the visuospatial type associated with the retrorolandic part of both hemispheres."

More currently Masure and Tzavaras (1976), using the Ghent test of overlapping figures plus a modified version of this test, were also able to demonstrate that posterior hemispheric lesions of either side were responsible for visuoperceptual defects. No preferential lesion lateralization was found. This observation contrasts with previous findings of DeRenzi et al (1966a).

Disorders of Recognition of Faces—Prosopagnosia Prosopagnosia, isolated as a specific form of visual agnosia, is a relatively recent discovery. In earlier periods of neuropsychological research, in the course of describing complex visual agnosias, some authors had observed that certain patients, unable to recognize objects, pictures, or colors or to orient themselves in familiar surroundings, were also unable to identify or to revisualize the faces of people, even the most familiar. The most famous of these observations are those of Charcot (1883c) and Wilbrand (1887); other, similar observations were reported by Milian (1932), Hoff and Pötzl (1937), and Donini (1939).

These disorders of visual recognition of human faces were thus present in a complex symptomatic ensemble and were not considered to represent a specific agnosic syndrome until 1947. In that year Bodamer, basing his conclusions on the study of three cases, isolated the defect of facial recognition from other disorders of visual recognition (of objects, forms, and color) and provided the new syndrome with a name—prosopagnosia. He attributed this particular deficit of visual recognition to an inability to appreciate the "visual category the most profound and genetically the most primitive in our perception." According to Bodamer recognition of general facial expression preceded vision of objects in the infant. Therefore, prosopagnosia was a regression to an infantile stage of perception of the external world in which visual attention cannot separate itself from the region of the eyes or the faces of other people.

However debatable Bodamer's interpretations may be, his publication in 1947 marks an important date in neuropsychology because it demonstrated the possibility of a selectivity within the disorders of visual recognition. Agnosia for objects could become manifest without agnosia for faces (here Bodamer cites Lissauer, 1890), and the reverse dissociation can also occur. This specificity of dissociation of visual recognition defects has been amply demonstrated since (see for example, Hécaen, 1972a).

Clinical Features   Essentially the disorder consists of an inability to recognize previously known people by relying only on visual perception of their faces. Differences from one face to another are recognized, but identification of the face cannot be achieved. In the majority of cases the disorder involves people who were well known to the patient before the onset of the illness (parents, close friends), as well as people newly met (doctors, nurses). The patient may even fail to recognize his own face in a mirror, if positional cues are suppressed. According to Bodamer (1947) the difficulty in recognizing faces is especially marked for the region incorporating the eyes and the bridge of the nose. Subsequent studies by Gloning and Quatember (1966, 1967) have provided experimental support for this clinical intuition. Details that are not an integral part of the face (e.g., color of hair, hair style, mustache, beard) are well perceived and may occasionally form the basis for identification. Patients often complain of not being able to revisualize faces. If they do succeed in revisualization, they provide a verbal description that is shallow, inadequate, and focused on elements extrinsic to the face itself, even for members of their own family. The disorder extends to include impaired recognition of pictures of famous people. Although some case reports indicate an impairment in recognition of facial expressions (e.g., anger, joy, sadness), in our own experience these expressions are identified.

Very quickly the patients learn to compensate for this defect, identifying people who were known to them either by visual cues, such as hair style or color, a scar or wart or other distinguishing mark on the face, clothing and accessories (e.g., glasses), silhouette and gestures or by nonvisual cues, such as the sound of the footsteps, and so forth.

In addition to this typical form other forms of defective facial recognition exist in which a distorted perception of faces (and only faces) occurs. This form may coexist with the preceding. These facial metamorphopsias are usually paroxysmal, although they may be permanent (Bodamer, 1947; Hécaen et al, 1957a, 1962). In a case reported by Hécaen et al (1957a) the distortion of faces occurred only with real faces and not with pictures because, as she said, "of the immobility of features."

Associated Clinical Findings   When lesions producing prosopagnosia are bilateral, it is not unusual to find other types of visual agnosia (objects, pictures, colors) in the total clinical picture. A statistical study evaluating 22 patients with agnosia for faces compared with 395 patients with unilateral retrorolandic lesions without prosopagnosia found the following associations. Significantly correlated with prosopagnosia were spatial dyslexia, spatial dyscalculia, visual field defects, dressing apraxia, and directional and vestibular defects. A negative correlation was found for aphasia and anarithmetia. No significant differences of sensory disorders or of intellectual deterioration were found between the two groups (Hécaen, 1969).

Thus approximately the same symptom complex of associated defects is found for prosapagnosia as for the spatial agnosias, which themselves are frequently associated with prosopagnosia. The association with loss of topographic memory (8 of 21 cases of prosopagnosia in the Hécaen, 1972b, series) may be of particular importance.

Anatomoclinical and Theoretical Considerations Diverse explanations have been offered to account for the syndrome. Stollreiter-Butzon (1950) considered prosopagnosia to be the result of a visual sensory defect that interfered with simultaneous perception of faces. For these authors it did not matter if the sensory defect was peripheral or central, although they did accept the role of a "general disorder of psychic synthesis" to explain the gnostic problem. For Faust (1955) prosopagnosia was neither a disorder of a specific visual category nor an elementary sensory defect. Although the defect was selective, he thought that the disorder was not limited to the human face. Rather, the disorder consisted of the difficulty in appreciating the element in any figure that provides individuality. Hécaen and de Ajuriaguerra (1952) asserted that some disorder of visual memory must play a fundamental role. They based their conclusions on the frequent association of prosopagnosia with disorders of topographical memory, the frequency of temporal lobe lesions, and the relatively global defects in revisualization. The hypothesis that prosopagnosia may represent a visual memory disorder has recently been supported by detailed, combined statistical and clinicoanatomic review by Meadows (1974).

As for the anatomic correlates of prosopagnosia, Bodamer (1947) believed that bilateral lesions were necessary. Since 1957 Hécaen et al, referring to anatomoclinical studies, the associated clinical symptoms, and statistical studies, have insisted on the role of right hemispheric lesions in the production of prosopagnosia. Nonetheless no anatomoclinical case has ever been reported with unequivocal prosopagnosia in which the lesions have been limited to the right hemisphere; they have always been bilateral (Bornstein, 1963; Lhermitte et al, 1972). With respect to intrahemispheric localization, anatomoclinical observations point to a right parietotemporo-occipital involvement. Meadows (1974) has argued more specifically that the critical structure in the right hemisphere is the inferior longitudinal fasciculus. A lesion here, he contends, may spare the visual association cortex while isolating it from necessary mnestic associations.

While accepting the necessary role of the right inferior longitudinal fasciculus, Benson et al (1974) argued that this lesion is not sufficient. Many patients, these authors contended, have lesions of the right visual association cortex, including both afferent and efferent pathways, but do not have prosopagnosia. Therefore, they assumed, additional pathology must be present. On the basis of a clinicoanatomic study plus review of the literature they proposed that prosopagnosia results from the combination of lesions affecting both the right inferior longitudinal fasciculus and the splenium of the corpus callosum. This latter lesion would prevent visual memories from passing from left visual association cortex to right.

Experimental Neuropsychological Studies The legitimacy of prosopagnosia as a syndrome and the proposed right hemispheric lateralization of lesions responsible for the symptom complex have been hotly disputed. Given that syndrome is relatively rare, and given that when the disorder appears it is often accompanied by a rich pattern of associated symptoms, it seemed necessary to consider by other means the problem of the recognition of human faces. This consisted, for the most part, of testing large numbers of patients with unilateral hemispheric lesions but without prosopagnosia on a variety of tests of facial recognition (matching or immediate memory). The supposition was that these tests might uncover a clinically silent defect.

DeRenzi and Spinnler (1966b) administered to groups of brain-damaged and normal subjects a test of immediate recall of photographs of faces previously unknown to the subjects. Photographs of chairs and line drawings were also presented, as a means of evaluating the hypothesis of Faust (1955), according to which prosopagnosia is not a specific perceptual disorder but is a general neuropsychological defect related to the inability to abstract the essential elements of a given category. On this test it was found that the ability to recognize faces is much more impaired following right than left hemispheric lesions. No correlation was found between performance scores on the tests of recognition of items in the groups of similar objects and scores on the facial recognition test. The authors concluded that the disorder of facial recognition was nothing more than a manifestation of a general disturbance of recognition of any relatively complex perceptual pattern.

In a subsequent study DeRenzi et al (1968c) further evaluated the role of memory in performances on facial recognition tasks. They found no significant differences between results on a test of immediate recall and one of delayed recall. On both tests, performances were significantly impaired in the group with right hemispheric lesions with visual field defects.

On two tests of facial recognition, one with photographs of people unknown to the subjects, the other with photographs of famous people, Warrington and James (1967) also found a prominent right hemispheric effect. Between the two tests no significant correlations existed on patient performance. These authors concluded from this that the two tests evaluated different functions. Following right temporal lesions, failures on the test of famous faces implied involvement of a mnestic factor; defective performance on this test approximated prosopagnosia as it is seen clinically. With the test of unfamiliar faces mean errors were greatest with right parietal lesions; defective performance on this test depended perhaps on a general perceptual disorder. The syndrome of prosopagnosia, thus, may result from two disturbances (mnestic and perceptual) due to two different lesions (temporal and parietal) in the right hemisphere. Additional support for right hemispheric involvement on a test of matching faces (in photographs) was provided by Benton and Van Allen (1968).

Milner (1958) administered tests of immediate recall and delayed recall of photographs of faces to subjects with right or left cortical ablations, especially of temporal lobes. She found that subjects with right temporal lobectomy had severe impairments of memory for photographs of the human face. In the delayed recall task, even when the delay period was not filled, the subjects were no better than when the period was filled. This observation suggested that right temporal lesions caused a specific defect in visual memory. By contrast, subjects with right frontal lobe ablations performed about as well as those with left-sided lesions. Too few subjects with parietal lesions were studied to allow comment on this anatomic region.

These various statistical studies all point to the same conclusion: that the right hemisphere plays a special role in determining deficits in facial recognition, at least on these tests. Questions still remain concerning the relative role of perceptual and mnestic factors, the intrahemispheric lesion site responsible for the disorders, the possibility that two defects may be responsible for the disorder of recognition, the specificity of faces as an isolated visual recognition problem, and especially the relationship of the deficits found on these statistical studies to the clinical syndrome of prosopagnosia.

Tzavaras, Hécaen, and Le Bras (1970) attempted to answer some of these questions by means of a series of matching tests of facial and object recognition under different conditions. The faces were either photographs or line drawings and were modified by changes in facial expression, lighting, or associated elements (hair, hat, etc.). Objects were either meaningless line drawings, photographs of objects in the same semantic category differing according to individual details, or objects shown under various degrees of shading. Twenty-five subjects with left hemispheric lesions, 26 with right, and 30 with no cerebral lesions took these tests. Results confirmed previous studies on the predominant role of the right hemisphere on deficits of recognition of the human face. A high correlation was found among deficits on all tests of facial recognition; no correlation was found between results on tests of facial recognition and results of the other tests.

The studies of facial recognition by Yin (1969) also support the specificity of this perceptual task. It is generally known that, for both children and adults, recognition of faces is more difficult when the faces are presented upside down. Taking this fact into account, Yin showed that this recognition difficulty was much greater when a subject had to select on multiple choice an upside-down face that had previously been presented in the normal position. This upside-down recognition defect also existed for objects that normally have a single orientation, but the defect was more severe for faces. In this task of delayed identification, Yin concluded that two factors were relevant. The first, a factor of familiarity, related to all visual representations, facial or not. The second, which was specific for human faces, may have been a loss of the "general impression" of the normally oriented face, when the face was upside down. An additional piece of evidence was provided by the same author to suggest that the human face is a specific perceptual complex. Photographs of faces were much more difficult to remember than photographs of objects under conditions of rapid presentation.

Yin (1970) continued similar research with posttraumatic brain-injured subjects. On a test of facial recognition, performances of subjects with right posterior lesions were inferior to those of subjects with unilateral lesions in any other part of the brain and to those of a control group. When the faces were presented in an upside-down position, subjects with lesions in all other locations were inferior to those with right posterior lesions and to controls. This dissociation between normal and inverted positions of presentation was not found with photographs of other familiar items.

Concordant results have been reported in other studies with normal subjects. For example, Rizzolatti et al (1970) studied discriminative reaction times to physiognomic and alphabetic stimuli presented tachistoscopically to the right or left visual field. The task was to push on a button when the stimulus presented corresponded to a previously learned stimulus. Reaction times to letters were significantly faster with stimuli presented in the right hemifield; reaction times to faces were faster with stimulus presentations in the left hemifield.

This type of experiment, although proving the superiority of the right hemisphere for treatment of information concerning faces, does not allow one to determine if the superiority is related to some particular qualities of the human face or if it is related more to task complexity. We could add that the perceptual superiority of the right hemisphere has been found in split-brain patients for a variety of complex stimuli: faces, meaningless drawings, and also familar, easily verbalizable drawings (Levy et al, 1972).

We believe that there is sufficient evidence to support the argument that disorders of visual recognition of human faces constitute a specific neuropsychological defect linked to right hemispheric lesions. Of interest in this regard is the observation of Warrington and James (1967) that two different factors (mnestic and perceptual) are at the basis of defective facial recognition. We must, however, emphasize that there is no good evidence allowing one to relate disorders of visual recognition of human faces as determined by these various studies to the clinical syndrome of prosopagnosia. In fact, Rondot and Tzavaras (1969) described the observation of a patient with clinical prosopagnosia who performed well on these standardized matching and memory tests of facial recognition (see also Assal, 1969; Benton and Van Allen, 1968).

Disorders of Color Recognition—Color Agnosia

Clinical Aspects   Under the rubric "color agnosia" several different aspects of disordered color identification have been included. True agnosia for colors may be situated at some stage between deficits in color perception that follow cortical blindness, and that may even be limited to a hemifield (Merle, 1908; Albert, et al, 1975b), and aphasia for color names. Color agnosia is characterized by two main features: (1) preservation of color perception, as determined by tests of color discrimination such as the tests of Ishihara, Pollack, Hardy, Rand Ritter, or Raylegt's equation, and (2) inability to select all colors of the same hue from a group of colored objects, to pick out or point to colors on command, to name colors in the absence of aphasia, and to evoke the specific colors of color-specific objects (e.g., tomato, sky, grass, etc.).

Clinically one is often hard pressed to find a disorder of color recognition as an isolated syndrome conforming to the criteria cited above. If isolated elements of the syndrome are found, they usually do not correspond to classical descriptions. In addition the lesion site responsible for the various defects may be the same regardless of clinical manifestation. In the series of brain-damaged patients with neuropsychological defects reported by Hécaen and Angelergues in 1963 disorders of color identification taken globally were present in 15 cases; in 9 of these 15 the left hemisphere was implicated, and in 8 of these 9 the occipital lobe was involved.

Since the end of the nineteenth century neuropsychologists have debated the nature of color agnosia. Some have proposed that defective color identification may in fact be the clinical manifestation of a disorder of language limited to the domain of colors (amnestic color blindness, Wilbrand, 1887). Others (e.g., Lewandowsky, 1908) suggested that the disorder reflected a "separation between the idea of the color and that of the object" and that language dysfunction was not the root cause. For Sittig (1921) the necessity was to differentiate between patients who have a disturbance of color sensation (i.e., who are color blind) and those who do not. If a patient cannot name or comprehend the name of a color, one may speak of amnesia for colors; if the patient is also unable to classify colored stimuli (e.g., to group different tints belonging to the same fundamental color group), then one may speak of color agnosia combined with an aphasic disorder.

True aphasia for color words is characterized by the situation in which the patient, who has no perceptual defect and is not aphasic in any other way, can neither name colors nor point to them on verbal command. Gelb and Goldstein (1920, 1924) considered that this aphasia for color names was a specific manifestation of a general disorder: the loss of categorical attitude in the domain of colors, the colors no longer retaining their traditional value as independent categories relative to the objects to which they are linked concretely.

The explanation provided by Geschwind (1965) for alexia was extended to disorders of color identification on the basis of a case studied in detail (Geschwind and Fusillo, 1966). This subject, an alexic who was able to name objects, pictured objects, and designs, was unable to name colors. He could, however, match colors and group them according to fundamental hue, independently of their brilliance or saturation. Colorimetric tests were normally performed. This patient had a left occipital lesion producing a right hemianopia, and a lesion of the posterior third of the corpus callosum. The argument provided by the authors was that the callosal lesion, by disconnecting visual areas in the right hemisphere from language areas in the left hemisphere, interfered with the association between color perception and verbalization of the name of the perceived color. However, color discriminations could take place in the intact right hemisphere. Thus tasks requiring the patient to evoke the name of the color of an object for which the name of the object was verbally presented (auditory-auditory intramodal association) and those requiring the ability to associate a color with the drawing of an object that had a characteristic odor (visuovisual intramodal association) were well accomplished by their patient. As for his preserved ability to name objects, the explanation provided was that, unlike words and colors, objects aroused somesthetic associations in the parietal area and that connections from right parietal area to left hemisphere were not disrupted. According to these authors, errors in color naming represented confabulations resulting from the absence of control of the language zone on the visual activity of the right occipital lobe, the only remaining cerebral region capable of visual activity. Some of the verbal behavior of split-brain subjects corresponds to this interpretation (Sperry and Gazzaniga, 1967; Dimond, 1972).

Studying three subjects with section of the splenium, Ikata et al (1974) found that, despite an almost total impossibility to name colors projected into the left visual field, the subjects could identify colors by nonverbal means equally well in either field. Similar observations were reported by Trevarthen (1974).

The disconnection hypothesis appears acceptable to account for the case described by Geschwind and Fusillo (1966), but it certainly cannot explain all cases of defective color identification, even when a verbal component dominates the clinical picture. For example, the disconnection hypothesis does not explain the symptoms of the patient described by Kinsbourne and Warrington (1964). This patient, whose color sensation and visual fields were normal, had severe naming problems, could not point to colors on command, could not provide the name of the appropriate color corresponding to an object when the name of the object was presented verbally, and could not color correctly drawings of items with characteristic colors. He could, however, recognize his errors. He was also unable to perform an associative learning task in which color names were paired with digits or objects, or another in which colored blocks were paired with nonverbal material. This patient was, however, able to acquire verbal associations that did not involve color names. For these authors the recognition defect for colors was possibly the result of an inability to evoke colors verbally. In such a case the deficit would consist, essentially, of an inability to associate color names with other information; this would be an association defect for color names rather than a visual-verbal disconnection syndrome. A patient with similar defects was described by Stengel (1948). Because this patient had no language deficit and because he had difficulty classifying colored swatches on Holmgreen's test, Stengel concluded that the defect was limited to color recognition.

A patient described by Mohr et al (1971) had defective color naming and impaired ability to match colors with their names, although color discrimination was normal. Errors on the various tests were not random; a certain relationship existed between stimulus and response. The authors felt that the deficit was perhaps limited to a loss of precision in the control normally exercised on behavior by isolated colored stimuli in the absence of other colors for comparison. The authors preferred the term *dys-relation* to that of *disconnection* between colors and their names.

By referring to a variety of different reports of cases of impaired color identification, we have tried to indicate that several different factors may be involved in the process of color recognition and that disturbance of any one of these factors may provoke a clinical defect of color recognition. One of these is, of course, color blindness, which may persist after an episode of cortical blindness. Linguistic and mnestic factors must also be evaluated before one can reliably speak of a truly gnostic defect.

Statistical Studies   DeRenzi and Spinnler (1967) studied these problems by presenting a series of tests to groups of brain-damaged and nonbrain-damaged subjects. The tests evaluated color perception, verbalization of colors, and the ability to color drawings of objects that had characteristic colors. This last test required not only the ability to discriminate colors but also the mnestic capacity for object-color relationships. Subjects with right hemispheric lesions had poorest performances on perceptual tasks; those with left hemispheric lesions performed poorly on the verbal tasks. On the coloring test aphasics performed most poorly, and scores were significantly correlated with scores on subtests of verbal comprehension and naming. These failures were present in some aphasics who had no defects on the perceptual tasks.

The authors concluded from these tests that the deficit of nonverbal association between objects and colors, even though correlated with aphasia, was the result of a general failure of associative skill, specific to left hemispheric lesions. The observation that four subjects had very low scores on color-naming tests without a particularly low score on tests of picture naming was interpreted as supporting the reality of a variety of amnestic aphasia limited to color names. By contrast, because they did not find any disorder of color recognition in the absence of perceptual or verbal defects, DeRenzi and Spinnler (1967) concluded that it was unlikely that color agnosia existed as an isolable syndrome.

Subsequent research by DeRenzi et al (1972) supported the conclusion that defective coloring of drawings having a characteristic color was associative. The experimental results confirmed the relationship between this particular coloring defect and aphasia, in the absence of impaired color discrimination. Tzavaras et al (1971) presented a similar battery of coloring tests to brain-damaged patients. Although they also found a relationship between aphasia and defective coloring of drawings having characteristic colors, they noted that some subjects with severe coloring defects were free of language troubles.

One conclusion acceptable to both the Milan and the Paris groups was that topographic proximity of two lesion sites responsible for the two disorders could account for their frequent, but not constant, association and that, while it was possible, it was not necessary to propose a functional relationship between the two disorders. The coloring test may have a heterogeneity of underlying mechanisms responsible for its adequate performance, and these mechanisms may selectively break down, depending on hemispheric lateralization and intrahemispheric location.

On the basis of a study of 42 subjects with posterior cerebral lesions Lhermitte et al (1969) drew conclusions directly opposite to those of DeRenzi and Spinnler (1967). A number of color-perceiving, color-matching, color-categorizing, and color-verbalizing tasks were employed. Chromatic vision, as determined by tests of matching and discrimination, was impaired only with (probable) bilateral posterior lesions. With unilateral hemispheric lesions, Lhermitte et al found either defects on the Farnsworth test only or defects on a cluster of tests including tests of verbal identification and recognition and tests of nonverbal evocation of colors.

Defective chromatic vision was thus present in three groups of brain-damaged subjects. In the group with bilateral lesions the defects seemed to represent a global deficiency in primary sensation. In the two other groups (unilateral right- or left-brain damage) the color defect either was specific for the blue-yellow axis or was the clinical manifestation of a loss of chromatic discrimination expressed exclusively in an organizational process. As for defective performances on pointing to command, naming, recognition, and evocation of colors, they could not be attributed directly to a language disorder, because the color defect occurred whether the task was verbal or nonverbal. The verbal errors were primarily linked to two chromatic features: the blue-yellow axis and the degree of saturation.

The authors interpreted these findings as indicating loss of the knowledge of colors as specific attributes of objects. The subject was agnosic for colors insofar as he could see them but not recognize them. Color agnosia was considered to be the regression from knowledge acquired concerning the link between colors and objects. Without denying the role of language in the acquisition of chromatic differentiations and in the formation of new associations between colors and objects, Lhermitte et al refused to accept the notion that language disorders underlie the defects of color agnosia.

Anatomic Aspects General agreement has resulted in attribution of deficits of color recognition to left hemispheric lesions, regardless of the nature of the deficit, with the exception of marked color vision defects. With the latter, bilateral lesions may be necessary (Lhermitte et al, 1969; Meadows, 1974). Only DeRenzi et al (1972) found a greater association of right hemispheric lesions with defects of color perception (matching, Ishihara), especially in subjects with visual field defects. They also found disorders of naming, pointing, and evocation for colors with right hemispheric lesions when these deficits were associated with perceptual troubles.

As for the intrahemispheric site of lesions responsible for color agnosia, an occipital lobe location is widely accepted. For Kleist (1933) the lesions that produced color agnosia are situated outside of the striate area and affect Brodmann area 19. A number of authors proposed a region including lateral gyri 02 and 03, the angular gyrus, and rarely, the first temporal gyrus (Sittig, 1921; Schuster, 1902; Peritz, 1918; Kleist, 1933). Faust (1955) suggested the base of the occipital lobe. In the Mohr et al (1971) case the lesions resulted from infarction in the distribution of the left posterior cerebral artery. Areas involved were the geniculate body, hippocampus, dorsolateral nucleus of the thalamus, and pulvinar; the entire extent of the lingual gyrus was undermined. Hécaen and Angelergues (1963) found that, of 11 cases in which the localization of lesions causing impaired color recognition could be ascertained, 8 involved the occipital lobe, and 6 of these in isolated fashion. In the

Lhermitte el al (1969) study, taking into consideration only vascular lesions, we find that, in 7 out of 7 cases of their group II (color agnosia), the infarction was in the territory of the posterior cerebral artery, whereas in only 3 of 13 cases was this true for group I (tritanopia or dyschromatopsia). A review of the anatomoclinical evidence together with his own clinical experience led Meadows (1974) to suggest a relationship between defective color perception in man and lesions of the anterior inferior part of the occipital lobe.

Theoretical Considerations   Divergent opinions exist concerning the reality of the syndrome of color agnosia, accepted by some, rejected by others. We believe that the arguments of those who deny the existence of color agnosia as a syndrome are not completely convincing. These arguments are based on studies of large series of patients selected only on the basis of hemispheric lateralization of lesion. In such series intrahemispheric localization of lesion is not precise, and this imprecision may skew the results. Clusters of associated neuropsychological defects, determined by such studies, may be the fortuitous result of anatomic proximity of sites responsible for different functions. In addition, if one considered individually the cases called "color agnosia," he would be struck by a certain similarity, as well as by certain peculiarities of the defective color recognition. Not a single case corresponds in all of its detail to what has been classically defined as color agnosia, or to aphasia for colors, cortical color blindness, or amnesia for specific attributes of colors.

We wonder if one should not ask a different question concerning defective color recognition. Are we dealing with defects in different fundamental functions that, by interfering with one specific behavioral capacity, confer a different final clinical form each time? The only means of answering this question is by anatomoclinical observation, including not only a behavioral evaluation of diverse behavioral activities but also precise anatomic localization of lesions. Random case reports leave too much room for individual variation. Given the rarity of the syndrome, the problem may remain insoluble, unless a systematic examination scheme is formulated, codified, and used by neuropsychologists in different laboratories.

The hypothesis implied in the question posed in the preceding paragraph may be considered as follows. If we take the example of amnesic aphasia limited to color names in a patient with no other evidence of language disorder, we would then have to assume a defect in a fundamental function (cf. Gelb and Goldstein, 1920, 1924) manifesting itself, for anatomic or other reasons, exclusively in the domain of colors, although characteristics of general disturbances in verbal evocation would be present. In like manner a deficiency in the association between an object and its color may be parallel to a deficiency in the association between an object and its sound. Instead of imagining that this deficiency is based on a specific aphasic disorder, one might envisage a specific association disorder resulting from a lesion in a cortical area responsible for a fundamental function of "association" but manifesting itself in one or another clinical form according to the direction and extent of the lesion's destruction. The qualifying term *amnesic* attributed to these disorders of color recognition is somewhat arbitrary and is certainly no more valid than the qualifying term *agnosic.* In fact the latter term is perhaps better because what is lost is the meaning of the color.

We are inevitably led to a consideration of the relation between language and color recognition. Certain studies done with normal subjects on the relationship between naming, discrimination, and recognition of colors are worth mentioning. Lenneberg (1961) found that discrimination of shades of colors was not linked to naming habits, when the task was simple and little demand was made on memory. By contrast, when the mnestic task was more difficult, naming habits played a greater role. According to these results one could presume that, in a color recognition task, our tendency to structure the colored material semantically may provide anchorage points on a continuum. Nevertheless codability (Brown and Lenneberg, 1954) is only one of the ways by which linguistic categorization intervenes in the process of recognition. A very low level of "codability" may equally be functioning in processes of hue memory (Burnham and Clark, 1955). Also worth noting is the observation that color naming is a stable function through wide variations of color intensity and exposure duration. Modifications of stability of color naming may, however, be brought about by changes in luminosity (S. L. Luria, 1967).

Coupling results from normal subjects with those from brain-damaged subjects, we may begin to see the influence of language on color recognition and the limits of this influence. It seems reasonable to accept that language disorders affect performance on tests of color recognition to different degrees depending on whether color discrimination is intact or impaired and depending on the nature and difficulty of the task. We can, ourselves, envisage a spectrum of disorders of color recognition ranging from those in which disturbances of language represent the essential feature to those in which the effect of language disturbance is reduced to a minimum; in fact, in the latter situations, recourse to language may facilitate recognition.

Disorders of Spatial Recognition—Spatial Agnosias

Historical Background   Loss of orientation, loss of sense of place, or loss of memory for place had been described with the earliest reports of psychic blindness but had not been isolated as a separate syndrome (Foerster, 1890; Wilbrand, 1892; Magnus, 1894; Dunn, 1895). Balint (1909), by his description of "psychic paralysis of gaze," demonstrated how important oculomotor disorders could be in defective exploration of space. It was not, however, until the studies of Holmes in 1918 and 1919 that the various defects that could be considered as concerning spatial perception were organized into separate and distinctive categories. He defined eight groups: (1) disorders of absolute localization of objects, (2) disorders of relative object location, (3) inability to compare dimensions of two objects, (4) difficulty of avoiding objects while walking and defective topographical memory, (5) impaired ability to count and group seen items, (6) inability to perceive movement of objects in a sagittal plane, (7) defective ocular movements, and (8) loss of stereoscopic vision.

Kleist (1933) described true spatial agnosia as being divided into the syndromes of opticosomatic agnosia; loss of topographical memory; disorders of relative localization of objects, linked to visual field defects; and "blindness for placement," or the inability to localize an object in its absolute position in space. At the same period of time a number of authors were emphasizing the importance of the right hemisphere in spatial organization (Pötzl, 1928; Lange, 1936; Dide, 1938).

Brain (1941a) proposed the following classification: (1) defective visual localization of objects (a) by amblyopia, (b) by displacement of fixation point in lateral homonymous hemianopia, or (c) by agnosia for spatial relations, bilateral or limited to a hemifield; (2) loss of stereoscopic vision; (3) agnosia for the left half of space; (4) visual alloesthesia; (5) loss of topographical memory; (6) visual disorientation secondary to object agnosia; and (7) mixed forms.

In the mid-1940s experimental methods were introduced. By such means Bender and Teuber (1947) distinguished disorders of perception of spatial relations from impaired general level of mental functioning in relationship to orientation in space. According to Critchley (1953) three aspects of spatial agnosia could be distinguished and seen clinically in isolated fashion: (1) disorders of spatial perception with respect to recognition of our three-dimensional world, (2) disorders of the concept of space with respect to the idea of our three-dimensional world, and (3) disorders of interdimensional manipulation of space, that is, loss of topographical memory, impaired orientation, unilateral spatial agnosia, and defective topographical concepts.

The entire approach to the question was transformed in the early 1950s when disorders of spatial organization were correlated with lesions in the posterior part of the nonspeech-dominant hemisphere (McFie et al, 1950; Hécaen et al, 1951, 1956). In these studies the accent was placed on the mutual relation between different clinical manifestations of disordered spatial recognition and various practic and somatognosic disorders. These observations, despite initial difficulty in acceptance, were subsequently confirmed both by results of experimental studies and by additional clinical observations on large series of patients. The polysensorial character of these disorders was emphasized and the nature of the functional deficits was explored (oculomotor disturbances, impaired sensorimotor feedback, etc.).

In this section we present a descriptive classification of various disorders of perception and manipulation of spatial information. We follow the outline originally proposed by Hécaen and de Ajuriaguerra (see Hécaen, 1972b): (1) disorders of spatial perception (absolute and relative localization), (2) defective manipulation of spatial information (loss of topographical concepts, unilateral spatial agnosia), (3) loss of topographical memory, and (4) Balint's syndrome. In subsequent sections we consider proposed mechanisms to explain these disorders.

Disorders of Spatial Perception   These functional defects represent most of the disorders classified by Holmes and Horrax (1919) as visual disorientation. Included are loss of ability to localize objects (absolute and relative), inability to compare object sizes, and loss of stereoscopic vision. At first it was believed that these disorders affected the entire visual field and resulted from bilateral lesions. Riddoch (1935), however, insisted that this type of disorder may be related to the visual field contralateral to a hemispheric lesion, and subsequent studies have shown that, in fact, this is the more usual situation. The disorder may even be seen in only one portion of the contralateral visual field.

Riddoch (1935) asserted that these higher order perceptual defects could occur in the absence of any hemianopic (sensory) defect. If, however, special tests are used, primary visual sensory defects may be demonstrated (Bender and Teuber, 1947; Bay, 1953). Using quantitative methods, Ratcliff and Davies-Jones (1972) found frequent deficits of visual localization in the field contralateral to a parietal lesion in either hemisphere. Deficits were even greater and were present in both fields following bilateral posterior lesions. Mild deficits were also present in the ipsilateral field with unilateral brain damage with or without hemianopia.

Bender and Teuber (1947) were particularly interested in the link between what they called disorders of visual perception of spatial organization and disorders of residual visual sensory function. Dynamic tests of vision, such as critical flicker fusion and perceptual capacity of stroboscopic movement, were used. They found phenomena of fluctuation, extinction, afterimage, and so forth, in those parts of the visual field that had been considered normal. By means of other tests, such as tests of pointing, bisection of lines in different positional orientations, perception of depth, and form and size of variable distances, they found that disturbances of spatial localization and visual illusions of form and size were associated with sections of the visual vield with deficient sensory function. They found that spatial disorientation occurred in three dimensions and that it was always accompanied by disorders of appearance, size, shape, and color of objects. These disorders were often limited to one quadrant and were usually in the neighborhood of scotomata of unequal density. For Bender and Teuber (1947) it was incorrect to speak of spatial disorders; they found no loss of spatial signs or symbols. They concluded that the defects represented the establishment of a new distribution of the equilibrium of forces in the cortical field.

These authors thus placed disturbances of lower level visual functions in the context of Gestalt theory. We, however, find it difficult to eliminate the important role played by other factors, such as impaired oculomotor function and sensory feedback, in the production of defective perception of depth or impaired localization of objects in space, or illusions of shape and size. Other authors (e.g., Kleist, 1933) have also stressed the significance of disturbed oculomotor function in the production of defective absolute localization of objects or of "blindness for place."

As for anatomic correlations, most authors have referred to lesions in the parieto-occipital areas in association with disorders of spatial perception (Holmes, 1918b; Riddoch, 1935; Lange, 1936). For others the lesional site is precisely in area 18 (Kleist, 1933; Pötzl, 1924). Still others localize the lesions in the calcarine regions (Quensel, 1931; Bay, 1950).

With respect to hemispheric lateralization we have previously stated that various visuospatial illusions, collected under the name of metamorphopsias, are preferentially determined by right hemispheric lesions. In 1969 Carmon and Bechtoldt invoked a similar lateralization for disturbances of absolute or relative localization and for impaired stereoscopic vision. These authors, studying groups of controls and subjects with unilateral brain damage, found that only those with right-brain damage had defects on stereoscopic tests of localization in depth of meaningless shapes. Loss of stereoscopic depth perception with right hemispheric lesions was also found by other authors. Durnford and Kimura (1971), studying normal subjects, found the right hemisphere to be superior for depth perception, as reflected by left hemifield superiority on perceptual tests derived from the Julesz stereograms.

A certain reserve must be maintained concerning interpretation of these results. Breitmeyer, Julesz, and Kropfl (1975), using dynamic random-dot stereograms, observed a left-field isotrophy between cortical hemifields. In addition more recent studies with brain-damaged subjects have not confirmed earlier results. Lehmann and Walchli (1975) found no significant lateralization effect on performance deficits with polaroid stereo depth perception tests. These authors concluded that general intellectual deficit was responsible for apparent perceptual defects. They contended that earlier studies had not adequately considered the variable of age as a factor producing perceptual deficits. A study by Tzavaras (in preparation), using the methods and materials of the Benton and Hécaen (1970) study, was also unable to demonstrate a significant lateralization effect.

These findings may be compared with those on tests of perception of verticality and horizontality (visual coordinates) in patients with cerebral lesions. The greatest deviations of subjective visual coordinates were found in subjects with right posterior lesions (Lenz, 1944; McFie et al, 1950; Hécaen et al, 1951; Tzavaras and Hécaen, 1971). Bender and Jung (1948) found, however, a more diffuse cerebral localization. By means of a simple and precise test DeRenzi et al (1970a,b) systematically studied the hemispheric contribution to exploration of space through the visual and tactile modalities. The subjects had to perceive the spatial orientation of a rod that could be placed in virtually any position. The group most impaired on this had right posterior lesions.

Disorders of Manipulation of Spatial Information   Under this rubric, borrowed from Critchley (1953), one may group a series of disorders concerning recognition and use of spatial information. In point of fact these disorders cannot be considered as pure visual agnosias, and Hécaen et al (1956) provided the term *apractognosia for spatial relations* as a better, more descriptive expression. The disorders of spatial recognition and/ use are closely associated with visuoconstructive deficits, spatial dyslexia, dysgraphia, and dyscalculia; and metamorphopsias, disorders of subjective visual coordinates, and hemiasomatognosias. These associated symptoms are recognized as the apractognosic syndrome of the right temporoparieto-occipital junction (Hécaen et al, 1956).

Unilateral Spatial Agnosia   In his studies on visual perception Poppelreuter (1914–1917, 1923) referred to unilateral visual inattention; this defect was also mentioned in the case report of Scheller and Seidemann (1931–1932). It was not, however, until the studies of Brain in 1941 that neglect of one side of space was related to right hemispheric lesions. In these studies Brain also discussed the intensity of visual neglect, describing patients who completely ignored everything on their left and who behaved as if this part of space did not exist. For Brain this disorientation for one half of space was linked to negligence for one half of the body, the schema of the external world and the body scheme being disturbed together.

In milder cases of unilateral spatial agnosia, the disorder may be demonstrated only when the patient is subjected to special tests. For example, in constructional or drawing activity, the patient may not reproduce the left half of the model; in tests of line crossing the subject may cross out only those lines on the right half of the page. In more severe cases the patient may draw or write only on the right side of a page, even spontaneously; in a complex picture he may see only those elements to the right; with a compound word he may read only the word on the right. For example, when shown a picture of a bicycle, a subject perceived only the elements to the right and called it a wheelbarrow; when shown the compound word *screwdriver*, he read it as

Neglect of left half of space in a patient with right parietal glioma.

"driver." Itemizing or counting the number of items on a single line or spread diffusely on a page is always in error, the patient ignoring elements on the left. In certain cases there is an absolute neglect of all stimuli presented to the left. In following a route, for example, the patient takes only those paths situated on the right. Even if the examiner is speaking, the patient may pay no attention to the examiner situated on his left and may reply as if the examiner were situated on his right. This may be so extreme as to produce a circling effect; in response to a stimulus on the left, the subject will turn to the right and continue turning to the right until he circles around to the source of the stimulus.

Unilateral neglect of space often extends beyond the visual modality and may include inappropriate responses to tactile and auditory stimuli as well. Somatognosic disorders related to the same side of the body, motor hemi-aspontaneity or hemiasomatognosia, may often accompany unilateral neglect. Other common associated disorders include left lateral homonymous hemianopia and oculomotor troubles (limitation of gaze, saccadic movements, gaze palsy). These associated defects are not necessary accompaniments of the syndrome. In some cases a permanent deviation of head and eyes toward the side of the lesion has been observed.

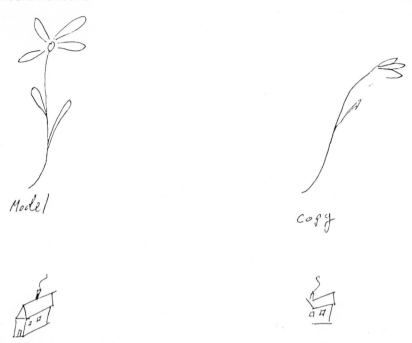

Neglect of left half of space in patient with right hemispheric infarction.

In a statistical study of patients with verified lesions Hécaen (1962) found the following defects to be significantly associated with unilateral spatial agnosia due to right hemispheric lesions: general deterioration of intellectual function, indifference to failures, hemianopia, oculomotor defects, sensory disturbances, constructional apraxia, dressing apraxia, loss of topographical orientation, spatial dyslexia, spatial dysgraphia, spatial dyscalculia, anarithmetia, and deviation of subjective visual coordinates. Gainotti (1968) also found that the significant clinical associations with unilateral spatial agnosia in subjects with right hemispheric lesions were visual field defects, sensory disorders, oculomotor deficits, hemiasomatognosias, intellectual deterioration, and affective indifference. Oxbury et al (1974) found that subjects with left-sided unilateral neglect were inferior on tests of visual perception and spatial analysis by comparison with subjects with right hemispheric lesions but without unilateral neglect.

Many authors since Brain have described unilateral spatial agnosia as relating almost exclusively to the left half of space. Hécaen (1962) has provided statistical evidence to support this view. For example, in one series of 413 patients with cortical lesions, of 59 patients with unilateral spatial agnosia, 51 had right hemispheric lesions, 4 left hemispheric, and 4 bilateral. In addition,

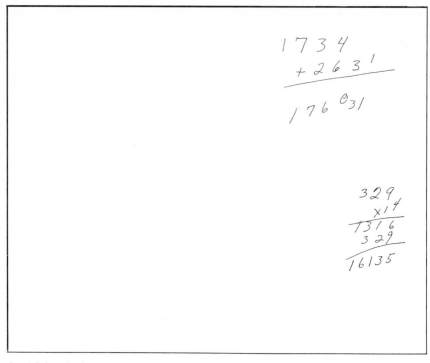

Spatial dyscalculia. Note tendency to crowd towards the right side of the page and incorrect placement of digits.

of these 4 subjects with unilateral spatial agnosia due to left hemispheric lesions, 3 were left-handed; and in the 4 subjects with bilateral lesions, neglect involved the left half of space (Hécaen and Angelergues, 1963). In a more recent analysis of right-handed patients with anatomically verified unilateral cortical lesions, Hécaen found 56 cases of unilateral spatial agnosia in 179 cases with right hemispheric lesions and 1 out of 286 subjects with lesions of the left hemisphere (see Hécaen, 1972a).

From the point of view of intrahemispheric localization, agreement seems general that the parietotemporo-occipital junction is the site responsible for this syndrome. In patients subjected to restricted cortical ablations the disorder was produced only when the supramarginal and angular gyri and posterior part of T_1 were included in the resection (Hécaen et al, 1956). In this series of patients with verified unilateral hemispheric lesions Hécaen (1962) found the presence of unilateral spatial agnosia with right hemispheric lesions to be significantly associated with damage to the occipital and parietal lobes but negatively correlated with frontal lesions.

The demonstration of visual attention cells in area 7 in primates has provided strong support for the data derived from human pathology (Hyvarinen and Poranen, 1974, Mountcastle et al, 1975). Single-cell studies showed the existence of cells that functioned by directing visual attention to objects of particular interest or with high motivational value. These cells were responsible for maintenance of fixation on stationary objects and for control of pursuit of moving objects. Destruction of an ensemble for such activity could account for visual neglect.

It seems, however, that posterior lesions are not the only lesions responsible for neglect. Frontal lesions may produce a form of visual inattention in man called pseudohemianopia (Silberpfennig, 1941). In such cases Chain et al (1972) noted defects of initiation of eye movements for gaze to the side contralateral to the lesion. This gaze defect was especially prominent with voluntary eye movements. Tracking movements and eye movements during reading were normal. Heilman and Valenstein (1972a) confirmed earlier reports suggesting that lesions producing frontal neglect were more often on the right.

As noted in the chapter on the frontal lobes, the role of frontal lobe lesions in the production of unilateral neglect in animals has been recognized for many years (Bianchi, 1895; Kennard, 1939; Kennard and Ectors, 1938; Welch and Stutteville, 1958). Frontal neglect in monkeys follows lesions limited to the oculomotor area. The defects become attenuated in 1 or 2 weeks but may be uncovered with careful testing of eye movements of visual fields (Latto and Cowey, 1971a,b).

Watson et al (1973) produced unilateral neglect in the monkey by cingulectomy. The authors tied a string of studies together to propose the hypothesis that neglect results from a disconnection of cortex from reticular activating system on the appropriate side. The argument is compelling. By itself, however, the hypothesis cannot explain the preponderance of right-sided lesions accepted clinically as causing unilateral neglect by contrast with left-sided lesions. Mountcastle et al (1975) suggest that frontal inattention may be a disconnection syndrome resulting from interruption of connections between area 7 and the frontal lobe.

In other animals, for example, cat, rat, contralateral "neglect" has been produced with lesions in a variety of locations. This neglect has always been considered to result from lesions affecting oculomotor projection pathways or centers for visual representation (Sprague and Meikle, 1965; Orem et al, 1973; Cowey and Bozek, 1974). When the neglect is polymodal, collicular regions (Kirvel et al, 1974) and lateral hypothalamus (Marshall and Teitelbaum, 1974) have also been implicated.

The special relationship between right hemispheric lesions in man and neglect of one side of space is not accepted by everyone. Denny-Brown and Chambers (1958) hold that, whereas unilateral spatial agnosia is seen more frequently following right hemispheric lesions, it may also occur following left-sided damage. Battersby et al (1960), after studying 120 brain-damaged subjects by means of a standard battery of perceptual tests, accepted that lesions of the temporoparieto-occipital areas may cause perceptual asymmetries, but they found only a slight, nonsignificant predominance of right-sided lesions in the production of this defect. This predominance, they believed, was artificial and resulted from the presence of aphasia in the left-sided lesions. The conclusions of these authors were partially supported by a more recent study of visual neglect involving the crossing out of lines on a sheet of paper placed before the subject. Right hemispheric lesions caused neglect only slightly more often than left hemispheric lesions did; however, the severity of the neglect was significantly greater with right-sided damage (Albert, 1973).

Additional studies have provided quantitative arguments concerning the preferential role of the right hemisphere in the production of this syndrome. Gainotti (1968) studied 110 subjects with unilateral hemispheric damage by means of a battery of four perceptual or writing tasks (Progressive Matrices, searching for items in a picture, copy of geometric figures, and copy of crosses). The diagnosis of unilateral spatial agnosia was made if a subject failed on three of the four tests. Of 30 subjects diagnosed as having unilateral spatial agnosia according to these criteria, 23 had lesions on the right, 7 on the left. This right-sided lateralization is even more marked if the intensity of the syndrome is considered. As with the study cited above (Albert, 1973), when the lesion was on the left, the defect involved mild inattention to the contralateral side; when the lesion was on the right, the contralateral neglect was severe. Statistical studies by Faglioni et al (1969b) also showed a significantly greater occurrence of visual hemi-inattention syndromes with retrorolandic lesions of the minor hemisphere. DeRenzi et al (1970a) examined the capacities for visual and tactile exploration of space in brain-damaged subjects. They found deficits in the contralateral field and in both modalities in all groups of subjects with unilateral hemispheric lesions by comparison with normal controls, but the deficits were significantly greater with right-sided lesions. Oxbury et al (1974) reported that 7 of 17 patients with right hemispheric lesions had unilateral spatial agnosia, while none of 15 patients with left hemispheric lesions had the syndrome.

By contrast Costa and Vaughan (1962), studying groups of brain-damaged subjects by approximately the same methods as Gainotti (1968), found no significant differences between the two sides. But the results of Costa et al may be skewed by the presence of left-handers in the population, 6 in the group with left hemispheric lesions, 2 in the group with right.

A different approach to the problem was taken by Leicester et al (1969). This approach, which will need verification, may perhaps resolve some of the problems concerning the lateralization of lesions causing unilateral inatten-tion syndromes. The test involved a matching-to-sample task, with the pre-sentations of stimuli in the auditory, visual, or tactile modalities occurring either simultaneously or after a delay. Choices for response were always vi-sual and were displayed on a 3 × 3 grid of back-lit panels. Stimulus material included isolated letters, trigrams, words, color names, colors, names of num-bers, numbers, and dots for counting.

Scores indicate the degree to which a tendency to neglect is present, de-termined by calculating the number of presses on panels on one side by comparison with the total number of presses. With this technique they found contralateral neglect in 14 of 18 subjects with left hemispheric lesions and in 6 of 6 subjects with right hemispheric lesions. Even in those cases in which neglect was present, it was manifested only on those tests using stimulus material difficult for the subject. Thus neglect was specific to both hemi-sphere and material. Left hemispheric lesions, but not right, produced con-tralateral neglect for isolated letters presented through the auditory channel. Neglect was found to be related to an inability to give correct responses either of a spatial or of a nonspatial type.

From their results these authors concluded that theoretically five different forms of contralateral neglect of space could exist. Two of these could appear in isolation from other symptoms and would thus represent a fundamental tendency to neglect. The other three would require the presence of other defects for the syndrome of neglect to become manifest. The first form of these last three syndromes would be the inability to provide a nonspatial response to objects presented in the field contralateral to the lesion; such would be the case in patients with left hemispheric lesions with language defects. The other two would find manifestations of neglect resulting either from difficulties in responding correctly to the spatial qualities of the objects themselves (their shapes) or from reduced ability to manipulate the spatial aspects of the task. Neglect of hemispace and hemicorporeal neglect would be the clinical corre-lates of these latter two disturbances and would be related to lesions of the minor hemisphere. Neglect in these cases would not be equivalent to the spatial deficit; because this hemisphere possesses spatial and somatognosic functions, the neglect would be manifested in these ways.

Heilman et al (1974) contend that the basic defect underlying the syn-dromes of neglect is a unilateral deficit in arousal mechanisms resulting from a corticolimbic-reticular activating system disconnection. Because of the fre-quent association between unilateral spatial agnosias and visual field defects, oculomotor defects, and impaired consciousness, it is natural that those au-thors who do not accept the preferential relationship of this syndrome to right hemispheric lesions would assume that unilateral spatial agnosia is the result of a combination of visual sensory and oculomotor deficits and reduced vigilance. Several statistical studies have, however, demonstrated that unilateral spatial agnosia, while often associated with these other defects, is not always and is not necessarily associated with them (Gainotti, 1968; Hécaen, 1972a; Albert, 1973).

Unilateral neglect may not be limited to the visual modality; auditory and tactile stimuli may be ignored, and motor hemiaspontaneity may occur. Thus, according to classical terminology, this syndrome is not truly one of agnosia, because the disorder involves more than a single sensory channel. Nonetheless, as demonstrated in the studies of tactile and visual spatial exploration of DeRenzi et al (1970a), the deficit causing the syndrome is not sensorimotor. The deficit is the result of impaired performance at a level higher than that of sensorimotor function; for these subjects, internal representations of space have become distorted.

Despite arguments to the contrary the bulk of the evidence from clinical experience and experimental studies supports the view that unilateral spatial agnosia is a syndrome related to right hemispheric dysfunction. This conclusion becomes more secure by addition of the following qualification: syndromes of neglect, if they are relatively mild or transient, may result from lesions of either hemisphere, but severe and long-lasting unilateral neglect is almost exclusively seen with right hemispheric lesions (Albert, 1973). Gainotti (1968), in his study of neglect in patients with unilateral brain damage, found that right-sided hemi-inattention syndromes not only were mild but also had different characteristics from those in the left field. In the right field the subjects could correct their errors if attention was stimulated; this was not true for errors in the left field. Hécaen et al (1952a) had previously noted that, with left-sided lesions, patients had difficulty closing off the right side of their drawings. Instead of neglecting the right side, these subjects persisted in working on the right side of the drawing without being able to complete the work accurately.

Loss of Topographical Concepts (Mental Maps)   The loss of the ability to conceptualize topographical relationships was mentioned by Marie et al (1922) in their description of planotopokinesia. Their patients were unable to orient themselves on a map. These disorders were particularly stressed in studies by McFie et al (1950) and Hécaen et al (1951). Subjects, when shown an unlabeled map, were unable to indicate locations of major cities or to indicate appropriate directions for traveling from one point to another, despite previous knowledge of the geographic area represented by the map. In a map of their own city they were unable to trace the route of a simple itinerary or to locate the region in which they lived.

At times it seemed as if these subjects were able to describe verbally the topographical relationships that they were unable to indicate on the map.

But as Benton (1969b) has pointed out, these verbal descriptions were poor and shallow, consisting of simple recitations of streets, squares, cities, and regions, with no true description of the relations between these various locations.

It is possible to analyze this disorder by quantitative means with the use of various special tests. For example, after drawing the outline of the examining room on a sheet of paper, the examiner may ask the subject to indicate the respective positions of windows, furniture, doors, and so forth. Maze running tests may also be used to quantitate the defect. If errors described on such tests are limited to one side of space, they may simply reflect the phenomena of hemi-inattention. It should be added that difficulties with topographical relations have usually been associated with other elements symptomatic of right parietotemporo-occipital junction lesions. However, a study by Benton et al (1975) on perception of line direction in patients with unilateral cerebral disease did not confirm the right hemispheric predominance for such deficits.

Semmes et al (1955, 1960) presented a route-finding test to subjects with traumatic brain injuries. The test involved specially prepared maps presented for visual or haptic association. The authors observed that subjects with parietal lobe lesions, right or left, had significant deficits on this test by comparison with normal subjects and those without parietal lesions. These observations do not correspond with data from clinical studies. Clinical experience strongly points to the major role of right posterior lesions in the production of

Geographic disorientation in patient with bilateral cerebrovascular pathology.

this syndrome (McFie et al, 1950; Hécaen et al, 1951; 1956; Hécaen, 1962). Experimental studies by Elithorn (1962, 1964), using a perceptual maze test, supported the clinical evidence.

Similarly Milner (1956), using a test of visually guided maze learning, and Corkin (1965), using a test of tactually guided maze learning, found evidence for a right hemispheric posteriorly located function necessary for doing these tasks. Results, similar on both sets of tests, thereby suggested that the function in question may be supramodal. Performances by subjects with right hemispheric lesions were significantly inferior to those by subjects with left-sided damage. Deficits for all groups were markedly increased when the hippocampus was included in the ablation; they were most severe when the hippocampal lesions were bilateral. With large right parietal lesions also the deficits were considerable. With small parietal lesions, however, either right or left, the deficits were not significant. Frontal lesions also impaired performance on these tests but apparently for different reasons.

The conclusions of these studies may be formulated as follows. (1) An impaired ability to learn a maze, independently of the sensory modality involved, appears following right hemispheric lesions. (2) The nature of the defect may vary according to intrahemispheric localization: (a) a true learning disorder specific for the right hemisphere (hippocampus), (b) a disorder of spatial orientation (large posterior right-sided lesions or large right parietal lesions), or (c) phenomena of perseveration or inability to follow rules (frontal lobe). These conclusions are consistent with clinical experience emphasizing the importance of right-sided lesions.

Additional studies support these conclusions. In a neuropsychological study of subjects with localized missile wounds of the brain (that is, with a population similar to that used in the Semmes et al, 1955, study), Newcombe (1969) evaluated responses on a visual test of maze learning. Performances were significantly impaired in the group with right-sided lesions by comparison with the group with left-sided lesions. The most severe impairments were found in the group with posterior, or more specifically parietal damage. Hécaen (1972b) found patients with right posterior lesions to be more impaired than those with left-sided damage on a route-finding task. Posterior lesions bilaterally caused greater deficits than anterior lesions. The defects associated with right hemispheric lesions were especially correlated with parietal damage.

But not all experimental data are in accord. Ratcliff and Newcombe (1973) studied brain-injured subjects with two tests: a visually guided maze-learning task and a route-finding task with a visually presented map as a guide. Subjects with right posterior lesions were impaired on the maze-learning task. Defective route finding was present only in the group with bilateral posterior lesions. A degree of uncertainty thus exists concerning the lateralization of brain damage responsible for these disorders, as well as the intrahemispheric localization. In a report of his own studies, Hécaen (1972b) cited disorders of topographical concepts as occurring in 27 of 174 patients with right hemispheric lesions (16%) and in 22 of 273 patients with left-sided lesions (8%, $p<0.01$). With respect to intrahemispheric localization significant correlations were found between the frequency of occurrence of these disorders and lesions of parietal and of occipital lobes.

In our opinion it seems reasonable to accept that right hemispheric lesions impair map orientation and maze learning by different mechanisms. Hippocampal lesions would affect the learning components; posterior parietal lesions would cause a loss of ability to respond to spatial cues. As for the observations of Semmes et al (1955, 1960) that the left hemisphere is involved in topographical concepts, it may be that, as Newcombe (1969) has suggested, deficits on their route-finding task following left hemispheric lesions were due to impaired ability to discriminate right from left. Another possibility is that, when a subject has to follow a map while walking along its directed path, he uses verbal cues; these, then, would be deficient with left-sided lesions.

It should be reiterated that 8% of patients with left hemispheric lesions in the Hécaen (1962) series had impairment of topographical concepts. With respect to intrahemispheric localization for the left hemisphere significant correlations were found between the frequency of impairment and lesions of parietal and of temporal lobe. Newcombe (1969) also reported a parietal predominance for production of deficit in those of her patients with left hemispheric involvement.

Loss of Topographical Memory (Spatial Orientation)   With this disorder a brain-damaged person is unable to orient himself in space. He is unable to identify and follow routes or to recognize familiar places. He has lost the ability to benefit from spatial cues that he uses, consciously or automatically, to guide him in his movement from one place to another. To move about, the patient must now construct a new system for guidance.

For example, the patients described by Meyer (1900) and Paterson and Zangwill (1944) were able to return home from trips by referring to tramway numbers, street signs, and other concrete cues such as the color of houses near their own. A patient described by Hécaen (1972b) complained that he "could no longer call to mind the location of streets with respect to his house." The patient described by Wilbrand (1892) clearly indicated this technique of using concrete cues for spatial orientation. To go from her own home to a friend's, she said, "I know that from here, from my house, I have to turn to the corner on the left, then I come to the cobblestone road, then I only have a few steps to go before coming to a store that I often go into. When I reach that store, I am more secure, because I know I'm on the right road. I continue as far as. . . . Oh my goodness, I reach that place with all the buses striped in red and white; and from there on, I'm stuck. I have to ask every two or three steps if I don't want to get lost." Patients specify that their problem is one of identification of routes or places. Even in familiar surroundings, the disorientation persists.

Sometimes the patients cannot evoke the image of familiar places; sometimes they can revisualize these places and provide a precise description. Occasionally neighborhoods and particular buildings, which had previously been familiar to the patient and which he no longer recognized since the onset of his illness, provoke a sentiment of strangeness and discovery, as if the patient were suddenly placed in an entirely new environment.

A certain degree of generalized amnesia, either of the fixation type (Jackson, 1932; Meyer, 1900; Paterson and Zangwill, 1944) or of a more extensive nature, has often been reported as an associated symptom. These mnestic defects may disappear or considerably diminish during the illness, while the orientation defects may persist. In one series full consciousness and lucidity were present in 7 of 15 subjects who were unable to use topographic cues to orient themselves in familiar surroundings or in the hospital.

We believe, thus, that the disorder consists essentially of an inability to recognize the identity of topographical cues. The category and even the style of buildings in the city or furniture in the house can be identified. A church, apartment building, table, or bed, for instance, can be recognized as such, but they have lost their usefulness as identifiable cues for spatial orientation, regardless of how familiar they may have been to the patient before his illness. In milder cases certain topographical cues learned and overlearned during a long period of time may still be usable, but the patient gets lost in a new environment, such as the hospital.

It is necessary to distinguish this disorder from a series of other disorders in which spatial disorientation devolves from other mechanisms. The subject may lose his way because he systematically neglects the left side of space; he may confuse left and right; in unfamiliar places he may be unable to build a mental map of the necessary route to follow. In these cases the nature of buildings in a city or furniture, doors, and windows in a room will permit him to correct his errors. Of course the mechanisms of temporospatial disorientation as seen in confusional states or Korsakoff's syndrome should also be excluded.

Loss of topographical memory is a rare syndrome. Hécaen et al (1952a) found it in only 15 of 398 patients with brain damage. The syndrome is rarely found in isolation, and its associated symptomatology is similar to that found with the syndrome of loss of topographical concepts. The symptoms of unilateral spatial agnosia are usual accompaniments, as well as constructional apraxia, and the spatial dyslexias, dyscalculias, and dysgraphias.

A particularly frequent association is agnosia for faces. In the 1963 series of Hécaen and Angelergues prosopagnosia was present in 8 of 11 patients with loss of topographical memory. This conjunction of two rare perceptual disorders naturally poses the problem of their possible common underlying basis. Buildings and faces have lost their individual, special identities, and single mnestic factor could be invoked to explain both disorders. When, however, this notion was examined experimentally by means of a test of recognition of photographs, no correlation was found between failures on recognition of faces and those on recognition of buildings. Moreover, although the frequency of occurrence of prosopagnosia is high in the presence of impaired topographical memory, the converse is not true. Only 36% of 22 patients with prosopagnosia also had loss of topographical memory. Nonetheless it is worth considering that these statistical studies do not tell the whole story. Just as it is possible for a patient with a manifest syndrome of prosopagnosia to perform well on standardized tests of matching pictures of faces, so it may be possible for these individual patients with this unusual syndrome to have a highly specific disorder of visual memory limited to faces and to topographical locations.

Concerning anatomoclinical correlations the majority of cases with autopsies had bilateral lesions. Some authors maintained that the left occipital lobe was dominant for this function (e.g., Foerster, 1890; Wilbrand, 1892; Sachs, 1895; Meyer, 1900). But others contended that the right hemisphere played the dominant role (Patterson and Zangwill, 1944; McFie et al, 1950). Of two patients with this syndrome operated on by Penfield the epileptic zone ablated was in the posterior portion of the right hemisphere. A detailed report by Pommé and Janny (1954) described a patient who developed a transient loss of topographical memory following a highly restricted, 3-centimeter excision of the right hemispheric angular gyrus region; the operation was conducted for excision of a more deeply located tumor. In their collected clinical experience Hécaen and Angelergues 1963 were able to confirm a right hemispheric localization in 8 of 12 cases. In all of their verified cases the occipital lobe was affected. More recently Ratcliff and Newcombe (1973) found deficits in topographical memory on a motor maze test only with subjects having bilateral posterior lesions. Patients with unilateral lesions did not differ from controls.

This review of anatomoclinical evidence and of experimental neuropsychological research at least partially substantiates the intuitions of clinicians, such as Reichardt (1907), Lange (1936), Dide (1938), and Pötzl (1924), who argued that the right hemisphere was important for the organization and recognition of spatial data. One cannot help but be struck by the fact that this functional specialization of the so-called minor hemisphere manifests itself in many ways, including disorders of elementary perception, perception of horizontality and verticality, and of depth, as well as disorders as complex as that of spatial disorientation in one's familiar surroundings or with symbolic spatial representations, as on a real or mental map. At all levels, from the simplest to the most complex, the impairment of spatial organization due to right hemispheric dysfunction is not limited to the visual modality but is manifested in other sensory modalities and also in gestural behavior.

DeRenzi et al (1970a,b) have argued that right hemispheric dominance for spatial activity is present only for elementary tasks (visual coordinates, perception of depth). When the task is more complex, right hemispheric lesions do not cause significantly more deficits than left-sided lesions. With highly complex tasks it is the posterior location of the lesions, right or left, that is linked to the deficit. At this level of function the contribution of each hemisphere may be different—mainly spatial for the right hemisphere and verbal for the left.

We believe that the various results presented here, both for elementary and for complex tasks, are not in harmony with this hypothesis. We do, however, agree with the notions, implicit in the hypothesis, that verbal "intellectual" functions and frontal lobe factors (e.g., related to visual attention) must be better defined for complete understanding of neuropsychological mechanisms of spatial perception.

That frontal lobe lesions cause disturbances in visual perception in animals has been recognized for many years (Bianchi, 1895; Kennard, 1939; Welch and Stutteville, 1958). In man the role of frontal lesions in visual perception has also been invoked. For example, for the perception of reversible figures, a diminution of reversals was observed following any unilateral lesion, left or right. The diminution was greater with right- than left-sided lesions and was greater still with frontal lesions of either hemisphere (Cohen, 1959).

A similar distribution of deficits was found by Albert and Hécaen (1971) on a test of visual perception of relative movement. A significant difference was noted between scores of normal persons and those of any brain-damaged group, the deficit being greater in the group with right-brain damage. In each group anterior lesions caused more severe defects than posterior lesions did. Greatest errors followed frontal lesions, right or left. Tzavaras et al (1972) analyzed scores of 35 subjects on two perceptual tasks: appreciation of visual coordinates and perception of relative movement. A high correlation of scores on both tests existed only for the group with right anterior lesions.

These studies provide evidence in favor of the proposition of Albert and Hécaen (1971) that at least two factors may underlie visuospatial perception and that these two factors may be dissociated by different lesions. One factor would be static, related to perception of position, and associated mainly with the right hemisphere but not exclusively its posterior portion. The other factor would be kinetic and would be associated with frontal lobe activity, both left and right. The participation of anterior cerebral regions in perceptual activity may find its explanation (cf. Teuber, 1961) in the mechanism of corollary discharge. This corollary discharge provides information about active movement of the subject to regions of the brain responsible for perception.

Balint's Syndrome

Clinical Aspects   In 1909 Balint described a new syndrome under the name *psychic paralysis of gaze*. The syndrome consisted of three essential elements: a characteristic disturbance of gaze, optic ataxia, and impaired "visual attention." *The disturbance of gaze* is manifested by the inability of the subject to orient his eyes at will toward a point in his peripheral field of vision, although in other situations in which higher cortical functions are not implicated, ocular motility is normal. *The optic ataxia* may be demonstrated by means of tests that document the inability of the subject to perform coordinated, conjugate voluntary eye movement when these are solely under visual control; when proprioception is the only means of control, eye movements may be executed correctly. *Impaired visual attention* refers to the situation that occurs when attention is normal for all stimuli except visual; for visual stimuli, attention is globally diminished. Only the strongest stimuli, that is, macular, succeed in penetrating to consciousness. Peripheral stimuli are not seen by the subject, even though his visual fields are normal and his peripheral visual apparatus is capable of functioning correctly. In addition the defective visual attention is more marked on the left, the subject's gaze always being directed spontaneously toward the right.

From the time of Balint's original observation until the early 1950s the only report of a case including all three elements of the syndrome was that of Holmes (1918a). In 1950 and 1954 Hécaen et al reported four observations of the syndrome, of which the first faithfully reproduced Balint's description. Since then, although the number of reports has been low, occasional observations have appeared in print.

Manifestations of the syndrome may be considered according to each of the three main aspects. Psychic paralysis of gaze refers to the inability to displace one's gaze voluntarily from the point of fixation. No peripheral stimulus is sufficient to capture visual attention. For example, one patient was offered a lit match to help him light his cigarette. The match was brought to within 3–4 centimeters from the end of the cigarette. The patient was looking at the tip of the cigarette held between his lips and was unable to respond visually to the presence of the flame. Cogan and Adams (1953) have called this peculiar paralysis of conjugate gaze "oculomotor apraxia." Their patient, when asked to name the color of the examiner's tie, gave the color of the tie being worn by another person, since the patient's gaze had been fixed on this other person's tie at the time the question was asked. A patient described by Allison et al (1969) poured water from a bottle onto the table next to the glass sitting on the table. When gaze has not become fixed, the patient's eyes may wander until they fall upon an object by chance and then fixate on that object.

Optic ataxia is revealed by the gross errors that occur when a subject wishes to grasp an object he is currently looking at. In Balint's case the disorder was lateralized, being much more severe for the right hand than for the left. In one of Hécaen's (1964) cases the errors were more severe with the left hand.

Spontaneous attention of the subject for any visual stimulus is markedly reduced. Visual attention tends to be concentrated on whatever passes directly into the axis of fixation. This disorder is manifested somewhat as a concentric narrowing of the field of attention. The patients are physically able to sweep a broad field with their gaze and will do it, if they have not fixed on a single object; in general, however, they do not scan broadly.

Luria et al (1963) described a patient who was normally capable of perceiving objects and geometric figures when presented singly, but he could not perceive several objects presented simultaneously. If two objects were presented tachistoscopically, he perceived one or the other but not both at the same time, unless they were identical objects or were fused into a single structure. For example, if a star composed of two overlapping triangles was presented as the stimulus, the subject always recognized the star, without reference to the triangles. If the triangles were drawn each with a different color, the patient perceived one or another of the triangles but never the star. This patient, with what Luria called a disorder of simultaneous visual synthesis, also had difficulties with spatial orientation, reading, picture interpretation, and visual perception of number.

Most striking in these clinical reports is the patient's fixation of gaze. But aside from the relatively rare syndrome we are discussing, fixation of gaze is not a rare phenomenon. It has been observed in a number of other conditions. Many authors have noted this disorder especially with respect to reading. Kleist (1933) described this problem, which he called weakness of peripheral gaze, in many states of cerebral dysfunction; he referred specifically to the difficulty in directing one's gaze toward a point in the periphery of the visual field when the gaze has already been fixed on a given point. Best (1917) commented on this problem with respect to perception of visual number; a patient is unable to enumerate a series of identical items. We believe that fixation of gaze is a symptom of an underlying disorder, and not the disorder itself. Gordon Holmes (1918) isolated the symptom and applied the name *spasmodic fixation of gaze*, first given by Gowers (1885). He compared this disorder to the spasmodic paralysis of a limb characterized by a reduction of strength, a diminution of voluntary movement, and a heightened tone, all of which together tended to immobilize the limb (or the gaze) in a particular position, difficult to overcome.

In our opinion Balint's syndrome is present only when all three elements appear in the clinical picture, even if one or another of them is transitory. The isolated finding of one or another of these elements is not enough for the diagnosis. Several reports have tended to describe partial aspects of Balint's syndrome, calling them "minor forms" of the syndrome (Hoff and Pötzl, 1935b; Cogan and Adams, 1953; Hécaen and de Ajuriaguerra, 1954; Faust, 1955; Luria et al, 1963; Botez et al, 1965; Tyler, 1968). In these minor forms fixation of gaze is less absolute; some ability for voluntary movement of gaze is preserved. The phenomenon of wandering gaze, preceding or following fixation of gaze, is less marked. In consequence patients may succeed in distinguishing and recognizing two almost identical objects presented simultaneously. In tests of perception of the number of items presented visually the subject's gaze is not limited to only those items that fall within the visual axis along a frontal plane. In these forms unilateral spatial neglect may be quite marked; optic ataxia is then predominant in the same field that is being neglected. Impairments of visual attention are not intense and tend to be variable.

Optic ataxia may appear in isolated fashion, most often unilaterally, and be either ipsilateral or contralateral to the lesion. Optic ataxia results from a defective transmission of visual information to the motor region and may, as a consequence, have different features, depending on the precise localization of the lesion within the crossed and uncrossed visuomotor pathways (Rondot, 1976). Boller er al (1975) hypothesized that impairment of visually guided movement in *both* visual fields requires at least two lesions, one in each hemisphere (or a unilateral lesion combined with a complete commissurectomy). These lesions would have to be placed so as to disconnect motor cortex from visual input. Tzavaras and Masure (1976) confirmed that a posterior parietal lesion could produce optic ataxia in the contralateral visual hemifield, and that the nature of the disorder was different depending on which hemisphere was damaged.

Electrooculographic studies have been used to investigate the two main features of oculomotor dysfunction: the wandering of gaze in the search for an object to fixate on and the rigidity of fixation once the object has, by chance, been discovered (Luria et al, 1963; Botez et al, 1965; Michel et al, 1965; Tyler, 1968; Allison et al, 1969). In Luria's (1963) case, pursuit movements for a luminous source were intact, but visual scanning was defective. In another study Michel et al (1965) found delayed oculomotor reaction time, ocular movements in all directions when a subject conducted a visual search, and a succession of low-amplitude movements during visual exploration of a picture; pursuit movements following a moving light in the darkness were, however, normal. Tyler (1968) found that the reflex response time for visual fixation following presentation of a picture was normal, but visual scanning was abnormal; no large saccades necessary for relating different portions of a visual scene were found.

Anatomic Considerations   In all clinical studies with associated anatomic confirmation, bilateral lesions were found (Balint, 1909; Hoff and Pötzl, 1935b; Hécaen et al, 1950, 1954; Michel et al, 1965; Porowski, 1965; Gloning et al, 1968). In all such cases lateral cortical lesions affecting parieto-occipital areas were demonstrated. The medial and inferior surfaces of occipital lobes were not necessarily involved.

In addition to the necessary role of bilateral parieto-occipital lesions, arguments have been put forth concerning the role of the frontal lobes. Holmes (1918a), referring to the frontal eye fields, area 8, believed that frontal lesions were necessary for production of spasmodic fixation of gaze. However, in some cases of Balint's syndrome, frontal lobe lesions have been demonstrated, and in other cases, they have not. Perhaps deeply seated lesions in the posterior portions of the hemispheres disconnect frontal from occipital regions, producing an effect equivalent to that caused by frontal lesions themselves. It seems, however, that the full syndrome in its severe and complete form requires frontal lesions associated with those located posteriorly (Hécaen et al, 1950).

Theoretical Considerations   For Balint (1909) the syndrome he was describing resulted from a defect in spontaneous attention related to the "psychic portion of the visual act."

The role of oculomotor disorders in the production of agnosic phenomena was retained by Holmes (1918b, 1919) and Pieron (1923) to explain phenomena of visual disorientation thought due to bilateral angular gyrus lesions. "One of the functions of these gyri," he asserted, "is the reflex adaptation of the eyes to peripheral stimuli, or the integrative coordination of afferent impressions which, because of efferent centers, produce appropriate ocular movements in response to retinal excitation." Kleist (1933) also stressed the importance of oculomotor disorders in these patients. In 11 of 53 patients with occipital lesions and "cortical blindness for place," inability to fixate and, occasionally, oculomotor ataxia were found. For these subjects, elements of peripheral portions of space could not be properly integrated into the central elements falling within the focus of visual attention. For Kleist (1933) disorders of visual attention and disorders of oculomotor function were merely two aspects of the same process.

Thus, by these bilateral lesions, wandering gaze, occurring when the subject wants to fixate, may be explained. To explain the fixation that follows the wandering, recourse must again be made to bilaterality of lesions. Frontal oculomotor centers exercise an inhibitory control on occipital centers. With a unilateral posterior lesion, frontal control can still be maintained, since occipital centers for vision in each hemisphere are connected. With bilateral lesions, frontal inhibitory control on the relationship between oculomotor influx and visual stimuli can no longer be maintained. Voluntary control of visual gaze is thus lost, and fixation comes under the influence of proprioceptive and other, nonfrontal mechanisms. The eyes are free to wander randomly.

During these disorganized excursions of eye movements, when an object falls into the central field of vision, the proprioceptive response that results acts on the frontal areas, with no counterbalancing effect from visual responses. Thereby gaze becomes fixed. To reinforce this fixation, one adds the relative impairment of responsiveness at a purely sensory level to stimuli appearing in the peripheral field. Holmes (1918a) emphasized especially the role of ocular and cephalic muscle afferents in the process of localization of objects with respect to one's body. For him visual stimuli provided only bidimensional images, but spatial localization depended on the link between visual and proprioceptive processes. This link represented the physiological equivalent of the psychological judgment that was dependent on this particular physiological activity.

The association of optic ataxia with psychic paralysis of gaze may be incorporated into the framework of the same theoretical explanation. Optic ataxia represents the disorganization of sensorimotor association mechanisms necessary for integration of spatial data. Thus one could understand why patients with psychic paralysis of gaze would also have difficulty with visual estimations of distance.

From the studies of Gelb and Goldstein (1924) we know that a spiral narrowing of the visual field occurs when a single region is stimulated during a prolonged interval. Other authors (e.g., Stein, 1928) have shown that the exhaustion that occurs in the region of excessive and prolonged stimulation may radiate toward unstimulated regions. It may be argued, from this, that if there exists a reduced functional capacity for peripheral field stimulation in Balint's syndrome, then repeated stimulation in the periphery produces a reaction of cellular exhaustion that radiates toward the central field; the patient may involuntarily react to this by constant ocular movement.

Kleist (1933) proposed that weakness of peripheral gaze, together with weakness of central gaze, are the necessary conditions underlying inability to maintain fixation, whereas weakness of peripheral gaze alone would underlie a tendency toward excessive fixation, for example, of the type of spasmodic fixation described by Holmes (1918a). As for the causes of weakness of peripheral gaze, they would find their origins in local fluctuations of excitability thresholds (in the sense defined by Stein, 1928). In such terms the question of Balint's syndrome would then be related to phenomena of extinction. Denny-Brown and Banker (1954) invoked a similar pathophysiological explanation. The visuospatial disorientations seen in Balint's syndrome and in related syndromes of perceptual impairment represented bilateral amorphosynthesis. They had to be distinguished from true agnosic phenomena, such as may be represented by the loss of topographical memory.

Luria et al (1963), referring to Pavlovian hypotheses, argued that the clinical defects, described in this section, resulted from a general functional weakening of parieto-occipital areas. Each focal zone of excitation within these cerebral regions inhibited the rest of the visual cortex by negative induction. When several stimuli were presented simultaneously, very few of these excitation foci were sufficiently functional to permit a perceptual response. The subject thus perceived only a limited aspect of the total stimulus.

Tyler (1968) contended that these perceptual disorders resulted from a combination of deficits of temporal and spatial recognition of visual stimuli plus disorders of oculomotor exploration. The portion of the visual field that remained functional was considerably reduced in efficiency by sensorimotor integration defects. Michel et al (1965) argued that the basic problem was a difficulty in modulating visual afferents as the inputs traveled from macular to peripheral fields and back.

Unit cell studies by Mountcastle et al (1975) on the properties of cells in areas 5 and 7 provide a basis for understanding human clinical pathological states. Bilateral lesions of these areas bring about a bilateral loss of visual attention and, at the same time, cause defects in the projection of the movement (optic ataxia). It seems that oculomotor and visuospatial sensory defects are intimately linked in the production of this syndrome, which alternates in manifestation between spasmodic fixation and wandering of gaze in visual search.

Theoretical Considerations and Conclusions

By the term *optic* (visual) *agnosia* we refer to a group of perceptual disorders concerning discrimination and recognition of objects, complex meaningful or meaningless forms, faces or their representations, and spatial information, limited to the visual modality. These perceptual disorders may be found in the absence of primary sensory defects, general intellectual deterioration, or confusion.

We exclude from the category of visual agnosia the nonrecognition of graphic signs (alexia); for us, this disorder represents a specific form of language defect concerned with the decoding of written signs. However, other authors have argued an opposing point of view. The posterior localization of lesions causing pure alexia and the absence of disorders of spoken language and of writing, other than of copying, have been used as evidence that pure alexia represents a specialized form of visual agnosia. Still other authors have contended that pure alexia, at least for some of its aspects, represents a disconnection syndrome resulting from a callosal lesion.

Descriptions of the different opticoagnostic disturbances have given such an impression of heterogeneity that one can easily understand the wall of resistance that has been built up against the very notion of agnosia. Rejection of a term considered to be dangerous seems legitimate, if acceptance of that term implies acceptance of a unitary process underlying a variety of separate mechanisms that individually or in combination produce the various clinical manifestations. We are willing to accept the term *agnosia*, with the understanding that for us it does not imply a single underlying neuropsychological process that, when damaged, leads to the different syndromes. If one considers the clinical features of the syndromes in isolation, in some cases there is monosensory involvement, in some cases polysensory; at times a memory component is prominent, at times a perceptual; occasionally language is a relevant factor and occasionally oculomotor function is; and so on.

Confronted with the multiplicity of disorders and mechanisms responsible for the disorders, can one successfully categorize? We believe so. Lateralization of lesions that produce the different syndromes provides a basis for systematization of clinical and experimental data. With right hemispheric lesions one finds disorders of recognition of complex forms, of human faces, and of spatial information. With left hemispheric lesions one finds disorders of recognition of graphic symbols, objects, pictures, and colors. In addition, with right hemispheric lesions, the disorders are often not limited to a single sensory modality; they may be polysensorial and integrated with gestural disorders, resulting in the syndrome of apractognosia (Hécaen et al, 1956).

Some authors (e.g., Kimura, 1963; Milner, 1969) hold that within each hemisphere the lesions disturb performance according to the nature of material presented. This hemisphere-dependent material specificity appears regardless of the test used—recognition, learning, or recall. If the material is verbal or easily verbalizable, the deficit manifests itself with left hemispheric lesions; if the material is nonverbal, the deficit follows right hemispheric lesions. This hemispheric difference is not limited to the visual systems, that is, is not modality specific.

Directed by the guidelines implicit in this brief introduction, we consider each of the major groupings of visual agnostic symptoms and examine the degree to which the facts correspond to this systematization.

Visual Object Agnosia

The clinical reality of agnosia for objects, despite its rarity, cannot be denied. The argument should concentrate more on the specificity of this syndrome as a disturbance in the appreciation of the meaning of seen objects. The contention of Bay (1950) that all defects in object identification depend exclusively on the combination of subtle disturbances of visual sensation and a reduced level of consciousness is difficult to defend. How can this argument be correct when cases of visual object agnosia without alexia appear in the neuropsychological literature? The visual sensory defect, in such a case, would have to be selective for big objects that can be seen and described but not recognized, whereas letters, numbers, and words can be seen and understood. One patient with visual object agnosia, unable to identify objects, letters, or colors, was nonetheless able to recognize faces of members of his family, even on small photographs (Hécaen and de Ajuriaguerra, 1956). Moreover, studies of Ettlinger (1956) failed to demonstrate a correlation between presence of visual agnosia and defective local adaptation of critical flicker fusion frequency. Recent case reports adequately prove that a disorder of visual recognition may be limited to objects or figurative pictures or to colors (Rubens and Benson, 1971; Lhermitte et al, 1973b; Hécaen et al, 1974). In exceptional cases visual object agnosia may even be present without alexia (Davidenkov, 1958; Albert et al, 1975a).

In some cases the argument has been that visual object agnosia is a disconnection syndrome: because of the (usual) right hemianopia, visual inputs reach only the right occipital lobe, and because of a lesion in the splenium of the corpus callosum, these inputs cannot be associated with the left hemispheric language areas and cannot be named. Dejerine proposed a disconnection hypothesis to explain one form of alexia. Although he described the callosal damage, he did not use that lesion to explain the dysfunction. He proposed that the white-matter lesion of the lingual lobule interrupted the pathways connecting the center for visual images (calcarine fissure) with the center for visual verbal images (angular gyrus). Geschwind (1965) modified this theory to explain impaired recognition of colors and objects. The clinicoanatomic arguments of Geschwind and his school have been supported, at least in part, by experimental studies of split-brain subjects (Sperry, Gazzaniga, and Bogen, 1969).

The disconnection theory cannot, however, apply to all cases. Hécaen (1972b), for example, cited the case of a patient with mild visual object agnosia with no right homonymous hemianopia. Some other argument must be used to explain this case, and others like it, because the visual inputs succeed in reaching the left hemisphere. In this case Hécaen stressed the dissociation occurring between defective recognition of meaningful designs and defective recognition of objects.

More recent observations (cited above) confirm the theoretical possibility of separating visual object agnosia from optic aphasia. In visual object agnosia subjects are unable to match objects in the same category, even though they can see and describe the objects. In addition, in several cases with object agnosia, the subjects had no disturbances of oral language, and, in fact, language seemed to compensate for the deficit.

DeRenzi et al (1966) rely for their conclusions on results of a statistical study of brain-damaged subjects with a series of "apperceptive" and "associative" tests. (The associative tests involved matching of real objects with pictures of similar, but nonidentical, objects in different colors and shapes.) Left hemispheric lesions caused defects on associative but not on perceptual tests. Right hemispheric lesions disturbed the perception of complex sensory inputs. These authors argued that right hemispheric lesions produced impairments comparable to Lissauer's apperceptive visual agnosia, while left hemispheric lesions produced defects comparable to Lissauer's associative visual agnosia. The patients with left-sided damage could not reach a conceptual level necessary for associating different sensory patterns and, thereby, allowing them to be recognized as members of the same conceptual reality. What they have lost is a higher gnostic function, the identification of meaning. DeRenzi et al (1966) emphasized that their patients with a severe degree of amnesic aphasia nonetheless performed well on the association test. This observation led them to believe that the defects on the association test could not be explained by naming difficulties. In addition the selectivity of recognition defect, as reported by certain authors (Lissauer, 1890; Hécaen and de Ajuriaguerra, 1956), was further evidence that this variety of associative agnosia was a disorder of identification of meaning.

Several more recent case reports have added weight to the evidence in favor of the clinical reality of the syndrome and have provided additional theoretical arguments. Hécaen et al (1974) described a man with visual object agnosia accompanied by alexia and color agnosia. Their patient could recognize forms, faces, and spatial information. He had no aphasia and no general intellectual deterioration. By means of an extensive series of tests, these authors demonstrated that the agnosia in this case was associative and that the underlying defect may have been related to a deficit of categorization of visual inputs. Albert et al (1975) described a patient who had visual object agnosia without alexia. Their findings provided evidence that two neuropsychological mechanisms were responsible for the disorder. One was an interhemispheric visual-verbal disconnection; the other was a specific categorization defect for visual, nonverbal, meaningful stimuli. Neither mechanism alone was sufficient; both were necessary.

Disorders of Recognition of Complex Shapes

These disorders result from right hemispheric lesions, when the shapes cannot be named or are not easily verbalizable. We have already indicated, however, that evidence exists that posterior lesions of either hemisphere may cause defective visual perception of forms (Poeck et al, 1973; Masure and Tzavaras, 1976).

The disturbance is not limited to identification but includes a memory component. Moreover, it is probably not modality specific. Whatever the sensory modality tested or the type of test employed, it is the nonverbal nature of the material that represents the essential element for the deficit to develop. DeRenzi has disagreed with this formulation. According to him right hemispheric lesions cause deficits on any complex perceptual task, whether the material is verbalizable or not. The function of the right hemisphere is to receive and compare, discriminate, and integrate visual inputs.

DeRenzi's results were obtained from studies of tests administered to large numbers of subjects with unilateral brain damage. Etiology of illness and sites of damage were varied. Milner's (1969) and Kimura's (1963) studies, on the other hand, were completed with patients who had undergone temporal lobectomies. Perhaps in the Milner and Kimura studies the mnestic factor was more prominent than in the DeRenzi studies. Right temporal lesions may exaggerate the memory component of a gnostic defect while more posteriorly located (parietal or parieto-occipital) lesions may exaggerate the perceptual component. As we have already seen, this dichotomy between mnestic and perceptual functions has been demonstrated in animals and depends on the anterior or posterior localization of an inferotemporal ablation.

It is also possible that identification of these shapes requires appreciation not only of their intrinsic orientation but also of their general orientation in space. If a general visuospatial factor is necessary to the recognition of these shapes, then the issue of visuomotor integration must be considered. Feature detectors necessary for visual form perception are not sufficient, by themselves, to provide spatial correlates of shapes or to allow separation of overlapping figures.

Another factor to consider is that of a differential pattern of cerebral organization of functional representations in each hemisphere. For example, Dorff et al (1965) found differences in tachistoscopic recognition in the right and left visual fields following unilateral temporal lobe removals. When the right temporal lobe was removed, disorders of visual discrimination involved the entire visual field. With left temporal lesions the defects of visual recognition involved only the contralateral visual field, and the right temporal lobe could provide normal perception over both fields. Goldman et al (1968) found that lesions situated outside the visual areas (e.g., temporal lobectomy) could impair fundamental sensory functions (e.g., critical flicker fusion frequency) and that, even at this level of elementary sensation, cerebral dominance was a relevant factor.

In addition it is known that cortical lesions, whatever their location, produce impairments of visual analytic abilities concerning the Gottschaldt hidden figures. However, deficits on this test are significantly greater in aphasics than in the other brain-damaged groups (Teuber and Weinstein, 1956; Russo and Vignolo, 1967). According to the hypotheses of both Milner and De-Renzi, deficits on this complex perceptual task should have been the result of right and not left hemispheric lesions. To interpret these results, one might have recourse to Gestalt theory, which states that the deficit observed is one of abstraction, an impaired ability to differentiate figure from ground specifically linked to language disorders.

Impaired Recognition of Faces

Prosopagnosia was first considered to be a recognition defect for one particular category of visual inputs (Bodamer, 1947), then a loss of the ability to determine what is common to similar items (Faust, 1955), then as one of the apperceptive disorders caused by right hemispheric lesions (DeRenzi et al, 1968c), and finally as a manifestation of a special type of memory loss (Warrington and James, 1967; Milner, 1969). Studies in developmental psychology have indicated that the human face has special perceptual qualities for the infant (Fantz, 1962). Studies in experimental neuropsychology have shown that subjects with right hemispheric lesions may have isolated disturbances in facial recognition, with no other disorder of complex discriminations.

The question must be asked, then, whether or not a mechanism, specific to human beings, exists that may be activated, created, developed, or liberated by perceptual inputs, if these inputs are presented at a critical period of cerebral development, and that orients subsequent learning activity according to individual experience but in a direction prescribed by an innate apparatus. Appreciation of the identity of human faces, if such a mechanism existed, would result from the application of a system of rules acting on visual inputs extracted by feature detectors. Agnosia for faces would be the clinical manifestation of a breakdown in the application of these rules. The specificity of the syndrome could thus be understood; a face would be recognized as belonging to the general category of human faces, but the individual identity of this face would not be appreciated. The disorder would be the result of impairment of a function represented in the right hemisphere, just as aphasia reflects impairment of a left hemispheric function.

Color Agnosia

Contemporary notions of agnosia for colors represent a range of interpretations. This syndrome is considered to be similar to object agnosia, or it may be a gnostic disturbance in which acquired knowledge concerning the relationship between colors and objects has been lost (Lhermitte et al, 1969), or it may be an optic aphasia for colors resulting from a disconnection syndrome (Geschwind, 1965; Oxbury et al, 1969), or it may be an associative conceptual defect linked to language disorders (DeRenzi and Spinnler, 1967).

As for disturbances of color perception due to cortical damage, for one group of neuropsychologists they are part of the general defective apperception syndrome resulting from right hemispheric lesions (DeRenzi and Spinnler, 1967); for another group they appear only following bilateral lesions and represent an elementary sensory disorder (Lhermitte et al, 1969).

Discordances are, thus, major, concerning interpretations of defective color perception. From these varied opinions one may be justified in proposing that disorders of recognition of colors may range in clinical manifestation and theoretical basis from simple loss of color vision to complex syndromes in which language plays the essential role. The possibility exists that, in the absence of loss of color vision or language disturbance, the meaning of colors in their relationship to language may be lost.

Disorders of Spatial Perception and Orientation

Despite their diversity some common elements may be discerned in this group of disorders. They do not concern only the visual modality; they involve motor performance as well, to the point that praxic and gnostic deficiencies become indissociable. They are caused mainly by right hemispheric lesions.

Defective stereoscopic vision, unilateral spatial agnosia, loss of topographical concepts, and loss of topographical memory—these all seem to represent different functional disorders. For orientation in one's town or home, one uses different cues from those used for orientation on a map or with a maze. Mnestic factors can, however, be identified in both sets of activity. Memory does not seem to play a role in disorders of stereoscopic vision or in neglect of one side of space. But the polysensorial nature of the disorder of unilateral spatial agnosia has been demonstrated in tests of spatial orientation at many levels (e.g., deficits in route finding, Semmes et al, 1955; perception of orientation of a short rod, DeRenzi et al, 1970a,b; maze learning, Corkin, 1965; Milner, 1965).

Representation of behavioral functions in the brain seems to be more diffuse in the right than in the left hemisphere (Semmes et al, 1960; Hécaen and Angelergues, 1963). Any right hemispheric lesion is thus capable of causing a general disturbance of spatial orientation. The manifestations may vary, however, according to site and extent of the lesion, according to the sensory modality being tested, and according to the nature of the test.

Studies of animal and human neuropsychology have demonstrated the importance of extravisual factors in visual perception. Optically guided behavior requires sensorimotor feedback to permit appropriate adaptations. Active motor behavior, so important in the course of development, is also important in the process of adapting to the constantly changing pattern of sensory inputs in the adult. We also know that considerable evidence exists to support the view that two visual systems exist, one cortical, of feature detectors, to say what has been seen; the other subcortical, to say where the item is. The latter system, phylogenetically older, controls visuomotor coordination.

We might tentatively suggest that a telencephalization of visual mechanisms takes place in man and that integration of sensory and motor data is made especially in the right hemisphere. Areas of delayed myelinization, that is, association areas, would be responsible for this integration; polymodal cellular responses have already been demonstrated in these areas. In the monkey we have evidence of posterior parietal specialization for allocentric orientation (Pohl, 1973) and of cells in area 7 highly specialized for spatial activity (Hyvarinen and Poranen, 1974). Mountcastle et al (1975) have proposed that syndromes caused in man and monkey by destruction of areas 5 and 7 may be understood "as deficits of volition, of the will to explore with hand and eye the contralateral half field of space, a deficit caused by the loss of the command operations for those explorations which exist in the parietal association cortex."

A cortical lesion would create a situation in which perception and its sensory motor feedback would no longer be properly correlated; arrival of information from corollary discharges would be suppressed. Thereby integration of basic perceptual data necessary for organization of one's recognition of space would be distorted, and the abstract representation of this organization would be impossible. The patient would experience visual illusions, alterations of spatial constants, and loss of the relationship between bodily position and the surrounding world. Experimental evidence of the effects of focal cerebral lesions on contralateral visuomotor adaptation to reversal and inversion of visual feedback supports our speculative suggestion (e.g., Meier, 1970). In a test of visually guided placement of three-dimensional objects in their respective matrices, lateral reversal of visual feedback provoked a deficit of visuomotor adaptation of the hand contralateral to the lesion especially for right hemispheric lesions. Another study with brain-damaged subjects showed that patients with right hemispheric lesions were impaired in their ability to use kinesthetic feedback to improve their performance on a posture maintenance test (Carmon, 1970).

The specifically visual nature of these disorders of spatial perception would be more prominent the more posterior the lesion is located. If the lesion were located more anteriorly, involving the anteromedial portion of the temporal lobe, a memory factor would become more prominent. Situated at the level of the anterior parietal lobe, the lesion may disrupt spatial aspects of gestural behavior, for example, writing, calculations, drawing, and constructions. A massive lesion of the association areas, by suppressing several sensorimotor afferents at the same time, might interfere with the normal development of sensory awareness of the opposite half of space; an impairment of vigilance, added to the perceptual disorder, might prevent compensation. By contrast a small lesion restricted to the parietotemporo-occipital junction might interfere only with the manipulation of complex spatial inputs or their abstract representations.

General Considerations

On the basis of a general neuropsychological concept of functional hemispheric asymmetry, we may attempt to interpret disorders of visual recognition. We tentatively propose that, with left hemispheric lesions, the various clinical manifestations of visual agnosia have a relationship, obvious or latent, to disorders of language, whereas, with right hemispheric lesions, these visual recognition disorders relate to a basic disturbance in the function of spatial orientation, itself dependent on defective sensorimotor coordination. Right hemispheric lesions, perhaps because of disruption of an innately directed, acquired set of perceptual rules, also determine disorders of recognition of the individuality of human faces.

Some authors prefer to see in the notion of functional hemispheric asymmetry a dichotomy dependent on the verbal or nonverbal nature of stimulus material. Others argue that the right hemisphere receives, discriminates, and organizes sensory information, while the left hemisphere names and semantically associates these data to apprehend their meaning. In an earlier statement on this general issue Hécaen and Angelergues (1963) systematized gnostic activity of the hemispheres thus: the right hemisphere identifies sensory inputs by discriminating among objects of the same categroy, the left hemisphere categorizes objects and classifies them according to a code.

Although reservations and qualifications must be introduced, certain comparisons between anatomoclinical studies in human beings and ablation studies in monkeys may be relevant. Accordingly monkeys with occipital ablations have been called "agnosic" (Humphrey, 1970); although they can see objects, the objects are apparently formless and without meaning. These monkeys are unable to abstract the attributes of the objects or to recognize them. Monkeys with inferotemporal lesions have lost size constancies (Humphrey and Weiskrantz, 1969). In man, bilateral occipital destruction provokes cortical blindness, but we have already cited evidence demonstrating that a certain type of "blind field" vision may be retained—vision in which the attributes of the object may not be recognizable. Visual agnosias in man may be related to lesions of occipital (and parieto-occipital) convexity, whereas visual illusions seem to result from modifications of size constancies brought about by temporal or parietotemporo-occipital junction lesions. In both instances, functional hemispheric asymmetry influences the clinical expression of the cerebral lesion.

Other studies from animal neuropsychology show that visuoperceptual disorders in monkeys are primarily the sequelae of lesions of the posterior portion of the inferotemporal region, the preoccipital sulcus appearing to be critical in this regard. Anterior temporal ablations produce predominantly mnestic defects, although this is less evident in monkeys than in man (Iwai and Mishkin, 1969; Iversen and Weiskrantz, 1964, 1967). Weiskrantz (1972) advanced the hypothesis that the posterior portion of the inferotemporal region functions to select and maintain attention on visual cues that have become relevant as the result of processing of foveal information, while the anterior inferotemporal region permits "the establishment of cohesive categories of visual events in the form of abstractions that can be exploited with economy by other parts of the nervous system."

The concordance between this hypothesis derived from animal experimentation and those based on most recent analyses of visual agnosia in man (i.e., Hécaen et al, 1974; Albert et al, 1975a) is striking. Both hypotheses relate deficits of visual recognition to disordered capacity for visual categorization and both suggest that a specific anatomic region, albeit different in monkey and man, may be responsible for categorization. It seems that the new and essential development in the functional cortical organization of the human brain resides in the factor of hemispheric specialization. Research with split-brain subjects, with inputs restricted to a single hemisphere, suggests that each hemisphere has a different manner of treating information. A formulation of these differences, such as that proposed by Trevarthen (1974) for information processing by the normal hemisphere of a split-brain subject, seems equally valid for explaining perceptual deficits resulting from unilateral lesions. The left hemisphere may assume command of the response for any task requiring verbal manipulation; the right hemisphere for tasks requiring wordless, perceptual manipulation.

It may be premature to attempt syntheses of available evidence concerning disorders of visual recognition; however, these efforts, by virtue of converging results from various sources, bear witness to the utility of the neuropsychological research they engender. By presenting visual stimuli under conditions of increasing task difficulty (e.g., temporal restrictions, reduction of cues, increase of complexity, etc.), researchers have been able to demonstrate perceptual deficits that are not immediately apparent, even with careful observation, in the clinical behavior of brain-damaged subjects. Localization, or at least hemispheric lateralization, of lesions responsible for these perceptual defects has been determined. The state of elementary visual function (critical flicker fusion, local adaptation, brilliance discrimination, etc.) has been studied in detail and placed in its proper relationship to higher order perceptual disturbances.

In fact experimental methods applied to large numbers of brain-damaged subjects have provided results much less in contradiction with each other and with anatomoclinical experience than one might have predicted, given the variety of clinical manifestations and, especially, the antithetical hypotheses provided to explain these case descriptions. What is missing from current human neuropsychology are studies of individual patients with pure and unquestionable clinical neurobehavioral syndromes evaluated systematically and intensively by means of the same batteries of tests used in the larger series of unselected brain-damaged subjects. By means of these evaluations the state of function of different sensory processes can be determined, and disparate interpretations can be modified or rejected.

It may also happen that a particular clinical symptom may appear without the patient's failing on the specialized tests that supposedly measure this function. This is the case, in fact, with prosopagnosia; some patients with clinical prosopagnosia have been found to perform as normal persons on tests of recognition of pictures of faces. The danger of measuring, not the deficit underlying a particular behavioral function, but aptitudes on an artificial test can be overcome only by constant return from the laboratory to the clinical observation of patient behavior. This observation provides the basis not only for development of theoretetical models but also for the means of testing these models.

It seems abundantly clear, by now, that the presence of confusional states or general intellectual impairment cannot be invoked to explain the high degree of specificity found for some disorders of visual recognition. Patients with certain specific visual agnosic syndromes may be perfectly lucid or may have normal visual recognition for stimuli not related to their specific defect; what is more, the great majority of confused or demented patients do not manifest the specific disorders of visual recognition defined by the visual agnosic syndromes. Nevertheless, to exclude the role of confusion or intellectual deterioration from the issue of symptom intensity or persistence, one must systematically analyze the relationship, especially by longitudinal studies of the interaction between respective patterns of evolution of the specific defect and the general impairment.

Acuteness or chronicity of lesion, etiologic nature of the lesion, extent of lesion, age of patient, handedness, and sex are additional factors too often ignored, although they may be responsible for certain contradictions in results so far presented. Only a standardization of examination techniques will allow a valid comparison of data from one laboratory to another, despite the danger of stagnation that such a standardization might imply. Only a systematic analysis of anatomoclinical evidence can support valid conclusions concerning specificity of defect, relevance of possible underlying mechanisms, and anatomic basis. The problem posed by rarity of certain varieties of agnosia can be resolved only in this manner. By postulating the contributory role of certain underlying mechanisms in the production of a particular clinical state, one may imagine being able to simulate the disorder in subjects who do not have the particular clinical defect in question but who nonetheless have a lesion in a region supposedly responsible for that defect; the results obtained may confirm or provide evidence against the contribution of these underlying mechanisms in the production of the perceptual disturbance.

FIVE
DISORDERS
OF AUDITORY
PERCEPTION

ANATOMIC AND PHYSIOLOGICAL CONSIDERATIONS

This section does not deal with peripheral or brain stem mechanisms related to encoding of auditory information. We do, however, consider certain experimental aspects of the cortical connections of auditory inputs.

Animal Studies

Since the early research of Woolsey and Walzl in the 1940s, many studies have been conducted on cats, dogs, and monkeys with the aim of defining the map of auditory cortical representation. In essence these studies have shown that cortical projections of the cochlear nerve are directed to several specific regions and that cortical representation of auditory inputs is tonotopic. In 1961 Woolsey summarized data relating to the organization of the cortical auditory system of the cat, with special reference to stimulation studies of the cochlear nerve and studies of evoked potentials. In the central auditory region of the cat four areas of cochlear representation were found, corresponding to a greater or lesser extent to the four cytoarchitectonic divisions of Rose: (1) the suprasylvian fringe *(SF)*, where low frequencies are represented anteriorly and high frequencies posteriorly; (2) auditory area I *(AI)*, corresponding to area *A*I of Rose, where high frequencies are represented in front, and low frequencies in back; (This tonotopic organization has been amply confirmed by microelectrode studies, for example, Whitfield and Evans, 1965; Goldstein et al, 1970). Area AI receives well-defined projections from the thalamus; (3) auditory area II (AII), subjacent to AI, in which the tonotopic relationships are less clear, but which seem to be in reverse order with respect to AI; (4) the region occupying the posterior two-thirds of the ectosylvian gyrus (Ep), where high frequencies are represented in the superior portion, low frequencies in the inferior.

Outside of the central auditory region, auditory responses have been found in the insular portion of the temporal lobe (Desmedt and Mechelse, 1959; Loeffler, 1958) and in the secondary sensory cortex (auditory area III of Tunturi). With the possible exception of area III of Tunturi and SF, all of these cortical auditory areas are interconnected. As for extrinsic connections of the auditory areas, corticocortical connections to polysensory regions have been found. In addition the regions of the anterior lateral and suprasylvian (associative) gyri as well as the precentral motor zone have been found to respond to auditory stimuli at a latency of 15 meters per second. These areas can also be activated by visual and somatic stimulation (by means of the thalamic pulvinar connection). A region of responses to auditory stimulation of long latencies is found in the secondary visual area.

Either ipsilateral or contralateral stimulation of the cochlea can be followed by evoked responses in all areas cited above. However, Rosensweig (1951) showed that lateralized sounds provoke larger evoked responses in the contralateral than in the ipsilateral hemisphere. With cochlear stimulation Gross et al (1967) have shown that contralateral cortical auditory zones respond over a wider area than ipsilateral. Also contralateral responses to cochlear stimulation are generally of greater amplitude than ipsilateral responses.

In more recent research on the representation of the cochlea within the primary auditory cortex in the cat, Merzenich et al (1975) found a disproportionate representation of the basal portion of the cochlea (high frequencies). They also stressed the high degree of correspondence between the extent of the field of primary auditory representation as it is defined physiologically and the extent of the field defined cytoarchitectonically (koniocortex). Katsuki (1961) recorded electrical responses of neurons isolated at different levels along the auditory pathways of the cat. Stimuli were acoustic signals, either continuous or in bursts. He found that analysis of complex sounds is partially carried out in the cochlea but that it continues at each step on the way to the cortex. Katsuki concluded that the analysis was completed at the level of the medial geniculate body, where the area of response is least extensive. (This latter point was not confirmed in a subsequent study by Kiang et al, 1965.) For Katsuki the responses at the cortical level were completely different. The various results were interpreted as demonstrating that intensities and fre-

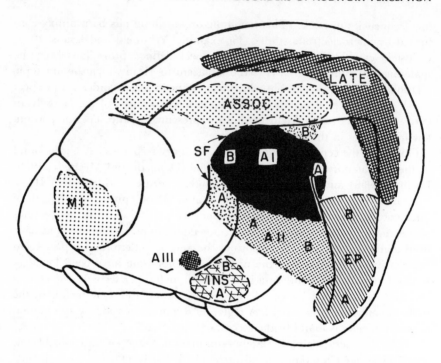

Summary of diagram of auditory response areas of cat cerebral cortex. The cochlea is represented anteroposteriorly from apex (A) to base (B) in the suprasylvian fringe area (SF); from base to apex in A I; from apex to base in A II; from base to apex dorsoventrally in EP; from base above to apex below in the insula (INS). A III = Tunturi's third auditory area, ASSOC = association cortex, LATE = visual area II which gave responses to auditory stimuli after long latencies (from Woolsey, 1960). Copyright 1960 by C. C. Thomas & Co., Springfield, Ill. Reproduced by permission.

quencies were discriminated at the level of the geniculate body, and other components of sound were analyzed in the cortex. At the cortical level the inhibitory interaction seen at peripheral and subcortical levels when two sound signals were presented simultaneously was not found; by contrast, an apparent facilitation effect was often observed. After stimulation by pulsed sound signals, cortical neurons often, but not always, responded with repetitive discharges corresponding to the frequency of the pulse. In this regard Katsuki referred to Helmholtz (1867), who hypothesized a close relationship between pulsed sounds and musical consonance. More recent studies by Watanabe and Katsuki (1974) using species-specific vocalizations as stimuli provide evidence suggesting that cortical cells (AI) integrate information related to various components of sound already analyzed in the thalamus.

Although these observations are still fragmentary, they are nonetheless sufficiently similar to those obtained for the visual system by Hubel and Wiesel (1962–1968) to allow consideration of analogous mechanisms of progressive discrimination of information from area to area (peripheral to central) with integration at each level of elements previously analyzed. Miller et al (1974), for example, studied different types of temporally complex responses of cortical auditory cells. In nearly half of the cells studied, response characteristics varied with specific changes in stimulus parameters. The authors concluded that responses of the auditory cells studied corresponded to individual characteristics of the stimulus in much the same way as complex cells in the visual system did.

However, a major difference between the two perceptual systems has been demonstrated: discrimination by units of the highest levels of the auditory system seems to be concerned primarily with temporal features of the stimulus, unlike that of the visual system, which, at the same levels, seems to be concerned with specificity of the stimulus. For example, Whitfield and Evans (1965) found cells in the auditory cortex of the cat that responded to modifications in frequency but not to continuous, monotonous sounds. Some cells responded to frequency modulation in the higher frequencies; others, to frequency modulations in the lower frequencies. Some auditory cortical neurons in the cat do not respond to auditory stimuli unless the animal is paying attention to the source of the sound (Hubel et al, 1959). Also contrary to an absolute parallelism between visual and auditory systems in structure and function are the results of single-cell studies by Goldstein et al (1970). These authors did not find a columnar organization of the cat's auditory cortex analogous to those found by others in the visual and somesthetic cortices. However, more recent results by Merzenich et al (1975) provide evidence in favor of a vertical unity of organization of the primary auditory area, these columns being perhaps asymmetric or irregular. Another way in which cells of primary auditory cortex differ from those of primary visual cortex is with respect to reactions to polymodal convergence. Auditory cells do not respond to a stationary visual stimulus (Stewart and Starr, 1970; de Ribaupierre et al, 1973), although visual cells may respond to acoustic stimulation (Murata et al, 1965; Spinelli et al, 1968).

An issue of considerable theoretical importance is that of auditory cell response to species-specific sounds. The early work of Whitfield (1967) demonstrating the capacity of certain auditory cells in the cat's brain to respond to glissando had already provoked the suggestion of "meow detectors" for this species. The question was intensively studied in the squirrel monkey, an animal with rich and well-described vocalizations (Ploog and Melnechuck, 1971). More than 80% of 213 cells in area T_1 of the squirrel monkey responded specifically to differing squirrel monkey vocalizations (Funkenstein et al, 1970; Wollberg and Newman, 1972). Type of response and probability of responding differed from cell group to cell group and even within a single cell according to the type of vocalization.

To define the acoustic features necessary for response of a single neuron, Wollberg and Newman (1972) suppressed certain temporal segments of the vocalization. Cells continued to respond to those incomplete calls that seemed to be the most specific to the species. Nonetheless the cells responded to other animal calls also, and the authors concluded that the specificity was not total. In a subsequent study they found that 89% of cells studied in the superior temporal gyrus responded to more than half of the vocal stimuli, whereas only 1 of 83 cells responded exclusively to a set of acoustically similar calls (Wollberg and Newman, 1973).

The authors interpreted these observations as suggesting that the cells were less like feature detectors than like tuned filters vis-à-vis specific acoustic parameters such as frequency, intensity, and rate of discharge. Particularly sensitive cells (passive filters) may be situated in small numbers in T_1 or may be located elsewhere. Selectivity depends not on the function of specific cells but on the activity of a neuronal ensemble that characterizes a specific vocalization by summation of outputs.

These vocalization-specific responses of auditory cortical cells remain stable despite experimental manipulation of level of consciousness by stimulation of mesencephalic reticular formation (Symmes and Newman, 1974). Auditory cell responses to specific animal calls seem to be independent even of the level of excitability of the cells themselves, in the waking state. The behavioral significance of these observations is that the response of cells to specific vocalizations cannot be attributed simply to a modification of attentional level and that this specificity must be considered as real.

From the behavioral point of view Neff (1961) and others have attempted to relate different features of auditory perception to different cortical auditory areas and their connections. After bilateral ablation of the cortical areas that receive projections from the medial geniculate body (i.e., areas AI, AII, Ep, and insulotemporal), the cat loses the discriminative functions of sound localization in space and responsiveness to changes in temporal pattern. If ablations of SII and of the suprasylvian gyrus are added to these lesions, the cat nonetheless retains responsiveness to sound onset and to changes in frequency and intensity. When subcortical lesions eliminate all cortical responsiveness, the cat can still discriminate intensities but not frequencies. Bilateral ablation of the insulotemporal region causes a severe deficit in the cat's ability to discriminate tone patterns, without abolishing its capacity to discriminate frequencies; this deficit may be partially reversible.

Neff has stressed that abilities for auditory discrimination that are preserved after ablation of the geniculocortical system are fundamentally different from those that are lost. Auditory discriminative abilities that are lost after ablation of this system are temporal. Such an ability for the discrimination of the temporal sequence of an auditory stimulus represents in animals a pattern of neuropsychological behavior that closely approximates verbal behavior of human beings.

Studies by other authors on the relationship of behavioral function to anatomic structure have extended the work by Neff. Cornwell (1967) demonstrated a loss of auditory pattern discrimination after insulotemporal lesions in cats and stressed that task difficulty was an important factor in loss or preservation of auditory discriminations following cortical lesions. Dewson (1964), studying human speech sound discrimination by cats, found that cats that demonstrated the ability for such discriminations lost it after insulotemporal lesions. Gersuni (1965) showed the cortical level to be capable of perceiving sounds of very brief duration.

When wide insulotemporal ablations are made in the cat, this animal can relearn temporal patterns of sounds modulated in ascending or descending frequency (Kelly and Whitfield, 1971), and it can discriminate sound onset-offset changes and modifications in frequency (Kelly, 1973). It cannot, however, discriminate pairs of pure sounds (high vs. low frequency). We may conclude that the auditory disability brought about by cortical lesions in the cat is not related to pattern complexity but rather to temporal configuration and the discontinuous nature of stimuli. These results also demonstrate that the two forms of discrimination (between sound patterns that are frequency modulated and between those that are pure) are processed differently by central auditory mechanisms. Ablation of associative or polysensorial areas, by contrast, causes no deficit in auditory discrimination (Kelly, 1974).

Insulotemporal ablations in the cat impair discrimination of changes in temporal sequence not only for auditory but also for visual and vibrotactile modalities (Colavita, 1972a,b). This deficit does not seem to be an inability to perceive the order of two successive stimuli as much as a disturbance in the global discrimination of patterns (Colavita, 1974). It could be argued that reduced attention span causes the deficit.

Considerable experimental work has also been conducted on monkeys. In the monkey cortical representation of the auditory system is found in the superior temporal gyrus. The posterior portion of the superior surface of this gyrus receives projections from the medial geniculate body, and this cortical region is composed of characteristic koniocortex elements. Again a tonotopic organization is present (Kennedy, 1955): low frequencies are located anteriorly; high frequencies, posteriorly. The horizontal representation of the cochlea on $A1$ has been confirmed in the macaque; in addition a vertical representation has been found (Merzenich and Brugge, 1973).

Anterior to this primary cortical auditory area is a region that receives projections from the posterior portion of the medial geniculate body; this area may be homologous to the insulotemporal region in the cat (Akert et al, 1959). The importance of the middle third of the superior temporal gyrus, of the opercular cortex, and of the middle two-thirds of the insular cortex has been emphasized with respect to reception of primary acoustic inputs (Massopust et al, 1970).

Degeneration studies by Mesulam and Pandya (1973) have provided more detailed information about the medial geniculate complex in the monkey. The parvocellular portion projects to auditory koniocortex ($A1$); the posterior parvocellular portion projects to rostral parakoniocortex, that is, the auditory association cortex of Akert. The parvocellular and magnocellular portions project to the secondary auditory cortex. Geniculate afferents are distributed preferentially in layer IV. The suprageniculate division does not seem to direct specific projections to the auditory cortex.

Efferent projections in the squirrel monkey have the following distribution (Forbes and Moskowitz, 1974). The supratemporal plane and the dorsolateral portion of the superior temporal gyrus both project to the medial geniculate body and inferior quadrigeminal tubercle but to different parts of these nuclei. If we consider the strict limitation of supratemporal plane projections to these two auditory nuclei, while the dorsolateral portion of the superior temporal gyrus projects to other regions as well, we may consider these two cortical regions as having distinct auditory functions. The supratemporal plane may be the primary auditory area, and the dorsolateral portion of the superior temporal gyrus may represent a secondary auditory zone. The insula, frontoparietal operculum, and ventrolateral portion of the superior temporal gyrus do not project to the two auditory nuclei and probably do not participate in auditory activity.

Pandya et al (1969) have also studied the intrahemispheric and interhemispheric connections of the neocortical auditory system in the rhesus monkey. They found that the primary auditory area that corresponds to area TC of von Bonin and Bailey is located in the planum supratemporale. Projections to this region are exclusively to association areas ipsilaterally (areas TA and TB) and to area TC on the contralateral side. Association area TA may be divided into anterior and posterior segments. Connections from the anterior segment project in a homotopic manner to the prefrontal region. From the posterior segment, projections run to frontal, parietal, and cingular regions. Interhemispheric connections of the anterior segment cross by way of the anterior commissures; those of the posterior cross by way of the corpus callosum.

Bilateral ablation of the auditory area and of the adjacent parietal and temporal cortex causes a complete and definitive loss of the ability to discriminate an auditory pattern learned preoperatively. Ablation of the zone defined by Akert as corresponding to the inferotemporal region of the cat and located anteriorly to the zone referred to above is also followed by loss of the same discriminative ability; however, in this case relearning is possible (Neff, 1961). After these cortical ablations, monkeys, as cats, are nonetheless capable of learning to respond to stimulus onset and to modifications of frequency and intensity.

Massopust et al (1970) found alterations in auditory discrimination threshold, relative to mean auditory frequencies, after ablations of the middle third of the superior temporal gyrus and adjacent insular and operculor cortex. This elevation of threshold seemed to be directly proportional to the lesion in the middle third of the superior temporal gyrus and to the volume of tissue destroyed. With lesions strictly limited to the superior temporal gyrus, threshold elevation was minimal. A general conclusion could be drawn that to obtain definitive deficits one must produce large cortical ablations not limited to the primary auditory area.

As with similar studies in the cat Dewson et al (1969) studied the effects of ablations of temporal cortex upon speech sound discrimination in the monkey. In the cat a permanent deficit was obtained after resection of insulotemporal cortex. In the monkey these authors attempted to obtain a permanent deficit by increasing task difficulty while limiting the lesion to the primary auditory area. The task was a discrimination of vocalic sounds ($/i/$–$/u/$). Bilateral destruction of the cortex of the planum supratemporale (see reference above) provoked a total inability to relearn a conditioned discrimination of these two sounds. By contrast a deficit in the ability to discriminate sounds from noises was mild and transitory. These studies demonstrate that lesions in the primary auditory areas provoke two types of auditory discrimination deficits: the discrimination of acoustic stimuli, for which temporal sequencing is an important variable, and the discrimination of acoustic stimuli characterized by their spectral complexity.

Dewson et al (1969) also found that bilateral lesions located somewhat anteriorly in the middle temporal cortex, that is, association areas receiving no direct projections from the geniculate bodies, could be followed by a similar deficit in the ability to discriminate vocalic sounds. This deficit, severe in the early postoperative period, is, however, reversible. These observations may be compared with those of Weiskrantz and Mishkin (1958) suggesting that a region within the middle temporal cortex is specialized for auditory discriminations. This region would be analogous to the inferotemporal region for visual discriminations. In the experiments of Dewson et al (1969), in which monkeys received lesions to primary auditory or auditory association cortex, no deficits were found in a task of visual discrimination learned preoperatively.

Using more advanced techniques, Dewson et al (1970) demonstrated a permanent deficit in discrimination of auditory sequences by a unilateral lesion limited to the superior temporal gyrus but not involving primary auditory cortex. This functional deficit was not attributable to a disorder in temporal auditory acuity and was considered by the authors to represent a memory defect. A subsequent study (Cowey and Dewson, 1972) confirmed the earlier results. The effect of unilateral removal of auditory "association" cortex in a single rhesus monkey was described. Performance on an auditory sequencing task was permanently impaired. This defect was more severe when input was to the ear contralateral to the ablation. Ablations in this location impaired auditory memory, and not auditory sensitivity. As we shall see in the clinical sections below, these experimental studies are particularly germane to our understanding of human auditory mechanisms.

Human Studies

Cytoarchitectonic and retrograde degeneration studies have provided data regarding the anatomic characteristics of the auditory zones in the human cortex. The cortical region that receives auditory input terminals is found in the first temporal gyrus and consists of Heschl's gyri or the transverse temporal gyri (von Economo's areas *TB, TC, TD;* Brodmann's areas 41, 42). Anteriorly in this area the structure resembles sensory koniocortex, although within rather broad limits of definition, according to von Bonin and Bailey. Nagino (1926) has indicated that Heschl's transverse gyri receive projections from the medial geniculate body and the temporal plane receives projections from the ventral portion of the geniculate region.

In addition to anatomic studies those based on techniques of experimental physiology and pathology have also provided information about man's auditory system. For example the famous cortical stimulation studies of Penfield proved the following. When the temporal cortex was directly stimulated (for example, during an operation), only stimulation of the anterior transverse gyrus of Heschl produced elementary hallucinations (noise, unformed sounds, murmurs). Penfield distinguished these elementary auditory sensations from modifications of sound perceptions, that is, experiential responses (Penfield and Perrot, 1963).

During neurosurgical operations Celesia and Puletti (1969) studied responses of varying cerebral regions to evoked potentials produced by click stimuli presented simultaneously to both ears. Consistent responses were limited to a small region of the planum supratemporale, a region corresponding to the anterior and posterior transverse gyri of Heschl. From this region they found potentials with short latency, reproducible over long periods of time and with polarity reversals between deep and superficial electrodes. In addition they also found low amplitude, longer latency responses with greater variability in the posterior two-thirds of the superior temporal gyrus. The authors wondered if these latter potentials merely represented a transmission

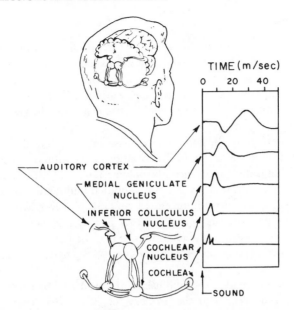

Human auditory pathway with corresponding click-evoked responses (from Galambos, 1975). Copyright 1975 by Raven Press, New York. Reproduced by permission.

effect or if they represented a secondary auditory area or auditory association area.

AUDITORY ILLUSIONS AND HALLUCINATIONS

We have already referred to the electrocortical stimulation studies of Penfield, studies that laid the groundwork for our understanding of the topography and character of auditory hallucinatory responses. In this section we elaborate on this work, in addition to providing other evidence from the clinical literature and from personal experience. Auditory illusions and hallucinations are much less frequent than such phenomena are in the visual system, and the anatomic problems raised by illusions and hallucinations in the auditory system are more difficult to clarify. This difficulty is in part related to the relative compactness of auditory centers and pathways. In clinical practice, when visual and auditory hallucinations are compared from the point of view of etiology, a specific etiologic agent or structural modification in the brain is found much more frequently with visual than with auditory hallucinations.

Auditory Illusions

To a certain extent auditory illusions may be considered similar to metamor-phopsias or visual illusions. Clinical complaints include descriptions of sounds heard as if they were louder or softer than normal; closer or more distant, to the point of disappearing; and as if there were an increase or decrease in the rhythm, a modification of tone or timbre, a strange or disagreeable quality, or a perseveration.

These phenomena of illusion are often associated with auditory hallucina-tions, in which case the auditory deformations may influence the hallucina-tion. Illusions may be simultaneously polymodal-visual and auditory. Com-bined sensory illusions, with or without combined hallucinations, are found in toxic states, especially drug induced. In general, however, when an organic basis underlies the illusion, it represents a paroxysmal event—an epileptic aura or equivalent. Rarely these paracusias may be permanent and may, for example, distort perception of musical inputs. Such cases must be distin-guished from amusias.

According to Penfield auditory illusions are produced by stimulation of the superior temporal gyrus near the primary receptive area. There is no domi-nance effect; stimulation of either hemisphere produces similar results.

Auditory Hallucinations

To facilitate discussion, we consider separately elementary and complex hal-lucinations. Complex hallucinations may be further subdivided into musical and verbal forms.

Elementary auditory hallucinations tend to be indistinct noises that the subject searches with difficulty to define: "a kind of murmur," "wind blow-ing," "trickling water," "a buzz," "a hum," "a whisper." At times these sounds have a rhythmic feature: the ticking of a clock, the rattling of an engine, the shots of a machinegun. The common feature of elementary hallu-cinations is their imprecision, which probably explains the multiplicity of images evoked by patients to describe them. Not unusual is the complaint of the repetitive, bothersome, and disagreeable nature of the experience. As a general rule patients recognize the pathological character of organically in-duced auditory hallucinations.

Nonetheless, even with elementary hallucinations, a more differentiated shape may emerge, with a richer sensorial quality. Patients will then report their experiences with greater emotional intensity, despite their knowledge of the pathological nature of the hallucination. These might be the sound of footsteps, a closing door, a dish breaking, clapping hands. The patient may describe in fine detail the acoustic features of the hallucination—timbre, intensity, rhythm, and so forth. At times the belief in the external provenance of the sound is so real that the patient attempts to verify the source. Elementary hallucinations may be the only manifestation of dysfunction in the auditory system, or they may precede or be associated with complex musical or verbal hallucinations.

Complex musical hallucinations vary in type. One variety is marked by stereotype; the same melodic theme returns in each hallucinatory experience. Sometimes the melodies are different. Occasionally one hears voices singing, without being able to distinguish the words; occasionally individual musical instruments are heard and, at times, an entire orchestra.

Musical hallucinations more frequently contain a clear sensorial quality than other auditory hallucinations do. The intensity is variable: songs and melodies are sometimes distant and attenuated, sometimes close and deafening; the intensity may change during a single hallucinatory episode, usually, in these cases, becoming progressively louder. The frequency, tonality, and timbre of the sounds may, at times, be so characteristic that the patient can ascribe the sound to a particular musical instrument. More often, however, the sensorial quality is less clear, and the subjects can speak only of the existence of "instrumental" or "choral" music. Equally it is not unusual for the description to be so imprecise or contradictory and for the subjective and affective aspects to be so strong that the examiner may conclude that the subject is reporting an experience that was not completely captured.

Auditory verbal hallucinations occur with varying complexity, from single words to complete sentences. Sometimes the hallucinations consist of orders or advice given to the subject, sometimes of conversations overheard, or of "voices crossing," and sometimes they have no real meaning. In some cases the association of an auditory hallucination with other symptoms (hallucinatory or not) may invest the hallucination with a special allure or meaning. A parallel phenomenon, paliacousia, may be related to auditory verbal hallucinations. In this condition the subject, in the course of a real conversation, seizes on a word or words from the conversation and hears them over and over again in hallucinatory fashion. The phenomenon in which a thought is "heard" repetitively, as an *idée fixe* that intrudes on other thoughts, is another associated condition.

In verbal hallucinations the clarity of sensation is less marked than in musical hallucinations; for the most part the acoustic features of the "heard" words are poorly described. Affective, rather than acoustic, qualities predominate. Nonetheless exceptions are found, and the subject can clearly define the sensory features of the hallucination.

Verbal hallucinations may precede or accompany aphasic phenomena. In some cases the aphasic disorder may manifest itself by means of the hallucination. Patients speak of hearing "incomprehensible words," "distorted sentences," "a foreign language."

For both verbal and musical auditory hallucinations significant associations have been observed with primary hearing deficits. Hallucinatory auras may be preceded by transitory deafness, then by auditory illusions, and finally by the hallucination. Hécaen and Ropert (1959), in a series of patients with auditory hallucinations, found these hallucinations to be isolated from other auditory symptoms in only 2 of 20 cases. In the 18 other cases the auditory hallucinations were associated with primary auditory perceptual defects (6), with visual hallucinations (5), with vestibular disorders (4), with disruptions of the body image (2), and with gustatory hallucinations (1). The constancy and stereotyped quality of the hallucinations experienced repeatedly by the subject in the course of successive auras are characteristic features.

The extent to which a subject believes his hallucinations depends not only on the type of hallucination (musical or verbal) but also on the context, the affective content, and the other pathological, illusional, or hallucinatory accompaniments. In general one may distinguish two major groups of complex musical or verbal hallucinations. In one group the hallucinations have a clear (external) sensorial quality, belief in the reality of the hallucination is immediate, and level of consciousness is normal. In the other, feelings of strangeness and *déjà vécu* predominate, and the state of consciousness is reduced. This latter condition is seen much less commonly in patients with auditory than in those with visual hallucinations.

By contrast Penfield and Perrot (1963) observed such auditory "dreamy states" following electrocortical stimulation of the temporal lobes. He calls these phenomena "experiential" auditory hallucinations; in such conditions the sound of voices is the most common hallucination, followed by sounds of music. Two-thirds of the voices were recognizable by the subjects, leading Penfield to conclude that such auditory hallucinations should be considered as being a part of the subject's prior experience. Although the voices probably *are* a part of the subject's past experience, we find the arguments to date inconclusive for proving that these auditory hallucinations should be considered as true *déjà entendu* phenomena.

Anatomoclinical Considerations

Auditory hallucinations associated with cortical lesions are almost exclusively manifestations of epilepsy. Their frequency has always been considered relatively low. For example, Strobos (1953), summarizing several series, reported a frequency of 1%. Hécaen and de Ajuriaguerra (1956), on the other hand, found auditory hallucinations in 8% of a series of 75 patients with temporal lobe tumors, and Bingley (1958), in 18% of his series. Courville (1928) contended that auditory hallucinations had localizing value for intracranial tumors, pointing to the temporal lobe. Bender and Diamond (1965) maintained, however, that the localizing value was not so clear. Hécaen (1972b) reported nine cases of which six had temporal lobe tumors.

As for hemispheric lateralization most authors agree that auditory hallucinations may result from lesions in either hemisphere. Nonetheless, in a series of 16 cases of auditory hallucinations for which the hemispheric lateralization could be confirmed, the left hemisphere was implicated in 13 (Hécaen, 1972b). For elementary hallucinations and for hallucinations associated with the dreamy state, each hemisphere was involved equally. However, for complex musical or verbal hallucinations with a clear external, sensory quality, all (10 cases) were produced by left hemispheric lesions.

Electrocortical stimulation studies performed at the time of operation have provided the clearest topographical picture. Auditory experiential responses (see above) were produced by stimulation of the zone of T_1, which surrounds Heschl's gyri and which corresponds to the audiopsychic cortex of Campbell. These phenomena were obtained more frequently in the nondominant than in the dominant hemisphere, although the difference was not statistically significant (Penfield and Perrot, 1963). The cortical areas from which such phenomena may be obtained by electrocortical stimulation extend further posteriorly on the lateral and superior aspects of T_1 on the right side than on the left.

In sum the main conclusions put forth for the neuropsychological problem of visual hallucinations are not easily borrowed for that of auditory hallucinations. Clinical reports are less abundant, descriptions less precise, and anatomic data less certain, because of the more restricted cortical limits of auditory pathways and projection zones. Nonetheless the model proposed for the visual phenomena may be considered as a working hypothesis for the auditory. We are thus able to distinguish elementary from complex hallucinations. Within the latter group we may separate sensorial from mnestic elements. The striking analogies between the hallucinations of patients with primary ocular pathology and those of patients with primary hearing defects must be underlined. It seems that in each instance a secondary hallucinatory embellishment is superimposed on the progressive sensory suppression.

CORTICAL DEAFNESS AND OTHER DEFECTS OF AUDITORY PERCEPTION

Anatomoclinical Aspects

Disturbances of auditory perception that result from temporal lobe lesions involving the transverse gyri of Heschl must be evaluated in the light of whether the lesion is unilateral or bilateral. Bilateral lesions produce deafness. Unilateral lesions in this area require special tests to demonstrate deficits (e.g., Jergen et al, 1969).

Concerning the clinical condition of cortical deafness Henschen (1920–

1922) reported findings from his personal experience and from a review of the world's literature. Of patients with vascular lesions with verified pathological anatomy he found nine with cortical deafness, all of whom had bilateral lesions of the transverse temporal gyri. Of 14 other cases with anatomic integrity of at least one of the transverse temporal gyri, none had complete deafness. From this Henschen concluded that the transverse temporal gyri are necessary for audition and that neither T_1, T_2, nor T_3 is responsible for elementary audition. We would add that bilateral subcortical lesions, involving the external capsule, that isolate the primary auditory cortex without directly involving this cortex may also produce total deafness (Le Gros Clark and Russell, 1938).

When we reviewed case reports of cortical deafness, we had difficulty finding any cases with unequivocal evidence of deafness due to cortical damage alone. This observation is similar to that of Lhermitte et al (1973a), who suggested that cortical deafness might not exist. For these authors, deafness following cortical lesions is usually transient, in which case it results from functional inhibition of the medial geniculate bodies. In the case of Le Gros Clark and Russell, retrograde degeneration of the geniculate bodies might have accounted for the deafness.

Anton (1898) observed that a patient may have total cortical deafness and act as if he were unaware of his deficit. We have already referred to this anosognosic behavior when speaking of cortical blindness. We shall find it again when we consider somesthetic defects.

Neuropsychological Aspects: Auditory Defects following Temporal Lobe Lesions

With occasional, almost anecdotal, exceptions, no deficits in human auditory perception had been commented on following unilateral temporal lobe lesions until the 1950s. Until then it had been generally concluded that the ipsilateral and contralateral auditory pathways were equipotential. In 1950 Grenier and Rohmer observed that after temporal lobectomy a postoperative deterioration in auditory discrimination was found, but this was a transitory defect. In 1951 Rosensweig provided an introduction to the modern understanding of the representation of the two ears at the auditory cortex. We shall make only brief reference to an expanding field of research that attempts to localize perceptual defects in the auditory pathways of brain-damaged subjects. Initial studies were based on the techniques of Chocholle et al, (1975), who used tonal audiometry tests in normal subjects to determine the time of auditory integration and the intensity threshold differential. Using similar tests, Maspetiol et al (1961) found abnormalities associated with unilateral temporal lesions. Karp et al (1969) studied the pure-tone threshold in a group of 19 subjects with left hemiplegia. Ten of the 19 had a unilateral left-ear hearing loss by comparison with the average threshold of a control group; right-ear thresholds were similar for the two groups.

Bocca et al (1955, 1958) developed a series of tests to evaluate auditory integration, and not simply auditory thresholds. Derived from tests of vocal audiometry, these tests involved recognition of words distorted by being passed through a low-pass filter or by being spoken at a rapid rate and also recognition of sentences presented with alternated rhythms. With such tests the authors demonstrated perceptual defects in the ear contralateral to a temporal lobe tumor. With double simultaneous auditory stimulation—words in one ear, white noise in the other—Shina (1959) was able to demonstrate impaired perception in the ear contralateral to a temporal lobectomy; without the masking effect, no deficit was found. Jergen and Meir (1960) found a similar deficit; in their study the masking effect was provided by presenting an unrelated conversation to the ear ipsilateral to the temporal lobe lesion. Subjects with hemispherectomies were deficient in their contralateral ears for words distorted by passage through a low-pass filter (Goldstein et al, 1970; Hodgson, 1967). Karasseva (1972) found perception thresholds for sounds of brief duration (less than 14 milliseconds) to be increased in the ear contralateral to a superior temporal lesion. Reaction times were increased in these subjects for brief auditory signals (1 millisecond) in the ear contralateral to the lesion, but not for long signals (120 milliseconds).

Using the Broadbent technique of binaural simultaneous presentation of digits, Kimura (1961a) found an auditory perception deficit in epileptics with temporal lobe lesions. On this verbal listening test, performances in both ears by epileptics with left-sided lesions were significantly inferior to those with right-sided lesions. After left temporal lobectomy a significant drop in performance by comparison with preoperative scores was found, whereas scores remained the same after right temporal lobectomy. If the relative competence of the two ears was compared by means of this test, in patients with left temporal lobectomy the auditory impairment was marked in the contralateral ear and mild in the ipsilateral ear; in patients with right temporal lobectomy there was a slight improvement in performance of the ipsilateral ear, which compensated for the mild impairment in the contralateral ear. In both groups the relative deficit of the contralateral ear was approximately equal. When Heschl's gyrus was included in the resection, the deficit in the contralateral ear was much greater. By way of comparison Kimura found no deficits on this test in patients undergoing frontal resections.

Heilman et al (1973) studied auditory perception in subjects with unilateral temporal lobectomy or with temporal lobe epilepsy with clear electroencephalographic focus. Speech discrimination was tested at varying signal-to-noise ratios. With noise the ear contralateral to the abnormal temporal lobe was impaired in discrimination. Performance was worse in the surgical than in the seizure group. The authors related the results to a defect in selective attention for auditory processing.

These various studies may be summarized as proving that, under special conditions of stimulus presentation, a unilateral temporal lesion causes a selective deficit in auditory perception in the ear contralateral to the lesion. Other studies have demonstrated the significant role played by cerebral dominance; the auditory deficit has been shown to relate to different types of stimulus material, depending on the hemisphere damaged. Swisher (1967), for example, found a heightened discriminative ability for intensity differences following left, but not right, temporal lobectomy. This increased sensitivity to variations in auditory intensity was not a permanent effect; by 1 year after the operation it had disappeared.

Another factor to be taken into consideration is the relative efficiency of ipsilateral and contralateral auditory pathways. Gordon (1975) studied this question in a group of subjects with complete forebrain commissurotomy using a vocal response time test. Callosal bisection and use of verbal stimuli and verbal response ensured exclusive use of the left hemisphere. Therefore, scores for the right and left ears respectively reflected performance by contralateral and ipsilateral pathways. He found that simple words were repeated faster, but no more accurately, when presented to the right ear than to the left. He concluded that the contralateral auditory pathway was more efficient than the ipsilateral, at least for this type of task.

Reports have appeared concerning disorders of localization of sounds in space following cerebral lesions. In the experimental animal such disorders have generally been found only with bilateral ablations of auditory cortex (Neff, 1961), and Strominger (1969) has shown that area AI plays the most important role. However, Moore et al (1974) have shown the trapezoid body to play a role in processing aspects of acoustic inputs necessary for sound localization, in particular, disparities in time and intensity. And Whitfield et al (1972) found that unilateral ablation of auditory cortex in the cat may cause a deficit in localization of sounds presented dichotically but with a temporal separation.

In man there is some indication that sound localization defects may occur with unilateral cortical lesions. Penfield and Evans (1934) found disturbances in localization of sounds on the left side of space in subjects who had undergone right temporal lobectomy. Similar observations were reported by Wortis and Pfeffer (1948) in a subject with a probable right hemispheric lesion.

Teuber and Diamond (1956) systematically studied the effects of brain injury in man on binaural localization of sounds with variable binaural clicks as stimuli: when intensity was held constant and only the interval of arrival of each of the clicks was varied, brain-injured subjects were always inferior to controls in sound localization. Right hemispheric lesions caused greater defects than left hemispheric lesions did. If the interval between clicks was held constant and the intensity of clicks varied, the results were similar, but a relatively constant error was made for the side of space opposite the lesion.

Sanchez-Longo and Forster (1957, 1958) studied the precision of sound localization in the horizontal plane. Blindfolded, the subject had to point to the source of a sound displaced on the arc of a perimeter. In 30 normal subjects no defect was found, and the precision of sound localization in the right and left auditory fields was the same. Of 21 subjects with temporal lobe lesions, 19 had defects in sound localization, especially in the field contralateral to the lesion. Of 21 additional subjects with cortical or subcortical lesions not involving the temporal lobes, only 4 had defects in sound localization.

Shankweiler (1961), attempting to verify the role of temporal lobe lesions in the capacity for localization of sound in space, employed a modification of the preceding tests. Subjects had to point to the source of an initial sound and say whether a second sound was to the right or left of the first. The position of the two sound boxes was systematically modified by varying angles along the arc of the perimeter. His conclusions contradicted those of Sanchez-Longo and Forster. Brain-damaged and control subjects did not differ from each other on the pointing-to-sound task, although they did differ on the discrimination of angular differences. Intrahemispheric localization of lesion did not play a significant role on either test. Hemispheric side of lesion did play a role: patients with right hemispheric lesions made more errors than did those with left hemispheric lesions on the pointing test, but there was no significant difference between the two groups on the angular differences test; Shankweiler concluded that free-field sound-localizing ability is not disturbed by cerebral lesions. The defects noted could be explained by impairments in short-term memory or general disorders of judgment. The specific defect found in the right-brain-damaged group was not due to an auditory disorder but could be explained by the disturbances in spatial orientation often found with posterior right hemispheric lesions.

AUDITORY AGNOSIAS

Anatomoclinical Aspects

The term *auditory agnosia* applies to the clinical condition of disturbed capacity to recognize the nature of heard, nonverbal, acoustic stimuli. Although the neurological literature contains many references to auditory agnosia, the term has not been used in a consistent manner. By the end of the 1800s clinical observations were reported of patients who, despite the preservation of reactions to acoustic stimulation, were unable to identify the meaning or nature of nonverbal sounds (psychic deafness), to distinguish tones or melodies (tone deafness, melody deafness, amusia), or to understand spoken words, although other language functions were intact (word deafness). Not rarely these various conditions were found together in the same patient.

By analogy with similar disorders in the visual modality, these auditory defects were considered to be agnosias, as opposed to elementary perceptual defects in the auditory system. The distinction, however, between auditory agnosia and other auditory perceptual defects is often difficult to establish, because of the close anatomic relationships between primary and secondary auditory reception zones. For some authors (e.g., Henschen, 1920–1922; Kleist, 1933, 1962) auditory agnosias may be subdivided into distinct clinical varieties relating to defective identification of sounds, music, or words, each type with its own, separate cortical representation. For others (e.g., Feuchtwanger, 1930) the recognition of music and words were inseparably linked by an underlying unitary process. The differentiation of sounds and tones could be made, however, at a more elementary sensory level, based on varying acoustic parameters. Rhythm, tempo, and, ultimately, memory of the various elements were essential to final recognition. The localization of lesions responsible for disorders of musical or verbal reception was, for Feuchtwanger, identical. Ombredane (1945, 1951) provided a similar conceptualization when he stated that the various auditory perceptual disorders may correspond to lacunae within the progressive integration of acoustic impressions in a chronological series. He added that other, not strictly acoustic, factors (acoustico-optic processes, auditory memory, affective components) may also intervene to provide special characteristics to the disorder of apprehension of meaningful, sonorous forms.

In this section we consider anatomicoclinical aspects of auditory agnosia according to the nature of material—sounds or music; pure word deafness is presented in the chapter on aphasia. We stress that the specific defects of auditory recognition under consideration may occur with preservation of other components of auditory perception and recognition.

Agnosia for Sounds

In this condition the patient is unable to recognize the meaning of nonverbal sounds. A variety of forms may be seen: the patient may confuse one sound for another; he may find all sounds to be similar (e.g., Laignel-Lavastine and Alajouanine, 1921, reported a patient for whom all sounds resembled a cricket singing); he may be unable to recognize speech, familiar sounds, and music, despite a preserved audiometric threshold (e.g., Chocholle et al, 1975); or he may have an isolated defect in recognition of nonverbal, meaningful sounds, despite preserved ability to recognize music and words (e.g., Albert et al, 1972). Intensity of sounds may be preserved but not quality. Some subjects recognize certain sounds better than others. The patient described by Klein and Harper (1956), for example, had more difficulty with sounds that had a musical nature (e.g., a tinkling glass, a bell ringing) than with those that did not (e.g., crumpling paper, striking a match).

With rare exceptions published cases of auditory agnosia for sounds have included evidence of either word deafness or amusia. Henschen (1920) and Kleist (1933) believed that pure auditory agnosia for sounds always occurred in association with one or the other of these related phenomena, although they conceded that the relative weight of the defect may be greater for sound agnosia. Kleist (1933, 1962) envisaged the possibility of a deafness for the temporal sequences of sounds.

Spreen, Benton, and Fincham (1965) presented an anatomoclinical observation of a patient with agnosia for sounds. No disorder of language reception was found. Unfortunately the recognition of music could not be explored, although a good performance was found on the loudness subtest of the Seashore battery. Audiometry revealed only a bilateral high-frequency hearing loss, normal for his age. These authors also cited a report by Nielsen and Sult (1939) of a patient who, despite preserved language reception, was unable to recognize a single familiar sound with the exception of the ticking of a watch. This subject was also unable to identify objects by touch or smell. According to Spreen et al (1965) these were the only two reported cases of agnosia for sounds in the absence of defective language reception. More recently Albert et al (1972) described a patient with good auditory thresholds for hearing who was unable to recognize the nature of heard, nonverbal, meaningful sounds; however, his auditory comprehension of spoken language was intact. As for music the patient performed poorly on the pitch discrimination, loudness, rhythm, and tempo subtests of the Seashore Measures of Musical Talents. Despite these defects the patient was 100% successful on a multiple-choice test of melody identification. These authors concluded that the patient was unable to establish a correspondence between the perceived nonverbal sound and its sensory or motor associations. Since the patient was unable to attach meaning to heard, nonverbal sounds but was able to attach meaning to heard word sounds, the authors put forth the theoretical position that there may be two central auditory processing mechanisms, one treating linguistic inputs, and the other, nonlinguistic inputs.

Elegant dichotic listening experiments by Cutting (1974) provide support for the hypothesis of two auditory processing mechanisms in the left hemisphere. One mechanism is linguistic and seems to deal with phonetic aspects of acoustic material; the other, independent of language, is involved with complex acoustic aspects of signals, analyzing abrupt changes in frequency.

From the anatomic point of view Henschen (1920) postulated a cerebral center in the temporal lobes for sound recognition but was unable to localize it. Since the destruction of the transverse gyri of Heschl provoked a complete deafness, Henschen concluded that the center must be located elsewhere. Kleist (1933, 1962) localized the center for sound recognition in areas 20 and 37 and concluded that bilateral lesions must be present to produce the syndrome. The autopsy in the case of Spreen et al (1965) demonstrated a massive, right hemispheric, frontotemporoparietal lesion also involving the insula. The corpus callosum and left hemisphere did not have lesions that could be implicated. Also in the case of Nielsen and Sult (1939) the lesions were located predominantly in the right hemisphere. No anatomic data were available in the case reported by Albert et al (1972), but clinical data were strongly suggestive of bilateral posterior temporoparietal lesions. Lhermitte et al (1972) described three cases of auditory agnosia. None of the three could appreciate words, music, or familiar sounds, but all could discriminate pure tones of differing intensity or frequency. Two patients, with pathological data available, had confirmed bilateral temporal lobe lesions; the other had clinical evidence of bitemporal damage.

At present we must conclude that the underlying anatomy of the syndrome of auditory agnosia for sounds is not clearly defined. Although the possibility exists that this syndrome is due to bilateral temporal lobe lesions, the role of a right hemispheric lesion alone, in the absence of left hemispheric damage, cannot yet be excluded.

Agnosia for Music—The Amusias

Observations of agnosia for music, receptive amusia, have not been abundant, and the diversity of examination techniques has rendered difficult the task of synthesis. From the earliest studies of aphasia (e.g., Bouillard, 1839) observations were recorded of preservation of musical abilities in aphasic musicians. In a detailed collection of published cases Henschen (1920) found that, of 65 patients with word deafness, receptive musical ability was spared in 45. At the same time he collected 16 cases of musical agnosia without language defect. He concluded from these data that the two functions were juxtaposed in the brain and not superposed. By contrast Feuchtwanger (1930) argued that not a single case of pure word deafness had been found to demonstrate a clear separation of musical and language representation. In his opinion, when amusia was absent in cases of Wernicke's aphasia, the defect was based on comprehension of the sense of the word and not on appreciation of the sound of the word.

To the present time we have been able to follow this argument while benefitting from the additional cases published. In fact it is difficult to find case descriptions of receptive amusia that are not associated with language disorder or perceptive disorder or paracusia. Nonetheless we still favor Henschen's argument, since there is a relatively large number of cases of sensory aphasia and even of pure word deafness in which the preservation of recognition of melodies is certain (e.g., Ingham and Nielsen, 1936; Luria et al, 1965; Wertheim 1969; Hécaen, 1972b; Assal, 1974; etc.).

Receptive amusia may be subdivided into several categories: tone deafness (inability to discriminate tones in a scale); melody deafness (inability to recall a melody into memory or to identify a heard melody); and disorders in perception of rhythm, measure, or tempo. It is easier to subdivide receptive amusias in theory than it is to find these various categories in pure form in practice. Some patients have been able to recognize various orchestral instruments by their timbre, to indicate wrong notes, and even to distinguish major and minor keys, while at the same time being totally unable to recognize familiar melodies (Bonvicini, 1905, Souques and Baruk, 1930; Wertheim and Botez, 1961). The reverse was true for a patient described by Wurtzen (1903); this patient could recognize familiar melodies but could not indicate wrong notes; judgment of amplitude was impaired and the sense of rhythm was lost. Liepmann's (1890) famous patient Gotstelle could at times identify a melody on the basis of its rhythm; he could not, however, discriminate neighboring tones on the scale, although he could distinguish notes if they were widely separated. Auditory agnosia may also be total, musical sounds themselves not being recognized as such (Shuster and Taterka, 1926). Such was the case with the patient described by Reinhold (1950); an excellent musician before the development of his cerebral lesion, the patient was agnosic for all auditory stimuli, including music, although he was capable of writing music to dictation.

Melody deafness may be present in two forms. In the first, which we consider to be true receptive amusia, recognition of melodies previously familiar to the patient is lost. This is a recognition defect, and it must not be confused with the inability to recall a melody into memory. In the second form of melody deafness, melodies lose their musical quality and may aquire a nonmusical, disagreeable character (Bernard, 1889). Music becomes a supplementary noise added to the others but with no special musical aspect. A former singer with such a defect complained of hearing "a screeching car" whenever he heard music (Foerster, 1936). When a piano was playing, the patient described by Quensel and Pfeiffer (1923) had the impression of hearing someone hammering on a metal sheet. All music heard by another patient, who had a right temporal glioma (Pötzl, 1937), had a "confused and disagreeable resonance" and a "strident, dissonant, and piercing" quality. In receptive amusias a wide range of preserved and lost musical capacities has been described (Gardner, 1975).

From the anatomic point of view lesions have been found principally in middle temporal regions and not, as Henschen (1920) proposed, in the temporal tips. In this regard the case reported by Segarra and Quadfasel (1961) should be cited. Their patient had destruction of both temporal tips with total aphasia and with preserved ability to sing. Lesions have generally been bilateral, but when they have been unilateral, they have been predominantly on the right. Unilateral right hemispheric lesions have been especially associated with paracusias. In the study by Dorgeuille (1966) three patients with tone deafness had verified lesions; two involved the temporal tip, one the middle temporal gyrus; all were in the left hemisphere.

Neuropsychological Aspects

The Seashore Measures of Musical Talents is a standardized battery of six subtests evaluating amplitude, sonority, rhythm, duration, timbre, and melodic memory. This battery was presented by Milner (1962a) to 27 subjects before and after temporal lobectomy (16 left, 11 right). No significant differences in performances were obtained from subjects preoperatively, regardless of the lesion side. Also no significant differences were found from subjects with left-sided lesions before and after left temporal lobectomy. However, a significant difference was found for subjects with right-sided lesions following right temporal lobectomy for the tests of duration, timbre, melodic memory, and loudness. These results were similar, whether or not Heschl's gyri were included in the operative procedure.

In 1966 Shankweiler studied the effects of unilateral temporal lobectomy on recognition and naming of familiar tunes. Recognition was evaluated by asking the subject to reproduce the tune by humming. Both groups of brain-damaged subjects (21 with right temporal lobectomy, 21 with left) were inferior to normal controls on both the naming and the recognition tasks. The right-brain-damaged group was significantly inferior to the left-brain-damaged group on melody recognition, but there was no significant difference between the two groups on naming of melodies. Shankweiler proposed that the naming deficit observed in the group with left temporal lobectomy was a result of verbal memory defect. The impaired performance by the group with right-brain damage, both on naming and on recognition, by comparison with the control group, should be subjected to further study. In a dichotic listening test, Shankweiler (1966) again found that subjects with right temporal lobectomy were inferior to subjects with left temporal lobectomy on a test of melody perception, although they were superior on a test of single-digit perception.

Milner (1962a, 1971) has continually emphasized that the differences in severity of auditory perceptual deficit depend on both the nature of the material (verbal or nonverbal) and the side of the lesion: auditory perception of verbal material is impaired with left temporal lobe lesions, and auditory perception of nonverbal material is impaired with right temporal lobe lesions. This has been a compelling argument. As we shall see below, however, data have been accumulating that both support and refute this argument, and additional models of hemispheric differences for auditory perception are being proposed.

A wealth of data has been obtained from normal persons by modifications of the Broadbent technique of dichotic listening. In general these studies have supported the contention that the right hemisphere is dominant for nonverbal auditory perception. In 1961 (a,b) Kimura showed that, when numbers are presented to both ears simultaneously, the numbers presented to the right ear (in right-handed subjects) are recalled better than those presented to the left ear. By contrast, when click stimuli are presented to both ears simultaneously, the appreciation of the number of clicks is better for the left ear in the same subjects for whom the perception of digits is better in the right ear. With dichotic presentation of melodies, a left ear superiority was also shown (Kimura, 1964). Curry and Rutherford (1967) found a left-ear dominance for familiar sounds; Chaney and Webster (1966) demonstrated a left-ear dominance for sonar signals. In 1970 Gordon found a left-ear superiority for perception of musical chords. In addition to supporting the argument that the right hemisphere is dominant for the perception of nonverbal sounds, these studies provide evidence that the crossed auditory pathways (e.g., left ear to right hemisphere) are more efficient or effective than the uncrossed.

With brain-damaged subjects Shankweiler (1966a,b) found that the left-ear superiority for melody perception on a dichotic test is lost when the subject's lesion is in the right temporal lobe. With lesions in the left temporal lobe, the left-ear dominance for melody perception is preserved. If Heschl's gyri were not included in the right temporal ablation, the same type of inter-auricular difference as with normal persons and left-brain-damaged subjects was found. If Heschl's gyri were included in the right temporal lobe operation, melodies presented to the right ear were recognized better than those presented to the left ear.

The independent identification of consonants and vowels presented to left and right ears of normal subjects has also been studied (Shankweiler and Studdert-Kennedy, 1967; Studdert-Kennedy and Shankweiler, 1970). Consonants showed a clear right-ear superiority. Vowels did not show a clear superiority for either ear. Spellacy and Blumstein (1970), in an elegant and important study, showed that left- or right-ear superiority for perception of vowels could be modified according to attentional set. When subjects were expecting to hear vowel sounds in a linguistic context, the right ear was dominant. When the same vowel sounds were presented in a nonlinguistic context, the left ear was superior. Shankweiler and Studdert-Kennedy (1967) showed that hemispheric lateralization was implicated in perception, not only of phonemic oppositions, but also of subphonemic, distinctive features (voicing, articulatory point).

Although language stimuli are found to be dealt with primarily by the left hemisphere, and nonverbal material by the right hemisphere, the right hemisphere may also predominate for the processing of prosodic features of language. Blumstein and Goodglass (1972) found the perception of stress to be available as a semantic cue in aphasia. Boller and Green (1972) found that intonation contours could subserve semantics in severe aphasia. Dichotic studies in normal persons have shown left-ear superiority for fundamental frequency (Wood et al, 1971) and, to a certain extent, for amplitude (Oscar-Berman et al, 1973).

A different theoretical approach has led some authors to consider another model of hemispheric function for perception. Rather than speak of the nature of the material (verbal vs. nonverbal), they speak of the quality of perceptual capabilities of each hemisphere. DeRenzi et al (1969b) and Vignolo (1969) propose that the right hemisphere functions in a perceptual/discriminative capacity, while the left hemisphere serves a cognitive/associative function. We have already seen how this theory applies to problems of visual perception (DeRenzi et al, 1966, 1967, 1968c, 1969b, 1970a, 1972). Vignolo (1969) has applied this theory to problems of auditory perception.

On the basis of an analysis of published cases of auditory agnosia, Vignolo (1969) suggested that a link exists between the deficit in recognition of the meaning of nonverbal sounds and the deficit in comprehension of spoken language following left hemispheric lesions. He proposed that disorders of recognition of sounds following right hemispheric lesions were qualititatively different from those due to left hemispheric lesions. In 1966 Spinnler and Vignolo found that patients with left hemispheric lesions, especially those with aphasia, were significantly worse than patients with right hemispheric lesions on a test of identification of the natural source of meaningful, nonverbal sounds. In a second study Vignolo (1969) evaluated functional hemispheric differences for auditory perception in brain-damaged subjects with a test in which subjects had to recognize the source of meaningful, nonverbal sounds and to discriminate meaningless auditory patterns. A dissociation of performance was found, depending on the hemisphere damaged: failure on tests of identification of meaningful sounds was specific to the group with left-hemisphere damage; discrimination of meaningless sounds was significantly impaired following right-hemisphere damage. In summarizing these results, Vignolo concluded that each hemisphere had a specific and different role to play in the process of auditory perception. The right hemisphere was responsible for the sensory discriminative aspects of auditory perception; the left hemisphere, for the semantic, associative aspects. The defect observed with left hemispheric lesions was associated with aphasia. Both the auditory associative defect and the aphasia resulted from an impaired ability to re-unite the different qualities or aspects of a single concept.

The studies by DeRenzi and Vignolo responded to contradictions in an earlier hypothesis, which stated that there was a dual functional hemispheric asymmetry depending on the verbal or nonverbal nature of stimuli. However, as attractive as the DeRenzi-Vignolo hypothesis may be in separating the hemispheres according to quality of function (perceptual/discriminative vs. semantic/associative), this hypothesis does not answer all outstanding questions. For example, one could argue that the recognition of melodies, which seems to be selectively impaired by right hemispheric lesions, could not be considered to be a purely perceptual discriminative task, but that a certain amount of associative decoding is involved. In addition, studies based on Vignolo's methodology (Albert et al, 1971) have not completely confirmed his findings. One study of auditory perception found no significant difference between right- and left-brain-damaged subjects on a task involving recognition of the semantic aspects of nonverbal, meaningful sounds (Albert, 1972b).

Another theoretical approach has been debated as an attempted explanation of hemispheric differences in auditory perception. Reduced to its simplest terms, this hypothesis holds that left temporal regions are better than right for making fine time discriminations (Teuber, 1969; Karasseva, 1972). The basic implication of this hypothesis is that auditory linguistic capacities depend on the ability of the brain to make such time discriminations; therefore the left hemisphere is better suited for language. By contrast those auditory activities that do not require fine time discriminations may be efficiently performed by the right hemisphere. A number of clinical and experimental studies provide evidence in favor of this point of view.

Efron (1963a,b,c), studying the perception of temporal order of tone stimuli in brain-damaged subjects, found that the conscious comparison of the time of occurrence of any two sensory stimuli required the use of the hemisphere that is dominant for language functions. He further observed that the judgment of simultaneity and the judgment of the correct sequence of sensory events were performed only after some information is transmitted to the hemisphere that is dominant for speech. He also noted that a defect in sequence discrimination was found only when there was some degree of aphasia present. These studies of perception of auditory sequences used tone or click stimuli. Studying auditory perception of verbal sequences, Goodglass et al (1970) and Albert (1972a) obtained results that support Efron's conclusions.

Swisher and Hirsh (1972) studied the effect of brain damage on the ability to order two temporally successive, brief, nonlinguistic stimuli. They found an impairment in the judgment of order of both auditory and visual signals after left-brain damage but not after right-brain damage. Similar results for auditory stimuli had been obtained by Carmon (1971). Using a dichotic test with normal subjects, Halperin et al (1973) found a right-ear superiority for binaurally presented tone sequences containing abrupt changes in frequency or duration.

Taken together, these studies indicate that "the left hemisphere is dominant for the capacity to maintain and utilize the sequential aspects of acoustic stimuli" (Albert, 1972a). For Hirsh (1967) any theory of auditory perception must include the concept of a temporal and sequential pattern that plays the same role in audition as gestalten in visual perception. Hirsch contends that a mechanism exists within the auditory system that is specifically adapted to place in correct order the elements of the structure of language.

In addition to the issue of auditory temporal sequencing there is the issue of auditory temporal resolution, or its opposite, auditory fusion. Studying auditory temporal discrimination, Van Allen et al (1966) found left-brain-damaged subjects to be less efficient than right-brain-damaged subjects. Lackner and Teuber (1973) found similar results on a click-fusion test. Patients with left-brain damage had abnormal fusion thresholds for dichotically presented clicks. At temporal separations at which normal persons heard two clicks, left-brain-damaged subjects heard one. This was most pronounced in aphasic patients. Albert and Bear (1974) described a word-deaf patient who had a rate-dependent linguistic processing defect limited to the auditory modality. Their patient had a severe auditory click-fusion defect, and the authors concluded that the clinical picture of word deafness in this patient was due in part to the defective ability for auditory temporal resolution and in part to a defective ability for auditory sequencing.

The left temporal lobe seems to be dominant for the ability to make fine time discriminations in the process of auditory perception (for temporal resolution and temporal sequencing), and this ability seems to be related to the dominance of the left hemisphere for language. But what of melodies and right hemispheric dominance? Studies on musical expression (Bogen and Gordon, 1971; Gordon and Bogen, 1974) may shed light on this question. These authors investigated hemispheric lateralization of singing in patients who had transient hemiplegia after intracarotid injection of sodium amylobarbitone. They found that after right carotid injection singing was markedly deficient, whereas speech remained relatively intact. Songs were sung in a monotone, devoid of correct pitch rendering; rhythm was much less affected. By contrast, singing was less disturbed than speech after left carotid injection.

These studies were interpreted as showing a differential hemispheric capacity for auditory processing of time-related stimuli. Auditory perception of speech may be related to the essential sequential nature of speech in small, temporally ordered units. Melodies, by contrast, according to these authors, are remembered and produced as intact wholes. The parts of these units are not pieced together tone by tone but rather are recalled all at once as a complete unit. The small, successively ordered speech units would be time dependent. The larger melodic lines would be time independent—that is, complete units unrelated to others. Although as yet unproved, this hypothesis has received support in a study by Blumstein and Cooper (1974). Two dichotic listening experiments were conducted to test for hemispheric lateralization of intonation contours. Filtered intonation contours from real speech gave a left-ear advantage on a perceptual matching task. Intonation contours from nonsense speech also gave a left-ear advantage. Thus the right hemisphere seems to be directly involved in the perception of intonation contours.

In sum we find that three major theoretical approaches have been used to explain auditory perceptual defects resulting from cerebral hemispheric damage. All depend on the neuropsychological concept of cerebral dominance. In one the left hemisphere is dominant for verbal material, the right, for nonverbal. In another the right hemisphere has a superior perceptual-discriminative skill, the left, a superior associative capacity. In the third the left hemisphere is responsible for fine time discriminations (e.g., temporal resolution and temporal sequencing), the right, for time-independent functions. Each of these three theoretical approaches responds, in its own way, to basic questions. Although occasionally in conflict over a specific research result, they are not necessarily mutually exclusive.

Some of the conflict seen between and among the three major theoretical approaches to understanding auditory perception may be resolved by considering the previous training and experience of subjects. Bever and Chiarello (1974) studied cerebral dominance in musicians and nonmusicians by means of a monaural listening test using melodic sequences as stimuli. Nonmusicians had better recognition scores with their left ear (i.e., right hemisphere); musicians had better right-ear (left hemisphere) scores. Thus different strategies may be used in recognition of melodic sequences, depending on the degree of musical education of the subjects. Nonmusicians seemed to identify tonal patterns by their general melodic contours, as gestalten. Musicians seemed to use an analytic approach to melodic recognition, evaluating the combination of elements that comprised the sequence.

These observations are in harmony with those of Papçun et al (1974), who performed a dichotic listening study with experienced and inexperienced Morse code listeners. Stimuli were letters presented by Morse code. For both groups of subjects a right-ear dominance was found for Morse code sequences that did not exceed seven elements. For sequences with greater then seven elements right-ear dominance was seen only with the experienced group; with the inexperienced group a left-ear superiority appeared. The authors concluded that the untrained group employed a different listening strategy when the sequences exceeded a critical limit. These subjects could no longer count the elements but resorted to a global perception of stimuli.

The role of psychological "set" has already been alluded to (e.g., Spellacy and Blumstein, 1970) with respect to the question of which ear responds better to an identical sound on a dichotic listening task. A study by Darwin (1974) dramatizes this effect. If the subject is unaware of the fact that some stimuli are meaningful words, but if he thinks that all stimuli are nonlinguistic (in this case the identification of pitch contours), the left ear predominates, even when real and meaningful words are presented.

Clinical neurobehavioral studies of amusia have generally been conducted with musicians or others with a high degree of musical education, whereas many neuropsychological dichotic listening studies of large groups of normal or brain-damaged subjects have not taken into consideration the level of musical education. Because of such skewing of subject selection it may be possible to explain certain contradictory data. Unilateral left hemispheric lesions may be accepted as causing amusia, and dichotic listening studies in normal persons or studies with the Seashore test in subjects with temporal lobectomy may suggest right hemispheric dominance for aspects of music.

SIX
DISORDERS
OF SOMESTHESIS
AND SOMATOGNOSIS

THE SOMESTHESIC SYSTEM

Anatomic and Physiological Considerations

As we indicated previously with respect to the other sensory systems, we do not intend these sections on anatomy and physiology to serve as major reviews. Rather, we wish to highlight selectively certain anatomic and physiological topics of special interest to neuropsychologists.

Peripheral Somesthetic System

Questions relating to modalities of somesthetic sensitivity, receptor specificity, and conduction pathways dominate the general issue of somesthesis to such an extent that we thought it essential to review briefly the evolution of knowledge in this area.

L. Müller (1826) in his "doctrine of specific nervous energy" considered the tactile sense as a single sensory system. Fibers coming from the skin carried information, regardless of the nature of the stimulus, and transferred this information to cerebral centers in the same manner as optic fibers, which transmitted different varieties of visual stimuli. In 1895 von Frey proposed that the tactile sense was composed of four separate elements, each responding to a different sensory modality, and each being served by a specific

277

cutaneous receptor. Following research by Blix (1884) and Donaldson (1885), von Frey provided the following systematization: light touch and pressure were attributed to Meissner's corpuscles; heat, to the end organs of Ruffini; cold, to Krause bulbs; and pain, to free nerve endings. This formulation was widely accepted, neurophysiologists speaking of a pressure sense, temperature senses (different for heat and cold), and a pain sense. During this same period Sherrington (1892) was studying the concept of the specificity of cutaneous receptors at a physiological level. He determined that a cutaneous receptor had a reduced threshold for a particular type of somesthetic stimulus and an elevated threshold for other types. At the anatomic level, difficulties raised by von Frey's propositions were immediately apparent. Goldscheider (1898), for example, violently rejected the notion of independence for touch and pain. Nonetheless Goldscheider accepted the existence of two separate tactile system mechanisms, one responding to pain and touch stimuli of equivalent intensity, the other responding to painful stimuli only at high excitation levels.

The hypothesis of von Frey fits well with the general line of nineteenth century psychophysical thought. This was based on Müller's doctrine, which accepted a unimodal relationship between stimulus parameters and psychological interpretation. Between 1905 and 1908 Head modified the concept of four modalities of cutaneous experience. In one study, done with Rivers, he evaluated the effects of peripheral nerve lesions by sectioning one of his own cutaneous nerves; he concluded that the skin was innervated by two anatomically distinct systems—protopathic and epicritic (Head and Rivers, 1905). Following nerve section, regeneration occured at different rates; certain cutaneous regions were served by only one of the two systems. Protopathic sensitivity depended on specific end organs grouped in the skin to form sensibility points. From those regions of the skin that contained only protopathic end organs, sensation had a tendency to radiate and to be referred to distant areas. From those regions of the skin that contained receptors to light touch and temperature, radiation and referral of sensation were less marked.

Sensitivity to light touch was found by Head to result from mechanisms different from those for heat, cold, and pain. With recovery of function following nerve regeneration the ability to appreciate temperature, tactile localization, and two-point discrimination returned. The sensitivity points for touch, described by Blix and von Frey, were found to be closely associated with hair roots and were different from sensitivity points for heat, cold, and pain. All protopathic end organs had a high threshold; epicritic end organs had a low threshold. To these observations Head added those of a noncutaneous system with an independent anatomophysiological organization responding to stimuli of movement or pressure. In situations in which the skin was rendered insensitive, this additional system could provide tactile localization by interpreting pressure stimuli.

Head did not assume, as earlier scientists did, that peripheral stimuli interacted directly in a one-to-one manner with central structures by way of peripheral conducting pathways to provide conscious knowledge of the stimulus. Psychological interpretations of physical stimuli were abstracted from the primary sensations but were not exact physiological counterparts of these sensations. Action of various levels of the nervous system on afferent inflow resulted in progressive integration of these inputs, and this was carried out by the mechanisms of specific combination and selective inhibition. Complex stimuli at the body's surface caused responses in end organs of the protopathic, epicritic, and deep systems—responses characteristic for each system. At the level of the first synapse the afferent impulses were regrouped into different pathways, each pathway carrying information of a particular sensory mode. Some inputs were facilitated and some inhibited, and the process was repeated all the way to the thalamus and cortex. At these two levels the inputs excited mechanisms responsible respectively for discriminative and affective aspects of the sensation. The thalamus represented a terminal center for fundamental aspects of sensation (touch, pain, temperature) and acted in complement with the cortex. The thalamus redistributed inputs on their way to the cortex and was in turn controlled by inhibitory cortical influences. If cortical influence was removed, the thalamic syndrome (an excessive response to affective stimuli) became manifest. The thalamic syndrome was analogous to the protopathic syndrome produced at the periphery (by contrast with the epicritic).

In 1924 Erlanger, Gasser, and Bishop discovered that conduction velocity of nervous system influx depended on the diameter of nerve fibers. New efforts were then made to establish a correlation between sensory modalities and each group of fibers (Gasser, 1935; Erlanger and Gasser, 1937; Bishop, 1946). Bishop (1946) declared that each category of sensory organs activated fibers of a specific diameter; a one-to-one correspondence could be drawn between a particular fiber diameter and a particular quality of conscious sensory experience. This affirmation was met with considerable theoretical and experimental criticism. Nonetheless it could be accepted that fiber diameter was correlated with anatomic locus in the spinal cord and with physiological threshold of receptive units and that central transmission pathways were responsible for particular types of information.

Anatomists and physiologists (e.g., Rose and Woolsey, 1949; Mountcastle, 1961) came to accept the epicritic protopathic dichotomy of Head, but in modified form and at a more central location, that is, at the level of central transmission pathways and thalamus. Two phylogenetically distinct systems were recognized. One was the spinothalamic system: the point of departure was in the simple and complex nerve endings of the skin and in the deeper structures; the nerve fibers were of small diameter, myelinated or not; the principal central transmission pathway was the paleospinothalamic tract; the central connections were in the reticular formation and the intrinsic thalamic nuclei; and the final transmission point was in the secondary cortical sensory projection area, S II (see below). The other was the lemniscal system: the point of departure was in the cutaneous and subcutaneous receptors represented by complex endings; the nerve fibers were of larger diamater, myelinated; the principal central transmission pathway was the medial lemniscal tract, which contained elements of the dorsal column, the neospinothalamic tract; the central connections were in the posterior ventral nuclei of the thalamus; and the final transmission point was in the primary cortical sensory region in the postcentral gyrus.

As for the specific functions of these two systems one can only be schematic, since in fact interactions and functional intercorrelations exist. The medial lemniscal-dorsal column system is primarily responsible for discriminative aspects of somatic sensitivity. In delicate and precise fashion it provides to higher cortical regions information about position, form or contour, and temporal change of the peripheral stimulus (Mountcastle, 1961). Receptive units are modality specific only in the lemniscal system; transmission is rapid and precise; receptive fields are small and stable; hemispheric representation is contralateral to the side of stimulus; and somatotopic representation is precise, with greater sensitivity for face and limbs. The extralemniscal spinothalamic system is primarily responsible for less precise aspects of somesthetic stimulation, as well as for the qualitative nature of peripheral events. Nociceptive and thermal stimuli are especially transmitted in this system, transmission is slow, localization is vague, receptive fields are large and unstable, hemispheric representation is bilateral for a unilateral stimulus, and no definite somatotopic organization has been found.

In contrast to this picture of somatosensory organization Weddell (1941a, b) proposed a different, antispecific thesis. By means of a series of comparative histological studies in different animal species, including man, Weddell and his collaborators observed a strikingly constant pattern of cutaneous sensory innervation. The so-called specialized receptors were highly organized into a specific pattern of distribution; they were found only in hairless cutaneous regions. Over most of the skin's surface area only two types of nerve terminals were found: these were naked terminals, either free or wrapped around the base of hair follicles. These authors provided evidence that regions of the skin that contained no Meissner's corpuscles, Krause bulbs, or Ruffini endings were nonetheless able to respond to all types of somesthetic stimulation. Individual nerve terminals did not correspond to a particular afferent nerve fiber; rather, there was an abundant overlapping of nerve terminals in the innervated cutaneous region. Thus Weddell (1941a,b) preferred to speak of overlapping sensory fields rather than sensitivity points. They rejected the existence of cutaneous sensory receptors specific to one modality, and they did not accept the concept of specific sensory transmission. Each cutaneous stimulation produced a specific pattern of nervous influx organized spatially and temporally, and it was this specifically organized pattern that was transmitted to the cortical centers.

More recent studies on the property of peripheral nerve fibers have demonstrated a receptor specificity. However, contrary to the original propositions of von Frey, their function seems to be based but little on their morphology. (But not all current research is in agreement on this point. Burgess and Perl [1973] suggest that receptor morphology and physiological characteristics may be related, for example, nociception and mechanoreception with Paccinian corpuscles.)

If one records the response of different fibers to a large number of different stimulus modalities, superficial or deep, one finds specificity of response to diverse stimulations, and this specificity is found at the level of the medullary cells. For Melzack and Wall (1962) the contradictions between the specificity and nonspecificity hypotheses are not absolute. These authors accept the notion of specialization of receptors for physiological variables; the influx is, however, represented as temporal patterns specific to each physiological variable. As for the association between fiber diameter and function Melzack and Wall believe that only a loose correlation exists. On the other hand they accept as proved the notion that central transmission pathways are specialized for carrying different types of information. They reject the proposition that a one-to-one correspondence exists between a particular stimulus dimension and a receptor type or that a one-to-one correspondence can be found between physiological specialization of central transmission pathways and particular psychological interpretations. They agree with Weddell that sensory perception depends on decoding of temporally and spatially organized information but observe that the theory advanced by the Oxford School does not explain how patterns of nervous influx originate from cutaneous receptors or how these patterns are interpreted centrally. To reconcile the specificity and nonspecificity hypotheses, Melzack and Wall provided the following propositions.

Cutaneous receptors transform physical characteristics of stimuli into temporal and spatial patterns of nervous influx; they do not, however, respond with modality specificity. At presynaptic terminal arborizations the temporal and spatial patterns produced by cutaneous stimulation undergo a filtering process. With variable thresholds for temporal summation, spatial summation, and adaptation, centrally located cells can detect and discriminate different aspects of the input patterns. This pattern discrimination concerns detection of influx from more than one afferent fiber at any one time; interconnections between afferent systems allow central cells to analyze multiple input patterns. The somesthetic system is a harmonious, unitary, integrated system composed of specialized elements. Each discriminable somesthetic perception is determined by a unique pattern of nervous influx.

Reviewing this hypothetical explanation of somesthesis, Wall (1970) noted that the dorsal columns were not so highly specialized as had previously been taught. Section of the dorsal columns in experimental animals, for example, did not necessarily abolish two-point discrimination, or discrimination of weight or texture, or vibratory or position sense. Wall concluded that deficits due to dorsal column lesions were not those of fine sensory discriminations but rather were deficits of capacities for exploratory behavior. The dorsal columns should be considered as transmission pathways for information derived from active, exploratory movements or from sequential analyses of stimuli. Functional discrimination would require additional information from other afferent pathways as well. This hypothesis concords with that of Semmes (1969) in which phylogenetically recent motor and sensory systems form a functional complex by means of which finesse of object manipulation and tactile exploration is established by a reciprocal interaction of somesthetic mechanisms on motor mechanisms, and vice versa.

Additional research by Melzack and Southmayd (1974) on the dorsal columns' contribution to anticipatory motor behavior confirmed earlier work suggesting that the dorsal columns receive precise tactile and proprioceptive information necessary for organization of motor activity underlying sequential movement. The dorsal columns are subjected to influences from the sensorimotor cortex, the cerebellum, and the reticular formation. Coulter (1974) studied sensory transmission through lemniscal pathways during voluntary movements in the cat and observed inhibition of afferent transmission in a highly specific manner. Certain redundant information, as specified by voluntary movements, was suppressed, allowing the remaining sensory information to be transmitted.

It seems that the dorsal columns form a necessary structural basis for maintenance of sequential motor behavior but may not be necessary for initiation of this behavior. In the monkey the posterior columns are necessary only for tactile discrimination of patterns when this discrimination requires active palpation of the pattern (Azulay and Schwartz, 1975). That is, the dorsal columns are implicated in tactile perception when a movement-related spatio-temporal transformation occurs.

Cortical Somesthetic System

Two regions are recognized as the main cortical sites responsible for somesthetic reception: primary somesthetic strip (SI) and secondary somesthetic zone (SII). However, the primary motor strip, the precentral motor cortex, and the supplementary motor cortex also participate in sensory activity. Penfield (1958b), studying man, found 25% of stimulation points producing a sensory response to be located in prerolandic cortex. Woolsey (1964), using evoked potentials and stimulation studies in monkeys, made similar observations. In contemporary terminology one is justified in speaking of the sensorimotor cortex.

The primary somatosensory strip is located in the postrolandic gyrus and corresponds to Brodmann's areas 3, 1, and 2. Evoked potential studies by Woolsey et al (1942, 1943) in a variety of animal species indicated the somatic representations for dermatomes to be grossly separable, although considerable overlap was found. Woolsey called this a point-to-area correspondence, rather than a point-to-point somatotopic relationship. The studies by Penfield (Penfield and Rasmussen, 1950; Penfield, 1958b) on the excitable cortex in conscious man are in general agreement with the findings of Woolsey. Penfield stressed that the sensory homunculus was similar to the motor homunculus, with the exception of the genitalia, which were found responsive only on the sensory strip.

Mountcastle (1961) demonstrated that the neurons of the somesthetic cortex were disposed in vertical columns that descended through all cellular fields. Each column, composed of cells responding to a single type of stimulation, seemed to represent a functional unit, and all the cells of a single column were linked to overlapping peripheral fields. Thus stimulation of one cutaneous point activated a multitude of cortical cells. In the cat, for instance, receptive fields of cortical cells were from 15 to 100 times larger than those innervated by dorsal root fibers (Puletti, 1959). In addition to this phenomenon of divergence from a cutaneous point stimulus to the cortex, the phenomenon of convergence was also found. By way of polysynaptic links many posterior root fibers could project to a single cortical cell. Cells from posterior column nuclei, ventral posterolateral thalamic complex, and postcentral gyrus were found to respond specifically to particular form or place stimuli for both superficial and deep sensation. Each of the somesthetic cortical cell columns was linked to one or another of these sensory submodalities. In the monkey the topographical distribution of these columns was as follows: area 3 was linked primarily to cutaneous sensitivity; area 2, to deep sensation; area 1, to both, as an intermediate form. Moreover, a transitional area within the cortical motor region 3a represented a region of afferent muscle projection (Powell and Mountcastle, 1959).

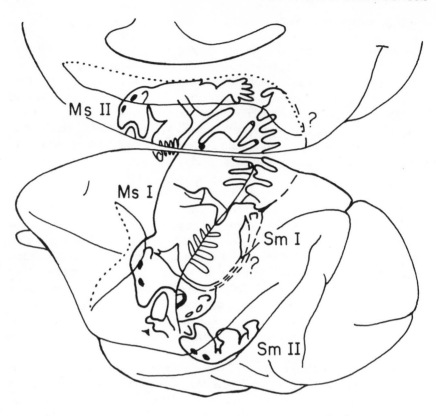

General arrangement of localization patterns in rolandic region of the monkey (from Woolsey, 1964). Copyright 1964 by University of Wisconsin Press, Madison. Reproduced by permission.

Dreyer et al (1974) studied projection pathways in the monkey following destruction of spinal pathways with subsequent analysis of cortical $S1$ neurons. A clear composite map could be constructed from this analysis, $S1$ comprising a central zone (areas 1 and 3) with cutaneous projections mainly through the cervical fasciculus gracilis, and anterior (area $3a$) and posterior (areas 1, 2) border zones receiving cutaneous and deep inputs by way of ascending pathways other than those of the dorsal columns. In the border zones there was a gradient with respect to composition of submodalities: closer to the center were cells for cutaneous sensitivity; more peripherally were those receiving mainly subcutaneous inputs. Body parts had a gross somatotopic organization in $S1$: distal portions of the body were represented

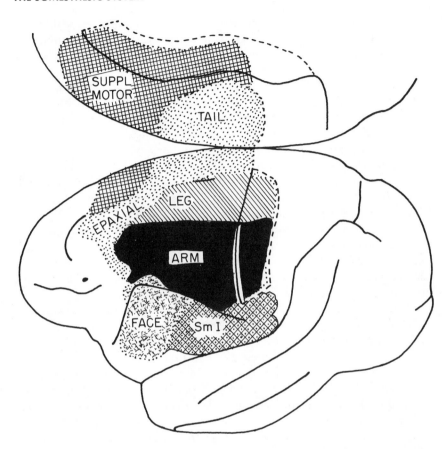

Regional boundaries for supplementary motor area, precentral motor area, and part of the postcentral sensory-motor field—SmI (from Woolsey, 1964). Copyright 1964 by University of Wisconsin Press, Madison. Reproduced by permission.

by fibers traversing the cervical fasciculus gracilis; proximal portions, by the dorsolateral fasciculus.

Studies by Bard (1938), Adrian (1941), Marshall (1951), Woolsey (1964), and others have identified a second somatosensory cortical projection area (SII) in experimental animals. Penfield (1958b) has found a similar region in man, situated on the superior bank of the sylvian fissure, occupying the inferior extension of the precentral gyrus. This area receives inputs, not only from the contralateral side of the body, but also from the ipsilateral. In man contralateral responses are clearly more frequent, but ipsilateral and bilateral responses are also seen. Cortical representation of body parts is grossly somatotopic with considerable overlapping.

The characteristics of sensations experienced by human beings with stimulation of SII are similar to the paresthesias experienced following stimulation of the postcentral gyrus. In addition, however, more complex sensations occur, including a desire to move, or a tendency to excute a particular motor behavior, occasionally associated with an inhibition of voluntary motor control, a paralysis, or a sudden loss of dexterity. From these observations Penfield concluded that this area plays a role in the control of voluntary movement, mainly on the contralateral side, but also bilaterally. Of interest is that ablation of this area produces neither sensory nor motor deficit.

Mountcastle (1961) has provided evidence to show that the secondary somesthetic area is the cortical locus for the representation of pain. Anatomic studies had already demonstrated that ablation of this cortical region was followed by degeneration in posterior thalamic nuclei (Rose and Woolsey, 1949), and physiological studies had shown that stimulation of the posterior thalamic nuclei produced responses in the secondary somesthetic area (Knighton, 1950). This region of the thalamus is known to respond to mechanical and nociceptive stimuli and is linked to receptive fields covering large areas but with no somatotopic representation.

These observations could be interpreted as indicating that the two major somatosensory transmission pathways from periphery to cortex—the spinothalamic and medial lemniscal systems—project to separate and distinct nuclear relay clusters, and from these different thalamic complexes to different cortical territories. The primary somatosensory area would receive inputs from the lemniscal system; the secondary somatosensory area, from the spinothalamic. In fact the situation is not quite so clear. For example, in the cat the spinothalamic system sends a portion of its fibers toward the nuclear relays that subserve the lemniscal system. In addition the secondary sensory cortex maintains a pattern of representation that is as precise as that found in the primary sensory cortex, and the columnar pattern of organization seen in SI is also seen in SII. One also finds cells in SII that are specific for modality and location. These results are inconsistent with the conclusion that SII receives only nonspecific pain stimulus relays from the posterior thalamus. Rather, a more consistent conclusion is that SII presents functional characteristics that relate to properties of both the lemniscal and the spinothalamic systems (Jones and Powell, 1969a,b). Evidence exists as well to show that the postcentral gyrus also contains some properties of the spinothalamic system (presence of cells with large receptive fields, responding to ipsilateral and contralateral stimuli and to nociceptive stimuli), although to a very small degree.

Despite objective anatomic and physiological evidence to the contrary, SI and SII had nonetheless been considered functionally distinct. One prinicpal reason is that ablations of SI caused deficits in tactile discrimination in experimental animals, but ablations of *S*II did not. A study by Glassman (1974a) suggests, however, that, when appropriate behavioral techniques are used, the dichotomy may collapse. He found a deficit in learning a cutaneous discrimination task of light touch among cats with resections of *S*II. Jones and Powell (1969a,b) studied ipsilateral and contralateral corticocortical connections of somatic sensory areas in the rhesus monkey. Both *S*I and *S*II have afferent and efferent connections with thalamic ventroposterolateral nuclei, with area 4, with the supplementary motor cortex, and with each other. But *S*I, not *S*II, sends fibers to area 5 in the parietal cortex, the region of monkey cortex considered by Penfield to be equivalent to the supplementary sensory area in man. Moreover *S*II receives fibers from *S*I and sends fibers to *S*I and the motor area. For these reasons Jones and Powell consider *S*II to be a polymodal sensory integration area. As for corticofugal fibers both *S*I and *S*II send projections to the ventrobasal nuclei of the thalamus, and from there by way of the pyramidal tract to the nuclei of the dorsal columns.

Werner and Whitsell (1973) have presented a major review of studies concerned with functional organization of the somatosensory cortex. Instead of looking at the projections to cortex of fiber pathways or peripheral cells, they studied relationships between linear arrays of cortical neurons and peripheral patterns constituted by the totality of respective fields of the same cortical cellular dispositions. In this way they attempted to discover general rules that presided over mapping phenomena.

They found that the corporeal periphery was represented topographically at the cortex by a particularly precise pattern. Each dorsal root projects to an anteroposterior band of cellular columns extending across all cytoarchitectonic divisions of *S*1. The sequence of receptive fields for each band of columns passes from the medial to the lateral part of the root. By virtue of the internal organization of the anteroposterior bands the totality of receptive fields represented by a continuous mediolateral array describes a continuous trajectory on the body. Because of the geometric, tridimensional properties of the body, and because of the bidimensional representation of the body in cortical organization, no simple, one-to-one correspondence can be established between somesthetic receptor organ and cortical projection area. One's impression of contiguity of two adjacent receptive fields can be maintained only by means of an interpretation amounting to topological equivalence, and then only if these two receptive fields belong to the same trajectory of dermatome.

Properties of cells in posterior parietal areas (5 and 7) have also been subjected to analysis (e.g., Burchfiel and Duffy, 1972; Sakata et al, 1973; Hyvarinen and Poranen, 1974). Cells responding to joint movements and possessing complex receptive fields were found in area 5 (Duffy and Burchfiel, 1971). These cells are maximally activated when a limb is placed in a coordinated, physiological posture such as flexion. Inputs from such cells could be effective in providing feedback information to the motor system.

Sakata et al (1973) found that area 5 cells discharge in response not only to rotation at a joint but also to cutaneous and deep touch stimulation. However, specific physiological differences distinguished responses of cells in area 5 from those of cells in primary somatosensory areas. The somesthetic influx to area 5 seemed already to have been treated at $S1$. Anatomically it had previously been established that area 5 receives projections from areas 3, 1, and 2.

A functional difference also seems to exist between areas 5 and 7 (Sakata et al, 1973; Hyvarinen and Poranen, 1974). This is supported by anatomic evidence, since no direct projections have been found between $S1$ and area 7, but a one-way projection exists from area 5 to area 7 (Jones and Powell, 1969a,b). Functionally most cells of area 5 respond only to somesthetic stimulation, whereas somesthetic and visual inputs are integrated in area 7. In addition a limited portion of the posterior parietal area, that is, the inferior lip of the interparietal sulcus, has been recognized as subserving vestibular function (Fredrickson et al, 1966, 1973). The integrative activity of posterior parietal areas for somesthetic, kinesthetic, visual, and vestibular function provides a physiological basis for spatial perception and visually guided control of movement.

Mountcastle et al (1975) studied properties of neurons in areas 5 and 7 in a detailed manner. In 11 monkeys they identified and analyzed 1451 neurons in the two cortical areas. The animals were subjected to detection or detection and grasp tasks; learning was based on operant conditioning techniques. Unit activity was also measured in response to passive movement at joints, cutaneous stimulation, muscle sensation to pressure, auditory stimuli, visual stimuli, and motivational factors.

Neurons of areas 5 and 7 could clearly be distinguished from those of somatosensory areas by differences in physiological activity in response to the several stimuli. Among the distinguishing characteristics were some of particular interest: cellular activity did not appear unless the animal projected his arm within the immediate extrapersonal space to obtain something needed or desirable (food if it was hungry, something to drink if it was thirsty). The majority of cells remained silent in the presence of active movement that was nonmotivated. Certain cells were related to manual manipulation and were specifically activated by active exploratory or grooming movements of either hand.

Distribution of differently reacting cells within the posterior parietal cortex was as follows. Neurons activated by passive movement of joints were present only in area 5. Cells responding to various types of visual activity (fixation or exploration of interpersonal space) were found only in area 7. Projection cells and cells of manual manipulation were more or less equally distributed in both areas 5 and 7. Functional organization of the cells was columnar, as in koniocortical areas.

Intramodal and intermodal convergences and interactions were demonstrated only rarely—too rarely to permit these authors to accept the traditional model of function attached to association areas, that is, successive integration. We might wonder, however, if the number of cells found to be activated in area 7 by the combination of movement and visual fixation or exploration was so small because the area studied may represent an intermediate step toward another cortical region.

The studies of Mountcastle et al (1975) thus demonstrate the existence of specialized neuronal ensembles in the posterior parietal association cortex. These cells are capable of receiving afferent signals that describe bodily position and movement. This cortical region provides the structural basis for a command system controlling motor behavior of limbs, hands, and eyes in extrapersonal space, especially for highly motivated goals.

Anatomic and physiological studies have led us far in our understanding of the somesthetic system. An additional dimension has been added by behavioral correlational studies following cortical ablations in monkeys. The remainder of this section deals with these studies.

As early as 1917 Minkowski studied the behavioral correlations of rolandic and parietal gyri. Ablations limited to the ascending parietal gyrus caused contralateral hemianesthesia with a predominant effect on touch and localization. Ablations of the parietal lobe with sparing of the ascending parietal gyrus caused a more severe and permanent contralateral hemianesthesia for superficial and deep sensation. The significance of the posterior parietal cortex for somesthesis was underlined by results of subsequent studies using placing response, hopping reaction, and cutaneous discrimination as measuring devices. The placing and hopping responses evaluated spatial aspects of sensation; the discrimination tests evaluated different somesthetic qualities (e.g., weight, roughness).

Bard (1938) found that ablations of postcentral cortex abolished placing reactions on the contralateral side, while ablations of the precentral gyrus impaired jumping responses. Kessler and Kennard (1940) determined that placing reactions were permanently abolished only after parietal lobectomy. As for disturbances of discrimination Ruch et al (1938) studied such defects experimentally in monkeys and chimpanzees (and also in man after parietal lobe lesion). Ablation of the postcentral gyrus caused an impairment in discrimination of weight and roughness in the chimpanzeee, and also in the monkey, but to a lesser degree. Identical results were obtained if the lesion involved posterior parietal, and not postcentral, gyri. With total parietal lobectomy the deficit was permanent and more severe. In the chimpanzee trained to discriminate geometric forms ablation of the posterior parietal cortex provoked a loss of this function; this loss was only partially compensated for by relearning. Peele (1944), confirming these results, added that posterior parietal areas were responsible for proprioception, and postcentral gyrus was responsible for cutaneous tactile sensitivity. In sum these early studies indicated that spatial aspects of cutaneous somesthesis were mediated by cortex of the postcentral gyrus, while stereognostic and proprioceptive aspects were mediated by posterior parietal cortex.

In 1951 Semmes-Blum demonstrated permanent deficits in somatosensory discrimination (three-dimensional geometric forms, roughness, weight, hardness) by ablating sypramarginal gyrus, prestriate cortex, and posterior temporal regions bilaterally in monkeys. Anteriorly located lesions caused more severe deficits. The loss was most apparent with difficult discrimination tasks; easy discriminations were preserved. She later observed that these deficits in monkeys resembled tactile agnosias described in man. In both animal and human cases, ataxia, motor clumsiness, and cutaneous anesthesia were all absent (Semmes, 1965). Similar behavioral defects were observed in monkeys with posterior parietal lesions that left intact the primary somatosensory reception cortex and the posterior temporal lobes (Pribram and Barry, 1956; Wilson, 1957; Ettlinger and Kahlsbeck, 1962). Wilson (1957, 1965) demonstrated more specifically that posterior parietal lesions caused a deficit in tactile learning without a deficit in visual learning, while inferotemporal ablations caused the reverse picture. The issue to be considered was thus whether the posterior parietal region was a tactile association area analogous to the visual association area of the inferotemporal region. Wilson indeed contends that the parietal cortex is necessary for full use of tactile inputs.

It is generally accepted that the defective tactile discrimination resulting from posterior parietal lesions is not dependent on deficits of elementary cutaneous sensitivity (Moffett et al, 1967). Of the three major disorders found following posterior parietal ablation—defective form discrimination, defective precision of prehensile manual grasping (Ettlinger and Kahlsbeck, 1962), and defective spatial analysis—no functional interrelations have been discerned. Attempts have, therefore, been made to find intraparietal-behavioral correlations by means of partial ablations in the posterior parietal region (Moffett et al, 1967). Excisions limited to the anterior end of the interparietal sulcus are associated with severe defects of tactile discrimination. However, any lesion, no matter how limited, in the posterior parietal area in general produces a defect in tactile discrimination, although less severe, and every large lesion incorporating the anterior interparietal area produces deficits that are even more severe than those due to the limited lesion described above. Thus, specific, intraparietal regions especially responsible for one of the three major deficits have not yet been found. In addition, lesions in the posterior parietal area produce disorders of spatial discrimination in the visual modality, as well as in the tactile (Bates and Ettlinger, 1960).

In a series of studies conducted over a 25-year period Semmes and her collaborators have attempted to refine our understanding of cortical mechanisms of somesthesis (Semmes et al, 1951–1975). Ablation of sensorimotor cortex was found to cause a delay in learning difficult tactile form discriminations with the limb ipsilateral to the lesion and, also on the same side, an elevation in differential threshold for roughness but not for size. Ablation of nonsensorimotor, posterior association cortex, with or without section of the corpus callosum, caused elevations of threshold for roughness and for size but no impairment of difficult tactile form discriminations with the limb contralateral to the lesion. However, ablation of the same, nonsensorimotor, parietal regions did cause a deficit in acquisition of strategies for learning discrimination problems, even for easily discriminable forms, but only for the contralateral hand. This deficit was more marked with callosal section.

Ridley and Ettlinger (1975) were unable to find anatomically isolated zones within the posterior parietal and prestriate regions (areas 5, 7, 19) that were selectively responsible for different tactile or visuospatial tasks. The possibility cannot be excluded that functional equipotentiality exists in the parietoprestriate area, although with anterior lesions in this area in the immediate postoperative period a deficit in tactile discrimination and in acquisition of a reversal task occurs. Semmes et al (1974) presented results of further studies of anterior postcentral lesions in monkeys. They had previously reported that monkeys with unilateral ablation of the hand area in the postcentral gyrus contralateral to the tested hand were severely impaired on tasks of somesthetic discrimination (Semmes and Porter, 1972). Yet earlier investigators (Ruch, Fulton, and Geruar, 1938; Orbach and Chow, 1959) had found different results: either moderate or no impairment after complete bilateral removal of postcentral gyri. The Semmes group produced the somesthetic deficit and studied the influence on the deficit of preoperative training, a 6-month recovery period, and complete or bilateral postcentral removals. None of these variables ameliorated the deficit. The authors suggested that in earlier studies the representation of finger tips near the bottom of the posterior bank of the central sulcus may have been spared. These observations are supported by findings of an additional study (Randolph and Semmes, 1974), which show that removals confined to the posterior bank, leaving the convexity of the postcentral gyrus largely intact, produce deficits almost as severe as the anterior postcentral removals do.

Randolph and Semmes (1974) have also studied the effect of limited cortical ablations in the somesthetic area representing the hand. When the posterior bank of the sylvian fissure, area 3, was destroyed, a deficit was present on all tests of tactile discrimination. When the posterior half of the postcentral gyrus was ablated, the deficit was restricted to tactile discrimination of corners (three-dimensional forms). When the lesion involved the anterior half of the posterior central gyrus, area 7, a deficit was found on tests requiring discrimination of texture (hardness, softness, smoothness, roughness). Area 3 was thus found to be most important for fine discrimination. When area 3 was destroyed, only gross tactile discriminations could be acquired, since posterior regions possessed more selective functions.

Ablation of frontal or temporal regions alone produced somesthetic deficits similar to those produced by larger, more nearly comprehensive hemispheric lesions, but this effect was not seen following ablations limited to the occipital lobe. The role of frontal and hippocampal lesions in the production of deficits of tactile learning was also shown (Orbach and Fischer, 1959; Ettlinger, 1960; Teitelbaum, 1974). Because frontal, hippocampal, and amygdalar lesions may cause a task-dependent learning deficit independent of sensory modality, Semmes et al (1969) believe that the tactile learning defect observed in the contralateral hand following frontal or temporal ablations with corpus callosal section is not truly modality specific. They interpret this defect as representing loss of the supramodal contribution to somesthesis normally provided by these lobes by means of corticocortical connections between them and the sensorimotor area responsible for the contralateral hand. An alternative interpretation is provided by Geschwind (1965), who suggests that the somesthetic defects may result from a corticolimbic disconnection in which somesthetic stimuli are disconnected from limbic (olfactory, gustatory, emotional) reinforcements. Yet another explanation is that of Konorski (1967), who speaks of a recent memory defect specific to the task and the sensory modality.

Cortical Somesthetic Defects

Cortical "Sensory" Loss

We owe the first descriptions of cortical somatosensory loss to Verger (1902) and Dejerine (1907, 1914). The Verger–Dejerine syndrome consists of a severe impairment in the ability to recognize by touch the attributes of an object (hardness, roughness, etc.), loss of tactile localization, loss of sense of position of a limb in space, loss of form discrimination, loss of two-point discrimination, and impairment of stereognosis. By contrast, peripheral sensitivities to touch, deep pressure, heat, cold, and pain are only minimally reduced and, at times, are clinically normal. Frequent clinicopathological correlations have confirmed the relation of these signs and symptoms to lesions of parietal cortex.

Disorders of sensation for touch, temperature, pain, and vibration are known to be rare following cortical lesions. Nonetheless Dejerine and Mouzon (1914) described such a case. Association of cortical lesions with loss of sensation for pain alone is more generally recognized (Cushing, 1909; Kleist, 1933; Marshall, 1951; Biemond, 1956). Biemond (1956) in particular believed that a region of the inferior parietal lobe, corresponding to SII as we have described it previously, received projections from the region of the thalamus responsible for treating pain stimuli. Penfield (1958b) added anatomoclinical arguments in favor of the supplementary sensory cortex, located on the medial, interhemispheric surface of the parietal lobe, as being the cortical zone responsible for pain. For Head (1920) pain sensitivity was almost never impaired from strictly cortical lesions. He drew a similar conclusion for thermal sensitivity, although he accepted an extensive neutral zone for which excitation was called neither hot nor cold, the discrimination of differences between the two temperature extremes being very difficult.

Head (1920) provided an extensive analysis of cortical sensory defects. He observed that light touch sensitivity was never completely lost but that there was such a variability in response to tactile stimulation of graduated intensity that the threshold for tactile perception could not be obtained. This response variability increased as the length of examination time increased; it seemed to result from an extreme fatiguability of "local" attention, since response remained accurate on the healthy side. Head also referred to a persistence of tactile sensations and a tendency for tactile hallucinations to explain the impossibility of obtaining an excitation threshold. Head and Holmes (1911) attached an extreme importance to the nature of the impairment of tactile discrimination—the ability to distinguish two simultaneous tactile sensations might be lost even though cutaneous touch sensitivity for a single stimulus was preserved. Localization of points of cutaneous stimulation was also impaired. Defective position sense and sense of passive movement were found to be most frequent following cortical somatosensory area lesions; these defects were most prominent distally in the involved limbs. Hallucinations of movement might also be present, complicating the clinical picture. Discrimination of form, dimensions of objects, volume, and stereognosis was often impaired, if not totally lost. In milder cases, sensation of roughness was spared, but even in the mildest cases the capacity to discern the structure of an object was lost. Vibratory sense was usually preserved.

From this analytic study Head concluded that the cortical somatosensory region was responsible for three main functions: (1) spatial recognition, made possible by use of the senses of passive movement, position, and topesthesia; (2) appreciation of tactile, thermal, or painful stimulus intensity differences; and (3) recognition of similarities and differences of objects, forms, weights, consistencies, and volumes. These three functions were not always altered to the same degree by cortical lesions; they were relatively independent. For

Head and Holmes an active participation of the totality of psychological function was required for these three aspects of human behavior to be fully carried out; that is, these three functions of sensory cortex were perceptual, not sensorial. The major conclusions of Head have had a great influence on subsequent studies of somatosensory function, even though they have not been wholeheartedly accepted by clinicians. In fact, in clinical behavioral neurology it is rare indeed to find the combinations of deficits in the manner defined by Head.

The topographical distribution of cortical anesthesias is variable. Hemianesthesia is the most common variety, the face often being spared. The sensory defect is most marked distally in the limbs, the upper being more severely involved than the lower. More rarely a pseudoradicular distribution is seen—radial in the arms or sciatic in the legs (Athanasio-Benisty, 1918; Foerster, 1936; Marshall, 1951). An unusual form involves small, isolated portions of the body surface, especially the hand (around the thumb) and face (around the mouth).

Subjective disorders of sensation due to cortical lesions are frequent. They occur as paroxysmal paresthesias, in migraine or in epilepsy, in which a characteristic "Jacksonian sensory march" may correspond to the somatotopic representation of the ascending parietal gyrus. Painful sensations of cortical origin are much less frequent; they have only rarely been produced by cortical stimulation. Permanent subjective disorders of sensation from cortical lesions are rarer still, and their localization is open to question. Published cases have mostly been due to tumors rather than to vascular lesions with clearly delimited pathology. Angelergues and Hécaen (1958), studying pain syndromes resulting from cerebral hemispheric lesions, observed a frequent association between auras of pain and auras of somatognosia that affected the same body part.

In addition to clinical descriptions and anatomoclinical correlations, a number of quantitative, systematic neuropsychological studies of somesthesis in man have appeared. Semmes et al (1960) studied two groups of subjects, those with missile wounds of the brain and controls. Modalities tested were cutaneous pressure, two-point discrimination, tactile localization, sense of passive movement, and discrimination of qualities of roughness, texture, size, and two-dimensional form. The observations of this study were at variance with earlier teachings. Sensory representation was found to be different, depending on the hemisphere damaged. Tactile sensation was more diffusely located in the right than in the left hemisphere. For example, sensory deficits of the right hand were clearly more frequent following a lesion of the left sensorimotor cortex than following lesions of any region of the left hemisphere except the left sensorimotor region. By contrast, sensory deficits of the left hand were no more frequent following right sensorimotor cortex lesions than following lesions elsewhere in the right hemisphere. The nature of the defect was different as well. Right-hand somesthetic defects seemed to be simply different degrees of the same fundamental problem; left-hand somesthetic defects reflected at least two qualitatively different problems: cutaneous pressure and tactile localization. As for somatic representation in the cortex, again differences were found. Lesions of the right sensorimotor cortex caused contralateral sensory deficits, lesions of the left sensorimotor cortex caused mainly ipsilateral sensory defects, with or without concomitant involvement of the contralateral limb. Vaughan and Costa (1962), with a series of sensory and motor tests administered to subjects with unilateral hemispheric damage, also found a greater prevalence of ipsilateral somatosensory deficits following left hemispheric lesions.

Other studies have not confirmed all the results of the Semmes et al report. Corkin et al (1970) evaluated the contrasting effects of postcentral gyrus and posterior parietal lobe excision on somatosensory thresholds. Permanent effects were found only with postcentral gyrus resection; the more severe deficits were associated with lesions involving the hand area. When the resection involved posterior parietal regions, without including the postcentral gyrus, no deficit was found. Similarly no sensory deficit was seen following resections limited to the precentral gyrus. No hemispheric differences were observed: ipsilateral sensory defects were found in 20 of the 50 subjects with parietal resection, the defect being significant only for tactile localization. In the presence of a postcentral gyrus lesion the severity of a contralateral deficit did not seem to be related to the existence of an ipsilateral deficit; rather the severity of the contralateral defect seemed more related to extent of lesion.

Boll (1974) studied the effects of lateralized cerebral lesions on tactile perception on the ipsilateral and contralateral sides of the body. Patients with right-brain damage had greater difficulties on either side of the body than patients did with left-brain damage. Moreover, total errors were greater in the group with right-brain damage. Boll concluded that the right hemisphere is preeminent in subserving tactile perception on both sides of the body.

In another study four children who had undergone hemidecortication for infantile hemiplegia were tested for tactile matching ability (Kohn and Dennis, 1974). Better tactile recognition was found with the hand ipsilateral to the hemidecortication than with the contralateral. On intermanual matching tasks, recognition of textures, but not shapes, was superior to that obtained with the contralateral hand alone. It was determined that recognition of ipsilaterally mediated tactile input could be modulated. In analyzing their data, the authors referred to behavioral and physiological studies indicating that mediation of somatic sensitivity in each lateral body half involves both cerebral hemispheres (see our anatomic and physiological review above and also Wall and Dubner, 1972). Unilateral brain damage can cause impaired sensitivity in both hands. The authors concluded that their evidence provided clinical support to the experimental data suggesting that somatosensory pathways project bilaterally.

Carmon and Benton (1969) studied tactile perception of direction and number in patients with unilateral cerebral disease. For either test, regardless of hemispheric lesion lateralization, the frequency of errors was greater on the contralateral than on the ipsilateral hand. For tactile number perception with the hand contralateral to the lesion no differences were found between brain-damaged groups. With the hand ipsilateral to the lesion, performance for both brain-damaged groups was statistically similar to that for controls. For tactile perception of direction, defects were severe with the contralateral hand for both brain-damaged groups and were present in the ipsilateral hand only in the group with right hemispheric lesions.

In a continuation study Fontenot and Benton (1971) compared subjects with left and right hemispheric lesions on a task of perception of the direction of tactile stimulation applied to the palms of the hands. Right-brain-damaged subjects had bilateral deficits; left-brain-damaged subjects had deficits only in the right hand. They tentatively concluded that the right hemisphere mediates spatial perception of tactile stimuli. In contrast with these results, however, were those of Carmon (1971) in a study of disturbances of tactile sensitivity in patients with unilateral cerebral lesions. He measured absolute pressure threshold, differential pressure threshold, and tactile resolution (two-point discrimination). Many patients with unilateral brain damage had bilateral sensory loss, whereas the left- and right-brain-damaged groups were equal for frequency of bilateral defects. These results in part confirm the earlier findings of Semmes et al (1960).

Split-brain studies have added experimental data. Milner and Taylor (1972) tested seven patients with surgical section of forebrain commissures for delayed matching of tactile patterns. In six the left hand was better than the right, a finding thereby demonstrating right hemispheric specialization for perception and recall of spatial patterns by touch.

The question of differences in hemispheric representation for somesthesis is thus not resolved. Differences of observations among various research teams may result in part from differences in etiologies of brain damage in subjects studied. We would agree with Carmon and Benton that it is with respect to the nature of the tactile performance that a bilateral effect of a unilateral lesion may be seen. For example, bilaterality of defect may result from right hemispheric damage if the discriminative task involves spatial direction. We might wonder if, by contrast, a bilateral defect in appreciating the meaning of language written on the skin would be more likely to result from a left hemispheric lesion.

Involvement of a spatial factor in tactile discrimination performance, associated with right hemispheric lesions, has been found by a number of authors. Corkin (1965) found such involvement in a test of tactually guided maze learning; DeRenzi and Scotti (1969) on a tactile form-board task. Semmes et al (1955) observed dissociated performances on the spatial aspects and the elementary sensory aspects of somesthetic tests in brain-damaged subjects. In reviewing earlier analyses, Semmes (1965) noted no significant association between somesthetic disorders of form discrimination and aphasia, defective motor control, or other cognitive defect. An impairment of spatial orientation was correlated with a defect in tactile form discrimination but not with defects of roughness, size, or texture discrimination. Defects of elementary tactile sensitivity were associated with disturbances in the discrimination of qualities of objects but were associated only with disturbances of tactile discrimination of forms if the lesion was lateralized to the right hemisphere.

In sum we may conclude that tactile discrimination of form depends on at least two factors, general spatial perception and elementary somesthesis. Defects in either of these two capacities may produce an impairment in tactile form discrimination, but such tactile impairment would be most severe when the two component factors are both deficient, as is seen with right hemispheric lesions. With left hemispheric lesions the several functional defects are more easily localized, but they do not seem to combine, as is the case with right hemispheric lesions. It may be possible to postulate the existence of two separate and independent areas in the left parietal region for the two factors. We would tentatively hypothesize that a different organization of functional representation exists in the two hemispheres, rather than simply a different degree of hemispheric dominance for a single function.

Pure Astereognosia

The problem of tactile asymbolia, pure astereognosia (loss of the ability to recognize the nature of an object by touch), was posed most clearly by Wernicke in 1895, although the astereognosias had already been distinguished from nonspecific anesthesias by earlier authors (Puchelt, 1844; Hoffman, 1885). Wernicke based his analyses on two cases with "tactile paralysis"; his proposition was analogous to what he had provided for aphasia. The disorder results from a lesion in the "center for tactile images." The tactile agnosias could be divided into primary agnosia and secondary agnosia, or asymbolia. In the former, one sees loss of primary identification, that is, of the ability to recognize tactile qualities of an object, because of an inability to evoke tactile images. In the latter, tactile asymbolia, the tactile memory images are not destroyed, but they cannot be associated with (i.e., they are disconnected from) other sensory representations, and the full significance of the object cannot be appreciated.

These notions of Wernicke were generally adopted, and subsequent authors presented case reports without paying much attention to details regarding the state of elementary somesthesis, until Dejerine (1907, 1914). Dejerine criticized these observations and, on the basis of personal case reports, declared that elementary somesthetic defects were a constant feature of every case of so-called pure astereognosia. As the history of studies on pure astereognosia unfolds, we see the battle lines drawn clearly between those who believed that elementary sensory defects were an integral and essential part of the syndromes of astereognosia and those who believed the opposite.

Experiences with soldiers who had received brain injuries during earlier wars and World War I supported the position of Wernicke (e.g., Raymond and Egger, 1906; Gerstmann, 1918; Campora, 1925). Other authors (e.g., J. Stein, 1924; Stein and von Weizsacker, 1926; Bay, 1944) stated that one-time examinations were unsatisfactory for determining the state of somesthetic function; elementary sensory deficits were best demonstrated by a dynamic, longitudinal evaluation of somesthesis. The observed disorders were said to be the result of quantitative modifications of sensory function, of a lability and inconstancy of sensory excitation arriving from the periphery in such a way that tactile recognition—a complicated, highly differentiated function— could be deranged by small lesions situated at different levels in the sensory system.

In 1935 Delay, basing his argument on Pavlov's conception of sensory analyzers, proposed a new model for classification of tactile agnosias. He criticized somewhat Head's views and accepted as cortical "sensory" skills only those activities related to interpretation of sensation as a function of intensity or extent of sensory input. If these functions were disrupted, the clinical picture of tactile agnosia was seen, with a basis in disordered cortical analyzers for intensity or extent. The total clinical picture could result either from an impairment of elementary sensation or from malfunction of the cortical analyzers. Ahylognosia, the loss of the capacity to differentiate structural components of objects, resulted from impairment of the intensity analyzers; amorphognosia, the loss of the capacity to differentiate forms, resulted from impairment of the analyzers of extent. Tactile asymbolia could develop as a third type of agnosia, if the cortical analyzers were not damaged; in this case the elementary qualities of an object were appreciated, but the significance of the whole was lost. This conceptualization recalls, of course that of Wernicke but with modified terminology.

Primary agnosias of intensity correspond, in Head's description, to impairments in the capacity to appreciate differences of intensity of tactile, thermal, pain, weight, and texture stimuli. The studies of Semmes et al described above indicate that these agnosias are not seen in the absence of disorders of elementary sensation. The same studies, by contrast, support the existence of a limited form of pure astereognosia, related to perception of extent, and corresponding in Head's description to impairments in the capacity to appreciate form and volume, or in Semmes's description to impairments in the skill of tactile spatial recognition. Before accepting the existence of pure astereognosia in any form, one must first demonstrate integrity of Head's three cortical sensory functions or Delay's two cortical sensory analyzers, since, as Wernicke indicated, the elementary tactile qualities of objects are always recognized, and only the underlying nature, the significance, of the object is not seized.

Clinical reports of pure astereognosia are rare, but they exist (Raymond and Egger, 1906; Bonhoeffer, 1918; Gerstmann, 1918; Campora, 1925; Guillan and Bize, 1932; Hécaen and David, 1945). In some cases the asymbolic picture precedes the appearance of elementary sensory defects, and in some cases it persists following regression of the elementary defects. The subject might eventually succeed in recognizing the object in the affected hand, but in such a case he succeeds by means of deduction; that is, instead of immediately recognizing the object, as he does with his unaffected hand, he analyzes its substance and form, pieces together the elements, and finally recognizes it, if the object is a common one. The case report of Hécaen and David (1945) is particularly instructive in this regard. The subject had no difficulty recognizing objects palpated with the left hand. When, for example, a key was placed in his affected right hand, the subject commented "It is a long object, round, an empty circle, of metal (long hesitation) a key!" Performance was similar with other objects placed in the right hand, although the subject was not always successful at the end. When this same subject was asked to draw a picture of an object placed in his right hand that he was unable to recognize, he was reasonably successful in making the drawing, and he could then recognize the object from the picture.

Despite the arguments in favor of the existence of a syndrome of pure astereognosia, arguments supported by rare but real and vivid case reports, two types of counterarguments are put forth by opponents: one deals with questions of elementary sensory defects, the other, with problems of modality-specific anomia.

The problem of elementary sensory defect was pursued by Bay (1944), who developed a similar theme by Stein and Weizsacker (1926). Bay denied that pure astereognosia exists and declared that published case studies were inadequate because of incomplete evaluation of elementary sensation. After analysis of six cases he drew four main conclusions. First lability of the tactile sensitivity threshold influenced tactile object recognition, because the coordination and constancy of tactile excitations were reduced. Second the essential problem was a loss of finesse of tactile impressions, and so errors in discrimination would naturally occur. Third the degree of "so-called agnosia" was parallel to the degree of impairment of elementary sensitivities. Finally the disorders of tactile recognition were an immediate and exclusive consequence of disorders of primary sensation. Supporting these conclusions were the results of the neuropsychological study by Corkin et al (1970). These authors found disorders of tactile object identification only in those brain-damaged subjects who had sensory deficits.

To counter these arguments we have recourse to details of case reports. In the Hécaen (1972b) case, for example, careful attention was paid to primary sensation. Exploration of primary sensation in a time-dependent, dynamic, longitudinal manner, as suggested by Stein and Weizsacker (1926), revealed neither lability of sensory threshold nor sensory perseveration. Touch, tactile discrimination, and appreciation of thickness were identical on both hands. The asymbolic hand had an altered threshold for pain reception, by comparison with the normal hand; the affected hand was also less sensitive in appreciating forms in a series going from ovoid to sphere. In the case reported by Delay (1935) no differences between the two hands were found for sensitivity thresholds for tactile pressure, pain, temperature, kinesthesis, and vibration, although tactile localization and discrimination were reduced in the affected hand. Nonetheless tactile recognition of the qualities of objects was preserved. In the light of these observations it would seem a weak argument to claim that sensory loss was the cause of the severe asymbolic defect.

The issue of modality-specific anomia provides a stronger argument against the existence of a syndrome of tactile asymbolia. This argument runs as follows: when an object is placed in the hand contralateral to the nondominant hemisphere, impulses successfully travel to the nondominant hemisphere, and tactile identification is normal. However, because of a lesion in the corpus callosum, impulses cannot travel from the somatosensory area of the nondominant hemisphere to the language zone in the dominant hemisphere; thus the object cannot be named. This syndrome, also called tactile aphasia, was envisaged from an early date (Claparede, 1906; Raymond and Egger, 1906) and has been revitalized in recent years by the anatomoclinical studies of Geschwind (Geschwind and Kaplan, 1962; Geschwind, 1965) and the split-brain studies of Sperry and Gazzaniga (1967).

The patient described by Geschwind and Kaplan (1962) had infarction of the anterior four-fifths of the corpus callosum. Thus the somatosensory area of the right hemisphere was separated from the language-dominant left hemisphere. Among other signs of the "anterior callosal disconnection syndrome" was evidence of tactile aphasia. Objects placed in the right hand were correctly named; objects placed in the left hand were misnamed (e.g., ball instead of watch, spoon instead of screw driver, etc.). The patient was able to draw or manually indicate usage of objects placed in her left hand, and she could correctly point with her affected left hand to the object she had misnamed, when it was shown to her with other objects on a multiple-choice test. Earlier case reports (Goldstein, 1916; Hoff 1931b) had already noted the presence of left-hand tactile "asymbolia" and its association with left-sided apraxia in patients with callosal lesions. The split-brain subjects of Sperry and Gazzaniga (1967) could not name, either orally or by writing, objects placed in their left hand; they provided whatever name happened to enter their mind. However, they were able to demonstrate knowledge of how the object should be used, by means of appropriate manipulations, and they could find the object by palpation of a group of objects, even after a delay of several minutes. The patients with tactile asymbolia reported by Delay (1935) and Hécaen and David (1945) could find an object by palpation on multiple choice if the object was first shown to them, if the object had previously been palpated by either hand, or if the name of the object was given.

In most cases reported, the tactile asymbolia was limited to the left hand; this corresponded to the tactile aphasia hypothesis. In the case of Hécaen and David (1945) the right hand was involved. However, this subject was left-handed and had only a mild and transitory aphasia following trauma to his left hemisphere; he easily regained his writing skills with his left hand. The subject described by Raymond and Egger (1906) also had right-hand involvement. However, handedness was not indicated, and this subject had only transitory, primarily anomic, language defects. Thus clinical observations are generally in favor of the hypothesis that tactile asymbolia is really tactile anomia resulting from disconnection between somesthetic regions and the zone of language.

Nonetheless case reports have been published for which the hypothesis of tactile anomia by disconnection could not possibly be correct. These are cases in which bilateral astereognosia is caused by a unilateral hemispheric lesion (e.g., Oppenheim, 1906; Goldstein, 1916; Foix, 1922). The anatomoclinical observation by Lhermitte and de Ajuriaguerra (1938) is an example: this patient was unable to identify objects by palpation with either hand, although primary qualities of objects could be identified by palpation, and, with the exception of two-point discrimination, elementary sensation was intact. Autopsy results showed evidence of temporal and parietal atrophy, very marked on the left, very mild on the right. In an earlier section we called attention to neuropsychological studies that demonstrate bilateral somatosensory defects from unilateral lesions (Semmes et al, 1960; Carmon, 1971; Wall and Dubner, 1972; Boll, 1974). The anatomoclinical reports may be more easily interpreted in the light of such studies.   .

Rather than answer questions, our review of somatosensory perceptual defects due to cortical lesions has highlighted existing contradictions and raised new questions. From the anatomic point of view, for example, the standard teaching that the posterior parietal area plays a primary role in somatosensory perceptual function has been thrown into doubt (Corkin et al 1970). Classically the tactile agnosias were related to lesions in a tactognostic zone of integration located in the posterior parietal region and not to lesions in the primary somesthetic strip. Animal experimentation seemed to confirm the role played by the posterior parietal region in somatosensory integration. However, Bay (1944) contended that the rolandic gyri were involved in the "so-called agnosias," and subsequent observations with postmortem verification have not contradicted this contention. Finally the corpus callosum must also be considered in any theory that tries to relate anatomy to tactile symbolic behavior.

As to hemispheric lateralization, current research raises additional questions. Unilateral lesions in either hemisphere have been found to produce either contralateral or bilateral stereognosic defects. Following right hemispheric lesions a supramodal spatial factor seems to express itself in certain bilateral disorders of tactile perception, in a manner similar to that found with the visual system. The observation of an association between defective spatial orientation in the visual modality and defective tactile discrimination of forms caused Semmes (1965) to reject the existence of a pure tactile agnosia, at least in the classical terms of a disorder specific to tactile integration. For Semmes the supramodal spatial factor is an essential nontactual element in astereognosis.

As for the associative-cognitive aspect of tactile asymbolia, one can only be intrigued by the simplicity of the disconnection hypothesis. An alternative proposal, not necessarily mutually exclusive, comes from the field of animal experimentation. Wilson (1957, 1965) suggests that a parietal tactile association area subserves tactile gnosis in the monkey. Destruction of this area impairs certain behavioral strategies. Significance, defined in the monkey by the reward system, cannot develop, even though elementary stimulus characteristics are appreciated. Defective discrimination of object qualities would not depend necessarily on a sensory deficiency but rather on a reduction of the possibilities for additional fixation on tactile stimuli. In a free-choice setting monkeys with posterior parietal ablations show preferences and aversions to tactile patterns in a manner similar to that of normal monkeys. As attractive as this hypothesis might be to explain pure tactile agnosia, other animal studies that do not show the same results offer serious difficulties for its adoption.

Additional research, not only on subjects with unilateral hemispheric lesions, but also on individual patients with tactile asymbolia, is necessary before questions of tactile agnosia can be answered. A promising line of research might be that proposed by Hécaen et al (1974) with respect to visual agnosia: that we might be dealing with a modality-specific inability to categorize. At least we can conclude that tactile agnosia is more than a simple disorder in elementary somatosensory function. The role played by spatial or verbal factors, or both, must be clarified before we can fully accept the reality of pure astereognosia—the inability to recognize the meaning of an object presented to the sense of touch.

SOMATOGNOSIS AND ASOMATOGNOSIA

Somatognosis (body schema, body image, image of self) refers to knowledge or sense of one's own body and bodily condition; asomatognosia is a loss of this knowledge. There has been an unfortunate tendency to enshroud the concept with vagueness. Despite a certain ambiguity inherent in the notion of somatognosis, the psychological reality of this concept has emerged clearly and concretely from clinical observation during the years. Certain behavior patterns, certain declarations of patients could be interpreted only as reflecting an impaired knowledge of the body.

In discussing this subject, we begin with concrete clinical data based on analyses of patients with cortical lesions. We divide disorders of body image into two groups: those that affect one side of the body, contralateral to the lesion, and those that affect both sides of the body. We examine the role of hemispheric lateralization of lesions, the associated symptomatology, and the behavior pattern of the brain-damaged subject. Finally we consider neuropsychological studies and theories designed to elucidate underlying mechanisms.

Anatomoclinical Aspects

Unilateral Asomatognosias

The first descriptions of unilateral asomatognosias—unawareness or denial of hemiplegia—were provided by Anton's clinical observations (1893, 1899). However, it was Babinski (1914) who clearly demonstrated that these unilateral defects could result from a focal cortical lesion and that primary sensory deficiencies could not explain the disorder.

Unilateral asomatognosia primarily affects the left side of the body in right-handed subjects with right hemispheric lesions. Cases have been described that are exceptions to this rule (Denny-Brown et al, 1952; Denny-Brown and Banker, 1954; Weinstein and Kahn, 1955; Weinstein, 1969), but in our experience these exceptions are rare, especially when the disorder is persistent. Paroxysmal or transient unilateral right-sided asomatognosia may, however, be seen. The incidence of unilateral or bilateral defects and their relation to hemispheric lateralization was reported by Hécaen (1968) from a series of 308 right-handed subjects with unilateral, retrorolandic lesions, right or left.

Hemisphere Damaged	Somatognosic Defect		
Right	Unilateral:	39/136 (29%)	
	Bilateral:	4/136 (3%)	
Left	Unilateral:	7/172 (4%)	
	Bilateral:	34/172 (20%)	

Anosognosia means unawareness or denial of illness. Somatognosic disturbances following right hemispheric lesions are generally seen as anosognosia,
or unawareness of a left hemiplegia. Frequently, but not exclusively, seen
after recovery from coma, the hemiplegic refuses to admit the reality of his
paralysis. If the examiner persists with the same request, the patient persists
with the same response. Every attempt to show the patient that one side of his
body is paralyzed is met with indifference or is grossly rebuffed. The patient
may accuse the doctor of exaggeration or error.

In a milder version of the same defect the patient does not deny his hemiplegia; he simply reacts to it with indifference. Hécaen et al (1954) described
a patient with this form. When asked to lift his left hand, the patient persistently lifted his right hand. When told that he was raising the wrong hand,
the patient replied with an indifferent air "I can't on the left; especially with
my arm." Even though he seemed to recognize his error, the patient again
responded with his right hand, when the original question was again posed.

These two varieties of asomatognosia—denial of hemiplegia (anosognosia)
and indifference to hemiplegia (anosodiaphoria)—form a part of the hemiasomatognosic syndrome (Lhermitte, 1939); in some instances they may be the
only elements of the neurobehavioral syndrome. The common characteristic
essential to either of these conditions is the failure to integrate one side of the
body into consciousness of the whole body. However varied the manifestations of the Anton–Babinski syndrome may be, study of the complete behavior pattern always reveals this one-sided reduction of the body image. At
times a patient may suffer from an acute and painful impression that one side
of his body has disappeared, and despite evidence to the contrary presumably
available to his sensory systems, he is uncertain of the integrity of his body. In
such a case the subject fails to recognize a portion of his body as being his
own and may attribute that body part to another person. For example, if the
examiner were to pick up this patient's paralyzed left arm, the patient would
declare that the arm in question belonged to the examiner.

A case of this sort was described by Olsen (1941). The patient denied her
left hemiplegia, declaring that her left arm and leg belonged either to the
doctor or to some other person sleeping in the same bed as she was. When she
was asked to verify visually that her left arm was indeed the direct continuation of her left shoulder, she replied, "My eyes and my feelings are not in

agreement; and I must believe what I feel. I sense by looking that they are as if they are mine, but I feel that they are not; and I cannot believe my eyes." Occasionally these feelings of missing body parts are accompanied by or provoke delirious or hallucinatory experiences (Ehrenwald, 1931a,b; Angyal and Frick, 1941).

From a purely descriptive point of view we would single out three behavioral features of the unilateral asomatognosias. Clinically each of these may be found in a more or less isolated form. However, as we have already indicated, they are more likely to be found together. (1) Anosognosia represents negation or denial of the motor deficit in the presence of left hemiplegia. (2) Hemiasomatognosia may range from simple neglect to total unawareness of one side of the body. (3) The feeling of absence of a body part or of one whole side of the body includes several variants: sentiments of strangeness, feeling that a body part does not belong, and phantom limbs.

Alloesthesia, although seen in other conditions, is a frequent behavioral feature of the unilateral asomatognosias. This phenomenon, which refers to displacement of a sensation, occurs when a stimulus applied to one side of the body is felt on the other side of the body, usually in a homologous region. Alloesthesia, in addition to its association with unilateral asomatognosia, has also been described in hysteria and in subjects with medullary lesions. It has been produced experimentally in animals by medullary section or by treatment with strychnine (Brown-Sequard, 1859, 1863; Mott, 1833; de Barenne and Dusser, 1916). In general, stimuli to one side of the body retain their essential qualities, even though appreciated on the other side of the body.

The clinical forms of alloesthesia may vary in extent and intensity and even with respect to the sensory modality involved. In the case described by Bender et al (1949a), for example, the following pattern was noted during recovery. First the alloesthetic phenomenon involved one side of the body except the leg; then the alloesthetic response became inconstant in the face; finally the residual defect involved only the arm and part of the trunk. In this residual state, under the influence of intravenous amytal, the patient again had an alloesthetic response for one entire side of his body. In milder residual forms (e.g., Kramer, 1915) the subject may have a tendency to mislocalize stimuli but always in the direction of the midline of the body. In addition to somatosensory alloesthesia one may also see a similar phenomenon of sensory displacement in the visual and auditory modalities.

A motor form of alloesthesia has also been described. Patients with hemiplegia may, under certain conditions, have spontaneous movements of their impaired limbs. In such situations the patients may feel as if the movements took place on the healthy side. A patient described by Brain (1941a) had the impression that the left side of his body was transposed to the right. "When I move my left hand," he said, "it seems as if I am using my right." This phenomenon may resemble kinesthetic hallucinations, which are frequently found when subjects deny the existence of a left hemiplegia. Asked to move the paralyzed limbs, the anosognosic may experience the sensation of voluntary movement in the impaired side and may be convinced that he has carried out the command, although in fact his limb has not moved.

More rarely it has been observed that nociceptive stimuli applied to the impaired side of the body may produce vegetative responses, unpleasant facial grimacing, and even normal verbal reactions, whereas the subject may make no effort with the healthy hand to drive away the painful stimulus. Neither the nature nor the location of the nociceptive stimulus is identified by the patient. This syndrome, called hemiagnosia for pain, is seen only in patients with significant reductions in the level of consciousness.

With respect to progression or regression of the unilateral asomatognosias the syndrome may persist unchanged for the life of the patient. In some cases, however, the disorder may be transient, appearing only during the acute phase of the illness. Slowly, after the acute phase of the illness, a progressive readaptation takes place, and the patients eventually accept the reality of their motor deficit and recover from their illusory experiences. Bender et al (1949b) noted that regression of anosognosic defects parallels recovery of function in other neurobehavioral categories. These authors observed that the last parts of the body to recover from the anosognosic defects are the distal portions of the extremities. They recorded that this topographical distribution of recovery from anosognosia was similar for recovery from alloesthesia, extinction, and phantom limb phenomena.

Additional clinical accompaniments have been described in association with unilateral asomatognosias. Pötzl (1924) referred to tonic disorders, such as conjugate deviation of the head and eyes, axial torsion of the trunk, and even turning of the whole body toward the right in a circling fashion. We have observed an anosognosic subject with a right parietal lesion who responded to stimuli on the left side (somesthetic, visual, and auditory) by turning to the right until he had circled around completely to the source of the stimulus. Primitive grasp reflexes may be found on the impaired side, and Denny-Brown et al (1952, 1954) have also noted avoidance reactions on the impaired hand.

In evaluating a series of patients with verified right hemispheric lesions, Hécaen (1972b) described significant correlations between unilateral somatognosias and confusional states, reduced levels of consciousness, indifference to failures, visual field defects, somatosensory disorders, a variety of motor impairments, spatial dyslexia, spatial dyscalculia, constructional apraxia, and dressing apraxia. Viewing these intercorrelations, one might be tempted to conclude that hemiasomatognosia is simply one of the elements of the posterior right hemispheric syndrome, that it is intimately linked to somatosensory and visuospatial disorders, and that its appearance is linked to an impairment of vigilance. Some caution is, however, warranted before we accept such conclusions. It is rare, for instance, to find somatognosias, by contrast with the frequency of cortical sensory disorders. Furthermore it is necessary to explain the rare cases reported of patients with unilateral disorders of body schema in the absence of any sensory disturbance whatsoever. On the other hand we would accept that some type of general mental impairment (confusion, intellectual deterioration, etc.) is an almost constant accompaniment of hemiasomatognosia. This general disorder of mental function could not be the sole cause of the defective body image, but it may well constitute one of the necessary conditions for the appearance of the somatognosic defect.

As for the anatomic basis of unilateral asomatognosias the bulk of evidence from published cases with anatomoclinical correlation supports the classical position in which the right hemisphere of right-handers is responsible. Less clear is the precise region within the right hemisphere. Nonetheless most authors agree that hemiasomatognosia, as defined by Lhermitte (1939), may result from a lesion of the right inferior parietal region, bordering the interparietal sulcus, the supramarginal gyrus, and the angular gyrus.

Subcortical structures have been implicated as regions that subserve specific features of the overall syndrome. Lesions of the thalamus or of the thalamoparietal peduncle have been associated with alterations in consciousness, alterations in pain perception, and perceptual modifications of a phantom limb variety (Pötzl, 1924; Hoff and Pötzl, 1931, 1935a; van Bogaert, 1934; von Stockert, 1934). Nielsen (1946) noted a relationship between thalamic lesions and indifference to hemiplegia. Hécaen (1972b) has stressed that simple denial of hemiplegia, in the absence of true disorders of knowledge of one's body image, may result from diencephalic lesions and may resemble the confabulatory states of subjects with Korsakoff's syndrome. He insisted, however, that lesions limited to the thalamus could produce only impressions of absence or loss of body parts or the feeling that a body segment did not really belong to the rest of the body. True disorders of recognition and knowledge of the body schema required parietal lobe involvement.

Bilateral Asomatognosias

These disorders, affecting both sides of the body, may result from single, unilateral hemispheric lesions. Three clinical conditions may be considered: Gerstmann syndrome, autotopognosia, and asymbolia for pain.

Gerstmann Syndrome The Gerstmann syndrome consists of the following four elements: finger agnosia, pure agraphia (without alexia), right-left disorientation, and acalculia. The central feature of the syndrome is finger agnosia, described by Gerstmann in 1924. In this first publication he considered

finger agnosia in isolated form to represent a circumscribed defect of orientation with respect to one's own body. Subsequently (in 1927) Gerstmann suggested that finger agnosia and agraphia represented a new syndrome. Finally
(in 1930) he enlarged the syndrome by adding right-left disorientation and
acalculia. Gerstmann believed that these four elements comprised a specific
neuropsychological syndrome with a single underlying cause.

Finger agnosia is characterized by an inability of subjects to recognize,
distinguish, draw, name, and choose on multiple choice different fingers,
either on their own hands or on those of the examiner. The patient may have
some difficulty with appropriate finger movements; he may move the wrong
fingers in response to verbal command; or with his eyes closed he may move
a finger other than the one touched by the examiner. Even with his eyes open
the patient may be unable to respond with a correct finger movement when
a finger is touched, although there is no evidence of weakness, apraxia, or loss
of fine finger movements. Such patients may, for example, be able to thread
a needle or play a piano. Errors are generally more marked with the three
middle fingers than with the thumb or little finger. The subject tends to be
unaware of or to deny his disability, making no effort to correct errors. This
lack of awareness of errors may regress with repeated testing.

Right-left disorientation is especially prominent with respect to one's own
body or that of the examiner. If a subject is asked, for example, to show his
right hand, he hesitates, becomes confused, and may show the left hand.
Appeal to visual or kinesthetic cues for determining the correct side is frequent. The agraphia is not supposed to be accompanied by aphasia or alexia.
Some authors accept this as apraxic agraphia (see the chapter on Aphasia),
and some place it in the category of constructional apraxia. Acalculia is
considered to be the least common element of the syndrome. Calculation
defects derive primarily from an inability to recognize the value of a number
in its appropriate numerical category (units, tens, hundreds, etc.), an impaired ability to manipulate numbers due to a loss of concepts for arithmetic
operations, and an impaired ability to establish the correct plan for resolving
the calculation problem. Ehrenwald (1931a,b) considers this to be a primary
impairment of skills basic to calculation.

Schilder (1923, 1935) maintained that the purely somatognosic defect of
nonrecognition of fingers could be associated with a variety of neurobehavioral defects—apractic, aphasic, and opticoagnosic. Constructional defects, he
thought, were frequently seen together with finger agnosia, and drawings
were impaired, especially drawings of people, and especially of face and
hands. We would stress that, from the clinical point of view, although the
four elements described above constitute the Gerstmann syndrome when they
are found together, each of the elements may be found independently of the
others. In such a case it would be inappropriate to speak of the Gerstmann
syndrome.

The Gerstmann syndrome is more often than not found as part of a clinical picture that includes a wide variety of other neuropsychological defects. Language disorders, especially amnesic aphasia, are particularly prominent. Right homonymous hemianopia is common; different types of visual agnosia have been reported. Constructional apraxia is the most frequently described associated defect.

In the years since it was first described, more and more authors have observed that the four elements of the Gerstmann syndrome are rarely found together isolated from other neuropsychological defects; some authors say never. It has not been unusual to find two or three, but not all four of the elements in the absence of additional defects. Despite these observations the Gerstmann syndrome had been an accepted neurobehavioral entity until the critical studies of Benton in 1961. In that year, in a paper entitled "The Fiction of the Gerstmann Syndrome," Benton raised serious questions about the theoretical significance of the Gerstmann syndrome. His argument ran as follows. If the Gerstmann syndrome is a natural combination of defects whose correlation derives from a single, underlying, basic neuropsychological disorder, the intercorrelational links among the four elements of the syndrome should be stronger than the correlational links between any one element of the syndrome and any neuropsychological defect not belonging to the syndrome.

On the basis of this hypothesis Benton studied 200 subjects, 100 with cortical lesions, 100 without. His test included the four elements of the Gerstmann syndrome, plus tasks of constructional praxis, reading, and visual memory. Results showed that correlations among the four elements of the syndrome were neither stronger nor weaker than correlations between any element of the syndrome and any of the other three functions. A cohesion index for the syndrome showed that the mean intercorrelation for the four elements of the syndrome (0.48) was similar to that of 34 other possible combinations among the results of the seven tests (between 0.48 and 0.54). Of the 100 brain-damaged subjects, and in particular of 12 with left parietal lesions, not a single subject had all four necessary elements and only those four.

Benton's argument appears, at first, to be founded on particularly solid ground. However, two critical cautionary notes should be considered before one accepts his conclusions. Hécaen (1972b) has indicated that right-left disorientation, certain types of dyscalculia and dysgraphia, and certain types of dyslexia may result from right hemispheric lesions. Since Benton considered performance deficits in a global manner, a new analysis should be done to evaluate deficits that might be associated exclusively with left parietal lobe lesions, the presumed site of causation of the syndrome. Geschwind (1973, personal communication) argues from the clinical point of view that it is precisely the rarity or lack of likelihood of finding certain deficits in combination with each other that defines a syndrome. That is, one would not expect

to find the four elements of the Gerstmann syndrome together in the randomly selected brain-damaged population. Therefore, one case observed with
these four elements together, in the absence of other neuropsychological defects, would be sufficient to establish the existence of the syndrome. For
Geschwind, rather than disprove the reality of the Gerstmann syndrome,
Benton's data confirm its existence. The observations of pure Gerstmann's
syndrome in children (Benson and Geschwind, 1970), may support this latter
conclusion.

Benton's study on the Gerstmann syndrome stimulated additional research
on the same topic. Kinsbourne and Warrington (1962a) supported the existence of the Gerstmann syndrome and reported that the basic underlying
disorder was in the knowledge of and recognition of limits of fingers. Also for
Ettlinger (1963) finger agnosia may have neuropsychological specificity as a
manifestation of a disorder of spatial orientation. He accepted the proposition
of Stengel (1944), which holds that the basic disorder is an inability of the
subject to relate objects to each other and to himself in a spatially meaningful
whole according to rules acquired through experience.

By contrast with these authors Poeck and Orgass (1964, 1966, 1969), in a
series of studies of subjects with cerebral damage tested by means of a neuropsychological battery including tests of verbal and nonverbal finger recognition, right-left orientation, general intellectual function, and verbal comprehension, concluded that aphasia was the common denominator underlying
the four elements of the Gerstmann syndrome. Errors on the nonverbal tests
of finger recognition, they believed, were the result of several factors, including general intellectual deterioration and defective visual retention. Gainotti
et al (1972) observed that finger agnosia, as judged by nonverbal tests, occurred as frequently with right as with left hemispheric lesions. They also
believed that general intellectual deterioration was a key factor in the genesis
of these disorders. Sauguet et al (1971) studied this problem in 80 brain-
damaged right-handed subjects who had no evidence of intellectual deterioration or confusion. They found that a significant proportion of subjects with
sensory aphasia performed poorly on both verbal and nonverbal tests. However, a small number of these subjects with sensory aphasia performed reasonably well on the tests of right-left orientation, finger recognition, and body-
part recognition, and two of these subjects performed all tests correctly. These
authors concluded that sensory aphasia might reasonably be considered a
necessary, but not sufficient, condition for the production of bilateral disorders of somatognosis.

From the point of view of anatomy, those authors who accept the existence
of the syndrome generally hold that the dominant parietal lobe, especially in
the region of the angular gyrus, is the anatomic region most likely to be
involved. The first case in which an anatomoclinical study of the Gerstmann

syndrome was reported showed a right hemispheric lesion in an ambidextrous patient (Hermann and Pötzl, 1926). Subsequent postmortem analyses indicated that responsible lesions were found in the left hemisphere. Lunn (1948), after reviewing the literature of cases with anatomic verification, concluded that no unequivocal case of Gerstmann syndrome had been produced by a lesion of the minor hemisphere, except in left-handers. Finger agnosia alone has, however, been found in a relatively small number of patients with right hemispheric lesions (Sauguet et al, 1971).

On the basis of studies of cases with vascular lesions Lange (1933) observed that the locus of lesion producing the Gerstmann syndrome was situated between 0_2 and the angular gyrus in the dominant hemisphere. Other authors (e.g., Heimburger, 1964) have maintained that the Gerstmann syndrome has no localizing value. Statistical analysis in the Sauguet et al (1971) study pointed up no significant correlation between intrahemispheric localization and the combination of disorders including finger agnosia and right-left disorientation. If we consider the question from the clinical point of view, we immediately recognize the value of the Gerstmann syndrome. Whether or not it really exists as a pure neuropsychological syndrome, an examiner can be reasonably certain that when all four elements of the Gerstmann syndrome appear in a single patient, with or without other defects, that patient is most likely to have a dominant hemisphere lesion, located in the parietal lobe, in or near the angular gyrus.

Autotopognosia Autotopognosia was described by Pick (1908, 1922) as a loss of the ability to localize and name body parts. Occasional reference to the syndrome and sporadic case reports have appeared subsequently. The general disorder of body part recognition occasionally regresses, leaving the clinical picture of finger agnosia and thus suggesting that these two agnosic disorders are linked. As with finger agnosia, autotopognosia may present different patterns according to its predominant, associated features: visual defects, apraxia, or aphasia.

Subjects have difficulty naming, finding, or pointing to body parts on themselves or on the examiner. The patients may have difficulty describing body parts, even when they can see or touch the parts. Placed before a mirror, the subjects still cannot point to or otherwise identify body parts. In some cases (Pötzl, 1924) they can point to midline body structures but cannot designate laterally located structures.

Hécaen (1972b) has called attention to a clear discrepancy between the ability of the subject to point to clothes or objects, despite his inability to point to body parts. One of his patients, for example, succeeded in pointing to a shirt, a collar, and other items of clothing but was unable to point to his neck or his foot. Another report of a similar case described a patient who was quick and accurate with response to questions about clothing (e.g., sleeve, zipper, etc.) but was totally unable to respond accurately to questions about body parts. When asked to "point to your arm," he stood up, looked around the room curiously, and sat down, spelling to himself "A-R-M, A-R-M." He finally said, "I'm sorry, I don't know that one" (Yamadori and Albert, 1973).

Subjects occasionally complain that they are unable to conceptualize elements of the human body, either in isolation or in their appropriate relationships to each other. This perturbation of revisualization of the human body is clearly seen in the gross inability of these patients to draw human figures, even stick figures.

On designs or pictures of whole bodies, patients have the same difficulties in naming or pointing to body parts. In some cases, however, subjects may succeed in pointing to parts of animals, especially if the name of the part is specifically linked to the animal, such as hoof, trunk, tusk, etc. In other cases the agnosia may extend to all living things (Nielsen, 1946).

By contrast with other reported cases the patient described by DeRenzi and Faglioni (1963) was able to describe and name body parts when the examiner showed them to him but was unable to point to body parts on verbal command. This subject, an engineer by profession, was also unable to point to various parts of his car. Subsequently DeRenzi and Scotti (1970) described another patient who was unable to point to body parts or parts of a bicycle on verbal command. However, this patient was able to name the same body or bicycle parts when they were designated by the examiner. He was also able to indicate purposeful errors made by an examiner in pointing to body parts at the oral request of a second examiner.

On the basis of these examinations DeRenzi has raised the question of whether autotopognosia is a reality or a fiction. He specifically has asked if the deficit is a disorder in the ability to deal with parts of a whole. That is, the whole may be dealt with properly, but the parts may not (DeRenzi, personal communication). According to such a proposition the human body would not be a special category to be dealt with in a special way. The case reported by Yamadori and Albert (1973) seems to refute this proposition. These authors described a patient with autotopognosia who was able to point to the various parts of whole objects (e.g., the parts of a pair of eyeglasses) without difficulty.

Some patients seem to be fully aware of their defect while others do not. Those who are unaware of their defect may suggest that the body part that they cannot designate has been lost. Thus the patient described by Pick (1908) looked for his own hands at the table or in bed, believing to have lost them. Gerstmann (1942) recounted that one of his patients thought her hands "were cut off because they were not being used." One of Hécaen's patients (1972b) accused the doctor of having taken away her hand.

From the point of view of anatomic correlations the lesions have often been bilateral. When the lesions have been unilateral, they have primarily been in the left hemisphere. This evidence may be additional support to the thesis that autotopognosia and finger agnosia are related.

Asymbolia for Pain   Asymbolia for pain was first described in 1927 by Schilder and Stengel as the absence of normal reactions to pain as a result of acquired cerebral lesions, in the presence of intact elementary sensation. In all about 20 cases fitting this description have been reported (Schilder and Stengel, 1930, 1931; Pötzl and Stengel, 1936; Rubins and Friedman, 1948; Hécaen and de Ajuriaguerra, 1950; Weinstein et al, 1955).

The response of the subject to a painful stimulus on either side of the body represents a peculiar modification of the normal reaction. Either the subject does not react, or his reaction is incomplete or insufficient. It seems as if he has not truly appreciated the nature of the stimulus. His facial expressions, his defense responses are reduced out of all proportion to the stimulus. In observing his own failure to respond appropriately, the subject may inflict pain on himself to test the astonishing abnormality. Occasionally the failure to react may extend beyond painful stimuli to include any stimulus that represents a dangerous situation. Schilder and Stengel called this latter situation asymbolia for danger.

Vegetative reactions to pain are preserved. Despite the impression given by the subject's behavior, he is nonetheless able to understand the nociceptive character of pain, as evidenced, for example, by his reaction to verbal threats. Elementary somatic sensitivity is not disturbed, and subjects can distinguish sharp from dull.

Asymbolia for pain is generally seen as part of a broader neuropsychological syndrome that includes sensory aphasia, apraxia, and disturbed orientation to one's own body. With respect to the type of aphasia associated with asymbolia for pain, Geschwind (1965, 1973) has contended that conduction aphasia is the variety usually found.

Anatomic localization of the lesion responsible for asymbolia for pain has not been definitely established. In most cases the lesion was lateralized to the left hemisphere; however, in a small number of cases the lesion was in the right hemisphere, even in right-handers. In cases with surgical or postmortem verification the lesion always involved posterior parietal areas and usually frontal areas as well. Schilder (1935) concluded that the responsible lesion was located in the region of the supramarginal gyrus in the dominant hemisphere. This localization was similar to that proposed by Geschwind (1965), who spoke of a subcortical (white matter) lesion in the parietal operculum of the dominant hemisphere. Hécaen and de Ajuriaguerra (1950) believed that the frontal lobe lesion, together with the parietal lobe lesion, might be necessary. Biemond (1956) suggested that the lesion might be situated in the secondary sensory area (see anatomic discussion above). By contrast to these authors, who proposed a specific cortical localization, and despite the characteristics of their own patient material (six cases with parietal lesions, two with temporal lesions), Weinstein et al (1955) denied the possibility that a specific localization existed for this syndrome.

As for the cause of this syndrome there are almost as many proposed mechanisms as there are cases reported. The absence of motor response to painful stimuli makes one think of apraxia. However, against this view is the general observation that apraxic patients respond normally to pain.

It would be natural to think that the basic disorder resides in some disturbance of sensation at an elementary level. However, patients with asymbolia for pain have not been found to have elementary somatosensory disorders; they can distinguish sharp from dull, and the asymbolia is bilateral.

Schilder and Stengel (1930) had noted disorders of attention in their patients. Rubins and Friedman (1948) commented on extinction phenomena and fluctuation in somatosensory responsiveness. For Weinstein et al (1955) these phenomena are critical: asymbolia for pain and other anosognosic syndromes represent a behavioral defect similar to that seen in Korsakoff's syndrome, in which modification of attention may have different neurobehavioral manifestations, depending on the premorbid personality of the brain-damaged subject.

After the original formulation of Schilder and Stengel (1931) a number of authors have considered this syndrome to represent a disorder of somatognosis (e.g., Critchley, 1953; de Ajuriaguerra and Hécaen, 1960). According to this conception a painful stimulus is not understood as relating to the body; therefore the body image is not called upon to respond in its own defense. In similar terms Brain (1965) said that the relationship between awareness of pain and the body schema was lacking. On the other hand Denny-Brown (1962) maintained that asymbolia for pain was not an agnosia but that it represented a bilateral disorder of morphosynthesis.

Pieron (1923) believed that asymbolia for pain was a manifestation of a specific agnosic defect—an "analgognosia or, better, an apractognosia for pain." The subject loses the comprehension of the significance of pain, just as the subject with visual agnosia loses that for objects or space. He contrasted analgognosia with analgothymia, which may be seen in certain mental disorders and, in particular, which may follow frontal lobotomy.

We believe that the body scheme must be disturbed in asymbolia for pain. As stated by Schilder and Stengel (1931), "pain must be brought into connection with recognition of the model of the body in order to be appreciated fully." In addition there may be some relation between disorders of the body image and limbic system function in the pathogenesis of this syndrome.

Geschwind (1965) has proposed that a disconnection between secondary sensory area and limbic system may underlie asymbolia for pain. This disconnection theory approach appears to be somewhat of an oversimplification; nonetheless, it does correspond, at least partially, with what is known of the syndrome.

Corporeal Illusions and Hallucinations

Phantom Limbs The "phantom limb" phenomenon refers to the perception of a missing body part, including all of the somesthetic characteristics (e.g., size, weight, length, position, and movement). Visual information, indicating absence of the limb, does not modify the somesthetic illusion. This phenomenon was described in early medical literature as occurring in individuals who had amputations of limbs (Descartes, 1662; von Haller, 1757–1766), and it has since been discussed in literally hundreds of publications. Our current discussion does not attempt to summarize all the relevant publications; for detailed reviews we refer tne reader to additional sources (see especially Hécaen and de Ajuriaguerra, 1952; Weinstein and Kahn, 1955; Frederiks, 1963; Weinstein, 1969).

The phenomenon is found following amputation of limbs or other body parts in 90–100% of cases, depending on the series (Frederiks, 1969; Weinstein et al, 1970). Amputation of limbs is not, however, the only condition that produces the phantom illusion. This effect is also seen after surgery on any part of the body (e.g., breast, eye), tooth extraction, mutilating diseases of the limbs, limb agenesis, and lesions of various parts of the nervous system.

Following amputation the illusion appears almost immediately and persists for relatively long periods of time (months or years). The position of the phantom limb, at first, is often the same as that of the limb before operation. However, the phantom limb may subsequently change its position, becoming more or less relaxed. A bizarre posture is not unusual. The sensation of movement of the phantom limb is common. Patients may still feel objects as being attached to the phantom, such as a ring on an amputated finger (Charcot, 1892). In the process of recovery the phantom limb may progressively become smaller and less well defined—an effect called telescoping (Gueniot, 1861; Weiss and Fishman, 1963).

In addition to the somesthetic illusion that a missing part is present, one also finds that subjects report sensations (such as pain, paresthesia, heat, cold, cramps, etc.) related to the phantom limb. The quality of illusory sensation is often vivid, especially in the early periods following amputation. Indeed phantom limb pain may be quite severe, posing a serious challenge for treatment.

It has generally been taught that the phantom limb phenomenon is less frequently encountered in mentally retarded subjects (Lhermitte, 1939) and in children with amputations. However, Simmel (1956) has reported the same frequency of phantom limbs in retarded and normal subjects. With respect to children statistical studies have confirmed earlier work indicating that the appearance of the phantom limb is a function of age. By 8 years of age the frequency of phantom limbs in children is similar to that in adults (Simmel, 1962; Weinstein et al, 1964). In cases of congenital aplasia of a limb it had been thought that phantom limbs did not occur (Pick, 1908, 1922). We now know, however, that phantom limbs may occur in such cases, although infrequently (Poeck, 1964; Weinstein et al, 1964; Vetter and Weinstein, 1967).

An intriguing aspect of this condition is the occurrence of somesthetic illusions related to body parts, without absence of the body part, following lesions of the nervous system. The illusions have different characteristics, depending on the location within the nervous system: peripheral nerve (Lurje, 1936); plexus (Mayer-Gross, 1929; Lhermitte and Sebillotte, 1938); cauda equina (Hécaen and David, 1945); spinal cord (Riddoch, 1917; Bors, 1951; Conomy, 1973); subcortical and cortica (Hécaen and de Ajuriaguerra, 1952; Frederiks, 1963). The frequency of illusion also varies with lesion level: exceptional in peripheral nerve lesions, rare in plexus lesions, and almost constant in spinal cord lesions, especially with cervical involvement (Weinstein, 1969).

Three principal theories may be isolated from all the proposed hypotheses to explain phantom limb phenomena: peripheral, central, and psychological. More and more evidence is combining to support the theory that phantom limbs result from a central neurological process. These include the fact that phantom limb phenomena may result from central nervous system lesions. The parts of the body that are most frequently, most persistently, and with most precision represented by phantom illusions are also those parts of the body that have the most extensive cortical representation. The phantom limb phenomenon may disappear following a cerebral lesion (Head and Holmes, 1911), and phantom limb pain may be successfully treated by operating on the parietal lobe (Fredriks, 1969). Observations of reorganization of sensory function at the amputated stump have shown a lower sensory discrimination threshold on the side of the stump by comparison with a homologous area on the healthy side (Teuber et al, 1949; Haber, 1956). Injection of calcium by the intravenous route produces a sensation of warmth in the phantom limb, even though circulation to the stump has been temporarily interrupted (Lhermitte, 1939).

Despite the arguments in favor of central neurological factors, it is difficult at this time to exclude the possibility that peripheral afferent impulses play a role in the production of the phantom limb phenomenon. Stimulation of the stump may reproduce the phantom or may heighten the effect of an already existing phantom. Surgical manipulation of a stump neuroma may cause disappearance of a phantom.

The psychological theory is based on the observations that phantom limbs may disappear after psychotherapy or hypnosis. Phantom limbs are, moreover, thought to be more intense and persistent in patients with certain personality characteristics, such as schizoid personalities. Although personality characteristics undoubtedly influence and interact with every neuropsychological defect, we believe the empirical data are sufficient to rule out psychological or personality factors as a sole cause of the phantom limb phenomenon.

At this stage we may temporarily conclude that the combination of partial sensory deprivation caused by the peripheral lesion, together with central neural reorganization provoked by this partial suppression of sensory information, may together act to produce the phantom limb phenomenon.

Paroxysmal Illusions and Hallucinations Paroxysmal alterations of somesthetic perception occur as auras preceding seizures, as epileptic equivalents, during migraine attacks, in the course of toxic or infectious illnesses, or as part of the recovery process following cerebral damage. Their occurrence is much more frequent than one would assume from a review of the literature. A variety of clinical forms may be seen, which may be grouped as follows— feelings of absence of a body part, illusions of corporeal displacement, phantom limb illusions, and autoscopic hallucinations.

The most frequently observed variety is the feeling of absence or loss of a body part. This may involve one-half of the body, one limb, or a portion of a limb. The loss is usually preceded by paresthesias in the affected body part, followed abruptly by the impression that the body part is missing, that it has disappeared, or that perhaps someone has cut it off. The subject calls on his other senses to overcome this astonishing impression. He looks at or palpates the body part that seems to be missing and often appreciates only after this additional sensory contact that the body part is indeed present. Ordinarily, paroxysmal sentiment of absence of a body part is quite brief. During the attack the subject, paradoxically, may have the impression that his missing body part is a part of someone else's body.

Illusions of corporeal transformation are frequently seen associated with discharging focal, cerebral lesions; they are also reported as phenomena associated with hallucinogenic drugs, such as marijuana or LSD. Clinically these disorders are manifested by alterations in somesthetic perception such that the subject believes his body to be heavier or lighter, of greater or lesser volume or density, taller or shorter, and so on. This syndrome, sometimes called macrosomatognosia or microsomatognosia, may affect the whole body; however, it is more often limited to a distal portion of a limb.

Illusions of corporeal displacement may occur as isolated phenomena, or they may accompany the sentiment of absence. They have been known in clinical neuropsychology for many years under the name "motor hallucinations." The clinical manifestations are feelings of lightness or levitation affecting either the whole body, half of the body, or one limb. In the case of a single limb the upper is involved more frequently than the lower. Such illusions have frequently been associated with visual or somesthetic hallucinations, with autonomic nervous system disturbances (flushing, warmth), and with feelings of anxiety. Perhaps the feelings of abnormal body position (e.g., Conomy, 1973) and of separation of parts should be placed in a similar category as illusions of corporeal displacement.

Paroxysmal phantom limb phenomena occur only rarely as manifestations of epilepsy. Following a paresthetic phase, the patient has the impression of having a supernumerary limb, usually in an abnormal position. This illusion generally, but not exclusively, involves the upper limb. Subjects speak of an extra arm or hand or even of several. This condition may be associated with visual illusions, such that the patient sees the extra limb.

The term *autoscopic hallucination* refers to the impression of seeing oneself, as in a mirror. As an epileptic phenomenon it is relatively rare; however, its frequency is not low in people taking hallucinogenic drugs. Two forms are recognized: in one the phenomenon is essentially visual; in the other, with or without a strong visual component, the subject transfers his many somatosensory impressions to his double. In the visual form of the syndrome the image may be transparent, opaque, or colored. The hallucinatory image is usually in front of the patient, but, in syndromes involving half of the body, it may be to one side.

Anatomic and pathophysiological correlations with these various paroxysmal somesthetic phenomena vary according to the complexity of the syndrome and the etiology. If we consider paroxysmal feelings of absence of body parts, we find that right hemispheric lesions predominate, at least in right-handers. However, the localization of lesions in the right hemisphere is not so constant with paroxysmal as with permanent absence syndromes. Of 51 cases either personally observed or reported in the literature, Hécaen and de Ajuriaguerra (1952) found 15 in which the sentiment of absence involved the right side of the body. Hemispheric lateralization of lesions is not so clearly defined for the other varieties of paroxysmal illusions involving body image. Nonetheless, in a review of Penfield's electrocortical stimulation studies, Hécaen (1956) found that all cortical points whose stimulation produced the illusory sensation of movement were in the right hemisphere.

With respect to intrahemispheric localization of lesions responsible for these various paroxysmal events the weight of the evidence favors the parietal region and in particular the posterior parietal region and interparietal sulcus

(Hécaen and de Ajuriaguerra, 1952; Hécaen, 1968, 1972b). If we analyze only those cases for which good anatomoclinical correlation is available, we may discern a somatotopic organization in the parietal lobe. Defect-producing lesions seem to be clearly divisible into two groups. A superior parietal group of lesions produces paroxysmal disorders of body part perception and awareness for the contralateral lower limb. A posterior inferior parietal group of lesions produces disorders affecting the contralateral upper limb.

Neuropsychological Considerations

Introduction

To understand the (still incomplete) notion of somatognosis, body schema, body image, and image of self, it is necessary first to understand how the concept emerged. In a vague, ill-defined manner the idea of a sense of one's body slowly and progressively separated itself from the idea of a sense of existence. The notion of body image underlay certain reflections on coenesthesis—the undifferentiated complex of organic sensation by which one is aware of the body and bodily condition.

Somatognosis was most easily understandable by reference to defects in a hypothetical mechanism that allowed one to be aware of and relate to his

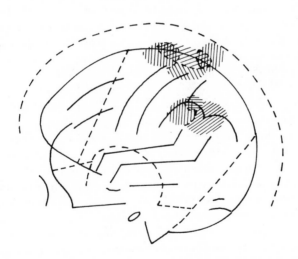

Sites of lesions (diagonal lines) in seven subjects with paroxysmal somatognosic disturbances. The lesions located in the superior regions produced illusions affecting the lower limb; those in the inferior cerebral regions caused disturbances in the upper limb (from de Ajuriaguerra and Hécaen, 1960). Copyright 1960 by Masson & Co., Paris. Reproduced by permission.

bodily image. In the context of psychasthenic personality disorders Krishaber (1873) spoke of perturbations of the "physical personality." Ribot (1897) emphasized the significance of these disorders of body sense in discussions of psychopathology of the personality. Bonnier (1905) observed that certain patients suffering from vertigo had abnormal perceptions of the spatial aspects of their own bodies; he referred to these disorders as hyposchematia, hyperschematia, paraschematia, and aschematia. This general theme was extensively developed by the burgeoning German school of neuropsychiatry. Wernicke (1906) adopted the term *somatopsyche* to indicate consciousness of one's own body. The term *body schema* was introduced by Pick (1922), who had attempted the first approximative neurological explanation in 1908. To explain disorders of localization of body parts, he hypothesized the existence of a spatial image of the body, constituted from primary sensory complexes. In 1914 Babinski presented observations of two patients who, despite an adequate level of intellectual functioning, ignored or neglected their hemiplegia. Similar observations had previously been reported by Anton (1893, 1899), but it was Babinski who clearly affirmed that such an anosognosic defect could result from a restricted cortical lesion.

In the course of his extensive studies on somesthesis, Head (Head and Holmes, 1911; Head, 1920) conceived of a model of the body—the postural scheme—that served as a standard against which sensations were compared. Schilder (1923) amplified and systematized Head's model: the body scheme was the totality of our internal and external experience, our complete knowledge of our own body, a knowledge resulting from the synthesis of multiple sensory impressions. Schilder accepted the existence of a cortical mechanism underlying the body scheme. Anatomoclinical studies of the Viennese School (Pötzl, 1924; Hoff, 1931; Engerth, 1932) supported Schilder's approach.

The studies of van Bogaert (1934) and Jean Lhermitte (1939) emphasized the significance of the concept of a body image, "independent of cutaneous and deep sensations," in the general consciousness of self. During the same period phantom limb illusions began to be interpreted according to this notion: the phantom limb represented persistence of an individual's consciousness of body image in its complete form, despite the physical diminution he may have undergone. Conrad (1932, 1933) provided a detailed and excellent analysis of the difficulties, contradictions, and ambiguities inherent in the notion of the body scheme as it had to be treated in neuropsychology. He then concluded that "consciousness of our body is an isolated whole, according to the terminology of Gestalt theory, in the world of our experiences and our actions." He conceived of the notion as a pure conceptual fact, with no relationship to our sensory world.

We can thus see that from the earliest attempts to describe and explain the notion of the body scheme two divergent tendencies emerged. In one the body scheme resulted from a successive and hierarchical elaboration and synthesis of primary sensory inputs. In the other the body scheme represented a complete and complex psychological knowledge transcending the basic sensory data. For the former theory the body scheme was the product of a physiological mechanism that gives us an overall feeling that corresponds to the real structure of our body. For the latter the body scheme was a psychological fact—the feeling that we have of our own body.

As we explore in subsequent sections the various explanations proposed to account for the different somatognosic syndromes seen clinically, we shall find the two main theoretical tendencies continued to our own period.

Unilateral Asomatognosias

From the first descriptions of anosognosia, attempts were made to explain away the syndrome by reducing it to a combination of associated symptoms. Thus Dejerine (1914) and Marie (1926) believed the syndrome to result from disorders of deep sensation. Denny-Brown rejuvenated such explanations with his concept of amorphosynthesis: as a result of a parietal lobe lesion the patient could not properly integrate and synthesize the numerous somatosensory inputs arriving from the contralateral side of the body (Denny-Brown, et al, 1952; Denny-Brown and Banker, 1954). According to such conceptions anosognosia would not represent a true agnosia, and the subject would not have lost his intact body image. Contemporary studies have supported this hypothesis by suggesting that parietal lobe damage, especially in the minor hemisphere, causes an impairment in the ability to use proprioceptive feedback concerning the spatial localization of body parts (Carmon, 1970; Levin, 1973).

Another attempt at neuropsychological explanation referred to the tonic disorders so frequently seen with hemiasomatognosic syndromes. For Pötzl the impression of somatic integrity depended on mechanisms related to control of posture and equilibrium (Pötzl, 1924; Pötzl and Stengel, 1936). This general hypothesis ran as follows. The predominance of rotatory influx coming from the intact hemisphere causes a rotation toward the right of one's kinesthetic image of the left side of the body. At the same time, and because of this, a dissociation occurs between the visual image and the kinesthetic image. As a result of this separation the left side of the body is projected in one's body image as being foreign to or as not belonging to the body.

Part of Denny-Brown's general theory included a reference to tonic disorder. The parietal lobe lesion produced a perceptual rivalry that in turn disrupted the equilibrium between tonic approach and avoidance reactions. Instead of these motor responses being in normal competitive balance, behavior would then be determined by the predominance of one of these motor reactions to diverse stimuli coming from the environment.

Other authors chose to emphasize the role of altered level of consciousness in the production of anosognosia, indicating that the syndrome resulted from a general disorder of mental functioning and was not related to a specifically localized or lateralized lesion. Redlich and Bonvicini (1908) thus suggested that associated with a decreased level of consciousness and attention was a defense mechanism of forgetting what was psychologically painful to the individual. In modern teminology Weinstein and Kahn (1955) adopted this conceptual approach, referring to asomatognosias as aspects of a "denial of illness," not only of the hemiplegia but also of all unpleasant circumstances. Later Weinstein (1969) accepted the fact that anosognosia was more frequently associated with the right than with left hemispheric lesions. He concluded, however, that left hemispheric lesions produced an insufficiency of metaphoric or gestural language and thus prevented the subject from expressing his confabulatory or denial type of behavior.

By contrast with these various theories, which of necessity rejected any significant association between anosognosia and hemispheric lateralization of lesion, other theories insisted on the anatomoclinical correlation. Schilder (1923, 1935) and Lhermitte (1939) contended that somatognosis was a psychological function represented unilaterally in the minor cerebral hemisphere and that hemiasomatognosia and anosognosia were neuropsychological defects resulting from lesions in this hemisphere. This theory is simply a tautological restatement of the observed anatomoclinical data; no useful physiological explanation of the mechanisms underlying the psychological function of somatognosis can be derived from such a theory.

Bilateral Asomatognosias

These syndromes are produced by lesions in the dominant hemisphere. Early theories were attempts to correlate structure (i.e., dominant parietal lobe) and function. Gerstmann (1927) proposed that finger agnosia should be considered as one of the bilateral asomatognosic syndromes; for this interpretation he received support from others (e.g., Engerth, 1932; Schilder, 1935). According to this theory the visual, tactile, and kinesthetic images of fingers may be separated from a global image of one's body. During the same scientific period other authors proposed that the elements of the Gerstmann syndrome were dependent on a fundamental neuropsychological defect related to the parietal lobe lesion and that finger agnosia was simply one manifestation of this basic defect. For Hermann and Pötzl (1926) the basic defect was apraxic; for Lange (1933) and Janota (1938) it was loss of the functional category of directionality in space and loss of spatial relations dependent on this category; for Ehrenwald (1931a,b) the basic defect included the spatial disorder plus a disorder in temporal ordering ability. Conrad (1932, 1933) considered the problem to be more general: loss of the capacity of appreciating the distinction between the whole and its parts. According to this theory the capacity for part-whole distinction is one of the fundamental capacities of cerebral activity; a cerebral lesion impairs this fundamental capacity, and the clinical manifestations of this capacity reflect the location of lesion.

More recent analyses have eschewed the older anatomofunctional approach and have concentrated on developmental aspects of the behavioral functions. Numerical concepts, it is said, develop from finger counting; thus finger agnosia and acalculia may be related deficits. This argument has an appealing ring, but genetic studies have not confirmed a special relationship between arithmetic capacity and knowledge of fingers (Benton, 1959; Poeck and Orgass, 1964).

Another analytic approach has rejected entirely the specificity of the syndrome. Benton (1961) accepts only an indirect connection between left parietal lesions and finger agnosia: by the intermediary of language disorders one finds loss of finger identification related to lesions of the dominant hemisphere. Poeck and Orgass (1966, 1969) have also rejected the concept that somatognosis is a normal, fundamental, psychological function. They argue that various bilateral somatognosic defects are too diverse in presentation to represent a single homogeneous concept. These defects, they continue, are the products of numerous, known neuropsychological disorders, the commonest of which is aphasia. With respect to autotopognosia they stress the combined roles of general deterioration of mental function and disorders of spatial orientation. In support of this analytic approach are the statistical studies of large numbers of randomly selected, brain-damaged patients subjected to standardized test protocols. Disorders of finger or other body part recognition do not stand out statistically as specific, isolated disorders. It would seem impossible, on the basis of such studies, to state that impaired verbalization does not play a role in finger agnosia or autotopognosia.

It is precisely in this regard that individual case studies provide useful clues to assist in unraveling the complexities of analysis. Hécaen (1972b) summarized three case studies of patients who had striking dissociations between their ability to recognize body parts and their ability to identify objects. All were right handed, with left parietal lesions. Language, both for naming and for comprehension, was nearly normal when tasks did not relate to fingers or other body parts. Failure was dramatic, however, when body parts had to be dealt with. Such observations clearly define the problem: either we are dealing with a specific defect within a general capacity to "know" one's body or we have a language disorder that is selective for a particular semantic category, that related to human body parts. Yamadori and Albert (1973) described a patient with autotopognosia and concluded that he had a "word category aphasia."

From the point of view of observable facts, whether or not one accepts the specificity of the Gerstmann syndrome, the symptoms of finger agnosia and autotopognosia are frequently associated, not only with agraphia, right-left disorientation, and acalculia, but also with constructional apraxia, ideomotor apraxia, conduction aphasia, and certain elements of alexia.

DeRenzi and Scotti (1970) described a patient with autotopognosia and interpreted his defects as reflecting an impaired ability to analyze the relations of a whole to its parts. The language disorders this patient displayed (inability to carry out complex commands, inability to recount a story), as well as the gestural disorders (inability to complete an act requiring a sequence of gestures), were also interpreted as reflecting the same basic defect. They refer to descriptions by Head (1926) of patients with semantic aphasia as providing precedent for their interpretation. This interpretative analysis is very much like that previously provided by Conrad (see above).

Luria (1966) proposed the following explanation of the function of the posterior parietal region. This area provides the cerebral mechanism necessary for the function of simultaneous synthesis. A lesion in this zone would affect the psychological activities dependent on simultaneous synthesis of visual, spatial, and kinesthetic influx and would also involve language function, depending on the lesion's extent.

We could summarize by proposing that in either hemisphere the posterior parietal lobe and the gyri abutting temporal and occipital lobes serve as regions of polysensory integration necessary for the elaboration of higher order perceptual activity combining vestibular, proprioceptive, kinesthetic, and visual information. In the left hemisphere this polysensory integration is influenced by interaction with language mechanisms. It may be that sensory inputs to the left hemisphere are first (or perhaps concurrently) integrated with linguistic activity. The principles of categorization would thus be imposed on experiential data at an early stage of information processing. There would then be a control zone more highly focalized in the left hemisphere permitting and ensuring categorization and programming of various behavioral functions.

Experimental Pathophysiology

Numerous experimental studies have elucidated the kinesthetic, visual, vestibular, and tactile components of somatognosis. Standard textbooks of physiological psychology review these studies. Alterations of somatognosis may be the result of modifications of sensory inputs in the normal subject or of suppression or distortion of these inputs in the subject with neurological disease.

The influence of many, varied factors on the sensation of changes of the normal body image has been amply demonstrated. Head (1920), for example, showed the significance of disorders of deep sensation; Ponzo (1911), the significance of muscular sensations. Longhi (1939) in a series of ingenious experiments described the interaction of tonic orientation with exteroceptive and interoceptive inputs. The Aristotle illusion, the Japanese illusion, the Kohstam phenomenon—all are evidence of the independence of body image from true body position when displacement is passive. The role of visual inputs has long since been accepted as proved by such experiments as those of Stratton (1897). He studied vision without inversion of the retinal image by means of a technique involving the wearing of prismatic lenses that inverted the external world. In such a condition the visual impression of bodily state was dissociated from tactile and kinesthetic impressions; adaptation occurred only secondarily. The influence of vestibular inputs was underscored by such studies as those of Bonnier (1905, cited above) or of Micalizzi (1949) in conditions of experimentally produced vertigo, or by experiments in an elevator (Schilder, 1935).

Experimental data on modifications of cerebral function and their relationship to somatognosis have also come from other sources. We have already alluded to the role of hallucinogenic agents (e.g., mescaline, lysergic acid) in provoking paroxysmal somatognosic illusions or hallucinations. Mention must also be made of the studies of sensory deprivation (see, for example, the reviews by de Ajuriaguerra, 1965; Zubek, 1970). Not only visual illusions and hallucinations but also disorders of body schema occurred; these changes were analogous to those found with subjects who had ingested hallucinogenic agents.

Illusions of change of body schema, in many of these studies, resulted from the absence of active body movements or occurred while no active body movements took place. In this regard one is reminded of effects that occur during relaxation therapy sessions: sensations of change in body size, movement, change of position, levitation, heaviness, lightness, extra limbs, division of body or body parts—all in the absence of active movement.

These studies underline the significance of reafferentation derived from activity in the external world. This reafferentation interacts with those central cerebral structures whose role it is to reorganize and compare inputs coming from within the body to a frame of reference developed over the years to organize one's spatiotemporal universe.

Conclusion

What conclusions can be drawn concerning the neuropsychological mechanisms underlying asomatognosias? Is it necessary to postulate a suprasensory psychological function whose very definition precludes research into underlying mechanisms? We believe that final conclusions are not yet available; too many problems demand experimental resolution. Nonetheless we believe that an attempt to synthesize available anatomic, clinical, and experimental data may reasonably be made.

We shall not attempt this synthesis for bilateral asomatognosias. Their dependence on disorders of language and spatial orientation or on general intellectual deterioration is too immediate to permit clear-cut separations of function. We reiterate, however, the outstanding question of whether or not a category-specific, linguistic defect for the semantic field of body parts exists.

We might also wonder about the possible existence of an internal representation for each hand that could serve as a template for rapid comparison of hands presented visually. According to one study (Cooper and Shepard, 1975), when an individual wants to determine if a hand he is looking at, regardless of its position or orientation in space, is right or left, he makes a transformation of a mental image or phantom of one of his own hands in such a way as to make this mental image coincide with the position of the hand he is looking at. If one accepted this hypothesis, he could perhaps add that the mechanisms that underlie these mental "phantoms," bilateral and distal, might be situated in the left hemisphere and that disturbance of these mechanisms might produce disorders of right-left orientation and of finger recognition, independently of disorders of language.

Unit cell studies of posterior parietal cortex support the conclusion that this region is an association area with two main functions (e.g., Burchfiel and Duffy, 1972; Sakata et al, 1973; Hyvarinen and Poranen, 1974; Mountcastle et al 1975). First this region provides a neural "image" of relations between different parts of the body by means of intramodal convergence. Second, by means of intermodal convergence, it provides an "image" of the position of the body in space with respect to objects in the surrounding space.

This leaves the problem of hemiasomatognosias—somatognosic defects affecting the side of the body contralateral to a cortical lesion. Anatomic data show a definite tendency for the right hemisphere to be the hemisphere damaged in such cases and for the intrahemispheric localization to involve the posterior parietal region. In the face of such clear lateralizing tendencies any attempt at interpretation must take into account the general question of cerebral dominance. Throughout this book we have emphasized evidence supporting the concept of functional hemispheric asymmetry. Language, spatial perception, and visual recognition depend on neural mechanisms that differ in each hemisphere. In addition to (or instead of) functional hemispheric asymmetries, one may also speak of a difference in hemispheric organization for behavioral activity: in the left hemisphere, functions would be represented more focally than in the right hemisphere; in the right hemisphere, functional representation would be concerned principally with the contralateral side of the body, while in the left hemisphere, functional representation would be concerned with both sides of the body.

Theories have been proposed that explain hemiasomatognosias as being due to disorders of sensation, to defects of vestibular or tonic function, or to psychic troubles. We believe each of these elements represents a part of the truth; hemiasomatognosias probably result from a variable combination of these elements. We are not, however, dealing with a simple addition of deficits. Hemiasomatognosia is more than, and different from, the sum of its component defects.

To interpret the unilateral asomatognosias, we again borrow von Holst's model of reafferentation (1954) in the form used by Teuber (1961b) and Held (1965). (See our previous discussion of this model in the section on visual perception.) It should be possible to extend this model to somatognosic illusions. For simplification in reworking this model, we limit ourselves to consideration of two types of sensory input—proprioceptive and visual. A lesion, depending on its localization, may suppress different aspects of afferent influx, may impair voluntary movement (with or without preservation of the corollary discharge), or may disrupt the central integrative mechanism. We would presume that the central integrative mechanism is predominantly organized in one of the hemispheres as a polysensory area into which the corollary discharge is directed.

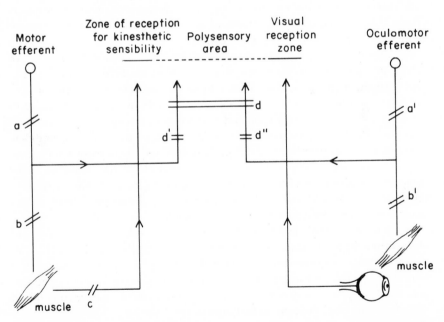

Diagramatic representation of possible lesion sites causing various forms of somatognosic defect, based on von Holst's theory of reafference (from Hécaen, 1972). Copyright 1972 by Larousse, Paris. Reproduced by permission.

The remainder of this discussion refers to the accompanying diagram. A lesion located at point (a) would cause an uncomplicated hemiplegia. A lesion at (b) would cause a hemiplegia with the impression of movement concurrent with a voluntary attempt to initiate movement; this impression would normally be corrected because of the integrity of the proprioceptive system. A lesion at point (c) produces loss of proprioceptive sensations. If there are lesions at both (b) and (c), despite a hemiplegia, the voluntary attempt to initiate movement could produce an uncorrected impression of movement and thereby cause anosognosia. Lesions at both (a) and (c) would cause hemiplegia and loss of proprioceptive sensation; this anesthesia would ordinarily be consciously appreciated by the patient. However, sensory deprivation to the polysensory integration area could result in a reorganization such that the patient did not appreciate his anesthesia; in such a situation the patient would experience a phantom limb illusion. Lesions at (b) and (d) cause a hemiplegia that the patient is aware of. With lesions located at (c) and (d), movement can take place, but without a corollary discharge and without proprioceptive feedback; in this case the patient would experience an impression of strangeness or nonbelonging of a body part. With an isolated lesion at point (d) the movement and its proprioceptive feedback exist, but the corollary discharge does not. A lesion located within the polysensory integration zone produces neglect of movement, because voluntary movement is not perceived as being voluntary; no amount of sensory input from the various sensory modalities can overcome this neglect.

As intriguing as this model may be for interpreting asomatognosias, we accept its worth only to the extent that it satisfies the following two exigencies. First the model should work for all cases of asomatognosia—personal or published—without exception; any exception would demand a reworking of the model. Second the model should be subjected to experimental verification. It should be possible to test this model, for example, by modifying different sensory inputs in subjects with different nervous system lesions, for example, modifications of proprioceptive inputs by passive movements or prolonged compression of a limb, of visual inputs by use of prisms, of vestibular inputs by constant and inconstant changes of position, or of level of consciousness by neuropharmacologic or sleep studies.

Hécaen (1972b) has examined the first of these two exigencies and concluded that the model does not completely satisfy the first condition. That is, although there is good correspondence between clinical experience and a hypothetical model for anosognosias and phantom limb phenomena, the correspondence is less satisfactory for hemiasomatognosia and sentiments of strangeness or nonbelonging of body parts.

The second condition, that of experimental verification, appears more promising, although quantitative studies of essentially subjective phenomena are notoriously difficult to obtain. Current research supports the view that modifications of sensory inputs produce somatognosic illusions primarily in the presence of right hemispheric lesions (Hécaen, 1972b, Tzavaras, personal communication). One is justified in asking, however, if the presence of aphasia in patients with left hemispheric lesions does not reduce the incidence of reported illusions for that group of subjects. Among the various types of sensory modifications so far employed, in a large majority of cases, only ischemia (limb compression) causes illusions. To date, visual modifications by the wearing of prisms have not provided conclusive results. Visual modifications do seem, nevertheless, to exaggerate pre-existing illusions. Reduction of attentional vigilance seems to be a critical necessity in the experimental setting, since no illusions are produced in the absence of some degree of confusion on the part of the subject. As for the type of illusions created by such experimentation we have found a wide range, including simple paresthesias, impression of increasing strength in a limb, feeling of heaviness, illusions of movement, phantom limbs, and sense of nonbelonging of a limb.

A different experimental approach to somatognosis has been taken by Melzack (e.g., Melzack and Bromage, 1973; Gross et al, 1974). One study analyzed phantom limb phenomena in 71 subjects undergoing operations on an arm and having brachial plexus anesthesia. With their motor and sensory nerves to the arm anesthetised, and when they closed their eyes, 67 of the 71 subjects experienced a phantom limb sensation similar to that of subjects with amputations, that is, clearly specified spatial situation of the arm, and paresthesias, voluntary and spontaneous movements. When they opened their eyes, the phantom limb suddenly became active and moved into and became a part of the real arm. The phantom disappeared completely and rapidly when motor and sensory function returned following recovery from anesthesia.

Another study tested the interaction of central and peripheral factors on localization of a limb in space. When eyes were closed, normal subjects perceived their immobile arm as being closer to the trunk than it really was. If the subject moved his unseen hand between trials, the position errors were exaggerated. In addition subjects complained of sensations of heaviness of the arm, warmth, tingling, and throbbing, and even of the feeling that parts of the limb were missing.

The authors concluded that perception of body parts depends on the interaction of stable central processes and transitory peripheral factors. Standard, preprogrammed spatial postures exist in limited number, around which other bodily positions distribute themselves. In a review of spatial information processing, Paillard (1974) presented similar conclusions concerning the existence of postural referents that serve as spatial codes for afferent stimuli permitting orientation of the body, location of points on the surface of the body, and guidance of movements in space. Melzack argues that certain central cellular pools become active when liberated from peripheral control, producing the sensation of spontaneous, involuntary, phantom movement. If voluntary movement is intended, but visual and proprioceptive feedback are missing, the movement is related to the phantom limb.

Although these results are incomplete and have been insufficiently elaborated, they are nonetheless sufficiently encouraging to warrant continuation of the psychophysiological exploration of the determining features of somatognosis.

SEVEN
DISORDERS
OF MEMORY

INTRODUCTION

This section is intended to provide a framework for our subsequent consideration of memory disorders; here we outline briefly some general aspects of normal memory and deal with the problem of definitions. In broad terms memory refers to the effects of previous perceptual experience on present behavior (Milner, 1968a). Within this more general statement we can incorporate the definition provided by J. Z. Young (1966) that memory is "a physical system by which there is made a record or representation of certain past events. It is in the nature of records to be consulted when future action has to be decided on." This chapter considers breakdowns at various points within this system.

Parameters of Memory

Temporal Factors

Short-term and long-term memories, recent and remote memories, primary and secondary memories—these and other terms have been employed to help clarify the various temporal relationships in memory processing. Instead of clarifying, however, they have occasionally obscured the picture because of inconsistencies in their use.

Milner (1968a) suggests that the expressions *short-term* and *long-term memories* are best used to designate hypothetical processes mediating retention, rather than categories of behavior. The short-term trace decays in a matter of sec-

331

onds when rehearsal is prevented; the long-term system is more permanent. Between the two is an unstable transition phase during which the memory trace is "consolidated." *Immediate memory* is a term defined behaviorally that refers to the amount of material that can be reproduced immediately after presentation.

The descriptive expressions considered in the preceding paragraph are consistent with the Waugh and Norman (1965) conception of the memory process as an orderly sequence of storage systems with different operating characteristics. Inputs may be transferred from sensory memory with a duration of a few hundred milliseconds to a primary memory system with a storage duration of several seconds and finally to a more permanent secondary memory system where information can be stored for minutes or years.

The greatest confusion in terminology arises with the introduction of the terms *recent* and *remote memories*. These expressions are clinically derived and have no direct relationship to underlying mechanisms of memory. They refer to a time scale of the patient's life (Milner, 1968a). In the amnestic syndrome (discussed below) a patient may have an anterograde or a retrograde amnesia. With an anterograde amnesia the patient is unable to learn new material and is thus unable to remember events of his life since the moment of onset of the defect. With a retrograde amnesia the patient has a variable difficulty in recalling events prior to the onset of the defect. This is often patchy, and usually memories for the early events of life are not lost. Thus one may speak of this patient's loss of memory for recent events by contrast with his preservation of memory for remote events. The clinical term *recent memory* should not be confused with the neuropsychological short-term memory process.

Remembering versus Forgetting

Recall, Recognition, and Acquisition of New Knowledge   Remembering is not necessarily the opposite of forgetting, and failure to remember is not necessarily the equivalent of forgetting, although there is undoubtedly overlap in underlying processes. This conception of memory provides a useful dichotomy that helps to highlight the multiplicity of underlying mechanisms. If we assume that the input has been adequately perceived, then remembering involves acquisition, registration, storage, and recall or recognition; forgetting involves loss, either active or passive.

In testing normal or pathological memory we use principally three techniques. Tests of free recall demand that the subject reproduce as much of the test material as he can. Tests of recognition demand that the subject recall previously presented stimuli by means of multiple-choice displays. Tests of learning usually involve repeated exposure to test material in such a manner that the subject gradually becomes more proficient in discriminating the old from the new.

Forgetting to Remember Some of us have had the experience of leaving the house with the intention of performing a particular task, being interrupted on the way, returning to the house after forgetting to perform the task, and remembering that the task had to be performed only after having returned. Such a normal process may be termed "forgetting to remember" and is more likely to be an alteration of selective attention than a defect of memory. When this occurs as a pathological defect of attention, it is often associated with frontal lobe pathology (see below in the chapter on the frontal lobes) or with certain types of subcortical diseases, especially those involving the reticular activating systems (Albert et al, 1974).

Material Specificity versus Modality Specificity

Not all memory disorders are alike. We have indicated above that in the amnestic syndrome a patient may have a memory loss for all aspects of certain events of his life. This general or global amnesia is defined in terms of time and not in terms of the elements of the event. It is also possible to define memories in terms of the characteristics of the event or stimulus to be remembered. Thus stimuli may be of a specific type of material: verbal or nonverbal, or stimuli may be presented to a specific sensory modality. By consequence, memory disorders may be general, as in the amnestic syndrome, or specific, associated with particular interhemispheric and intrahemispheric lesions. In subsequent sections of this chapter we consider memory disorders according to these two major subdivisions: general or specific.

Clinical Considerations

Neurology and Neuropsychology

With respect to memory disorders the concerns of the neurologist and the neuropsychologist often coincide, and work performed by one often aids the other. Both must attempt to distinguish memory disorders from disorders of attention, of perception, and of general intellectual impairment. Both must attempt to establish that the memory disorder has an organic and not a psychogenic basis. When one is assessing disorders of memory, one must sample a wide range of other intellectual functions before concluding that memory has been selectively involved. For example, language impairment on an aphasic basis can disturb performance on material-specific (verbal vs. nonverbal) tests.

Disorders of perception may occur together with disorders of memory, and attempts must be made to distinguish them. Presenting similar material through different sensory channels and different material through similar sensory channels may at times be useful. Another technique is a version of that proposed by Peterson and Peterson (1959). Patients are presented with stimuli to a particular sensory channel and then required to recall the stimuli immediately after presentation (nondelay) or after one of various post-stimulus delays (3, 6, 9, 12, 15, or 18 seconds) during which the patient has to count backward to prevent rehearsal. If a patient demonstrates normal identification under the nondelay condition but is impaired for delay conditions, failures in the short-term memory process are indicated. If, however, the patient is impaired on the nondelay as well as the delay conditions, perceptual processes may be more critical.

Recovery of Function

Some patients, as for example, alcoholic Korsakoff patients, may retain their memory defect for life. Others, as for example, some patients with posttraumatic amnesias, may recover from their amnesia, at least partially and often totally. The nature, extent, and rate of recovery from amnesia are legitimate subjects for study. Indeed study of such topics may lead to the development of new forms of therapy for patients with memory defects. The conditions under which an amnesic patient may learn (e.g., state-dependent learning) and the cues that may aid such learning (e.g., categorical cues and references to the task, Gardner et al, 1973) are useful guides to therapy programs. Patten (1972) has already described a plan for memory therapy that has been successfully employed in a small group of amnesic patients.

GENERAL DISTURBANCES OF MEMORY—THE AMNESTIC SYNDROME

Korsakoff's Syndrome

Clinical Features

In 1887 S. S. Korsakoff described what he considered to be a new disease entity, "cerebropathia toxemia psychica," having both peripheral and central nervous system manifestations. The peripheral signs were those of a diffuse, symmetrical distal neuropathy. The central signs were primarily those of memory defect. Frequently studied since Korsakoff's earliest reports (1887, 1889a,b), the syndrome that now bears his name has come to refer to the central, neurobehavioral disorder, for it has long since been recognized that the central and peripheral manifestations may be separated. The Korsakoff syndrome is now accepted as a neurological disorder manifested by impaired recent memory (an anterograde amnesia with disturbed ability to learn new material), together with a patchy and variable retrograde amnesia, but with relative preservation of early memories; confabulation is a frequent, but not essential, part of the clinical picture.

This disorder is distinguishable from confusional states by clarity of consciousness and intact perception, and from the dementias by the relatively good preservation of other intellectual capacities. In 1901 Bonhoeffer established the following clinical criteria for the diagnosis: memory defect for current events, retrograde amnesia, disorientation, and confabulation. With minor variations in emphasis of one or the other sign the syndrome has remained in essentially the same form to the present. An additional feature stressed by Zangwill (1966a) and also referred to by Korsakoff (1889b) is a striking lack of insight. Zangwill indicates that the deficiency of insight may underlie the peculiar defects in reasoning and judgment described by Pick (1915).

Anatomic and Physiological Considerations

The clinical features described in the preceding section may result from a wide variety of pathological causes, including metabolic or nutritional deficiencies (in particular the B-complex vitamins), exogenous toxins, central nervous system infections, tumors, trauma, vascular lesions, and surgically induced lesions. The common factor producing the Korsakoff syndrome is not the etiologic agent but the location of the lesion.

In a monograph reviewing the syndrome due primarily to chronic alcoholism with resultant nutritional deficiencies, Victor, Adams, and Collins (1971) found that the dorsomedial nuclei of the thalamus were always involved, and the mamillary bodies were almost always involved. This anatomic formulation has not met with universal acceptance. Involvement of the mamillary bodies, first stressed by Gamper (1928), is considered to be constant by Delay and Brion (1969). These authors, while accepting the importance of lesions of the dorsomedial nucleus of the thalamus, do not consider lesions of this region to be essential to the syndrome. Depending on the cause (see below) various other regions of the brain (hippocampus, fornix, anterior thalamus) have also been implicated.

Neuropsychological Aspects of the
Alcoholism-Induced Korsakoff's Syndrome

Numerous studies have been done with groups of amnesic subjects, occasionally with conflicting results. One possible explanation for the differences in results is that different patient populations have been used and that these different groups may have had different anatomic loci of their lesions. A lesion at one point within the memory pathways may provoke a different effect on the processes of memory than a lesion at another point. In the remainder of this section we consider neuropsychological studies done with groups of patients with Korsakoff's syndrome due to alcoholism. In subsequent sections we consider other groups of amnesic subjects.

In several studies with alcoholic Korsakoff's patients Butters, Cermak, Goodglass, and their collaborators have attempted to define the nature of the amnesic defect. In 1971 they compared the effects of cortical damage and alcoholic subcortical damage on short-term visual and auditory memory (Samuels et al, 1971b). In a preliminary experiment using the Peterson and Peterson technique (1959) they found that Korsakoff's patients were like patients with right hemispheric damage in that both groups had severe memory defects on all visual tasks; however, unlike the right-brain-damaged group, the Korsakoff's group also had memory defects on auditory tasks. Subsequent qualitative analysis of the differences in response patterns of Korsakoff and cortically damaged patients with quantitatively similar memory defects indicated that the Korsakoff patients made more perseverative-type errors.

To evaluate the extent of memory loss in Korsakoff patients, Cermak et al (1971) had three groups of subjects perform in a short-term memory distractor technique design (Peterson and Peterson, 1959). The groups were alcoholic Korsakoff's patients, alcoholics with no brain damage, and nonalcoholics with no brain damage. Results showed that the retention span for Korsakoff's patients deteriorated more rapidly than that for either of the other two groups. Recognition testing revealed that more of the original trace was present than could be recalled. The authors demonstrated that, although some material could be transferred into and maintained in long-term memory, the Korsakoff's patients also had evidence of impairment in the long-term memory system.

This research group then examined short-term memory disorders of alcoholic Korsakoff's patients for evidence of material and modality specificity (Butters et al, 1973b). Verbal and nonverbal memory tasks employing the visual, auditory, and tactile modalities were administered to Korsakoff's patients and to alcoholic and nonalcoholic control subjects. In all three modalities the Korsakoff's patients demonstrated normal short-term retention of nonverbal materials but severe memory defects for verbal material. They concluded that their findings were consistent with the hypothesis that failures in verbal encoding underlay their patients' memory difficulties.

Conflicting results regarding the nature of the memory defect in Korsakoff's patients have been reported. Cermak and Butters (1972) indicated that the memory deficits exhibited by alcoholic Korsakoff's patients were related to an increased sensitivity to interference from previously presented material. They felt that this hypersensitivity to interference reflected a failure to encode new material. On the other hand Warrington and Weiskrantz (1971) found that the Korsakoff's patient's increased sensitivity to proactive inhibition was not due to a failure in encoding or organizational processes. These authors were able to demonstrate preservation of a perceptual learning task in amnesic subjects. On a test of recognition of fragmented designs, modified from an earlier test by Gollin (1960), amnesics had improved recognition scores 1 hour after initial presentation of stimuli, even though they could not remember ever having performed the task before.

To determine the extent of the Korsakoff's patient's ability to encode semantically meaningful verbal material, Cermak et al (1973a) presented four experiments. The first experiment showed that the Korsakoff's patient is aided by category cues following a 1-minute retention interval. The remaining experiments, which also employed cuing techniques, demonstrated that Korsakoff's patients, with instructions, can encode on acoustic, associative, and semantic levels. When left to their own preferences, however, these Korsakoff's patients relied upon acoustic and associative encoding. The authors concluded that the failure to employ semantic encoding strategies spontaneously was perhaps an underlying factor in the overall inability to retain verbal material.

We have indicated above that among the clinical features of the Korsakoff syndrome was a peculiar disturbance in reasoning and judgment. Oscar-Berman (1973) evaluated this process by comparing patients with Korsakoff's syndrome, other brain-damaged subjects, and normal controls on a set of visual discrimination tasks designed to test focusing behavior and hypothesis testing. Results showed that Korsakoff's patients were able to formulate and use hypotheses but that their strategies did not lead to correct solutions. Rather, they perseverated with one strategy even after receiving indications of its inappropriateness. This pattern of results occurred even in the presence of memory aids, suggesting that Korsakoff's patients may have impaired cognitive function independent of their retention deficits.

Amnesias Associated with Surgical and Other Lesions of the Hippocampal Formation

Clinical Features

The critical role of the hippocampal formation in mnemonic processes was firmly established by the reports of Scoville and Milner (1957) and Penfield and Milner (1958), which indicated that bilateral damage to the hippocampus produced a "severe and generalized defect in memory involving continuous anterograde amnesia for the events of daily life together with some retrograde amnesia for the period preceding the critical brain lesions" (Milner, 1968a).

The operations in these cases were performed in patients who had serious psychiatric disturbances (psychosurgery) or who had intractable seizures. Thus the neurobehavioral defects observed may be related in part to the long-standing psychiatric or neurological disease. However, the fact that surgical lesions in similar regions consistently produce similar patterns of memory defect militates against this argument.

Formal psychological testing in these cases revealed severe anterograde and some retrograde amnesia, with preservation of early memories and technical skills. There were no deteriorations in general intelligence and no complex perceptual disturbance. There was no loss of attention, concentration, or reasoning ability. No linguistic defects were observed.

Anatomic and Physiological Considerations

Surgical procedures in the Scoville cases were radical, involving the medial surfaces of both temporal lobes, extending posteriorly for a distance of 8 centimeters from the temporal tips, and destroying the anterior two-thirds of the hippocampus and the hippocampal gyrus. The degree of memory loss appeared to depend on the extent of hippocampal removal. In the operations described above, the memory loss was particularly severe; bilateral removal of only the uncus and amygdala did not appear to cause memory impairment. A case of unilateral inferior temporal lobectomy with radical posterior extension to include the major portion of the hippocampus and hippocampal gyrus showed no lasting memory loss.

In 1961 Victor et al described a case of a patient who suffered a severe amnesia and visual field defects in association with occlusion of both posterior cerebral arteries. During a period of 5 years this patient retained a profound deficit in recent memory despite the preservation of a "bright normal" level on intelligence testing. He also had an incomplete retrograde amnesia, although remote memory for distant events was spared. The significant pathology was an old bilateral infarction involving the hippocampal formation, fornix, and mamillary body. The uncus, amygdaloid body, and terminal digitations of the hippocampus were unaffected on either side. Korsakoff's syndrome resulting from bilateral lesions in the territory of the posterior cerebral arteries has been recognized since the observation of Dide and Botcazo in 1902. In that case an occipital syndrome (alexia and visual field defect) was added to the anterograde amnesia, confabulation, and disorientation. The case of Victor et al is remarkable in that "intelligence" was preserved.

Benson, Segarra, and Albert (1974) have described the clinical and neuropathological findings in a similar case. The memory disorder of this patient slowly improved over a 6-month period but never returned to normal. Pathological examination revealed infarction bilaterally in the distribution of both posterior cerebral arteries, in particular involving the inferomedial surfaces of both temporal lobes. Castaigne et al (1966) noted similar amnesic states associated with bilateral thalamic infarction.

Neuropsychological Aspects

In an attempt to investigate more systematically the learning ability of patients with bilateral hippocampal lesions, by preference choosing tasks that were not primarily verbal, Milner (1965) studied the capability of these subjects on a test of visually guided maze learning. The maze-learning performance of these subjects was compared with that of normal subjects and of subjects with other cortical lesions. The task chosen was a stylus-maze problem of the stepping-stone kind, the subjects being trained over many trials until they could traverse the maze without error. The subjects with bilateral hippocampal lesions were the most severely impaired, one subject showing no progress in 215 trials. With respect to this latter subject, experience in the latter part of the maze interfered with effective rehearsal of the first part of the path. This subject, who seemed to rely entirely on verbal rehearsal, had to start each new trial as if it were a fresh problem.

Using the same methodology, Corkin (1965) evaluated tactually guided maze learning in subjects with bilateral hippocampal lesions. Again these subjects were severely impaired. But such motor learning was always possible with the patient H.M., who was severely impaired on all other learning tasks. On one motor task H.M. even demonstrated complete retention several days after learning the task (Corkin 1968).

To clarify the nature of the memory defect, Drachman and Arbit (1966) studied five patients with known or presumed bilateral lesions of the hippocampal regions. Two memory tasks were devised in which the length of a memorandum could be gradually increased from subspan to supraspan lengths. They found that the patients' immediate memory spans were normal compared with controls. However, the patients had severe impairment in learning supraspan memoranda, even after many repetitions. The authors concluded from these results that hippocampal lesions produced impairment of storage ability; no perseverative-type errors were noted.

In an attempt to differentiate various types of memory disorder associated with different lesions within the memory system, Lhermitte and Signoret (1972) studied patients with amnesia due to alcoholism and patients with amnesia due to encephalitis. The authors reported that postencephalitic patients had severe anterograde amnesia but performed well on sequential tests, while alcoholic Korsakoff's patients were able to store information but failed on the sequential tests.

Traumatic Amnesias

Clinical Features

Most reports on the memory disorders that follow head injuries emphasize the temporal features of the amnesia (see, for example, Russell and Nathan,

1946; Whitty and Zangwill, 1966; I. S. Russell, 1971). If there is considerable variation in the duration of one or another of the key symptoms comprising the postconcussion amnesic syndrome, nonetheless, the general clinical pattern appears to be constant. The typical picture of concussion is a transient loss of consciousness followed by a period of confusion and impaired memory. Integral features are a shrinking temporary retrograde amnesia, a short period of permanent retrograde amnesia, and a longer period of post-traumatic amnesia (Fisher, 1966). Depending on the severity of the head injury some of these clinical features may be long lasting or even permanent (Zangwill, 1943, 1946b; Williams and Zangwill, 1952).

Anatomic and Physiological Considerations

Since most of these patients recover, we have no good evidence to support an anatomic or pathophysiological correlation. Several possibilities may nonetheless be raised. Any severe acceleration-deceleration injury involving the skull causes a sudden movement of intracerebral structures, and certain regions are preferentially damaged. In particular the temporal tips and the undersurfaces of the temporal lobes are often found to be contused in cases of fatal head injuries.

Symonds (1962) suggests that there may be direct traumatic physical alteration of nerve cells and axons in the white matter of both hemispheres following head injury. This is somewhat supported by Stritch (1961), who felt that severe head injury produced a stretching of some nerve fibers and a rupture of others. The fibers that are stretched, rather than torn, could eventually recover some function, perhaps accounting for the reversibility of some of the defects.

Neuropsychological Aspects

Benson and Geschwind (1967) reported the detailed observation of shrinking retrograde amnesia in a young man with a post-traumatic memory disorder. In this patient there was a rapid recovery of the ability to learn new material followed by a slower but progressive shortening of the retrograde amnesia. The retrograde amnesia diminished in a patchy, rather than smooth, manner, leaving islands of memory loss surrounded by regions of intact memory. These observations were similar to those described previously by Russell and Nathan (1946). Benson and Geschwind considered the retrograde amnesia to represent a retrieval defect, rather than a loss of established memories; the post-traumatic amnesia, they felt, most likely represented a failure to establish new memory traces. They considered it possible that the retrieval process depends on the same system that is necessary for laying down new memories.

In this way they explained the fact that the shrinking of retrograde amnesia runs generally parallel to the recovery of recent memory function.

Yarnell and Lynch (1970, 1973) studied four young athletes immediately after concussion in a football game and compared the immediate postconcussion test results with results on memory testing minutes later. The examination consisted of asking the athletes several questions concerned with the game and repeating these questions at short intervals thereafter. The striking finding was that all four players immediately recalled what had happened ("I got hit") and could recall the events in the seconds preceding the injury. On re-examination within 3 to 20 minutes all four had lost the immediate pretraumatic information.

These observations are in marked contrast with other reports of post-traumatic amnestic syndromes, all of which indicate only that there is a consistent loss of memory for the brief period of time immediately preceding the injury and for the injury itself (Whitty and Zangwill, 1966). The explanation for the different observations is that Yarnell and Lynch, by virtue of their presence on the sidelines, could be on the playing field within seconds after impact.

The interpretation provided by Yarnell and Lynch is as follows. Since immediate preconcussion information was retrievable when the patients were questioned within seconds after injury, the information must have been stored by some short-term process. The finding that these memories were then lost in a time span of 3 to 20 minutes after concussion implies that fixation or consolidation into long-term memory is an ongoing process and is damaged by the physical effects of a concussive injury.

Transient Amnesias

Amnesias Associated with Electroconvulsive Therapy

Electroconvulsive therapy has an adverse effect on memory, both for events preceding the shock (retrograde effect) and for those experienced after it (anterograde effect). The severity and duration of these amnesias depend on a number of variables, including the intensity of electrical stimulation, the placement of the electrodes (unilateral or bilateral), the number and interval of shocks, the age of the patient, the clinical diagnosis, and the use of concomitant anesthetic, tranquilizing, or muscle-relaxing medication.

Retrograde Effects   After every shock, patients experience a period of amnesia for the few seconds preceding it, similar to the retrograde amnesia following concussions (Williams, 1966). The events forgotten are usually independent of psychological importance but are closely related to the onset of the seizure, those last experienced being most easily forgotten. Mayer-Gross

(1943) and Williams (1950) have, however, shown that visual stimuli presented within a few seconds before the onset of the seizure can be picked out on a test of multiple choice or with prompting, even though most patients would deny any recollection of these stimuli.

In addition to amnesia for events immediately preceding the shock, many patients complain of forgetfulness of remote events. Names of persons and places are particularly vulnerable (Brody, 1944) and may persist for a long time after the series of treatments has been completed. The memory losses may be patchy (Ebtinger, 1958) and may thus resemble the retrograde losses seen in post-traumatic amnesias (Williams and Zangwill, 1952). A "shrinking" of the retrograde amnesia usually takes place; the pattern of shrinkage is not always time related, from past to present, but consists rather of a filling in between islands.

Recovery of verbal memory (vocabulary) is dependent on word frequency. Rochford and Williams (1962) found a very close parallel between difficulty or rarity of a word and time elapsing between treatment and recall of the word. For example, the word *comb* could be named by 90% of post-ECT patients within 2 minutes of being able to give their own names, while the "teeth" of the comb could not be named until 12 minutes later.

Anterograde Effects   Williams (1966) has clearly described the early phase of mental activity following ECT. First, patients are disoriented, confused, and unable to answer questions coherently. Stimuli presented to them at this time are forgotten almost immediately, and after final recovery of orientation the patients have no recollection of events occurring at this time. Subsequent restitution of memory for past events is gradual, personal orientation returning before that for place and time.

Regarding long-term effects of treatment there is some difference of opinion. Many clinicians have personal experience with post-ECT patients who have persistent memory disorders. As a rule, however, ability to learn new material usually returned to its pretreatment level by several weeks after termination of the treatment (Zubin and Barrera, 1941).

Amnesias Induced by Anesthesia

In 1799 Humphrey Davy described the amnesic effect of nitrous oxide. Since then, and in rapidly increasing numbers, anesthetic agents have been found that affect memory. Of considerable interest to observers (Brunn, 1963; Gruber and Reed, 1968; Crawford et al, 1969; Sia, 1969; Terrell et al, 1969; Cherkin and Harroun, 1971;) is the fact that postoperative recall of events during the operation is not always prevented by seemingly adequate anesthesia. However, paradoxically, recall of operative events may be prevented by light anesthesia, during which time the patient is responsive to conversation (Mazzia and Rand, 1966; Terrell et al, 1969). That memories can be formed despite anesthesia is supported by the evidence that anesthetized rats (Berger, 1970) and anesthetized rabbits (Lico et al, 1968) can learn. It must, however, be understood that surgical anesthesia is not a single state of consciousness; rather, variable levels of consciousness are maintained during the operation.

The effect of anesthesia on the consolidation of a memory trace is equally variable. One minute after information input, memory consolidation is invulnerable to weak anesthesia (Cherkin and Harroun, 1971) but is still vulnerable to stronger anesthesia. One hour after information input, only deep anesthesia can disrupt the consolidation process (Alperin and Kimble, 1967). Mazzia and Randt (1966) found that, in patients who were shown a picture during light anesthesia when the ability for eye centering was lacking, the picture could be recalled for up to 60 seconds but not thereafter. This finding is reminiscent of the observations of Yarnell and Lynch (described above in the section on traumatic amnesias), who reported retention of a pretraumatic event for minutes following a head injury, with subsequent loss of this memory. We can tentatively conclude that anesthetic amnesia results from a modification of sensory reception together with disruption of the processes of memory consolidation.

The Syndrome of Transient Global Amnesia

In 1958 and 1964 Fisher and Adams defined a hitherto unrecognized neurological syndrome of which the cardinal feature was a sudden and transient loss of memory, which they labeled transient global amnesia. Since then many similar cases have been reported (Shuttleworth and Morris, 1966; Symonds, 1966; Heathfield et al, 1973; etc.). The clinical signs and symptoms are characteristic, and the syndrome is difficult to confuse with any other. The onset is sudden, without any premonitory symptoms and usually without apparant precipitating cause. There may be a brief, mild degree of clouding of consciousness at the beginning. The major feature is amnesia, both anterograde and retrograde. The episode usually lasts for several hours (although it may last 2–3 days) and ends in complete recovery. The retrograde amnesia may cover a short (hours) or relatively long (weeks) time span, but this rapidly shrinks, leaving a brief permanent retrograde amnesia equivalent in duration to the anterograde amnesia. The subject is otherwise quite well—even during the attack insight is retained; speech is normal; and there is no loss of personal identity, usually no loss of spatial memories, and no impairment of other neuropsychological activity.

Few neuropsychological studies have been conducted during the attack, and, since the patients usually survive the incident, few anatomic studies are available. Clinical studies have, however, provided information regarding the presumed anatomic and physiological substrata of these episodes. In a careful evaluation of 31 patients with sudden loss of memory Heathfield, Croft, and Swash (1973) found two-thirds (19 cases) to have the syndrome of transient global amnesia. Of these 19 patients, 8 had recurrent episodes, and 9 had clear-cut evidence of a vascular cause, whether the amnesic episodes were single or recurrent. These authors concluded that most episodes of transient global amnesia resulted from bilateral temporal lobe or thalamic lesions, and that ischemia in the territory of the posterior cerebral artery circulation was the cause.

The Amnestic Syndrome—Summary

Clinical and Neuropsychological Features

A remarkable conclusion gradually emerges from analyses of the general disturbances of memory: regardless of the cause the clinical features of the amnestic syndrome are virtually always the same. These features include principally an impairment of recent memory, with preservation of the ability for immediate recall (e.g., digit span) and preservation of remote memories. There is a time-limited anterograde amnesia, and a retrograde amnesia that, if at first extensive, shrinks in a characteristic manner, not smoothly from past to present but in patchy fashion.

From the point of view of neuropsychological research, however, more variability has been discovered. Amnesic subjects are not so forgetful as was once thought (Warrington and Wieskrantz, 1970). Learning and retention of motor skills, such as rotary pursuit and tracking tasks, are possible if not altogether normal (Corkin, 1968). They can use partial cues for retrieving verbal material (Warrington and Weiskrantz, 1970). Even over a long period of time they can retain verbal materials that have been adequately rehearsed (Talland, 1965; Cermak, Butters, and Goodglass, 1971); they have adequate short-term memory for nonverbal stimuli (Butters et al, 1973b); when given two sets of cues (reference to the task and category cues), they demonstrate adequate recall of verbal material (Gardner et al, 1973). Thus, whereas earlier studies succeeded in demonstrating the characteristics of functions that were lost, current studies seem determined to demonstrate the characteristics of capacities that are preserved.

The Anatomy of Memory

The similarity of clinical signs and symptoms of the amnestic syndrome, whatever its etiology, impels a belief that the same anatomic areas are being altered from their normal function, either by primary structural damage or by secondary physiological modification. In this sense one is justified in talking about the "anatomy of memory." By this we do not imply that the memory traces are actually laid down in these anatomic regions; rather, this system operates in such a way as to facilitate storage of previous experience in other parts of the brain.

The anatomic and physiological considerations discussed above may now be synthesized to afford a general anatomic scheme underlying memory. The structures essential for the process are the hippocampal formations within the temporal lobes (that is, the hippocampal or parahippocampal gyrus, and the hippocampus of Ammons Horn), the mamillary bodies, and certain thalamic nuclei within the diencephalon (anterior nuclear complex and dorsomedial nucleus). A continuous pathway of connections may be drawn: from the hippocampal gyrus along afferent fibers to the hippocampus, thence along efferent fibers in the fornix to the mamillary bodies; from here along the mamillothalamic tract to the anterior thalamic nuclei; thence to the cingulate gyrus; and finally from the cingulate gyrus to the hippocampal gyrus (Brierly, 1966). This memory pathway is apparently continuous and as such forms one of the inner circuits of the limbic system (Papez, 1937), which, in a larger sense, is responsible for the reception, elaboration, and control of emotional and visceral activity.

Either bilateral hippocampal or bilateral diencephalic damage can cause a defect in recent memory and a retrograde amnesia. Bilateral destruction of the fornix, the major pathway between these two regions, has also been found to produce a similar defect in memory (Sweet et al, 1959). Delay and Brion (1969) contend that any bilateral lesion, even asymmetric, of the "memory circuit" produces Korsakoff's syndrome.

SPECIFIC DEFECTS OF MEMORY

Memory Disorders Associated with Temporal Lobe Lesions

In the preceding section we discussed general disorders of learning and retention caused by lesions of the hippocampal formation, the mamillary bodies, or the dorsomedial nuclei of the thalamus or their connections. In this section we consider specific, rather than general, memory disorders and their associated anatomic relationships. Associated with unilateral temporal lesions there are specific memory deficits for certain types of material, and these deficits differ depending on which hemisphere is involved. These deficits have been found to be independent of the modality of stimulus presentation, and they become manifest regardless of the nature of the memory task, be it recall, delayed recognition, or learning.

These disorders of material-specific memory have been demonstrated by several different research groups, and in particular by the work of B. Milner and her collaborators (1958, 1962, 1967, 1968a,b). Many of their studies have attempted to evaluate the neuropsychological effects of right or left unilateral temporal lobectomies, with and without hippocampal involvement.

Verbal Memory Defects following Left Temporal Lobectomy

In her earliest works Milner showed that nonaphasic subjects with left temporal lobectomies had defective verbal memories by comparison with subjects with right temporal lobectomies. Verbal memory defects were demonstrated in the auditory modality even with a test of immediate retention in which a short paragraph was read aloud to the subject for immediate recall, but the defects were clearly more marked in a test of recall following a 1-hour delay during which time the subject was occupied with other tests. Deficits were also found on tests of auditory associative learning (reviewed in Milner and Teuber, 1968).

With visuoverbal learning and retention tasks a significant impairment was again seen following removal of the left temporal lobe. Tasks included a test in which the subject had to write a short story 40 minutes after having read it, a verbal paired-associates learning test presented in the visual modality, and a test requiring recognition of recurrent visuoverbal stimuli (words, numbers, nonsense syllables) appearing in a group of other similar stimuli that were not recurrent. These various verbal memory deficits, auditory and visual, were present not only in the immediate postoperative period but also 1 year after the operation.

In evaluating the results, Milner emphasized the role of the hippocampal regions, since the deficits were more severe when the temporal ablation included these structures. Nevertheless she did not exclude the possibility that lesion size—the volume of tissue destroyed or removed—may have played a role, for she found similar deficits with large parietal lobe lesions and with the larger temporal ablations that reached Heschl's gyri, even without including hippocampal structures. In this latter regard, however, we should add a note of caution: the larger left temporal lesions and large left parietal lesions may have been associated with a mild aphasia that could have influenced the results.

Nonverbal Memory Defects following Right Temporal Lobectomy

In 1963 Kimura demonstrated that subjects with right temporal lobectomy were significantly impaired by contrast with left temporal lobectomized subjects on a task requiring visual recognition of recurrent meaningless designs appearing in a group of other designs that were not recurrent. However, unlike the results with verbal stimuli, described above in the previous section, which were abnormal regardless of the sensory modality, the results with nonverbal stimuli were clearly abnormal only when the input was visual. For example, with a similar methodology (recognition of recurrent stimuli) but with an auditory input (bird songs), the impairment of sound recognition following right temporal lobectomy was more marked than that following left-sided lesions, but the difference was not statistically significant. For the tactile modality Corkin (1965) used a similar methodology and found no defect in the group with temporal lesions.

Thus, if we limit ourselves to this particular test methodology, we find that the sensory channel plays a determining role in nonverbal memory after right temporal lobectomy. It may be that the complexity of the stimulus material is different for the different sensory modalities and that different cues may be used to recognize the recurrent stimuli.

Nonetheless, other tests have also demonstrated impairment of nonverbal memory after right temporal lobectomy. Milner (1968a) found such a deficit, using a delayed matching task with photographs of faces.

Deficient capacity for nonverbal learning has been found after right temporal lobectomy whether the sensory modality was visual or tactile (Corkin, 1965; Milner, 1965). In a maze-learning task the number of trials to criterion and the number of errors were significantly greater following right-sided ablations. Of particular interest is that these significant differences appeared only when the hippocampal region was removed. Performance of subjects with right temporal ablations not including the hippocampal regions was not significantly different from that of subjects with left-brain damage. In addition, within the group of subjects with right temporal ablations, the subgroup with hippocampal excision required significantly more trials to learn the maze than did the subgroup in which the hippocampus was spared.

Memory Defects following Lesions to Specific Intratemporal Regions

We have already indicated that maze learning in both the visual and tactile modalities is impaired after right temporal lobectomy only if the hippocampal region is excised. Subsequent research has confirmed and refined these observations, adding to our understanding of the relation of different segments of the hippocampal formation to specific mnemonic capabilities.

Corsi (1972) studied memory defects in subjects with temporal lobectomies, dividing his subject population into four subgroups for each hemisphere: (1) with hippocampus intact, (2) with excision of the pes hippocampi, (3) with excision of the pes hippocampi and about 1 centimeter of the body of the hippocampus, and (4) with radical ablation of the entire hippocampal region. These brain-damaged subjects and normal controls were presented four tests of information retention and recall, two verbal, two nonverbal.

The verbal tests included a modification of the Peterson and Peterson technique, in which the subject had to recall three consonants after an interval occupied by verbal activity; and a modification of the Hebb technique, involving cumulative learning of a sequence of recurrent numbers exceeding the subject's memory span. The nonverbal tests used similar techniques: recall of the position of a cross on a line after an occupied or unoccupied delay interval (Posner Test), and reproduction of a sequence by pointing in the correct order to a series of blocks, the order having been previously established and learned by the subject.

All subgroups with left temporal lobectomy had significant impairment on the task of delayed recall of consonants. On the task involving learning sequences of recurrent digits, the left-brain-damaged groups were similarly impaired, except for the subgroup with intact hippocampus, whose performances were normal. In each case the severity of the deficit was directly related to the extent of hippocampal damage—the greater the hippocampal involvement, the greater the verbal memory deficit.

The two tests of nonverbal learning and retention showed similar results but with damage to the other hemisphere, while the subjects with left-brain damage performed as well as controls, those with right temporal resections being significantly impaired. For the right-brain-damaged group the intensity of the spatial learning deficit and, to a lesser degree, of the visual recall deficit was related to the extent of hippocampal involvement.

We thus see confirmed the influence of intratemporal structures (uncus, amygdaloid nucleus, hippocampus, parahippocampal gyrus) on the process of consolidation of information. These structures have a selective influence on learning and retention according to the specific type of material received (verbal or nonverbal) and depending on the functional specialization of each hemisphere.

Supporting Evidence and Inconsistencies

In sum the earlier studies of Milner and her collaborators demonstrated material-specific deficits of retention, delayed matching, and learning, according to the hemisphere that had suffered a temporal lobectomy. With left-sided ablations she found impairment of delayed verbal retention, of paired-associates learning, and of recognition of recurrent verbal stimuli, after both visual and auditory presentation. With right-sided ablations she found deficits of recognition of recurrent nonverbal visual stimuli, of delayed matching of photographs of faces, and of maze learning, after visual and tactile cues.

While it would be intriguing to conclude that the left temporal lobe is the dominant region for verbal memory, regardless of sensory modality, and the right temporal lobe is the dominant region for nonverbal memory, regardless of sensory modality, this conclusion is not supported by all available evidence. Even from Milner's own results the test of recognition of recurrent nonverbal stimuli, if presented in the auditory or tactile modality, showed no significant differences in subject groups with right or left temporal lobectomy. Only in the visual modality was a material-specific memory defect found on this test after right temporal resection.

Additional discordant results have been reported. V. Meyer (1959), studying subjects with temporal lobe excisions, observed deficits in verbal retention and verbal learning in subjects with left temporal lobectomies, but these deficits were present only in the auditory modality. The same author found no impairment of paired-associates learning (geometric designs) with either tactile or visual presentation regardless of the side of the excision.

Boller and DeRenzi (1967) presented visual memory tests consisting of paired-associates learning of meaningful designs (easily verbalizable) and of meaningless designs (less easily verbalizable) to groups of brain-damaged subjects. They found a significant deficit for both types of material in the group with left-brain damage.

Samuels, Butters and Fedio (1972) evaluated short-term memory disorders following temporal lobe removals in human beings to assess the issue of modality specificity versus material specificity and side of lesion. They presented subjects with visual stimuli (geometric patterns, consonant trigrams) or auditory stimuli (consonant trigrams) and then required the subjects to recall stimuli after varying delay periods according to the method of Peterson and Peterson (1959). The results of their study provide evidence for modality-specific short-term memory storage in the temporal lobes: subjects with both right and left temporal lobectomies showed severe deficits in auditory memory for verbal material but normal performance on visuoverbal and visual nonverbal tasks.

Butters et al (1970) had previously found that patients with right parietal lesions had deficient retention of visual but not auditory material regardless of the nature of the material. Thus Samuels et al (1972) concluded that there are modality-specific, anatomically separate short-term memory stores for audition and vision, with auditory memory mediated by the temporal lobes and visual memory by the parietal, whether the material is verbal or nonverbal.

Against these results and in favor of the role of the right hemisphere in nonverbal memory processing are the results of Dee and Fontenot (1973). They investigated the role of memory as a factor in producing perceptual asymmetry in normal persons; they used tachistoscopic presentation of complex visual figures to either the right or the left visual field, followed by a delayed recognition task involving these figures. They found that longer retention intervals increased left visual field (right hemisphere) superiority for recognition of these figures, and they concluded that the left visual field superiority for the complex visual forms arose from hemispheric differences in memory rather than from purely perceptual processes.

These results are consistent with those of Halliday et al (1968), who found that nonbrain-damaged depressed patients showed selective impairment of verbal learning and retention as a result of having electroconvulsive shock applied unilaterally to the left side of the cranium, and selective impairment in nonverbal retention when the shock was applied to the right side of the cranium.

Milner (1968a) concluded that the contradictory observations most likely resulted from differences in patient population and test construction.

Memory Disorders Associated with Frontal Lobe and Callosal Lesions

In a relatively small number of studies specific memory disorders have been found associated with frontal lobe lesions. But the various neuropsychological features of frontal lobe damage, such as perseveration, impaired initiative and spontaneity, and defective sensory-motor integration, cause one to doubt that specific memory processes are involved, unlike the situation with temporal lobe lesions.

Milner (1965) found impairment of maze learning following frontal lobe damage. Corkin (1965) used the method of recognition of recurrent tactile stimuli; she presented meaningless forms to one or the other hand of subjects with various cortical excisions. Defects were found only in the groups with frontal lesions, left or right, and only for the hand contralateral to the lesion. The observed defects in these two studies may reflect perseveration and inability to follow rules rather than specific memory defects. Prisko (1963) presented groups of brain-damaged subjects a test of "composed stimuli" based on a technique used by Konorski (1967) with animals. In this test the subject must indicate if two stimuli in the same modality, separated by a 60-second interval, are the same or different. In both the visual and auditory modalities deficits were found only in the subjects with frontal excisions. It may be possible to explain these findings by relating the underlying deficit to the defect in delayed response found in monkeys with dorsolateral frontal lesions (see the chapter on frontal lobe disorders).

With respect to callosal lesions Zaidel and Sperry (1974) found that 10 commissurotomized patients (8 complete, 2 partial) had reduced scores on a battery of six standardized memory tests. The impaired memory may have been due in part to extra-commissural brain damage; however, the loss of interhemispheric connections may have been responsible for some of the memory impairment. Data suggested that processes mediating the initial encoding of engrams and the retrieval and readout of contralateral engram elements involved hemispheric cooperation and were dependent on intact commissural function.

Memory Disorders following Electrocortical Stimulation

Depending on the hemisphere involved, different memory defects have been demonstrated after electrocortical temporal lobe stimulation (Ojeman et al, 1968, 1971). Verbal and nonverbal material and several stimulus test techniques were employed. One test consisted of the projection of sequences of photographs of familiar objects; the subjects were asked to name each object and recall the name of the immediately preceding object. Another test involved the projection of groups of complex, meaningless designs, one of which served as the model, the others of which served as a multiple-choice set from which the subject had to select a design identical to the model. Immediately after this selection the subject was shown another set of designs from which he had to select the design similar to that selected in the preceding set. A third type of projection was an oddity problem: from three geometric figures of which two were identical, the subject had to select the figure that was different. Defective immediate verbal memory appeared with left hemispheric stimulation, and defective immediate nonverbal memory appeared following right hemispheric stimulation.

Defects of memory were further classified as anterograde errors, that is, errors appearing several seconds after the stimulation had ceased; retrograde errors, that is, errors occurring during stimulation but with correct recall responses after stimulation had ceased; and mixed errors, which occurred both before and after stimulation. Stimulation of the left posterior temporoparietal during provoked verbal retrograde-type errors, while stimulation of the anterior temporal region produced verbal anterograde errors. For these authors anterograde errors result from interference during registration; retrograde errors, from a deficit in recall.

A similar dissociation of error types was also seen for nonverbal material when the stimulation involved the right hemisphere. With anterior temporal stimulation they found post-stimulation errors in recognition of material correctly matched during the stimulation. With posterior temporoparietal stimulation subjects were unable to recognize visual patterns that they had perceived and matched several seconds earlier.

These results confirm and expand evidence of memory defects found following cortical ablation studies: there is a material specificity according to the hemisphere involved. In addition there seem to be two separate temporal lobe mechanisms in memory processing: one deals with memory consolidation and is situated in the anterior temporal region; the other deals with recall and is situated in the posterior temporal region.

Memory Disorders following Subcortical Electrical Stimulation

Using techniques of electrical stimulation similar to those described in the preceding section but applying these techniques to subcortical structures, Ojeman and Fedio (1968) have been able to demonstrate specific memory-processing defects according to the regions stimulated. They found both aphasic disorders and disorders of short-term verbal memory after stimulation of certain sections of the left thalamus (pulvinar, posterocentromedian portion of ventrolateral nucleus). No such defects were found with stimulation of the right pulvinar or the left anteroinferior thalamic region.

The disorder of recall was of verbal material presented 4 seconds before stimulation, and the disorder appeared during stimulation. For verbal material presented while the subject was being stimulated, with the request for recall to be made during the same period of stimulation, recall capability was less impaired. Subsequent recall of material presented during a period of stimulation was also only mildly impaired.

Stimulation of other subcortical regions produced varied results. Stimulation of right or left parietal white matter provoked a moderate mnestic deficit, while stimulation of right or left temporal white matter did not. Stimulation of left, but not right, cingulum caused verbal memory defects without the anomic type of response found with left pulvinar stimulation. Analysis of errors showed that this deficit was primarily one of recall, while the deficit from the pulvinar region was primarily one of registration.

There is also a suggestion of material-specific memory disturbance involving the mamillothalamic tract and the zone incerta, depending on which side is stimulated. Stimulation of this zone on the right was found to produce alterations in nonverbal short-term memory in a single subject, but no defect in verbal memory was observed.

CONCLUSION

We are justified in asking if the clinical and experimental evidence on human memory disorders may permit some general conclusions. In particular we wonder about the relationship between what we have called specific disturbances of memory and general disturbances of memory. In a grossly schematic way we might say that specific memory defects represent syndromes of unilateral hippocampal damage while general memory defects (i.e., the amnestic syndrome) represent behavioral disturbances resulting from bilateral hippocampal damage or dysfunction. Is the amnestic syndrome (i.e., the syndrome resulting from bilateral hippocampal damage) a consequence of two unilateral hippocampal syndromes, or is there a qualitative rather than quantitative difference between general and specific memory disorders?

It seems to us that the amnestic syndrome represents the combination of two unilateral hippocampal syndromes. The striking neuropsychological deficit found in the amnestic syndrome may be best explained by the suggestion that patients with bilateral hippocampal lesions are unable to use either verbal or nonverbal cues as mnemonic aids.

McGaugh (1966) has discussed time-dependent processes in memory with specific reference to the "tri-trace" system of memory storage (Flexner et al, 1963; Barondes and Cohen, 1966; Agranoff et al., 1965; Deutsch and Hamburg, 1966). According to McGaugh (1966) there may be at least three kinds of traces involved in memory storage: one for immediate memory, one for short-term memory that develops within a few seconds or minutes and lasts for several hours, and one that consolidates slowly and is relatively permanent. McGaugh's evidence was derived from animal experimentation. We believe that evidence from human studies is consistent with this time-dependent tri-trace system of memory storage.

Thus we have evidence that immediate memory may be selectively impaired while longer memory storage processes may function (e.g., Luria, 1966; Shallice and Warrington, 1970; Warrington and Shallice, 1969; Tzortzis and Albert, 1974). An additional memory system (which may be called short-term memory as defined in the preceding paragraph) may be impaired, as in the alcoholic Korsakoff's syndrome. In this case one finds intact immediate memory, intact long-term memory, but impaired short-term memory with inability to learn new information (e.g., Seltzer and Benson, 1974). This memory system and its related memory defects may be material specific and possibly also modality specific (Butters et al, 1974). Finally one may find defects in the long-term memory system(s), especially with clinical conditions that have a more diffuse pattern of cerebral involvement, such as Alzheimer's disease.

EIGHT
DISORDERS
DUE TO FRONTAL
LOBE PATHOLOGY

INTRODUCTION

"The riddle of the frontal lobes," "the problem of the frontal lobes," "unity and diversity of frontal lobe function"—behind these research titles and others of similar allure, scientists have attempted for nearly a century to unravel the "hidden secrets" relating the frontal lobes to human intellectual functioning. Before 1900, prior to the development of systematic analyses of frontal lobe functions, individual cases were reported of striking behavioral alterations associated with frontal lobe pathology. Often cited is the case of Velpeau and Delpech reported by Lhermitte (1929): a 66-year-old man entered Charity Hospital in Paris for treatment of a minor urinary tract problem. The surgeons were astonished by his abnormal behavior; he was always talking about strange ideas and would make inappropriate remarks and jokes. Autopsy demonstrated bilateral frontal lobe tumors. Of equal renown is the "American Crowbar Case." The patient Phineas P. Gage was the victim of an accident in which a crowbar penetrated from the left angle of the jaw to the frontal region, exiting through the skull near the sagittal suture. He lived 12 years after this injury. Dr. Harlowe (cited by Ferrier, 1878), commenting on the profound transformations in Gage's personality, observed: "As for intelligence and intellectual manifestation, he is a child; as for passions and instincts, he is a man."

354

Since the turn of the century systematic analyses of behavioral alterations in human beings with frontal lobe pathology due to trauma, tumors, infections (especially syphilitic), vascular accidents, and surgical interventions (lobectomies, lobotomies, topectomies) have permitted the development of a semiology of frontal lobe syndromes. A new period in experimental research on the frontal lobes was signaled by the publications of Jacobsen in the mid-1930s concerning functions of the frontal association areas in nonhuman primates. Today laboratories of neuropsychology are defining with greater and greater precision specific functional modifications and their anatomic correlates.

This chapter deals first with information derived from animal experimentation, and then with the human "frontal lobe syndromes." When we refer to "frontal lobes," we are speaking of the voluminous portion of the frontal lobes anterior to, and exclusive of, the precentral (Rolandic) gyrus.

ANIMAL EXPERIMENTATION

Functional Deficits following Frontal Lobe Lesions

Deficient Delayed Response

In 1935 and 1936 Jacobsen presented his results of ablation studies of prefrontal regions in the monkey. This marked the beginning of a new epoch in experimental research on the frontal lobes. Jacobsen demonstrated that ablation of prefrontal areas produced a deficit on tests requiring a delayed response, while tests of immediate discrimination showed no deficit. For Jacobsen these results implied an alteration in immediate memory.

Although much subsequent experimental research has tended to refute Jacobsen's explanation for his findings, few authors dispute his results. Most agree that deficits on delayed-response tests are found following frontal lobe lesions. Malmo (1942) found that, if the animal was kept in the dark during the delay period, subsequent responses were correct. For Malmo these results indicated that retroactive inhibition, rather than immediate memory, played a predominant role in delayed-response tests involving vision. Riopelle and Chumkian (1958) supported Malmo's position by demonstrating that monkeys with frontal lesions performed as well as normal monkeys on concurrent learning tasks.

Gross and Weiskrantz (1964) promulgated a new version of the older "immediate memory" hypothesis. They showed that monkeys with frontal lesions are incapable of using information stored in short-term memory and lose access to this information at the moment of its entry into short-term memory. Their hypothesis suggested that these animals were deficient on tasks of single discrimination—tasks that could be learned in a single session—while they had less difficulty with tasks requiring several days to learn, even though these tasks involved more complicated discriminations.

Impaired Delayed Alternation in Space

In addition to provoking a deficit on simple delayed-response tasks, frontal lesions were found to cause an impairment in the capacity for delayed alternation in space (Jacobsen and Nissen, 1937). Again differences of opinion were voiced concerning the nature of this functional deficit. Such lesions were shown to disturb the stereotyped response sequence of normal monkeys in a task requiring simple search with several boxes (Meyer and Settlage, 1958). It was felt that kinesthetic or tactile cues, or both, formed one of the elements of a behavioral sequence necessary for delayed response.

Nonetheless a selective deficit in proprioceptive or kinesthetic activity was not considered a sufficient explanation for such functional disturbances as impaired object reversal discrimination (Harlow and Dagnon, 1943) or impairment on an operant conditioning program involving alternate rhythm-pattern learning (Pribram, 1961a). In this latter experiment the animal had to press a lever 40 times after a red signal; then it had to press the lever 40 times after a green signal; then it had to wait 4 minutes and then begin again. In the second stage of the experiment the animal had to press the bar according to a pattern of alternation, without the lights being used as a signal. Monkeys with frontal lesions failed this task, while normal monkeys and monkeys with temporal lesions succeeded.

Basing his conclusions on results of a series of tests performed with cats and dogs with frontal lesions who were able to move freely in the examining cages, Konorski (1967) felt that the deficits of delayed response and delayed alternation seen in animals with frontal lesions were linked to a disorder in the use of spatiokinetic images. In the period preceding the trials on the spatial alternation task, the animal is seen to be incapable of directing itself toward the rewarded stimulus by means of kinesthetic information from the prior response and without the help of exteroceptive cues.

This concept of a "kinesthetic agnosia" for spatial relations is also accepted by Stamm (1970, 1971). A series of visual discrimination and delayed alternation experiments in monkeys with frontal lesions allowed this author to conclude that frontal lesions produce two types of deficit: one, perseveration, is transitory; the other, kinesthetic agnosia, is permanent, except under particular experimental conditions. He added that the animal with frontal lesions is always able to complete a motor sequence in itself and that the kinesthetic agnosia consists, not of a difficulty in establishing pertinent kinesthetic cues, but rather of a difficulty of carrying out motor acts in relation to these cues.

Perseveration

Once experimental studies with monkeys with frontal lesions were started, research teams began to observe the problem of perseveration. Harlow and Settlage (1948) reported that monkeys with frontal lesions tended to persist in choice responses that had become inappropriate to the resolution of an ongoing problem, maintaining responses that had earlier been adequate to the task. This perseverative attitude was particularly clear when testing sessions were alternated between object discrimination and position discrimination requirements. Responses learned as appropriate to the object discrimination task were used on the position discrimination task and vice versa. For Harlow (1950a,b,c) frontal lesions in monkeys caused two types of functional errors, one related to "perseveration of the stimulus," the other to "displacement of response."

During a several-year period Mishkin and Rosvold and their collaborators attempted to define with more precision the nature of the defect in monkeys with frontal lesions. In 1961 Brush, Mishkin, and Rosvold reported their results with tests of visual discrimination in monkeys with frontal and inferotemporal lesions. They found learning skills to be impaired in both groups of brain-damaged monkeys by comparison with controls, but the nature of the functional deficit was different depending on the location of the lesion. The inferotemporal lesions provoked learning difficulties because of disturbances in visual discrimination, while the frontal lesions prevented monkeys from abandoning previously established preferences and aversions.

Pursuing this line of reasoning, these authors conducted an additional experiment in which preferences or aversions for objects were induced experimentally. Individual stimuli were presented with or without reward; subsequently these stimuli were paired on a discrimination task with "indifferent" stimuli, that is, items that were the least selected on a previous experiment involving preference. If rewards were associated with stimuli that had previously been preferred, the animal with frontal lesions was like the normal animal. However, if it became necessary to suppress a prior preference or aversion to obtain the reward, the animal with frontal lesions failed, while monkeys with inferotemporal lesions and normal monkeys did not.

A series of similar experiments revealed a diversity of perseverative-type errors. These results led Mishkin and his collaborators (1962–1964) to conclude that the different deficits observed in monkeys with frontal lesions were not due to perseveration of responses or "perseveration of the stimulus." Rather, they concluded that a more general disturbance of central attitude was occurring, a perseveration of central processes of mediation. Denying that a simple unitary formulation could account for the multiplicity of deficits seen in monkeys with frontal lesions, Mishkin (1964) nonetheless proposed that these animals had a greater persistence, or even inertia, of their initial central attitude.

Pribram and his collaborators (1964) described two opposing elements underlying the errors of monkeys with frontal lesions: one was the tendency to change response when a new stimulus was introduced, the other was perseveration of a previous response when the problem was modified. Pribram proposed the hypothesis that there existed a "working memory," that is, a mechanism that extracted from the permanent memory stock those patterns of nervous activity that allowed the immediate use of inputs. The frontal lesion, by interfering with the temporary combination of stimuli with these previously stored patterns of nervous activity, interfered with behavioral flexibility and thus produced perseveration, among other deficits of behavioral function.

For Pribram (1969) flexibility or rigidity involved inhibitory processes at two levels: neuronal and behavioral. The frontal lobe contributed to the "registration" portion of the orienting reaction by maintaining a stable organization of inputs coming from the body. For any new event to be "registered," that is, incorporated into the life of the organism, it had to be attached to a stable and organized base. Without such a stability within the organism, any behavioral flexibility would be impossible; the behavior would be bound to the stimulus or would be perseverative. A frontal lesion, thus, would interfere with the "registration" component of the orienting reaction and would shift the organism in the direction of "treatment of inputs"; that is, the new stimulus would not be assimilated, and the organism would remain stimulus bound.

Distractibility and Hyperactivity

Experiments subsequent to those of Jacobsen suggested that the abnormality of delayed response may have been the result of impaired attention to the stimulus, or distractibility, rather than of an abnormal short-term memory. Finan (1942), for example, showed that, if immediately before the delay, one gave the monkey with a frontal lesion a reward for a response, the delayed response was satisfactorily accomplished.

Many authors reported hyperactivity in the behavior of monkeys with frontal lesions (Richter and Hines; 1938; French; 1938–1947; Harlow, 1952; Orbach and Fisher, 1959). Rather than speak of hyperactivity, other authors referred to hyperreactivity. Thus Ruch and Shenkin (1943) noted that the activity of monkeys with frontal lesions increased in the presence of an observer. Malmo (1942) also provided evidence in this direction: if barbiturates were given to reduce hyperactivity, monkeys would have normal performances on tests of delayed response. Pribram et al (1952) showed that "frontal monkeys" could perform normally on delayed response tasks after administration of insulin or the suppression of feedings. He presumed that by increasing their "appetite" in this manner he increased their attention to the placement of the food stimulus. Isaac and De Vito (1958) and Gross and Weiskrantz (1964) demonstrated that placing the monkeys in the dark during the delay period improved their performance.

However, despite the influence that hyperactivity seems to have on attention, arguments have been put forth to show that hyperactivity per se is neither necessary nor sufficient to account for the deficit of delayed response seen in monkeys with frontal lesions (Pribram, 1950; Lawicka and Konorski, 1961; Miles and Blomquist, 1960; Weiskrantz, Mihalovic, and Gross, 1962). In addition, hyperactivity, or perhaps hyperreactivity, has also been considered to be a disorder of higher levels of cortical inhibition, with several different possible explanations provided: as a failure of inhibition of inappropriate responses, as a disinhibition of inhibitory cortical reflexes (Brutowski, Konorski, and Lawicka, 1956), or as an absence of inhibition of orienting responses that thus become stronger and more resistant to extinction (Konorski, 1967).

Evidence in favor of the interpretation that frontal lobe lesions produce an attentional deficit related to learning has been provided by Buffery (1967) on the basis of his experiments with baboons. If a negative (unrewarded) object is added daily to a discrimination task in which the positive (rewarded) stimulus remains the same, the baboon with a frontal lesion makes more errors in direct proportion to the increased number of new stimuli. His tendency is to explore the novel stimulus rather than to seek the reward associated with the familiar object.

Kimble et al (1965) indicated that frontal lesions provoked distractibility in monkeys because of an impairment in habituation. These observations are supported by those of Grueninger et al (1965), who found a reduction in the electrodermal response in monkeys with frontal lesions when new stimuli were introduced, despite the presence of signs of alertness on the electroencephalogram and despite the preservation of the peripheral mechanisms necessary for the production of the electrothermal response. Subsequently Grueninger and Pribram (1969) subjected monkeys with frontal lesions and control monkeys to a behavioral task interrupted by visual or auditory distractors. The effect of distraction was greater with the monkeys with lesions.

Deficits of Sensory-Motor Integration

Questions of whether or not frontal lesions provoke disorders of sensory function or of sensory-motor integration have been raised by several authors. Denny-Brown (1951), for example, considered the frontal lobe to be the principal executive organ of optically guided behavior. He demonstrated that an animal with ablation of its frontal lobe or temporal lobe became hyperresponsive to tactile or proprioceptive stimuli. With frontal ablations the animal would be indifferent to visual stimuli and hyperresponsive to auditory, while the converse was true for animals with temporal ablations. In all cases the normal control animal maintained a balanced response to the several stimuli. Thus, for Denny-Brown, the frontal syndrome represented the result of the loss of normal responsivity to an adequate stimulus together with a hyperresponsivity to other stimuli.

The position is only partially supported by research of Harlow (1950a,b,c) and Pribram (1952, 1954). They found no difficulty in visual discrimination after frontal lesions when the tasks were easy, unlike the results found after inferotemporal lesions. However, with complex tasks of visual discrimination the monkeys with frontal lesions were deficient in their performances.

Concerning the auditory modality, several authors have noted a deficit after lateral frontal ablations (Blum, 1952; Weiskrantz and Mishkin, 1958; Rosvold and Mishkin, 1960). Gross and Weiskrantz (1962, 1964) demonstrated that this deficit was clearly dissociable from the deficit of simple delayed reaction and that it could not be attributed to task complexity or to procedural methodology, since with similar procedures in the visual modality, deficits were not seen. Furthermore, this deficit in function within the auditory modality could not be based on an elevation in the auditory discrimination threshold, which Iverson and Mishkin (1970) found to be normal.

Polymodal sensory disturbances have also been described following frontal lesions. Welch and Stutteville (1958) produced a change in behavior which is characterized by unresponsiveness to stimuli of various kinds on the opposite half of space. The features of this disorder resembled very closely those of unilateral neglect as seen in man. The lesions causing such behavioral changes were small and localized to the depth of the posterior part of the superior limb of the arcuate sulcus. The changes were transient, and all sensory modalities were involved.

Heilman and his collaborators (see Watson et al, 1973) were also successful in producing a contralateral neglect syndrome in monkeys with frontal lesions. In their study neglect to all sensory stimuli was produced in the monkeys' left hemifield by right anterior cingulectomy. Because the cingulate gyrus projects to the mesencephalic reticular formation, they held that cingulectomy interrupted the corticolimbic reticular activating pathway and produced neglect by causing a unilateral defect in the alerting response to sensory stimuli.

Mechanisms Underlying the Functional Deficits: Anatomic and Physiological Considerations

Functions Associated with Major Anatomic Regions of the Frontal Lobes

Gross lesions of the frontal lobes, as we have seen, produce certain well-defined functional deficits. However, the very existence of a great variety of hypotheses proposed to account for these deficits indicates that the underlying mechanisms of these deficits are still unclear. Perhaps the first question is whether the observed deficits are based on a disorder of a single cerebral process or whether each deficit depends on a different mechanism. Analysis of behavioral changes caused by well-localized lesions within precise and different regions of a single frontal lobe has aided in answering that question.

The *dorsolateral frontal zone*, especially the region around the *sulcus principalis*, has been considered the critical region for deficits of delayed alternation in space. Rosvold and Szwarcbart (1964), for example, demonstrated that even small lesions within that zone would provoke maximal deficits, while lesions elsewhere provoked less severe deficits, or deficits that recovered after a new learning period, or deficits with only the most complex tasks. The borders and depths of the sulcus principalis are the primary loci of the deficit (Mishkin, 1957; Gross and Weiskrantz, 1962). Dorsolateral lesions that do not encroach upon the sulcus principalis produce only a mild and transitory deficit (Gross and Weiskrantz, 1962); however, a lesion of the entire dorsolateral, prefrontal cortex provokes a greater deficit than a lesion of the sulcus principalis alone does.

Orbitofrontal lesions, on the other hand, are associated with disturbances on a task involving successive visual discriminations. If that task is taught preoperatively, retention of that skill is lost following the lesion. Dorsolateral lesions do not, however, provoke such a deficit (Brutowski, Mishkin, and Rosvold, 1963) Rosvold and Mishkin (1960) also found that orbitofrontal lesions are associated with significantly more perseverative-type errors than dorsolateral lesions are, although lesions in both loci produce perseveration. On tests of reversal in space those authors found deficits of equal intensity following orbitofrontal and dorsolateral lesions, whereas with tests of object reversal, the orbitofrontal lesions were more significant. From these various studies Mishkin (1964) concluded that, even though animals with dorsolateral and orbitofrontal lesions had similar deficiencies on the tests of reversal in space, there were nonetheless different causes for the errors seen: for the animals with orbital lesions the deficit depended on the feature of alternation; for those with dorsolateral lesions the spatial factor played a greater role.

In 1969 Mishkin, Vest, Waxler, and Rosvold tested the hypothesis that perseverative errors seen following lateral frontal lesions were due to the *ventrolateral region's* ordinarily being included in the lateral ablations. They studied object alternation and spatial alternation in two groups of animals— those with lesions of the lateral region sparing the ventrolateral cortex, that is, the region beneath the sulcus principalis, and those with orbital lesions including the ventrolateral portion. The restricted lateral lesion produced a permanent deficit on the spatial alternation task but not on the object alternation task. The animals with orbital and ventrolateral lesions, on the other hand, failed both alternation tasks. Mishkin et al (1969) concluded from these results that the alternation deficit found after gross prefrontal ablations was composed of two separable deficits: one, due to a dorsolateral lesion, depended on the spatial aspects of the task; the other, due to ventral lesions, depended on the factor of reversal.

In 1970 Iverson and Mishkin reported their results of studies with animals subjected to ablation of the *inferior frontal convexity*. They contended that lesions in this region were supramodal. Within the auditory sphere a greater number of trials were needed by these animals than by animals with lesions elsewhere in the frontal lobe to relearn a differentiation task. The deficit that followed a limited lesion was similar to that seen following total orbital ablation (Lawicka et al, 1966). Beyond the auditory sphere, lesions limited to the inferior frontal convexity caused deficits of greater or lesser severity on tasks involving object reversal, pattern discrimination, and spatial alternation. For Iverson and Mishkin the observed deficits were based on a difficulty in learning to suppress the response to a negative stimulus. They felt that the perseverative tendencies seen following large dorsolateral or orbital lesions were due to involvement of the inferior lateral region.

Functions Associated with Anatomic Subsections of the Major Frontal Regions

The frontal lobe was thus divided anatomically and functionally into several regions: dorsolateral, orbital, ventrolateral, or inferior frontal. Following the lead of earlier researchers, others tried to define with even greater precision the locus of functional deficits within these frontal regions. Butter (1969) attempted to demonstrate the precise locus within the orbital cortex that was responsible for perseveration. He found that medial posterior orbital lesions produced an impairment in the ability to extinguish a rewarded instrumental response but no deficit on tasks of object reversal discrimination, equal in severity to that produced by total orbital ablations. Lateral orbital lesions also caused deficits in spatial reversals.

Concerning function within the dorsolateral cortex, Butters and Pandya (1969) have tried to locate the specific focus responsible for the capacity of delayed alternation in space. They resected different portions of the sulcus principalis and discovered that the functional deficit of delayed alternation in space was caused by small lesions limited to the middle third of the sulcus. They added that this small region is the only prefrontal tissue that does not receive corticocortical projections (Pandya and Kuypers, 1969). Butters et al (1971b) further indicated that functional deficits are not produced with lesions of the superior or inferior borders of the sulcus; they occur only when the lesions include both banks of the sulcus.

Goldman and Rosvold (1970) also evaluated the effect of different dorsolateral lesions on two spatial tasks, one dealing with delayed alternation in space; the other, a conditional position response task not involving delay. Ablation of the sulcus principalis caused a deficit in the delayed task, while ablation of the arcuate sulcus produced a disturbance in the immediate spatial response. These results, together with findings by other experimenters (e.g., Gross and Weiskrantz, 1962; Stepien and Stamm, 1970), have led Goldman and Rosvold to the conclusion that the sulcus principalis constitutes a neural center for spatial memory. Delayed spatial alternation tasks can be successfully carried out because the monkey can be guided by the memory of positional (proprioceptive) information from prior responses, and the sulcus principalis is responsible for this activity.

Stamm (1973), building on a series of frontal lobe studies with collaborators (Wegener and Stamm, 1966; Stepien and Stamm, 1970), attempted to demonstrate a functional dissociation between the inferior and arcuate segments of dorsolateral prefrontal cortex. He first trained monkeys on successive visual discriminations or on an auditory conditional position response task and then made bilateral lesions in segments of dorsolateral cortex. A double dissociation was obtained: on the visual discrimination task severe impairments were found after ablations of the segment inferior to the sulcus principalis but not after superior dorsolateral or arcuate ablations; on the conditional response test, impairments were found after ablations of the arcuate segments but not after inferior dorsolateral ablations. Although he concluded that the sulcus principalis is implicated in the mediation of tasks involving spatial differentiation, he proposed that the inferior prefrontal segment functions in response inhibitions and that the arcuate cortex mediates associations between the orienting and instrumental responses.

By studying unit activity in the prefrontal cortex of monkeys during delayed-response tasks, some authors have been able to demonstrate the existence of cells that discharge in a specific and differential fashion depending on the time within the total performance of the task (Kubota and Niki, 1971; Fuster, 1973; Niki, 1974a,b). Excitatory or inhibitory modifications of cellular discharges from the principalis region or from the anterior cingulate region were found to vary with time of presentation of cues, delay period, and time of response. No such changes were found with cells in the parietal region. According to Fuster (1973) these modifications did not occur on trials carried out in the absence of cues, and they were attenuated if the animal was distracted.

Niki (1974a,b) found that prefrontal unit activity associated with delayed alternation was related to direction of response. Different discharge patterns appeared during the delay period according to whether the choice was on the right or on the left. This directional selectivity of prefrontal units could be considered as relative, rather than absolute, insofar as the discharge patterns varied with respect to the required direction of choice between cues and not with respect to the position of cues in their relationship to the right or left of the animal's body.

Teuber (1972) attempted to summarize much of the anatomic and physiological work relating to functions of granular prefrontal cortex in primates. His analysis provided the conception of a "two-fold gradient of functional specialization: up-down and back-to-front." The up-down gradient goes from dorsolateral frontocortical removals to orbitofrontal lesions. Dorsolateral cortex lesions cause deficits on delayed-response and related tasks; inferior convexity lesions mainly cause defects on object reversal tasks; orbitofrontal lesions often cause disturbances in emotional reactivity and interfere with appropriate behavior in social groups (see chapter on emotion, where these issues are treated in greater detail).

The back-to-front gradient refers to a pattern of changing performances related to lesions located at different points along a horizontal plane running in an anterior-posterior direction along the dorsolateral frontal surface. Symptoms related to *spatial* aspects of certain tasks result from lesions confined to the transitional, dysgranular cortex between the limbs of the arcuate sulcus, whereas symptoms related to *mnemonic* aspects of the tasks result from lesions situated further anteriorly in the midportion of the sulcus principalis. With the former set of lesions the presence of a delay is irrelevant; with the latter set of lesions the presence of delay is crucial to the nonperformance of the task.

We should add that capacities for delayed response are highly variable, depending on the species. In the monkey prefrontal lesions cause severe deficits on tasks of delayed response or spatial alternation. These deficits are either absent altogether or are less severe and less persistent in chimpanzees with the same lesions (Jacobsen, 1936; Blum, 1952) and in cats (Warren, 1964). The capability of man to perform delayed-response tasks is so much better than the capability of the best of the nonhuman animals (rhesus monkey) that one is compelled to assume that the difference must be qualitative rather than simply quantitative.

Effects of Bilateral versus Unilateral Lesions

It is important to point out that all results of ablation studies so far described in this chapter were obtained from animals subjected to bilateral ablations. Studies with unilateral ablations have also been done. In 1960 Rosvold and Mishkin observed that unilateral ablation of the monkey's dorsolateral cortex caused a severe disturbance in the acquisition of a delayed response. Warren and his collaborators (1969) confirmed these results, although they noted that the deficit was less marked than that seen following bilateral lesions. However, they further observed that a unilateral lesion did not affect the ability to learn spatial reversals. In addition they demonstrated a relationship between the volume of the lesion and the severity of the functional deficit. They found no difference in the deficit, depending on which hemisphere was damaged and on whether or not the hemisphere was "dominant" in relation to the preferred hand of the monkey. Fuster and Alexander (1971) also found a transient deficit of delayed response following unilateral freezing of the monkey's dorsolateral cortex; they noted that this deficit was less marked than that observed following bilateral freezing lesions.

Studies of prefrontal lobe functions were performed by Yamaguchi and Myers (1972) in split-brain monkeys. They found little deterioration in ability to transfer delayed response and delayed alternation from one hemisphere to another. However, transfer to a go-no go task of color discrimination was abolished. Memories for bodily orientation patterns and for temporal and spatial movement sequences were not found to be lateralized, by contrast with exteroceptive cues used for discrimination tasks.

Functional interhemispheric differences may exist in prefrontal areas of the monkey. Stamm et al (1975) recorded electrocortical potentials in monkeys that had learned a delayed spatial response skill with one or the other hand. They observed that a single prefrontal area was more likely to be involved in mediation of delayed response independently of the responding hand than the precentral area, in which activation appeared only on the side contralateral to the responding hand. These intrahemispheric differences did not seem to be related to a dominance of the prefrontal region but rather to experimental conditions that favored the prevalence of one hemisphere over the other.

Corticosubcortical (Frontolimbic) Associations

The deficit on delayed-response tests is not produced exclusively by frontal lobe lesions. Experiments have shown this deficit to appear following certain subcortical lesions as well, and a corticosubcortical system is considered to regulate this function (Rosvold and DelGado, 1956; Rosvold et al, 1958,

Battig et al, 1962; Rosvold and Szwarcbart, 1964; Rosvold, 1972). The prefrontal lesion causes the most severe deficit, but nearly similar deficits are seen following lesions of the head of the caudate nucleus, and less severe deficits follow lesions of the hippocampus and subthalamic structures. Rosvold refers to this as the "frontal lobe system."

Some disagreement has occurred concerning the specific subcortical structures involved. According to Rosvold destruction of the dorsomedial nuclei, which have well-known projections to different regions of the frontal lobes (Akert, 1964), does not produce a defect in delayed alternation response in the cat. Warren and Akert (1960), on the other hand, indicate that lesions of the dorsomedial nuclei do cause such defects. Schulman (1964) demonstrated a deficit on delayed response in the monkey with lesions involving the dorsomedial nuclei; however, the lesions were extensive, and other functional deficits were also provoked. Dealing with the problem of prism adaptation, Bossom (1965) demonstrated similar defects following ablations of the frontal lobe or of the head of the caudate nuclei—visual adaptation to prisms was abolished in the monkey with lesions in these two loci, while it was preserved in control animals and in monkeys with other cerebral lesions.

The anatomic studies of Nauta and his collaborators (1954, 1958, 1961, 1962, 1964, 1971, 1972), performed over a 20-year period, permit a clearer understanding of frontolimbic relationships. Anatomically the frontal lobe is characterized by its multiple connections with the limbic system and in particular by its direct connections with the hypothalamus (Nauta, 1971). Within this multiplicity of connections, separate primary association systems stand out: the dorsolateral prefrontal cortex associated with the hippocampus, the orbitofrontal cortex associated with the amygdaloid complex. These two major frontolimbic association systems seem sufficiently distinct anatomically to suggest that they may be responsible for different aspects of behavioral integration. For Nauta (1971) the frontal cortex may be considered as the major, although not the only, neocortical representative of the limbic system. The reciprocal anatomic relationship between frontal lobe regions and limbic regions suggests that the frontal cortex both monitors and modulates limbic mechanisms.

Cerebral Plasticity

Among the factors with significant influence on functional deficits following brain damage is cerebral plasticity. Critical aspects of cerebral plasticity include age-dependent effects, the role of single-stage versus serial lesions, and task-dependent effects. In a subsequent chapter we discuss cerebral plasticity in some detail.

DATA FROM HUMAN PATHOLOGY

Clinical "Frontal Lobe" Syndromes

"My hypothesis is that the frontal lobes are the seat of coordination and fusion of the incoming and outgoing products of the several sensory and motor areas of the cortex." This hypothesis was proposed in 1895 by Bianchi, after he observed the behavior of animals with frontal lobe excisions. In like manner scientists since then have observed the behavior of human beings with frontal lobe lesions and have proposed hypotheses to account for this behavior. The influence of animal experimentation has been keenly felt by those who have attempted to analyze and evaluate the human frontal lobe syndromes. The remainder of this chapter deals with these attempts at analysis of frontal lobe behavior in man.

This section is descriptive and is based on personal experience together with a synthesis of clinical reviews (see, for example, Denny-Brown, 1951; Angelergues et al, 1956; Benson and Geschwind, 1975). Despite the anatomic specificity of known corticocortical and corticosubcortical connections involving different portions of the frontal lobes, the nature of clinical material has been such as to prevent the development of a definite clinicoanatomic specificity. It is premature, we believe, to attempt to correlate specific behavioral deficits in human beings with specific regions within the frontal lobes. On the other hand it is possible to categorize or group the behavioral defects, correlating them with frontal lobe damage, without further specifying which area of the frontal lobe has been damaged. Lesions of the frontal lobes may be associated with personality disorders, alterations of motor activity, disorders of cognitive function, and paroxysmal disorders.

Personality Disorders

Frequently one sees an apparent heightening of affective tone, with euphoria and lack of concern for the present or the future. This behavioral change does not, however, necessarily reflect a true alteration of mood. Such patients, in the midst of apparent euphoria, often state that they are not at all happy. A puerile or silly attitude may be maintained, often with an inappropriate use of pretentious language. Erotic behavior, sexual exhibitionism, or lewd remarks are not rare. Euphoric excitation may take on an atypical hypomanic aspect, "moria": the patient, overexcited, manifesting erotic behavior, bothers the examiner with inappropriate jokes and caustic or facetious remarks (*Witzelsucht*).

The diverse aspects of excitation and euphoria are rarely permanent. In general they appear episodically, superimposed on an underlying background of abulia and apathy. The euphoric periods may alternate with periods of apparent depression. True depression, however, is rarely seen; rather, a picture of asthenia and akinesia imitates a true depression. A disorder of activity, rather than of affectivity, is the hallmark.

Loss of impulse control, manifested by outbursts of irritability, is common. These outbursts may be the first behavioral change noted; often they reach such a degree of violence that they force a family to institutionalize the patient.

Alterations of Motor Activity

Lack of initiative or spontaneity is a characteristic feature of frontal lobe pathology. This is linked to a general diminution of motor activity. The patient no longer voluntarily carries out the necessary daily activities of life, such as getting out of bed in the morning, washing or dressing himself, feeding himself, or even urinating or defecating in the toilet. These latter activities may be performed at any time or place, without regard for the social consequences. The actual ability to do the various activities of daily living is not impaired—the patient is not paralyzed, apraxic, or confused. When he is vigorously urged to do something, he can do it. What is impaired is the ability to initiate spontaneously a desired or an automatic motor task.

This rupture between the patient and the external world, this diminution of activity in manipulating real objects, and this reduction of interpersonal exchange are what appear to be a loss of interest on the part of the patient. Whether there is a true loss of interest or an apparent loss of interest due to an impairment of spontaneous initiation of activity, the effect on the examiner remains the same.

Disorders of Cognitive Function

Loss of the "esthetic" sense and loss of "abstracting" ability are considered to be early signs of frontal lobe dysfunction. Underlying these cognitive defects are disorders of attention and memory. From the first examination of the patient, the disorder of attention is noticeable; it is necessary to repeat questions and orders several times to obtain a response.

The disorder of memory may be of two types. One type is primarily a disorder of recent memory, similar to that seen in the Korsakoff syndrome, in which remote events may be better preserved and recalled than recent events. The other type of memory defect is more a forgetfulness than a true memory disorder. In this situation the patient "forgets to remember" certain information he has preserved in his memory. This defect seems to be one of lack of initiative to recall elements that have not truly been forgotten. In many ways this defect is similar to the lack of spontaneity or initiative seen in the motor

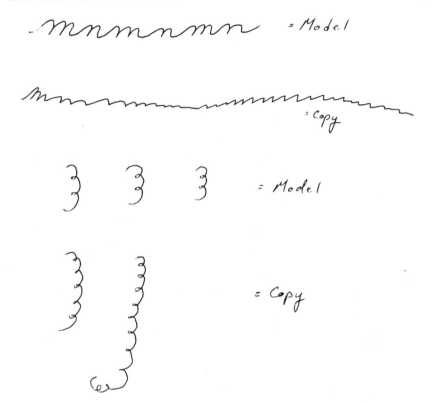

Perseveration on tasks of repetitive writing in a patient with a right frontal lobe gunshot wound.

system. If these patients are given enough time, or if they are urged with sufficient vigor, they recall items and events of which they had previously denied knowledge.

Paroxysmal Disorders

Paroxysmal disturbances of mental functioning are rare. Occasionally one sees abrupt and transitory periods of disorientation. Rarely, brief episodes of visual or olfactory hallucinations have occurred following frontal lobe damage. This may be related to lesions of the olfactory or optic nerves. Patients have infrequently complained of periods during which they were able to think about only, and seemed to be forced to think about only, a single idea or thought or topic. These paroxysmal disturbances may represent epileptic equivalents.

Neuropathological Studies

Tumors

The history of systematic studies of clinicoanatomic correlations of behavioral disorders with frontal lobe tumors has shown a clear trend. The earliest reports (e.g., Schuster, 1902; Pfeifer, 1910) were efforts to describe general psychiatric syndromes associated with cerebral tumors. Symptoms and signs included torpor, irritability, and depression. No attempt was made to define specific "frontal-lobe" behavior. It was noted, however, that "general mental symptoms" did seem to occur earlier in the course of the illness if the tumor was frontal.

Subsequent research tended to isolate specific behavioral abnormalities, such as memory disturbance, euphoria, and loss of initiative, and relate these behavioral abnormalities to frontal lobe change rather than to general cerebral dysfunction (Kolodny, 1929; Frazier, 1936). Finally attempts were made to localize within the frontal lobes the various clinical abnormalities found (Cushing and Eisenhardt, 1938; Morsier and Rey, 1945; Messimy, 1948).

A summary of the various studies relating frontal lobe tumors to behavioral abnormalities would include the following material. Disorders of mental functioning occur in 60–90% of cases in which cerebral tumors involve the frontal lobes. It is not yet possible to correlate specific behavioral syndromes with tumoral invasion of specific regions of the frontal lobes. The general defects of behavior following frontal lobe damage by tumors may include any combination of signs or symptoms described above in the clinical sections. However, the rate of growth of the tumor does have an effect on symptomatology. Slowly growing frontal tumors are characterized primarily by apathy, akinesia, and loss of spontaneity or initiative. Personality changes may be quite marked. Rapidly growing frontal tumors are more often associated with torpor or with confusional states.

Trauma

In his famous textbook of pathology, Kleist (1934) described alterations of mental functioning following frontal lobe trauma. He included, in particular, psychomotor disturbances: loss of initiative, lack of "motor spontaneity," depression, and mutism. Goldstein (1936a,b, 1944) cited defects of attention and memory, affective indifference, and akinesia. Jarvie (1954) considered the chief feature of frontal lobe trauma to be a disinhibition that permanently altered the patient's personality in such a way as to reduce his control of socially acceptable behavior.

A classical study of subjects with penetrating missile wounds of the brain was that of Feuchtwanger (1923, cited in Teuber, 1964). After World War I he systematically contrasted behavior patterns of 200 subjects with frontal gunshot wounds and 200 others whose known gunshot wounds had entered the skull outside of the frontal region. Frontal lesions, on the whole, had less effect on intelligence, on categorizing, and on a variety of complex reaction time tasks than lesions in other areas. He found no specific intellectual, attentional, or memory changes. The more pervasive changes were those of mood and attitude, ranging from euphoria, with occasional depression, "to a curious form of other-directedness" on the part of the patient—an incapacity for making plans. Feuchtwanger felt these changes to be independent of the motor changes: restlessness, hyperkinesias, or more rarely, slowing and torpor.

None of the changes was obligatory. He found no changes at all in 13 of the 200 with frontal damage. Feuchtwanger concluded that the primary alteration was in the sphere of voluntary action and in the ability to evaluate situations.

To these studies we would add the not infrequently observed syndrome of akinetic mutism, which appears after bilateral frontal lobe trauma. In this syndrome, also referred to as coma vigil, the patient is able to move but does not; he is able to speak but does not. He lies in bed, mute and immobile, with eyes open and with random, wandering eye movements. For brief periods the eyes may fix on a moving object and follow it. Rare spontaneous or responsive movements may be made; rare sounds and single words may be heard. We have observed remarkable recoveries, especially in younger patients, after several years in this state.

Neurosurgical Intervention

Frontal Lobectomies Ordinarily one expects valuable clinicoanatomic information from lobectomies. In the case of the frontal lobes, however, the information has been contradictory. Several authors report no deficit whatsoever, after unilateral frontal lobectomy; others note "inability to concentrate," "impairment of synthetic or organizational ability," "loss of initiative" (see Angelergues et al, 1956). Rylander (1939), in a good review of the topic, including 32 of his own cases, concluded that frontal lobectomies were associated with behavioral modifications in almost every case: reduction of affective response inhibition, tendency to euphoria, emotional instability, impairment of attention, and reduction of initiative. In a follow-up study (1943) he indicated that disorders of mental functioning were clearly more marked after frontal lobectomy than after ablation of any other lobe.

In a subject who had severe behavioral problems from trauma to the prefrontal regions, Hebb (1945) observed that prefrontal lobectomy performed by Penfield resulted in the complete abolition of these behavioral problems.

Psychological tests revealed considerable improvement by comparison with the preoperative state. The patient had no further problems with social adaptation except for a relative indifference to his distant future.

Frontal Lobotomies   From the moment of their introduction by Moniz and Lima in 1935 (see Moniz, 1936, 1937) frontal lobotomies for the treatment of mental illness created a storm—first a storm of enthusiasm, then a storm of rejection reaching almost taboo proportions, and now, especially in the United States, a new storm of controversy revolving around the political-medical-social issue of psychosurgery. From a strict neuropsychological point of view, little useful scientific information relating frontal lobe lesions to human behavior can be gleaned, chiefly because of the preexisting mental disorders in patients undergoing frontal lobotomies.

According to the precise region of the brain attacked (orbital or orbitofrontal regions, cingulum, etc.), one could nevertheless expect to see certain behavioral characteristics of the lobotomized patient: loss of initiative, apathy, some euphoric tendencies, simplification of social interactions, and loss of concern for the future (Moniz, 1937; Greenblatt, 1950; Fulton, 1951; Meyer and Beck, 1954).

Proposed Mechanisms Underlying the Functional Deficits—Based on Anatomoclinical Correlations

Many authors have used anatomoclinical correlations as a basis for theories of frontal lobe function. Vincent (1928) and Hebb (1945) believed that a "disorganization of cerebral function" created by the presence of the frontal lobe lesion was responsible for the mental abnormalities. Total removal of the lesion, by unilateral or bilateral frontal lobectomy, would return the patient to normal.

Most authors felt, however, that the presence of a lesion or ablation of a frontal lobe produced the same effect. Brickner (1934) believed that the basic disorder in the frontal lobe syndrome was a deficit in the highest levels of associative processing, a reduction in the capacity for synthesis, upon which all other abnormalities depended.

Kurt Goldstein (1936a,b, 1944) thought that the fundamental disorder underlying the features of the frontal lobe syndromes was an inability to grasp the entirety of a complex situation or to differentiate one complex situation from another. This apparent identity of differing complex situations produced indifference and a pathological alteration of emotional reactions. For Goldstein the observed disorders of motor activity and social conduct resulted from a response by the patient to fragments of a situation and not to the whole. The inability to comprehend the whole situation caused a failure to recognize the key features of that situation: an impairment in the capacity to extract the essential figures from a background. The end result was a regression from the abstract attitude toward the concrete.

Other authors spoke of disorders of vigilance (Halstead, 1947) or of inhibition (Arnot, 1952). Angelergues et al (1956) warned against the imposition of *a priori* theoretical conceptions, preferring to refine the clinical descriptions and thus provide a solid clinical base for detailed neuropsychological analyses.

Neuropsychological Studies

Functional Deficits following Frontal Lobe Lesions in Man

In the first portion of this chapter we reviewed the functional deficits following frontal lobe lesions in animals. These deficits include disorders of delayed response and delayed alternation in space, perseveration, distractibility and hyperactivity, and deficits of sensory-motor integration. It is possible that some or all of these abnormalities underlie the behavioral alterations of the human frontal lobe syndromes. However, results of studies with human beings have not always been as consistent as results with animals.

Basing their work on the techniques and results of experimental (animal) neuropsychology, researchers have attempted to find the fundamental neuropsychological defects underlying the behavioral alterations in human beings with frontal lobe pathology. Results have been contradictory and difficult to interpret. Thus Ghent, Mishkin, and Teuber (1962) could not find a deficit in delayed reaction among subjects with frontal lobe trauma. Chorover and Cole (1966) did demonstrate disturbed performance in human beings on a test of delayed alternation, but the deficits were present with any cerebral lesion and not specifically frontal.

On the Wisconsin Card Sorting Test, on which the subject must repeatedly change his principal line of reasoning to solve a problem, the performance of 25 subjects with frontal lobe resections, right or left, was significantly inferior to that of control subjects. The frontal deficit was manifested by an inability of the subject to overcome a previously established response pattern. A tendency to perseveration, previously demonstrated in "frontal" animals, was thus shown to be present in human beings with frontal lobe lesions (Milner, 1963).

Brenda Milner subjected large numbers of subjects with cerebral ablations for epileptogenic cortical scars to a series of verbal and nonverbal tests (see her review article, Milner, 1971). She indicated that subjects with frontal lobe lesions had difficulty distinguishing the degree of recency of an item among a series of presented items. Prisko (cited by Milner, 1971) had previously shown that frontal lobectomy impaired the subject's ability to perform on a delayed paired-comparison task. In this task the subject must suppress the memory of earlier trials and compare the present stimulus only with the one that immediately preceded it. Prisko's data suggested that frontal lesions prevented the subject from keeping the different trials apart. On verbal and nonverbal recency tasks Milner and Corsi (Milner, 1971) established that frontal lobectomy produced a disturbance in the temporal ordering of events but that the impaired performance, verbal or nonverbal, was different according to the side of the lesion. Lesions of the left frontal lobe produced a deficit on the verbal tests; lesions of the right frontal lobe, a deficit on the nonverbal task.

Milner had previously demonstrated other hemispheric asymmetries following frontal lobe lesions: left frontal lobe lesions were associated with deficits on a verbal fluency task, while right frontal lesions were associated with deficits on a maze-learning task. In regard to verbal fluency tests Ramier and Hécaen (1970) found deficits following either right or left frontal lobe lesions; however, the deficits were much more marked when the lesion was on the left. Milner tentatively concluded that a common defect underlies the various functional abnormalities observed: impairment of the ability to suppress the interference effect of a previous action on a current task.

Indications of specific disturbances in sensory processing or sensory motor integration following frontal lesions in man have also been reported. Heilman and Valenstein (1972) have described six cases of unilateral neglect (failure to respond to one of the stimuli when two stimuli are presented simultaneously and bilaterally) in patients with lesions restricted to the frontal lobes. All of these patients had right frontal lesions—three dorsolateral and three medial. These results are reminiscent of similar findings in other animals with experimentally induced frontal lesions (Bianchi, 1895; Kennard, 1939; Welch and Stutteville, 1958). For Heilman and his collaborators (1970, 1971a, 1972a) the neglect represents an attentional defect caused by a disconnection within the frontolimbic-reticular activating system.

With regard to the parceling of the human frontal lobes to demonstrate an association of specific behavioral defects with specific intrafrontal anatomic regions, only suggestive studies have been concluded. Thus Milner (1968a) has pointed out that human performance on certain sorting tasks may be more impaired with dorsolateral frontal lesions than with lesions elsewhere in the frontal lobes. Luria (1966), on the other hand, has indicated that disturbances of impulse control may be more related to orbital and medial lesions than to other frontal damage.

Thus whereas the neuropsychological deficits following frontal lesions in man are not as readily observed as the behavioral deficits in monkeys with frontal lesions, nonetheless specific deficits can be found in man. Of particular interest is that some of the deficits in man are seen to be related to the issue of cerebral dominance, a problem that has not yet been found to be of serious consideration in nonhuman animals.

Proposed Mechanisms Underlying the Functional Deficits—Based on Neuropsychological Studies

During this century many valuable theoretical contributions to our understanding of frontal lobe functions in man have been provided (e.g., Goldstein, 1936a, 1944; Hebb, 1945; Denny-Brown, 1951; Teuber, 1964a, 1972; Milner, 1968a, 1971; Pribram, 1969; Luria, 1971, 1972; Nauta, 1971, 1972a, etc.). In this section we refer chiefly to hypotheses of Teuber, Luria, and Nauta.

For Teuber the frontal lobe contributes to the control of behavior by originating anticipatory discharges (corollary discharges) that attain sensory structures, preparing them for the motor activity that is about to occur. Because of the reception of these corollary discharge signals, the sensory systems can compare the expected results of the action with the intention of the subject. This theory would account for observed functional deficits in frontal lobe animals; the absence of comparable deficits in man would be explained by his capacity for verbal mediation as an additional regulator of motor activity. In man the frontal lobe deficits would be manifested not only as problems of control of reflexive movement or posture but also as deficits in the regulation of their voluntary control. By such a hypothesis the grasping or groping reflexes seen after frontal lesions could be explained.

Teuber based his theoretical analyses on a series of studies done on subjects with war-missile-induced cerebral lesions. In these studies there were 90 subjects with frontal lesions, 142 subjects with other cerebral lesions, and 118 normal controls. The subjects with frontal lobe lesions were specifically impaired on four perceptual-motor tasks involving posture and movement. These tasks were a visuospatial task requiring appreciation of verticality (Teuber and Mishkin, 1954); a study of reversible figures, that is, the double Necker cube (Cohen, 1959); a test of visual searching; and a test of personal body orientation in space (Semmes et al, 1963).

In a subsequent analysis of Teuber's results, as well as of the results of others, Nauta (1971) speculated that a frontolimbic relationship could be centrally involved in the phenomenon of "behavioral anticipation" and that the anticipatory selection process would be severely impaired following frontal lesions. Nauta related this concept to Teuber's "corollary discharge" hypothesis but added limbic mechanisms to the basic hypothesis. Teuber's proposition postulated an effector function of the frontal lobe, even though that function acted primarily on perception rather than movement. Nauta asked if a wider aspect of the frontal lobe syndrome could not also be explained in terms of a corollary discharge. He proposed that the frontal lobes effected a presetting, not only of exteroceptive processing mechanisms, but also of those mechanisms dealing with interoceptive information. This presetting activity could then establish a temporal sequence of affective reference points and thereby provide, by means of their sequential order, both the general course and the temporal stability of complex goal-directed forms of behavior.

Nauta supported his position by observing, from the results of neuropsychologists, that the frontal lobe disorder was characterized primarily by a derangement of behavioral programming. He commented that one of the essential functional deficits of the patient with frontal lobe damage lies in an inability to maintain a normal "stability-in-time" in his behavior.

The interpretation proposed by Luria as an explanation of frontal lobe dysfunction has certain points of similarity with that of Teuber and Nauta (Luria, 1966). For Luria frontal lobe lesions provoke a disturbance in the programming of one's diverse activities; there is impairment in the final intended action because of a lack of information provided during the elaboration of the action. Thus the frontal lobes regulate the "active state" of the organism, control the essential elements of the subject's intentions, program complex forms of activity, and constantly monitor all aspects of activity. The regulatory function of the frontal lobes is effected by a constant comparison between the effect of an action and its program of origin: if there is a correspondence, the action is completed; if there is no correspondence, the action continues until the desired effect and the necessary correspondence are obtained. This mechanism is based on a system of "feedback afferents." Consequently, frontal lobe signs do not represent a disorder of sensation or perception, of language, or of primary motor or reflex activity. Rather, they represent disorders of regulation of activity and correction of errors.

Disorders of regulation of activity are manifested clinically by apathy and akinesia. In milder cases, instead of responding correctly to the command, the subject cannot maintain his attention, and the desired program of action is replaced by a stereotyped motor response. The physiological basis for these observations can be demonstrated by a study of the autonomic components of the orienting reaction. In the case of a lesion other than frontal these autonomic responses evaluated by plethysmography and electrodermal reaction may be disturbed, but any verbal command gives the stimulus a new signal value and brings about a reappearance of the orienting reaction. On the other hand, in the case of a frontal lesion, the autonomic components of the orienting reaction are suppressed or diffused, and verbal instructions do not bring about their reappearance. In similar fashion in frontal lobe patients electroencephalographic expectation waves (contingent negative variations) do not appear after verbal instruction.

Additional clinical manifestations of the loss of frontal lobe regulatory control are the phenomena of motor impersistence and perseveration. For example, it may be difficult for a patient repeatedly to open and close his eyes or to open and close his fist; on the other hand, once started, it may be difficult for the patient to stop these activities. Luria concludes that these phenomena are indications that the subject has "ceased to be controlled by the prescribed program and has passed under the influence of non-pertinent factors." It becomes impossible for the patient to create a complex and selective system of connections to control the active movement. The necessary program is replaced by inert stereotypies. With a series of ingenious motor tests of increasing complexity (simple motor response to a conditioned signal, conditioned choice reaction, reactions in conflict, and successive actions in direct or alternating series) Luria has been able to demonstrate the impairment of regulation of voluntary acts that are no longer subject to verbally formulated programs.

Certain aspects of perceptual and intellectual activity may also be impaired following frontal lobe lesions. If a visual or tactile perceptual task is relatively simple, it may be done accurately. If, however, the perception requires a preliminary analysis during which the subject must make a correct choice among several reasonable possibilities, the disorder becomes manifest. Such is also the case for disorders of arithmetic, other tasks of problem solving, and other intellectual activities.

As for memory disorders these are demonstrated most clearly when two memory tasks are given one after another in a short period of time. The items and associations from one task interfere with those of the other. For Luria the frontal lobe memory disorders are related, at least in severe cases, to defects of attention, temporospatial disorientation, and confabulation.

Problems are posed by the clinical material Luria used for his studies, and for these reasons a certain prudence is warranted before one accepts his hypotheses. Most of his observations are based on cases with massive frontal tumors that quite possibly extended beyond the limits of the frontal lobes both in depth and on the cortical surface. Several of his patients must have had increased intracranial pressure, confounding the clinical and experimental picture. In addition many of the experimental results put forth by Luria to support his arguments are purely qualitative. No comparative studies with normal controls or with brain-damaged subjects with nonfrontal lesions are presented. Denny-Brown, in a review of Luria's work, was struck by the significant role played by perseveration in the impaired performance of Luria's patients. The perseveration was of a sufficient severity to have accounted for many of the reported behavioral abnormalities. Yet perseveration cannot be considered an abnormality limited exclusively to frontal lobe lesions. It remains to be proven that posterior cerebral (nonfrontal) lesions produce a perseveration that affects different behavioral functions than that produced by frontal lesions.

These criticisms in no way reduce the intrinsic value of the interpretative analyses or examining techniques presented by Luria. Rather they are intended to stimulate an experimental evaluation of his theories. To confirm a general hypothesis of frontal lobe function, it will be necessary to apply systematically a standardized battery of tests to large numbers of subjects with relatively limited and well-localized cerebral lesions in varied locations.

NINE
CEREBRAL PLASTICITY AND RECOVERY OF FUNCTION

REORGANIZATION AND REPLACEMENT

Much of the content of this book, up to now, has been concerned with patterns of behavioral dysfunction associated with cerebral damage. The concepts of cerebral localization of function and functional hemispheric asymmetry have been explicitly and implicitly considered as basic to any interpretative analysis of these neuropsychological defects. However, to consider the questions of cerebral localization and dominance without due regard for modifications of behavior brought about by recovery of function would be a mistake. In fact such functional recovery can at times be so great as to throw into doubt the very notion of cerebral localization. Early in the history of neuropsychology, from the time that the principle of cerebral localization of function was introduced, a problem was already posed: the more or less complete reappearance of function following destruction of anatomic zones considered to be specifically responsible for that function provided arguments in favor of the antilocalizers, the group that believed that the initial abnormality of function was simply the result of inhibitory influences.

Thus the localizationists had to account for functional recovery after circumscribed lesions. The arguments in this early period centered primarily on reappearance of movements following destruction of the motor zone. Currently popular explanations for recovery of function, such as taking over of function by another cerebral structure (vicarious function or replacement) or cerebral reorganization, were either explicitly formulated or proposed in embryonic form in some of these earlier hypotheses.

Theories of functional replacement refer to the taking over of function by the opposite hemisphere, by neighboring cortical regions, or by subcortical structures. With respect to recovery of higher cortical functions in animals or man, the notion of replacement refers to other cortical structures that do not ordinarily participate in the behavioral activity but that may assume the function by virtue of their connections with the specific area destroyed.

According to von Monakow (1914) effects of recovery vary depending on the functional role of the structures originally damaged. He divided such structures into two anatomofunctional groups: those responsible for immediate execution (motor, sensory), having precise neural substrates; and those responsible for elaboration of neural excitations over a period of time (as with the higher cortical functions), having more extensive neural substrates. In the first group the effect of a lesion is permanent, in the second group the effects of lesions occur only in the early stage.

He called the early effects "diaschisis," that is, "a dynamic inhibitory effect at a distance, originating in the region of the lesion, and spreading to distant regions connected to the lesion by direct fiber pathways." Diaschisis affects all cells presumed to be involved in the same function. The inhibitory process affects those elements of the function that are newest, most recently organized, least solidly fixed in structure, and most voluntary; older aspects of the function are more resistant to these inhibitory phenomena.

Von Monakow contended that aphasias, apraxias, and agnosias were especially transitory. He stressed that localizationists systematically ignored the frequent negative cases (cases in which a lesion in an anatomic region presumed to be responsible for a particular function did *not* cause an impairment in this function). For him readaptation following cerebral lesion was a global process of the brain.

For Goldstein (1939) release from the inhibitory effects of diaschisis does not explain recovery of function. In fact there is no true recovery of function, just a modification of adaptation. The function is no longer performed according to the same strategy; behavioral detours, a roundabout way, are adopted to ensure continuation of those functions most important from an organismic point of view. This functional reorganization takes place only if it is absolutely impossible for the function to be carried out in the ordinary manner. In the case of an elementary disorder of neurological function cerebral reorganization does not occur.

Despite considerable research performed since these earlier theories were proposed, the same notions are current today, although under different names. Following Rosner (1970) we could suggest regrouping proposed mechanisms for recovery of function into two major, nonexclusive categories: re-establishment and reorganization.

Re-establishment postulates a redundant representation of a psychological capacity within an anatomic center or specialized region. Following an initial phase of inhibition, the intact portions recuperate their normal mode of functioning. Numerous experimental studies in animals have supported this view. Chow (1968), for example, in a study in cats destroyed 85% of optic nerves and enough visual cortex to cause degeneration of 85% of the geniculate bodies. Nonetheless these cats preserved brilliance and pattern discriminations learned preoperatively. Experimental arguments have been presented to support this principle of redundancy even in fiber pathways. However, the principle of redundancy in the central nervous system has been rejected by Young (1966), among others, because, according to him, it runs counter to the principle of economy that governs development in the course of evolution. A counterargument states that redundancy provided a means of ensuring greater functional efficiency.

Reorganization assumes that a function is controlled by several centers, either symmetrically located in each hemisphere or located asymmetrically in different parts of the nervous system. Functional recovery takes place when a center in relationship to the one that was destroyed takes over the activities of the damaged region. For example, if we consider recovery of language function following cortical lesions, we could refer to Penfield's (1958a) hypothesis of three separate areas of varying significance devoted to this function. When the principal zone (posterotemporal region) is destroyed, the two other zones (Broca's area and supplementary motor cortex), which had been of lesser importance until the destruction of the principal zone, now assume (or at least partially assume) the role of the principal zone. According to the concept of reorganization one would envisage a functional system composed of several regions (cortical/subcortical). Certain of these regions would be more important than others, and their destruction would cause a more pronounced and longer lasting defect. The undamaged portions of the system could take over all or part of the behavioral function.

In this regard, with respect to language, we might wonder if compensation takes place by additional activity of the right hemisphere, as must be assumed in certain cases with left hemispherectomy. Hécaen and de Ajuriaguerra (1952) observed almost total recovery of ability to read in patients subjected to left occipital lobectomy. However, these latter cases do not completely prove the capacity of the right hemisphere to take over language function, because in those cases in which the lesion involved more than the occipital lobe, recovery was not good. For this reason these authors could not exclude the possibility of vicarious function in regions adjacent to the occipital lobes, for those subjects with limited occipital lobectomies.

Reorganization may take place at different levels: from modifications of general adaptation (invoked by Goldstein) to the appearance of new strategies of physiological mechanisms themselves. These latter strategies consist of "behavioral maneuvers" (Goldberger, 1972) and can even be found after section of peripheral nerves (Sperry, 1966–1967). This type of reorganization is especially evident in the vestibular system. Following unilateral labyrinthectomy, compensation follows the readjustment of equilibrium between excitatory and inhibitory influences on the cellular activity of vestibular nuclei (Precht, 1974). Dischgans et al (1973) have shown that the remarkable recovery that follows bilateral vestibular ablation results from reorganization of motor function together with development of functional connections between the motor centers for head and eyes. These centers are functionally independent in the intact animal.

Russian neuropsychologists have developed a concept of recovery of function that is based on principles of reorganization. Studies by Asratyan (1966), Anokhin (1949), and Bernshtein (1947, 1957) have attempted to define characteristics of functional reorganization in the peripheral nervous system for elementary functions. They consider these functions to be complex adaptive processes accomplished by functional systems that integrate structural units and act as coordinating entities. Such functional systems could not exist without a constant afferent influx of information concerning the state in which the individual finds himself. Each system possesses its specific afferent field (receptor group) that ensures the requisite information. Compensation may occur when one system comes to the aid of a damaged system, the receptors of the healthy system substituting for those of the damaged system to provide the necessary afferent information.

Luria (1966) drew on these hypothetical models plus those of Vygotsky (1962, 1965) to define mechanisms of reorganization related to more complex psychological functions. Because of the functional and structural differentiations that develop in the cortex of man and higher primates, each behavioral function, according to Luria, derives from activity of both a primary and a secondary cerebral region, and each of these regions interacts with the other in diverse ways. Processes of reorganization differ, depending on whether the lesion affects a cortical region primarily responsible for reception or projection or whether the lesion involves association cortex. If the latter, the nature of reorganization would depend on the type of associative integration performed.

"Whereas in a lesion of the primary areas, all the motor or receptor components of a given functional system may suffer; a lesion of the secondary integration area destroys one of the basic elements necessary for the creation of integrated afferent fields; and the whole functional system will invariably suffer (although the motor or sensory composition of the action may remain unchanged). This disintegration of the system can be compensated either by internal reorganization of its preserved elements or by the replacement of the lost cerebral link by another which is still intact. This task of reintegration of the functional system can be undertaken, not by means of facilitating impulses originating from non-specific cortical areas, but by including in the functional system such areas as are able to compensate in one form or another for the lost elements, or to enable a given problem to be solved by new methods. This can be done, for in the course of development, complex intersystematic relationships are created on the basis of deliberately objective action and speech which permit completely new relationships between the higher centers. This modified task may thus lead to the creation of new functional systems; and almost any area of the cerebral cortex may be included in a particular functional system in order to reintegrate the disturbed activity of the brain" (Luria, 1963).

When the lesion involves association cortex, reorganization is effected only with the active participation of the patient and only after a long period of re-education that helps to develop methods for detour. If, for example, the patient is unable to analyze a series of stimuli because of the destruction of one system, re-education may help him use these same stimuli within the framework of another functional system by conferring a distinctive sign value to the stimuli. When total destruction of a system occurs, as one may see with peripheral lesions, an intersystem compensation may take place. Under such conditions the component that is totally lost is replaced by another that takes over the role of the lost element in the reintegrated system.

REGENERATION

Until most recently, interpretations of mechanisms of recovery of function combined theorizing with occasional physiological support. Little anatomic evidence was provided, and central nervous system regeneration in vertebrates was excluded from consideration, despite sporadic reports in its favor (e.g., Windle, 1940; Liu and Chambers, 1958). Current studies have, however, demonstrated evidence of central nervous system regeneration following lesions. Collateral reinnervation may proceed from intact axons from the synaptic sites left empty by degeneration of sectioned fibers (Goodman and Horel, 1967; Raisman, 1969; Moore, Bjorklund, and Steveni, 1971; Lynch and Crane, 1972; Raisman and Field, 1973; etc). Frank regeneration of sectioned axons in the central nervous system has also been found (Bjorklund and Steveni, 1972). Axonal regeneration seems to be most readily demonstrable in catecholamine-containing mesencephalic systems and in systems rich in indolamines. Certain proteins, such as nerve growth factor, favor this regeneration as clearly in central as in peripheral fibers (Bjorklund and Steveni, 1972).

Although it is still difficult to indicate what the functional consequences of these collateral sproutings may be, in some cases it has been shown that the neural interaction that results may interfere with function (e.g., recuperation of spinal reflexes: McCough et al, 1958). Moreover collateral sprouting may not turn out to be a general phenomenon but rather a process limited to specific systems.

Furthermore other mechanisms may be involved in recuperation, such as denervation hypersensitivity. According to this hypothesis, proposed in 1949 by Cannon and Rosenblueth, denervated elements become hypersensitive to the inhibitory or excitatory action of chemical agents or of neural influx. Effects of denervation have been demonstrated especially in effector organs of the autonomic nervous system, but more and more precise evidence is being provided to indicate the existence of this phenomenon in the central nervous system as well.

Sharpless (1964, 1969) suggested that the effects of denervation hypersensitivity result either from the nonutilization or from the degeneration of presynaptic elements. Denervation of a structure must involve not only the suppression of inputs that normally arrive at that structure but also a modification of the normal influence exerted by a nerve ending by its metabolism. Hypersensitivity, it is suggested, would result either from increased sensitivity of the postsynaptic component of neural transmission or from a delay in the inactivation of transmitter substance.

It seems to us that a model of denervation hypersensitivity implies, more generally, an augmentation over time of the sensitivity of postsynaptic structures to the chemical stimulation of the normal transmitter or to any other chemical agent. Recent studies (Nygren et al, 1974; Bird and Aghajanian, 1975) have provided histochemical, neurochemical, and functional arguments in favor of the existence of denervation hypersensitivity in the septal region.

As a final point we may add that functional recovery has been linked in certain situations to the pre-existence of "silent" synapses that attain functional efficiency only in response to the presence of a destructive lesion or the appearance of deafferentation. The activation of these previously suppressed or silent synapses might bring about a reorganization of connections that could produce some degree of functional compensation (Wall and Egger, 1971; Merrill and Wall, 1972).

MULTISTAGED LESIONS

By referring to studies on reorganization, replacement, and regeneration, we have been able only to highlight old theories and recent experimental trends. The gulf between anatomic or physiological data and behavioral phenomena is still too great to bridge comfortably. In trying to bring these two bodies of information closer together, one must consider other factors that may increase or decrease possibilities for functional restoration. These may relate to the lesion (nature, extent, etc.) or to the subject (species, prelesion and postlesion state, age, etc.). Among these various factors that may influence recovery of function, we consider two that have been the subject of considerable attention in recent years: one is the sequential (serial, progressive) character of lesions in adults; the other is the degree of cerebral maturation at the time of lesion onset.

With respect to the former an initial series of experiments seemed to prove that placing lesions in several stages, by contrast with producing the same final lesion in a single surgical procedure, resulted in a less marked functional defect. This effect of functional sparing by multistaged lesions was found in different animal species, in different cerebral regions, and with different behavioral tasks. Ades and Raab (1946a,b; 1949) observed sparing of a pattern discrimination retention task in monkeys after sequential (multistaged) ablation of prestriate areas, even though deficits on this task appeared if the lesions were made simultaneously. Also noted was a greater degree of motor recovery when ablation of motor areas was done in several stages rather than in a single-stage operation (Ades and Raab, 1946a,b; Travis and Woolsey, 1956). Other authors demonstrated that, in the rat subjected to bilateral serial ablations of posterior neocortical regions, conditioned avoidance responses were preserved, whether the interoperative stimulus was visual (Meier, 1970; Meyer, Isaac, and Maher, 1958), auditory (Isaac, 1964) or chemical (Cole et al, 1967), whereas these avoidance responses were lost if the bilateral ablations were performed simultaneously.

Petrinovitch and Bliss (1966) systematically re-evaluated these latter experiments, confirming the major observations. They found that simultaneous bilateral occipital lesions in rats produced a deficit on a previously learned brilliance discrimination task, whereas successive lesions did not produce this deficit, provided that the rats were kept in a normally lighted environment or that the rats were exposed to the task again during the interval between the two operations. If the rats were kept in the dark during the interval between the two operations, their performance on the lightness-darkness discrimination task was as poor following the two-stage operation as following the one-stage. A study by R. Thompson (1960) did not completely confirm these results. He found no differences in light discrimination after one-stage or two-stage operations on occipital cortex in the rat except for the condition in which the rats continued to practice the task during the interoperative interval. To explain these contradictory findings, Petrinovitch and Carew (1969) referred to lesion size—large in the Thompson experiments, smaller in theirs. These authors, with a new group of rats, again showed that keeping the rats in a lighted environment during the interoperative period was sufficient to maintain the previously learned skill.

D. G. Stein et al (1969, 1976) described their results of several studies on recovery of function, again concluding that two-stage operations produced less deficit than one-stage operations. These authors operated on frontal, hippocampal, and amygdaloid regions in rats; tested a variety of behavioral tasks; and did not retrain during the interoperative period.

By contrast other experimenters have not found such differences between serial and simultaneous operations. McIntyre and Stein (1973) found sparing in the multistage procedures only on two of the four behavioral tests studied following partial destruction of the amygdaloid complex. Isaacson and Schmaltz (1968) and Dawson et al (1973) did not find sparing following multistage lesions of the hippocampus. Greene et al (1970) found sparing following two-stage lesions of the fornix of the rat, but these rats were nonetheless inferior to controls.

In the monkey Rosen et al (1971) found a sparing effect on two of three behavioral tasks (delayed response and place reversal) after serial (four-stage) lesions of the sulcus principalis: for the third task (spatial alternation), results were ambiguous. On the other hand the same research teams failed to demonstrate sparing effect of serial lesions of the lateral orbital cortex.

The results of these diverse experiments are sufficiently consistent, despite a certain percentage of negative findings, to support the hypothesis that some sort of functional organization takes place more clearly with multistage than with simultaneous or single-stage operations. In a general review Finger et al (1973) consider the following variables critical for the sparing effect of serial lesions: duration of interoperative interval, presence of practice or nonspecific stimulation in the interoperative interval, nature of the behavioral task, site of lesion, and period of time allotted postoperatively before the animal is retested, whether for the one-stage or for the multistage operations.

Two other variables should probably also be considered: age and sex. Stein (1976) pointed out that rats with two-stage frontal lobe lesions showed different performances on a task of spatial alternation according to their age. The older rats (2 years) had much poorer performances than the younger rats (90 days). The role of sex in functional recovery following multistage operations was demonstrated by Teitelbaum (1974). On a learning task involving repetitive spatial discriminations, male rats showed complete recovery following serial frontal ablations, while female rats did not recover.

As for animal species Finger et al (1973) do not consider this a critical variable, since the sparing effect of serial lesions has been found in mice, rats, cats, and monkeys. These authors suggest that, in man also, slowly progressive lesions produce less marked functional deficits than acute lesions do.

Concerning anatomic regions in which the effects of multistage lesions are seen, although arguments have been put forth supporting the view that functional sparing may occur with subcortical lesions, Levere and Weiss (1973) contend that the sparing effect is limited to neocortical structures. These authors found no sparing effect on a reversal task in rats with two-stage dorsal hippocampal lesions. They hypothesized that interoperative functional reorganization is independent of the task but is linked to the specific anatomic region involved. Only the neocortex can be reorganized. Such recovery as may be seen following subcortical lesions would, according to this hypothesis, be related to relatively stable behavioral functions that were unlearned; functional recovery would be associated with general recovery. With respect to this hypothesis it is of interest that operative mortality is greater with large simultaneous ablations than with serial ablations of the same final size, both cortically and subcortically (Adametz, 1959).

Not only absolute but also relative differences of functional recovery may depend on lesion site. In a study with monkeys, serial dorsolateral frontal lobe ablation effected only a partial recovery on a task of delayed alternation but a complete recovery on two other tasks (Rosen et al, 1971). After subsequent studies of the orbitofrontal areas Butters et al (1973a) observed that to interpret differences in functional recovery it was necessary to take into account the different behavioral functions for which different frontal zones are responsible.

Interpretation of these various sets of data is still difficult. Is one justified in proposing a single explanatory hypothesis to account for recovery of function, or is it necessary to assume that different principles of reorganization are involved, depending on variables such as localization of lesion, extent and depth of lesion, or interoperative conditions? There are already sufficient experimental data to allow the conclusion that interoperative conditions (practice, stimulation, etc.) are not essential variables. This leads to the conclusion that some natural process is occurring, initiated by the first lesion.

Ades and Raab (1946b) proposed that destruction of a portion of nervous tissue used for a particular functional integration provoked a process of reorganization that extended beyond the hemisphere in which the process started. When the second surgical intervention destroyed the remaining tissue—tissue that had previously been critical for the function—preservation of the function implied that this particular behavioral task no longer depended on one specialized group of neurons but had become the general property of all parts of the nervous system with which the lesioned site had connections. If this is indeed the case, that the first lesion has such a stimulating effect on CNS reorganization, then one might suppose that the first lesion produced a deficit that was compensated for by activation of some reserve system. Studies in the rat (Greene et al, 1970) and in the monkey (Warren et al, 1969; Cowey and Dewson, 1972; Stamm et al, 1975) tend to support this hypothesis: a unilateral lesion may cause a mild deficit from which the animal may recover.

Finger et al (1973) provide several different explanations for recovery of function, explanations that are not necessarily mutually exclusive. These include structural reorganization (axonal sprouting, denervation hypersensitivity, hormonal factors), reorganization by substitution of function, functional re-establishment (greater inhibitory shock from simultaneous lesions), and role of cerebral structures functionally related to the destroyed zone.

In our opinion none of these explanations alone can account for all the available experimental data. In addition it seems difficult, if not impossible, to reject completely the notion that certain anatomic regions may be "critical" for certain specific behavioral functions. For subcortical lesions the interpretation that recovery is related to wearing off of the effect of shock seems adequate. However, with respect to cortical lesions we would tentatively accept the explanation of either or both of substitution of function or structural regeneration, activated by changes associated with the first operation.

Studies of recovery of function in human beings have generally been clinically based. It has been classical dogma since Jackson (1932) to teach that slowly progressive lesions produce less marked functional deficits than lesions of acute onset do. In fact it is a common clinical observation that lesions of abrupt onset are often associated with severe symptoms, whatever the interpretation of their cause (inhibition, "cerebral shock," diaschisis) or the structural changes involved (vascular pathology, vasospasm, edema). However, only after the initial clinical stage has passed can the relationship between lesion and deficit be appreciated. Only then can subsequent functional recovery be evaluated. It is inappropriate to compare the functional effects of lesions of acute onset that subsequently remain unchanged (e.g., cerebrovascular accidents) and slowly progressive lesions (e.g., tumors). To study the effects of rapidity of lesion onset on appearance of functional deficits, it is necessary to compare lesions that are in the same pathological category but with different rates of progression (e.g., rapidly progressive tumors such as glioblastomas vs. slowly progressive tumors such as low-grade astrocytomas).

We have undertaken to make a gross comparison of this type, despite the possibilities for error in such an analysis owing to the presence of many, often uncontrollable variables. The following data cannot, therefore, be considered as providing a basis for definitive hypotheses; they may, however, be indicative. In subjects of equivalent ages, with lesions of similar localization and extent but with lesions of different rapidity of evolution (3 weeks to 6 months for one group, 3 to 30 years for the other), no significant differences in focal symptomatology appeared. This was true not only for elementary motor or sensory functions but also for higher cortical functions. Our findings were, however, different in two specific subject groups: patients with lesions localized to Broca's area and patients in whom the tumor started during childhood. In these two subject groups we found some evidence that functional compensation may occur if the lesion has a slow rate of progression.

One is justified in questioning the relevance of comparisons between human beings and animals. Slowly progressive lesions in human beings may not be similar to multistage lesions in animals. Vascular lesions in man, appearing in successive stages in symmetrical regions of the hemispheres, are more comparable, but these are, of course, exceptionally rare. Nonetheless cases have been reported of thrombosis of first one and then the other posterior cerebral artery. Clinically one usually finds a picture of cortical blindness, whether the lesions were produced in one or two stages. Rare cases of cortical deafness or pure word deafness have also been reported and may occur following serial lesions in right and left temporal lobes. This absence of sparing in humans may, however, be due to the fact that the majority of such cases concern adult, usually elderly, subjects. Stein (1976) has shown that in the aged rat one does not find the same sparing after serial frontal lesions as in the adult, but younger, rat. Anatomic observations have caused Stein to suggest that similar structures do not support the same activities with increasing age. Plasticity of the central nervous system, in such a case, would not be limited to the period of cerebral maturation.

LESIONS IN THE IMMATURE BRAIN

The state of maturation of the nervous system at the moment a focal lesion occurs is a major factor affecting eventual recovery from functional deficits caused by the lesion. We have already considered this issue in the sections devoted to acquired aphasia in childhood. In animals considerable research has been done, especially in recent years, on the effects of lesions in different cerebral regions in different animal species before complete maturation of the brain.

Primary Motor and Sensory Regions

Kennard (1936, 1938, 1942) studied effects of unilateral or bilateral ablations of motor and premotor areas in monkeys and chimpanzees less than 4 weeks old. No paresis was immediately observable, and, when paresis finally appeared as the animal developed, it was much less severe than that found after similar operations in adults. Ablation of neighboring cerebral zones considerably aggravated the motor deficit in the young monkeys but not in the adults. From these observations Kennard concluded that a direct relationship exists between age and capacity for CNS reorganization that allows integration of motor performance by cortical structures remaining after destruction of areas 4 and 6. This capacity was not limited to the first months of life but was found to continue, while slowly and progressively diminishing, during the first 2 years of life. Functional restoration was never complete, however, neither in the young nor in the adult monkey, because in both groups a permanent impairment in performing isolated finger movements remained. Lawrence and Hopkins (1972) made the same observation after bilateral pyramidotomies in neonatal monkeys.

Varying results have been reported with studies of motor function in other species. In the rat Hicks and D'Amato (1970) observed that hemispherectomy caused little deficit in either the neonate or the adult. In neonates, however, ability to run remained normal, while in adults the stride component was lost.

Ablation of somatosensory regions in the neonatal cat caused no impairment in roughness discrimination, but this sensory discrimination was lost following similar ablations in adults (Benjamin and Thompson, 1959). By contrast comparable ablations in neonatal cats did not spare tactile placement or hopping reactions (Glassman, 1973).

Mixed results have also been obtained in studies of visual function following striate cortex lesions in young and adult animals. Earlier studies found functional sparing in kittens to such an extent that their visual performance was indistinguishable from that of controls (Doty, 1961). These observations were supported by others (Wetzel et al, 1965). However, Doty (1973), in reconsidering the question, suggested that the ablation may have been insufficiently large to cause complete degeneration of the geniculate bodies; in adults he observed that very large cortical ablations were needed to suppress cortical visual function.

Negative results were also reported from studies with rats (Bland and Cooper, 1969; Bauer and Hughes, 1970; Thompson, 1970). In the newborn hamster striate lesions retard learning of pattern discriminations, whereas in adults these discriminations are retarded to a greater degree or are lost completely (Schneider, 1969). Additional negative results were reported after occipital lobe ablations in monkeys (Weiskrantz, 1963); although discriminations of lightness intensity seemed to be better in the young than in the adult following operation.

In the auditory system Sharlock et al (1963) found preservation of the capacity to discriminate durations of tones in newborn cats after ablation of auditory cortex. This capacity was lost in adult cats with similar operations.

Association Areas

The effect of functional sparing found with lesions in young, as opposed to adult, animals has also been found with association area ablations. However, results have been more or less clear, depending on which areas were involved. Lesions of prefrontal regions have most consistently shown the effect of sparing; lesions elsewhere, less consistently. For example, ablation of inferotemporal regions showed ambiguous results: partial sparing in young monkeys with two-stage operations, compared with eventual compensation of defects in adult monkeys (Raisler and Harlow, 1965). Others have observed sparing of visual or auditory discriminations in newborn monkeys (Kling and Tucker, 1968) or kittens (Colavita, 1972a) as opposed to adult animals of the same species.

Data on sparing of functional capacities after frontal lobe lesions in immature monkeys are most abundant. Harlow et al (1970) found complete or almost complete preservation of capacity for delayed response after bilateral dorsolateral frontal (area 9) ablations in monkeys of 5 days and 5 months. In the latter group, maturation of the function of delayed response had already appeared but was incomplete. In subsequent experiments this same research team showed that, even with larger ablations, such as lobectomies, no deficit in delayed response appeared if the operation was performed in the first half of the first year. A continuum in sparing of function occurred, relative to size of lesion and age of animal at the time of operation (Harlow et al, 1970). These conclusions were confirmed in experiments conducted more recently.

Harlow et al (1970) found that lesion size was a critical variable and that an age limit of 12 months existed for preservation of certain functions. Harlow interpreted these results as showing that, since frontal ablation in immature monkeys resulted in sparing of ability for delayed response, the mechanisms that underlie this ability must develop in another cerebral region (caudate nucleus?). In addition, since monkeys operated on at 18 and 24 months have less deficit than those operated on at 12 months, the development of intellectual capacities must aid the older monkeys in resolving delayed-response problems, despite loss of the specific mechanism for this ability. Maturation of supplementary mechanisms allows resolution of these problems, albeit in a less efficient manner. In animals operated on at 12 months, a deficit appears in the ability to learn object discriminations; this deficit does not appear in animals operated on much earlier or later. It would seem that this function is spared after operations in the younger animals, and some alternative mechanism develops for the older animals.

Goldman, Rosvold, and Mishkin (1970) re-evaluated the question from several different points of view, and their results shed new light on the issue of cerebral plasticity in young animals. They performed total prefrontal lobectomies on monkeys aged from 2 to 3 months, and from 18 to 24 months. Learning three tasks—delayed response, delayed alternation response, and visual discrimination—was begun 10 months after the lobectomies. In learning the delayed-response task, 2- to 3-month-old monkeys were significantly impaired by comparison with nonoperated monkeys of the same age; however they were much less impaired on this task than monkeys operated on at an older age were. In the older monkeys no learning was possible. On the visual discrimination task more trials were necessary for both groups of lobectomized monkeys than for controls. The learning of a delayed alternation response was impaired in all operated monkeys, but performances were better in those subjected to operation at a younger age.

These results confirm those of Harlow with respect to cerebral plasticity of the developing brain. Nonetheless this plasticity does not appear to be absolute, since the young monkeys with ablations were retarded by comparison with unoperated controls. The retardation may be related to extent of the lesion, since in the experiments of Harlow et al (1970) and Tucker and Kling (1967), ablations did not include the orbital cortex.

Thus it may be reasonable to conclude that combined ablations of orbital and dorsolateral cortex in the newborn monkey prevent the complete compensation seen after ablation of dorsolateral cortex alone. Orbital ablations in adults produce deficits of delayed response that are less severe than those produced by lesions of the sulcus principalis. It seems logical, therefore, to assume that the orbital region consists of neural tissue capable of taking over the function of delayed response when the primary neural zone responsible for this function is destroyed.

Nevertheless, Goldman et al (1970) envisage a hypothesis other than that relating to the vicarious role of orbital cortex. They stress that, in their studies of prefrontal ablations, learning of delayed response was retarded, and deficits of delayed alternation and visual discrimination also appeared. In their adult monkeys, deficits in delayed alternation were as severe after orbital as after dorsolateral lesions. These authors concluded that the functional deficits were due to ablations of the orbital region, whose functions were not compensated.

Mishkin (1957) found that deficits in delayed alternation depended on two mechanisms that differed according to lesion site—orbital or dorsolateral. The dorsolateral function was that of spatial alternation and could be partially compensated if the lesion occurred early in the animal's life. The orbital function contributed to all learning tasks and was not compensated with precocious lesions. Supporting this interpretation Goldman et al (1970) provided data from isolated orbital or dorsolateral lesions. Performances of monkeys with orbital lesions at 2 months were similar to those of monkeys with comparable lesions at an older age. On the other hand, performances following dorsolateral lesions were better for the younger than for the older group.

Goldman et al (1971), in additional studies, presented more direct evidence in favor of this hypothesis. They studied performances of monkeys of different ages (1 to 2 months vs. 18 to 24 months) 10 months after operations that included either total prefrontal lobectomies, dorsolateral frontal ablations, or orbital cortex ablations. Functions tested were delayed spatial response, delayed spatial alternation, visual object discrimination, and reversal of object discriminations. When young, unoperated control monkeys were compared with young monkeys with dorsolateral resections, no significant differences were found on tests of delayed response and delayed alternation. However, considerable individual variation was observed. On these two tests all operated groups, young and old, had similar performances. For the test of reversal of object discrimination, no deficit appeared in any group in which the orbital region was spared. A significant delay in visual discrimination was noted for the young monkeys with dorsolateral resection but not for the older monkeys with similar lesions. With one qualification all animals with orbital lesions had similar deficits on the four tests. The qualification was that young lobectomized monkeys with or without isolated orbital lesions were less deficient than adolescent monkeys. In the older monkeys dorsolateral and orbital effects were additive; this combining of defects did not occur in younger monkeys.

These general observations are subject to certain exceptions. Goldman (1970) had already reported that some infant monkeys with dorsolateral resections had severe deficits on tasks of delayed alternation in space and that some infant monkeys with orbital resection were able to learn the task of delayed alternation. Subsequent studies helped resolve these contradictions. Testing of the same animals 3 months after the initial testing period revealed differences in late learning ability in the "orbital" versus the "dorsolateral" groups. Infant monkeys with orbital lesions were able to relearn the delayed alternation task; infant monkeys with dorsolateral lesions were inferior to controls (Goldman, 1970; Miller et al, 1973).

Basing her interpretations on the various results cited, Goldman (1971) proposed a new theory of recovery of function. For any given area, after its ablation in the immature animal, recovery of function depends on the mode of maturation of structures that are functionally related to that area. If these functionally related cortical systems are "uncommitted," that is, functionally immature, at the moment the lesion is produced, they are plastic and can thereby assume the functions of the destroyed area. If these functionally related areas are already engaged or have attained a state of relative maturation, they are unable to take over the function. The diverse experiments suggest that orbital cortex becomes functionally mature at an earlier age than dorsolateral frontal cortex. "Uncommitted" in infancy, the dorsolateral cortex possesses the capacity for compensation; however, this capacity does not manifest itself until this cortical region matures. This is evidenced by the fact that monkeys with orbital lesions do not recover ability for delayed alternation until they reach 24 months of age. The converse is not true, however, suggesting that the orbital region is already too mature at the time of dorsolateral ablation at age 1 month to assume the function lost. Combined ablation of both orbital and dorsolateral cortices impairs any recuperation. One does not see a deterioration of performance so much as a failure to improve as controls improve.

Tucker and Kling (1967) had found a sparing effect for delayed response in neonatal monkeys with total prefrontal ablation but did not find sparing if the caudate nucleus was also destroyed. From this they concluded that the caudate nucleus participated, together with the dorsolateral frontal cortex, in delayed response activity in young monkeys. According to Goldman's hypothesis, however, the caudate nucleus is the only structure responsible for this function in infancy, because the dorsolateral cortex, by virtue of its state of immaturity, does not yet participate in this function. With maturation of the cortex the role of the caudate nucleus diminishes, although it always contributes to performance of delayed-response tasks (Goldman and Rosvold, 1972).

Archipallium and Subcortical Structures

The majority of reports concerning cerebral plasticity following archipallial or subcortical lesions indicate that lesions placed in these structures during the neonatal or perinatal period are not followed by evidence of functional sparing. Nevertheless, even here one finds contradictory evidence. Thus Kling (1962, 1965, 1966) found no modification of normal affective, sexual, or oral behavior in various animal species subjected to bilateral amygdalectomies at birth, and Isaacson et al (1968) found partial functional sparing on several tests in kittens. By contrast severe functional deficits were found by other authors after subcortical lesions in newborn animals (e.g., septal lesions in the rat—Johnson, 1972; Schoenfeld et al, 1974; ventromedial thalamic lesions and hypothalamic lesions in the rat—Frohman and Bernadis, 1968; Bernadis and Frohman, 1971a,b).

It would seem that functional sparing after subcortical lesions is not so certain as that after cortical lesions in immature animals. Johnson (1972) explains this difference by the fact that subcortical structures are more clearly delimited and that behaviors dependent on subcortical structures are more stereotyped and species specific. The cortex, by contrast, exhibits behavioral flexibility. The significant differences in structural maturation between cortex and subcortical zones may also play a role; morphogenesis continues after early cortical destruction. Nonetheless, however imperfect or partial it may be, some functional compensation has been shown to occur after subcortical lesions in newborn animals (Schneider, 1969).

Cerebral Plasticity in the Developing Brain

What general conclusions, if any, can be drawn from the various studies in animals and man concerning cerebral plasticity in the developing brain? An initial conclusion must be that available data are less clear and more contradictory now than they might have seemed after the pioneer studies of Kennard (1936, 1940). No general law can be formulated to explain functional sparing after cerebral lesions, however limited, in immature animals. Each case must be considered on its own.

Partial synthesis of data may, nonetheless, be considered. In the first place it seems that problems related to cortical and subcortical lesions may be separated. Functional sparing is rare and incomplete after subcortical lesions, with the exception perhaps of amygdaloid and quadrigeminal plate lesions. At the cortical level, evidence favors the existence of a greater possibility for functional reorganization following lesions, especially in reception and projection areas.

However, this phenomenon, even at the cortical level, cannot be accepted as universal. Doty (1971, 1973), for example, reversed his opinion concerning the excellent vision of cats following striate cortex lesions; he now accepts that deficits are similar after ablations in the neonate and in the adult if the lesion is sufficiently large. In addition physiological and behavioral studies have demonstrated such precision of relationships between central and peripheral elements that it becomes difficult to conceive of how a veritable sparing of function could come about (Lawrence and Kuypers, 1968a,b). Even though the motor defects are less severe in infant monkeys by comparison with adults after motor area ablations (Kennard, 1940), the infant monkeys after operation never acquire motor precision of the distal extremities.

With respect to association areas the earlier studies (e.g., Harlow et al, 1952) supported the existence of cerebral plasticity, and subsequent studies (e.g., Goldman, 1970) confirmed this opinion. One may accept that neural structures that are still functionally immature and that are functionally related to cortical zones destroyed in the neonatal period may take over the function of these destroyed zones. Observations in man have shown evidence of a certain degree of plasticity in the developing brain (see, for example, the section above on childhood aphasia), but they have equally shown the limits of this plasticity. Human cerebral structures may be already committed from a very early age, if not from birth, to functions for which they are responsible in the adult state. One cannot be certain that a particular behavioral task is being done in the same way by the normal person as by the individual who had received a lesion while his brain was still immature. An additional question concerns the expense of cerebral plasticity: sparing of a particular function may take place only at the price of deficits in other functions. The mass of remaining cerebral tissue may be inadequate to the task of performing all behavioral activity with normal efficiency. Despite these powerful reservations and qualifications, there is nevertheless sufficient evidence to support the notion that cerebral plasticity exists in human beings to a greater degree in the developing than in the adult state.

What are the conditions and mechanisms of this functional sparing in the developing brain? We are still far from knowing what conditions favor the development of plasticity. Age and the factor of critical periods of development must certainly play a role, as well as lesion size. In children, for example, it is the large lesions, even if unilateral, that impede regression from aphasia. One might suggest that interaction of two factors—lesion localization in the center of the region responsible for a function and lesion volume sufficiently great to involve neighboring zones (the field within which the function might be reorganized)—could prevent any veritable recuperation. Perhaps also, with maturation, functional representation becomes less highly focalized and less highly lateralized to a single hemisphere.

Other conditions may also be considered. The factor of prior experience may play a more important role than had been previously thought. Indications to this effect are already available (e.g., the role of "handling" in young animals, Johnson et al, 1968). Other variables have been suggested. Hein (1971), for example, on the basis of studies of sensory deprivation and of destruction of visual areas in the kitten, proposed that the conditions necessary for the newborn to acquire visuomotor coordination skills were the same as those necessary for restoration of these skills after destruction of visual cortex.

The nature of the task remains a known variable whose elements have yet to be clarified. Kling and Tucker (1968) suggested that absence of a sparing effect was related to task complexity. Goldman et al (1971), however, refuted this opinion, indicating that the animals studied by Kling and Tucker had been tested at too young an age, at an age at which the tested function had not yet appeared even in the normal animal. Isaacson et al (1968) found certain functions to be compensable, others not, in the newborn cat after hippocampal lesions. They proposed that the compensable functions (compensable by drug administration or by modifications in learning conditions) depend on multiple anatomophysiological systems permitting diverse strategies, while the noncompensable functions were linked to single, definite, and precise anatomophysiological systems.

If this last suggestion is verified by future research, the result will be to invalidate the concept of cerebral plasticity, since this suggestion refers to a readjustment or adaptation to the existence of a deficit by modification of the milieu or conditions of neural functioning, rather than by reorganization, functional replacement, or regeneration. This form of readjustment may be such that performances may be superior in operated than in control animals (Colavita, 1974).

As for mechanisms underlying functional sparing we are still at the level of speculation. Regeneration of tissue may be relevant. Phenomena of regeneration have been demonstrated in the central nervous system, even in adults (Liu and Chambers, 1958; Raisman, 1969a,b; Bernstein and Bernstein, 1971; Moore et al, 1971; Lynch, 1973), and correlations have been drawn between these regenerative phenomena and behavioral functions.

Along the same lines of reasoning are the older observations concerning compensatory hypertrophy of the ipsilateral pyramid in cases of cerebral infantile hemiplegia (Dejerine, 1914). Dejerine had even reported that in such cases, in which medullary decussation of the enlarged remaining pyramid occurred, a small segment of this tract separated itself from the rest and descended as a compact fiber bundle on the homolateral side of the spinal cord. These earlier observations have been more recently reconfirmed (Verhaart, 1950; Scales and Collins, 1972). Related observations were made in rats subjected to hemispherectomy at birth (Hicks and d'Amato, 1970). These animals did not develop defects in rapid locomotion, as adult hemispherectomized rats do, and the authors believed that this functional sparing was due to the existence of an uncrossed corticospinal tract in the younger operated animals. Analogous results have been reported from other laboratories (Leong and Lund, 1973; Castro, 1975a,b).

However, given the fact that neoconnections formed after cerebral lesions are often abnormal, it becomes difficult to imagine how they could be counted on to re-establish function. Schneider has even asked if some regenerative phenomena do not interfere with compensation. Studies by Raisman (1969b) have demonstrated that, after destruction of an anatomic system, synaptic sites are freed and that involvement of these unoccupied synaptic sites by sprouting from another anatomic system does not favor a true functional restoration. Nevertheless studies with evoked potentials have shown that these neoconnections function (Lynch et al, 1972, 1973); one can only speculate about their compensatory nature.

Another possibility for functional recovery in newborn animals with cerebral lesion is that of abnormal embryogenic axonal generation, rather than real regeneration. This, at least, is the suggestion of Sechzer (1974), who studied rats of 140 days of age that had been subjected to surgical section of the medial portion of the corpus callosum 24 hours after birth. In one of the hemispheres he found a group of callosal fibers spreading ventrally toward the superior portion of the septum. In this case the date of maturation of each structure and the date of the onset of the lesion would be of extreme importance. One could envisage a re-establishment of normal connections associated with its appropriate functional sparing, even before morphogenesis begins.

In any event these generations or regenerations are found in axons only. We can understand that neoconnections may develop after section of fiber tracts, but how can one conceive of an anatomic regeneration to explain compensation for destruction of cell bodies themselves? At least to the present time there has been no convincing evidence of regeneration of destroyed cell bodies in the central nervous system. One is forced to conclude that other cells are capable of assuming the function of destroyed cells that in the normal adult would be specifically responsible for a particular behavior.

Chemical factors must also be implicated in recovery of function, especially since they have been shown to be involved with axonal sprouting. The neonatal lesion may provoke chemical changes that themselves affect the process of regeneration. We wonder if denervation hypersensitivity is more prominent or active in the immature animal than in the mature. Research suggests that the answer to this question may be positive. Lynch et al (1972, 1973a,b) found a proliferation of cholinergic fibers in deafferented zones considerably more massive and rapid in the immature rat than in the adult. Electrophysiological evidence has also demonstrated the functional character of these connections (Lynch et al, 1973a,b).

Neural regeneration has, so far, been limited to certain systems, and chemical factors may be regulating this regeneration. In fish and amphibians, for example, Sperry (1950) has postulated that specific chemotactic mechanisms may guide regenerating axons toward their points of termination. More general chemical factors may also be operating, such as nerve growth factor, whose action is now known to be general within the central nervous system.

Is it possible to relate experimental data on cerebral plasticity derived from animal studies to evidence of cerebral plasticity in man? We think that for many reasons (e.g., lack of anatomic precision in human beings) this is a very difficult, if not impossible, task. Nonetheless some studies in humans have provided food for thought. For example, perinatal lesions that are presumably lateralized seem to determine the same types of hemisphere-dependent deficits as in the adult, and yet aphasia acquired in childhood regresses to a much greater degree than it does in adulthood.

Aside from these studies are the systematic neuropsychological analyses of normal and brain-damaged children (e.g., the experiments of Teuber and Rudel, 1962, 1967). In these valuable studies the authors contrasted performances of these different groups of children with performances of adults with focal cerebral lesions. Examples of these contrasting performances are relevant. On the Gottschaldt Hidden Figures Test, failure occurred in adults with cerebral lesions in any location but was particularly frequent in patients with aphasia. On the other hand, failure by children on this test was significantly correlated with severe motor impairment. No significant differences occurred between normal and brain-damaged groups of children on the Aubert Test (correction of a luminous line to the vertical position when the body was tilted), whereas adults with frontal lobe lesions performed poorly. Ability to localize the sources of visual or auditory stimuli was impaired in all brain-damaged groups, adult and child. Normal children made more errors on this test the younger they were, but brain-damaged children made more errors than normal children did. No correlation was found between poor performance and lesion localization or level of intelligence; however, the larger the lesion, the larger the error score. Correction of body position with eyes closed is a test that demonstrated no significant differences of performance between normal and brain-damaged adults but a significant difference between normal and brain-damaged children.

From studies such as these Teuber and Rudel (1967) concluded that three different phenomena could be observed related to brain damage at an early age in human beings: (1) The lesion causes an immediate and definitive functional deficit. (2) The effect of the lesion suffered in childhood does not manifest itself until adulthood. (3) Deficits caused by the lesion and manifested in childhood tend to diminish and even disappear with the passage of time. As for cerebral equipotentiality for perceptual processes the authors believe that this principle applies to certain performances but not to all.

Any review of cerebral plasticity should take into consideration similarities between effects of lesions in the immature brain and effects of serial lesions. In each case functional sparing is found associated with cortical lesions. With subcortical lesions functional sparing (perhaps of a different sort from that found with cortical lesions) has been more frequently reported following serial than following precocious ablations. Task dependency is also seen in both situations. For example, the experiments of Butters et al (1971b, 1973a) with serial lesions revealed the same differences between dorsolateral frontal functions and orbitofrontal functions as the experiments of Goldman et al (1970, 1971) with early lesions did.

Is cerebral plasticity simply a facilitatory phenomenon that occurs in the absence of cerebral maturation or that results from the sequential nature of the lesion? That is, in adults who suffer a single lesion, does the same type of recovery of function take place, but at a slower rate or to a lesser degree? In the immature brain with a single lesion, as in the adult brain with sequential lesions, behavioral reorganization may be more easily established. In the former case, destruction of cerebral tissue may not produce an immediate deficit, because the performance for which that tissue is ordinarily responsible in the adult has not yet entered the behavioral repertoire. In the latter case, remaining cerebral structures may be able to carry on the task, with a different degree of efficiency or another mechanism. Finally one must ask if the initial lesion in the adult brain initiates morphological or chemical changes that assist compensatory regenerative phenomena analagous to similar changes that occur in the immature brain.

LIMITS TO RECOVERY OF FUNCTION

We have seen the great potentialities of cerebral structures for functional recovery, especially from effects of lesions in the immature brain. We have also emphasized the capacities of the adult nervous system to adapt itself to modifications of input stimuli. However great the possibilities for restoration or rearrangement, we must also stress the limits to recovery imposed by an already existing cerebral organization. This organization is established, it would seem, at least in its general lines before any external influence, but the potentialities are not realized until adequate stimuli have been furnished.

Observations made in neonates demonstrate their perceptual and motor skills, and even coordination sufficient to allow imitation. It is almost as if subsequent experience encourages a refinement of innate skills and an adaptation to environment, rather than fostering the acquisition of new skills. These neonatal capacities seem to recede during a period of growth and development, only to reappear later in behavioral patterns considerably removed from their original forms.

The experiments of Hubel and Wiesel (1963) on properties of visual cortical cells of the newborn kitten seemed to be almost completely contradicted by results of others (Hirsh and Spinnelli, 1971; Blakemore and Cooper, 1970; Barlow and Pettigrew, 1971) demonstrating the significant influence of experience on the properties of these cells. These later authors have modified their opinions, however, returning somewhat to the earlier conclusions of Hubel and Wiesel (e.g., Blakemore, 1974; Pettigrew, 1974a,b. See especially the review by Stryker and Sherk, 1975). Current study reaffirms the suggestion of Hubel and Wiesel (1968, 1974a,b) that task-specific cells exist from birth or that certain groups of cells exist that can develop only certain functional relationships, given appropriate stimulation, during maturation. Nevertheless development under the influence of environment bears witness to the great plasticity of connections. Each of these conditions is as necessary as is each, alone, insufficient. The influence of experience on the developing visual system, for example, can manifest itself only according to the initial dispositions of the system. The establishment of the normal adult visual system is based on innate dispositions, the influence of maturation, and adequate environmental stimuli received at an appropriate period, which may be of brief duration depending on the visual task in question.

Ethologists have shown that specific stimulations release innate liberator mechanisms. This is followed by a special type of learning, called imprinting. Imprinting occurs only during a specified developmental period, often of brief duration, and in a highly defined context. This form of learning remains quite stable throughout life, and its characteristics are species specific. Imprinting is a process that leads to "instinctual" recognition and reaction mechanisms, which may be complemented and adjusted by experience (Thorpe, 1950). This special type of learning has been correlated with particular biochemical changes (Horn, Rose, and Bateson, 1973a,b).

Clearly the hypothesis of innate mechanisms underlying language, so popular in the 1960s, is no longer maintained in its absolute form. Nonetheless, it is of interest to point out the studies that show that newborn infants perceive sounds of language the same way as adults do (Eimas et al, 1970) or that anatomic asymmetry of the planum temporale in right and left hemispheres exists in the fetus and newborn child (Teszner et al, 1972; Wittelson and Pallis, 1973; Wada et al, 1975). It would seem, thus, that human beings have available to them at birth an ensemble of innate dispositions necessary for ensuring the appearance of language, if verbal stimuli are presented at the appropriate period of development; these stimuli release latent mechanisms that permit or facilitate learning.

This learning necessarily depends on capacities for recognition, and here, again, the interaction of innate mechanisms and experiential factors may be supposed. In the recognition of forms we might suggest that innate mechanisms exist that permit detection of invariant elements from an infinite collection of forms and thereby provide a classification scheme for objects in the external world, regardless of transformations they might undergo. In addition, during various learning periods the individual creates an alphabet for himself on the basis of which he may identify objects to which he has previously been exposed or, for that matter, that he may presuppose.

TEN
CONCLUSIONS

In the field of human neuropsychology there are still too many outstanding questions to permit real conclusions. Nonetheless, it is possible to attempt a synthesis of available data on selected aspects of cerebral functioning. The problems we touch on here have all been discussed to a greater or lesser degree in earlier chapters. There, however, stress was laid on special characteristics related to each specific functional defect. In this chapter, in a schematic manner, we systematize general aspects of neuropsychology and thereby, it is hoped, expose and clarify major underlying issues.

CEREBRAL LOCALIZATION OF FUNCTION

In the introduction to this volume we noted how conceptions of cerebral localization evolved. After Broca (1861) and Fritsch and Hitzig (1870) laid the foundations of the doctrine, anatomically and physiologically oriented clinicians multiplied centers and connecting pathways almost beyond counting. Reaction, ushered in by Marie (1906), triumphed during the period between the two world wars, principally owing to the efforts of Goldstein (1919, 1936, 1939) and Lashley (1937). The global view of the Gestalt theorists was, in its turn, countered by reaction. Development of new examining techniques and new research methodologies confirmed localizationist theories, if not from an atomistic, at least from a regional topographical point of view. Even associationist theories, popular in the late nineteenth century, have been revitalized by contemporary split-brain studies.

Modern research goals have not, however, been simply to confirm neuropsychological theories of a previous century, nor even to refine these earlier observations with greater precision. The notion of cerebral localization of

402

function has acquired additional dimensions in direct proportion to the increased knowledge of basic neurophysiological principles, to the extent that phenomena of cerebral plasticity and recovery are considered, and to the extent that performance factors are added to the total equation.

Rare cases with unusual neuropsychological features and with anatomic verification of lesion site are no longer the end point of analysis; nor do they form the basis for acceptance or rejection of cerebral localization. Large numbers of normal and brain-damaged subjects are tested systematically. Statistical analyses of results allow a certain degree of confidence to the modern critic of earlier clinical intuitions. The principle of double dissociation (Teuber, 1961) offers a partial, but essential, guarantee of validity to these statistical analyses, necessary because with large numbers of subjects formal anatomic verification of lesion sites is often lacking.

Single-cell recording techniques have demonstrated the extent to which cerebral localization may be precise, and the extreme degree to which single sensory cells may be specialized in response to specific stimulus characteristics. The mosaic organization of efferent zones in the depths of the cortex also bears witness to a similar localizationist rigor. For example, using intracortical microstimulation techniques, Rosen and Asanuma (1972) have demonstrated the existence of precise cortical points with very low thresholds, grouped in zones with a columnar organization, each responding directly, selectively, and differentially to a movement of each of the finger joints. These authors also refer to a precise and systematic relationship between peripheral input and efferent effect in the columns. An equally rigorous motor localization pattern of anatomobehavioral relations has been provided by Kuypers and Lawrence (1968), who found that any lesion of the corticospinal tract causes an irreversible loss of isolated fine finger movements.

Despite these examples of precise and highly differentiated localizations, results of other studies suggest that cerebral localization of function is an extremely complex phenomenon. Thus Philips (1960–1967), for example, has shown that the control of muscles by the CNS is achieved by means of motor units of organization and that, at the neural level, efferent inputs converge on corticospinal cells, exercising either an excitatory or an inhibitory control. At the periphery of the motor unit, intramuscular afferent receptors have been found, a finding suggesting a certain degree of involuntary control of movement by reflex feedback mechanisms, and at the cortical level polysensory convergence affects 92% of neurons in the motor area (of the cat, Buser and Imbert, 1972). Motor cells of the pyramidal system seem to exist with at least three different functional correlations: (1) pyramidal cells with focal and permanent fields, acting specifically to move segments of the contralateral limb and reacting to particular types of stimulation; (2) others with permanent but widespread fields, reacting to bilateral, often nonspecific, stimulation; and (3) and a third group of pyramidal cells with labile fields (Brooks, Rudomin, and Slayman, 1961). Current research suggests that corticofugal neurons constitute the common pathway leading from the cortex; at the cell bodies of these neurons, numerous differentiated peripheral inputs are integrated. The neurons form an interconnected system of cortical reflexes that become the starting point for any movement, while further development and elaboration of the movement is controlled by the arrival of feedback afferents.

Cortical representation of motor function can no longer be considered to reside exclusively in the precentral gyrus (area 4). It is more in keeping with research data to speak of sensorimotor zones with varying degrees of motor or sensory predominance. The precentral region and supplementary motor cortex are sensorimotor zones with motor predominance; the postcentral region and secondary sensory cortex have sensory predominance. In each of these different areas, bodily representation is different.

With respect to the sensory system we also know, for example, that single cells that react specifically to certain visual stimuli may also respond nonspecifically to other sensory stimuli and that this nonspecific effect can modify the ability of these cells to respond to the specific visual stimulus (Morell, 1967).

Thus, at the same time that contemporary research has demonstrated an extreme degree of cortical cellular localizationism with particular precision, the variety and number of integrations that take place at the surface of individual sensory or motor cells, and the multiplicity of cortical regions in which these motor or sensory cells are found, force a total reconsideration of the principle of cerebral localization of function. Classic conceptions are now untenable.

In our opinion these complex interrelations among cortical neurons do not negate the concept of functional localization. They simply indicate that cerebral regions do not function in isolation. Each cerebral zone may contain diverse functional potentialities while remaining primarily responsible for certain specific behavioral skills. Destruction of one cerebral zone would not necessarily bring about a change in ability to perform these other skills, which, although related to this damaged zone, are not dependent on it. If one cerebral region normally receives inputs necessary to carry out its functions from another cerebral region, and if the first region is deprived of these inputs for whatever reason, it may continue to function. In this case the level of functioning of the undamaged region may be inferior to its normal level (but our gross neuropsychological tests may be incapable of registering the change in performance), or the undamaged region may make more than normal use of inputs coming from other undamaged regions with which it had always been in contact.

Another major factor for consideration is that of lesion size. Large cerebral lesions have a nonspecific effect manifested by general lowering of efficiency. This mass effect, although overemphasized by Lashley and rejected by many subsequent workers, is being reconsidered. For example, in animals with complete callosal and optic chiasm section, learning a visual discrimination task with one eye closed (the inputs being thereby limited to one hemisphere) is much less rapid than in normal animals, who retain the possibility of interhemispheric transfer (Sechzer, 1973). Those learning defects that result from the dysfunction of a large mass of cerebral tissue seem to be especially prominent when complex cognitive tasks are involved, rather than simple sensory discriminations (Robinson and Voneida, 1973).

Studies of hemidecortication in the rat suggest that the defect of instrumental learning that results is not due to a qualitative modification of learning processes but reflects a quantitative deviation from normal learning (Plotkin and Russell, 1969a,b). The deficit seems to derive from a reduction of the normal redundancy of cortical neurons in information processing. If input redundancy is increased by modification of the duration and temporal structure of the conditional stimulus, the deficit may be compensated for.

Nonspecific effects of cerebral lesions have also been found in human beings. For instance, even though subjects with lesions in one particular cerebral locus may perform more poorly than subjects with lesions in other loci on a given behavioral task, the subjects in the latter groups are often found to perform more poorly than nonbrain-damaged controls. Hécaen (1972b) reviewed 10 studies of cerebral localization of function in brain-damaged subjects and found the following: although deficits of function were significantly correlated with one hemisphere (depending on the behavioral task in question), scores obtained by the group of subjects with lesions in the other hemisphere were significantly inferior to those of controls in six of the studies and were clearly, but not significantly, inferior in three other studies.

In addition to the nonspecific mass effect of a lesion in any part of the brain, one must also take into account the mass effect of a lesion in a specific region whose function has already been established. This aspect of the phenomenon of cerebral localization may be better understood by reference to the notion of "center" and "field" elaborated by Mishkin (1966), Gross et al (1967), and Moffet et al (1967) in studies of delayed alternation and auditory or tactile discrimination. A limited cerebral zone is essential for execution of a task; destruction of this zone produces a severe deficit in task performance. Destruction of cerebral tissue in the neighborhood of the focal zone responsible for the task may also provoke deficits in the same performance, but these defects are milder. When a large lesion envelops both the central zone and its surrounding field, the deficit is maximal.

We believe that this gradient model of functional fields, each containing a critical central zone, may apply to human beings as well as other animals.

With such a model one could explain varying clinicopathological phenomena: the mass effect of lesions involving a given field, the real compensation that follows cerebral destruction not touching the critical zone, and the relative severity of defects produced by small lesions located in the critical center. Thus, whenever an individual is afflicted by a cerebral lesion, evaluation of his defect must take into consideration the focal effect, the field effect, and the mass effect. These several factors interact with each other and with the factor of cerebral dominance, whereby the influence of the lesion might be manifested predominantly for a particular type of stimulus material or a particular means of stimulus processing.

Luria (1966), following the line established by Vygotsky, has also proposed a conception of localization of function. Behavioral tasks are the responsibility of functional systems that achieve their goals by means of a complex organization incorporating the activity of different cerebral zones. Each zone contributes a specific portion of the overall performance. If àny one of the regions contributing to the total behavioral performance is destroyed, that performance is impaired, but the nature of the impairment varies, according to which of the participating regions has been damaged.

The associationist model of cerebral function, as elaborated by Wernicke (1874), has been rejuvenated in the past decade by the anatomoclinical studies of Geschwind (1965) and the experimental studies of Sperry (1966, 1967), Myers (1961), and Gazzaniga (1970) on human beings and animals with complete or partial section of forebrain commissures. According to this model, behavioral defects are interpreted not only in relation to lesions in cerebral centers but also in relation to lesions that interrupt pathways connecting the centers to each other. Because of damage to these pathways, information that normally passes from one cerebral region to another for appropriate transformations and integrations cannot be transmitted properly.

Despite popular opinion to the contrary Lashley (1937) provided and defended one of the localizationist arguments. At this stage in his career he argued, not so much against the principle of cerebral localization, as against mentalist interpretations of this principle. These interpretations, which suggested that particular cortical centers were the seat of specific psychological functions, were based exclusively on logical analyses of behavioral traits. Basing his conclusions on experimental observations, Lashley noted that behaviorally similar functional defects could result from focal lesions in different parts of the brain, whereas behaviorally different functional defects could result from lesions within a single cortical field.

Thus he embarked on a program designed to define isolated physiological mechanisms corresponding not to behavioral effects but to neural processes associated with diverse integrative activities. He succeeded in distinguishing mechanisms regulating response intensity from those regulating spatial processing. He also proposed the existence of a time-related mechanism that regulated serial order in behavior. He provided a final synthesis of his many research investigations, concluding that there is enough evidence "to indicate that the spatial distribution of excitations in a nervous center can form the basis of several types of integration, such as the regulation of intensity of the discharge, establishment of fields of force determining spatial orientation, and the control of serial timing of activity. Each of these functions implies a different mechanism of organization and, consequently, a spatial separation of fields in which the different processes operate. Clinical and experimental data indicate that the dissociation of functions resulting from cerebral lesions is in harmony with the assumption that cerebral localization is determined by the separation of these incompatible mechanisms" (Lashley, 1937).

From this model proposed by Lashley at least two basic neuropsychological principles emerge. First, beneath the constellation of behavioral disorders resulting from a single focal cerebral lesion, one may seek a deficit of a single neural mechanism that underlies the various functional defects. Second, although one may believe that he is dealing with a single behavioral defect with a single underlying cause, it may be possible to fractionate the abnormal performance into separate elements, each of which is related to a different lesion site.

From our point of view, we would agree with those who reject the notion that the brain is a mosaic of clearly delimited centers, each of which is responsible for a precise psychological function. We would envisage, rather, a system comprising relatively large cerebral regions, each possessing diverse potentialities that, in the normally functioning brain, are combined to provide the basis for a given behavioral skill.

However, studies in animal neuropsychology have provided evidence of cerebral zones, extremely limited in extent, whose bilateral destruction causes a highly specific functional deficit. Thus, for example, with respect to defective delayed alternation, when the frontal lobe lesions are ventrolateral, the defect is limited to spatial aspects of the task; when the lesions are orbital, the defect is global (Mishkin et al, 1969). Initial studies with delayed response in monkeys reported the defect as being due to destruction of the entire prefrontal region; subsequently the defect was produced by lesions of the sulcus principalis; finally, the defect has been shown to result from limited lesions localized to the middle third of the sulcus principalis.

In addition to these anatomobehavioral correlational studies, as we have previously discussed, neurophysiological studies have also demonstrated highly specific correlations between electrocerebral activity and execution of a behavioral task. We have, for example, already cited results of Hyvarinen and Poranen (1974) and Mountcastle et al (1975) on the extreme specificity of cellular response from posterior parietal (associative) cortex in the monkey and its relationship to motor and sensory functions of the opposite side of the body. Cells in this region respond when a sensory stimulus of interest to the animal, situated in a given vicinity of space around the animal, falls within the animal's limits of reach, either for manual manipulation or for ocular pursuit. Some of these cells respond only when there is a convergence of tactile and visual stimuli, for example if the animal's gaze turns to the cutaneous receptive field. Others react only if the stimulus is novel. The authors underline the relationship between these neurophysiological observations in animals and the clinical observations of spatial disorientation in human beings with posterior parietal lesions.

Anatomic and physiological studies have provided evidence in favor of the notion of cerebral localization. Neurochemical evidence is now beginning to accumulate as well. For example, the functional correlates of neural pathways rich in excitatory and inhibitory neurotransmitters, such as catecholamines or gamma aminobutyric acid, are being elucidated.

Thus we find a discordance between two main lines of neuropsychological data—human and animal. Evidence from animal studies indicates a more highly focalized, mosaic-like pattern of cerebral localization. Must we conclude from this discordance that the study of abnormal behavior in brain-damaged human beings has not yet been sufficiently thorough to demonstrate fundamental defects hidden beneath the performance disorders that we observe? Do these observed performance disorders result from the interaction of several different basic defects caused by a lesion of sufficient size to interfere with the normal activity of several critical zones, several centers?

We would suggest that there is a danger in relying too heavily on results obtained from animal studies, even from primates, for theories of human neuropsychology. Human cerebral organization is characterized above all by functional (and perhaps morphological) hemispheric asymmetry. It may be that in nonhuman animals the principle of functional bilaterality (as opposed to functional hemispheric asymmetry) may be associated with an extreme focalization of function in each hemisphere. By contrast, in human beings the focalization may be less precise, each hemisphere being responsible instead for a specific functional activity. Perhaps also, the principles of localization within each hemisphere and of interhemispheric interaction are different according to the type of function considered. In the final section of this book, we analyze this problem in greater detail.

CEREBRAL DOMINANCE

Cerebral dominance or, better, functional hemispheric asymmetry is the hallmark of the human brain. In earlier chapters we observed how this concept developed, following Broca's affirmation that the left hemisphere was responsible for the function of spoken language. Primarily owing to neuropsychological studies of practic and gnostic function conducted after the Second World War, the notion of left hemispheric dominance little by little gave way to one of asymmetric organization and control of functions between the two hemispheres. Demonstration of impairment of behavioral capacities following right hemispheric lesions, especially for somatognosis, spatial orientation, and constructional abilities impelled reconsideration of the role of the right hemisphere. No longer could the right side of the brain be considered "mute," "minor," "passive," or "subordinate." Further study firmly established the relevance of the right hemisphere, not only for spatial activities but also for recognition, recall, and learning of certain types of stimulus material and in certain aspects of perceptual processing.

We could schematically summarize the major, known functional roles of each hemisphere as follows. Left hemispheric lesions produce various types of aphasia; ideational, ideomotor, and constructional apraxias; bilateral asomatognosias; and visual agnosias for objects and colors. With respect to some of these defects, as we have already noted, disorders of language may underlie apparent agnosias or apraxias. Those agnosias and apraxias resulting from left hemispheric lesions but not due to language defect per se may be manifestations of impairments in other functional systems of communication or reception (e.g., gestural codes, associative functions, specific forms of recognition, etc.). Extensive and varied studies in normal and brain-damaged subjects have amply confirmed the preeminence of left hemispheric mechanisms for processing verbal material, regardless of the input channel used and regardless of the linguistic level of presentation.

Essentially the left hemisphere contains the neural substrate necessary for language; systems necessary for nonverbal forms of communication, such as gestures; and systems for perception of sensory stimuli that can be verbally labeled without difficulty. We should also note that, when subjects with lesions of either hemisphere are compared on tests of "abstraction," those with left hemispheric lesions perform significantly more poorly. Deficits on such tests are not necessarily linked to the language defects.

By contrast the syndromes caused by right hemispheric lesions are characterized by disorders of spatial orientation (manifested in several areas: constructions, drawings, written language, written calculations, spatial memory, topographical notions); by hemifield inattention to extracorporeal space (unilateral spatial agnosia) and to the body (hemiasomatognosia); by a particular form of visual agnosia, agnosia for faces (prosopagnosia); and by deficits in perception or recall of nonverbal material and material containing a complex perceptual structure. With the exception of the last group of deficits cited, the other disorders associated with right hemispheric lesions seem to have in common a polysensory nature and to be concerned principally with

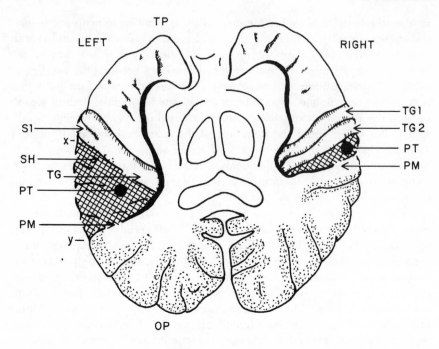

Asymmetry of human planum temporale. Upper surfaces of human temporal lobes exposed. Note larger planum temporale (PT) on left. TP = temporal pole. OP = occipital
pole. x and y = ends of Sylvian fissure. SI = sulcus intermedius. SH = Heschl's sulcus. PM
= posterior margin of planum temporale. TG = transverse gyrus. In this brain there is a
single transverse gyrus on the left and two on the right. Copyright 1968 by American
Association for the Advancement of Science, Washington, D.C. Reproduced by permission.

half of space or of the body. According to some authors (e.g., Milner), the
deficits seem to involve material for which a verbal label can only be attached with difficulty. These disorders become manifest regardless of the nature of the task (learning, retention, identification) and regardless of the
sensory modality used for stimulus presentation.

The following statement summarizes and serves as an initial approxima-
tion of the preceding observations: the left hemisphere is responsible essentially for verbal functions and abstracting ability; the right hemisphere, for
nonverbal, perceptual, and spatial functions.

Functional hemispheric asymmetry was thus supported by evidence from
anatomoclinical studies, systematic human neuropsychology, and experimental psychology. However, basic anatomic and electrophysiological evidence
for interhemispheric differences had been lacking until modern times. As
recently as 1962 von Bonin concluded a review of anatomic evidence concerning hemispheric differences by asserting that such evidence was minimal

at best. However, in 1968 Geschwind and Levitsky, basing their approach on previous observations by Flechsig (1901), von Economo (1925), and von Economo and Horn (1930), studied 100 adult brains and demonstrated that the surface of the planum temporale was significantly greater on the left than on the right. This structural asymmetry was confirmed in other laboratories (Teszner et al, 1972; Witelson and Pallis, 1973; Wada et al, 1975). Wada et al (1974) also found structural differences between the hemispheres for Broca's area, but the evidence is less certain for this area than for the planum temporale.

As for electrophysiological evidence, although the method of evoked potentials is subject to many technical difficulties, nonetheless it seems reasonable to accept that over each hemisphere during periods of information processing, physical events are recorded that differ, depending on whether the information being processed is verbal or nonverbal (Wood, Goff, and Day, 1971; Morrell and Salamy, 1971). In addition, click stimuli evoke greater potentials over right temporal derivations than over left, whereas, conversely, auditory verbal stimuli evoke greater responses over left temporal derivations, than over right (Cohn, 1971).

A question arises about the nature of this hemispheric specialization and about the possibility that the two hemispheres function in complementary fashion. For some authors such as Milner (1968) the functional difference between the hemispheres relates to the material being treated, verbal or nonverbal, whatever the modality of presentation and whatever the task required (learning, memory, recognition). We have already cited the work of Corsi (1972) showing hemispheric differences for verbal versus nonverbal material on short-term memory tests following hippocampal lesions. On another task, maze learning according to appropriate rules, deficits from frontal lesions occur only when the lesions are in the right hemisphere (Milner, 1965). Similar results were found with a test of ability to appreciate the recency of presentation of an item: deficits appeared following lesions in the left frontal lobe only if the series of items was verbal; with right frontal lesions, deficits occurred only if the series of items was nonverbal (Milner, 1971).

Another point of view on the nature of interhemispheric differences is that they reside in the mode of treatment exercised by each hemisphere on information. Hécaen and Angelergues, in a 1963 study of visual agnosia, advanced the hypothesis that deficits resulting from right hemispheric lesions were due to defects in the ability to isolate similar objects from each other in a given category, while deficits resulting from left hemispheric lesions were due to defective ability to categorize. DeRenzi et al (1969) attributed a role of discrimination and organization of sensory data to the right hemisphere, and to the left hemisphere the role of naming and associating the data to permit appreciation of significance.

Split-brain studies provided a new opportunity to study behavioral characteristics and underlying mechanisms of each hemisphere. For Nebes (1971) the right hemisphere is charged with the responsibility for organizing information in its total, Gestalt form. From this it follows that the right hemisphere should be superior on all tasks requiring conceptualization of the whole of a stimulus configuration, when presented with poorly verbalizable, fragmentary information. He reported results of two experiments that showed the right hemisphere to be better than the left on tasks involving association of a part to its whole, regardless of the modality of presentation or the intermodal or intramodal nature of the task.

In other split-brain studies Levy, Treverthen, and Sperry (1972) compared the capacity of the two hemispheres to perceive and respond. Their experiments used the tendency of each hemisphere to effect perceptual completion of patterns across the midline. Stimuli consisted of chimeric figures, created by union of the right half of one figure and the left half of another, presented tachistoscopically. Human faces, familiar objects, serially connected patterns composed of crosses and squares, and nonverbalizable, branchlike patterns were employed. Because each hemisphere completed the half-image that it saw, a situation of conflict between the hemispheres was created. Responses were either by naming, in the absence of pictures, or by pointing to a complete picture, either with the left hand or with the right. The right hemisphere was superior for all tasks requiring a manual pointing response; the left hemisphere was superior when a verbal response was required.

These results may be interpreted as demonstrating a right hemispheric predominance for the primitive perceptual capacity of apprehension of form; the left hemisphere may be poorly organized for such a function. When a verbal response is required, the left hemisphere becomes dominant, and information is processed differently, in a more analytic fashion associated with a search for distinctive characteristics that may be verbally tagged. For these authors we are not dealing with a simple predominance in competition between the two hemispheres but with a fundamental difference in their methods of processing information.

From additional studies using the same technique, Levy (1974) observed that, in the presence of such chimeric figures, when a conceptual categorization had to be accomplished to achieve a match, it was always the left hemisphere that made this categorization. (Under special conditions the right hemisphere, which spontaneously tried to make visual categorizations by matching according to shape, also succeeded in making conceptual categorizations.) Trevarthen (1974), on the basis of these and other split-brain studies, defined the role of the left hemisphere as follows: "Any requirement to say what the object was, to think in words without speaking, or to reason about the meaning of the object in a context of objects of different appearance causes the left hemisphere to assume command of response. . . ."

Thus we see that the hemispheres are able to process information in differ-

ent ways according to the demands of the situation. An individual, by varying his strategies, may call into service one or the other hemisphere to produce results that appear similar but that are obtained by different mechanisms. Previous experience may encourage him to use one strategy over
another, emphasizing activity of one hemisphere at the expense of the other.
We have already cited experiments of dichotic listening that support this
point; treatment of material presented (melodies, Morse Code) may depend
more on one or the other hemisphere according to the previous experience of
the subject with the material (Papçun et al, 1974; Bever and Chiarello,
1975).

We can perhaps better understand the normal complementary action of
the two hemispheres by analyzing the patterns of competition found in split-
brain subjects. The corpus callosum plays a principal role in this complementary action, permitting coordination, if not unification, of information treated
differently in each hemisphere. Parellel processing of information may be
carried out in each hemisphere for certain performances; one hemisphere
may initiate processing activity, while a different and slower processing may
occur in the other hemisphere to guarantee maintenance of the performance
(Dimond and Beaumont, 1974). According to Kinsbourne (1974), the hemispheres collaborate in control of attention in two ways: they control its disposition in space by establishing an appropriate balance between opponent
directions, and they guide its focus by establishing preattentive structuring of
the field and attentive focusing within it in an appropriate temporal sequence.

A recent dichotic listening study by Calderon (1976) elegantly demonstrated the existence of parallel processing. Conflicting dichotic stimuli of
verbal material in one ear and musical stimuli in the other ear were presented to normal subjects. Under conditions of simultaneous verbal and tonal
processing, she found a right-ear advantage for words and a left-ear advantage for tonal patterns. She concluded that the two hemispheres may independently process the components of complex stimuli, selecting that component for which each is dominant.

Kinsbourne's (1973) "attentional" hypothesis of cerebral dominance may
also be relevant. According to this hypothesis one hemisphere becomes active
and the other inhibited (as determined by the direction of gaze) depending
on the task to be accomplished. Orienting behavior toward one side of space
is linked to hemispheric lateralization of the mental activity to be carried out.
With silent verbal mental activity the eyes turn to the right; with silent
spatial mental activity the eyes turn to the left.

This hypothesis is at least partially supported by contemporary research.
Morais and Bertelson (1973) and Morais (1974, 1975) found that, in dichotic
listening experiments, when the subject is deliberately deceived with respect
to the spatial origin of stimuli and when, because of this, he directs his atten-

tion toward the presumed source, lateral perceptual asymmetry may be eliminated. In a study with native-born Israelis and Arabs, who read from right to left, and European-born or American-born Israeli immigrants, who read from left to right, Albert (1975) found significant impairment in the native-born Israeli and Arab groups on a task demanding a spatial response to a verbal command. Basing his interpretation on Kinsbourne's "attentional" hypothesis of cerebral dominance, he argued that lifelong reading habits may facilitate or impede interhemispheric integration for combined verbal-spatial tasks, depending on the characteristics of reading habits.

At this point we are justified in asking a question that probes more deeply into the structural basis of functional hemispheric asymmetry: what is the relationship of cerebral localization to cerebral dominance—or more specifically: are the special capacities of each cerebral hemisphere products of each hemisphere in its entirety, or do they depend on certain zones, more or less well defined within each hemisphere?

Anatomical studies have found the left planum temporale to be larger than the right; no comparable anatomic enlargement that might explain functional superiority has yet been found in the right hemisphere. By contrast a certain amount of evidence has emerged to support the notion of a different type of distribution of functional zones within each hemisphere. According to this notion the left hemisphere would have greater focalization of functional regions and would be responsible for bilateral representation of the body; the right hemisphere would have a more diffuse, less highly focalized distribution of functional regions and would be responsible for unilateral (contralateral) representation of the body (Semmes et al, 1960, Hécaen and Angelergues, 1963; Semmes, 1965). If one may, as it now seems, speak of certain anatomic zones within each hemisphere as being primarily responsible for specific functions, one must also take cognizance of the participation of neighboring anatomic regions in the same functions, although this participation is to a lesser degree. These anatomofunctional arrangements suggest the existence of an intrahemispheric functional gradient.

Results of subcortical stimulation studies seem to indicate that functional specialization, observed and confirmed at the cortical level, may also exist at the subcortical level (Ojeman et al, 1968, 1971). Thus one may postulate that, in addition to a horizontal intrahemispheric functional representation, there is a vertical, corticosubcortical representation. Cortical neural mechanisms of one hemisphere would be responsible for a particular performance, and subcortical structures connected to these cortical zones would participate in the realization of the performance, creating a complex, corticosubcortical functional system specific to each hemisphere. Such functional systems have already been demonstrated in nonhuman primates between sulcus principalis and anterodorsal portions of the caudate nucleus (Divac et al, 1967); between orbitofrontal regions and ventrolateral portions of the caudate nucleus (Butters and Rosvold, 1962); and between inferotemporal cortex and the tail of the caudate nucleus (Divac et al, 1967).

In addition one cannot exclude the possibility that the so-called minor hemisphere may intervene to maintain a performance when the major hemisphere becomes unable to exercise this function, or the minor hemisphere may be able to carry out certain features of the function.

Whatever hypothesis one accepts to explain functional hemispheric asymmetries (hemispheric specialization vis-à-vis material presented, or different modes of treating information), it is clear that this hemispheric asymmetry of neural mechanisms is not seen with all forms of cognitive activity. Several different types of interhemispheric interaction may be found, according to the functions under consideration. Basing our own suggestions on a systematization proposed by Piercy (1964) and taking into account more recent data, we wish to propose an outline of the different types of interhemispheric functioning.

1   Symmetrical regions in each hemisphere may have the same function, but in relation to the opposite half of the body. This type of hemispheric functioning is seen with elementary motor and sensory functions. However, even with these elementary functions, this principle is not absolute.

2   Each of the symmetrical cerebral regions may possess identical functions. Not too many years ago, this was the role ascribed to the two frontal lobes. Now, however, as we have seen, at least some defects of frontal lobe function must be considered in terms of hemispheric lateralization of frontal lesions (Corsi, 1972; Milner, 1965). Nevertheless, there are some indications supporting the existence of symmetrical deficits from frontal lesions. For example, defective verbal fluency, even though maximal with left frontal lesions, is also present with right frontal lesions (Ramier and Hécaen, 1970; Perret, 1974). Similar results were found with a test of verbal recency (Milner, 1971).

3   A simple duplication of function, as seen in animal neuropsychology with equipotentiality of symmetrical regions, is seen only in certain conditions in man. These conditions are manifested behaviorally as anterograde amnesias, as in the Korsakoff syndrome, and result in almost all cases from bilateral hippocampal lesions. Even in such conditions, however, we have noted that unilateral hippocampal lesions may cause material-specific learning disabilities depending on lateralization of lesion.

4   Hemispheric interaction may be hierarchical. One hemisphere is dominant, and a lesion of this hemisphere determines functional disability. A lesion in a symmetrical region in the other hemisphere causes either no deficit or a very insignificant one in this particular functional sphere. This is the

functional relation generally accepted for language. We should add that bilateral apraxias, ideomotor or ideational, are also determined primarily by left hemispheric lesions.

5 A type of functional asymmetry that can be divided into three subtypes, may exist for a certain number of behavioral performances.

a A qualitative difference may be found between deficits according to the hemisphere damaged. For example, with right hemispheric lesions one finds unilateral spatial agnosia, defects in picture interpretation, and defects in auditory discrimination of nonverbal material, while with left hemispheric lesions, evocation and learning of verbal material are disturbed.

b Differences in task performance may be only quantitative. Perhaps, as some authors maintain, this is the case for certain visuoconstructive defects, in which lesions in either hemisphere produce similar defects qualitatively, differences being manifested only in frequency and intensity.

c The deficit may concern the same function in each hemisphere, but with a different topographical disposition. For example, following right hemispheric lesions, somatognosic defects involve the contralateral half of the body; following left hemispheric lesions, knowledge of one's body is disturbed bilaterally. It has also been observed that elementary tactile, auditory, or visual defects may affect both sides of the body following left hemispheric lesions, but such defects are contralateral when lesions are in the right hemisphere.

Founding his model on the formulation described above, Hécaen (1971, 1972) proposed a systematization of interhemispheric activity based on two functional categories: instrumental and fundamental. Instrumental functions are defined as serving as tools for human beings to understand the external world, to communicate with each other, and to perform voluntary actions. Only the instrumental functions involve hemispheric asymmetries. Fundamental functions are represented bilaterally and symmetrically. Performance of fundamental functions is independent of both instrumental activity and sensory modalities; however, performance of instrumental functions is dependent on fundamental function.

On reconsideration of the above formulation, and taking into account more recent data, we believe that this model should be slightly modified. Certain symmetrical regions of the two hemispheres may have similar (instrumental) functions, although to different degrees. When one of these regions is damaged, the behavioral skill impaired as a result of the damage may be carried out to a limited extent by action of the symmetrical region in the other hemisphere, even if the behavioral skill falls within the specific domain of the damaged hemisphere.

A final problem we wish to consider in this section is that of the origin of hemispheric specialization. How is one to deal with the question of ontogeny of cerebral dominance? Is hemispheric asymmetry present from the moment the human brain is formed, or is it acquired during the process of maturation? Three types of evidence are available to help answer these questions: studies of acquired aphasias in childhood, psychometric studies in subjects who had received neonatal cerebral lesions, and anatomic studies of hemispheric asymmetries in the fetus and neonate.

As we have previously discussed, research on acquired aphasia in childhood favors the existence of a certain degree of interhemispheric equipotentiality for language representation during the period of cerebral maturation. The critical period during which transfer may be possible lasts, according to Lenneberg (1967), until about the time of puberty. Other studies, however, would suggest that the terminal date for language transfer equipotentiality is considerably younger (Hécaen, 1975).

By contrast the two other types of evidence strongly support the notion that hemispheric specialization is established at an extremely young age and may even be innate. Psychological studies in subjects who had received unilateral hemispheric lesions in the neonatal or perinatal period reveal hemisphere-specific deficits that are similar to those found in adults with unilateral brain damage. That is, one finds defective verbal skills following left hemispheric lesions, and defective nonverbal skills (especially on spatial tasks) following right hemispheric lesions (McFie, 1961; Fedio and Mirsky, 1965; Woods and Teuber, 1973; Rudel et al, 1974).

The remaining argument is drawn from examination of fetal and neonatal brains (Tezner et al, 1972; Wittleson and Pallis, 1973; Wada et al, 1975). These studies reported findings similar to those in adult brains (Geschwind and Levitsky, 1968); that is, there is an asymmetry between the right and left planum temporale, the posterior language area, in favor of the left. Wada et al (1974) point out, however, that the differences are less marked in the fetus or neonate than in the adult. Thus, it seems that anatomic hemispheric asymmetries in the language region exist in the fetus and become more marked with maturity.

The discordant results described here—equipotentiality versus early specialization—may be somewhat attenuated by observations of recent studies. Among the factors affecting displacement of language representation from one hemisphere to the other, in addition to age, is lesion site. Milner (1974), by means of the Wada test, found that, despite large lesions occurring at an early age, language was still represented in the left hemisphere if the temporoparietal region was not damaged. By contrast, in the event of a lesion, even a small one, in the temporoparietal region, language representation was transferred to the right hemisphere. Reorganization may thus take place within a single hemisphere; in this case differences in maturation of various areas within the zone of language may play a role. In addition, language displacement to the right hemisphere may, in some cases, be partial (Nebes and Sperry, 1971). Finally we wish to make allusion to the unusual case of a child deprived of all verbal communication from 20 months to 13 years of age (Fromkin et al, 1974). Despite the return to a normal life, this child has acquired only a limited amount of language. Dichotic listening studies showed that only the right hemisphere was treating material, verbal or non-verbal. The problem of a critical period of maturation affecting transfer of language representation from one hemisphere to the other may now be posed in a different manner: perhaps without adequate stimulation during maturation, a preformed cerebral zone may not be able to acquire its functional capacities.

Is functional hemispheric asymmetry specific to human beings, or can precursors of this phenomenon be found in lower levels of the phylogenetic scale? Although some studies have shown asymmetry in birds (Notebolm, 1970) and mice (Collins and Ward, 1970), these facts seem rather distant from human cerebral dominance. On the other hand, split-brain studies in the cat (Webster, 1972; Robinson and Voneida, 1973) and especially in the monkey (Gazzaniga, 1963; Trevarthen, 1965; Butler and Francis, 1973; Doty and Yamaga, 1973; Hamilton et al, 1974) suggest that elements of such a specialization may exist, although not yet in a systematic manner. These elements may represent the earliest forms of an evolutionary pattern leading, finally, to human cerebral dominance.

REFERENCES

Adametz, J. H., Rate of recovery of functioning in cats with rostral reticular lesions, *J. Neurosurg.*, **16**, 85–97, 1959.

Ades, H. W. and Raab, D. H., Effects of extirpation of parastriate cortex on learned visual discrimination in monkeys, *J. Neuropath. Exp. Neurol.*, **5**, 60–66, 1946a.

Ades, H. W. and Raab, D. H., Recovery of motor function after two stage extirpation of area 4 in monkeys, *J. Neurophysiol.*, **9**, 55–60, 1946b.

Ades, H. W. and Raab, D. H., Effects of pre-occipital and temporal decortication in learned visual discrimination in monkeys, *J. Neurophysiol.*, **12**, 101–108, 1949.

Adler, A., Disintegration and restoration of optic recognition in visual agnosia, analysis of a case, *Arch. Neurol. Psychiatr.*, **51**, 243–259, 1944.

Adler, A., Course and outcome of visual agnosia, *J. Nerv. Ment. Dis.*, **3**, 41–51, 1950.

Adrian, E. D., Afferent discharges to the cerebral cortex from perhipheral sense organs, *J. Physiol.*, **100**, 159–191, 1941.

Agranoff, B. W., Davis, R. M. and Brink, J. J., Chemical studies on memory fixation in goldfish, *Brain Res.*, **1**, 303–309, 1966.

Ajax, E. T., Dyslexia without agraphia, *Arch. Neurol.* (Chicago), **6**, 645–652, 1967.

Ajuriaguerra, J. de, "Discussion," in S. Wapner and H. Werner (eds.), *The Body Percept*, Random House, New York, 1965, pp. 82–106.

Ajuriaguerra, J. de and Hécaen, H., *Le cortex cerebral*, 2nd ed., Masson et Cie, Paris, 1960.

Ajuriaguerra, J. de, Hécaen, H. and Angelergues, R., Les apraxies: varietes cliniques et lateralisation lesionnelle, *Rev. Neurol.*, **102**, 566–594, 1960.

Akelaitis, A. J., Studies on the corpus callosum V: Homonymous defects for colour, object and letter recognition (homonymous hemiamblyopia) before and after section of the corpus callosum, *Arch. Neurol. Psychiat.*, **48**, 108–118, 1942a.

Akelaitis, A. J., Studies on the corpus callosum VI: Orientation (temporal-spatial gnosis) following section of the corpus callosum, *Arch. Neurol. Psychiat.*, **48**, 914–937, 1942b.

Akelaitis, A. J., A study of gnosis, praxis, and language following section of the corpus callosum, *J. Neurosurg.*, **1**, 94–102, 1944.

Akelaitis, A. J., Risteen, W. A., Herren, R. Y. and van Wagenen, W. P., Studies on the corpus callosum III. A contribution to the study of dyspraxia following partial and complete section of the corpus callosum, *Arch. Neurol. Psychiat.*, **47**, 971–1007, 1942.

Akert, K., "Comparative anatomy of frontal cortex and thalamofrontal connection," in J. M. Warren, and K. Akert, (eds.), *The Frontal Granular Cortex and Behavior,* McGraw-Hill, New York, 1964, pp. 372–396.

Akert, K., Woolsey, C. N., Diamond, I. T. and Neff, W. D., "The cortical projection area of the posterior pole of the medial geniculate body," in *Macaca mulatta, Anat. Rec.,* 134–242, 1959.

Alajouanine, Th. and Lhermitte, F., Les troubles des activities expressives du langage dans l'aphasie, leurs relations avec les apraxies, *Rev. Neurol.,* 102, 604–629, 1960.

Alajouanine, Th. and Lhermitte, F., Acquired aphasia in children, *Brain,* 88, 653–662, 1965.

Alajouanine, Th., Ombredane, A. and Durand, M., *Le Syndrome de désintegration phonétique dans l'aphasie,* Masson et Cie, Paris, 1939.

Alajouanine, Th., Castaigne, P., Lhermitte, F., Escourolle, R. and Ribaucourt, B. de, Etude de 43 cas d'aphasie post traumatique. Confrontation anatamo-clinique et aspects evolutifs, *L'Encephale,* 46, 3–45, 1957.

Alajouanine, Th., Lhermitte, F. and Ribaucourt-Ducarne B., Les alexies agnosiques et aphasiques, in *Les Grandes Activities du lobe occipital,* Masson et Cie, Paris, 1960.

Albert, M. L., Auditory sequencing and left cerebral dominance for language, *Neuropsychologia,* 10, 245–248, 1972a.

Albert, M. L., Aspects of auditory language comprehension following cerebral damage, *Langages,* 7, 37–51, 1972b.

Albert, M. L., A simple test of visual neglect, *Neurol.,* 23, 658–664, 1973.

Albert, M. L. and Bear, D., Time to understand. A case study of word deafness with reference to the role of time in auditory comprehension, *Brain,* 97, 383–394, 1974.

Albert, M. L. and Hécaen, H., Relative movement perception following unilateral cerebral damage, *Trans. Am.Neurol. Assoc.,* 96, 200–202, 1971.

Albert, M. L., and Obler, L. K., Mixed polygot aphasia, paper presented at Academy of Aphasia. Victoria, B. C., Canada, October, 1975.

Albert, M. L., Benson, D. F., Goldblum, M. C. and Hécaen, H., Mechanisms of auditory comprehension II, Cerebral dominance, *Trans. Amer. Neurol, Assoc.,* 96, 132–135, 1971.

Albert, M. L., Sparks, R., von Stockert, T. and Sax, D., A case of auditory agnosia: Linguistic and nonlinguistic processing, *Cortex,* 8, 427–443, 1972.

Albert, M. L., Yamadori, A., Gardner, H. and Howes, D., Comprehension in alexia, *Brain,* 96, 317–328, 1973.

Albert, M. L., Sparks, R. and Helm, N., Melodic intonation therapy for aphasia, *Arch. Neurol.* 29, 130–131, 1973.

Albert, M. L., Feldman, R. G. and Willis, A. L., The subcortical dementia of progressive supranuclear palsy, *J. Neurol. Neurosurg. Psychiat.,* 37, 121–130, 1974.

Albert, M. L., Reches, A. and Silverberg, R., Associative visual agnosia without alexia, *Neurol.,* 25, 322–326, 1975a.

Albert, M. L., Reches, A. and Silverberg, R., Hemianopic color blindness, *J. Neurol. Neurosurg. Psychiat.,* 38, 546–549, 1975b.

Allison, R. S., Hurwitz, L. J., White, J. Graham, and Wilmot, T. J., A follow-up study of a patient with Balint's syndrome, *Neuropsychologia,* 7, 319–334, 1969.

Alperin, H. P. and Kimble, D. P., Retrograde amnesic effects of diethyl ether and bis (trifluoroethyl) ether, *J. Comp. Physiol. Psychol.,* 63, 168–171, 1967.

Anderson, K. V. and Symmes, D., The superior colliculus and higher visual function in the monkey, *Brain Res.,* 13, 37–52, 1969.

Anderson, K. V. and Williamson, M. R., Visual pattern discrimination in cats after removal of superior colliculi, *Psychon. Sci.* 24, 125–127, 1971.

Angelergues, R. and Hécaen, H., La douleur au cours des lesions des hemispheres cerebraux, *J.*

de Psychol. Norm. et Pathol., **93**, 42–70 and 184–204, 1958.

Angelergues, R., Hécaen, H. and Ajuriaguerra, J. de, Les troubles mentaux au cours des tumeurs du lobe frontal, *Ann. Med. Psychol.*, **113**, 577–642, 1956.

Angelergues, R., Ajuriaguerra, J. de and Hécaen, H., La negation de la cecite au cours des lesions cerebrales, *J. Psychol.*, **4**, 381–404, 1960.

Angelergues, R., Hécaen, H., Djindjian, R. et al, Un cas d'aphasie croisee, *Rev. Neurol.*, **107**, 543–545, 1962.

Angyal, L. von and Frick, F., Beitrage zur Anosognosie und zur Regression des Phantomgliedes, *Z. ges. Neurol. Psychiatr.*, **173**, 440–447, 1941.

Anokhin, P. K., *Problems in Higher Nervous Activity*, Izd. Akad. Med., Nauk SSSR, Moscow, 1949.

Anton, G., Beitrage zur klinischen Beurteilung zur Localisation der Muskelsinnstorungen im Grosshirn, *Z. Heilk*, **14**, 313–348, 1893.

Anton, G., Über Herderkrankungen des Gehirns, welche vom Patienten selbst nicht wahrgenommen werden, *Wien. klin. Wschr.*, **11**, 227–229, 1898.

Anton, G., Über die Selbstwahrnehmung der Herderkrankungen des Gehirns durch den kranken der Rindenblindheit und Rindentaubheit, *Arch. Psychiat.*, **32**, 86–127, 1899.

Archibald, Y. M., Wepman, J. M. and Jones, L. U., Performance on non-verbal cognitive tests following unilateral cortical injury to the right and left hemispheres, *J. Nerv. Ment. Dis.*, **145**, 25–36, 1967.

Arnot, R., A theory of frontal lobe function, *Arch. Neurol. Psychiat.* **67**, 487–495, 1952.

Arrigoni, G. and DeRenzi, E., Constructional apraxia and hemispheric locus of lesion, *Cortex*, **1**, 170–197, 1964.

Asratyan, A.; cited in Luria, A., 1966.

Assal, G., Regression des troubles de la reconnaissance des physionomies et de la memoire topographique chez un malade opéré d'un hematome intracerebral parieto-temporal droit, *Rev. Neurol.*, **121**, 184–185, 1969.

Assal, G., Troubles de la reception auditive du langage lors de lesions du cortex cerebral, *Neuropsychologia,,* **3**, 12, 399–401, 1974.

Assal, G., Ramier, A. M., A sentence generation test in patients with unilateral cerebral lesions, Paper presented at International Neuropsychological Symposium, Cambridge, England, June 1970.

Assal, G., Chopins, G. and Zander, E., Isolated writing disorders in a patient with stenosis of the left internal carotid artery, *Cortex*, **6**, 241–248, 1970.

Athanasio-Benisty, *Les Lesions de la zone rolandique par blessure de guerre, contribution a l'etude clinique des localisations cerebrales*, Vigot freres, Paris, 1918.

Attardi, D. G. and Sperry, R. W., Preferential selection of central pathways by regenerating optic fibers. *Exp. Neurol.*, **7**, 46–64, 1963.

Azulay, A. and Schwartz, A. S., The role of the dorsal funiculus of the primate in tactile discrimination, *Exp. Neurol.*, **2**, 46, 315–332, 1975.

Babinski, J., Contribution a l'etude des troubles mentaux dans l'hemiplegie cerebrale (anosognosie), *Rev. Neurol.*, **27**, 845–847, 1914.

Bailey, P. and von Bonin, G., *The Isocortex of Man*, University of Illinois Press, Urbana, 1951.

Baker, E., Berry, T., Gardner, H., Zurif, E. et al, Can linguistic competence be dissociated from natural language functions? *Nature*, **254**, 609–619, 1975.

Balint, R., Die seelenlahmung des "Schauens," *Mtschr. f. Psych. u. Neur.*, **1**, 25, 51–81, 1909.

Baldwin, M. and Hofman, A., "Hallucinations," in P. J. Vinken and G. W. Bruyn, (eds.), *Handbook of Clinical Neurology* 4, North Holland Publishing Company, Amsterdam, 1969, pp. 327–339.

Bard, P., Studies on the cortical representation of somatic sensibility, *Bull. N.Y. Acad. Med.*, 14, 585–607, 1938.

Barlow, H. B. and Pettigrew, J. D., Lack of specificity of neurons in the visual cortex of young kittens, *J. Physiol.* (London), 218, 98–100, 1971.

Barnes, P. J., Smith, L. M. and Latto, R. M., Orientation to visual stimuli and the superior colliculus in the rat, *Q. J. Exp. Psychol.*, 22, 239–247, 1970.

Barnet, A. B., Manson, J. I. and Wilner, E., Acute cerebral blindness in childhood: Six cases studied clinically and electrophysiologically, *Neurol.*, 43, 1147–1156, 1970.

Barondes, S. H. and Cohen, H. D., Puromycin effect on successive phases of memory storage, *Science*, 151, 594–595, 1966.

Barraquer-Bordas, C., Mendilaharsu, C., Peres-Serra, J., Acevedo-de-Mendilaharsu, S. and Granveciana, J. M., Estudio de dos casos de afazia cruzada en pacientes manidextros, *Acta Neurol. Latinoamer.*, 9, 140–148, 1963.

Barrett, A. M., A case of pure word deafness with autopsy, *J. Nerv. Ment. Dis.*, 37, 73–92, 1910.

Bartlett, J. R. and Doty, R. W., Response of units in striate cortex of squirrel monkey to visual and electrical stimuli, *J. Neurophysiol.*, 37, 621–641, 1974.

Basser, L. S., Hemiplegia of early onset and the faculty of speech with special reference to the effects of hemispherectomy, *Brain*, 85, 427–460, 1962.

Basso, A., DeRenzi, E., Faglioni, P. et al, Neuropsychological evidence for the existence of cerebral areas critical to the performance of intelligence tasks, *Brain*, 96, 715–728, 1973.

Bastian, H. C., Disorders of speech, *Brit. Foreign Med-Chir. Rev.*, 43, 69, 209, 470, 1869.

Bastian, H. C., *Aphasia and Other Speech Defects*, H. K. Lewis, London, 1898.

Bateman, F., *On Aphasia, or Loss of Speech, and the Localization of the Faculty of Articulate Language*, Churchill, London, 1890.

Bates, J. A. V. and Ettlinger, G., Posterior biparietal ablations in the monkey, *Arch. Neurol.*, 3, 172–192, 1960.

Battersby, W. S., The regional gradient of critical flicker frequency after frontal or occipital injury, *J. Exp. Psychol.*, 42, 59–68, 1951.

Battersby, W. S., Wagman, I. H., Karp, E. and Bender, M. B., Neural limitations of visual excitability: Alterations produced by cerebral lesions, *Arch. Neurol.*, 3, 24–42, 1960.

Bazhin, L., Meerson, Y. and Tonkonogii, I., On distinguishing signal from noise by patients with visual agnosia and visual hallucinations, *Neuropsychologia*, 11, 319–325, 1973.

Battig, K., Rosvold, H. E. and Mishkin, M., Comparison of the effects of frontal and caudate lesions on discrimination learning in monkeys, *J. Comp. Physiol. Psychol.*, 55, 458–463, 1962.

Bauer, J. H. and Hughes, K. R., Visual and nonvisual behaviors of the rat after neonatal and adult posterior neocortical lesions, *Physiol. Behav.* 5, 427–441, 1970.

Bauer, W. and Beck, D. M., Intellect after cerebrovascular accident, *J. Nerv. Ment. Dis.*, 120, 379–384, 1954.

Bay, E., Zum problem der taktilen Agnosie, *D. Ztschr. f. Nervenk.* 156, 1–3, 64–96, 1944.

Bay, E., Agnosie und Funktionswandel, *Monogr. Gesamtgeb. Neurol. Psychiatr.*, 73, 1–94, Springer, Berlin, 1950.

Bay, E., Der gegenwartige Stand der Aphasie-Forschung, *Folia Phoniatrica*, 4, 9–30, 1952.

Bay, E., Disturbances of visual perception and their examination, *Brain*, 76, 515–551, 1953.

Bay, E., Die corticale dysarthrie und ihre Beziehungen zur sog. motorischen Aphasie, *Dtsch. Ztschr. Nervenhk.*, 176, 553–594, 1957.

Bay, E., Aphasia and non-verbal disorders of language, *Brain*, 85, 411–426, 1962.

Bender, B. G., Spatial interactions between the red-and-green-sensitive colour mechanisms of the human visual system, *Vision Res.*, 13, 2205–2218, 1973.

Bender, H. and Jung, R., Awbeichungen der subjektiven optischen Vertikalen und Horizontalen bei Gesunden und Hirnverletzen, *Arch. f. Psych.*,181, 193–212, 1948.

Bender, M. B. and Diamond, S. P., An analysis of auditory perceptual defects with observations on the localization of function, *Brain,* **88,** 675–686, 1965.

Bender, M. B. and Teuber, H. L. Phenomena of fluctuation, extinction and completion in visual perception, *Arch. Neurol. Psychiatr.,* **55,** 627–658, 1947.

Bender, M. B. and Teuber, H. L., Disturbances of visual perception following cerebral lesions, *J. Psychol.,* **28,** 223–233, 1949.

Bender, M. B., Schapiro, M. F. and Teuber, H. L., Allesthesia and disturbance of the body schema, *Arch. Neurol. Psychiatr.,* **62,** 222–231, 1949a.

Bender, M. B., Wortis, S. B. and Gordon, G. G., Disorder in body image: Anosognosia, in *Rapports du Ve Congres Neurologique International II,,* Paris, 1949b.

Benedikt, M., Über Aphasie, Agraphie und verwandte pathologische Zustande, *Wien Med. Pr.,* **6,** 897–899, 923–926, 945–948, 997–999, 1020–1022, 1063–1070, 1094–1097, 1139–1142, 1167–1169, 1189–1190, 1264–1265, 1865.

Benjamin, R. M. and Thompson, R. F., Differential effects of cortical lesions in infant and adult cats on roughness discrimination, *Exp. Neurol.,* **1,** 305–321, 1959.

Benson, D. F., Psychiatric aspects of aphasia, *Brit. J. Psychiat.,* **123,** 555–566, 1973.

Benson, D. F. and Barton, M., Constructional disability, *Cortex,* **6,** 19–46, 1970.

Benson, D. F. and Geschwind, N., Shrinking retrograde amnesia, *J. Neurol. Neurosurg. Psychiat.,* **30,** 539–544, 1967.

Benson, D. F. and Geschwind, N., "The Alexias," in P. J. Winken, and G. W. Bruyn, (eds.), *Handbook of Clinical Neurology,* North Holland Publishing Co., Amsterdam, 1969.

Benson, D. F. and Geschwind, N., Developmental Gerstmann syndrome, *Neurol.,* **20,** 293–298, 1970.

Benson, D. F. and Geschwind, N., "Aphasia and Related Disturbances," in A. B. Baker (ed.), *Clinical Neurology,* Harper and Row, New York, 1972.

Benson, D. F. and Geschwind, N., "Psychiatric Conditions Associated with Focal Lesions in the Nervous System," in S. Arieti, (ed.), *American Handbook of Psychiatry IV,* Basic Books, Boston, 1975, pp. 208–243.

Benson, D. F. and Greenberg, J. P., Visual form agnosia: A specific defect in visual recognition, *Arch. Neurol.,* **20,** 82–89, 1969.

Benson, D. F., Brown, J. W. and Tomlinson, E. B., Varieties of alexia: Word and letter blindness, *Neurol.,* **21,** 951–957, 1971.

Benson, D. F., Sheremata, W. A., Bouchard, R., Segarra, J. M., Price, D. and Geschwind, N., Conduction aphasia, *Arch. Neurol.,* **28,** 339–346, 1973.

Benson, D. F., Segarra, J. and Albert, M. L., Visual agnosia-prosopagnosia, A clinicopathological correlation, *Arch. Neurol.,* **30,** 307–310, 1974.

Benton, A. L., *Right-Left Discrimination and Finger Localization, Development and Pathology,* Hoeber-Harper, New York, 1959.

Benton, A. L., The fiction of the "Gerstmann syndrome," *J. Neurol. Neurosurg. Psychiatr.,* **24,** 176–181, 1961.

Benton, A. L., The visual retention test as a constructional praxis task, *Confin. neurol.* (Basel), **22,** 141–155, 1962.

Benton, A. L., Contributions to aphasia before Broca, *Cortex,* (Milano), **1,** 314–327, 1964.

Benton, A. L., Differential behavioral effects in frontal lobe disease. *Neuropsychologia,* **6,** 53–60, 1968.

Benton, A. L., "Constructional Apraxia: Some Unanswered Questions," in A. L. Benton (ed.), *Contributions to Clinical Neuropsychology,* Aldine, Chicago, 1969a, pp. 129–141.

Benton, A. L., "Disorders of Spatial Orientation," in J. P. Vinken, and G. N. Bruyn, (eds.), *Handbook of Clinical Neurology III,* North Holland Publishing Co., Amsterdam, 1969b, pp. 212–228.

Benton, A. L. and Hécaen, H., Stereoscopic vision in patients with unilateral cerebral disease, *Neurol.* (Minneapolis), **20**, 1084–1088, 1970.

Benton, A. L. and Joynt, R. J., Early descriptions of aphasia, *Arch. Neurol.*, **3**, 205–221, 1960.

Benton, A. L. and Van Allen, M. W., Impairment in facial recognition in patients with cerebral disease, *Cortex*, **4**, 344–358, 1968.

Benton, A. L., Hutcheon, J. F., and Seymour, E., Arithmetic ability, finger-localization capacity and right-left discrimination in normal and defective children. *Am. J. Orthopsychiatr.*, **21**, 756–766, 1951.

Benton, A. L., Hannay, J. and Varney, N., Visual perception of line direction in patients with unilateral brain disease, *Neurol.*, **25**, 907–910, 1975.

Berger, B. D., Learning in the anesthetized rat, *Fed. Proc.*, **29**, 749, 1970.

Bergmann, P. S., Cerebral blindness, *Arch. Neurol. Psych.*, **78**, 568–584, 1957.

Bergson, H., *Matiere et memoire*, Alcan, Paris, 1896.

Beringer, K. and Stein, J., Analyse eines Falles von "reiner" Alexie, *Ztschr. Neurol. Psychiat.*, **123**, 472–478, 1930.

Berlucchi, G., Sprague, J. M., Levy, J. et al, Pretectum and superior colliculus in visually guided behavior and in flux and form discrimination in the cat, *J. Comp. Physiol. Psychol.*, **78**, 123–172, 1972.

Berman, O. M., The effects of dorsalateral-frontal and ventrolateral orbitofrontal lesions on spatial discrimination learning and delayed response in two modalities, *Neuropsycholgia*, **13**, 237–247, 1975.

Bernadis, L. L. and Frohman, L. A., Plasma growth hormone responses to electrical stimulation of the hypothalamus in the rat, *Neuroendocrinol.*, **7**, 193–201, 1971a.

Bernadis, L. L. and Frohman, L. A., Effects of hypothalamic lesions at different loci on development of hyperinsulinemia and obesity in the weaning rat, *J. Comp. Neurol.*, **141**, 107–115, 1971b.

Bernard, P., *De l'aphasie et de ses diverses formes*, Lecrosnier et Babe, Paris, 1889.

Bernhardt, M., Über die spastische cerebrale paralyse im Kindersalter (Hemiplegia spastisca infantilis) nebst einem Excurse über "Aphasie bei Kindern," *Virchows Archives für Anatomie und Physiologie*, **102**, 1885.

Bernhardt, M., Neuropathologische beobachtungen. *Dtsch Arch. klin. Med.*, **22**, 362–367, 1878.

Bernheim, H., 1886, cited in Hécaen, H., "Introduction a la . . .," 1972.

Bernshtein, N. A., On the construction of movements [in Russian], "Medecina" Publishing House, Moscow, 1947.

Bernshtein, N. A., Some actual problems of regulation of motor acts [in Russian], *Questions of Psychology*, No. 6, 1957.

Bernstein, J. J. and Bernstein, M. E., Axonal regeneration and formation of synapses proximal to the site of lesion following hemisection of the rat spinal cord, *Exp. Neurol.*, **30**, 336–351, 1971.

Best, F., Hemianopsie und Seelenblindheit bei Hirnverletzungen, Albrecht v. Graefes, *Arch. Opthal.*, **93**, 49–150, 1917.

Bever, T. G. and Chiarello, R. J., Cerebral dominance in musicians and nonmusicians, *Science*, **185**, 357–359, 1974.

Bianchi, L., The functions of the frontal lobes, *Brain*, **18**, 497–530, 1895.

Biemond, A., The conduction of pain above the level of the thalamus opticus, *Arch. Neurol. Psychiat.*, **75**, 231–244, 1956.

Bingley, T., Mental symptoms in temporal lobe epilepsy and temporal lobe gliomas, *Acta Psychiat. et Neurol.*, **195**, Suppl. 120, 33, 1958.

Bird, S. J. and Aghajanian, G. K., Denervation supersensitivity in the cholinergic septohippocampal pathway: a micro ontophoretic study, *Brain Res.* **100**, 355–370, 1975.

Birkmayer, W., Hirnverletzungen. Mechanismus, Spatkomplikationen, Funktionswandel, Springer-Verlag, Wien, 1951.

Bishop, G. H., Neural mechanisms of cutaneous sense, *Physiol. Rev.*, **26**, 77–102, 1946.

Bisiach, E., Perceptual factors in the pathogenesis of anomia, *Cortex*, **2**, 90–95, 1966.

Bizzi, E., Discharge of frontal eye field neurons during saccadic and following eye movements in unanaesthetized monkeys, *Exp. Brain Res.*, **6**, 69–80, 1968.

Bjorklund, A. and Steveni, U., Nerve growth factor: Stimulation of regeneration growth of central noradrenergic neurons, *Science*, **175**, 1251–1253, 1972.

Blake, L., The effect of lesions of the superior colliculus on brightness and pattern discrimination in the cat, *J. Comp. Physiol. Psychol.*, **52**, 272–278, 1959.

Blakemore, W. F., Pattern of remyelination in the CNS, *Nature*, **249**, 577, 578, 1974.

Blakemore, W. F., Remyelination of the superior cerebellar peduncle in old mice following demyelination induced by cuprizone, *J. Neurol. Science*, **22**, 121–126, 1974.

Blakemore, C. and Cooper, G. F., Development of the brain depends on the visual environment, *Nature* (Lind), **228**, 477–478, 1970.

Bland, B. H. and Cooper, R. M., Posterior neodecortication in the rat: Age at operation and experience, *J. Comp. Physiol. Psychol.*, **69**, 345–354, 1969.

Blix, M., Experimentelle Beitrage zur Losung der Frage über die specifische Energie der Hautnerven (1 and 2), *Ztschr. f. Biol.*, Bd. xx, S. 141, 1884.

Blum, R. A., Effects of subtotal lesions of frontal grandular cortex on delayed reaction in monkeys, *Arch. Neurol. Psychiat.*, **67**, 375–386, 1952.

Blum-Semmes, J. S., Chow, K. L. and Pribram, K. H., A behavioral analysis of the organization of the parieto-temporo-preoccipital cortex, *J. Comp. Neurol.*, **93**, 53–100, 1950.

Blumstein, S., *A Phonological Investigation of Aphasic Speech*, Mouton, The Hague, 1973.

Blumstein, S., The use and theoretical implications of the dichotic listening technique for investigating distinctive features, *Brain and Language*, **1**, 337–350, 1974.

Blumstein, S. and Cooper, W. E., Hemispheric processing of intonation contours, *Cortex*, **10**, 146–158, 1974.

Blumstein, S. and Goodglass, H., Perception of stress as a semantic cue in aphasia, *JSHR*, **15**, 800–806, 1972.

Bocca, E., Clinical aspects of cortical deafness, *Laryngoscope*, **68**, 301–315, 1958.

Bocca, E., Calearo, C., Cassinori, V. and Migliavocca, F., Testing "cortical" hearing in temporal lobe tumours, *Acta oto-laryngol.*, **45**, 289–304, 1955.

Bodamer, J., Die Prosopagnosie, *Arch. Psychiat. u. Zeitsch. Neur.*, **179**, 6–54, 1947.

Bogen, J. E., The other side of the brain. I. Dysgraphia and dyscopia following cerebral commissurotomy, *Bull. Los Angeles Neurol. Soc.*, **32**, 73–105, 1969.

Bogen, J. E. and Gordon, H. W, Musical tests for functional lateralization with intra carotid amobarbital, *Nature* (London), **230**, 524–525, 1971.

Bogen, J. E. and Vogel, P. J., Cerebral commissurotomy: A case report, *Bull. Los Angeles Neurol. Soc.*, **27**, 169, 1962.

Boll, T. J., Right and left cerebral hemisphere damage and tactile perception: Performance of the ipsilateral and contralateral sides of the body, *Neuropsychologia*, **12**, 235–238, 1974.

Boller, F., Destruction of Wernicke's area without language disturbance. A fresh look at crossed aphasia, *Neuropsychologia*, **11**, 243–246, 1973.

Boller, F. and DeRenzi, E., Relationship between visual memory defects and hemispheric locus of lesion, *Neurol.* (Minneapolis), **17**, 1052–1058, 1967.

Boller, F. and Green, E., Comprehension in severe aphasics, *Cortex*, **8**, 382–394, 1972.

Boller, F., Cole, M., Kim, Y., Mack, J., Patawaran, C., Optic Ataxia: Clinico–Radiological Correlations with the EMIscan, *JNNP*, **38**, 954–958, 1975.

Bonhoeffer, K., Casuistische Beitrage zur Aphasielehre. II. Ein Fall von Apraxie und sogenannter transcorticaler sensorischer Aphasie, *Arch. F. Psychiat.*, **37**, 800–825, 1903.

Bonhoeffer, K., Partielle reine Tastlahmung, *Mtschr. Psychiat. Neurol.*, **43**, 141–145, 1918.

Bonnier, P., L'Aschematie, *Rev. Neurol.*, **54**, 605–609, 1905.

Bonvicini, G., Subcorticale sensorische Aphasie, *J. Psychiat. Neurol.*, **26**, 126–229, 1905.

Bornstein, B., "Prosopagnosia," in Z. Halpern (ed.), *Problems of Dynamic Neurology*, Jerusalem Post Press, Jerusalem, pp. 283–318, 1963.

Bors, E., Phantom limbs of patient with spinal cord injury, *Arch. Neurol. Psychiatr.*, **66**, 610–631, 1951.

Bossom, J., The effect of brain lesions on prisan adaptation in monkeys, *Psychonom. Sci.*, **2**, 45–46, 1965.

Botez, M. I., *Afazia si sindroamele corelate in procesele expansive intracraniene* [Rumanian], Ed. Acad. Rep. Popul. Romine, Bucarest, 1962.

Botez, M. I., Two visual systems in clinical neurology: Readaptive role of the primitive visual system in visual agnostic patients, *Eur. Neurol.*, **2**, 13, 101–122, 1975.

Botez, M. I., Serbanescu, T., Petrovici, I. and Vernea, I., "Clinical and Electroculographic Findings in Balint's Syndrome and Its Minor Forms," in *Rapports du 8ᵉ Congress International de Neurologie*, **3**, Vienna, 183–187, 1965.

Bouillaud, J., Recherches cliniques propres a dé montrer que la perte de la parole correspond à la lesion des lobules anterieurs du cerveau et a confirmer l'opinion de M. Gall sur le siege de l'organe du langage articulé, *Arch. ges. Med.*, **8**, 25–45, 1825.

Bouillaud, M., 1839; cited by Bouillaud, M., in *Bulletin de l'Academie royale de Medecine*, *Iᵉʳ trimestre*, 699–719, 1848.

Bouman, L. and Grunbaum, A., Experimentell-psychologische Untersuchungen zur Aphasie und Paraphasie, *Ztschr. fur die gesamte Neurol. und Psychiat.*, **96**, 481–538, 1925.

Bower, T. G. R., Broughton, J. M. and Moore, M. K., *Percept. Psychophys.*, **9**, 193, 1970.

Brain, R., Visual disorientation with special reference to the lesions of the right cerebral hemisphere, *Brain* **64**, 244–272, 1941a.

Brain, R., Visual object-agnosia with special reference to the gestalt theory, *Brain*, **64**, 43–62, 1941b.

Brain, R., *Speech Disorders* (2nd ed.) Butterworths, London, 1965.

Bramwell, B., On crossed aphasia, *Lancet*, June 3, 803–805, 1899.

Breitmeyer, B., Julesz, B. and Kropfl, W., Dynamic random-dot stereograms reveal up-down anisotropy and left-right isotropy between cortical hemifields, *Science*, **187**, 269–270, 1975.

Bremer, F., Global aphasia and bilateral apraxia due to an endothelioma compressing the gyrus supra marginalis, *Arch. Neurol. Psychiat.*, **5**, 663–669, 1921.

Brickner, R., An interpretation of frontal lobe function based upon the study of a case of partial bilateral frontal lobectomy, *Res. Publ. Assoc. Res. Nerv. Ment. Dis.*, **13**, 259–351, 1934.

Brierly, J. B., "The Neuropathology of Amnesic States," in C. W. M. Whitty and D. L. Zangwill (eds.), *Amnesia*, Butterworths, London, 1966, pp. 134–149.

Brindley, G. S., The variability of the human striate cortex, *J. Physiol.* (London), **225**, 1972.

Brindley, G. S. and Janota, I., Observations on cortical blindness and on vascular lesions that cause loss of recent memory, *J. Neurol. Neurosurg. Psychiat.*, **5**, 38, 459–464, 1975.

Brindley, G. S., Gautier Smith, P. C. and Lewin, W., Cortical blindness and the functions of the nongeniculate fibers of the optic tracts, *J. Neurol. Neurosurg. Psychiat.*, **32**, 259–264, 1969.

Broadbent, D. E., The role of auditory localization in attention and memory span, *J. Exp. Psychol.*, **47**, 191–196, 1954.

Broca, P., Perte de la parole. Ramollissement chronique et destruction partielle du lobe anterieur gauche du cerveau, *Bull. Soc. Anthrop., Paris*, **2**, 219, 1861a.

Broca, P., Remarques sur le siege de la faculte du langage articulé suivie d'une observation d'aphemie, *Bull. Soc. Anat., Paris*, **6**, 330, 1861b.

Broca, P., Sur la faculte du langage articulé, *Bull. Soc. Anthr., Paris,* **6,** 337–393, 1865.

Brodmann, K., *Vergleichende Lokalisationslehre der Grosshirnrinde,* Barth, Leipzig, 1909.

Brody, J., 1944; cited in *Amnesia,* C. W. M. Whitty and O. L. Zangwill (eds.), Butterworths, London, 1966.

Brooks, V. B., Rudomin, P., and Slayman, C. L., Sensory activation of neurons in the cat's cerebral cortex, *J. Neurophysiol.,* **24,** 286–301, 1961.

Brooks, V. B., Rudomin, P., and Slayman, C. L., Peripheral receptive fields in the cat's cerebral cortex, *J. Neurophysiol.* **24,** 302–325, 1961.

Brown, R. W. and Lenneberg, E. A., A study in language and cognition, *J. Abnorm. Soc. Psychol.,* **49,** 454–462, 1954.

Brown, J. W. and Wilson, F. R., Crossed aphasia in a dextral. A case report, *Neurol.* (Minneapolis), **23,** 907–911, 1973.

Brown-Sequard, E., Experiences nouvelles sur la transmission des impressions sensitives dans la Moelle epiniere, *J. Physiologie,* **2,** 65, 1859.

Brown-Sequard, E., Recherches sur la transmission des impressions dans la Moelle epiniere, *J. Physiologie,* **6,** 124, 232, 581, 1863.

Brown-Sequard, E., Lectures on the physiology and pathology of the nervous system, *Lancet,* **2,** 593, 659, 755, 821, 1868.

Brunn, J. T., The capacity to hear, understand, and remember experiences during chemoanesthesia, *Am. J. Clin. Hypnosis,* **6,** 27–30, 1963.

Brush, E. S., Mishkin, M. and Rosvold, H. E., Effects of object preferences and aversions on discrimination learning in monkeys with frontal lesions, *J. Comp. Physiol. Psychol.,* **54,** 319–325, 1961.

Brutkowski, S. and Dabrowska, K., Prefrontal cortex control of differentiation of behavior in dogs, *Acta Biol. Exp.,* **26,** 425–439, 1966.

Brutkowski, S., Konorski, J., Lawicka, W. et al., The effect of the removal of the frontal poles of the cerebral cortex on motor conditioned reflexes, *Acta Biol. Exp.,* **17,** 311–320, 1956.

Brutkowski, S., Mishkin M. and Rosvold, H. E., "Positive and Inhibitory CR's in Monkeys after Ablation of Orbital or Dorsolateral Surface of the Frontal Cortex," in E. Gutman, and P. Hnik, (eds.), *Central and Peripheral Mechanisms in Motor Functions,* Czech. Acad. Sci., Prague, 1963, pp. 133–141.

Bryden, M. P., Tachistoscopic recognition, handedness, and cerebral dominance, *Neuropsychologia,* **3,** 1–8, 1965.

Buerger, A. A., Gross, C. G. and Rocha-Miranda, C. E., Effects of ventral putamen lesions on discrimination learning by monkeys, *J. Comp. Physiol. Psychol.,* **86,** 440–446, 1974.

Buffery, A. W. H., Learning and memory in baboons with bilateral lesions of frontal or inferotemporal cortex, *Nature,* **214,** 1054–1056, 1967.

Buisseret, P. and Imbert, M., Visual cortical cells: Their development properties in normal and dark reared kittens, *J. Physiol.,* **255,** 511–525, 1976.

Burchfiel, J. E. and Duffy, F. H., Muscle afferent input to single cells in primate somatosensory cortex, *Brain Res.,* **45,** 241–246, 1972.

Burgess, P. R. and Perl, E. R., "Cutaneous Mechano-receptors and Nociceptors," in A. Iggo (ed.), *Somatosensory Systems, Handbook of Sensory Physiology II,* Springer-Verlag, Berlin, Heidelburg, New York, 1973, pp. 29–78.

Burgmeister, J. J., Tissot, R. and de Ajuriaguerra, J., Les Hallucinations visuelles des ophtalmopathes, *Neuropsychologia,* **3,** 9–38, 1965.

Burnham, R. W. and Clark, J. R., A test of hue memory, *J. Appl. Psychol.,* **15,** 73–86, 1955.

Buscher, J. de, Agnosie visuelle pour les objets animés et inanimés: Achromatognosie incomplete apres deux lésions vasculaires consecutives chez un hypertendu de 56 ans, *Acta Neurological et Psychiatrica Belgica,* **55,** 221–281, 1955.

Buser, P. and Imbert M., "Sensory Projections to the Motor Cortex in Cats: a Microelectrode Study," in W. A. Rosenblith (ed.), *Sensory Communication,* M.I.T. Press, Cambridge, Mass., and Wiley, New York, 1961, pp. 607–626.

Butler, C. R. and Francis, A. C., Specialization of the left hemisphere in baboon—evidence from directional preferences, *J. Nutr. Sci. Vitaminol.* (Tokyo), **20,** 351–354, 1974.

Butter, C. M., The effect of discrimination training on pattern equivalence in monkeys with inferotemporal and lateral striate lesions, *Neuropsychologia,* **5,** 27–40, 1966.

Butter, C. M., Impairment in selective attention to visual stimuli in monkeys with inferotemporal and lateral striate lesions, *Brain Res.,* **12,** 374–383, 1969.

Butter, C. M., Visual discrimination impairments in rhesus monkeys with combined lesions of superior colliculus and striate cortex, *J. Comp. Physiol. Psychol.,* **5,** 87, 918–929, 1974a.

Butter, C. M., Effect of superior colliculus, striate and prestriate lesions on visual sampling in rhesus monkeys, *J. Comp. Physiol. Psychol.,* **5,** 87, 905–917, 1974b.

Butters, N. and Pandya, D., Retention of delayed-alternation effect of selective lesions of sulcus principalis, *Science,* **165,** 1271–1273, 1969.

Butters, N., Barton, M. and Brody, B. A., Role of the right parietal lobe in the mediation of cross-modal associations and reversible operations in space, *Cortex,* **6,** 174–190, 1970.

Butters, N., Cermak, L. S. and Goodglass, H., The extent of memory loss in Korsakoff patients, *Neuropsychologia,* **9,** 307–315, 1971a.

Butters, N., Pandya, D., Sanders, K. et al, Behavioral deficits in monkeys after selective lesions within the middle third of sulcus principalis, *J. Comp. Physiol. Psychol.,* **78,** 8–14, 1971b.

Butters, N., Butter, C., Rosen, J. et al, Behavioral effects of sequential and one stage ablations of orbital prefrontal cortex in monkey, *Exp. Neurol.,* **39,** 204–214, 1973a.

Butters, N., Lewis, R., Cermak, L. and Goodglass, H., Material-specific memory deficits in alcoholic Korsakoff patients, *Neuropsychologia,* **11,** 291–299, 1973b.

Butters, N., Lewis, R. and Cermak, L. S. et al, Material-specific memory deficits in alcoholic Korsakoff patients, *J. Nutr. Sci. Vitaminol.* (Tokyo), **20,** 291–299, 1974.

Bychowski, Z., Über die Restitution der nach einem Schadelschuss verlorengegangenen Sprachen bei einem Polyglotten, *Mtschr. Psychiat. Neurol.,* **45,** 184–201, 1919.

Bychowski, Z., Über das Fehlen der Wahrnehmung der eigenen Blindheit bei zwei kriegsverletzen, *Neur. Centralblatt.,* **106,** 354–357, 1920.

Calderon, M., Doctoral dissertation at Boston University, 1976.

Campbell, A. W., *Histological Studies on the Localization of Cerebral Function,* Cambridge University Press, Cambridge, England, 1905.

Campora, G., Astereognosis: Its causes and mechanism, *Brain,* **18,** 65–71, 1925.

Cannon, D. F. and Rosenblueth, A., The supersensitivity of denervated structures, MacMillan, New York, 1949.

Caplan, L., An investigation of some aspects of stuttering-like speech in adult dysphasic subjects, *J. S. Afr. Speech Hear. Assoc.,* **19,** 52–66, 1972.

Cardu, B., Ptito, M., Dumont, M. and Lepore, F., Effects of ablations of the superior colliculi on spectral sensitivity in monkeys, *Neuropsychologia,* **13,** 297–306, 1975.

Carmon, A., Impaired utilization of kinesthetic feedback in right hemispheric lesions. Possible implications for the pathophysiology of "motor impersistence," *Neurol.* (Minneapolis), **20,** 1033–1038, 1970.

Carmon, A., Disturbances of tactile sensitivity in patients with unilateral cerebral lesions, *Cortex,* **7,** 83–97, 1971.

Carmon, A., and Bechtoldt, H., Dominance of the right cerebral hemisphere for stereopsis, *Neuropsychologia,* **7,** 29–40, 1969.

Carmon, A. and Benton, A. L., Tactile perception of direction and number in patients with unilateral cerebral disease, *Neurol.,* **19,** 525–532, 1969.

REFERENCES

Castaigne, P., Buge, A., Cambier, J., Escourelle, R., Brunet, P. and Degos, J. D., Demence thalomique d'origine vasculaire par ramollissement bilateral, limite au territoire du pedicule retro-mamillaire: a propos de deux observations clinique, *Rev. Neurol.,* 114, 89–107, 1966.

Castro, A. J., Ipsilateral corticospinal projections after large lesions of the cerebral hemisphere in neonatal rats, *Exp. Neurol.,* 46, 1–8, 1975a.

Castro, A. J., Tongue usage as a measure of cerebral cortical localization in the rat, *Exp. Neurol.,* 47, 343–352, 1975b.

Celesia, G. G. and Puletti, F., Auditory cortical areas of man, *Neurol.,* 19, 211–220, 1969.

Cermak, L. S. and Butters, N., The role of interference and encoding in the short-term memory deficits of Korsakoff patients, *Neuropsychologia,* 10, 89–95, 1972.

Cermak, L. S., Butters, N. and Goodglass, H., The extent of memory loss in Korsakoff patients, *Neuropsychologia,* 9,, 307–315, 1971.

Cermak, L. S., Butters, N. and Gerrein, J., The extent of the verbal encoding ability of Korsakoff patients, *Neuropsychologia,* 11, 85–94, 1973a.

Cermak, L. S., Lewis, R., Butters, N. et al, Role of verbal mediation in performance of motor tasks by Korsakoff patients, *Percept. Mot. Skills,* 37, 259–262, 1973b.

Chain, F., Chedru, F., Leblanc, M. and Lhermitte, F., Renseignements fournis par l'enregistrement du regard dans les pseudo hemianopsie d'origine frontale chez homme, *Rev. EEG and Neurophysiol. Clin. de langue francaise,* 2, 223–232, 1972.

Chaney, R. E. and Webster, J. C., Information in certain multidimensional sounds, *J. Ac. Soc. Am.,* 47, 447–455, 1967.

Chapanis, N. P., Utmatsu, S., Konigsmark, B. and Walker, A. E., Central phosphenes in man: A report of three cases, *Neuropsychologia,* 10, 27–42, 1972.

Charcot, J. M., "Sur un cas de cécité verbale," in *Lecons sur les maladies du systeme nerveux,* Vol. 3 of *Oeuvres Completes de J. M. Charcot,* Delahaye & Lecrosnier, Paris, 1877.

Charcot, J. M., Des differentes Formes de l'aphasie et de la cécité verbale, *Progr. Med.* (Paris), 11, 441–444, 1883a.

Charcot, J. M., Des varietés de l'aphasie. De la cécité des mots, *Progr. Med.* (Paris), 11, 469–471, 1883b.

Charcot, J. M., Un Cas de suppression brusque et isolee de la vision mentale des signes et des objets (formes et couleurs), *Progr. Med.,* 11, 568, 1883c.

Charcot, J. M., "Physiologie et pathologie du moignon; a propos d'un homme ampute du bras gauche," in *Lecons du mardi a la Salpetriere,* 1, 344–355, 1892.

Chedru, F. and Geschwind, N., Disorders of higher cortical function in acute confusional states, *Cortex,* 8, 395–411, 1972.

Cherkin, A. and Harroun, P., Anaesthesia and memory processes, *Anaesthesiol.,* 34, 469–474, 1971.

Chesher, E. C., Some observations concerning the relation of handedness to the language mechanism, *Bull. Neurol. Inst. N.Y.,* 4, 556–562, 1936.

Chocholle, R., Chedru, F., Botte, M. C. et al, Etude psychoacoustique d'un cas de "surdite corticale," *Neuropsychologia,* 2, 13, 163–172, 1975.

Chomsky, N., *Aspects of a Theory of Syntax,* The MIT Press, Cambridge, Mass., 1965.

Chorover, S. L. and Cole, M., Delayed alternation performances in patients with cerebral lesions, *Neuropsychologia,* 4, 1–7, 1966.

Chow, K. L., Further studies on selective ablation of associative cortex in relation to visually mediated behavior, *J. Comp. Physiol. Psychol.,* 47, 194–198, 1954.

Chow, K. L., Visual discriminations after extensive ablation of optic tract and visual cortex, *Brain Res.,* 9, 363–366, 1968.

Claparede, E., La perception stereognostique. *Internat. Med. Biol.* (Paris), 1, 432–437, 1898.

Claparede, E., Agnosie et asymbolie, *Rev. Neurol.*, **14**, 803–805, 1906.

Clarke, B. and Zangwill, O., A case of "crossed aphasia" in a dextral, *Neuropsychologia*, **3**, 81–86, 1965.

Cogan, D. G. and Adams, R. D., A type of paralysis of conjugate gaze (ocular motor apraxia), *Arch. Ophthalmol*, **50**, 434–442, 1953.

Cohen, L., Perception of reversible figures after brain injury, *AMA Arch. Neurol. Psychiat.*, **81**, 765–775, 1959.

Cohen, D. and Hécaen, H., Remarques neurolinguistiques sur un cas d'agrammatisine, *J. de Psych.*, **3**, 273–296, 1965.

Cohen, D., Dubois, J., Gauthier, M., Hécaen, H. and Angelergues, R., Aspects du fonctionnement du code linguistique chez les aphasiques moteurs, *Neuropsychologia*, **1**, 165–177, 1963.

Cohn, R., Differential cerebral processing of noise and verbal stimuli, *Science*, **172**, 599–601, 1971.

Colavita, F. B., Auditory cortical lesions and visual pattern discrimination in cats, *Brain Res.*, **39**, 437–447, 1972a.

Colavita, F. B., Insular temporal lesions and visual pattern discrimination in cats, *Brain Res.*, **39**, 432–437, 1972b.

Colavita, F. B., Insular-temporal lesions and vibro-tactile temporal pattern discrimination in cats, *Physiol. Behav.*, **13**, 215–218, 1974.

Cole, D. D., Sullins, W. R. and Isaac, W., Pharmacological modifications of the effects of spaced occipital ablations, *Psychopharmacol.*, **11**, 311–316, 1967.

Collignon, R., Hécaen, H. and Angelergues, R., A propos de 12 cas d'aphasie acquise de l'enfant, *Acta Neurol. et Psychiat. Belgica*, **68**, 245–277, 1968.

Collins, R. L. and Ward, R., Evidence for an asymmetry of cerebral function in mice tested for audiogenic seizures, *Nature* (London), **226**, 1062–1063, 1970.

Colonnier, M. L., "The Structural Design of the Neocortex," in J. C. Eccles (ed.), *Brain and Conscious Experience*, Springer-Verlag, New York, 1966, pp. 1–23.

Conomy, J. P., Disorders of body image after spinal cord injury, *Neurol.* (Minneapolis), **23**, 842–850, 1973.

Conrad, K., Versuch einer psychologischen Analyse des Parietalsyndroms, *Mtschr. f. Psychiatr. Neurol.*, **84**, 28–97, 1932.

Conrad, K., Das korperschema, Eine kritische Studie und der Versuch einer Revision, *Ztschr. Neurol. Psychiatr.*, **147**, 346–369, 1933.

Conrad, K., Über den Begriff der Vorgestalt und seine Bedeutung fur die Hirnpathologie, *Nervenarzt*, **18**, 289–293, 1947.

Conrad, K., Über Aphasische Aprachstorungen bei hirnverletzen Linkshander, *Nervenarzt*, **20**, 148–154, 1949.

Conrad, K., New problems of aphasia, *Brain*, **77**, 491–509, 1954.

Cooper, L. A. and Shepard, R. N., Mental transformations in the identification of left and right hands, *J. Exp. Psychol. (Hum. Percept.)*, **1**, 104, 48–56, 1975.

Corkin, S., Tactually guided maze learning in man: Effects of unilateral cortical excisions and bilateral hippocampal lesions, *Neuropsychologia*, **3**, 339–352, 1965.

Corkin, S., Acquisition of motor skill after bilateral medial temporal-lobe excision, *Neuropsychologia*, **3**, 6, 255–265, 1968.

Corkin, S., Milner, B. and Rasmussen, T., Somatosensory thresholds. Contrasting effects of postcentral gyrus and posterior parietal lobe excisions, *Arch. Neurol.*, **23**, 41–58, 1970.

Cornwell, P., Loss of auditory pattern discrimination following insular temporal lesions in cats, *J. Comp. Physiol. Psychol.*, **63**, 165–168, 1967.

Corsi, P. M., Human memory and the medial temporal region of the brain, Thesis, McGill University, Canada, 1972.

Costa, R. D. and Vaughan, H. G., Performance of patients with lateralized cerebral lesions, I.

Verbal and perceptual tests, *J. Nerv. Ment. Dis.*, **184**, 162–168, 1962.

Coulter, J. D., Sensory transmission through lemniscal pathway during voluntary movement in the cat, *J. Neurophysiol.*, **5**, 37, 831–845, 1974.

Courtney, J., Davis, J. M. and Solomon, P., Sensory deprivation: The role of movement, *Percept. Mot. Skills*, **13**, 191–199, 1961.

Courville, C. B., Auditory hallucinations provoked by intracranial tumors, *J. Nerv. Ment. Dis.*, **67**, 265–274, 1928.

Cowey, A. and Bozek, T., Contralateral "neglect" after unilateral dorsomedial prefrontal lesions in rats, *Brain Res.*, **72**, 53–63, 1974.

Cowey, A. and Dewson, J. H., Effects of unilateral ablation of superior temporal cortex on auditory sequence discrimination in *Macaca mulatta*, *Neuropsychologia*, **10**, 279–289, 1972.

Cowey, A. and Gross, C. G., Effects of foveal prestriate and inferotemporal lesions on visual discrimination by rhesus monkeys, *Exp. Brain Res.*, **11**, 128–144, 1970.

Cowey, A. and Weiskrantz, L., A comparison of the effects of inferotemporal and striate cortex lesions on the visual behavior of rhesus monkeys, *Quart. J. Exp. Psychol.*, **19**, 246–253, 1967.

Cragg, B. G. and Ainsworth, A., The topography of the afferent projections in the circumstriate visual cortex of the monkey studied by the Nauta method, *Vision Res.*, **9**, 737–747, 1969.

Crawford, J. S., Harley, N. F., Bland, E. P. et al., Awareness during anesthesia, *Brit. Med. J.*, **1**, 508, 1969.

Critchley, M., Anterior cerebral artery and its syndromes, *Brain*, **53**, 120–165, 1930.

Critchley, M., *The Parietal Lobes*, E. Arnold & Co., London, 1953.

Critchley, M., "Speech and Speech-Loss in Relation to the Duality of the Brain," in V. Mountcastle (ed.), *Interhemispheric Relations and Cerebral Dominance*, Johns Hopkins University Press, Baltimore, 208–213, 1962.

Critchley, M., The neurology of psychotic speech, *Brit. J. Psychiat.*, **40**, 353–364, 1964.

Crockett, H. G. and Estridge, N. M., Cerebral hemispherectomy, *Bull. Los Angeles Neurol. Soc.*, **16**, 71–87, 1951.

Cronholm, B. and Molander, L., Memory disturbances after ECT, *Acta Psychiat. Neurol. Scand.*, **40**, 211, 1964.

Curry, F. K. W., A comparison of left-handed and right-handed subjects on verbal and non-verbal dichotic listening tasks, *Cortex*, **3**, 343–352, 1962.

Curry, F. K. W. and Rutherford, D. R., Recognition and recall of dichotically presented verbal stimuli by right- and left-handed persons, *Neuropsychologia*, **5**, 119–126, 1967.

Cushing, H., A note upon the faradic stimulation of the postcentral gyrus in conscious patients, *Brain*, **32**, 44–54, 1909.

Cushing, H., Distortions of visual fields in cases of brain tumor, *Brain*, **44**, 341, 1922.

Cushing, H. and Eisenhardt, L., *Meningiomas*, Charles C. Thomas, Springfield, Ill., 1938.

Cutting, J. E., Two left hemisphere mechanisms in speech perception, *Perception and Psychophysics*, **16**, 601–612, 1974.

Dalby, D. A., Meyer, D. R. and Meyer, P. M., Effects of occipital neocortical lesions upon visual discriminations in the cat, *Physiol. Behav.* **5**, 727–734, 1970.

Darley, F., "Language Rehabilitation," in A. L. Benton (ed.), *Behavioral Change in Cerebrovascular Disease*, Harper and Row, New York, 1970.

Darley, F. L., Aronson, A. E. and Brown, J. R., Motor speech signs in neurologic disease, *Med. Clin. N. Amer.*, **52**, 835–844, 1968.

Darley, F. L., Treatment of acquired aphasia, *Adv. Neurol.*, **7**, 111–145, 1975.

Darley, F. L., Aronson, A. E. and Brown, J. R., Clusters or deviant speech dimensions in the dysarthrias, *JSHR*, **12**, 462–496, 1969a.

Darley, F. L., Aronson, A. E. and Brown, J. R., Differential diagnostic patterns of dysarthria, *JSHR*, **12**, 246–269, 1969b.

Darwin, C. J., "Ear Differences and Hemispheric Specializations," in F. O. Schmidt and F. G. Worden (eds.), *Neurosciences Third Study Program*, MIT Press, Cambridge, Mass., 1974, pp. 57–63.

Davidenkoff, S. N., "Visual Agnosias," in *Clinical Lectures in Nervous Diseases* [in Russian], State Publishing House of Medical Literature, Leningrad, 1958.

Davy, H., Amnesic effect of nitrous oxide, 1799, cited in Cherkin, A. and Harroun, P., 1971.

Dawson, R. G., Conrad, L. and Lynch, G., Single and two-stage hippocampal lesions: A similar syndrome, *Exp. Neurol.*, **40**, 263–272, 1973.

Dax, M., Lesions de la moitie gauche de l'encephale coincidant avec trouble des signes de la pensee (lu a Montpellier en 1836), *Gaz. Hibd. 2ieme serie*, **2**, 1865.

Deal, J. and Darley, F., The influence of linguistic and situational variables on phonemic accuracy in apraxia of speech, *JSHR*, **15**, 639–653, 1972.

Dee, H. L. and Fontenot, D. J., Cerebral dominance and lateral differences in perception and memory, *Neuropsychologia*, **11**, 167–173, 1973.

de Barenne, J. and Dusser, J. G., Experimental research on sensory localizations in the cerebral cortex, *Quart. J. Exp. Physiol.*, **9**, 355–390, 1916.

Dejerine, J., Sur un cas de cécité verbale avec agraphie, suivi d'autopsie, *Mem. Soc. Biol.*, **3**, 197–201, 1891.

Dejerine, J., Contribution à l'etude anatomoclinique et clinique des différentes varietes de cécité verbale, *C. R. Soc. Biol.* **4**, 61–90, 1892.

Dejerine, J., A propos de l'agnosie tactile, *Rev. Neurol.*, **15**, 781–784, 1907.

Dejerine, J., Discussion sur l'aphasie, *Rev. Neurol.*, **16**, 611, 974, 1908.

Dejerine, J., Semeiologie des affections du systeme nerveux, Masson et Cie, Paris, 1914.

Dejerine, J. and Andre-Thomas, J., Un Cas de cécité verbale avec agraphie suivi d'autopsie, *Rev. Neurol.*, **12**, 655–664, 1904.

Dejerine, J., and Dejerine, S., Sur l'hypertrophie compensatrice du aisceau pyramidal du côté sain dans un cas d'hémiplégie cérébrale infantile. *Rev. Neurol.*, **10**, 642–646, 1902.

Dejerine, J. and Mouzon, S., Un nouveau type de syndrome sensitif cortical observé dans un cas de monoplegie corticale dissociée, *Rev. Neurol.*, **2**, 388–392, 1914.

Dejerine, J. and Serieux, J., *C. R. Soc. Biol.;* cited by Henschen, 1920–1922.

Dejerine, J. and Vialet, N., Sur un cas de cécité corticale, *C. R. Soc. Biol.*, **11**, 983, 1893.

Delay, J., *Les astereognosies, Pathologie du toucher*, Masson et Cie, Paris, 1935.

Delay, J. and Brion, S., *Les Demences tardives*, Masson et Cie, Paris, 1962.

Delay, J. and Brion, S., *Le Syndrome de Korsakoff*, Masson et Cie, Paris, 1969.

Dement, W. C. and Kleitman, N., Cyclic variations in EEG during sleep and their relation to eye movements, bodily motility and dreaming, *Electroencephal. Clin. Neurophysiol.*, **9**, 673–690, 1957.

Denney, D. and Adorjani, C., Orientation specificity of visual cortical neurons after head tilt, *Exp. Brain Res.*, **14**, 312–317, 1972.

Denny-Brown, D., *The Frontal Lobes and Their Function. Modern Trends in Neurology*, Butterworth, London, 1951.

Denny-Brown, D., The nature of apraxia, *J. Nerv. Ment. Dis.*, **126**, 1, 9–33, 1958.

Denny-Brown, D., "Discussion," in V. B. Mountcastle (ed.), *Interhemispheric Relations and Cerebral Dominance*, The Johns Hopkins University Press, Baltimore, 1962, pp. 242–252.

Denny-Brown, D., "The Physiological Bases of Perception and Speech," in H. Halpern, (ed.), *Problems of Dynamic Neurology*, Jerusalem Post Press, Jerusalem, 1963, pp. 1–33.

Denny-Brown, D. and Banker, B., Amorphosynthesis from left parietal lesion, *Arch. Neurol. Psychiat.*, **71**, 301–313, 1954.

Denny-Brown, D. and Chambers, R. A., Visual-motor function in the cerebral cortex, *J. Nerv. Ment. Dis.*, **121**, 288–289, 1955.

Denny-Brown, D. and Chambers, R. A., The parietal lobe and behavior, *Res. Publ. Assoc. Nerv. Ment. Dis.*, **36**, 35–117, 1958.

Denny-Brown, D., Meyer, J. S. and Horenstein, S., The significance of perceptual rivalry resulting from parietal lobe lesion, *Brain*, **75**, 433–471, 1952.

DeRenzi, E., Deficit gnosici, prassici, mnestici, e intellettivi nelle lesion: emisferiche unilaterali, in Att: XVI Congresso Nazionale di Neurologia, Pensiero Scientifico, Roma, 1967.

DeRenzi, E. and Faglioni, P., L'Autotopagnosia, *Arch. di psicologia, neurologia e psichiatria*, **24**, 1–34, 1963.

DeRenzi, E. and Scotti, G., The influence of spatial disorders in impairing tactual discrimination of shapes, *Cortex*, **5**, 53–63, 1969.

DeRenzi, E. and Scotti, G., Autotopognosia: Fiction or reality? *Arch. Neurol.*, **23**, 221–227, 1970.

DeRenzi, E. and Spinnler, H., Visual recognition in patients with unilateral cerebral disease, *J. Nerv. Ment. Dis.*, **142**, 513–525, 1966a.

DeRenzi, E. and Spinnler, H., Facial recognition in brain-damaged patients. An experimental approach, *Neurol.*, **16**, 145–152, 1966b.

DeRenzi, E. and Spinnler, H., Impaired performance on color tasks in patients with hemispheric damage, *Cortex*, **3**, 194–216, 1967.

DeRenzi, E., Faglioni, P., Savoiardo, M. and Vignolo, L. A., The influence of the hemispheric side of the cerebral lesion on abstract thinking, *Cortex*, **2**, 399–420, 1966.

DeRenzi, E., Pieczulo, A. and Vignolo, L. A., Ideational apraxia: A quantitative study, *Neuropsychologia*, **6**, 41–52, 1968a.

DeRenzi, E., Faglioni, P. and Scotti, G., Tactile spatial impairment and unilateral cerebral damage, *J. Nerv. Ment. Dis.*, **146**, 468–475, 1968b.

DeRenzi, E., Faglioni, P. and Spinnler, H., The performance of patients with unilateral brain damage on face recognition tasks, *Cortex*, **4**, 17–34, 1968c.

DeRenzi, E., Faglioni, P. and Scotti, G., Impairment of memory for position following brain damage, *Cortex*, **5**, 274–284, 1969a.

DeRenzi, E., Scotti, G. and Spinnler, H., Perceptual and associative disorders of visual recognition. Relationship to the side of the cerebral lesion, *Neurology*, **19**, 634–642, 1969b.

DeRenzi, E., Faglioni, P. and Scotti, G., Hemispheric contribution to exploration of space through the visual and tactile modality, *Cortex*, **6**, 191–203, 1970a.

DeRenzi, E., Faglioni, P. and Scotti, G., Loss of the ability to perceive the spatial orientation of a rod after posterior right brain damage, Communication presented at a meeting of the EBBS, Oxford, England, Sept., 1970b.

DeRenzi, E., Faglioni, P., Scotti, G. et al, Impairment of color sorting behavior after hemispheric damage: An experimental study with the Holmgren skein test, *Cortex*, **8**, 147–163, 1972.

DeRenzi, E., Faglioni, P., Scotti, G. et al, Impairment in associating color to form, concomitant with aphasia, *Brain*, **95**, 293–304, 1972.

Desmedt, J. E. and Mechelse, K., Mise en évidence d'une quatrième aire de projection acoustique dans l'écorce cérébrale du chat, *J. Physiol.*, **51**, 448–449, 1959.

Deutsch, J. A. and Hamburg, G., Anticholinesterase-induced amnesia and its temporal aspects, *Science*, **151**, 221–223, 1966.

DeValois, R. L., "Central Mechanisms of Color Vision," in R. Jung (ed.), *Handbook of Sensory Physiology Central Visual Information Part A,* Springer-Verlag, Berlin, Heidelberg, New York, 1973, pp. 209–253.

Dews, P. B. and Wiesel, T. N., Consequences of monocular deprivation on visual behavior in kittens, *J. Physiol.*, **206**, 437–455, 1970.

Dewson, J. H., Speech sound discrimination by cats, *Science*, **144**, 555–556, 1964.

Dewson, J. H., Pribram, K. and Lynch, J. C., Effects of ablations of temporal cortex upon speech sound discrimination in the monkey, *Exp. Neurol.*, **24**, 579–591, 1969.

Dewson, J. H., Cowey, A. and Weiskrantz, L., Descriptions of auditory sequence discrimination by unilateral and bilateral cortical ablations of superior temporal gyrus in the monkey, *Exp. Neurol.*, **28**, 529–548, 1970.

Diamond, I. T. and Hall, W. C., Evolution of neocortex, *Science*, **164**, 251–262, 1969.

Dichgans, J., Bizzi, E., Murasso, P., and Tagliasio, V., Mechanisms underlying recovery of eye-head coordination following bilateral labyrinthectomy in monkeys, *Exp. Brain Res.*, **18**, 548–562, 1973.

Dide, M., Les Désorientations temporospatiales et la préponderance de l'hemisphere droit dans les agnosies-akinesies proprioceptives, *L'Encephale*, **2**, 276–294, 1938.

Dide, M. and Botcazo, H., Amnesie continue, cécité verbale pure, perte du sens topographique, ramollissement double du lobe lingual, *Rev. Neurol.*, **10**, 676–680, 1902.

Dimond, S., *The Double Brain*, Williams & Wilkins Co., Baltimore, 1972.

Dimond, S. and Beaumont, G., Hemisphere function and paired-associate learning *Brit. J. Psychol.*, **65**, 275–278, 1974.

Divac, I., Rosvold, H. E. and Szwarcbart, M. K., Behavioral effects of selective ablation of the caudate nucleus, *J. Comp. Physiol. Psychol.*, **63**, 184–190, 1967.

Dobelle, W. N. and Mladejorsky, M. G., Phosphenes produced by electrical stimulation of human occipital cortex, and their application to the development of a prosthesis for the blind, *J. Physiol.* (London), **2**, 243, 553–576, 1974a.

Dobelle, W. N. and Mladejorsky, M. G., The directions for future research on sensory prostheses, *Trans. Amer. Soc. Artif. Intern. Organs*, **20B**, 425–429, 1974b.

Dobelle, W. H., Mladejorsky, M. G. and Garvin, J. P., Artificial vision for the blind: electrical stimulation of visual cortex offers hope for functional prosthesis, *Science*, **183**, 440–444, 1974.

Donaldson, H. H., On the temperature-sense, *Mind*, **10**, 339, 1885.

Donini, F., Su di un caso di aprasia construttiva con grave disorientamento esospaziale e perdita della facolta del riconiscemento della fisinomia della persone, *Note Psichiatre*, **68**, 469–485, 1939.

Dorff, J. E., Mirsky, A. F. and Mishkin, M., Effects of unilateral temporal lobe removals in man on tachistoscopic recognition on left and right visual fields, *Neuropsychologia*, **3**, 39–52, 1965.

Dorgeuille, C., Introduction a l'étude des amusies, 170 pages dactylographiées, These, Paris, 1966.

Doty, R. W., "Functional Significance of the Topographical Aspects of the Retinocortical Projection," in R. Jung and H. Kornhuber (eds.), *Neurophysiologie und Psychophysik des visuellen Systems*, Springer-Verlag, Berlin, 1961, pp. 228–245.

Doty, R. W., Survival of pattern vision after removal of striate cortex in the adult cat, *J. Comp. Neurol.*, **143**, 341–370, 1971.

Doty, R. W., "Ablation of Visual Areas in the Central Nervous System," in R. Jung, (ed.), *Handbook of Sensory Physiology*, Vol. III 3 B, *Central Processing of Visual Information*, Springer-Verlag, Berlin, 1973, pp. 438–541.

Doty, R. W. and Yamaga, K., Maze behavior in macaques, *Amer. J. Phys. Anthropol.*, **38**, 403–405, 1973.

Dow, R. S., Some novel concepts of cerebellar physiology, *Mt. Sinai J. Med.*, (New York), **41**, 103–119, 1974.

Dow, B. M. and Dubner, R., Visual receptive fields and responses to movement in an association area of cat cerebral cortex, *J. Neurophysiol.*, **32**, 773–784, 1969.

Drachman, D. A. and Arbit, J., Memory and the hippocampal complex, II. Is memory a multiple process?, *Arch. Neurol.*, **15**, 52–62, 1966.

Dreyer, D. A., Schneider, R. J., Metz, C. B. et al, Differential contributions of spinal pathways to body representation in post-central gyrus of *Macaca mulatta*, *J. Neurophysiol.*, **37**, 119–145, 1974.

Dubois, J., Hécaen, H., Angelergues, R., Maufras du Chatelier, A., and Marcie, P., Etude neurolinguistique de l'aphasie de conduction, *Neuropsychologia*, **2**, 9–44, 1964.

Dubois, J., Mazars, G., Marcie, P. and Hécaen, H., Etude des performances aux epreuves linguistiques des sujets atteints de syndromes parkinsoniens, *L'Encephale*, **55**, 496–513, 1966.

Dubois, J., Hécaen, H. and Marcie, P., L'agraphie "pure," *Neuropsychologia*, **7**, 271–286, 1969.

Dubois, J., Hécaen, H., Cunin, M. et al, Analyse linguistique d'énonces d'aphasiques sensoriels, *J. Psychol.*, **2**, 185–190, 1970.

Dubois-Charlier, F., Etude neurolinguistique de l'alexie pure (These IIIe cycle, Faculte des Lettres et Sciences Humaines, Paris Est.), 1970.

Dubois-Charlier, F., Approche neurolinguistique du probleme de l'alexie pure, *J. Psychol.* **1**, 39–68, 1971.

Dubois-Charlier, F., A note on literal alexia, *Internat. J. Ment. Health*, **1**, 11–14, 1972a.

Dubois-Charlier, F., A propos de l'alexie pure, *Langages*, **25**, 76–94, 1972b.

Dusser de Barenne, J. G., "The Labyrinthine and Postural Mechanisms," in *Handbook of General Experimental Psychology*, 1934, pp. 204–246.

Duensing, F., Raumagnostische und ideatorisch-apraktische Storung des Gestaltenden Handelns, *Dtsch. Z. Nervenhk.*, **170**, 72–94, 1953.

Duffy, F. H. and Burchfiel, J. L., Eye morement related inhibition of primate visual neurons, *Brain Res.*, **89**, 121–132, 1975.

Dunn, T., Double hemiplegia with double hemianopsia and loss of geographical centre, *Transactions of the College of Physicians of Philadelphia*, **16**, 45–55, 1895.

Durnford, M. and Kimura, D., Right hemisphere specialization for depth perception reflected in visual field differences, *Nature*, **231**, 394–395, 1971.

Ebtinger, R. *Aspects psycho-pathologiques du post electrochoc.*, Colmar, Alsatia, France, 1958.

Efron, R., The effect of handedness on the perception of simultaneity and temporal order, *Brain*, **86**, 261–284, 1963a.

Efron, R., The effect of stimulus intensity on the perception of simultaneity in right- and left-handed subjects, *Brain*, **86**, 285–294, 1963b.

Efron, R., Temporal perception, aphasia, and *déjà vú*, *Brain*, **86**, 403–424, 1963c.

Ehrenwald, H., Anosognosie und Depersonalisation. Ein Beitrag zur Psychologie der linkseitig hemiplegischen, *Nervenartz*, **112**, 240–244, 1931a.

Ehrenwald, H., Storung der Zeitauffassung der raumlichen Orientierung des Zeichnens und des Rechnens bei einem Hirnverletzen, *Ztschr. Neurol. Psychiatr.*, **132**, 518–569, 1931b.

Eidelberg, E., Kreinick, C. J. and Langescheid, C., On the possible functional role of afferent pathways in skin sensation, *Exp. Neurol.*, **47**, 419–432, 1973.

Eimas, P., Siqueland, E., Jusczyr P., and Vigorito J., Speech perception in infants, *Science*, **171**, 303–306, 1971.

Eisenson, J., Language dysfunctions associated with right brain damage, *Acti del VIIe Congresso Internationale de Neurologia*, Rome, 1961.

Elithorn, A., Intelligence, perceptual integration and the minor hemisphere syndrome, *Neuropsychologia*, **2**, 327–332, 1964.

Engerth, G., Zeichenstorungen bei Patienten mit Autotopagnosie, *Z. ges. Neurol. Psychiatr.*, **143**, 381–402, 1932.

Erlanger, J. and Gasser, H. S., *"Electrical Signs of Nervous Activity,* University of Pennsylvania Press, Philadelphia, 1937.

Erlanger, J., Gasser, H. S. and Bishop, G. H., The compound nature of the action current of nerve as disclosed by the cathode ray oscillograph, *Amer. J. Physiol.*, **70**, 624–666, 1924.

Ervin, S. and Osgood, C., "Psycholinguistics: A Survey of Theory and Research Problems," in C. Osgood and F. Sebeok (eds.), *Psycholinguistics, J. Abn. Soc. Psychol., Suppl.* 1954a.

Ervin, S. and Osgood, C., "Second Language Learning and Bilingualism," in C. Osgood and F. Sebeok (eds.), *Psycholinguistics, J. Abn. Soc. Psychol., Suppl.*, 139–146, 1954b.

Ethelberg, F., On changes in circulation through the anterior cerebral artery, *Acta Psychiat. et Neurol. Scandinavica,* Suppl., **75,** 1951.

Ettlinger, G., Sensory deficits in visual agnosia, *J. Neurol. Neurosurg. Psychiat.,* **19,** 4, 297–308, 1956.

Ettlinger, G., The description and interpretation of pictures in cases of brain damage, *J. Ment. Sci.,* **106,** 1337–1346, 1960.

Ettlinger, G., Defective identification of fingers, *Neuropsychologia,* **1,** 39–45, 1963.

Ettlinger, G., Apraxia considered as a disorder of movements that are language-dependent: Evidence from cases of brain bi-section, *Cortex,* **5,** 285–289, 1969.

Ettlinger, G. and Kahlsbeck, J. E., Changes in tactual discrimination and in visual reaching after successive and simultaneous bilateral posterior parietal ablations in the monkey, *J. Neurol. Neurosurg. Psychiat.,* **25,** 256–268, 1962.

Ettlinger, G., Jackson, C. V. and Zangwill, O. L., Dysphasia following right temporal lobectomy in a right-handed man, *J. Neurol. Neurosurg. Psychiat.,* **18,** 214–217, 1955.

Evarts, E. V. and Nissen, H. W., Test of abstract attitude in chimpanzees following ablation of prefrontal cortex. *Arch. Neurol. Psychiat.,* **69,** 323–331, 1953.

Ewert, J. P., Neural mechanisms of prey-catching and avoidance behavior in the toad (*Bufo bufo* L), *Brain Behav. Evol,* **1–4,** 36–56, 1970.

Exner, S., *Untersuchungen über die Lokalisation der Funktionen in der Grosshirnrinde des Menschen,* W. Braumuller Wien, 1881.

Faglioni, P., Gatti, B., Paganoni, A. M. et al, A psychometric evaluation of developmental dyslexia in Italian children, *Cortex,* **5,** 15–26, 1969a.

Faglioni, P., Scotti, G. and Spinnler, H., Impaired recognition of written letters following unilateral hemispheric damage, *Cortex,* **5,** 120–133, 1969b.

Faglioni, P., Spinnler, H. and Vignolo, L. A., Contrasting behavior of right and left hemisphere damaged patients on a discriminative and semantic task of auditory recognition, *Cortex,* **5,** 366–389, 1969c.

Fant, C. G. M., *Acoustic Theory of Speech Production,* Mouton, The Hague, 1960.

Fantz, R. L., Ordy, J. M. and Udelf, M. S., Maturation of pattern vision in infants during the first six months, *J. Comp. Physiol. Psychol.,* **55,** 907–916, 1962.

Faust, C., *Die zerebralen Herdstorungen bei Hinterhauptsverletzungen und ihre Beurteilung,* G. Thieme Verlag, Stuttgart, 1955, pp. 111.

Fedio, P. and Mirsky, A. F., Selective intellectual deficits in children with temporal lobe or centrencephalic epilepsy, *Neuropsychologia,* **7,** 287–300, 1969.

Fedio, P. and van Buren, M., Memory and perceptual deficits during electrical stimulation in the left and right thalamus and parietal subcortex, *Brain Lang.,* **1, 2,** 78–100, 1975.

Ferrier, D., *The Functions of the Brain,* 2nd ed., Smith, Elder, and Co., London, 1878.

Feuchtwanger, E., "Die Funktionen des Stirnhirns, ihre Pathologie und Psychologie," Monogr. aus: O. Foerstr and K. Williams (eds.), *Gesget, Neurol. Psychiat.,* Springer-Verlag, Berlin, Heft 38, 4–194, 1923.

Feuchtwanger, E., "Amusie, Studien zur pathologischen Psychologie der akustischen Wahrnehmung und Vorstellung und ihrer Strukturgebiete besonders in Musik und Sprache," *Monograph aus dem Gesamtgeb. der Neur. u. Psych.,* J. Springer, Berlin, 1930.

Finkelnburg, R., Vortrag in der Niedernheim Gessellschaft der Aerzte, Bonn, Berlin, *Klin. Wochenschr.,* **7,** 449, 1870.

Finan, J. L., Delayed response with pre-delay reinforcement in monkeys after removal of the frontal lobe, *Amer. J. Psychol.,* **55,** 202–214, 1942.

Finger, S., Walbran, B. and Stein, D. G., Brain damage and behavioral recovery: Serial lesion phenomena, *Brain Res.,* **63,** 1–18, 1973.

Fisher, C. M., Concussion amnesia, *Neurol.* (Minneapolis), **16,** 826–830, 1966.

Fisher, C. M. and Adams, R., Transient global amnesia, *Trans Amer. Neurol. Assoc.,* **83,** 143–145, 1958.

Fisher, C. M. and Adams, R., Transient global amnesia, *Acta Neurol. Scand., Suppl.* 9, 1964.

Fleschig, P., Developmental localisation of the cerebral cortex in the human subject, *Lancet,* **2,** 1027–1029, 1901.

Flexner, J. B., Flexner, L. B. and Stellar, E., Memory in mice as affected by intracerebral puromycin, *Science,* **141,** 57–59, 1963.

Fontenot, D. J. and Benton, A. L., Tactile perception of direction in relation to hemispheric locus of lesion, *Neuropsychologia,* **9,** 83–88, 1971.

Foerster, O., Beitrage zur Pathologie der Sehbahn und der Sehsphare, *J. Psychol. Neurol.,* **39,** 463, 1928.

Foerster, O., "Sensible corticale felder," *Bumke Foersters Handbuch der Neurologie,* Vol. 6, pp. 358–448, 1936.

Foerster, R., Über Rinderblindheit, Albrecht v. Graefs, *Arch. Ophthalm.,* **36,** 98–108, 1890.

Foix, C., Contribution a l'étude de l'apraxie ideomotrice, *Rev. Neur.,* **1,** 285–298, 1916.

Foix, C., Sur une variete de troubles bilateraux de la sensibilite par lesion unilaterale du cerveau, *Rev. Neurol.,* **29,** 322–331, 1922.

Foix, Ch., "Aphasies," in G. Roger, F. Widal and P. J. Teissier (eds.), *Nouveau Traite de Medecine,* Masson et Cie, Paris, **18,** 135–213, 1928.

Foix, Ch. and Hillemand, P., Role vraisemblabe du splenium dans la pathogenie de l'alexie pure par lesion de la cerebrale posterieure, *Bull. et Mem. Soc. Med. Hop. Paris,* **41,** 393–395, 1925.

Forbes, B. F. and Moskowitz, N., Projections of auditory responsive cortex in the squirrel monkey, *Brain Res.,* **67,** 239–254, 1974.

Fraisse, P., Noizet, G. and Flament, C., "Frequence et familiarite du vocabulaire," in *Problemes de Psycholinguistique,* P. U. F., Paris, pp. 157–167, 1962.

Franz, S. I., On the functions of the cerebrum: The frontal lobes, **8,** 1–22, 1902.

Franz, S. I., New phrenology, *Science,* **35,** 321–328, 1912.

Frazier, C., Tumor involving the frontal lobe alone, *Arch. Neurol. Psychiat.,* **35,** 525–571, 1936.

Fredricks, J. A. M., Anosognosie et hemiasomatognosie, *Rev. Neurol.,* **109,** 585–597, 1963.

Fredricks, J. A. M., "Disorders of the Body Schema," in P. J. Vinken and G. W. Bruyn (eds.), *Handbook of Clinical Neurology, IV,* North Holland Publishing Co., Amsterdam, 1969, pp. 207–240.

Fredrickson, J. M., Figge, U., Scheid, P. and Kornhuber, H. H., Vestibular nerve projection to the cerebral cortex of the rhesus monkey, *Exp. Brain Res.,* **2,** 318–327, 1966.

Fredrickson, J. M., Kornhuber, H. H. and Goode, R. C., Nystagmus, diagnostic significance of recent observations, *Arch. Otolaryng.,* **89,** 504–511, 1968.

Fredrickson, J. M., Kornhuber, H. H. and Schwartz, D. W. F., "Cortical projections of the vestibular nerve," in H. H. Kornhuber (ed.), *Vestibular System, Handbook of Sensory Physiology* VI, Springer-Verlag, Berlin, Heidelberg, New York, 1973, pp. 565–582.

Freedman, S. J., Perceptual changes in sensory deprivation: Suggestions for a conative theory, *J. Nerv. Ment. Dis.,* **132,** 17–21, 1961.

Freedman, S. J., "Experimental Deafferentation in Man," in J. de Ajuriaguerra (ed.), Georg et Cie, Geneva; Masson et Cie, Paris, 1965, pp. 79–88.

French, G., "The Frontal Lobes and Association," in J. M. Warren and K. Akert (eds.), *The Frontal Granular Cortex and Behavior,* McGraw-Hill, New York, 1964, pp. 56–72.

French, J. D., Hernandez-Peon, R. and Livingston, R. B., Projections from cortex to cephalic brainstem (reticular formation) in monkeys, *J. Neurophysiol.,* **18,** 74–95, 1955.

Freud, S., *Zur Auffassung der Aphasien,* Deuticke, Wien, 1891.

Freud, S., "Die Infantile Cerebrallahmung," in G. Nothnagel, *Specielle Pathologie und Therapie IX,* Holder, Vienna, 1897.

Freund, C. S., Über optische Aphasie und Seelenblindheit, *Arch. Psychiat. Nervenkhr.*, **20**, 276–297, 1888.

Fritsch, G. and Hitzig, G., Über die elektrische Erregbarkeit des Grosshirns, *Arch. Anat. Physiol.*, **4**, 300–332, 1870.

Frohman, L. A. and Bernardis, L. L., Growth hormone and insulin levels in weaning rats with ventromedial hypothalamic lesions, *Endocrinol.*, **82**, 1125–1132, 1968.

Fromkin, V. A., Krashen, S., Curtiss, S., Rigler, D. and Rigler, M., The development of language in Genie: A case of language acquisition beyond the critical period. *Brain and Lang.*, **1**, 81–108, 1974.

Fry, D. B., Phonemic substitutions in an aphasic patient, *Lang. and Speech*, **2**, 52–61, 1959.

Fulton, J. F., Forced grasping and groping in relation to the syndrome of the premotor area, *Arch. Neurol. Psychiat.*, **31**, 27–42, 1937.

Fulton, J., *Frontal Lobotomy and Affective Behavior*, Norton, New York, 1951.

Funkenstein, H. H., Winter, P. and Nelson, P. G., Unit response to acoustic stimuli in the cortex of awake squirrel monkeys, *Fed. Proc.*, **29**, 394, 1970.

Fuster, J. M., Unit activity in prefrontal cortex during delayed-response performance: Neuronal correlates of transient memory, *J. Neurophysiol.*, **36**, 61–78, 1973.

Fuster, J. M. and Alexander, G. E., Neuron activity related to short-term memory, *Science*, **173**, 652–654, 1971.

Gainotti, G., Les manifestation de negligence et d'inattention pour l'hemiespace, *Cortex*, **4**, 64–91, 1968.

Gainotti, G., Messerli, P. and Tissot, R., Qualitative analysis of unilateral spatial neglect in relation to laterality of cerebral lesion, *J. Neurol. Neurosurg. Psychiat.*, **35**, 545–550, 1972.

Gall, F. and Spurzheim, G., *Anatomie et Physiologie du Systeme Nerveux en General et du Cerveau en Particulier avec des Observations sur la Possibilité de Reconnaitre Plusieurs Dispositions Intellectuelles et Morales de L'homme et des Animaux par la Configuration de Leurs têtes*, 4 vol., F. Schoell, Paris, 1810–1819.

Gamper, E., Zur Frage der Polioencephalities haemorrhagica der chronischen Alkoholiker. Anatomische Befunde beim alkoholischen Korsakow und ihre Beziehungen zum klinischen Bild, *Dtsch. Z. Nervenhk*, **102**, 122–129, 1928.

Ganz, L. and Haffner, M. E., Permanent perceptual and neurophysiological effects of visual deprivation in the cat, *Exp. Brain Res.*, **20**, 67–87, 1974.

Ganz, L., Hirsch, H. V. and Tieman, S. B., The nature of perceptual deficits in visually deprived cats, *Brain Res.*, **44**, 547–568, 1972.

Gardner, H., *The Shattered Mind*, Knopf, New York, 1975.

Gardner, H. and Zurif, E., Bee but not be: Oral readings of single words in aphasia and alexia, *Neuropsychologia*, **2**, 13, 181–190, 1975.

Gardner, H., Boller, F., Moreines, J. and Butters, N., Retrieving information from Korsakoff patients, *Cortex*, **9**, 165–176, 1973.

Gardner, R. A. and Gardner, B. T., Teaching sign language to a chimpanzee, *Science*, **165**, 664–672, 1969.

Gascon, G., Victor, D. and Lambrosco, C. T., Language disorders, convulsive disorder and electroencephalographic abnormalities. Acquired syndrome in children, *Arch. Neurol.*, **28**, 156–162, 1973.

Gasser, H. S., Conduction in nerves in relation to fiber type, *Res. Publ. Assoc. Nerv. Ment. Dis.*, **15**, 35–59, 1935.

Gazzaniga, M. S., Effects of commissurotomy on preoperatively learned visual discrimination, *Exp. Neurol.*, **8**, 14–19, 1963.

Gazzaniga, M. S., Cross-cuing mechanisms and ipsilateral eye-hand control in split-brain monkeys, *Exp. Neurol.*, **23**, 11–17, 1969.

Gazzaniga, M. S., *The Bisected Brain,* Appleton-Century Crofts, New York, 1970.

Gazzaniga, M. S., Changing hemisphere dominance by changing reward probability in split-brain monkeys, *Exp. Neurol.,* **33**, 412–419, 1971.

Gazzaniga, M. S., Discrimination learning without reward, *Physiol. Behav.* **11**, 121–123, 1973.

Gazzaniga, M. S. and Hillyard, S. A., Language and speech capacity of the right hemisphere, *Neuropsychologia,* **9**, 273–280, 1971.

Gazzaniga, M. S. and Sperry, R. W., Language after section of the cerebral commissures, *Brain,* **90**, 131–148, 1967.

Gazzaniga, M. S., Bogen, J. E. and Sperry, R. W., Some functional effects of sectioning the cerebral commissures in man, *Proc. Natl. Acad. Sci.,* **48**, 1765–1769, 1962.

Gazzaniga, M. S., Bogen, J. E. and Sperry, R. W., Observations on visual perception after disconnexion of the cerebral hemispheres in man, *Brain,* **88**, 221–236, 1965.

Gazzaniga, M. S., Bogen, J. E. and Sperry, R. W., Dyspraxia following division of the cerebral commissures, *Arch. Neurol.,* **12**, 606–612, 1967.

Gazzaniga, M. S., Glass, A. V., Sarno, M. T. et al, Pure word deafness and hemispheric dynamics: A case history, *Cortex,* **9**, 136–143, 1973.

Gelb, A., Remarques generales sur l'utilisation des donnees pathologiques pour la psychologie et la philosophie du langage, *Journal de Psychologie XXXᵉ annee,* **30**, 403–429, 1933.

Gelb, A. and Goldstein, K., *Psychologische Analysen hirnpathologischer Falle,* Barth, Leipzig, 1920.

Gelb, A. and Goldstein, K., Über Farbenamnesie, *Psychol. Forsch.,* **6**, 127–186, 1924.

Gendrin, A. N., *Traite philosophique de medecine pratique,* Vol. 1, Germer Bailliere, Paris, 1838.

Gerstmann, J., Reine taktile agnosie, *Mtschr., Psychiat. Neurol.,* **44**, 329–343, 1918.

Gerstmann, J., Figeragnosie. Eine umschriebene Storung der Orientierung am eigenen Korper, *Wien. Klin. Wschr.,* **37**, 1010–1012, 1924.

Gerstmann, J., Figeragnosie und isolierte Agraphie, ein neues Syndrom, *Ztschr. Neurol. Psych.,* **108**, 152–177, 1927.

Gerstmann, J., Zur Symptomatologie der Hirnlasionem im Übergangsgebiet der unteren Parietal und mitteren Occipitalwindung, *Nervenarzt,* **3**, 691–695, 1930.

Gerstmann, J., Problems of imperception of disease and of impaired body territories with organic lesions; relations to body scheme and its disorders, *Arch. Neurol. Psychiat.,* **48**, 890–913, 1942.

Gerstmann, J. and Schilder, P., Über eine besondere Gangstorung bei Stirnhirnerkrankung, *Wien. Med. Wschr.,* **76**, 97–102, 1926.

Gersuni, G. V., Organization of afferent flow and the process of external sign discrimination, *Neuropsychologia,* **3**, 95–110, 1965.

Geschwind, N., "The Anatomy of Acquired Disorders of Reading," in J. Money (ed.), *Reading Disability,* Johns Hopkins University Press, Baltimore, 1962.

Geschwind, N., "Brain Mechanisms Suggested by Studies of Interhemispheric Connections," in F. Darley and C. Millikan (eds.), *Brain Mechanisms Underlying Speech and Language,* Grune & Stratton, New York, 1963, pp. 103–108.

Geschwind, N., Disconnexion syndromes in animals and man, *Brain,* **88**, 237–294, 585–644, 1965.

Geschwind, N., Wernicke's contribution to the study of aphasia, *Cortex,* **3**, 449–463, 1967a.

Geschwind, N., The varieties of naming errors, *Cortex,* **3**, 97–112, 1967b.

Geschwind, N., "Problems in the Anatomical Understanding of the Aphasias," in A. L. Benton (ed.), *Contributions to Clinical Neuropsychology,* Aldine, Chicago, 1969, pp. 107–128.

Geschwind, N., "Clinical Syndromes of the Cortical Connections," in D. Williams (ed.), *Modern Trends in Neurology,* Butterworths, London, 1970a, pp. 29–40.

Geschwind, N., "Language Disturbances in Cerebrovascular Disease," in A. Benton (ed.), *Behavioral Changes in Cerebrovascular Disease,* 1970b, pp. 29–36.

Geschwind, N., The organization of language and the brain, *Science,* **170**, 940–944, 1970c.

Geschwind, N., Review of: Luria, A. R., *Traumatic Aphasia, Lang.,* **48**, 755–763, 1972a.

Geschwind, N., Disorders of the higher cortical function in children, *Clin. Proc. Children's Hosp.*, **28**, 261–272, 1972b.

Geschwind, N., Anatomical evolution and the human brain, *Bull. Orton, Soc.*, **22**, 7–13, 1972c.

Geschwind, N., "The Brain and Language," in G. A. Miller (ed.), *Communication, Language and Meaning*, Basic Books, New York, 1973, pp. 61–72.

Geschwind, N. and Fusillo, M., Color-naming defects in association with alexia, *Arch. Neurol.*, **15**, 137–146, 1966.

Geschwind, N. and Howes, D., "Quantitative Studies of Aphasic Language," in D. Rioch and E. Weinstein (eds.), *Disorders of Communication, Proceedings of Association for Research in Nervous and Mental Diseases*, **42**, Williams and Wilkins, Baltimore, 1964, pp. 229–244.

Geschwind, N. and Kaplan, E., A human cerebral deconnection syndrome, *Neurol.*, **12**, 675, 1962.

Geschwind, N. and Levitsky, W., Human brain: Left-right asymmetries in temporal speech regions, *Science*, **161**, 186–187, 1968.

Geschwind, N., Quadfasel, F. A. and Segarra, J. M., Isolation of the speech area, *Neuropsychologia*, **6**, 327–340, 1968.

Gesner, J. A. P., *Sammlung von Beobachtungen aus der Arzneygelahrtheit und Naturkunde*, C. G. Beck, Nordlingen, 1769–1776.

Ghent, L., Mishkin, M. and Teuber, H. L., Short term memory after frontal lobe injury in man, *J. Comp. Phys. Psychol.*, **55**, 705–709, 1962.

Gibson, J. J., *The Senses Considered as Perceptual Systems*, Houghton-Mifflin, Boston, 1966.

Glass, A. V., Gazzaniga, M. S. and Premack, D., Artificial language training in global aphasias, *Neuropsychologia*, **11**, 95–103, 1973.

Glassman, R. B., Similar effects of infant and adult sensorimotor cortical lesions on cats' posture, *Brain Res.*, **63**, 103–110, 1973.

Glassman, R. B., Functional recovery of the lesions of the nervous system. IV. Structural correlation of recovery in adult subjects. Equipotentiality and sensorimotor function, *Neurosc. Res. Program Bull.*, **12**, 246–249, 1974a.

Glassman, R. B., Selection process in living systems: Role in cognitive construction and recovery from brain damage, *Behav. Sci.*, **19**, 149–165, 1974b.

Gloning, K. and Quatember, R., Methodischer Beitrag zur Untersuchung der Prosopagnosie, *Neuropsychologia*, **4**, 133–141, 1966.

Gloning, K. and Quatember, R., Über Anwendung und Bedeutung einer Untersuchungsreihe der Sprachentwicklung bei aphasischen Patienten, *Nervenarzt*, **38**, 315–317, 1967.

Gloning, I., Gloning, K., Seittelberger, F. and Tschabitscher, H., Ein Fall von reiner Wortblindheit mit Obduktionsbefund, *W. Z. Nervenk.*, **12**, 194–215, 1955.

Gloning, I., Gloning, K. and Hoff, H., "Aphasia—a Clinical Syndrome," in L. Halpern (ed.), *Problems of Dynamic Neurology*, Jerusalem Post Press, Jerusalem, 1963, pp. 63–70.

Gloning, I., Gloning, K. and Tschabitschen, Über einen obduzierten Fall von optischer Korperschemastorung und Heautoskopie, *Neuropsychologia*, **1**, 217, 1963.

Gloning, I., Jellinger, K., Sluga, W. and Weingarten, K., Über Uhrzeitagnosie, *Arch. Psychiat. Nervenkhr.*, **198**, 58–95, 1963.

Gloning, I., Gloning, K. and Hoff, H., Neuropsychological symptoms and syndromes in lesions of the occipital lobe and the adjacent areas, Gauthier-Villars, Paris, 1968.

Gloning, K., Trappl, R., Heiss, W. D. et al, Eine experimentall-statische Untersuchung zur Prognose der Aphasie, *Nervenarzt*, **40**, 491–494, 1969.

Gogol, D., *Aphasie, Apraxie, Agnosie*, 1874; cited by R. Thiele in *Bumke Handb. Geisteskrankh. VI*, Springer, Berlin, 1928, pp. 243–365.

Goldberger, M. E., Restitution of function in the CNS: The pathologic grasp on *Macaca mulatta*, *Exp. Brain Res.*, **15**, 79–96, 1972.

Goldblum, M. C., Analyse des responses de denomination chez les aphasiques, *Langages*, **25**, 66–75, 1972a.

Goldblum, M. C., Unpublished data, 1972b.

Goldblum, M. C. and Albert, M. L., Phonemic discrimination in sensory aphasia, *Internat. J. Ment. Health*, **1**, 25–29, 1972.

Goldman, P. S., Functional development of the prefrontal cortex in early life and the problem of neuronal plasticity, *Exp. Neurol.*, **32**, 366–387, 1971.

Goldman, P. S. and Rosvold, H. E., Localization of function within the dorsolateral prefrontal cortex of the rhesus monkey, *Exp. Neurol.*, **27**, 291–304, 1970.

Goldman, P. S. and Rosvold, H. E., The effects of selective caudate lesions in infant and juvenile rhesus monkeys, *Brain Res.*, **43**, 53–66, 1972.

Goldman, P. S., Lodge, A., Hammer, L. R., Semmes, J. and Mishkin, M., Cortical flicker frequencies after unilateral temporal lobectomy in man, *Neuropsychologia*, **6**, 355–364, 1968.

Goldman, P. S., Rosvold, H. E. and Mishkin, M., Evidence for behavioral impairments following prefrontal lobectomy in the infant monkey, *J. Comp. Physiol. Psychol.*, **70**, 454–463, 1970.

Goldman, P. S., Rosvold, H. E., Vest, B. et al, Analysis of the delayed alternation deficit produced by dorsolateral prefrontal lesions in the rhesus monkey, *J. Comp. Physiol. Psychol.*, **77**, 212–220, 1971.

Goldman-Eisler, F., A comparative study of two hesitation phenomena, *Lang. and Speech*, **4**, 18–26, 1961a.

Goldman-Eisler, F., The significance of change in the rate of articulation, *Lang. and Speech*, **4**, 171–174, 1961b.

Goldman-Eisler, F., Continuity of speech utterance, its determinants and significance, *Lang. and Speech*, **4**, 220–231, 1961c.

Goldman-Eisler, F., The distribution of pause durations in speech, *Lang. and Speech*, **4**, 232–236, 1961d.

Goldscheider, A., *Gesammelte Abhandlungen*, Leipzig, 1898.

Goldstein, K., Der makrokopische Hirnbefund in meinen Falle von linksseitiger motorischer Apraxie, *Neur. Centralblatt.*, **28**, 898–906, 1909.

Goldstein, K., Über kortikale Sensibilitatsstorungen, *Neurol. Zblt.*, **19**, 825–827, 1916.

Goldstein, K., *Die transkorticale Aphasien*, Gustov Fischer, Jena, 1917.

Goldstein, K., *Die Behandlung, Fursorge und Begutachtung der Hirnverletzten*, Vogel, Leipzig, 1919.

Goldstein, K., The significance of the frontal lobes for mental performances, *J. Neurol. Psychiat.*, **17**, 27–56, 1936a.

Goldstein, K., The mental changes due to frontal lobe damage, *J. Psychol. Neurol. Psych.*, **17**, 27–56, 1936b.

Goldstein, K., *The Organism*, American Book Publishers, New York, 1939.

Goldstein, K., The mental changes due to frontal lobe damage, *J. Psychol.*, **17**, 187–208, 1944.

Goldstein, K., *Language and Language Disturbances*, Grune & Stratton, New York, 1948.

Goldstein, K., L'analyse de l'aphasie et l'etude de l'essence du langage, *J. Psychologie*, **30**, 430–496, 1953.

Goldstein, M., Abeles, M., Daly, R. L. and McIntosh, J., Functional architecture in cat primary auditory cortex: Tonotopie organization, *J. Neurophysiol.*, **33**, 188–197, 1970.

Goldstein, M. N., Joynt, R. J. and Goldblatt, D., Word blindness with intact central visual fields. A case report, *Neurol.* (Minneapolis), **21**, 873–876, 1971.

Gollin, E. S., Developmental studies of visual recognition of incomplete objects, *Percept. Mot. Skills*, **11**, 289–298, 1960.

Goltz, F., Über die Verrichtungen des Grosshirns, *Pflugers Arch. ges. Physiol.*, **51**, 570–614, 1892.

Goodglass, H., Developmental comparison of vowels and consonants in dichotic listening, *JSHR*, **16**, 744–752, 1973.

Goodglass, H. and Blumstein, S., *Psycholinguistics and Aphasia,* Johns Hopkins University Press, Baltimore, 1973.

Goodglass, H., Geschwind, N., "Language Disorders (Aphasia)," in E. C. Carterette, and M. Friedman (eds.), *Handbook of Perception,* Academic Press, New York, 1976.

Goodglass, H. and Kaplan, E., Disturbance of gesture and pantomime in aphasia, *Brain,* **86,** 703–720, 1963.

Goodglass, H. and Kaplan, E., Assessment of aphasia and related disorders, Lea and Febiger, Philadelphia, 1972.

Goodglass, H. and Quadfasel, F. A., Language laterality in left-handed aphasics, *Brain,* **77,** 521–548, 1954.

Goodglass, H., Klein, B., Carey, P. and Jones, K., Specific semantic word categories in aphasia, *Cortex,* **2,** 74–89, 1966.

Goodglass, H., Gleason, J. B. and Hyde, M. R., Some dimensions of auditory language comprehension in aphasia, JSHR, **13,** 595–606, 1970.

Goodman, D. C. and Horel, J. A., Sprouting of optic tract projections in the brain stem of the rat, *J. Comp. Neurol.,* **127,** 71–88, 1967.

Gordinier, H. C., A case of brain tumor at the base of the second left frontal circonvolution, *Amer. Med. Sci.,* **117,** 526–535, 1899.

Gordon, B., The superior colliculus of the brain, *Sci. Am.,* **227,** 6, 72–82, 1972.

Gordon, H. W., Hemispheric asymmetries in the perception of musical chords, *Cortex,* **6,** 387–398, 1970.

Gordon, H. W., Comparison of ipsilateral and contralateral auditory pathways in callosum-sectioned patients by use of a response time technique, *Neuropsychologia,* **13,** 9–18, 1975.

Gordon, R. W. and Bogen, J. E., Hemispheric lateralization of singing after intracarotid sodium amyloborbitone, *J. Neurol. Neurosurg. Psychiat.,* **37,** 727–738, 1974.

Gouras, P., Trichromatic mechanisms in single cortical neurons, *Science,* **168,** 489–492, 1970a.

Gouras, P., Electroretinography: Some basic principles, *Invest. Ophthal.,* **9,** 557–569, 1970b.

Gowers, W., *Lectures on the Diagnosis of Diseases of the Brain,* Churchill, London, 1885.

Graveleau, D., Cécité corticale. A propos d'une observation, datylographiees, These, Paris, 1956, 87 pp.

Greenblatt, M., *Studies in Lobotomy,* Grune & Stratton, New York, 1950.

Greenblatt, S. H., Alexia without agraphia or hemianopia. Anatomical analysis of an autopsied case, *Brain,* **96,** 307–316, 1973.

Greene, E., Saporta, S. and Walters, J., Choice bias from unilateral hippocampal or frontal lesions in the rat, *Exp. Neurol.,* **29,** 534–545, 1970.

Greene, E., Stauff, C., and Walters, J., Recovery of function with two stage lesions of the Fornix, *Exptl. Neurol.,* **37,** 14–22, 1972.

Grenier, G. F. and Rohmer, F., Semiologie cochleovestibulaire, *Rev. Oto-neuro-ophtalmologie,* **22,** 243–272, 1950.

Grewel, F., Aphasia and linguistics, *Folia Phoniatrica,* **3,** 100–105, 1951.

Gross, C. G., "Visual Functions of Infero-Temporal Cortex," in R. Jung (ed.), *Handbook of Sensory Physiology VII/3, Central Visual Information B,* Springer-Verlag, New York, 1973, pp. 451–482.

Gross, C. G. and Weiskrantz, L., Evidence for dissociation of impairment on auditory discrimination and delayed response following lateral frontal lesions in monkeys, *Exp. Neurol.,* **5,** 453–476, 1962.

Gross, C. G. and Weiskrantz, L., "Some Changes in Behavior Produced by Lateral Frontal Lesions in the Macaque," in J. M. Warren and K. Akert (eds.), *The Frontal Granular Cortex and Behavior,* McGraw-Hill, New York, 1964, pp. 74–101.

Gross, C. G., Chorover, S. L. and Cohen, S. M., Caudate, cortical, hippocampal and dorsal thalamic lesions in rats: Alternation and Hebb-William maze performance, *Neuropsychologia,* **3,** 53–68, 1965.

Gross, N. B., Small, A. M. and Thompson, D. D., Response to contralateral and ipsilateral auditory stimulation from the same cortical areas, *Brain Res.,* **5**, 250–262, 1967.

Gross, C. G., Bender, D. B. and Rocha-Miranda, C. E., Visual receptive fields of neurons in the cortex of the monkey, *Science,* **166**, 1303–1306, 1969.

Gross, C. G., Bender, D. B. and Rocha-Miranda, C. E., "Inferotemporal cortex, a single unit analysis," in F. O. Schmitt and F. G. Worden (eds.), *The Neurosciences: Third Study Program,* MIT Press, Cambridge, Mass., 1974, pp. 229–238.

Gruber, R. P. and Reed, D. R., Postoperative anterograde amnesia, *Brit. J. Anaesth.,* **40**, 845–851, 1968.

Grueninger, W. E. and Pribram, K. H., Effects of spatial and nonspatial distractors on performance latency of monkeys with frontal lesions, *J. Comp. Physiol. Psychol.,* **68**, 203–209, 1969.

Grueninger, W. E., Kimble, D. P., Grueninger, J. and Levine, S., GSR and corticosteroid response in monkeys with frontal ablations, *Neuropsychologia,* **3**, 205–216, 1965.

Grunbaum, A. A., Aphasie und Motorik, *Z. ges. Neurol. Psychiat.,* **130**, 385–412, 1930.

Gueniot, M., D'une hallucination du toucher (ou heterotopie subjective des extremities) particuliere a certains amputes, *J. Physiol.* (Paris), **4**, 416–430, 1861.

Guillan, G. and Bize, P. R., Astereognosie pure par lesion corticale parietale traumatique, *Rev. Neurol.,* **1**, 502–509, 1932.

Guiot, G., Hertzog, E., Rondot, P. and Molina, P., Arrest or acceleration of speech evoked by thalamic stimulation in the cou.se of stereotaxic procedure for Parkinsonism, *Brain,* **84**, 363–379, 1961.

Guttman, E., Aphasia in children, *Brain,* **65**, 205–219, 1942.

Haaxma, R. and H. G. Kuypers, Intrahemispheric cortical connexions and visual guidance of hand and finger movements in the Rhesus monkey, *Brain,* **98**, 239–260, 1975.

Haber, W. B., Observations on phantom limb phenomena, *Arch. Neurol. Psychiatr.,* **75**, 624–636, 1956.

Halliday, A. M., Davison, K., Browne, M. W. et al., A comparison of the effects on depression and memory of bilateral E.C.T. and unilateral E.C.T. to the dominant and nondominant hemispheres, *Brit. J. Psychiat.,* **114**, 997–1012, 1968.

Halperin, Y., Nachshon, I. and Carmon, A., Shift of ear superiority in dichotic listening to temporally patterned nonverbal stimuli, *J. Acoust. Soc. Am.,* **53**, 46–50, 1973.

Halstead, W., *Brain and Intelligence,* University of Chicago Press, Chicago, 1947.

Hamilton, C. R., Tieman, S. B. and Farrell, W. S., Jr., Cerebral dominance in monkeys, *Neuropsychologia,* **12**, 193–197, 1974.

Hara, K., Cornwell, P. R., Warren, J. M. and Webster, I., Posterior extramarginal cortex and visual learning by cats, *J. Comp. Physiol. Psychol.,* **87**, 884–904, 1974.

Harlow, H. F., Performance of Catonluni monkeys on a series of discrimination reversal problems, *J. Comp. Physiol. Psychol.,* **43**, 231–240, 1950a.

Harlow, H. F., Learning and satiation of response in intrinsically motivated complex puzzle performance by monkeys, *J. Comp. Physiol. Psychol.,* **43**, 289–294, 1950b.

Harlow, H. F., Analysis of discrimination learning by monkeys, *J. Exp. Psych.,* **40**, 26–39, 1950c.

Harlow, H. F., "Functional Organization of the Brain in Relation to Mentation and Behavior," in S. Cobb (ed.), *The Biology of Mental Health and Disease,* Hoeber, New York, 1952, pp. 244–253.

Harlow, H. F. and Dagnon, J., Problem solution by monkeys following bilateral removal of the prefrontal areas. I. The discrimination and discrimination-reversal problems, *J. Exp. Psychol.,* **32**, 351–356, 1943.

Harlow, H. F. et al., Analysis of frontal and posterior association syndromes in brain-damaged monkeys, *J. Comp. Psychol.,* **30**, pp. 419–429, 1952.

Harlow, H. F. and Settlage, P. H., Effect of extirpation of frontal areas upon learning performance of monkeys, *Res. Publ. Assoc. Res. Nervous Mental Dis.,* **27**, 446–459, 1948.

Harlow, H. F., Doris, R. T., Settlage, P. H. and Meyer, D. R., Analysis of frontal and posterior association syndromes in brain-damaged monkeys, *J. Comp. Physiol. Psychol.*, **45**, 419–429, 1952.

Harlow, H. F., Thompson, C., Blomquist, A. and Schilte, K., Learning in Rhesus monkeys after varying amounts of prefrontal lobe destruction during infancy and adolescence, *Brain Res.*, **18**, 343–353, 1970.

Hartmann, F., Beitrage zur Apraxielehre, *Mtschr. Psychiat. Neurol.*, **21**, 97–118, 248–270, 1907.

Haslerud, G. H. and Clark, R. E., On the reintegrative perception of words, *Amer. J. Psychol.*, **70**, 97–101, 1957.

Hassler, R., "Thalamic Regulation of Muscle Tone and the Speed of Movements," in D. Pupura and M. Yahr (eds.), *The Thalamus*, Columbia University Press, New York, 1966, pp. 419–436.

Hayes, K. S. and Hayes, C., *Proc. Amer. Phil. Soc.*, **95**, 105, 1951.

Hayes, K. S. and Hayes, C., *J. Comp. Physiol. Psychol.*, **45**, 450, 1952.

Hayes, K. S. and Hayes, C., in J. A. Govan (ed.), *The Non-human Primates and Human Evolution*, Wayne University Press, Detroit, 1955, p. 110.

Head, H., *Studies in Neurology* (2 vol.), Oxford University Press, London, 1920.

Head, H., *Aphasia and Kindred Disorders of Speech*, Cambridge University Press, England, 1926.

Head, H. and Holmes, G.,Sensory disturbances from cerebral lesions, *Brain*, **34**, 102–254, 1911.

Head, H., Rivers, W. H. R. and Sherren, J., The afferent nervous system from a new aspect, *Brain*, **28**, 99, 1905.

Heathfield, K. W., Croft, P. B. and Swash, M., The syndrome of transient global amnesia, *Brain*, **96**, 729–736, 1973.

Hebb, D. O., Man's frontal lobe: A critical review, *Arch. Neurol. Psychiat.*, **54**, 10–24, 1945.

Hebb, D. O., *A Textbook of Psychology*, Saunders, Philadelphia, 1966.

Hécaen, H., "L'Asymbolie a la douleur," in *La douleur et les douleurs*, Masson et Cie, Paris, 1956, pp. 259–265.

Hécaen, H., "Clinical Symptomology in Right and Left Hemisphere Lesions," in V. B. Mountcastle (ed.), *Interhemispheric Relations and Cerebral Dominance*, Johns Hopkins University Press, Baltimore, 1962, pp. 215–243.

Hécaen, H., "Mental Symptoms with Tumors of the Frontal Lobe," in J. M. Warren and K. Akert (eds.), *The Frontal Granular Cortex and Behavior*, McGraw-Hill, New York, 1964, pp. 335–352.

Hécaen, H., Approche semiotique des troubles du geste, *Langages*, **5**, 67–83, 1967a.

Hécaen, H., Aspects des troubles de la lecture (alexies) au cours des lesions cerebrales en foyer, *Word*, **23**, 265–287, 1967b.

Hécaen, H., "Essai d'interpretation des asomatognosies en pathologie corticale," in M. M. Velasco-Suarez and F. Escobedo (eds.), *Lobulo Parietal*, Instituto National de Neurologie, Mexico, 1968, pp. 141–156.

Hécaen, H., "Aphasic, Apraxic, and Agnosic Syndromes in Right and Left Hemisphere Lesions," in P. Vincken and G. Bruyn (eds.), *Handbook of Clinical Neurology*, Vol. 4, North Holland Publishing Co., Amsterdam, 1969a, pp. 291–371.

Hécaen, H., Essai de dissociation du syndrome de l'aphasie sensorielle, *Rev. Neurol.*, **120**, 229–231, 1969b.

Hécaen, H., (ed.), *Neuropsychologie de la perception visuelle*, Masson et Cie, Paris, 1972a.

Hécaen, H., *Introduction a la neuropsychologie*, Larousse, Paris, 1972b.

Hécaen, H., Donnees nouvelles sur la dominance hemispherique, *Annee Psychologique*, **73**, 611–634, 1973.

Hécaen, H., Acquired aphasia in children and the ontogenesis of hemispheric functional specialization, *Brain and Lang.* **3**, 114–134, 1976.

Hécaen, H. and de Ajuriaguerra, J., L'apraxie de l'habillage, ses rapports avec la planotopokmesie et les troubles de la somatognosie, *L'Encephale*, **35**, 113–114, 1942–1945.

Hécaen, H. and de Ajuriaguerra, J., Asymbolie a la douleur, étude anatomoclinique, *Rev. Neurol.*, **83**, 300–302, 1950.

Hécaen, H. and de Ajuriaguerra, J., *Meconnaissances et hallucination corporelles*, Masson et Cie, Paris, 1952.

Hécaen, H. and de Ajuriaguerra, J., Balint's syndrome (Psychic paralysis of visual fixation and its minor forms), *Brain*, **77**, 373–400, 1954.

Hécaen, H. and de Ajuriaguerra, J., *Les troubles mentaux au cours du tumeurs intracraniennes*, Masson et Cie, Paris, 1956.

Hécaen, H. and de Ajuriaguerra, J., *Les gauchers, prévalence manuelle et dominance cerebrale*, P.U.F., Paris, 1963.

Hécaen, H. and Albert, M. L., "Disorders of Mental Functioning Related to Frontal Lobe Pathology," in D. F. Benson and D. Blumer (eds.), *Psychiatric Aspects of Neurologic Disease*, Grune & Stratton, New York, 1975, pp. 137–149.

Hécaen, H. and Angelergues, R., Etude anatamo clinique de 280 cas de lesions retrolandiques unilaterales des hemispheres cerebraux, *L'Encephale*, **6**, 533–562, 1961.

Hécaen, H. and Angelergues, R., Agnosia for faces, *Arch. Neurol.*, **7**, 92–100, 1962.

Hécaen, H. and Angelergues, R., *La Cécité psychique*, Masson et Cie, Paris, 1963.

Hécaen, H. and Angelergues, R., "Localisation of Symptoms in Aphasia," in A. U. S. de Reuck and M. O'Connor (eds.), *Disorders of Language*, Churchill, London, 1964, pp. 223–246.

Hécaen, H. and Angelergues, R., Neuropsychologie des dysfonctionnemente des lobes occipitaux, *Proc. 8th Int. Congr. Neurol.*, Vienna **3**, 29–45, 1965.

Hécaen, H. and Assal, G., A comparison of construction deficits following right and left hemispheric lesions, *Neuropsychologia*, **8**, 289–304, 1970.

Hécaen, H. and Consoli, S., Analyse des troubles du langage au cours des lesions de l'aire de Broca, *Neuropsychologia*, **11**, 377–388, 1973.

Hécaen, H. and David, M., Syndrome parietale traumatique: asymbolie tactile et hemiasomatognosie paroxystique et douloureuse, *Rev. Neurol.*, **77**, 113–123, 1945.

Hécaen, H. and Dubois, J., *La Naissance de la neuro-psychologie du langage (Textes et Documentes)*, Flammarion, Paris, 1969.

Hécaen, H. and Garcia Badaaco, J., Les Hallucinations visuelles au cours des ophtalmopathies et des lesions des nerfs et du chiasma optique. *Evol. Psychiatr.*, **21**, 157–159, 1956a.

Hécaen, H. and Garcia Badaaco, J., Semeiologie des hallucinations visuelles en clinique neurologique, *Acta Neurol. Lat. Amer.*, **2**, 23–57, 1956b.

Hécaen, H. and Gimeno, A., L'Apraxie idéomotrice unilaterale gauche, *Rev. Neurol.*, **102**, 648–653, 1960.

Hécaen, H. and Goldblum, M., "Etudes neurolinguistiques sur l'aphasie sensorielle," in Perez de Francisco (ed.), *Dimensiones de la psiquiatria contemporanea*, Fournier, S. A. Mexico, 1972.

Hécaen, H. and Gruner, J., Alexie verbale pure avec integrite du corps calleux, Colloque sur les Syndromes de Disconnexion chez l'homme, Lyon, 1974.

Hécaen, H. and Kremin, H., "Neurolinguistic Research on Reading Disorders from Left Hemisphere Lesions: Aphasic and 'Pure' Alexias," in *Studies in Neurolinguistics II*, H. A. and H. Whitaker, (eds.), Academic Press, New York, 1976.

Hécaen, H. and Marcie, P., "Disorders of Written Language following Right Hemisphere Lesions: Spatial Dysgraphia," in S. Dimond and L. Beaumont (eds.), *Hemisphere Function in the Human Brain*, Paul Elek, London, 1974, pp. 345–366.

Hécaen, H. and Ropert, R., Hallucinations auditives au course de syndromes neurologiques, *Ann. Med. Psychol.*, **117**, 257–306, 1959.

Hécaen, H. and Sauguet, J., Cerebral dominance in left-handed subjects, *Cortex*, **7**, 19–48, 1971.

Hécaen, H., David, M. and Talairach, J., Membres fantomes par compression traumatique de la queue de cheval; disparition apres liberation des racines, *Rev. Neurol.*, **77**, 146, 1945.

Hécaen, H., de Ajuriaguerra, J., David, M., Rouques, M. B. and Dell, R., Paralysie psychique du regard de Balint au cours de l'evolution d'une leuco-encephalite type Balo, *Rev. Neurol.*, **83**, 81–104, 1950.

Hécaen, H., de Ajuriaguerra, J. and Massonet, J., Les troubles visuo constructifs par lesions parieto-occipitales droites. Role des perturbations vestibulaires, *L'Encephale*, **1**, 122–179, 1951.

Hécaen, H., de Ajuriaguerra, J. and David, M., Les deficits fonctionels apres lobectomie occipitale, *Mtschr. Neurol. und Psychiat.*, **123**, 239–291, 1952.

Hécaen, H., de Ajuriaguerra, J., Magis, G. and Angelergues, R., Le probleme de l'agnosie des physionomies, *L'Encephale*, **47**, 322–355, 1952.

Hécaen, H., Dubois-Poulsen, M., Magis, G. and de Ajuriaguerra, J., Consequences visuelles des lobectomies occipitales, *Annales d'oculistique*, **185**, 305–347, 1952.

Hécaen, H., de Ajuriaguerra, J., Le Guillant, H. and Angelergues, R., Delire centre sur un membre fantome chez un hemiplegique gauche par lesion vasculaire avec anosognosie, *Evolution Psych.*, **12**, 273–279, 1954.

Hécaen, H., Penfield, W., Bertrand, C., and Malmo, R., The syndrome of apractognosia due to lesions of the minor cerebral hemisphere, *Arch. Neurol. Psychiat.*, **75**, 400–434, 1956.

Hécaen, H., Angelergues, R., Bernhard, C. and Chiarelli, J., Essai de distinction des modalitees cliniques de l'agnosie des physionomies, *Rev. Neurol.*, **96**, 125–144, 1957.

Hécaen, H., de Ajuriaguerra, J. and Angelergues, R., Les Troubles de la lecture dans le cadre des modifications des functions symboliques, *Psychiat. Neurol.*, **124**, 97–129, 1957.

Hécaen, H., Angelergues, R., Djinjan, R. and Hazan, J., Un Cas d'aphasie croisee chez une droitiere (Thrombose de l'artere sylvienne droite), *Rev. Neurol.*, **107**, 543–545, 1962.

Hécaen, H., Angelergues, R. and Douzenis, J. A., Les Agraphies, *Neuropsychologia*, **1**, 179–208, 1963.

Hécaen, H., Marcie, P., Dubois, J. and Angelergues, R., Les realisations due langage chez les madades Heints de lesions de l'hemisphere droit, *Neuropsychologia*, **3**, 217–247, 1965.

Hécaen, H., Dubois, J. and Marcie, P., Aspects linguistiques des troubles de la vigilance au cours des lesions temporales anterointernes droite et gauche, *Neuropsychologia*, **5**, 311–328, 1967.

Hécaen, H., Dubois, J. and Marcie, P., Les désorganisations de la reception des signes verbaux dans l'aphasie sensorielle, *Revue d'Acoustique*, 287–304, 1968.

Hécaen, H., Dubois, J. and Marcie, P., L'agraphie "pure." *Neuropsychologia* **7**, 271–286, 1969.

Hécaen, H., Marcie, P., Constans, J. P. and Chodkiewicz, J. P., Etude spectrographique de la parole chez deux malades apres ablation de meningiome du pied de F3 gauche, *Rev. Neurol.*, **120**, 350–352, 1969.

Hécaen, H., Mazurs, G., Ramier, A. et al, Aphasie croiseé chez un sujet droitier bilingue, *Rev. Neurol.*, **1**, **124**, 319–323, 1971.

Hécaen, H., Tzortzis, C. and Masure, M. C., Troubles de l'orientation spatiale dans une épreuve de recherche d'itinéraires lors des lésions corticales unilatérales, *Perception*, **1**, 325–330, 1972.

Hécaen, H., Goldblum, M. C., Masure, M. C. et al, Une Nouvelle Observation d'agnosie d'objet. Deficit de l'association, ou de la categorisation, specifique de la modalite visuelle? *Neuropsychologia*, **12**, 447–464, 1974.

Heilman, K. M., Ideational apraxia—a redefinition, *Brain*, **96**, 861–864, 1973.

Heilman, K. and Valenstein, E., Frontal lobe neglect in man, *Neurol.*, **22**, 660–664, 1972a.

Heilman, K. and Valenstein, E., Auditory neglect in man, *Arch. Neurol.*, **26**, 32–35, 1972b.

Heilman, K. M., Pandya, D. N. and Geschwind, N., Trimodal inattention following parietal lobe ablations, *Trans. Amer. Neurol. Assoc.*, **95**, 259–261, 1970.

Heilman, K. M., Pandya, D. N., Karol, E. A. et al, Auditory inattention, *Arch. Neurol.*, **24**, 323–325, 1971a.

Heilman, K. M., Safron, A. and Geschwind, N., Closed head trauma and aphasia, *J. Neurol. Neurosurg. Psychiat.*, **34**, 265–269, 1971b.

Heilman, K. M., Harrer, L. C. and Wilder, B. J., An audiometric defect in temporal lobe dysfunction, *Neurol.* (Minneapolis), **23**, 384–386, 1973.

Heilman, K., Watson, R. T. and Schulman, H. M., A unilateral memory defect, *J. Neurol. Neurosurg. Psychiat.*, **37**, 790–794, 1974.

Heilman, K. M., Scholes, R. and Watson, R. T., Auditory affective agnosia. Disturbed comprehension of affective speech, *J. Neurol. Neurosurg. Psychiat.*, **38**, 69–72, 1975.

Heimburger, R. F., Demyer, W. and Reitan, R. M., Implications of Gerstmann's syndrome, *J. Neurol. Neurosurg.. Psychiat.*, **27**, 52–57, 1964.

Hein, A., "Labile Sensorimotor Coordination," in N. S. Scrimshaw and J. E. Gordon (eds.), *Malnutrition, Learning and Behavior*, MIT Press, Cambridge, Mass., 1968.

Hein, A., "L'Acquisition de la coordination perceptromotrice et sa reacquisition après lesion du cortex visuel," in H. Hécaen (ed.), *Neuropsychologie de la perception visuelle*, Masson et Cie, Paris, 1972, pp. 123–136.

Hein, A. and Diamond, R. M., Independence of the cat's scotopic and photopic systems in acquiring control of visually guided behavior, *J. Comp. Physiol. Psychol.*, **76**, 31–38, 1971a.

Hein, A. and Diamond, R. M., Contrasting development of visually triggered and guided movements in kittens with respect to interocular and interlimb equivalence, *J. Comp. Physiol. Psychol.*, **76**, 219–224, 1971b.

Heindenhain, A., Beitraq zur kenntnis der Seelenblindheit, *Mtschr. Psychiat.*, **1**, 449–468, 1919.

Held, R., Exposure history as a factor in maintaining stability of perception and coordination, *J. Nerv. Ment. Dis.*, **132**, 26–32, 1961.

Held, R., Plasticity in sensory-motor systems, *Sci. Am.*, **213**, 84–94, 1965.

Held, R., Dissociation of visual functions by deprivation and rearrangement, *Psychol. Forsch.*, **31**, 338–348, 1968.

Held, R., Development of spatially coordinated movements, *Brain Res.*, **71**, 247–248, 1974.

Held, R. and Bauer, J. A., Visually guided reaching in infant monkeys after restricted rearing, *Science*, **155**, 718–720, 1967.

Held, R. and Bauer, J. A., Development of sensorially guided reaching in infant monkeys, *Brain Res.*, **71**, 265–271, 1974.

Held, R. and Freedman, S., Plasticity in human sensorimotor control, *Science*, **142**, 455–462, 1963.

Held, R. and Hein, A., Movement-produced stimulation in the development of visually guided behavior, *J. Comp. Physiol. Psychol.*, **56**, 872–876, 1963.

Helmholtz, H., 1867; cited by R. Held, 1961.

Henschen, S. E., *Klinische und anatomische Beitrage zur Pathologie des Gehirns*, Nordiske Bokhandeln, Stockholm, 1920–1922.

Henschen, S. E., On the function of the right hemisphere of the brain in relation to the left hemisphere in speech, music, and calculation, *Brain*, **49**, 110–123, 1926.

Hernandez-Peon, R., "Reticular Mechanisms of Sensory Control," in W. A. Rosenblith (ed.), *Sensory Communication*, MIT Press, Cambridge, Mass., and Wiley, New York, 1961, pp. 497–520.

Herrmann, G. and O. Pötzl, *Über die Agraphie und ihre lokaldiagnostischen Beziehungen*, S. Karger, Berlin, 1926.

Herrmann, G. and Pötzl, O., *Die optische alaesthesie*, Berlin, S. Karger, 1928.

Hicks, S. P. and D'Amato, C. S., Motor-sensory and visual behavior after hemispherectomy in newborn and mature rats, *Exp. Neurol.*, **29**, 416–438, 1970.

Hillier, W. F., Total left cerebral hemispherectomy for malignant glioma, *Neurol.*, **4**, 718–722, 1954.

Hinshelwood, J., *Letter, Word, and Mind-Blindness*, H. K. Lewis, London, 1900.

Hirsh, I., "Information Processing in Input Channels for Speech and Language: Significance of Serial Order of Stimuli," in C. Millikan and F. Darley (eds.), *Brain Mechanisms Underlying Speech and Language*, Grune & Stratton, New York, 1967.

Hirsch, H. U. B. and Spinelli, D. N., Modification of the distribution of receptive field orientation in cats by selective visual exposure during development, *Exp. Brain Res.*, **12**, 504–527, 1971.

Hodgson, W. R., Audiological report of a patient with left hemispherectomy, *J. Speech and Hear. Dis.*, **32**, 39–45, 1967.

Hoeppner, T., Letter: Trophic effects of striatal neuron denervation, *Amer. J. Psychiat.*, **131**, 831–832, 1974.

Hoff, H., Zur Frage der formalen Gestaltung optischer Halluzinationen in hemianopischen Gesichtefeld, *Z. ges. Neurol. Psychiat.*, **137**, 453–457, 1931a.

Hoff, H., Balkentumor mit linksseitiger Astereognosis und Apraxie, *D. Ztschr. f. Nervenhk*, **123**, 89–100, 1931b.

Hoff, H., Die Lokalisation der Aphasie, *Rep. 7th Internat. Congr. Neurol.* (Rome), 455–468, 1961.

Hoff, H. and Pötzl, O., Über eine optisch-agnostische Stonung des "Physionomie-Gedachtnisses," *Ztschr. ges. Neurol. Psychiat.*, **52**, 173–218, 1925.

Hoff, H. and Pötzl, O., Experimentielle Nachbildung von Anosognosie, *Ztschr. Neurol. Psychiat.*, **137**, 722–734, 1931.

Hoff, H. and Pötzl, O., Über Storungen des tiefensehens bei zerebraler metamorphopsie, *Mtschr. Psychiat.*, **90**, 305, 1935a.

Hoff, H. and Pötzl, O., Über ein neues parieto-occiptaler syndrom (Seelenlahmung des Schauens Storung des korperschemas Wegfall der zentralen Schens), *Jhrb. Psychiat. Neurol.*, **52**, 173–218, 1935b.

Hoff, H. and Pötzl, O., Über Polyopie und gerichtele hemianopische Halluzinationen, *Jhrb. Psychiat. Neurol.*, **54**, 55–88, 1937.

Hoff, H., Gloning, I. and Gloning, K., Über Alexie, *Z. Nervenhlk*, (Wien), **10**, 149–162, 1954.

Hoffman, H., Stereognostische Versuche, angesllellf zur Ermi Helangder Elemente des Gefahlssinnes, aus denen die Vorstellungen des korps vin Raume gebildet werden, *Dtsch. Arch. klin. Med.*, **36**, 398–426, 1885.

Hoffman, K. P. and Straschill, M., Influences of cortico-tectal and intertectal connections on visual responses in the cat's superior colliculus, *Exp. Brain Res.*, **12**, 120–131, 1971.

Holmes, G., Disturbances of vision by cerebral lesions, *Brit. J. Ophthalmol.*, **2**, 353–384, 1918a.

Holmes, G., Disturbances of visual orientation, *Brit. J. Ophthalmol.*, **2**, 449–468, 506–516, 1918b.

Holmes, G. and Horrax, G., Disturbances of spatial orientation and visual attention with loss of stereoscopic vision, *Arch. Neurol. Psychiat.*, **1**, 385–407, 1919.

Horel, J. A., and Misantone, L. J., The Kluver-Bucy syndrome produced by partial isolation of the temporal lobe, *Exp. Neurol.* **42**, 101–112, 1974.

Horn, G., Stechler, G. and Hill, R. M., Receptive fields of units in the visual cortex of the cat in the presence and absence of bodily tilt, *Exp. Brain Res.*, **15**, 113–132, 1972.

Horn, G., Rose, S. P. and Bateson, P. P., Experience and plasticity in the central nervous system, *Science*, **181**, 506–514, 1973a.

Horn, G., Rose, S. P. and Bateson, P. P., Monocular imprinting and regional incorporation of tritiated uracil into the brains of intact and split-brain chicks, *Brain Res.*, **56**, 227–237, 1973b.

Horrax, G., Visual hallucinations as a cerebral localizing phenomenon, *Arch. Neurol. Psychiat.*, **10**, 532, 1923.

Horrax, D. and Putnam, J., Distortions of the visual field in cases of brain tumors, *Brain*, **55**, 499–522, 1932.

Howes, D. and Green, E., Naming defects in conduction aphasia, Paper presented at Academy of Aphasia, 1972.

Hubel, D. H. and Wiesel, T. N., Receptive fields, binocular perception and functional architecture in the cat's visual cortex, *J. Physiol.*, **160**, 106–154, 1962.

Hubel, D. H. and Wiesel, T. N., Receptive fields in striate cortex of very young visually inexperienced kittens, *J. Neurophysiol.*, **26**, 994–1002, 1963.

Hubel, D. H. and Wiesel, T. N., Receptive fields and functional architecture in two non-striate visual areas (18 and 19), *J. Neurophysiol.*, **28**, 229–289, 1965.

Hubel, D. H. and Wiesel, T. N., Receptive fields and functional architecture of monkey striate cortex, *J. Physiol.*, **195**, 215–243, 1968.

Hubel, D. H. and Wiesel, T. N., The period of susceptibility to the physiological effects of unilateral eye closure in kittens, *J. Physiol.*, **206**, 419–436, 1970.

Hubel, D. H. and Wiesel, T. N., Sequence regularity and geometry of orientation columns in monkey striate cortex, *J. Comp. Neurol.*, **158**, 267–293, 1974a.

Hubel, D. H. and Wiesel, T. N., Uniformity of monkey striate cortex: A parallel relationship between field size, scatter and magnification factor, *J. Comp. Neurol.*, **158**, 295–305, 1974b.

Hubel, D. H., Calvin, O. H., Rupert, A. and Galambos, R., "Attention" units in the auditory cortex, *Science*, **129**, 1279–1280, 1959.

Humphrey, N. K., What the frog's eye tells to the monkey's brain, *Brain Behav. Evol.*, **2**, 324–337, 1970.

Humphrey, N. K., Vision in a monkey without striate cortex: A case study, *Perception*, **3**, 241–255, 1974.

Humphrey, N. K. and Weiskrantz, L., Vision in monkeys after removal of striate cortex, *Nature*, **215**, 595–597, 1967.

Humphrey, N. K. and Weiskrantz, L., Size constancy in monkeys with I. T. lesion, *Quart. J. Exp. Psychol.*, **25**, 225–228, 1969.

Humphrey, M. E. and Zangwill, O. L., Dysphasia in left handed patients with unilateral brain lesions, *J. Neurol. Neurosurg. Psychiat.*, **15**, 184–193, 1952.

Hyvarinen, J. and Poranen, A., Function of the parietal associative area 7 as revealed from cellular discharges in alert monkeys, *Brain*, **97**, 673–692, 1974.

Ikata, M., Sugishita, M., Toyokura, Y., Yamada, R., and Yoshioka, M., Etude sur le syndrome de disconnection visuo-linguale apres la transection du corps calleux. Troubles de la verbalisation des informatione visuelles dans l'hemisphere miniar, *J. Neurol. Sci.*, **23**, 421–432, 1974.

Imbert, M. and Buisseret, P., Receptive field characteristics and plastic properties of visual cortical cells in kittens reared with or without visual experience, *Exp. Brain Res.*, **22**, 25–30, 1975.

Ingham, S. D. and Nielsen, J. M., Interpretation dissociated from recognition of visual verbal symbols illustrated by case of complete major (left) temporal lobectomy, *Proc. Amer. Neurol. Assoc.*, **61**, 1936.

Ingle, D., Two visual mechanisms underlying the behavior of fish, *Psychol. Forsch.*, **31**, 44–51, 1967.

Ingram, D., The acquisition of the English verbal auxiliary and copula in normal and linguistically deviant children, *ASHA Monogr.* **18**, 5–14, 1974.

Irigaray, L., Approche psycholinguistique de langage des dements, *Neuropsychologia*, **5**, 25–52, 1967.

Irigaray, L., *La Langage des déments*, Mouton & Co., The Hague, 1973.

Isaac, W., Role of stimulation and time in the effects of spaced occipital ablations, *Psychol. Rep.*, **14**, 151–154, 1964.

Isaac, W. and De Vito, J., Effect of sensory stimulation on the activity of normal and prefrontal lobectomized monkeys, *J. Comp. Physiol. Psychol.*, **51**, 172, 1958.

Isaacson, R. L. and Schmaltz, L. W., Failure to find savings from spaced, two stage destruction of hippocampus, *Comm. Beh. Biol., PTA,* **1**, 353–359, 1968.

Isaacson, R. L., Nonneman, A. J. and Schmaltz, L. W., "Behavioral and Anatomical Sequels of Damage to the Infant Limbic System," in R. L. Isaacson (ed.), *The Neuropsychology of Development: A Symposium,* Wiley, New York, 1968, pp. 41–78.

Isserlin, M., Über Agrammatismus, *Ftschr. ges. Neurol. u. Psych.*, **75**, 332–410, 1922.

Iversen, S. D. and Mishkin, M., Perseverative interference in monkeys following selective lesions of the inferior prefrontal convexity, *Exp. Brain Res.*, **11**, 376–386, 1970.

Iversen, S. D. and Weiskrantz, L., Temporal lobe lesions and memory in the monkey, *Nature*, **201**, 740–742, 1964.

Iversen S. D. and Weiskrantz, L., Perception of redundant cues by monkeys with inferotemporal lesions, *Nature*, **214**, 241–243, 1967.

Iwai, E. and Mishkin, M., Further evidence on the locus of the visual area in the temporal lobe of the monkey, *Exp. Neurol.*, **25**, 585–594, 1969.

Jackson, J. H., Clinical remarks on cases of defects of expression (by words, writing, signs, etc.) in diseases of the nervous system, *Lancet*, **1**, 604–605, 1864.

Jackson, J. H., *Selected Writings*, **2**, J. Taylor (ed.), Hodder and Stoughton, London, 1932.

Jacobsen, C. F., An experimental analysis of the frontal association areas in primates, *Arch. Neurol. Psychiat.*, **33**, 558–569, 1935.

Jacobsen, C. F., Studies of cerebral function in primates. I. The functions of the frontal association areas in monkeys, *Comp. Psychol. Monogr.*, **13**, whole of No. 63, 1936.

Jacobsen, C. F. and Nissen, H. W., Studies of cerebral function in primates. IV. The effects of frontal lobe lesions on the delayed alternation habit in monkeys, *J. Comp. Physiol. Psychol.*, **23**, 101–112, 1937.

Jakobson, R., *Kindersprache, Aphasie und allgemeine Lautgesetze,* Universitets Arsskrift, Uppsala, Sweden, 1941.

Jakobson, R., Toward a linguistic typology of aphasic impairments, in A. U. S. de Reuck and M. O'Connor (eds.), *Disorders of Language,* Churchill, London, pp. 21–42, 1964.

Jakobson, R., On visual and auditory signs, *Phonetica*, **2**, 216–220, 1964b.

Jakobson, R. and Halle, M., *Fundamentals of Language,* Mouton et Cie, The Hague, Netherlands, 1956.

Jakobson, R., Fant, G. M. and Halle, M., *Preliminaries to Speech Analysis: The Distinctive Features and Their Correlates,* MIT Press, Cambridge, Mass., 1963.

Janota, O., Sur l'apraxie constructive et sur les troubles de l'aperception et de l'expression des rapporte spatiaux, *L'Encephale* **33**, 173–211, 1938.

Jarvie, H., Frontal lobe disinhibition, *J. Neurol. Neurosurg. Psychiat.*, **17**, 14–32, 1954.

Jeannerod, M. and Chouves, G., Saccadic displacements of the retinal image: Effects on the visual system in the cat, *Vision Res.*, **13**, 161–169, 1972.

Jeannerod, M. and Sakai, K., Occipital and geniculate potentials related to eye movements in the unanaesthetized cat, *Brain Res.*, **19**, 361–377, 1970.

Jergen, J. F. and Meir, M., 1960; cited by B. Milner, 1962a.

Jergen, J., Weikers, N. J., Sharbrough, F. W., III et al, Bilateral lesions of the temporal lobe. A case study, *Acta Otolaryng.* (Stockholm), Suppl. **258**, 1+, 1969.

Johns, D. F. and Darley, F. L., Phonemic variability in apraxia of speech, JSHR, **13**, 556–583, 1970.

Johnson, D. A., Developmental aspects of recovery of function following septal lesions in the infant rat, *J. Comp. Physiol. Psychol.*, **78**, 331–348, 1972.

Johnson, T. L., Rosvold, H. E. and Mishkin, M., Projecting from behaviorally defined sectors of the prefrontal cortex to the basal ganglia septum, and diencephalon of the monkey, *Exp. Neurol.*, **21**, 20–34, 1968.

Jones, E. G. and Powell, T. P. S., Connexions of the somatic sensory cortex of the rhesus monkey. I. Ipsilateral cortical connexions. *Brain*, **92**, 477–502, 1969a.

Jones, E. G. and Powell, T. P. S., Connexions of the somatic sensory cortex of the rhesus monkey. II. Contralateral cortical connexions. *Brain*, **92**, 717–730, 1969b.

Jouvet, M., "Neurophysiology of the States of Sleep," in G. C. Quatron, T. Melnechunk and F. O. Schmitt, (eds.), *The Neurosciences*, Rockefeller University Press, New York, 1967, pp. 529–544.

Jouvet, M., "Coma and Other Disorders of Consciousness," in P. J. Vinken and G. W. Bruyn (eds.), *Handbook of Clinical Neurology*, Vol. 3, North Holland Publishing Co., Amsterdam, 1969, pp. 62–79.

Jung, R., "Neuronal Integration in the Visual Cortex and Its Significance for Visual Information," in W. A. Rosenblith (ed.), *Sensory Communication*, MIT Press, Cambridge, Mass., and Wiley, New York, 1961, pp. 627–674.

Kaas, J. H., Hall, W. C., Killackey, H. and Diamond, I. T., Visual cortex of the tree shrew (*Tupia glis*): Architectonic subdivisions and representations of the visual field, *Brain Res.*, **42**, 491–496, 1972.

Kaplan, E. F., Gestural representation of implement usage: An organismic-developmental study, *Dissertation Abstracts*, **29**, (6-B), 2193–2194, 1968.

Karasseva, T. A., The role of the temporal lobe in human auditory perception, *Neuropsychologia*, **10**, 227–231, 1972.

Karp, E., Belmont, I., and Birch, H. G., Unilateral hearing loss in hemiplegic patients, *J. Nerv. Ment. Dis.*, **148**, 83–86,1969.

Katsuki, Y., "Neural Mechanism of Auditory Sensation," in W. A. Rosenblith (ed.), *Sensory Communication*, MIT Press, Cambridge, Mass., and Wiley, New York and London, 1961, pp. 561–583.

Keating, E. G., Loss of visual control of the forelimb after interruption of cortical pathways, *Exp. Neurol*, **41**, 635–648, 1973.

Keating, E. G. and Horel, J. A., Effects of prestriate and striate lesions on performance of simple visual tasks, *Exp. Neurol.*, **35**, 322–336, 1972.

Kellogg, W. and Kellogg, L., *The Ape and the Child*, McGraw-Hill, New York, 1933.

Kelly, J. B., The effects of insular and temporal lesions in cats on two types of auditory pattern discrimination, *Brain Res.*, **62**, 71–87, 1973.

Kelly, J. B., Localization of paired sound sources in the rat: Small time differences, *J. Acoust. Soc. Amer.*, **55**, 1277–1284, 1974.

Kelly, J. B. and Whitfield, I. C., Effects of auditory cortical lesions on discriminations of rising and falling frequency-modulated tones, *J. Neurophysiol.*, **34**, 802–816, 1971.

Kennard, M. A., Age and other factors in motor recovery from precentral lesions in monkeys, *Amer. J. Physiol.*, **115**, 138–146, 1936.

Kennard, M. A., Reorganization of motor function in the cerebral cortex of monkeys deprived of motor and pre-motor areas in infancy, *J. Neurophysiol.*, **1**, 477–496, 1938.

Kennard, M., Alteration in response to visual stimuli following lesions of frontal lobe in monkeys, *Arch. Neurol. Psychiat.* (Chicago), **41**, 1153–1165, 1939.

Kennard, M. A., Relation of age to motor impairment in man and in subhuman primates, *Arch. Neurol. Psychiat.*, **44**, 377–397, 1940.

Kennard, M. A., Cortical reorganization of motor function: Studies on a series of monkeys of various ages from infancy to maturity, *Arch. Neurol. Psychiat.*, **8**, 227–240, 1942.

Kennard, M. and Ectors, L., Forced circling in monkeys following lesions of frontal lobes, *J. Neurophysiol.*, **1**, 45–54, 1938.

Kennard, M., Viets, H. and Fulton, J., The syndrome of the premotor cortex in man, *Brain,* **57,** 411–434, 1934.

Kennedy, F., The symptomatology of temporo-sphenoidal tumors, *Arch. Internat. Med.,* **8,** 317–350, 1911.

Kennedy, F., Stock-brainedness, the causation factor in the so-called "crossed aphasias," *Amer. J. Med. Sci.,* **6,** 849–859, 1916.

Kennedy, F., 1955; cited by W. D. Neff, 1961.

Kerschensteiner, M., Hartje, W., Orgass, B. and Poeck, K., The recognition of simple and complex realistic figures in patients with unilateral brain lesion, *Arch. Psychiat. Nervenkhr.,* **216,** 188–200, 1972.

Kessler, M. and Kennard, M. A., Studies of motor performance after parietal ablations in monkeys, *J. Neurophysiol.,* **3,** 248–257, 1940.

Kiang, N. Y. S., Watanabe, T., Thomas, E. C. and Clark, L. F., *Discharge Patterns of Single Fibers in Cat's Auditory Nerve,* MIT Press, Cambridge, Mass., 1965.

Killackey, H., Wilson, M. and Diamond, I. T., Further studies of the striate and extrastriate visual cortex in the tree shrew, *J. Comp. Physiol. Psychol.,* **81,** 45–63, 1972.

Kimble, D. P., Bagshaw, M. and Pribram, K. H., The GSR of monkeys during orienting and habituation after selective partial ablation of the cingulate and frontal cortex, *Neuropsychologia,* **3,** 121–128, 1965.

Kimura, D., Some effects of temporal lobe damage on auditory perception, *Canad. J. Psychol.* **15,** 156–165, 1961a.

Kimura, D., Cerebral dominance and the perception of verbal stimuli, *Canad. J. Psychol.* **15,** 166–171, 1961b.

Kimura, D., Right temporal lobe damage, *Arch. Neurol,* **8,** 264–271, 1963.

Kimura, D., Left-right differences in the perception of melodies, *Quart. J. Exp. Psychol.,* **14,** 355–358, 1964.

Kimura, D., Manual activity during speaking. I. Right-handers, *Neuropsychologia,* **11,** 45–50, 1973a.

Kimura, D., Manual activity during speaking. II. Left-handers, *Neuropsychologia,* **11,** 51–55, 1973b.

Kimura, D., The asymmetry of the human brain, *Sci. Amer.* **228,** 70–78, 1973c.

Kimura, D. and Archibald, Y., Motor functions of the left hemisphere, *Brain,* **97,** 337–350, 1974.

Kinsbourne, M., Eye and head turning indicate cerebral lateralization, *Science,* **179,** 539–541, 1972.

Kinsbourne, M., Cognitive deficit and the aging brain: A behavioral analysis, *Internat. J. Aging Hum. Dev.,* **5,** 41–49, 1974a.

Kinsbourne, M., Direction of gaze and distribution of cerebral thought processes, *Neuropsychologia,* **12,** 279–281, 1974b.

Kinsbourne, M., The ontogeny of cerebral dominance, *Ann. N.Y. Acad. Sci.,* **263,** 250–255, 1975a.

Kinsbourne, M., Models of learning disability: Their relevance to remediation, *Canad. Med. Assoc. J.,* **113,** 1066–1069, 1975b.

Kinsbourne, M. and Rosenfield, D., Agraphia selective for written spelling, *Brain and Lang.,* **1,** 215–225, 1974.

Kinsbourne, M. and Warrington, E. K., A study of finger agnosia, *Brain,* **85,** 47–66, 1962a.

Kinsbourne, M. and Warrington, E. K., A disorder of simultaneous form perception, *Brain,* **85,** 461–486, 1962b.

Kinsbourne, M. and Warrington, E. K., Observations in colour agnosia, *J. Neurol. Neurosurg. Psychiat.,* **27,** 296–299, 1964.

Kirvel, R. D., Greenfield, R. A. and Meyer, D. R., Multimodal sensory neglect with radical unilateral posterior isocortical and superior colliculus ablation, *J. Comp. Physiol. Psychol.,* **87,** 156–162, 1974.

Klein, R. and Harper, J., The problem of agnosia in the light of a case of pure word deafness, *J. Ment. Sci.*, **102**, 112–120, 1956.

Kleist, K., Der gang und der gegenwurtige Stand der Apraxie-forschung. *Ergebn. Neurol. Psychiat.*, **1**, 342–452, 1912.

Kleist, K., Über Leitungs aphasie und grammatische Storungen, Mtschr. Psychiat. Neurol., **40**, 118–199, 1916.

Kleist, K., in O. Schjernings (ed.), *Handbuch der argblichen Erfahrungen*, Barth, Leipzig, 1922.

Kleist, K., Gehirpathologische und lokalisatorische Ergebnisse 4. Mitteilung über motorische Aphasien, *J. F. Psychol. u. Neur.*, **40**, 338–346, 1930.

Kleist, K., *Gehirnpathologie*, Barth, Leipzig, 1934.

Kleist, K., *Sensory Aphasia and Amusia*, Pergamon Press, Oxford, England, 1962.

Kleitman, N., *Sleep and Wakefulness*, University of Chicago Press, Chicago, 1963.

Kling, A., Amygdalectomy in the kitten, *Science*, **137**, 429–430, 1962.

Kling, A., Behavior and somatic development following lesions of the amygdala in the cat, *J. Psychiat. Res.*, **3**, 263–273, 1965.

Kling, A., Ontogenetic and phylogenetic studies on the amygdaloid nuclei, *Psychosom. Med.*, **28**, 155–161, 1966.

Kling, A. and Green, P. C., Effects of neonatal amygdalectomy in the maternally reared and maternally deprived macaque, *Nature*, **213**, 742–743, 1967.

Kling, A. and Tucker, T. J., "Sparing of Function following Brain Lesions in Neonatal Monkeys," in R. Isaacson (ed.), *Neuropsychology of Development*, Wiley, New York, 1968, pp. 121–149.

Kluver, H., "Mechanisms of Hallucination," in *Studies in Personality*, McGraw-Hill, New York, 1942, pp. 175–207.

Kluver, H. and Bucy, P. C., "Psychic blindness" and other symptoms following temporal lobectomy in rhesus monkeys, *Amer. J. Physiol.*, **119**, 352, 353, 1937.

Kluver, H. and Bucy, P. C. Preliminary analysis of function of the temporal lobes in monkeys, *Arch. Neurol. Psychiat.*, **42**, 979–1000, 1939.

Knighton, R. S., Thalamic relay nucleus for the second somatic receiving area of the cerebral cortex of the cat. *J. Comp. Neurol.*, **92**, 183–191, 1950.

Knox, C. and Kimura, D., Cerebral processing of non-verbal sounds in boys and girls, *Neuropsychologia*, **8**, 227–237, 1970.

Kohler, I., Über Aufban und Wordlungen der Wahrnehmungswelt, *Sitzber Osters. Akadwisc.*, **227**, 1–118, 1951.

Kohler, W. and Wallach, H., Figurial after effects: An investigation of visual processes, *Proc. Amer. Phil. Soc.*, **88**, 269–357, 1944.

Kohn, B. and Dennis, M., Somatosensory functions after cerebral hemidecortication for infantile hemiplegia, *Neuropsychologia*, **12**, 119–130, 1974.

Kolodny, A., Symptomatology of tumor of the frontal lobe, *Arch. Neurol. Psychiat.* (Chicago), **21**, 1107–1127, 1929.

Konorski, J., *Integrative Activity of the Brain: An Interdisciplinary Approach*, University of Chicago Press, Chicago, 1967.

Konorski, J., *Conditioned Reflexes and Neuron Organization*, Hafner, New York, 1968.

Kooi, K. A. and Sharbrough, F. W., Electrophysiological findings in cortical blindness. Report of a case, *Electroencephal. Clin. Neurophysiol.*, **20**, 260–263, 1966.

Korsakow, S. S., Disturbance of psychic function in alcoholic paralysis and its relation to the disturbance of the psychic sphere in multiple neuritis of non-alcoholic origin, *Vestnik Psichiatrii*, IV, 1887; cited in Victor, M., Adams, R., and Collins, G., 1971.

Korsakow, S. S., Psychic troubles associated with polyneuritis. Psychosis polyneurotica. Cerebroputhia psychica toxoemica [in Russian], *Med. Obozren*, **31**, No. B, 1889a. English translation in *Neurol.* (Minneapolis), **5**, 394–407, 1955.

Korsakow, S. S., Etude medico psychologique sur une forme des maladies de la memoire, *Rev. Phil.* **28**, 501–530, 1889b.

Kramer, G., Alloasthesie und fehlende Wahrnehmung der gelahinten korperhalfle bei subcortikalem Hirnherd, *Neurol. Zentralbl.,* **34**, 287–288, 1915.

Krashen, S., Lateralization, language learning, and the critical period. Some new evidence, *Lang: Learning,* **23**, 63–74, 1973.

Krause, F., Die sehbahn in chirurgischen Beziehung und die faradischen Reizung der Sehzentrums, *Klin. Wschr.,* **3**, 15–24, 1924.

Kremin, H. and Goldblum, M. C., Etude de la compréhension syntaxique chez les aphasiques, *Linguistics,* **154/155**, 31–46, 1975.

Krishaber, *La Neuropathie cerebrocardiaque,* G. Masson et Cie, Paris, 1873.

Kubota, K. and Niki, H., Prefrontal cortical unit activity and delayed alternation performance in monkeys, *J. Neurophysiol.,* **34**, 337–347, 1971.

Kussmaul, A., Les troubles de la parole (trad. par A. Rueff, Paris, 1884).

Kuypers, H. G. J. M., Szwarcbart, M. K., Mishkin, M. and Rosvold, H. E., Occipitotemporal cortico-cortical connections in the Rhesus monkey, *Exp. Neurol.,* **11**, 245–262, 1965.

Lackner, J. R. and Teuber, H. L., Alterations in auditory fusion thresholds after cerebral injury in man, *Neuropsychologia,* **11**, 409–415, 1973.

Lagrange, H., Bertrand, I. and Garcin, R., Cécité corticale par ramollissement des deux cunei, *Rev. Neurol.,* **1**, 417–427, 1929.

Laignel-Lavastine, M. and Alajouanine, T., Un cas d'agnosie auditive, *Rev. Neurol.,* **37**, 194–198, 1921.

Lambert, F. and Fillenbaum. S., A pilot study of aphasia among bilinguals, *Canad. J. Psychol.,* **12**, 28–34, 1959.

Landau, W. M. and Kleffner, F. R., Syndrome of acquired aphasia with convulsive disorder in children, *Neurol.* (Minneapolis), **7**, 523, 1957.

Landau, W. and Kleffner, R., (cited in Worster-Drought, 1971), *Dev. Med. Child Neurol.,* **13**, 563–571, 1971.

Lange, J., Probleme der Fingeragnosie, *Ztschr. Neurol. Psychiat.,* **47**, 594–610, 1933.

Lange, J., Agnosien und Apraxien, *Handbuch der Neurol. Burnke-Foerster,* **6**, 807–960, 1936.

Lashley, K. S., *Brain Mechanisms and Intelligence,* University of Chicago Press, Chicago, 1923.

Lashley, K., The mechanism of vision. XII. Nervous structures concerned in the acquisition and retention of habits based on reactions to light, *Comp. Psychol. Monographs,* **11**, 43–79, 1935.

Lashley, K. S., Functional determinant of cerebral localization, *Arch. Neurol. Psychiat.,* **38**, 371–387, 1937.

Latto, R. and Cowey, A., Fixation changes after frontal eye-field lesions in monkeys, *Brain Res.,* **30**, 25–36, 1971a.

Latto, R. and Cowey, A., Visual field defects after frontal eye-field lesions in monkeys, *Brain Res.,* **30**, 1–24, 1971b.

Lawicka, W., Proreal syndrome in dogs, *Acta Neurobiol. Exp.,* **32**, 261–276, 1972.

Lawicka, W. and Konorski, J., The effect of prefrontal lobectomies on the delayed response in cats, *Acta Biol. Exp.,* **21**, 141–156, 1961.

Lawicka, W., Mishkin, M., Kreiner, J. and Brutkowski, S., Delayed response deficit in dogs after selective ablation of the proreal gyrus, *Acta. Biol. Exp.,* **26**, 309–322, 1966.

Lawrence, D. G. and Hopkins, D. A., Developmental aspects of pyramidal motor control in the Rhesus monkey, *Brain Res.,* **40**, 117–118, 1972.

Lawrence, D. G. and Kuypers, H. G., The functional organization of the motor system in the monkey. I. The effects of bilateral pyramidal lesions, *Brain,* **91**, 1–14, 1968a.

Lawrence, D. G. and Kuypers, H. G., The functional organization of the motor system in the monkey. II. The effects of the descending brain stem pathways, *Brain,* **91**, 15–36, 1968b.

Le Beau, J. and Wolinetz, E., Le phenomene de perséveration visuelle, *Rev. Neurol.*, **99**, 525–534, 1958.

Lebrun, Y., "Recovery in polyglot aphasics," in Y. Lebrun and R. Hoops, (eds.), *Recovery in Aphasics,* Swets and Zeitlinger, Amsterdam, 1976.

Lecours, A. R. and Lhermitte, F., Phonemic paraphasias: Linguistic structures and tentative hypothesis, *Cortex*, **5**, 193–228, 1969.

Lefevre, A. and Branco, F., Contribuicquo para o estudo da psicopatologia da afusio em criancas (these, Sao Paolo), 1 vol. (50 pp.), Sao Paolo, Brazil, 1950.

Le Gros Clark, W. E. and Russell, R. W., Cortical deafness without aphasia, *Brain*, **61**, 375–383, 1938.

Lehiste, I., "Some Acoustic Characteristics of Dysarthria," *Biblioteca Phonetica,* Basel, Switzerland, 1968.

Lehmann, D. and Walchli, P., Depth perception and location of brain lesions, *J. Neurol.*, **209**, 157–164, 1975.

Leicester, J., Sidman, M., Stoddard, L. T., and Mohr, J. P., Some determinants of visual neglect, *J. Neurol. Neurosurg. Psychiat.*, **32**, 580–587, 1969.

Leischner, A., Über die Aphasie der Mehr-sprachigen, *Arch. Psychiat.* (LPZ), **118**, 731–775, 1948.

Lenneberg, E. H., Color naming, color recognition, color discrimination: A reappraisal, *Percept. Mot. Skills*, **12**, 275–382, 1961.

Lenneberg, E. H., *Biological Foundation of Language,* Wiley, New York, 1967.

Lenz, H., Raumsinnstorungen bei Hirnverletzungen, *Dtsch. Z. Nervenhk.*, **157**, 27–64, 1944.

Leong, S. K. and Lund, R. D., Anomalous bilateral corticofugal pathways in albino rats after neonatal lesions, *Brain Res.*, **62**, 218–221, 1973.

Leporé, F., Cardu, B., Rasmussen, T. and Malino, R. B., Rod and cone sensitivity in destriate monkey, *Brain Res.*, **93**, 203–222, 1975.

Lettvin, J. Y., Maturana, H. R., McCulloch, W. S. and Pitts, W. A., What the frog's eye tells to the frog's brain, *Proc. Inst. Rad. Engr.*, **47**, 1940–1951, 1959.

Levere, T. and Weiss, J., Failure of seriatim dorsal hippocampal lesions to spare spatial reversal behavior in pets, *J. Comp. Physiol. Psychol.*, **82**, 205–210, 1973.

Levin, H. S., Motor impersistence and proprioceptive feedback in patients with unilateral cerebral disease, Neurol. (Minneapolis), **23**, 833–841, 1973.

Leventhal, A. G. and Hirsh, H. U. B., Cortical effect of early selective exposure to diagonal lines, *Science*, **190**, 902–904, 1975.

Levy, J., Trevarthen, C. and Sperry, R. W., Reception of bilateral chimeric figures following hemispheric disconnexion, *Brain*, **95**, 61–78, 1972.

Lewandowsky, M., Über abspaltung des Farbensinnes, *Mtschr. Psychiat.*, **23**, 488, 1908.

Lhermitte, F. and Beauvois, M. F., A visual-speech disconnexion syndrome. Report of a case with optic aphasia, agnosia, alexia and colour agnosia, *Brain*, **96**, 695–714, 1973.

Lhermitte, F. and Signoret, J. L., Analyse neuropsychologique et differenciation des syndromes amnesiques, *Rev. Neurol,* **126**, 161–178, 1972.

Lhermitte, F., Lecours, A. R. and Ouvry, B., Essai d'analyse structurale e des paralexies et des paragraphies. Rapport preliminaire, *Acta Neurol. Belg.* **67**, 1021–1044, 1967.

Lhermitte, F., Chain, F., Aron, D., Leblanc, M. and Souty, O., Les troubles de la vision des couleurs dans les lesions posteueures du cerveau, *Rev. Neurol.*, **121**, 5–29, 1969.

Lhermitte, F., Chain, F., Escourolle, R. et al, Etude anatomo-clinique d'un cas de prosopagnosie, *Rev. Neurol.*, **126**, 329–346, 1972.

Lhermitte, F., Lecours, A. R. and Ducarne, B. et al, Unexpected anatomical findings in a case of fluent jargon aphasia, *Cortex*, **9**, 436–449, 1973a.

Lhermitte, F., Chedru, F., and Chain, F., A propos d'un cas d'agnosie visuelle, *Rev. Neurol.*, **128**,301–322, 1973b.

Lhermitte, J., Le lobe frontal, *L'Encephale,* **24,** 87–118, 1929.

Lhermitte, J., *L'Image de notre corps, Nouvelle Revue Critique,* Paris, 1939.

Lhermitte, J. and de Ajuriaguerra, J., Hallucinations visuelles et lesions de l'appareil visuel, *Ann. Med. Psychol.,* **94,** 321–351, 1936.

Lhermitte, J. and de Ajuriaguerra, J., Asymbolie tactile et hallucinations du toucher, *Etude anatomoclinique. Rev. Neurol,* 492–495, 1938.

Lhermitte, J. and Nicolas, T., Sur la maladie d'Alzheimer, un observation clinique, *Ann. Med. Psychol.,* **1,** 435–448, 1923.

Lhermitte, J. and Sebillotte, R., Le membre fantome dans les lesions graves du plexus brachial, *Rev. Neurol.,* **70,** 488–492, 1938.

Lhermitte, J., Levy, G. and Kyriaco, N., Les perturbations de la representation spatiale chez les apraxiques. A propos de deux cas cliniques d'apraxie, *Rev. Neurol.,* **2,** 586–600, 1925.

Lhermitte, J., de Massary, J. and Kyriaco, N., Le role de la pensee spatiale dans l'apraxie, *Rev. Neurol.,* **2,** 895–903, 1928.

L'Hermitte, R., Hécaen, H., Dubois, J., Culioli, A. and Tabouret-Keller, A., Le probleme de l'aphasie des polyglottes-remarques sur quelques observations, *Neuropsychologia,* **4,** 315–329, 1966.

Liberman, A. M., Cooper, F. S., Shankweiler, D. P., and Studdert-Kennedy, M., Perception of the speech code, *Psychological Rev.,* **74,** 431–461, 1967.

Lichtheim, L., 1881: cited in Lichtheim, 1885.

Lichtheim, L., 1884; cited in Lichtheim, 1885.

Lichtheim, L., Über Aphasie, *Dtsch. Arch. klin. Med.,* **36,** 204, 1885.

Lico, M. C., Hoffman, A., and Covian, M. R., Autonomic conditioning in the anesthetized rabbit, *Phys. Behav.,* **3,** (5) 673–675, 1968.

Liepmann, H., "Ein Fall von reiner Sprachtaubheit," in *Psychiatrische Abhendungen,* Breslau, Poland, 1890.

Leipmann, H., Das krankheitshild der Apraxie (motorischen Asymbolie), *Mtschr. Psychiat.,* **8,** 15–44, 102–132, 182–197, 1900.

Liepmann, H., Die linke Hemisphare und das Handeln, *Munch. Med. Wschr.* **49,** 2375–2378, 1905.

Liepmann, H., *Drei Aufsatze aus dem Apraxiegebeit,* 1 vol., Karger, Berlin, 1908a.

Liepmann, H., Über die agnostischen Storungen, *Neur. Zbl.,* **27,** 609–617, 1908b.

Liepmann, M. and Pappenheim, M., Über einen Fall von sogenantes Leitungsaphasie mit anatomischen Befund, *Ztschr. ges. Neurol. Psychiat.,* **27,** 1–41, 1915.

Lissauer, H., Ein Fall von Seelenblindheit nebst einen Beitrag zur Theorie derselben, *Arch. f. Psychiat.,* **21,** 222–270, 1890.

Liu, C-N, and Chambers, W. W., Intraspinal sprouting of dorsal root axons, *Arch. Neurol. Psychiat.,* **79,** 46–61, 1958.

Loeffler, J. D., 1958; cited by Woolsey, 1961.

Longhi, A., La schema corporeo: indagini cliniche et an alisi initia, *Arch. Psychol. Neurol. Psiciat. et psicoterapia,* **1–2,** 47–189, 1939.

Lowenstein, K. and M. Borchardt, Symptomatologie und Electrische Reizung bei einer Schussverletzung des Himtshauptlappens, *Dtsch. Ztschr. Nervenhk.* **58,** 264–270, 1918.

Lund, M., Epilepsy in association with intracranial tumours, *Acta Psychiat. Neurol. Scand.,* Suppl. No. 81, 149, 1952.

Lunn, V., *Om Legernsbevidstheden Belyst ved Nogle Forstyrrelser of den normale oplevelsesmaade,* E. Munksgaard, Copenhague, Denmark, 1948.

Luria, A. R., *Traumatic Aphasia,* Academy of Medical Sciences Press, Moscow, 1947.

Luria, A. R., Restoration of functions after brain trauma [in Russian]. Academy of Medical Science Press, Moscow, 1948; Pergamon Press, London, 1963.

Luria, A. R., Brain disorder and language analysis, *Lang. and Speech,* **1,** 14–34, 1958.

Luria, A. R., Disorders of simultaneous perception in a case of bilateral occipitoparietal brain injury, *Brain,* **82,** 437–449, 1959.

Luria, A. R. *Restoration of Function after Brain Injury,* Macmillan, New York, 1963.

Luria, A. R., "Factors and Forms of Aphasia," in A. U. S. de Reuck and M. O'Connor (eds.), *Disorders of Language,* Churchill, London, 1964, pp.143–161.

Luria, A. R., Two kinds of motor perseveration in massive injury of the frontal lobes, *Brain,* **88,** 1–10, 1965a.

Luria, A. R., Aspects of aphasia, *J. Neurol. Sci.,* **2,** 278–286, 1965b.

Luria, A. R., *The Higher Cortical Function in Man,* Basic Books, New York, 1966.

Luria, A. R., The functional organization of the brain, *Sci. Amer.,* **222,** 66–72, passim, 1970.

Luria, A. R., "The Origin and Cerebral Organization of Man's Conscious Action," *Proc. XIV Int. Congr. Psychol.* (London, 1969), Dorset Press, Dorchester, 1971, pp. 37–52.

Luria, A. R., Aphasia reconsidered, *Cortex,* **8,** 34–40, 1972.

Luria, A. R., Towards the mechanisms of naming disturbance, *Neuropsychologia,* **11,** 417–421, 1973.

Luria, A. R. and Homskaya, E., "Disturbance in the Regulative Role of Speech with Frontal Lobe Lesions," in S. M. Warren and K. Akert (eds.), *The Frontal Granular Cortex and Behavior,* McGraw-Hill, New York, 1964.

Luria, A. R. and Tsectova, L. S., *Le^c Troubles de la Resolution de Problemes. Analyse Neuropsychologique,* Gauthier-Villars, Paris, 1967.

Luria, A. R., Pravdena-Vinarskaya, E. N., and Yarbus, A. L., Disorders of the ocular movements in a case of simultagnosia, *Brain,* **86,** 219–228, 1963.

Luria, A. R., Isvetkova, L. S. and Futer, J. C., Aphasia in a composer, *J. Neurol. Sci.,* **2,** 250–262, 1965.

Luria, S. L., Color name as a function of stimulus-intensity and duration, *Amer. J. Psychol.,* **80,** 14–27, 1967.

Lurje, Zur Lehre vom korperschema, *Zbl. ger Neurol. Psychiat.,* **81,** 468, 1936.

Lynch, G., The formation of new synaptic connections after brain damage and their possible role in recovery of function, in *Neuroscience Res. Progr. Bull.,* "Functional Recovery after Lesions of the Nervous System," 1973, pp. 228–233.

Lynch, G. and Crain, B., Increased generalized activity following lesions of the caudal reticular formation, *Physiol. Behav.,* **8,** 747–750, 1972.

Lynch, G., Matthews, D. A., Mosko, S. et al, Induced acetylcholinesterase-rich layer in rat dentate gyrus following entorhinal lesions, *Brain Res.,* **42,** 311–318, 1972.

Lynch, G., Deadwyler, S. and Cotman, G., Postlesion axonol growth produces permanent functional connections, *Science,* **180,** 1364–1366, 1973a.

Lynch, G., Smith, R. L., Mensah, P. et al, Tracing the dentate mossy fiber system with horseradish peroxidase histochemistry, *Exp. Neurol.,* **40,** 516–524, 1973b.

Maas, O., Fall von linkseitiger Apraxie mit Bemerkenswerter Sensibilitatstorung, *Neur. Zbl.,* **29,** 962–967, 1910.

Magito, A. and E. Hartmann, La cécité corticale, *Revue oto-neuro-oculistique,* **5,** 81–114, 1927.

Magnus, H., Ein Fall von Rindenblindheit. *Dtsch. med. Wschr.,* **20,** 4, 1894; cited by Soury, J., *Le Systeme nerveux central,* Carre et Naud, Paris, 1899.

Malmo, R. B., Interference factors in delayed response in monkeys after removal of frontal lobes, *J. Neurophysiol.,* **5,** 295–308, 1942.

Malmo, R B., Effects of striate cortex ablation on intensity discrimination and spectral intensity distribution in the rhesus monkey, *Neuropsychologia,* **4,** 9–26, 1966.

Marcie, P., Writing disorders in 47 left-handed patients with unilateral cerebral lesions, *Internat. J. Ment. Health,* **1,** 30–38, 1972.

Marcie, P., Hécaen, H., Dubois, J., and Angelergues, R., Les troubles de la realisation de la parole au cours des lesions de l'hemisphere droit, *Neuropsychologia*, **3**, 217–247, 1965.

Marg, E. and Dierssen, G., Reported visual percepts from stimulation of human brain during therapeutic surgery, *Comp. Neurol.*, **26**, 57–75, 1965.

Marie, P., Revision de la question de l'aphasie: la voisieme circonvolution frontale gauche ne joue aucun role special dans la fonstion du langage, *Sem. med.* (Paris), **21**, 241–247, 1906a.

Marie, P., Revision de la question de l'aphasie. Que faut-il penser des aphasies sous corticales (aphasies pures)? *Sem. med.* (Paris), **42**, 493–500, 1906b.

Marie, P., Revision de la question de l'aphasie: l'aphasie de 1801 a 1866; essai de critique historique sur la genese de la doctrine de Broca, *Sem. med.* (Paris), **48**, 565–571, 1906c.

Marie, P., *Travaux et Memoires*, Masson et Cie, Paris, 1926.

Marie, P. and Chatelin, C., Les troubles visuels dus aux lesions des voies optiques intrecerebrales et de la sphere visuelle corticale dans les blessures du crane par coup de feu, *Rev. Neurol.*, **28**, 882–925, 1915.

Marie, P. and Foix, C., Les aphasies de guerre, *Rev. Neurol.*, **24**, 53–87, 1917.

Marie, P. and Foix, C., Phenomenes dits apraxiques avec lesions du lobe parieto-temporal gauche, *Rev. Neurol.*, **1**, 275–277, 1922.

Marie, P. and Guillain, G., Le faisceau pyramidal dans l'hémiplégie infantile, hypertrophie compensatrice du faisceau pyramidal, *Rev. Neurol.*, **11**, 293–298, 1903.

Marie, P., Bouttier, H., and Bailey, P., La planotopokinesie. Etude sur les erreurs d'execution de certains mouvements dans leurs rapports avec la representation spatiale, *Rev. Neurol.*, **1**, 505–512, 1922.

Marinesco, G., Grigoresco, D., and Axentes, S., Aphasie croisee, aphasie de Wernicke avec hemiplegie et hemianopsie homonyme laterale gauches chez un droitier, *Revue Belge des Sciences Medicales*, **4**, 2, 1932.

Marquis, D. G., Effects of removal of the visual cortex in mammals with observations on the retention of light discrimination in dogs, *Assoc. Res. Nerv. Ment. Dis.*, **13**, 558–592, 1934.

Marshall, J., Sensory disturbances in cortical wounds with special reference to pain, *J. Neurol. Neurosurg. Psychiat.*, **14**, 187–204, 1951.

Marshall, J. C. and Newcombe, F., Syntactic and semantic errors in paralexia, *Neuropsychologia*, **4**, 169–176, 1966.

Marshall, J. F. and Teitelbaum, P., Further analysis of sensory inattention following lateral hypothalamic damage in rats, *J. Comp. Physiol. Psychol.*, **86**, 375–395, 1974.

Maspes, P. L., Le Syndrome experimental chez l'homme de la section du splenium du corps calleux. Alexie visuelle pure hemianopsique, *Rev. Neurol.*, **80**, 100–113, 1948.

Maspetiol, R., Semette, D., and Mathieu, C., Etude clinique des troubles auditifs dans les lesions corticales, *Sem. Hop. Paris*, 37, 1229–1234, 1961.

Massaro, D. W., Preperceptual images, processing time, and perceptual units in auditory perception, *Psychol. Rev.*, **79**, 124–145, 1972.

Massopust, L. C., Wolin, L. R. and Frost, V., Increase in auditory middle frequency. Discrimination thresholds after cortical ablations, *Exp. Neurol.*, **28**, 299–307, 1970.

Mayer-Gross, W., Ein Fall von Phantomarm nach Plexus zerreissung, *Nervenarzt.*, **2**, 65–72, 1929.

Mayer-Gross, W., Some observations of apraxia, *Proc. Roy. Soc. Med.* **28**, 1203–1212, 1935.

Mayer-Gross, W., Further observations on apraxia, *J. Ment. Sci.*, **82**, 744–762, 1936.

Mayer-Gross, W., Retrograde amnesia, *Lancet*, **2**, 603–605, 1943.

Masure, M. C. and Tzavaras, A., Perception de figures entrecroisees par des sujets atteints de lesions corticales unilaterales, *Neuropsychologia*, **14**, 371–374, 1976.

Mazzia, V. D. B. and Randt, C., Amnesia and eye movements in first stage anesthesia, *Arch. Neurol.*, **14**, 522–525, 1966.

McCough, G. P., Austin, G. M., Lin, C. N. and Lise, C. Y., Sprouting as a cause of spasticity,

J. Neurophysiol., **21**, 205–216, 1958.

McFie, J., Intellectual impairment in children with localized postinfantile cerebral lesions, *J. Neurol. Neurosurg. Psychiat.*, **24**, 361–365, 1961.

McFie, J. and Piercy, M. F., The relation of laterality of lesion to performance on Weigl's sorting test, *J. Ment. Sci.*, **98**, 299–305, 1952a.

McFie, J. and Piercy, M. F., Intellectual impairment with localized cerebral lesions, *Brain*, **75**, 292–311, 1952b.

McFie, J., Piercy, M. F. and Zangwill, O. C., Visual spatial agnosia associated with lesions of the right cerebral hemisphere, *Brain*, **73**, 167–190, 1950.

McGaugh, J. L., Time dependent processes in mummy storage, *Science*, **153**, 1351–1358, 1966.

McIntyre, M. M. and Stein, D. G., Differential effects of one versus two-stage amygdaloid lesions on activity, exploratory and avoidance behavior in the albino rat, *Behav. Biol.*, **9**, 451–465, 1973.

Meadows, J. C., Disturbed perception of colours associated with localized cerebral lesions, *Brain*, **97**, 615–632, 1974.

Meier, M. J., Effects of focal cerebral lesions in contralateral visuomotor adaptation to reversal and inversion of visual feedback, *Neuropsychologia*, **8**, 269–280, 1970.

Melzack, R. and Bromage, P. R., Experimental phantom limbs, *Exp. Neurol.*, **39**, 261–269, 1973.

Melzack, R. and Southmayd, S. E., Dorsal column contributions to anticipatory motor behavior, *Exp. Neurol.*, **42**, 274–281, 1974.

Melzack, R. and Wall, P. D., On the nature of cutaneous sensory mechanisms, *Brain*, **85**, 331–356, 1962.

Merle, P., Aphasie et hemiachromatopsie, *Rev. Neurol.*, **21**, 1129–1136, 1908.

Merrill, E. G. and Wall, P. D., Factors forming the edge of a receptive field: The presence of relatively ineffective afferent terminals, *J. Physiol.* (London), **226**, 825–846, 1972.

Merzenich, M. M. and Brugge, J. F., Representation of the cochlear partition of the superior temporal plane of the macaque monkey, *Brain. Res.*, **50**, 275–296, 1973.

Merzenich, M. M., Knight, P. L. and Roth, G. L., Representation of cochlea within primary auditory cortex in the cat, *J. Neurophysiol.*, **38**, 231–249, 1975.

Messimy, R., Faits experimentaux et cliniques concernant les fonctions des lobes prefrontaux, *Ann. Med.*, **49**, 69–85, 1948.

Mesulam, M. M. and Pandya, D. N., The projections of the medial geniculate complex within the sylvian fissure of the rhesus monkey, *Brain Res.*, **60**, 315–333, 1973.

Meyer, A. and Beck, E., *Prefrontal Leucotomy and Related Operations: Anatomical Aspects of Success or Failure*, Charles C. Thomas, Springfield, Ill., 1954.

Meyer, D. R. and Settlage, P. H., Analysis of simple searching behavior in the frontal monkey, *J. Comp. Physiol. Psychol.*, **51**, 408–410, 1958.

Meyer, D. R., Isaac, W. and Maher, R., The role of stimulation in spontaneous reorganization of visual habits, *J. Comp. Physiol. Psychol.*, **51**, 546–548, 1958.

Meyer, J. S., and Barron, D. W., Apraxia of gait: a clinicophysiological study, *Brain*, **83**, 261–284, 1960.

Meyer, O., Ein-und doppel seitige homonyme Hemianopsie mit Orientierungs-storungen, *Mtschr. Psychiat. Neurol.*, **8**, 440–456, 1900.

Meyer, V., Cognition changes following temporal lobectomy for relief of temporal lobe epilepsy, *AMA Arch. Neurol. Psychiat.*, **81**, 299–309, 1959.

Meyers, B. and McLeary, R. A., Interocular transfer of a pattern discrimination in pattern deprived cats, *J. Comp. Physiol. Psychol.*, **570**, 16–21, 1964.

Meyers, R., Relation of "thinking" and language: An experimental approach using dysphasic patients, *Arch. Neurol. Psychiat.* (Chicago), **60**, 119–139, 1948.

Meynert, A.; cited by H. Liepmann, 1900.

Micalizzi, F., Lo schema corporeo in soggetti con fanzione labirintica assimetrica, *Acta Neurologica*, **4**, 377–406, 1949.

Michael, J. A. and Ichinose, L. Y., Influence of oculo-motor activity on visual processes, *Brain Res.*, **22**, 249–253, 1970.

Michel, F., Jeannerod, M. and Devic, M., Trouble de l'orientation visuelle dans les trois dimensions de l'espace (a propos d'un cas anatomique), *Cortex*, **1**, 441–446, 1965.

Milian, G., Cécité morphologique, *Bull. Acad. Med.*, **107**, 664, 1932.

Miles, R. C. and Blomquist, A. J., Frontal lesions and behavioral deficits in monkey, *J. Neurophysiol.*, **23**, 471–484, 1960.

Miller, E. A., Goldman, P. S. and Rosvold, H. E., Delayed recovery of function following orbital prefrontal lesions in infant monkeys, *Science*, **182**, 304–306, 1973.

Miller, J. M., Benton, R. D., O'Connor, T. et al, Response pattern complexity of auditory cells in the cortex of unanaesthetized monkeys, *Brain Res.*, **69**, 101–113, 1974.

Milner, B., Visual recognition and recall after right temporal lobe excision in man, *Neuropsychologia*, **6**, 191–210, 1958a.

Milner, B., Psychological defects produced by temporal lobe excision, *Res. Publ. Assoc. Res. Nerv. Ment. Dis.*, **36**, 244–257, 1958b.

Milner, B., "Laterality Effects in Audition," in *Interhemispheric Relations and Cerebral Dominance*, Johns Hopkins University Press, Baltimore, 1962a, pp. 177–195.

Milner, B., Les troubles de la memoire accompagnant des lesions hippocampiques bilaterales, *Physiologie de l'hippocampe*, CNRS, Paris, 1962b, pp. 257–272.

Milner, B., Effects of different brain lesions on card sorting, *Arch. Neurol.* (Chicago), **9**, 90–100, 1963.

Milner, B., Visually guided maze learning in man: Effects of bilateral hippocampal, bilateral frontal, and unilateral cerebral lesions, *Neuropsychologia*, **3**, 317–338, 1965.

Milner, B., Disorders of memory after brain lesions in man: Preface: Material-specific and generalized memory loss, *Neuropsychologia*, **6**, 175–179, 1968a.

Milner, B., Visual recognition and recall after right temporal lobe excision in man, *Neuropsychologia*, **6**, 191–209, 1968b.

Milner, B., Differences in behavioral effects of right and left temporal lesion, 9e International Congress of Neurology, New York, 1969.

Milner, B., Interhemispheric differences in the localisation of psychological processes in man, *Brit. Med. Bull.*, **27**, 272–277, 1971.

Milner, B., Functional recovery after lesions of the nervous system. 3. Developmental processes in neural plasticity. Sparing of language functions after early unilateral brain damage, *Neurosci. Res. Program Bull.*, **12**, 213–217, 1974a.

Milner, B., "Hemispheric Specialization: Scope and Limits," in F. O. Schmitt and F. G. Worden (eds.), *The Neurosciences: Third Study Program*, MIT Press, Cambridge, Mass., 1974b, pp. 75–89.

Milner, B. and Taylor, L., Right hemisphere superiority in tactile pattern recognition after cerebral commissurotomy: Evidence for nonverbal memory, *Neuropsychologia*, **10**, 1–15, 1972.

Milner, B. and Teuber, H. L., "Alteration of Perception and Memory in Man," in L. Weiskrantz (ed.), *Analysis of Behavioral Changes*, Harper and Row, New York, 1968, pp. 268–375.

Milner, B., Branch, C. and Rasmussen, Th., Evidence for bilateral speech representation in some non-right handers, *Trans. Amer. Neurol. Assoc.*, **91**, 306–308, 1966.

Milner, B., Taylor, L. and Corkin, S., Tactual pattern recognition after different unilateral cortical excisions, Paper read at 38th Annual Meeting of EPA, Boston, 1967.

Milner, B., Corkin, S. and Teuber, H. L., Further analysis of the hippocampal amnesic syndrome: 14-year follow-up study of HM, *Neuropsychologia*, **6**, 215–234, 1968.

Milner, B., Taylor, L. and Sperry, R. W., Lateralized suppression of dichotically presented digits after commissural section in man, *Science*, **161**, 184–186, 1968.

Minkowski, M., Etude sur la physiologie des circonvolutions rolandiques et parietales, *Schweiz, Arch. Neurol. Psychiat.*, **1**, 389–459, 1917.

Minkowski, M., "On Aphasia in Polyglots," in L. Halpern (ed.), *Problems of Dynamic Neurology*, Jerusalem Post Press, Jerusalem, 1963, pp. 119–161.

Mishkin, M., Visual discrimination performance following partial ablations of the temporal lobe. II. Ventral surface vs. hippocampus, *J. Comp. Physiol. Psychol.*, **47**, 187–193, 1954.

Mishkin, M., Effects of small frontal lesions on delayed alternation in monkeys, *J. Neurophysiol.*, **20**, 615–622, 1957.

Mishkin, M., "Preservation of Central Sets after Frontal Lesions in Monkeys," in J. M. Warren and K. Akert (eds.), *The Frontal Granular Cortex and Behavior*, McGraw-Hill, New York, 1964, pp. 219–241.

Mishkin, M., "Visual Functions beyond Striate Cortex," in R. W. Russell (ed.), *Frontiers of Physiological Psychology*, Academic Press, New York, 1966, pp. 93–116.

Mishkin, M., "Cortical Visual Areas and Their Interactions" in A. G. Karczman and J. C. Eccles (eds.), *Brain and Human Behavior*, Springer-Verlag, Berlin, 1972, pp. 187–208.

Mishkin, M. and Hall, H., Discrimination along a size continuum following ablation of the inferior temporal convexity in the monkeys, *J. Comp. Physiol. Psychol.*, **48**, 97–101, 1955.

Mishkin, M., Prockop, E. S. and Rosvold, H. E., One-trial discrimination learning in monkeys with frontal lesions, *J. Comp. Physiol. Psychol.*, **55**, 178–181, 1952.

Mishkin, M., Vest, B., Waxler, M. and Rosvold, H. E., A re-examination of the effects of frontal lesions on object alternation, *Neuropsychologia*, **7**, 357–364, 1969.

Moffett, A., Ettlinger, G., Morton, H. B. and Piercy, M. F., Tactile discrimination performance in the monkey: The effect of ablation of various subdivisions of posterior parietal cortex, *Cortex*, **3**, 59–96, 1967.

Mohr, J. P., Leicester, J., Stoddard, L. T. and Sidman, M., Right hemianopsia with memory and color deficits in circumscribed left posterior cerebral artery territory infarction, *Neurol.* **21**, 1104–1113, 1971.

Mohr, J. P., Wattes, W. C. and Duncan, G. W., Thalamic hemorrhage and aphasia, *Brain Lang.*, **2**(1), 3–17, 1975.

Monbrun, A. and Gautrand, G., 1920; cited in Brindley et al, 1969.

Moniz, E., *Tentatives Operatoires, dans le Traitement de Certaines Psychoses*, Masson et Cie, Paris, 1936.

Moniz, E., Prefrontal leucotomy in the treatment of mental disorders, *Am. J. Psychiat.*, **93**, 1379–1385, 1937.

Monrad-Krohn, G. H., Dysprosody or altered "melody of language," *Brain*, **70**, 405–415, 1947.

Moore, R. Y., Bjorklund, A. and Stenevi, U., Plastic changes in the adrenergic innervation of the rat septal area in response to denervation, *Brain Res.*, **33**, 13–35, 1971.

Moore, C. N., Casseday, J. H. and Neff, W. D., Sound localization: The role of the commissural pathways of the auditory system of the cat, *Brain Res.*, **82**, 13–26, 1974.

Morais, J. and Bertelson, P., Laterality effects in dichotic listening, *Perception* **2**, 107–111, 1973.

Morais, J. and Bertelson, P., Spatial position versus ear of entry as determinant of the auditory laterality effects: A stereophonic test, *J. Exp. Psychol. Hum. Percep. and Perf.*, **1**, 253–262, 1975.

Morax, P. V., "La cécité corticale," in T. Alajouanine (ed.), *Les Grands Activités du Lobe Occipital*, Masson et Cie, Paris, 1960.

Morel, F., Les scotomes positifs et les hallucinations visuelles du delirium tremens, *Rev. Oto-Neuro-Ophtalmo*, **11**, 81–88, 1933.

Morrell, F., "Electrical Signs of Sensory Coding," in G. C. Quatron, T. Melnechuk and F. O. Schmitt (eds.), *The Neurosciences*, Rockefeller University Press, New York, 1967, pp. 452–468.

Morrell, L. K. and Salamy, J. G., Hemispheric asymmetry of electrocortical responses to speech stimuli, *Science,* **174,** 164–166, 1971.

Morlaas, J., Contribution a l'etude de l'apraxie, These, Paris, 1928, A. Legrand (ed.).

Morsier, G. de and Rey, A., Le syndrome psychologique dans les tumeurs des lobes frontaux, *Monatss. fur Neurol. u. Psychiat.,* **110,** 293–308, 1945.

Mott, F. W., Results of hemisection of the spinal cord in monkeys, *Phil. Trans. Roy. Soc.,* **1,** 1833, 1892.

Mountcastle, V. B., Modalities and topographic properties of single neurons of cat's sensory cortex, *J. Neurophysiol.,* **20,** 408–434, 1957.

Mountcastle, V. B., "Some Functional Properties of the Somatic Afferent System," in W. A. Rosenblith (ed.), *Sensory Communication,* MIT Press, Cambridge, Mass., 1961, pp. 403–436.

Mountcastle, V. B., Lynch, J. C., Georgopoulos, A., Sakata, H. and Acuna, C., Posterior parietal association cortex of the monkey. Command functions for operations within extra-personal space, *J. Neurophysiol.,* 871–908, 1975.

Mullan, S. and Penfield, W., *AMA Arch. Neurol. Psychiat.,* **81,** 269, 1959.

Müller, J., *Zur vergleichenden Physiologie des Gesichtssinnes,* 1826.

Munk, H., *Über die Functionen der Grosshirnrunde,* (17 papers 1877–1889), Hirschwald, Berlin, 1890.

Murata, K., Cramer, H. and Bach-Y-Rita, P., Neuronal convergence of noxious acoustic and visual stimuli in the visual cortex of the cat, *J. Neurophysiol.,* **28,** 1223–1239, 1965.

Murphy, E. H., Ranney Mize, R., Schecter, S., Visual discrimination following infant and adult ablation of cortical areas 17, 18, and 19 in the cat, *Exp. Neurol.* **49,** 386–405, 1975.

Myers, R. F., "Corpus Callosum and Visual Gnosis," in A. Fessard, (ed.), *Brain Mechanisms and Learning,* Blackwell, Oxford, England, 1961, p. 180.

Nagafuchi, M., 1974; cited by D. Ingram. Cerebral speech lateralization in young children, *Neuropsychologia,* **13,** 103–105, 1975.

Nagino, I., Anatomische Untersuchungen über die zentralen Akutischen. Bahnen beim Menschen and Grund des studiums sekundärer Degenerationen, *Schweiz. Arch. Neurol. Neurochir. Psychiat.,* **17,** 229–259, 1926.

Nathan, P. W., Facial apraxia and apraxic dysarthria, *Brain,* **70,** 449–478, 1947.

Nauta, W. J. H., Fiber degeneration following lesions of the amygdaloid complex in monkeys, *J. Anat.* (London), **95,** 515–531, 1961.

Nauta, W. J. H., Neural associations of the amygdaloid complex in the monkey, *Brain,* **85,** 505–520, 1962.

Nauta, W. J. H., "Some Efferent Connections of the Prefrontal Cortex in the Monkey," in J. M. Warren and K. Akert (eds.), *The Frontal Granular Cortex and Behavior,* McGraw-Hill, New York, 1964, pp. 297–409.

Nauta, W. J. H., Hippocampal projections and related neural pathways to the midbrain in the cat, *Brain,* **88,** (81), 319–340, 1965.

Nauta, W. J. H., The problem of the frontal lobe: A reinterpretation, *J. Psychiat. Res.,* **8,** 167–187, 1971.

Nauta, W. J. H., Neural associations of the frontal cortex, *Acta Neurobiol. Exp.,* **32,** 125–140, 1972a.

Nauta, W. J. H., "The Central Visceromotor System: A General Survey," in C. H. Hockman (ed.), *Limbic System Mechanisms and Autonomic Function,* Charles C. Thomas, Springfield, Ill., 1972b, pp. 21–38.

Nauta, W. J. H. and Bucher, V. M., Efferent connections of the striate cortex in the albino rat, *J. Comp. Neurol.,* **100,** 257–286, 1954.

Nauta, W. J. H. and Kuypers, H. G. J. M., "Some Ascending Pathways in the Brain's Firm Reticular Formation," in M. M. Jasper, L. D. Procter, R. S. Knighton, W. C. Noshay and R. T. Costello (eds.), *Reticular Formation of the Brain,* Little, Brown, Boston, 1958, pp. 1–30.

Nauta, W. J. H. and Mehler, W. R., Some efferent connections of the lentiform nucleus in monkey and cat, *Anat. Res.,* **139,** 260, 1961.

Nauta, W. J. H. and Whitlock, D. G., "An Anatomical Analysis of the Nonspecific Thalamic Projection System," in E. D. Adrian, F. Bremer and A. Jasper (eds.), *Brain Mechanisms and Consciousness,* Blackwell, Oxford, England, 1954, pp. 81–116.

Nebes, R. D., Superiority of the minor hemisphere in commissurotomized man for the perception of part-whole relations, *Cortex,* **7,** 333–349, 1971a.

Nebes, R. D., Handedness and the perception of part-whole relationship, *Cortex,* **7,** 350–356, 1971b.

Nebes, R. D. and Sperry, R. W., Hemispheric deconnection syndrome with cerebral birth injury in the dominant arm area, *Neuropsychologia,* **9,** 247–259, 1971.

Neff, W. D., "Neural Mechanisms of Auditory Discrimination," in V. Mountcastle (ed.), *Sensory Communication,* MIT Press, Cambridge, Mass., Wiley, New York and London, 1961, pp. 259–278.

Newcombe, F., *Missile Wounds of the Brain,* Oxford University Press, London, 1969.

Newcombe, F., Marshall, J. C., Camvick, P. J. and Hiorus, R. W., Recovery curves in acquired dyslexia, *J. Neurol. Sci.,* **24,** 127–133, 1974.

Newcombe, F., Oldfield, C. and Wingfield, R., Object naming by dysphasic patients, *Nature,* **207,** 1217–1218, 1964.

Newcombe, F. and Ratcliff, G., Handedness, speech lateralization, and ability, *Neuropsychologia,* **11,** 399–407, 1973.

Newman, J. D. and Wolberg, Z., Multiple coding of species specific vocalizations in the auditory cortex of squirrel monkeys, *Brain Res.,* **54,** 287–304, 1973.

Newman, J. D. and Wolberg, Z., Response of single neurons in the auditory cortex of squirrel monkey to variants of a single cell type, *Exp. Neurol.,* **40,** 821–824, 1973.

Nielsen, J. M., Unilateral cerebral dominance as related to mind blindness: Minimal lesion capable of causing visual agnosia for objects, *Arch. Neurol. Psychiat.,* **38,** 108–135, 1937.

Nielsen, J. M., *Agnosia, Apraxia, Aphasia: Their Value in Cerebral Localization,* 2nd ed., Hoeber, New York, 1946.

Nielsen, J. M. and Raney, R. B., Symptoms following surgical removal of major (left) angular gyrus, *Bull. Los Angeles Neurol. Soc.,* **3,** 42–46, 1938.

Nielsen, J. M. and Sult, C. W., 1939; cited by Spreen, Benton, and Fincham, 1965.

Niki, H., Differential activity of prefrontal units during right and left delayed response trials, *Brain Res.,* **70,** 346–349, 1974a.

Niki, H., Prefrontal unit activity during delayed alternation in the monkey. I. Relation to direction of response, *Brain Res.,* **68,** 185–196, 1974b.

Niki, H., Prefrontal unit activity during delayed alternation in the monkey. II. Relation to absolute versus relative direction of response, *Brain Res.,* **68,** 197–204, 1974c.

Nobile J. and d'Agata, M. P., Il mancato riconoscimento dello propria cecita (sintamo di Anton), *Revista Neurologica,* **21,** 93–123, 1951.

Noda, H., Freedman, R. B., Jr. and Grenzfeldt, O. D., Neuronal correlates of eye movements in the visual cortex of the cat, *Science,* **175,** 661–664, 1972.

North, E., Unpublished data, 1971.

Nothnagel, 1887; cited by H. Liepmann, 1900.

Nottebohm, F., Ontogeny of bird song, *Science,* **167,** 950–956, 1970.

Nygren, L-G., Fuxe, K., Jonson, G. and Olson, L., Functional regeneration of 5-hydroxy tryptamine nerve terminals in the rat spinal cord following 5, 6 dihydroxy-tryptamine induced degeneration, *Brain Res.,* **78,** 377–394, 1974.

Obler, L. K., Albert, M. L., and Gordon, H., Asymmetrical cerebral dominance for language in fluent bilinguals, Paper presented at Academy of Aphasia, Victoria, B.C., Canada, October, 1975.

Ogle, J. W., Aphasia and agraphia in St. George's Hospital, *Rep. Med. Res. Coun.* (London), **2,**

83–122, 1867.

Ojemann, G. and Fedio, P., Effect of stimulation of the human thalamus and parietal and temporal white matter on short-term memory, *J. Neurosurg.*, **29**, 51–59, 1968.

Ojemann, G., Fedio, P. and van Buren, J., Anomia from pulvinar and subcortical parietal stimulation, *Brain*, **91**, 99–116, 1968.

Ojemann, G. A., Blick, K. I. and Ward, A. A., Jr., Improvement and disturbance of short term verbal memory with human ventrolateral thalamic stimulation, *Brain*, **94**, 225–240, 1971.

Ojemann, G. A., Hoyenga, K. B. and Ward, A. A., Jr., Prediction of short term verbal memory disturbance after ventrolateral thalamotomy, *J. Neurosurg.*, **35**, 203–210, 1971.

Okada, S., Hanada, M., Hattori, H. and Shoyama, T., A case of pure word deafness. About the relation between auditory perception and recognition of speech sounds, *Studia Phonologica*, **3**, 58–65, 1963–1964.

Olsen, C. W. and Ruby, C., Anosognosia and autotopognosia, *Arch. Neurol. Psychiat.*, **46**, 340–345, 1941.

Ombredane, A., Sur le mécanisme de l'angrthrie, *J. Psychologie Normale et Pathologique*, **61**, 940–955, 1926.

Ombredane, A., *Etudes de psychologie medicale.* I. *Perception et langage*, Atlantica Editorial, Rio de Janeiro, 1945.

Ombredane, A., *L'Aphasie et L'elaboration de le Pensee Explicite*, P.U.F., Paris, 1951.

Oppenheim, H., Über einen bemerkswerten Fall von Tumorcerebr, *Berlin Med. Wschr.*, **19**, 1001–1004, 1906.

Orbach, L. and Chow, K. L., Differential effects of resections of somatic areas I and II in monkeys, *J. Neurophysiol.*, **22**, 195–203, 1959.

Orbach, J. and Fantz, R. L., Differential effects of temporal neocortical resections on over-trained and non overtrained visual habits in monkeys, *J. Comp. Physiol. Psychol.*, **51**, 126–129, 1958.

Orbach, J. and Fischer, G. L., Bilateral resections of frontal granular cortex, *Arch. Neurol.*, **1**, 78–86, 1959.

Orban, G., Wissaert, R. and Callens, M., Influence of brainstem oculomotor area stimulation on single unit activity in the visual cortex, *Brain Res.*, **17**, 351–354, 1970.

Orem, J., Schlag-Rey, M., and Schlag, J., Unilateral visual neglect and thalamic intralaminar lesions in the cat, *Exp. Neurol.*, **40**, 784–797, 1973.

Oscar-Berman, M., Goodglass, H. and Chirlow, D. G., Perceptual laterality and iconic recognition of visual materials by Korsakoff patients and normal adults, *J. Comp. Physiol. Psychol.*, **82**, 316–321, 1973.

Oxbury, J. M., Campbell, D. C. and Oxbury, S. M., Unilateral spatial neglect and impairment of spatial analysis and visual perception, *Brain*, **97**, 551–564, 1974.

Oxbury, J. M., Oxbury, M. and Humphrey, N. K., Varieties of colour anomia, *Brain*, **92**, 847–860, 1969.

Paillard, J., "Le Traitement des Informations Spatiales," in *De l'espace corporel a l'espace écologique. Symposium de l'association de psychologie scientifique que de langue francaise.* P.U.F., Paris, 1974, pp. 7–30.

Pandya, D. N. and Kuypers, H. G. J. M., Cortico-cortical connections in the Rhesus monkey, *Brain Res.*, **13**, 13–36, 1969.

Pandya, D. N., Hallet, M. and Mukherjee, S. K., Intra and interhemispheric connections of the neocortical auditory system in the Rhesus monkey, *Brain Res.*, **14**, 49–66, 1969.

Papçun, G., Krashen, S., Terbeek, D. et al, Is the left hemisphere specialized for speech, language and-or something else? *J. Acoust. Soc. Amer.* **55**, 319–327, 1974.

Papez, J. W., A proposed mechanism of emotion, *Arch. Neurol. Psychiat.* (Chicago), **38**, 725–743, 1937.

Parkinson, D., Rucker, C. W. and McCraig, W., Visual hallucinations associated with tumors of the occipital lobe, *Arch. Neurol. Psychiatr.*, **68**, 66–68, 1952.

Pasik, P. and Pasik, T., Further studies on extrageniculostriate vision in the monkey, *Trans, Amer. Neurol. Assoc.*, **93**, 262–264, 1968.

Pasik, P. and Pasik, T., Extrageniculostriate vision in the monkey. V. Role of accessory optic system, *J. Neurophysiol.*, **36**, 450–457, 1973a.

Pasik, T. and Pasik, P., Extrageniculostriate vision in the monkey. IV. Critical structures for light vs. no light discrimination, *Brain Res.*, **56**, 165–182, 1973b.

Patten, B. M., The ancient art of memory. Usefulness in treatment, *Arch. Neurol.*, **26**, 25–31, 1972a.

Patten, B. M., Modality specific memory disorders in man, *Acta Neurol. Scand.*, **48**, 69–86, 1972b.

Paterson, A. and Zangwill, O. L., Disorders of visual space perception associated with lesions of the right cerebral hemisphere, *Brain*, **67**, 331–358, 1944.

Pavlov, I. P., *Complete Collected Works* Vols. 1–6, Izd. Akad. Nank. SSSR, Moscow and Leningrad, 1949.

Peele, T. L., Acute and chronic parietal lobe ablation in monkeys, *J. Neurophysiol.*, **7**, 247–269, 1944.

Penfield, W., Functional localization in temporal and deep sylvian areas, *Res. Publ. Assoc. Nerv. Ment. Dis.*, **36**, 210–227, 1958a.

Penfield, W., *The Excitable Cortex in Conscious Man*, Charles C. Thomas, Springfield, Ill., 1958b.

Penfield, W. and Evans, J., Functional defects produced by cerebral lobectomies, *Publ. Assoc. Res. Nerv. Ment. Dis.*, **13**, 352–377, 1934.

Penfield, W. and Jasper, H., *Epilepsy and the Functional Anatomy of the Human Brain*, Little, Brown, Boston, 1954.

Penfield, W. and Milner, B., Memory deficit produced by bilateral lesions in the hippocampal zone, *AMA Arch. Neurol. Psychiat.*, **79**, 475–497, 1958.

Penfield, W. and Perrot, P., The brain's record of auditory and visual experience, *Brain*, **86**, 595–696, 1963.

Penfield, W. and Rasmussen, T., *The Cerebral Cortex of Man*, MacMillan, New York, 1950.

Penfield, W. and Roberts, L., *Speech and Brain Mechanisms*, Princeton University Press, Princeton, N.J., 1959.

Perenin, M. T. and Jeannerod, M., Residual vision in cortically blind hemifields, *Neuropsychologia*, **13**, 1–7, 1975.

Perret, E., The left frontal lobe of man and the suppression of habitual responses in verbal categorical behavior, *Neuropsychologia*, **12**, 323–330, 1974.

Peritz, G., Zur pathophysiologie des rechnens, *Dtsch. Z. Nervenhk.*, **61**, 1918.

Peron, N. and Goutner, V., Alexie pure sans hemianopsie, *Rev. Neurol.*, **76**, 81–82, 1944.

Peterson, L. R. and Peterson, M. J., Short term retention of individual verbal items, *J. Exp. Psychol.*, **58**, 193–198, 1959.

Petrinovitch, L. and Bliss, D., Retention of a learned brightness discrimination following ablation of the occipital cortex in the rat, *J. Comp. Physiol. Psychol.*, **61**, 136–138, 1966.

Petrinovitch, L. and Carew, T. J., Interaction of neo-cortical lesion size and interoperative experience in retention of a learned brightness discrimination, *J. Comp. Physiol. Psychol.*, **68**, 451–454, 1969.

Pettigrew, J. D., The effect of visual experience on the development of stimulus specificity by kitten cortical neurones, *J. Physiol.* (London), **237**, 49–74, 1974a.

Pettigrew, J. D., Trophic functions of the neuron. VI. Other trophic systems. The effect of selective visual experience of stimulus trigger features of kitten cortical neurons, *Ann. N.Y. Acad. Sci.*, **228**, 393–405, 1974b.

Pfeifer, B., Les troubles psychiques dans les tumeurs cerebrales, *Arch. Psychol.*, **47**, 558–591, 1910.

Piaget, J., *La Naissance de L'intelligence,* Nestle, Neuchatel, Switzerland, 1935.

Piaget, J., Les praxies chez l'enfant, *Rev. Neurol.,* **102,** 551–565, 1960.

Pick, A., *Studien über motorische Apraxie und ihr nahestehenden Erscheinungen,* Deuticke, Leipzig, 1905.

Pick, A., *Über Storungen der Orientierung am eigenen korper. Arbeiten aux der deutschen Psychiatrischen Universitat-klinik in Prag,* Karger, Berlin, 1908.

Pick, A., *Die agrammatischen Sprach storungen,* Springer, Berlin, 1913.

Pick, A., Beitrag zur pathologie des denkverlantes beim Korsakow, *Z. ges. Neurol. Psychiat.,* **28,** 344–383, 1915.

Pick, A., Storung der Orientierung am eigenen korper. Beitrag zur Lehre von Bewusstein des eiginen korpers, *Psychol. Forschung,* **1,** 303–318, 1922.

Pierce, C. S., "Speculative Grammar," in *Collected Papers,* **2,** 129. Harvard University Press, 1932 (cited by R. Jakobson, On visual and auditory signs, *Phonetica,* **2,** 216–220, 1964.

Piercy, M., The effects of cerebral lesions on intellectual function; a review of current research trends, *Brit, J. Psychiat.,* **110,** 310–352, 1964.

Piercy, M., "Neurological Aspects of Intelligence," in P. J. Vinken and G. W. Bruyn (eds.), *Handbook of Clinical Neurology,* Vol. 3, North Holland Publishing Co., Amsterdam, 1969, pp. 296–342.

Piercy, M. and Smith, V. O., Right hemisphere dominance for certain nonverbal intellectual skills, *Brain,* **85,** 775–790, 1962.

Piercy, M., Hécaen, H. and de Ajuriaguerra, J., Constructional apraxia associated with unilateral cerebral lesion, left and right cases compared, *Brain,* **83,** 225–242, 1960.

Pieron, H., *Le Cerveau et la Pensée,* F. Alcan, Paris, 1923.

Pieron, H., Le Toucher. Traite de physiologie nerveuse, **10,** 1055–1228, 1934.

Pitres, A., Consideration sur l'agraphie. A propos d'une observation nouvelle d'agraphie motrice pure, *Rev. Med.,* **4,** 855–873, 1884.

Pitres, A., Etude sur l'aphasie chez les polyglottes, *Rev. Med.,* **15,** 873–899, 1895.

Pitres, A., *L'Aphasie Amnesique et Ses Varietés Cliniques,* Alean, Paris, 1898.

Ploog, D. and Melnechuck, T., "Are Apes Capable of Language?" *Neurosci. Res. Progr.,* Brookline, Mass., 1971.

Plotkin, H. C. and Russell, I. S., Unilateral cortical spreading depression and escape learning, *Physiol. Behavior,* **18,** 395–399, 1969.

Poeck, K., Phantoms following amputation in early childhood and in congenital absence of limbs, *Cortex,* **1,** 269–275, 1964.

Poeck, K., "Modern Trends in Neuropsychology," in A. L. Benton (ed.), *Contributions to Clinical Neuropsychology,* Aldine, Chicago, 1969, pp. 1–29.

Poeck, K. and Orgass, B., Die Entwicklung des korperschemas bei kindern im Alter von 4–10 Jahren, *Neuropsychologia,* **2,** 109–130, 1964.

Poeck, K. and Orgass, B., Gerstmann's syndrome and aphasia, *Cortex,* **2,** 421–436, 1966.

Poeck, K. and Orgass, B., An experimental investigation of finger agnosia, *Neurol.* **19,** 501–507, 1969.

Poeck, K., Hartje, W., Kerschensteiner, M. et al, Sprach verstandnisstorungen bei aphasischen und nicht aphasischen Hirnkranken. *Dtsch. Med. Wschr.,* **98,** 139–147, 1973.

Poggio, G. F., Baker, F. H., Mansfield, R. J. W., Sillito, A. and Grigg, P., Spatial and chromatic properties of neurons subserving foveal and parafoveal vision in Rhesus monkey, *Brain Res.,* **100,** 25–60, 1975.

Pohl, W., Dissociation of spatial discrimination deficits following frontal and parietal lesions in monkeys, *J. Comp. Physiol. Psychol.,* **82,** 227–239, 1973.

Pommé, B. and Janny, P., Trouble de la mémoire topographique consecutif a une intervention sur l'hemisphere non dominant, *Rev. Neurol.,* **91,** 307–308, 1954.

Ponzo, M., Recherches sur la localisation des sensations tactiles et des sensations dolorfiques,

Arch. Ital. Biol., **55,** 1–14, 1911.

Poppel, E., Held, R. and Frost, D., Letter: Residual visual function after brain wounds involving the central visual pathways in man, *Nature,* **243,** 295–296, 1973.

Poppelreuter, W., *Die psychischen Schadigungen durch kopfschuss in kriege,* 2 vols., Voss, Leipzig, 1914–1917.

Poppelreuter, W., Zur Psychologie und Pathologie der optischen Wohr nehmung, *Ztschr. ges. Neurol. Psychiat.,* **83,** 26–152, 1923.

Porowski, S., "Observations on Balint's Syndrome," *Rapports du 8ᵉ Congres Neurologique Intern. III,* Vienne, 1965, pp. 197–200.

Pötzl, O., Über die Storungen der Selbst wahrnehmung bei linksseitiger Hemiplegie, *Ztschr. Neurol. Psychiat.,* **93,** 117–168, 1924.

Pötzl, O., Zur kasuistik der Wortblindheit-Notenblindheit. *Mtschr. Psychiat. Neurol.,* **66,** 1–12, 1927.

Pötzl, O., *Die optisch-agnostischen Storungen,* F. Deuticke, Leipzig-Wien, 1928.

Pötzl, O., Aphasie und Mehrsprachigkeit, *Ztschr. ges. Neurol. Psychiat.,* **124,** 145–162, 1930.

Pötzl, O., Zur pathologie der amusie. *Wien. klin. Wschr.* **20,** 175, 1937.

Pötzl, O. and Stengel, E., Über das syndrom Leitungsaphasie-Schmerzasymbolie, *J. Psychiat. Neurol.,* **53,** 174–207, 1936.

Powell, T. P. S. and Mountcastle, V. B., The cyto-architecture of the post central gyrus of the monkey *Macaca mulatta, Bull. Johns Hopkins Hosp.,* **105,** 108–131, 1959.

Precht, W., "Characteristics of Vestibular Neurons after Acute and Chronic Labyrinthine Destruction," 451–462 in H. H. Kornhuber (ed.), *Handbook of Sensory Physiology VI Vestibular System 2, Psychophysics Applied Aspects and General Interpretations,* Springer Verlag, Berlin, Heidelberg, New York, 1974, pp. 451–462.

Premack, D., Language in chimpanzee? *Science,* **172,** 808–822, 1971.

Pribram, K. H., Some physical and pharmacological factors affecting delayed response performance of baboons following frontal lobotomy, *J. Neurophysiol.,* **13,** 373–382, 1950.

Pribram, K. H., "The Intrinsic Systems of the Forebrain," in J. Field, H. W. Magoun and V. E. Hall (eds.), *Handbook of Physiology, Neurophysiology,* Vol. 2, American Physiological Society, Washington, D.C., 1960a.

Pribram, K. H., "A Review of Theory in Physiological Psychology," in *Ann. Rev. Psychol.,* vol. II, *Annual Reviews,* Palo Alto, Calif., 1960b.

Pribram, K. H., A further experimental analysis of the behavioral defect that follows injury to the primate frontal cortex, *Exp. Neurol.* **3,** 432–466, 1961a.

Pribram, K. H., "Limbic System," in D. E. Sheer (ed.), *Electrical Stimulation of the Brain,* University of Texas Press, Austin, 1961b, pp. 1323–1344.

Pribram, K. H., The primate frontal cortex, *Neuropsychologia,* **7,** 259–266, 1969.

Pribram, K. and Barry, J., Further behavioral analysis of parieto temporo preoccipital cortex, *J. Neurophysiol.,* **19,** 99–106, 1956.

Pribram, K. H., Spinelli, D. and Reitz, S. L., The effects of radical disconnexion of occipital and temporal cortex on visual behavior of monkeys, *Brain,* **92,** 301–312, 1969.

Pribram, K. H., Mishkin, M., Rosvold, H. E. and Kaplan, S. J., Effects on delayed response performance of lesions of dorsolateral and ventromedial frontal cortex of baboons, *J. Comp. Physiol. Psychol.,* **45,** 565–575, 1952.

Pribram, K. H., Ahumada, A., Hartog, J. and Roos, L. A., A progress report on the neurological processes disturbed by frontal lesions in primates, in J. M. Warren and K. Akert (eds.), *Frontal Granular Cortex and Behavior,* McGraw-Hill, New York, 1964, pp. 28–52.

Prisko, L., Short term memory in focal cerebral damage, Unpublished Doctoral Thesis, McGill University, Canada, 1963.

Puchelt, F., Über partielle Empfindungs lahmung, *Heidelberg Med. Annalen,* **10,** 485, 1844.

Puletti, F., 1959; cited by V. B. Mountcastle, 1961.

Quensel, F., Ein Fall von rechtsseitger Hemianopsie mit Alexie und zentral bedingtern monokularem Doppellsehen. *Mtschr. Psychiat. Neurol.* **65**, 173–207, 1927.

Quensel, F., "Die Erkrankungen der hoheren optischen Zentren," *Kurzes Handbuch der Ophtalmologie,* Shieck-Brickner, VI, 1931.

Quensel, P. and Pfeiffer, R. A., Über reine sensorische amusie, *Ztschr. Neurol. Psychiat.,* **81**, 311–330, 1923.

Raisler, R. L. and Harlow, M. F., Learned behavior following lesions of posterior association cortex in infant, immature and pre-adolescent monkeys, *J. Comp. Physiol. Psychol.,* **60**, 167–174, 1965.

Raisman, G., A comparison of the mode of termination of the hippocampal and hypothalamic efferents to the septal nuclei as revealed by electron microscopy of degeneration, *Exp. Brain Res.,* **7**, 317–343, 1969a.

Raisman, G., Neuronal plasticity in the septal nuclei of the adult rat, *Brain Res.,* **14**, 25–48, 1969b.

Raisman, G. and Field, P. M., A quantitative investigation of the development of collateral reinnervation after partial deafferentiation of the septal nuclei, *Brain Res.,* **50**, 241–264, 1973.

Ramier, A., Les apports de la methods d'ecoute dichotique a l'etude de l'asymetrie fonctionnelle hemispherique, *Langages,* **25**, 6–28, 1972a.

Ramier, A. M., Etude des troubles de la denomination lors des lesions corticales unilaterales, These du 3ᵉᵐᵉ cycle, Nauterre-Paris X, 1972b.

Ramier, A. M. and Hécaen, H., Role respectil des atteintes frontales et de la lateralisation lesionnelle dans les deficits de la "fluence verbale," *Rev. Neurol.* (Paris), **123**, 17–22, 1970.

Randolph, M. and Semmes, J., Behavioral consequences of selective subtotal ablations in the postcentral gyrus of *Macaca mulatta, Brain Res.,* **70**, 55–70, 1974.

Ratcliff, G. and Davies-Jones, A. B., Defective visual localization in focal brain wounds, *Brain,* **95**, 49–60, 1972.

Ratcliff, G. and Newcombe, F., Spatial orientation in man: Effects of right-left and bilateral posterior cerebral lesions, *J. Neurol. Neurosurg. Psychiat.,* **36**, 448–454, 1973.

Raymond, F. and Egger, M., Un cas d'aphasie tactile, *Rev. Neurol.,* **14**, 371–375, 1906.

Redlich, E. and Bonvicini, G., Über das Fehlen der Wahrnehmung der Eigenen Blindheit bei Hirnkrankheiten, *Jb. Psychiatr.,* **20**, 1–33, 1908.

Redlich, F. and Dorsey, J. F., Denial of blindness by patients with cerebral diseases, *Arch. Neurol. Psychiat.,* **53**, 407–417, 1945.

Reichardt, M., *Die Stonungen der Optisch-raumticken Funktionen des Erkennes und Wiedererkennens. Allgemeine und Spezielle Psychiatrie,* First Ed., G. Fischer, Iena, 1907.

Reinhold, M., A case of pure auditory agnosia, *Brain,* **73**, 203–223, 1950.

Ribaupierre, F. de, Goldstein, M. H. and Yenikomshian, G., Lack of response in primary auditory neurons to visual stimulation, *Brain Res.,* **52**, 370–373, 1973.

Ribot, T., *Les Maladies de la Memoire,* Libraire Germer Bailliere, Paris, 1883.

Ribot, T., *Maladies de la Personalite,* Alcan, Paris, 1897.

Richter, C. and Hines, M., Increased spontaneous activity produced in monkeys by brain lesions, *Brain,* **61**, 1–8, 1938.

Riddoch, G., Dissociation of visual perceptions due to occipital injuries, with special reference to appreciation of movement, *Brain,* **40**, 15–47, 1917.

Riddoch, G., Visual disorientation in homonymous half-fields, *Brain,* **58**, 376–382, 1935.

Riesen, A. H., "Plasticity of Behavior: Psychological Aspects," in H. F. Harlow and C. N. Woolsey (ed.), *Biological and Biochemical Bases of Behavior,* University of Wisconsin, Madison, 1958, pp. 425–450.

Riklan, M. and Cooper, I. S., Psychometric studies of verbal functions following the lornic lesions in humans, *Brain Lang.*, **2**,(1), 45–64, 1975.

Riklan, M. and Levita, E., Psychological studies of thalamic lesions in humans, *J. Nerv. Ment. Dis.*, **150**, 251–265, 1970a.

Riklan, M. and Levita, E., Psychological and electroencephalographic relationships in crysthalamectomy for Parkinsonism, *Percept. Mot. Skills*, **30**, 799–810, 1970b.

Riklan, M., Levita, E., Zimmerman, J. et al, Thalamic correlates of language and speech, *J. Neurol. Sci.*, **8**, 307–328, 1969.

Riklan, M., Levita, E., Samra, K. et al, Psychological functions in relation to lesion size and site in cryothal amectomy for Parkinsonism, *Percept. Mot. Skills*, **28**, 723–734, 1969.

Ridley, R. M. and Ettlinger, G., Tactile and visuo-spatial discrimination performance in the monkey: The effects of total and partial posterior parietal removals, *Neuropsychologia*, **13**, 191–207, 1975.

Riopelle, A. J. and Chumkian, G. A., The effect of varying the intertrial interval in discrimination learning by normal and brain-operated monkeys, *J. Comp. Physiol. Psychol.*, **51**, 119–125, 1958.

Riopelle, A. J., Alper, R. G., Strong, P. N. and Ades, H. W., Multiple discrimination and patterned string performance of normal and lobectomized monkeys, *J. Comp. Physiol. Psychol.*, **46**, 145–149, 1953.

Rizzolatti, G. and Tradardi, V., Pattern discrimination in monocularly reared cats, *Exp. Neurol.*, **33**, 181–194, 1971.

Rizzolatti, G., Tradardi, V. and Camarda, R., Unit responses to visual stimuli in the cat's superior colliculus after removal of the visual cortex, *Brain Res.*, **24**, 336–339, 1970a.

Rizzolatti, G., Umilta, C. A. and Berlucchi, G., Simple and choice reaction times to lateralized visual stimuli in normal stimuli, *Brain Res.*, **24**, 557–558, 1970b.

Rizzolatti, G., Umilta, C., and Berlucchi, G., Opposite superiorities of the right and left cerebral hemispheres in discriminative reaction time to physiognomical and alphabetical material, *Brain*, **94**, 431–442, 1971.

Robinson, J. S. and Voneida, T. J., Hemisphere differences in cognitive capacity in the split brain cat, *Exp. Neurol.*, **38**, 123–134, 1973.

Rocha-Miranda, C. E., Bender, D. B., Grors, C. G. et al., Visual activation of neurons in infero-temporal cortex depends on striate cortex and forebrain commissures, *J. Neurophysiol.*, **38**, (3), 475–491, 1975.

Rochford, G. and Williams, M., The development and breakdown of the use of names, *J. Neurol. Neurosurg. Psychiat.*, **25**, 222–233, 1962.

Rondot, P., "Le Geste et Son Controle Visuel, Ataxie Visuo Motrice," in H. Hécaen and M. Jeannerod (eds.), *Du Controle Moteur a L'organisation du Geste*, Masson et Cie, Paris, (in press).

Rondot, P. and Tzavaras, A., La prosopagnosie apres vingt annees d'etudes cliniques et neuro-psychologiques, *J. Psychol. Norm. Path.*, **2**, 133–165, 1969.

Rose, F., De l'apraxie des muscles céphaliques, *Sem. Med.*, **18**, 193–198, 1908.

Rose, J. E. and Woolsey, C. N., Organization of the mammalian thalamus and its relationship to the cerebral cortex, *E. E. G. Clin. Neurophysiol.*, **1**, 391–400, 1949.

Rosen, I. and Asanuma, H., Peripheral afferent inputs to the forelimb area of the monkey motor cortex: Input-output relations, *Exp. Brain Res.*, **14**, 257–273, 1972.

Rosen, J., Stein, D. and Butters, N., Recovery of function after serial ablation of prefrontal cortex in the Rhesus monkey, *Science*, **173**, 353–356, 1971.

Rosensweig, M. R., Representations of the two ears at the auditory cortex, *Amer. J. Physiol.* **167**, 147–158, 1951.

Rosner, B. S., Brain functions, *Ann. Rev. Psychol.*, **21**, 555–594, 1970.

Rosvold, H. E., The frontal lobe system: Cortical-subcortical interrelationships, *Acta Neurobiol.*

Exp., **32,** 439–460, 1972.

Rosvold, H. E. and Delgado, J. M. R., The effect on delayed-alternation test performance of stimulating or destroying electrically structures within the frontal lobes of the monkey's brain, *J. Comp. Physiol. Psychol.,* **49,** 356–372, 1956.

Rosvold, H. E. and Mishkin, M., Severity of deficit following unilateral and bilateral prefrontal lesions in monkeys and chimpanzees, 31st Ann. Meet. EPA, New York, 1960.

Rosvold, H. E. and Scwarcbart, M. K., "Neural Structures Involved in Delayed-response Performance," in J. M. Warren and K. Akert (eds.), *The Frontal Granular Cortex and Behavior,* McGraw-Hill, New York, 1964, pp. 1–25.

Rosvold, H. E., Mishkin, M. and Szwarcbart, M. K., Effect of subcortical lesions on visual discrimination and single alternation performance, *J. Comp. Physiol. Psychol.,* **51,** 437–441, 1958.

Rubens, A. B. and Benson, D. F., Associative visual agnosia, *Arch. Neurol.,* **24,** 305–316, 1971.

Rubins, J. L. and Friedman, E. D., Asymbolia for pain, *Arch. Neurol. Psychiatr.,* **60,** 554–573, 1948.

Ruch, T. C. and Shenkin, H. A., The relation of area 13 on the orbital surface of the frontal lobe to hyperactivity and hyperphagia in monkeys, *J. Neurophysiol.,* **6,** 349–360, 1943.

Ruch, T. C., Fulton, F. J. and German, W. J., Sensory discrimination in monkeys, chimpanzee, and man after lesions of the parietal lobe, *Arch. Neurol. Psychiat.,* **39,** 919–937, 1938.

Rudel, R. G., Denckla, M. B. and Spalten, E., The functional asymmetry of Braille letter learning in normal, sighted children, *Neurol.* (Minneapolis), **24,** 733–738, 1974.

Rudel, R. G., Teuber, H. L. and Twitchell, T. E., Levels of impairment of sensorimotor functions in children with early brain damage, *Neuropsychologia,* **12,** 95–108, 1974.

Rumbaugh, D. M., Paper presented at Int. Cong. Anthro. Ethno. Sci., Chicago, Ill., August 1973.

Rumbaugh, D. M. and Gill, T. V., Reply to Mistber-Lachman, J. L. and R. Lachman, *Science,* **185,** 972–973, 1974.

Rumbaugh, D. M., Gill, T. V. and Glasersfeld, E. C. von, Reading and sentence completion by a chimpanzee, *Science,* **182,** 731–733, 1973.

Russell, I. S., Neurological basis of complex learning, *Brit. Med. Bull.* **27,** 278–285, 1971.

Russell, R. and Espir, M. L., *Traumatic Aphasia,* Oxford University Press, Oxford, England, 1961.

Russell, W. R., "The Traumatic Amnesias," in P. J. Vinken and G. W. Bruyn, (eds.), *Handbook of Clinical Neurology,* Vol. 3, North Holland Publishing Co., Amsterdam, 1969, pp. 293–295.

Russell, W. R. and Nathan, P. W., Traumatic amnesia, *Brain,* **69,** 280–300, 1946.

Russell, W. R. and Whitty, Ch. W. M., Studies in traumatic epilepsy. III. Visual fits, *J. Neurol. Neurosurg. Psychiat.,* **18,** 79–96, 1955.

Russo, M. and Vignolo, L., Visual figure-ground discrimination in patients with unilateral cerebral disease, *Cortex,* **3,** 113–127, 1967.

Rylander, G., *Personality Changes after Operations on the Frontal Lobes. A Clinical Study of 32 Cases,* E. Munksgaard, Copenhagen, 1939.

Rylander, G., *Mentality Changes after Excision of Cerebral Tissue,* Einar Munksgaard, Copenhagen, 1943.

Sachs, H., Dos Gehirns des Forsterschen Rinden-blinden, *Arb. Psychiat. Klinik Breslau,* **2,** 1895; cited by Benton, 1969.

Saenger, A., Ein Fall von dauernder zerebraler erblindung nach hinterhauptnerletzung, *Zbl. Neurol. Psychiat.,* **38,** 210, 1919.

Sakata, H., Takaoka, Y., Kawarasaki, A. et al, Somatosensory properties of neurons in the superior parietal cortex (area 5) of the Rhesus monkey, *Brain Res.,* **64,** 85–102, 1973.

Samuels, I., Butters, N. and Goodglass, H., Visual memory deficits following cortical and limbic lesions: Effect of field of presentation, *Physiol. Behav.*, **6**, 447–452, 1971a.

Samuels, I., Butters, N. and Goodglass, H., A comparison of subcortical and cortical damage on short term visual and auditory memory, *Neuropsychologia*, **9**, 293–306, 1971b.

Samuels, I., Butters, N. and Fedio, P., Short term memory disorders following temporal lobe removals in humans, *Cortex*, **8**, 283–298, 1972.

Sanchez-Longo, L. P., Forster, F. M. and Aut, T. L., A clinical test for sound localization and its application, *Neurol.*, **7**, 655–663, 1957.

Sanchez-Longo, L. P. and Forster, F. M., Clinical significance of impairment of sound localization, *Neurol.*, **8**, 119–125, 1958.

Sanford, H. S. and Bair, H. J., Visual disturbances associated with tumours of the temporal lobe, *Arch. Neurol. Psychiat.*, **42**, 21–24, 1939.

Sarno, M. T., A survey of 100 aphasic Medicare patients in a speech pathology program, *J. Amer. Geriat. Soc.*, **18**, 471–480, 1970.

Sato, S. and Dreifuss, F. E., Electronencephalographic findings in a patient with developmental expressive aphasia, *Neurol.* (Minneapolis), **23**, 181–185, 1973.

Satz, P., Laterality effects in dichotic listening, *Nature* (London), **218**, 277–278, 1968.

Satz, P., Fennelle, E. and Jones, M. B., Comments on a model of the inheritance of handedness and cerebral dominance, *Neuropsychologia*, **7**, 101–103, 1969.

Sauguet, J., Benton, A. L. and Hécaen, H., Disturbances of the body schema in relation to language impairment and hemispheric locus of lesion *J. Neurol. Neurosurg. Psychiatr.*, **34**, 496–501, 1971.

Scales, D. A. and Collins, G. H., Cerebral degeneration with hypertrophy of the contralateral pyramid, *Arch. Neurol.*, **26**, 186–190, 1972.

Scheller, H., Über das wesen und die abgenzung optischagnostischer storungen, *Nervenartz*, **22**, 187–190, 1951.

Scheller, H. and Seidemann, H., Zur frage der optischraumlichen agnosie, *Mtschr. Psychiat. Neurol.*, **81**, 97–188, 1931–1932.

Schenk, V. W., Troubles des phonemes en cas d'aphasie sensorielle, *L'Encephale*, **42**, 158–169, 1953.

Schilder, P., *Das kroper Schema; ein Beitrag zur Lehre vom Bewusstsein des eigerenen korpers*, J. Springer, Berlin, 1923.

Schilder, P., *The Image and Appearance of the Human Body*, Routledge and Kegan Paul, London, 1935.

Schilder, P. and Stengel, E., Das krankheits bild der Schmerzasymbolie, *Ztschr. Neurol. Psychiat.*, **129**, 250–279, 1930.

Schilder, P. and Stengel, E., Schmerzasymbolie, *Ztschr. Neurol. Psychiat.*, **132**, 367–370, 1931.

Schilder, P., Pasik, P. and Pasik, T., Extrageniculostriate vision in the monkey. 3. Circle vs. triangle and "red vs. green" discrimination, *Brain Res.*, **32**, 383–398, 1971.

Schilder P., Pasik, P. and Pasik, T., Extrageniculostriate vision in the monkey. *Exp. Brain. Res.*, **14**, 436–448, 1972.

Schiller, F., Aphasia studied in patients with missile wounds, *J. Neurol. Neurosurg. Psychiat.*, **10**, 183–197, 1947.

Schiller, P. H., Stryker, M., Cynader, M. et al, Response characteristics of single cells in the monkey superior colliculus following ablation or cooling of visual cortex, *J. Neurophysiol.*, **37**, 181–194, 1974.

Schmidt, J., De oblivione lectionis ex apoplexia salva scriptione, *Miscellanea Curiosa Medico-Physica Academiae Naturae Curiosocum*, **4**, 195–197, 1676.

Schneider, G. E., Contrasting visuomotor functions of tectum and cortex in the golden hamster, *Psychol. Forsch.*, **31**, 52–62, 1967.

Schneider, G. E., Two visual systems, *Science*, **163**, 895–902, 1969.

Schoenfeld, T. A., Hamilton, L. W. and Gandelman, R., Septal damage during the maturation of inhibitory responding: Effects in juvenile and adult rats, *Dev. Psychobiol.*, 7, 195–205, 1974.

Schuell, H. and Jenkins, J. J., The nature of language deficit in aphasia, *Psychol. Rev.*, 66, 45–67, 1959.

Schuster, P., *Psychische storungen bei Hirntumoren*, Enke, Stuttgart, 1902.

Schwartzroin, P. A., Cowey, A. and Cross, C. G., A test of an "efferent model" of the function of inferotemporal cortex in visual discrimination, *Electroenceph. Clin. Neurophysiol.*, 27, 594–600, 1969.

Scoville, W. B. and Milner, B., Loss of recent memory after bilateral hippocampal lesions, *J. Neurol. Neurosurg. Psychiat.*, 20, 11–21, 1957.

Sechzer, J. A., Axonal regeneration or generation after corpus callosum section in the neonatal rat, *Exp. Neurol.*, 45, 186–188, 1974.

Seelert, H., Beitrag sur kenntnis der Ruckbildung von Apraxie, *Mtschr. Psychiat. Neurol.*, 48, 125–149, 1920.

Seglas, J., *Des Troubles du Langage Chez les Alienes*, Rueff et Cie, Paris, 1892.

Segarra, J. M. and Quadfasel, F. A., Destroyed temporal lobe tips—preserved ability to sing with total aphasia, *Proceed. of VII Int. Congr. of Neur. II*, Rome, 1961.

Seltzer, B. and Benson, D. F., The temporal pattern of retrograde amnesia in Korsakoff's disease, *Neurol.*, 24, 527–530, 1974.

Semmes, J., A non-tactual factor in astereognosis, *Neuropsychologia*, 3, 295–315, 1965.

Semmes, J., Protopathic and epicritic sensation. A reappraisal, in A. L. Benton (ed.), *Contributions to Clinical Neuropsychology*, Aldine, Chicago, 1969, pp. 142–171.

Semmes, J. and Porter, L., A comparison of pre-central and post-central cortical lesions on somatosensory discrimination in the monkey, *Cortex*, 8, 249–264, 1972.

Semmes, J., Mishkin, M. and Denel, R. K., Somesthetic discrimination learning after partial non-sensorimotor lesions in monkeys, *Cortex*, 5, 331–350, 1969.

Semmes, J., Porter, L. and Randolph, M. C., Further studies of anterior postcentral lesions in monkeys, *Cortex*, 10, 55–68, 1974.

Semmes, J., Weinstein, S., Ghent, L. and Teuber, H. L., Spatial orientation in man after cerebral injury: Analysis by locus of lesion, *J. Psychol.*, 39, 227–244, 1955.

Semmes, J., Weinstein, S., Ghent, L. and Teuber, H. L., *Somatosensory Changes of the Penetrating Head Wounds in Man*, Harvard University Press, Cambridge, Mass., 1960.

Semmes, J., Weinstein, S., Ghent, L. and Teuber, H. L., Correlates of impaired orientation in personal and extrapersonal space, *Brain*, 86, 747–772, 1963.

Semmes-Blum, J., Cortical organization in somesthesis: Effects of lesions in posterior associative cortex on somatosensory function in *Macaca mulatta*, *Comp. Psychol. Monogr.*, No. 105 20, 219–249, 1951.

Shallice, T. and Warrington, E. K., Independent functioning of verbal memory stores: A neuropsychological study, *Quart. J. Exp. Psychol.*, 22, 261–273, 1970.

Shankweiler, D. P., Performance of brain-damaged patients on two tests of sound localization. *J. Comp. Physiol. Psychol.* 54, 375–381, 1961.

Shankweiler, D., Effects in recognition of familiar tunes after unilateral temporal lobectomy, Paper given at E.P.A. Meeting, New York, 1966a.

Shankweiler, D., Effects of temporal lobe damage on perception of dichotically presented melodies, *J. Comp. Physiol. Psychol.*, 62, 115–122, 1966b.

Shankweiler, D., "Language Rehabilitation," in A. L. Benton, (ed.), *Behavioral Change in Cerebrovascular Disease*, Harper and Row, New York, 1970, pp. 72–76.

Shankweiler, D. and Harris, K. S., An experimental approach to the problem of articulation in aphasia, *Cortex*, 2, 277–292, 1966.

Shankweiler, D. and Studdert-Kennedy, M., Identification of consonants and vowels presented to left and right ears, *Quart. J. Exp. Psychol.*, **19**, 59–63, 1967.

Shankweiler, D., Harris, K. S. and Taylor, M. L., Electromyographic studies of articulation in aphasia, *Arch. Phys. Med. and Rehab.* **49**, 1–8, 1968.

Sharlock, D. P., Tucker, T. J. and Strominger, N. L., Auditory discrimination by the cat after neonatal ablation of the temporal cortex, Science, **141**, 1197–1198, 1963.

Sharpless, S. K., Reorganization of function in the nervous system—use and disuse, *Ann. Rev. Physiol.*, **26**, 357–388, 1964.

Sharpless, S. K., "Isolated and Deafferented Neurons: Disuse Supersensitivity," in H. H. Jasper, A. A. Ward, and A. Pope (eds.), *Basic Mechanisms of the Epilepsies*, Little, Brown, Boston, 1969, pp. 329–348.

Sherman, S. M., Visual fields of cats with cortical and tectal lesions, *Science*, **185**, 355–357, 1974a.

Sherman, S. M., Permanence of visual perimetry deficits in nonocularly and binocularly deprived cats, *Brain Res.*, **73**, 491–501, 1974b.

Sherrington, C. S., Examination of the peripheral distribution of the fibres of the posterior roots of some spinal nerves. Part I, *Phil. Trans. Roy. Soc.*, **183B**, 641, 1892.

Sherrington, C. S., On the spinal animal, *Medico-Chirurgical Trans.*, **132**, 449, 1899.

Sherrington, C. S., *The Integrative Action of the Nervous System*, Scribner, New York, 1906.

Shina, 1959; cited by B. Milner, 1962.

Shoumaker, R. P., Bennett, D. R., Bray, F. F. et al, Clinical and EEG manifestations of an unusual aphasic syndrome in children, *Neurol.* (Minneapolis), **24**, 10–16, 1974.

Schulman, S., Impaired delayed response from thalamic lesions, *Arch. Neurol.*, **11**, 447–499, 1964.

Shuster, P. and Taterka, H., Beitrag zur Anatomie und klinik der reinen Wort taubheit, *Ztschr. Neurol. Psychiat.*, **105**, 498–538, 1926.

Shuttleworth, E. C. and Morris, C. E., The transient global amnesia syndrome, *Arch. Neurol. Psychiat.*, (Chicago), **15**, 515–520, 1966.

Sia, R. L., Consciousness during general anaesthesia, *Anaesth. Analg.* (Cleveland), **48**, 363–366, 1969.

Silberpfennig, J., Contribution to the problem of eye movements. III. Disturbances of ocular movements with pseudo-hemianopsia in frontal lobe tumors, *Confin. Neurol.*, **4**, 1–13, 1941.

Simmel, M., On phantom limbs, *Arch. Neurol. Psychiat.* (Chicago), **75**, 637–647, 1956.

Simmel, M., Phantom experiences following amputation in childhood, *J. Neurol. Neurosurg. Psychiat.*, **25**, 69–78, 1962.

Sittig, O., Storungen un Verhalten gegenuber Farben bei Aphasischen, *Mtschr. Psychiat.*, **49**, 63, 1921.

Sittig, O., Über apraktische Agraphie, *Arch. f. Psychiat. u. Nervenhk*, **91**, 470–473, 1930.

Sittig, O., Über Apraxie eine klinische studie Abh. aus der Neur, *Psychiat. Psych. u. ihr. Grenz.*, Karger, S., Verlag, Berlin, **63**, 1–248, 1931.

Sjogren, T., Sjogren, H. and Lindgren, A. G. H., Morbus Alzheimer and morbus Pick. A genetic, clinical, and pathoanatomical study, *Acta Psychiat. et Neurol.*, Scand. 1952, Suppl. 82.

Smith, A., Speech and other functions after left dominant hemispherectomy, *J. Neurol. Neurosurg. Psychiat.*, **29**, 467–471, 1966.

Smith, A. and Sugar, O., Development of above normal language and intelligence 21 years after left hemispherectomy, *Neurol.* (Minneapolis), **25**,(9), 813–818, 1975.

Snyder, M. and Diamond, I. T., The organization and function of the visual cortex in the tree shrew, *Brain Behav. Evolut.*, **1**, 244–288, 1968.

Soper, H. V., Diamond, I. T. and Wilson, M., Visual attention and inferotemporal cortex in Rhesus monkeys, *Neuropsychologia*, **13**, 409–420, 1975.

Souques, A. and H. Baruk, Autopsie d'un cas d'amusie (avec aphasie) chez un professeur de piano, *Rev. Neurol.*, **37**, 545–556, 1930.

Sparks, R., Helm, N. and Albert, M., Aphasia rehabilitation resulting from melodic intonation therapy, *Cortex*, 10(4), 303–316, 1974.

Spear, P. D. and Braun, J. J., Pattern discrimination following removal of visual neocortex in the cat, *Exp. Neurol.*, 25, 331–348, 1969.

Spellacy, F. and Blumstein, S., The influence of language set on ear preference in phoneme recognition, *Cortex*, 6, 430–440, 1970.

Sperry, R. W., Neural basis of the spontaneous optokinetic response produced by visual inversion, *J. Comp. Physiol. Psychol.*, 93, 482–489, 1950.

Sperry, R. W., Neurology and the mind-brain problem, *Amer. Sci.*, 40, 291–312, 1952.

Sperry, R. W., Corpus callosum and interhemispheric transfer in the monkey, (Macaca mulatta), *Anat. Rec.*, 297, 1958, 1931.

Sperry, R. W., Cerebral organization and behavior, *Science*, 133, 1749–1757, 1961.

Sperry, R. W., Mental unity following surgical disconnection of the cerebral hemispheres, *Harvey Lect.*, 62, 293–323, 1966–1967.

Sperry, R. W., "Plasticity of Neural Maturation," in M. Locke (ed.), *Emergence of Order in Developing Systems*, Academic Press, New York, 1968a.

Sperry, R. W., Hemisphere deconnection and unity in conscious awareness, *Amer. Psychol.*, 23, 723–733, 1968b.

Sperry, R. W. and Gazzaniga, M. S., "Language following Surgical Disconnection of the Hemispheres," in C. Millikan and F. Darley (eds.), *Brain Mechanisms Underlying Speech and Language*, Grune & Stratton, New York, 1967, pp. 108–115.

Sperry, R. W., Gazzaniga, M. S. and Bogen, J. E., "Interhemispheric Relationships: The Neocortical Commissures; Syndromes of Hemisphere Disconnection," in P. J. Vinken and G. W. Bruyn (eds.), *Handbook of Clinical Neurology*, North Holland Publishing Co., Amsterdam, 1969, pp. 273–290.

Spinelli, D. N. and Barrett, T. W., Visual receptive field organization of single units in the cat's visual cortex, *Exp. Neurol.*, 24, 76–98, 1969.

Spinelli, D. N., Starr, A. and Barrett, T. W., Auditory specificity in unit recordings from cat's visual cortex, *Exp. Neurol.*, 22, 75–84, 1968.

Spinnler, H. and Vignolo, L. A., Impaired recognition of meaningful sounds in aphasia, *Cortex*, 2, 337–349, 1966.

Sprague, J. M., Interaction of cortex and superior colliculus in visually guided behavior in cat, *Science*, 153, 1544–1547, 1966.

Sprague, J. M. and Meikle, T., The role of the superior colliculus in visually guided behavior, *Exp. Neurol*, 11, 115–146, 1965.

Sprague, J. M., Berlucchi, G. and Dibernardino, A., The superior colliculus and pretectium in visually guided behavior and visual discrimination in the cat, *Brain Behav. Evol.*, 3, 285–294, 1970.

Spreen, O., Benton, A. L. and Fincham, R. W., Auditory agnosia without aphasia, *Arch. Neurol.*, 13, 84–92, 1965.

Spreen, O., Benton, A. L. and Van Allen, M. W., Dissociation of visual and tactile naming in amnesic aphasia, *Neurol.* 16, 807–814, 1966.

Stamm, J. S., Dorsolateral frontal ablations and responses processes in monkeys, *J. Comp. Physiol. Psychol.*, 70, 437–447, 1970.

Stamm, J. S., Functional dissociation between the inferior and arcuate segments of dorsolateral prefrontal cortex in the monkey, *Neuropsychology*, 11, 181–190, 1973.

Stamm, J. S. and Weber Levine, M. L., Delayed alternation impairment following selective prefrontal cortical ablations in monkeys, *Exp. Neurol.*, 33, 263–278, 1971.

Stamm, J. S., Gadiotti, A. and Rosen, S., Interhemispheric functional differences in prefrontal cortex of monkeys, *J. Neurobiol.*, 6, 39–49, 1975.

Stanley, W. C. and Jaynes, J., The function of the frontal cortex, *Psychol. Rev.*, **56**, 18–32, 1949.

Stein, B. E. and Magalhaes-Castro, B., Effects of neonatal cortical lesions upon the cat superior colliculus, *Brain Res.*, **83**, 480–485, 1973.

Stein, B. E., Magalhaes-Castro, B. and Kruger, L., Relation between visual and somatic organization in the cat superior colliculus, *Soc. for Neuroscience Abst.*, No. 655, 1972.

Stein, B. E., Magalhaes-Castro, B. and Kruger, L., Superior colliculus: Visuotopic-somatopic overlap, *Science*, **189**, 224–226, 1975.

Stein, D. G. and Firl, A. C., Brain damage and reorganization of function in old age, *Exp. Neurol.*, **52**, 157–167, 1976.

Stein, D. G., Rosen, J. J., Gramadel, J. and Mishkin, D., Cerebral nervous system recovery of function, *Science*, **166**, 528–530, 1969.

Stein, J., Untersuchungen in der Neurologie. II. Über Sensibilitatsprufunger Nervenarzt **1**, 529–532, 1928.

Stein, J., Nachempfindungen bei Sensibilitatsstorungen, *R. Ztschr. f. Nervenlik.* **80**, 218–233, 1924.

Stein, J., "Pathologie der Wahrnehmung," in *Bumke Hanbuch fur Geisteskrankheiten*, I. Springer, Berlin, 1928.

Stein, J. and Weizsacker, v. von, Über klinische sensibilitatsprufungen, *D. Arch. f. klin. Med.* (Heidelberg), **151**, 230–253, 1926.

Steinbach, M. J., Eye tracking of self-moved targets: The role of efference, *J. Exp. Psychol.*, **82**, 366–376, 1969.

Steinbach, M. J., Aligning the eye to the actively or passively positioned hand, *Perception and Psychophysics*, **8**, 287–288, 1970.

Steinthal, H., 1971; cited by Thiele, R., "Aphasie, Apraxie, Agnosie," *Bunke Handb. Gersteskrank*, Springer, Berlin, 1928.

Stengel, E., Loss of spatial orientation, constructional apraxia and Gerstmann's syndrome, *J. Ment. Sci.* **90**, 753, 1944.

Stengel, E., The syndrome of visual alexia with colour agnosia, *J. Ment. Sci.*, **94**, 46–58, 1948.

Stengel, E., Psychopathology of dementia. *Proc. Roy. Soc. Med.* **57**, 911–914, 1964.

Stengel, E. and Lodge-Patch, I. E., "Central" aphasia associated with parietal symptoms, *Brain*, **78**, 401–416, 1955.

Stengel, E. and Zelmanowicz, J., Über Polyglotle Motor Aphasie, *Z. Neurol. Psychiat.* **149**, 291–301, 1933.

Stepien, I. and Stamm, J. S., Impairments on loco-motor task involving spatial opposition between cue and reward in frontally ablated monkeys, *Acta Neurobiol. Exp.*, **30**, 1–12, 1970.

Stewart, D. L. and Starr, A., Absence of visually influenced cells in auditory cortex of normal and congenitally deaf cats, *Exp. Neurol.*, **28**, 525–528, 1970.

Stollreiter-Butzon, L., Zur Frage der Prosopagnosie, *Arch. Psychiat. Nervenhk.*, **184**, 1–27, 1950.

Stone, L., Paradoxical symptoms in right temporal tumor, *J. Nerv. Ment. Dis.*, **79**, 1–13, 1934.

Stratton, G. M., Vision without inversion of the retinal image, *Psychol. Rev.*, **4**, 341–360 and 463–481, 1897.

Strauss, H., Über konstrucktive Apraxie, *Mtschr. f. Psychol.*, **56**, 65–124, 1924.

Stritch, S., Shearing of nerve fibers as a cause of brain damage due to head injury, *Lancet*, **2**, 443–448, 1961.

Strobos, R. J., Tumors of temporal lobe, *Neurology*, **3**, 752–760, 1953.

Strohmayer, W., Über subkortikale alexie mit agraphie und apraxie, *Dtsch. Z. Nervenhk.*, **24**, 372–380, 1903.

Strominger, H. L., Subdivisions of auditory cortex and their role in localization of sound in space, *Exp. Neurol.*, **24**, 348–362, 1969.

Strub, R. and Gardner, H., The repetition deficit in conduction aphasia: Amnestic or linguistic? *Brain and Lang.*, **1**, 241–257, 1974.

Stryker, M. P. and Sherk, H., Modifications of cortical orientation selectivity in the cat by restricted visual experience, a reexamination, *Science*, **190**, 904–906, 1975.

Studdert-Kennedy, M. and Shankweiler, D., Hemispheric specialization for speech perception, *J. Acoust. Soc. Amer.*, **48**, 579–594, 1970.

Subirana, A., La Droitersie. *Arch. Suisses Neurol. Psychiat.*, **69**, 321–359, 1952.

Subirana, A., "Handedness and Cerebral Dominance," in P. J. Vinken and G. W. Bruyn (eds.), *Handbook of Clinical Neurology*, Vol. 4, North Holland Publishing Co., Amsterdam, 1969, pp. 248–273.

Sutherland, N. S.; cited in C. Millikan and F. Darby, 1967.

Sutherland, N., Shape discrimination in rat, octopus, and goldfish, *J. Comp. Physiol. Psychol.*, **67**, 160–176, 1969.

Sweet, W. H., Talland, G. A. and Ervin, F. R., Loss of recent memory following section of fornix, *Trans. Amer. Neurol. Ass.*, **84**, 76, 1959.

Swisher, L. P., Auditory intensity discrimination in patients with temporal lobe damage, *Cortex*, **3**, 179–193, 1967.

Swisher, L. and Hirsh, I. J., Brain damage and the ordering of two temporally successive stimuli, *Neuropsychologia*, **10**, 137–152, 1972.

Symmes, D., Flicker discrimination by brain-damaged monkeys, *J. Comp. Physiol. Psychol.*, **60**, 470–473, 1965.

Symmes, D. and Newman, J. D., Discrimination of isolation peep variants by squirrel monkeys, *Exp. Brain Res.*, **19**, 365–376, 1974.

Symonds, C. P., Concussion and its sequelae, *Lancet*, **1**, 1–5, 1962.

Symonds, C., Disorders of memory, *Brain*, **89**, 625–644, 1966.

Taine, H., *L'Intelligence*, 11th Ed., Hachette et Cie, Paris, 1906.

Talland, G. A., *Deranged Memory. A Psychonomic Study of the Amnesic Syndrome*, Academic Press, London-New York, 1965.

Teitelbaum, H., A comparison of effects of orbito frontal and hippocampal lesions upon discrimination learning and reversal in the cat, *Exp. Neurol.*, **9**, 452–462, 1964.

Teitelbaum, P., Functional recovery after lesions of the nervous system. V. Neural plasticity and behavioral recovery in the central nervous system. The use of recovery of function to analyze the organization of motivated behavior in the nervous system, *Neurosci. Res. Program Bull.*, **12**, 255–260, 1974.

Terbraak, J. W. G., Shenk, W. V. D. and Van Vliet, A. G. M., Visual reactions in a case of long lasting cortical blindness, *J. Neurol. Neurosurg. Psychiat.*, **34**, 140–147, 1971.

Terrell, R. K., Sweet, W. O., Gladfelter, J. H. et al, Study of recall during anaesthesia, *Anaesth. Analg.* (Cleveland), **48**, 86–90, 1969.

Teszner, D., Etude anatomique de l'asymetrie droite-gauche du planum temporale. These pour le Doctorat en Medecine, Univ. Paris, 1972.

Teszner, D., Tzavaras, A., Gruner, J. and Hécaen, H., L'asymetrie droite-gauche du planum temporale, a propos de l'etude anatomique de 100 cerveaux, *Rev. Neurol.*, **126**, 444–449, 1972.

Teuber, H. L., "Some Alterations in Behavior after Cerebral Lesions in Man," in *Evolution of Nervous Control*, AAAS, Washington, 1959, 157–194.

Teuber, H. L., Sensory deprivation, sensory suppression and agnosia: Notes for a neurologic theory, *J. Nerv. Ment. Dis.*, **132**, 32–43, 1961a.

Teuber, H. L., "Perception," in J. Field, H. W. Magoun and V. E. Hall (eds.), *Handbook of Physiology-Neurophysiology*, III, American Physiological Society, Washington, 1961b, pp. 1595–1668.

Teuber, H. L., "The Riddle of Frontal Lobe Function in Man," in J. M. Warren and K. Akert (eds.), *The Frontal Granular Cortex and Behaviour*, McGraw-Hill, New York-London, 1964a, pp. 416–441.

Teuber, H. L., "Discussion," in A. V. S. de Reuch and M. O'Connor (eds.), *Disorders of Language,* Churchill, London, 1964b, pp. 177–180.

Teuber, H. L., "Alterations of Perception of the Brain Injury," in J. C. Eccles (ed.), *Brain and Conscious Experience,* Springer, New York, 1966a.

Teuber, H. L., Effects of occipital lobe lesion on pattern vision, *Suppl. 8th Internat. Cong. Neurol.,* **3,** 79–102, 1966b.

Teuber, H. L., The frontal lobes and their function. Further observations on rodents, carnivores, subhuman primates and man, *Internat. J. Neurol.,* **5,** 232–300, 1966c.

Teuber, H. L., Disorders of memory following penetrating missile wounds of the brain, *Neurol.* (Minneapolis), **18,** 287–288, 1968.

Teuber, H. L., "Neglected Aspects of the Post-traumatic Syndrome," in E. Walker, W. F. Caveness and M. Critchley (eds.), *The Late Effects of Head Injuries,* Charles C. Thomas, Springfield, Ill., 1969, pp. 13–34.

Teuber, H. L., Unity and diversity of frontal lobe functions, *Acta Neurobiol. Exp.,* **32,** 615–656, 1972.

Teuber, H. L. and Diamond, S., Effects of brain injury in man on binaural localization of sounds, Paper read at 27th Ann. Meeting of Eastern Psychol. Assoc., Atlantic City, N.J. 1956.

Teuber, H. L. and Mishkin, M., Judgment of visual and postural vertical after brain injury, *J. Psychol.,* **38,** 161–168, 1954.

Teuber, H. L. and Rudel, R., Behavior after cerebral lesions in children and adults, *Dev. Med. and Child Neurol.,* **4,** 3–20, 1967.

Teuber, H. L. and Weinstein, S., Ability to discover hidden figures after cerebral lesions, *Arch. Neurol. Psychiat.* (Chicago), **76,** 369–379, 1956.

Teuber, H. L., Battersby, W. S. and Bender, M. B., Performance of complex visual tasks after cerebral lesions, *J. Nerv. Ment. Dis.,* **114,** 43–429, 1951.

Teuber, H. L., Battersby, W. S. and Bender, M. B., *Visual Field Defects after Penetrating Missile Wounds of the Brain,* Harvard University Press, Cambridge, 1960.

Teuber, H. L., Krieger, H. P. and Bender, M. B., Reorganization of sensory function in amputation stumps: Two point discrimination, *Fed. Proc.* **8,** 1, 1949.

Thompson, R., Retention of a brightness discrimination following neocortical damage in the rat, *J. Comp. Physiol. Psychol.,* **53,** 212–215, 1960.

Thompson, V. E., Visual decortication in infancy in rats, *J. Comp. Physiol. Psychol.,* **72,** 444–451, 1970.

Thorpe, W. H., "The Concepts of Learning and Their Relation to Those of Instinct," in *Physiological Mechanisms in Animal Behavior,* Cambridge Univ. Press, Cambridge, England, 1950, pp. 387–408.

Tikofsky, R. S., A comparison of the intelligibility of esophageal and normal speakers, *Folia Phoniat.* (Basel), **17,** 19–32, 1965.

Tissot, R., Lhermitte, F. and Ducarne, B., Etat intellectuel des aphasiques. Essai d'une nouvelle approche a travers des epreuves perceptives et operatoires, *L'Encephale,* **52,** 285–320, 1963.

Tissot, R., Mounin, G., and Lhermitte, F., *L'Agrammatisme,* Dessart, Bruxelles, 1973.

Tissot, R., Constantinidis, J. and Richard, J., *La Maladie de Pick,* Masson et Cie, Paris, 1975.

Travenec, J., Problemy afasie, alexie, agrafie, *Acta Univ. palack. Olomucensis,* Suppl. 2, 1958.

Travis, A. M. and Woolsey, C. N., Motor performance of monkeys after bilateral partial and total cerebral decortications, *Amer. J. Phys. Med.,* **35,** 273–310, 1956.

Tresher, J. H. and Ford, F. R., Colloid cyst of the third ventricle, *Arch. Neurol. Psychiat.,* **37,** 959–973, 1937.

Trevarthen, C. B., "Functional Interactions between the Cerebral Hemispheres of the Split-Brain Monkey,'" in G. Ettlinger (ed.), *Functions of the Corpus Callosum,* Churchill, London, 1965, pp. 24–40.

Trevarthen, C., Two mechanisms of vision in primates, *Psychol. Forsch.,* **31,** 299–337, 1968.

Trevarthen, C., Experimental evidence for a brain-stem contribution to visual perception in man, *Brain Behav. Evol.,* **3,** 338–352, 1970.

Trevarthen, C., "Functional Relations of Disconnected Hemispheres with the Brain Stem and with Each Other: Monkey and Man," in M. Kinsbourne and W. L. Smith (eds.), *Hemispheric Disconnection and Cerebral Function,* Charles C Thomas, Springfield, Ill. 1974, pp. 187–207.

Trost, J. E. and Canter, G. J., Apraxia of speech in patients with Broca's aphasia: A study of phoneme production accuracy and error patterns, *Brain and Lang.,* **1,** 63–79, 1974.

Trousseau, A., De l'aphasie, maladie decrite recemment sons le nom impropre d'aphemie, *Gaz. Hop* (Paris), **37,** 1864.

Trousseau, A., De l'aphasie, *Clin. Med.,* (Holel Dieu de Paris), **14,** 669–729, 1877.

Tucker, T. J. and Kling, A., Differential effects of early and late lesions of frontal granular cortex in the monkey, *Brain Res.,* **5,** 377–389, 1967.

Tyler, H. R., Abnormality of perception with defective eye movements (Balint's syndrome), *Cortex,* **4,** 171, 1968.

Tzavaras, A. and Hécaen, H., Etude des coordonnees visuelles subjectives au cours des lesions corticales unilaterales, *Rev. Neurol.,* **125,** 458–461, 1971.

Tzavaras, A., Albert, M. L. and Hécaen, H., Essai de dissociation des deficits de la perception spatiale elementaire au cours de lesions corticales, *Rev. Neurol.,* **129,** 60–62, 1972.

Tzavaras, A., Hécaen, H. and Le Bras, H., Le probleme de la specificite du deficit de la reconnaissance du visage humain lors des lesions hemispheriques unilaterales, *Neuropsychologia,* **8,** 403–417, 1970.

Tzavaras, A., Hécaen, H. and Le Bras, H., Trouble de la vision des couleurs après lésions corticales unilatérales, *Rev. Neurol.,* **124,** 316–402, 1971.

Tzavaras, A. and Masure, M., Aspects differents de l'ataxie optique, *Lyon Médical,* **236,** 673–683, 1976.

Tzortzis, C. and Albert, M. L., Impairment of memory for sequences in conduction aphasia, *Neuropsychologia,* **12,** 355–366, 1974.

Urbaitis, J. C. and Meikle, T. H., Relearning a dark-light. Discrimination by cats after cortical and collicular lesions, *Exp. Neurol.,* **20,** 295–311, 1968.

Van Allen, M., Benton, A. L. and Gordon, M. C., Temporal discrimination in brain damaged patients, *Neuropsychologia,* **4,** 159–167, 1966.

van Bogaert, L., L'hallucinose pedonculaire, *Rev. Neurol.,* **69,** 608–617, 1927.

van Bogaert, L., Sur la pathologie de l'image de soi, *Ann. Med. Psychol.,* **92,** 519–555, 744–759, 1934.

van Bogaert, L. and Martin, P., Sur deux signes du syndrome de desequilibration frontale. L'Apraxie de la marche et l'atonie statique, *L'Encephale,* **24,** 11–18, 1929.

van Buren, J. M., Confusion and disturbance of speech from stimulation in vicinity of the head of the caudate nucleus, *J. Neurosurg.,* **20,** 148–157, 1963.

van Buren, J. M., The question of thalamic participation in speech mechanisms, *Brain Lang.,* **2,** 31–44, 1975.

van Thal, J., Polyglot aphasics, *Folia Phoniatrica,* **12,** 123–128, 1960.

van Woerkom, La signification de certains elements de l'intelligence dans la genese des troubles aphasiques, *J. Psychol.,* **18,** 730–751, 1921.

Vaughan, H. G. and Costa, L. D., Performances of patients with lateralized cerebral lesions. II. Sensory and motor tests, *J. Nerv. Ment. Dis.,* **134,** 237–243, 1962.

Vaughan, H. G. and Gross, C. G., Cortical responses to light in unanesthetized monkeys and their alteration by visual system lesions, *Exp. Brain Res.,* **8,** 19–36, 1969.

Velpeau, A. and Delpech, A.; cited in J. Lhermitte, Le lobe frontale, *L'Encephale,* **24,** 87–118,

Human Neuropsychology

Hécaen, Henri + Albert, Martin L. (1978) John Wiley & Sons Inc. Toronto

32 44 45-46 390-399 412-418
142,76 82-84 72-93

32
82-83
82-94 - gesture
76
41-42
44-47

1929.

Velzeboer, C. M. J., Bilateral cortical hemianopsia and optokinetic mystagmus, *Ophthalmologica*, **123**, 187–188, 1952.

Verger, H., Sur la valeur semeiologique de la stereo-agnosie, *Rev. Neurol.*, **2**, 1201–1205, 1902.

Verhaart, W., Hypertrophy of peduncle and pyramid as a result of degeneration of contralateral corticofugal fiber tracts, *J. Comp. Neurol.*, **92**, 1–15, 1950.

Vetter, R. J. and Weinstein, S., The history of the phantom in congenitally absent limbs, *Neuropsychologia*, **5**, 335–338, 1967.

Victor, M., Adams, R. D. and Collins, G. H., *The Wernicke-Korsakoff Syndrome*, F. A. Davis Co., Philadelphia, 1971.

Victor, M., Angerine, J. B., Mancall, E. L. and Fisher, C. M., Memory loss with lesions of hippocampal formation, *Arch. Neurol.* **5**, 244–263, 1961.

Vignolo, L., Evolution of aphasia and language rehabilitation, *Cortex*, **1**, 344–352, 1964.

Vignolo, L. A., "Auditory Agnosia: A Review and Report of Recent Evidence," in A. L. Benton (ed.), *Contributions to Clinical Neuropsychology*, Aldine, Chicago, 1969, pp. 172–208.

Vincent, C., Diagnostic des tumeurs comprimant le lobe frontal, *Rev. Neurol.*, **1**, 801–884, 1928.

Vincent, C., David, M. and Puech, P., Sur l'alexie. Production du phenomene a la suite de l'extirpation d'une tumeur de la corne occipitale due ventriate lateral gauche, *Rev. Neurol.*, **72**, 262–272, 1930.

Vital-Durand, F., Eye movements are necessary for the development of visually guided behavior, *Exp. Brain Res.*, **23**, 211, 1975, Suppl.

Vogt, C. and Vogt, O., Allgemeinere ergebnisse unserer Hirnforschung, *J. Psychol. Neurol.* (Leipzig), **25**, 277–462, 1919.

von Bonin, G., "Anatomical Asymmetries of the Cerebral Hemisphere," in V. Mountcastle (ed.) *Interhemispheric Relations and Cerebral Dominance*, Johns Hopkins University Press, Baltimore, 1962.

von Dongen, H. R. and Prooglever-Fortuyn, D., Drawing with closed eyes, *Folia Psychiat. Neurol. Neurochir.*, **71**, 275–280, 1968.

von Economo, C. and Horn, L., r.he *Z. ges. Neurol. Psychiat.*, **130**, 678, 1930.

von Economo, C. and Koskinas, G. N., *Die Cytoarchitektonik der Hirnrinde des erwachsenen Menschen*, J. Springer, Wien, Berlin, 1925.

von Frey, M., Beitrage zur Sinnes physiologie der Haut Berichle u.d. Verhandlungen d.k. Sachs, *Gesellschaft d. Wissensch.*, **2 S**, 166, 1895.

von Haller, A., *Elementa physiologiae corporis humain* (8 vols), 1757–1766.

von Holst, E., Relations between the central nervous system and the peripheral organs, *Brit. J. Animal Behav.*, **2**, 89–94, 1954.

von Holst, E., Aktice Leistungen der meschlichen Gesichtswahrnehinung, *Studien Generale*, **10**, 231–243, 1957.

von Holst, E. and Mittelstaedt, H., Das Reafferenzprinzip, *Naturwiss*, **37**, 464–476, 1950.

von Monakow, C., *Gehirnpathologie*, Nothnagel, Wien, 1897.

von Monakow, C., *Gehirnpathologie*, 2nd ed., Vienna, Alfred Holder, 1905.

von Monakow, C., *Über Lokalisation de Hirnfunktionen*, 1 vol. (34 pp.), Verlag, von Bergmann, Wiesbaden, 1910.

von Monakow, C., *Die Lokalisation im Grosshirn und der Abbau der Funktion durch cortikale*, Herde, Wiesbaden, 1914.

von Monakow, C. and Mourque, R., *Introduction Biologique a L'etude de la Neurologie et de la Psychiatrie*, Alcan, Paris, 1928.

von Noorden, G. K., Dowling, J. E. and Ferguson, D. C., Experimental amblyopia in monkeys. I. Behavioral studies of stimulus deprivation amblyopia, *Arch. Ophtalmol.*, **84**, 206–214, 1970.

von Stauffenberg, W., Über Seelenblindheit, *Arb. hirn-anatom. Institut Zurich Wiesbaden*, **8**, 1–212,

1914.

von Stauffenberg, W., Klinische und anatomische Beitrage zur kenntnis der aphasischen, agnostischen, und apraletischen Symptome, *Z. chr. ges. Neurol. Psychiatr.*, **93**, 71, 1918.

von Stockert, G., Lokalisation und klinische differenzierung des symptoms der Nichtwahrnehmung einer korperhalfle, *Dtsch. Z. Nervenhk.*, **134**, 1–13, 1934.

von Stockert, T. R., Recognition of syntactic structure in aphasic patients, *Cortex*, **8**, 323–335, 1972.

von Stockert, T. R., Ein neues konzept zum Verstandnis der cerebralen Sprachstorungen, *Nervenarzt*, **45**, 94–97, 1974.

Vygotsky, L. S., *Thought and Language*, MIT Press, Cambridge, Mass., 1962.

Vygotsky, L. S., Psychology and localization of functions, *Neuropsychologia*, **3**, 381–386, 1965.

Wada, J. and Rasmussen, T., Intra-carotid injection of sodium amytal for the laterlization of cerebral speech dominance, *J. Neurosurg.*, **17**, 266–282, 1960.

Wada, J. A., Clarke, R. and Hamm, A., Cerebral hemispheric asymmetry in humans. Cortical speech zones in 100 adults and 100 infant brains, *Arch. Neurol.*, **32** (4), 239–246, 1975.

Wade, M., The effect of sedatives upon delayed response in monkeys following removal of the prefrontal lobes, *J. Neurophysiol.*, **10**, 57–61, 1947.

Walker, A. E., *The Primate Thalamus*, University of Chicago Press, Chicago, Ill., 1938.

Wall, P. D., The sensory and motor role of impulses travelling in the dorsal columns toward the cerebral cortex, *Brain*, **93**, 505–524, 1970.

Wall, P. D. and Dubner, R., Somatosensory pathways, *Ann. Rev. Physiol.*, **34**, 315–336, 1972.

Wall, P. D. and Egger, M. D., Formation of new connexions in adult rat brain after partial deafferentation, *Nature* (London), **232**, 542–545, 1971.

Ware, C. B., Diamond, I. T. and Casagrande, V. A., Effects of ablating the striate cortex on a successive pattern discrimination: Further study of the visual system in the tree shrew *(Tupaia glis)*, *Brain Behav. Evol.*, **9**(4), 264–279, 1974.

Warren, J. M., "The Behavior of Carnivores and Primates with Lesions in the Prefrontal Cortex," in J. M. Warren and K. Akert (eds.), *The Frontal Granular Cortex and Behavior*, McGraw-Hill, New York, 168–191, 1964.

Warren, J. M., Discrimination of mirror images by cats, *J. Comp. Physiol. Psychol.*, **69**, 9–11, 1969.

Warren, J. M. and Akert, K., Impaired problem solving by cats with thalamic lesions, *J. Comp. Physiol. Psychol.*, **57**, 207–211, 1960.

Warren, J. M. and Akert, K. (eds.)., *The Frontal Granular Cortex and Behavior*, McGraw-Hill, New York, 1964, pp. 313–331.

Warren, J. M., Contant, L. W. and Cornwell, P. R., Cortical lesions and response inhibition in cats, *Neuropsychologia*, **7**, 245–257, 1969.

Warrington, E. K., "Constructional Apraxia," in P. Vincken, G. Bruyn (eds.), *Handbook of Clinical Neurology*, North Holland Publishing Co., Amsterdam, 1969, pp. 67–83.

Warrington, E. K., Perception of naturalistic stimuli in patients with focal brain lesions, *Brain Res.*, **31**, 370, 1971.

Warrington, E. K., Neurological disorders of memory, *Brit. Med. Bull.* **27**, 243–247, 1971.

Warrington, E. K. and James, M., Disorders of visual perception in patients with localized cerebral lesions, *Neuropsychologia*, **5**, 253–266, 1967a.

Warrington, E. and James, M., An experimental investigation of facial recognition in patients with unilateral cerebral lesion, *Cortex*, **4**, 17–34, 1967b.

Warrington, E. K. and Pratt, R. T. C., Language laterality in left handers assessed by unilateral ECT, *Neuropsychologia*, **11**, 423–428, 1973.

Warrington, E. K. and Shallice, T., The selective impairment of auditory verbal short-term memory, *Brain*, **92**, 885–896, 1969.

Warrington, E. K. and Weiskrantz, L., Amnesic syndrome: Consolidation or retrieval? *Nature*

(London), **228**, 628–630, 1970.

Warrington, E. K. and Weiskrantz, L., Organisational aspects of memory in amnesic patients, *Neuropsychologia*, **9**, 67–73, 1971.

Warrington, E. K., James, M. and Kinsbourne, M., Drawing disability in relation to laterality of lesion, *Brain*, **89**, 53–92, 1966.

Watanabe, T. and Katsuki, Y., Response patterns of single auditory neurons of the cat to species specific vocalization, *Jap. J. Physiol.*, **24**, 135–155, 1974.

Watson, R. T., Heilman, K. M., Cauthen, J. C. et al, Neglect after cengulectomy, *Neurol.*, **23**, 1003–1007, 1973.

Waugh, N. C. and Norman, D. A., Primary memory, *Psych. Rev.*, **72**, 89–104, 1965.

Webster, W. G., Functional asymmetry between the cerebral hemispheres of the cat, *Neuropsychologia*, **10**, 75–87, 1972.

Wechsler, A. F., Transient left hemialexia, *Neurol.*, **22**, 628–633, 1972.

Wechsler, A. F., Weinstein, E. A. and Antin, S. P., Alexia without agraphia. A clinical and radiological study of three unusual cases, *Bull. Los Angeles Neurol. Soc.*, **37**, 1–11, 1972.

Weddell, G., The pattern of cutaneous innervation in relation to cutaneous sensitivity, *J. Anat.* (London), **75**, 346–367, 1941a.

Weddell, G., The multiple innervation of sensory spots in the skin, *J. Anat.* (London), **75**, 441–446, 1941b.

Wegener, J. G. and Stamm, J. S., Behavior flexibility and the frontal lobes, *Cortex*, **2**, 188–201, 1966.

Weigl, E. and Bierwisch, M., Neuropsychology and linguistics: Topics of common research, *Found. of Lang.*, **6**, 1–18, 1970.

Weinreich, U., *Languages in Contact: Findings and Problems.* Publication No. 1, Linguistic Circle, New York, 1953.

Weinstein, E. A. and Kahn, R. C., *Denial of Illness, Symbolic and Physiological Aspects*, Charles C. Thomas, Springfield, Ill. 1955.

Weinstein, E. A. and Keller, N. J. A., Linguistic patterns of misnaming in brain injury, *Neuropsychologia*, **1**, 79–90, 1963.

Weinstein, E. A., Kahn, R. C., and Slate, W. H., Withdrawal, inattention and pain asymbolia, *Arch. Neurol. Psychiatr.*, **74**, 245–248, 1955.

Weinstein, S., "Differences in Effects of Brain Wounds Implicating Right or Left Hemispheres: Differential Effects on Certain Intellectual and Complex Perceptual Functions," in V. H. Mountcastle (ed.), *Interhemispheric Relations and Cerebral Dominance*, John Hopkins University Press, Baltimore, 1962, pp. 159–176.

Weinstein, S., "Neuropsychological Studies of the Phantom," in A. L. Benton (ed.), *Contributions to Clinical Neuropsychology*, Aldine, Chicago, 1969, pp. 73–106.

Weinstein, S., Sersen, E. A. and Vetter, R. J., Phantoms and somatic sensation in cases of congenital aplasia, *Cortex*, **1**, 276–290, 1964.

Weinstein, S., Vetter, R. J., Shapiro, G. et al, The effects of brain damage on the phantom limb, *Cortex*, **5**, 91–103, 1969.

Weinstein, S., Vetter, R. J. and Sersen, E. A., Phantoms following breast amputation, *Neuropsychologia*, **8**, 185–197, 1970.

Weisenburg, T. and McBride, K. E., *Aphasia: A Clinical and Psychological Study*, Commonwealth Fund, New York, 1935.

Weiskrantz, L., Contour discrimination in a young monkey with striate cortex ablation, *Neuropsychologia*, **1**, 145–164, 1963.

Weiskrantz, L., Behavioural analysis of the monkey's visual nervous system, *Proc. Roy. Soc. Lond.* (Biol.), **182**, 427–455, 1972.

Weiskrantz, L., "The Interaction Between Occipital and Temporal Cortex in Vision: An Overview," in F. O. Schmitt and F. G. Worden (eds.), *The Neurosciences Third Study Program.* M.I.T. Press, Cambridge, Mass., 1974, pp. 189–204.

Weiskrantz, L. and Mishkin, M., Effect of temporal and frontal cortical lesions on auditory discrimination in monkeys, *Brain*, 81, 406–414, 1958.

Weiskrantz, L., Mihailovic, L. and Gross, C. G., Effects of stimulation of frontal cortex and hippocampus in behavior in the monkey, *Brain*, 85, 487–504, 1962.

Weiskrantz, L., Warrington, E. K., Sanders, M. D. et al., Visual capacity in the hemianopic field following a restricted occipital ablation, *Brain*, 97, 709–728, 1974.

Weiss, S. A. and Fishman, S., Extended and telescoped phantom limbs in unilateral amputees, *J. Abnorm. Soc. Psychol.*, 66, 489–497, 1963.

Weizsacker, V. Von, Pathophysiologie der Sensibilitat, *Dtsch. Z. Nervenhk.*, 101, 184–211, 1928.

Welch, K. and Stutteville, P., Experimental production of neglect in monkeys, *Brain*, 81, 341–347, 1958.

Wepman, J., Dimensions of language performance in aphasia, *JSHR*, 4, 220–232, 1961.

Wepman, J. M. and Jones, L. V., "Studies in Aphasia: A Psycholinguistic Method and Case Study," in E. C. Carterette (ed.), *Brain Functions* Vol. 3: *Speech and Language Communication*, University of California Press, Los Angeles, 1966, pp. 141–171.

Wepman, J. M., Bock, R. D., Jones, L. and Van Pelt, D., Psycholinguistic study of aphasia: A revision of the concept of anomia, *Speech Hear. Dis.*, 21, 468–477, 1956.

Werner, G. and Whitsell, B. L., "Functional Organization of the Somatosensory Cortex," in A. Iggo (ed.), *Somatosensory Systems, Handbook of Sensory Physiology*, Vol. 2, Springer-Verlag, Berlin, Heidelburg, New York, 1973, pp. 621–700.

Wernicke, C., *Der aphasische symptomenkomplex*, M. Cohn and Weigert, Breslau, Poland, 1874.

Wernicke, C., *Lehrbuch der gehirnkran kheiten. Tragweite der aphasie*, Theodor Fischer, Kassel and Berlin, 1881.

Wernicke, C., 1884; cited by H. Liepmann, 1900.

Wernicke, C., *Grundriss der Psychiatrie: Psychophysiologische Einleitung*, Verlag, Leipzig, 1894.

Wernicke, C., Zwei Falle von Rindenlasion. *Arb. aus d. Psychiat. klin. in Breslau*, 11, 35, 1895.

Wernicke, C., Ein Fall von isolierter Agraphie. *Mtschr. Psychiat. Neurol.* 13, 241–265, 1903.

Wernicke, C., *Grundriss der Psychiatrie*, G. Thieme Verlag, Leipzig, 1906.

Wertheim, N., "The Amusias," in P. J. Vinken and G. W. Bruyn, (eds.), *Handbook of Clinical Neurology*, Vol. 4, North Holland Publishing Co., Amsterdam, 1969, pp. 195–206.

Wertheim, N. and Botez, J. I., Receptive amusia, a clinical analysis, *Brain*, 84, 19–30, 1961.

Westphal, S., Über einen Fall von "amnestischer Aphasie," Agraphie und Apraxie nebst eigenartigen Storungen des Erkennens und Vorstellens im Auschluss ar eine eklamptische Psychose, *Dtsch. Med. Wschr.*, 34, 2326, 2327, 1908; *Allg. Z. Psychiat.*, 66, 187–192, 1909.

Wetzel, A. B., Thompson, V., Horel, J. and Meyer, P. M., Some consequences of perinatal lesions of the visual cortex in the cat, *Psychon. Sci.*, 3, 381, 382, 1965.

Whitaker, H., A model for neurolinguistics, *Occasional Papers*, 10, Colchester: University of Essex, 1971.

Whitfield, I. C., Coding in the auditory nervous system, *Nature*, 213, 756–760, 1967.

Whitfield, I. C. and Evans, E. F., Responses of auditory cortical neurosis to stimuli of changing frequency, *J. Neurophysiol.*, 28, 655–672, 1965.

Whitfield, I. C., Crawford, J., Ravizza, R. et al, Effects of unilateral ablation of auditory cortex in cat on complex sound localization, *J. Neurophysiol.*, 35, 718–731, 1972.

Whitty, C. W. M. and Zangwill, O. L., "Traumatic Amnesia," in C. W. M. Whitty, and O. L. Zangwill (eds.), *Amnesia*, Butterworths, London, 1966: pp. 92–108.

Wiesel, T. N. and Hubel, D. H., Extent of recovery from effects of visual deprivation in kittens, *J. Neurophysiol.*, 28, 1060–1072, 1965.

Wilbrand, H., *Die Seelenblindheit al Herderichemungen und ihre Beziehungen zur homonymen Hemianopsie*, *zur Alexie und Agraphie,* Bergmann, Wiesbaden, 1887.

Wilbrand, H., Ein Fall von Scelenblindheit und Hemianopsie mit SectionsBefund, *Dtsch. Ztschr. Nervenhk.,* **2,** 361–387, 1892.

Williams, M., Memory studies in ECT, *J. Neurol. Neurosurg. Psychiat.,* **13,** 30, 314–322, 1950.

Williams, M., "Memory Disorders Associated with Electroconvulsive Therapy," in C. W. M. Whitty and O. L. Zangwill (eds.), *Amnesia,* Butterworths, London, 1966, pp. 134–149.

Williams, M. and Zangwill, O. L., Memory defects after head injury, *J. Neurol. Neurosurg. Psychiat.,* **15,** 54–58, 1952.

Wilson, I. G. H., A case of bilateral cortical blindness, *J. Neurol. Psychiat.,* **6,** 42–45, 1925.

Wilson, M., Effects of circumscribed cortical lesions upon somesthetic and visual discrimination in the monkey, *J. Comp. Physiol. Psychol.,* **50,** 630–635, 1957.

Wilson, M., Tactual discrimination learning in monkeys, *Neuropsychologia,* **3,** 353–362, 1965.

Wilson, M., Inferotemporal cortex and the processing of visual information in monkeys, *Neuropsychologia,* **6,** 135–140, 1968.

Wilson, M., Wilson, W. A., Jr. and Sunenshine, H. S., Perception, learning and retention of visual stimuli by monkeys with inferotemporal lesions, *J. Comp. Physiol. Psychol.,* **65,** 404–412, 1968.

Wilson, M. E., Cragg, B. G., Ainsworth, A. et al, Projections from the medial geniculate body to the cerebral cortex in the cat, *Brain Res.,* **13,** 462–475, 1969.

Wilson, S. A. K., A contribution to the study of apraxia, *Brain,* **31,** 164–216, 1908.

Wilson, S. A. K., Concussion injuries of the visual apparatus in warfare of central origin, *Lancet,* **2,** 1–5, 1917.

Winckelgren, B. G. and Sterling, P., Influence of visual cortex on receptive fields in the superior colliculus of the cat, *J. Neurophysiol.,* **32,** 16–23, 1969.

Windle, W. F., *Physiology of the Fetus,* Saunders, Philadelphia, 1940.

Wittelson, S. F. and Pallis, W., Left hemisphere specialization for language in the newborn, *Brain,* **96** 641–646, 1973.

Wollberg, Z. and Newman, V. D., Auditory cortex of squirrel monkey. Response patterns of single cells to species specific vocalizations, *Science,* **175,** 212–214, 1972.

Wolpert, I., Über das Wesen der literalen Alexie, *Mtschr. Psychiat. Neurol.,* **75,** 207–266, 1930.

Wood, C. C., Goff, W. R. and Day, R. S., Auditory evoked potentials during speech perception, *Science,* **173,** 1248–1251, 1971.

Wood, C. C., Spear, P. D. and Braun, J. J., Effects of sequential lesions of suprasylvian gyri and visual cortex on pattern discrimination in the cat, *Brain Res.,* **66,** 443–466, 1974.

Woods, B. T. and Teuber, H. L., Early onset of complementary specialization of cerebral hemispheres in man, *Trans. Amer. Neurol. Assoc.* **98,** 113–117, 1973.

Woolsey, C. N., "Cortical Localization as Defined by Evoked Potential and Electrical Stimulation Studies," in G. Schaltenbrand and C. N. Woolsey (eds.), *Cerebral Localization and Organization,* University of Wisconsin Press, Madison and Milwaukee, 1964, pp. 17–26.

Woolsey, C. N., Marshall, W. H. and Bard, P., Representation of cutaneous tactile sensibility in the cerebral cortex of the monkey as indicated by evoked potentials, *Bull. of the Johns Hopkins Hospital,* **70,** 399–441, 1942.

Woolsey, C. N., Marshall, W. H. and Bard, P., Note on the organization of the tactile sensory area of the cerebral cortex of the chimpanzee, *J. Neurophysiol.,* **6,** 287–292, 1943.

Worster-Drought, C., An unusual form of acquired aphasia in children, *Dev. Med. Child Neurol.,* **13,** 563–571, 1971.

Wortis, S. and Pfeffer, A., Unilateral auditory spatial agnosia, *J. Nerv. Ment. Dis.,* **108,** 181–186, 1948.

Wurtz, R. H., Response of striate cortex neurons to stimuli during rapid eye-movements in the monkey, *J. Neurophysiol.,* **32,** 975–986, 1969a.

Wurtz, R. H., Comparison of effects of eye movements and stimulus increments on striate cortex neurons of the monkey, *J. Neurophysiol.*, **32**, 987–994, 1969b.

Wurtz, R. H. and Goldberg, M. E., Superior colliculus cells responses related to eye movements in awake monkeys, *Science*, **171**, 82–84, 1971.

Wurtzen, C. H., Einzelne formen von amusie, durch beispiele beleuchet, *Dtsch. Ztschr. Nervenhk.*, **24**, 465–473, 1903.

Wyke, B., Recent advances in the neurology of phonation: Phonatory reflex mechanisms in the larynx, *Brit. J. Disord. Commun.*, **2**, 2–14, 1967.

Wyke, M., Alterations of size constancy associated with brain lesions in man, *J. Neurol. Neurosurg. Psychiat.*, **23**, 253–261, 1960.

Wyke, M., The effects of brain lesions on the learning performance of a bimanual coordination task, *Cortex*, **7**, 59–72, 1971.

Yamadori, A. and Albert, M. L., Word category aphasia, *Cortex*, **9**, 83–89, 1973.

Yamaguchi, S. Y. and Myers, R. E., Failure of discriminative vocal conditioning in Rhesus monkey, *Brain Res.*, **37**, 109–114, 1972.

Yarnell, P. R. and Lynch, S., Retrograde amnesia immediately after concussion, *Lancet*, **1**, 863, 864, 1970.

Yarnell, P. R. and Lynch, S., The "ding": amnestic states in football trauma, *Neurol.* (Minneapolis), **23**, 196, 197, 1973.

Yin, R. K., Looking at upside down faces, *J. Exp. Psychol.*, **81**, 141–145, 1969.

Yin, R. K., Face recognition by brain-injured patients: A dissociate ability, *Neuropsychologia*, **8**, 395–402, 1970.

Young, J. Z., *The Memory System of the Brain*, University of California Press, Berkeley, 1966.

Young, R. M., *Mind, Brain and Adaptation in the Nineteenth Century*, Oxford, Clarendon, 1970.

Zaidel, E., Unilateral auditory language comprehension on the Token Test following cerebral commissurotomy and hemispherectomy, *Neuropsychologia*, **15**, 1–13, 1977.

Zaidel, E., Auditory vocabulary of the right hemisphere after brain bisection or hemidecortication, *Cortex*, **12**, 191–211, 1976.

Zaidel, D. and Sperry, R. W., Memory impairment after commissurotomy in man, *Brain*, **97** (2), 263–272, 1974.

Zaidel, D. and Sperry, R. W., Some long-term motor effects of cerebral commissurotomy in man, *Neuropsychologia*, **15**, 42–48, 1977.

Zangwill, O. L., Clinical tests of memory impairment, *Proc. Roy. Soc. Med.* **36**, 576, 1943.

Zangwill, O. L., Some clinical applications of the Rey-Davis Performance Test, *J. Ment. Sci.*, **92**, 19–26, 1946a.

Zangwill, O. L., Some qualitative observations on verbal memory in cases of cerebral lesions, *Brit. J. Psychol.*, **37**, 8–14, 1946b.

Zangwill, O. L., La probleme de l'apraxie idéatoire, *Rev. Neurol.*, **102**, 595–603, 1960.

Zangwill, O. L., "Intelligence in Aphasia," in A. V. S. de Reuck and M. O'Connor (eds.), *Disorders of Language*, Churchill, London, 1964, pp. 261–274.

Zangwill, O. L., "The Amnesic Syndrome," in C. W. M. Whitty and O. L. Zangwill (eds.), *Amnesia*, Butterworth, London, 1966a, pp. 77–91.

Zangwill, O., Psychological deficits associated with frontal lobe lesions, *Internat. J. Neurol.*, **5**, 395–402, 1966b.

Zangwill, O. L., L'apraxie ideatoire. Expose presente au Seminaire de Neuropsychologie, E.P. H.E., Paris, 1967a.

Zangwill, O. L., The Grunthal-Storing case of amnesic syndrome, *Brit. J. Psychiat.*, **113**, 113–128, 1967b.

Zaporozhets, A. V., *Development of the Child's Voluntary Movements*, Izd. Akad. Pedagog. Nauk RSFSR, Moscow, 1960.

Zeigler, D. K., Word deafness and Wernicke's aphasia, *Arch. Neurol. Psychiat.* (Chicago), **67**, 323–331, 1952.

Zeki, S. M., Representation of central visual fields in prestriate cortex of monkey, *Brain Res*, **14**, 217–291, 1969.

Zeki, S. M., Interhemispheric connections of prestriate cortex in monkey, *Brain Res.*, **19**, 63–76, 1970.

Zeki, S. M., Colour coding in Rhesus monkey prestriate cortex, *Brain Res.*, **53**, 422–427, 1973a.

Zeki, S. M., Comparison of the cortical degeneration in the visual regions of the temporal lobe of the monkey following section of the anterior commissure and the splenium, *J. Comp. Neurol.*, **148**, 167–175, 1973b.

Ziskind, E. and Ausburg, Th., Hallucinations in sensory deprivation (method or madness?), *Dis. Nerv. Syst.*, **28**, 721–726, 1967.

Zollinger, R., Removal of the left cerebral hemisphere, *Arch. Neurol. Psychiat.*, **34**, 1055–1064, 1935.

Zubek, J. P., Effects of prolonged sensory and perceptual deprivation, *Brit. Med. Bull.*, **20**, 38–42, 1964.

Zubek, J. P., *Sensory Deprivation: Fifteen Years of Research*, Appleton-Century-Crofts, New York, 1970.

Zubin, J. and Barrera, S. E., Effect of ECT on memory, *Proc. Soc. Exp. Biol. & Med.*, **48**, 596, 1941.

Zurif, E. B. and Bryden, M. P., Familial handedness and left-right differences in auditory and visual perception, *Neuropsychologia*, **7**, 179–188, 1969.

Zurif, E. B. and Caramazza, A., "Psycholinguistic Structures in Aphasia, Studies in Syntax and Semantics," in H. Whitaker and H. Whitaker (eds.), *Studies in Neurolinguistics*, Adademic Press, New York, 1976.

Zurif, E. B. and Ramier, A. M., Some effects of unilateral brain damage on the perception of dichotically presented phoneme sequences and digits, *Neuropsychologia*, **10**, 103–110, 1972.

Zurif, E. B., Caramazza, A. and Myerson, R., Grammatical judgments of agrammatic aphasics, *Neuropsychologia*, **10**, 405–417, 1972.

Zurif, E., Green, E., Caramazza, A. and Goodenough, L. C., Grammatical intuitions of aphasic patients: Sensitivity to functors, *Cortex*, **12**, 183–186, 1976.

AUTHOR INDEX

SUBJECT INDEX